R. Gupta's®

POPULAR MASTER GUIDE

# RPF & RPSF

Railway Protection Force & Railway Protection Special Force

# Constable

## Recruitment Exam

*Useful for*

- Constable (Exe)
- Constable (Ancillary)
- Driver Grade III

**2027**
EDITION

RAMESH PUBLISHING HOUSE, NEW DELHI

***Published by***
O.P. Gupta *for* Ramesh Publishing House

***Admin. Office***
12-H, New Daryaganj Road, Opp. Officer's Mess,
New Delhi-110002 ✆ 23275224, 23245124

**E-mail:** info@rameshpublishinghouse.com
**For Online Shopping:** www.rameshpublishinghouse.com

***Showroom***
• Balaji Market, Nai Sarak, Delhi-6 ✆ 23282525 📱 9354373464
• 4457, Nai Sarak, Delhi-6, ✆ 23918938



**Book Code: R-1398**

**ISBN: 978-93-5012-097-2**

**Price: ₹ 310**

**Printed at: B.K. Offset, Delhi**

# CONTENTS

Previous Years' Paper

## Railway Protection Force & Railway Protection Special Force

# RPF/RPSF—CONSTABLE

## Recruitment Exam-2025

(Exam held on 10-03-2025)

**1.** Arjun can do a piece of work in 4 hours. Kartik can do it in 48 hours. With the assistance of Ishan, they completed the work in 3 hours. In how many hours can Ishan alone do it?

1. 17
2. 16
3. 18
4. 15

**2.** Evaluate:

41 – [36 – {48 ÷ 2 – (5 – 10 ÷ 2) ÷ 3}]

1. 30
2. 29
3. 28
3. 31

**3.** Calculate the smallest five-digit number divisible by 9, 11 and 21.

1. 10390
2. 10385
3. 10830
4. 10395

**4.** Evaluate:

$$\sqrt{\left(17+\sqrt{\left(56+\sqrt{\left(60+\sqrt{\left(9+\sqrt{(49)}\right)}\right)}\right)}\right)}$$

1. 5
3. 4
3. 8
4. 2

**5.** If the distance between A and B is 1084 Km. From A, Vishal goes to B with speed 104 km/h and return to A with the speed 112 km/h. Find the average speed of Vishal. (rounded off to two decimal place)

1. 110.64 km/h
2. 110.52 km/h
3. 102.18 km/h
4. 107.85 km/h

**6.** Three partners invested in a business in the ratio 6 : 7 : 9. They invested their capitals for 7 months, 3 months and 9 months, respectively. What was the ratio of their profits?

1. 15 : 7 : 27
2. 13 : 7 : 27
3. 17 : 7 : 27
4. 14 : 7 : 27

**7.** Two banks, A and B, offered loans at 3.5% and 6% per annum, respectively. Chetan borrowed an amount of ₹ 420000 from each bank. Find the positive difference between the amounts of simple interest paid to the two banks by Chetan after 2 years.

1. 20500
2. 22000
3. 22500
4. 21000

**8.** Train A leaves station M at 7:30 AM and reaches station N at 2:30 PM on the same day. Train B leaves station N at 9:30 AM and reaches station M at 2:30 PM on the same day. Find the time when Trains A and B meet.

1. 11:35 AM
2. 11:30 PM
3. 07:08 AM
4. 01:43 PM

| **1.** 2 | **2.** 2 | **3.** 4 | **4.** 1 | **5.** 4 | **6.** 4 | **7.** 4 | **8.** 1 |
|---|---|---|---|---|---|---|---|

**9.** A bus travelling at 56 km/h completes a journey in 16 hours. At what speed will it have to cover the same distance in 8 hours?

1. 112 km/h 2. 118 km/h
3. 106 km/h 4. 103 km/h

**10.** If 40% of $k$ is 10 less than 1200% of 10, then $k$ is:

1. 235 2. 275
3. 315 4. 255

**11.** The cost price of 30 articles is the same as the marked price of $x$ articles. If the profit is 20%, then find the value of $x$.

1. 35 2. 20
3. 25 4. 30

**12.** Two types of rice costing ₹ 50 per kg and ₹ 70 per kg are mixed together to make a blend that costs ₹ 60 per kg. In what ratio should the two types of rice be mixed?

1. 2 : 3 2. 4 : 3
3. 3 : 2 4. 1 : 1

**13.** The prices of three items are ₹ 120, ₹ 150 and ₹ 180. On these items, respectively, 20%, 10% and 5% profits are earned. The overall profit on the items is ........%.

1. $10\frac{1}{3}$ 2. $8\frac{1}{3}$
3. $8\frac{2}{3}$ 4. $10\frac{2}{3}$

**14.** The simplified value of the expression

$$\frac{0.75^2 - 0.25^2}{2} \times \frac{2.5^2 - 1.5^2}{4} \times \frac{1}{0.25}$$ is:

1. –1 2. 0.5
3. 1 4. –0.5

**15.** The sum of 8 numbers is 888. Find their average.

1. 112 2. 109
3. 110 4. 111

**16.** 2 men can complete a piece of work in 15 days while 5 women can do it in 14 days. In how many days can 7 women and 3 men complete it?

1. 8 days 2. 5 days
3. 6 days 4. 3 days

**17.** A hollow spherical shell is made of a metal of density 9 g/cm$^3$. Its internal and external radius are 10 cm and 13 cm, respectively. What is the weight (in kg) of the shell? $\left(\text{take } \pi = \frac{22}{7}\right)$

1. 46.67 2. 45.144
3. 42.144 4. 46.2

**18.** The average of first 138 even numbers is:

1. 139.5 2. 139
3. 140 4. 138.5

**19.** Find the volume of a given cone with height of 14 cm and diameter of the circular base of 6 cm. $\left(\text{use } \pi = \frac{22}{7}\right)$

1. 130 cm$^3$ 2. 132 cm$^3$
3. 232 cm$^3$ 4. 396 cm$^3$

**20.** Find the value of $18^{-13} \div 18^{18} \times 18^{-3}$

1. $18^{-29}$ 2. $18^{-34}$
3. $18^{-41}$ 4. $18^{-40}$

**21.** The price of milk was increased by 15% last year and this year, there is again an increment of 12% in the price. Two years ago, the price was ₹ 60, now the price of the milk is ₹ ............ .

1. 77.82 2. 78.72
3. 77.28 4. 78.27

| | | | | | | |
|---|---|---|---|---|---|---|
| **9.** 1 | **10.** 2 | **11.** 3 | **12.** 4 | **13.** 4 | **14.** 3 | **15.** 4 |
| **16.** 2 | **17.** 2 | **18.** 2 | **19.** 2 | **20.** 2 | **21.** 3 | |

**22.** After 56 litres of petrol was poured into an empty storage tank, it was still 10% empty. How much petrol (in litres, rounded off to two decimal place) must be poured into the storage tank in order to fill it?

1. 62.22
2. 57
3. 63.22
4. 61.22

**23.** An article is sold at a profit of 17%. If the selling price is doubled, the profit will be:

1. 34%
2. 200%
3. 68%
4. 134%

**24.** In what ratio should sugar costing ₹ 84 per kg be mixed with sugar costing ₹ 51 per kg so that by selling the mixture at ₹ 90.2 per kg, there is a profit of 10%?

1. 32 : 3
2. 31 : 2
3. 33 : 3
4. 35 : 2

**25.** The area of a trapezium is 330 $cm^2$, if the lengths of its parallel sides are 24 cm and 20 cm, find the distance between the parallel sides.

1. 15 cm
2. 10 cm
3. 20 cm
4. 25 cm

**26.** The sum of five numbers is 655. The average of the first two numbers is 77 and the third number is 129. Find the average of the remaining two numbers?

1. 187
2. 207
3. 206
4. 186

**27.** A merchant fixes the sale price of his goods at 90% above the cost price. He sells his goods at 18% discount. His percentage of profit is:

1. 55.8%
2. 59.6%
3. 58.5%
4. 53.7%

**28.** What is the greatest common divisor of 90, 1020 and 2340?

1. 5
2. 45
3. 10
4. 30

**29.** The population of a small city decreased every year due to water contamination. The present population of the town is 1,39,650. Last year, the migration was 2%, and the year before last, it was 5%. What was the population of the city two years ago?

1. 1,55,000
2. 1,45,000
3. 1,25,000
4. 1,50,000

**30.** A pipe A can fill a cistern in 12 hours, while pipe B can fill it in 8 hours. In how much time will the cistern be filled, if both pipes A and B are opened together?

1. 4 hours 48 minutes
2. 4 hours 12 minutes
3. 3 hours 54 minutes
4. 3 hours 26 minutes

**31.** A sum of ₹ 8,000 is invested at an annual interest rate of 12% compounded half-yearly for 2 years. Calculate the compound interest earned at the end of 2 years.(Rounded off to the nearest integer)

1. ₹ 2,100
2. ₹ 2,150
3. ₹ 2,280
4. ₹ 2,200

**32.** The least number which should be added to 6424 so that the sum is exactly divisible by 8, 9 and 12 is:

1. 26
2. 56
3. 36
4. 46

**33.** A 242 m long train crosses a man walking at a speed of 9.5 km/h in the opposite direction in 24 seconds. What is the speed (in km/h) of the train?

1. 23.8
2. 22.4
3. 26.8
4. 28.3

| | | | | | |
|---|---|---|---|---|---|
| **22.** 1 | **23.** 4 | **24.** 2 | **25.** 1 | **26.** 4 | **27.** 1 |
| **28.** 4 | **29.** 4 | **30.** 1 | **31.** 1 | **32.** 2 | **33.** 3 |

**34.** An amount of ₹ 968 is divided among three persons in the ratio of 16 : 13 : 15. The difference between the largest and the smallest shares (in ₹) in the distribution is:

1. 85
2. 28
3. 66
4. 20

**35.** Find the value of $\frac{62}{4} - 7 \times 2.5 + \sqrt[3]{2197}$.

1. 9.5
2. 14
3. 12.5
4. 11

**36.** Six people T, U, V, W, X, and Y are sitting in a straight row facing north. Only one person sits between W and V when counted from the left of V. Y sits third to the right of V. U sits to the immediate left of X. How many people sit between T and X?

1. Two
2. One
3. Four
4. Three

**37.** What should come in place of the question mark (?) in the given series?

57 70.4 88.8 112.2 140.6 ?

1. 182.2
2. 174
3. 188
4. 168.8

**38.** Select the set in which the numbers are related in the same way as are the numbers of the following sets.

(NOTE : Operations should be performed on the whole numbers, without breaking down the numbers into its constituent digits. E.g. 13 – Operations on 13 such as adding/ subtracting/multiplying etc. to 13 can be performed. Breaking down 13 into 1 and 3 and then performing mathematical operations on 1 and 3 is not allowed.)

(6, 11, 19)
(7, 12, 21)

1. (17, 23, 43)
2. (12, 17, 31)
3. (8, 13, 29)
4. (10, 5, 7)

**39.** Identify the figure given in the options which when put in place of '?' will logically complete the series.

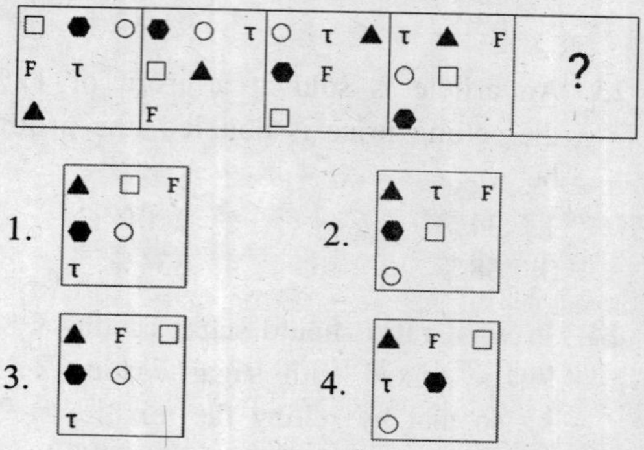

**40.** What should come in place of the question mark (?) in the given series?

32 36 47 51 62 66 ?

1. 76
2. 78
3. 77
4. 70

**41.** Y, A, K, S, E, N, and T are sitting around a circular table facing the centre. A sits second to the left of K. S sits second to the right of K. Only one person sits between S and E. T sits second to the right of Y. Only one person sits between E and N. Who sits to the immediate left of E?

1. K
2. A
3. S
4. T

**42.** Which of the following letter-number clusters will replace the question mark (?) in the given series to make it logically complete?

FOR 16, JIV 29, NCZ 42, RWD 55, ?

1. VQH 68
2. WQI 70
3. NCZ 68
4. NQZ 70

| **34.** 3 | **35.** 4 | **36.** 1 | **37.** 2 | **38.** 2 | **39.** 4 | **40.** 3 | **41.** 4 | **42.** 1 |
|---|---|---|---|---|---|---|---|---|

**43.** Select the pair that follows the same pattern as the one followed by the two set of pairs given below. Both pairs follow the same pattern.

BDF : GKK

GIK : LPP

1. ADE : EHI
2. MQT : QVX
3. JLO : NPQ
4. CMJ : HTO

**44.** Based on the English alphabetical order, three of the following four letter-clusters are alike in a certain way and thus form a group. Which letter-cluster DOES NOT belong to that group?

(Note: The odd one out is not based on the number of consonants/vowels or their position in the letter-cluster.)

1. NUB
2. IPW
3. VCI
4. GNU

**45.** This question is based on the five, three-digit numbers given below.

(Left) 458 652 483 617 456 (Right)

(Example- 697 – First digit = 6, second digit = 9 and third digit = 7)

(NOTE: All operations to be done from left to right.)

What will be the resultant if the third digit of the highest number is added to the second digit of the lowest number?

1. 7
2. 11
3. 9
4. 12

**46.** EGKN is related to PQVX in a certain way based on the English alphabetical order. In the same way, WUCB is related to HENL. To which of the given options is DYJF related, following the same logic?

1. POIU
2. OIUP
3. PIOU
4. OUPI

**47.** What should come in place of the question mark (?) in the given series based on the English alphabetical order?

PRU NPS LNQ JLO ?

1. HJN
2. HIN
3. HJM
4. HIM

**48.** In a certain code language, 'tea and coffee' is coded as 'nm hg bv' and 'tea is better' is coded as 'mn vb hg'. How is 'tea' coded in the given language?

1. bv
2. vb
3. nm
4. hg

**49.** Identify the option that when put in place of the question mark (?) will logically complete the series.

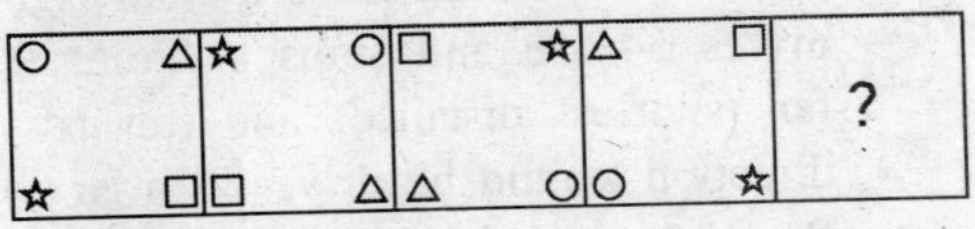

1. 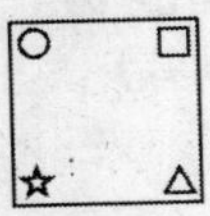
2. 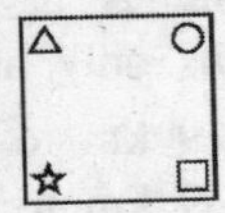
3. 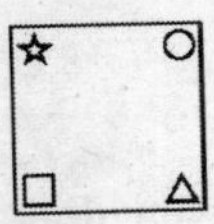
4. 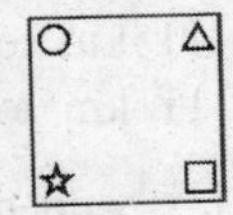

**50.** If you subtract the number formed by reversing the digits of 74 from the number 74 itself, what is the result?

1. 27
2. 12
3. 0
4. 36

**51.** In a certain code language, 'how was exam' is coded as 'xp or hg' and 'exam is tough' is coded as 'fs xp wl'. How is 'exam' coded in the given language?

1. fs
2. or
3. xp
4. hg

| **43.** 4 | **44.** 3 | **45.** 1 | **46.** 2 | **47.** 3 | **48.** 4 | **49.** 4 | **50.** 1 | **51.** 3 |
|---|---|---|---|---|---|---|---|---|

**52.** In a certain code language, 'MOTION' is coded as '121345' and 'SLOW' is coded as '1689'. What is the code for 'O' in the given code language?

1. 6
2. 1
3. 3
4. 4

**53.** What should come in place of the question mark (?) in the given series?

86 94 110 142 ? 334

1. 205
2. 206
3. 208
4. 204

**54.** Mr. Tigiri starts from Point A and drives 16 km towards west. He then takes a left turn, drives 17 km, turns right and drives 18 km. He then takes a right turn and drives 28 km. He takes a final right turn, drives 34 km and stops at Point P. How far (shortest distance) and towards which direction should he drive in order to reach Point A again? (All turns are 90-degree turns only unless specified.)

1. 9 km to the east
2. 9 km to the west
3. 11 km to the north
4. 11 km to the south

**55.** If 1 is added to each even digit and 3 is subtracted from each odd digit in the number 2935874, how many digits will appear more than once in the new number thus formed?

1. None
2. Two
3. Three
4. One

**56.** Read the given statements and conclusions carefully. Assuming that the information given in the statements is true, even if it appears to be at variance with commonly known facts, decide which of the given conclusion(s) logically follow(s) from the statements.

**Statements:**

All priests are teachers.

Some priests are singers.

**Conclusions:**

(I) Some singers are teachers.

(II) Some singers are priests.

1. Both conclusions (I) and (II) follow
2. Only conclusion (I) follows
3. Only conclusion (II) follows
4. Neither conclusion (I) nor (II) follows

**57.** Read the given statements and conclusions carefully. Assuming that the information given in the statements is true, even if it appears to be at variance with commonly known facts, decide which of the given conclusions logically follow(s) from the statements.

**Statements:**

All breads are donuts.

Some donuts are muffins.

No muffin is a fruit.

**Conclusions:**

(I) No bread is a fruit.

(II) Some muffins are breads.

1. Only conclusion (II) follows
2. Both conclusions (I) and (II) follow
3. Neither conclusion (I) nor (II) follows
4. Only conclusion (I) follows

**58.** All 48 people are standing in a row facing North. Sridesh is 31st from the right end while Niraj is 26th from the left end. How many people are there between Sridesh and Niraj?

1. 8
2. 5
3. 6
4. 7

| **52.** 2 | **53.** 2 | **54.** 4 | **55.** 1 | **56.** 1 | **57.** 3 | **58.** 4 |
|---|---|---|---|---|---|---|

**59.** Mr. Z starts from Point A and drives 3 km towards the north. He then takes a right turn, drives 2 km, turns right and drives 4 km. He then takes a right turn and drives 5 km. He takes a final right turn, drives 1 km and stops at Point P. How far (shortest distance) and towards which direction should he drive in order to reach Point A again? (All turns are 90° turns only unless specified.)

1. 2 km towards the south
2. 2 km towards the north
3. 1 km towards the west
4. 3 km towards the east

**60.** Refer to the following series and answer the question (all numbers are single digit numbers only).

(Left) 3 5 9 7 8 6 6 8 7 2 6 1 4 5 6 2 9 1 1 9 1 (Right)

How many such even digits are there each of which is immediately preceded by an odd digit and also immediately followed by an even digit?

1. Three 2. Two
3. One 4. Four

**61.** Based on the English alphabetical order, three of the following four letter-clusters are alike in a certain way and thus form a group. Which letter-cluster DOES NOT belong to that group?

(Note: The odd one out is not based on the number of consonants/vowels or their position in the letter-cluster.)

1. KHMQ 2. AXCH
3. PMRV 4. HEJN

**62.** Seven students, Q, R, S, T, W, X and Y, are sitting in a straight line facing north. Only R sits to the left of Q. Only four people sit between R and X. Only W sits between S and T, and S is not an immediate neighbour of X. How many people sit between Y and S?

1. One 2. Four
3. Two 4. Three

**63.** Refer to the following number and symbol series and answer the question that follows. Counting to be done from left to right only.

(Left) 7 $ % 5 & 8 2 @ 4 & 3 Ω 1 * 9 £ # 6 (Right)

If all the symbols are dropped from the series, which of the following will be fifth from the right?

1. 9 2. 3
3. 2 4. 4

**64.** FOR is related to CLO in a certain way. In the same way, POT is related to MLQ. To which of the following is RUN related, following the same logic?

1. KRO 2. UXQ
3. ORK 4. QXU

**65.** Eden ranked 21st from the bottom and 14th from the top in his class. How many students are there in his class?

1. 34 2. 33
3. 31 4. 32

**66.** Read the given statements and conclusions carefully. Assuming that the information given in the statements is true, even if it appears to be at variance with commonly known facts, decide which of the given conclusions logically follow(s) from the statements.

**Statements:** Some apples are rocks.
Some peanuts are crows.
All rocks are crows.

**Conclusions:**

(I) Some rocks are peanuts.
(II) Some crows are apples.

1. Only conclusion (II) follows.
2. Neither conclusion (I) nor (II) follows.
3. Both conclusions (I) and (II) follow.
4. Only conclusion (I) follows.

| **59.** 4 | **60.** 1 | **61.** 2 | **62.** 4 | **63.** 4 | **64.** 3 | **65.** 1 | **66.** 1 |
|---|---|---|---|---|---|---|---|

**67.** Which of the following letter-number clusters will replace the question mark (?) in the given series to make it logically complete?

ADB 1, EHF 4, ILJ 16, MPN 64, ?

1. QTR 256 2. QRT 128
3. QTR 32 4. QTR 128

**68.** In a certain code language,

A + B means 'A is the wife of B'

A – B means 'A is the brother of B'

A × B means 'A is the mother of B'

A ÷ B means 'A is the father of B'

Based on the above, how is P related to T if 'P + Q ÷ R – S × T'?

1. Mother-in-law 2. Granddaughter
3. Mother 4. Grandmother

**69.** In a certain code language,

A : B means 'A is the son of B'

A = B means ' A is the wife of B'

A * B means 'A is the brother of B'

A ? B means 'A is the father of B'

Based on the above, how is F related to N if 'F * A : L ? E = N'?

1. Wife's brother 2. Wife's sister
3. Wife's father 4. Wife's son

**70.** What is the difference between the number 49 and the number obtained by adding 4 to each digit of 49?

1. 789 2. 760
3. 657 4. 764

**71.** Which of the following is India's longest national waterway?

1. National Waterway 3 (NW 3)
2. National Waterway 2 (NW 2)
3. National Waterway 4 (NW 4)
4. National Waterway 1 (NW 1)

**72.** When was the Appellate Tribunal for Electricity established in India?

1. 2003 2. 2002
3. 2005 4. 2009

**73.** Which of the following promotes cross-border movement of resources?

1. Import restrictions
2. Foreign direct investment
3. Quotas
4. Tariffs

**74.** What was the year-on-year (Y-o-Y) growth in HDFC Bank's total deposits as of Q2 FY25?

1. 5% 2. 10%
3. 20% 4. 15%

**75.** When was the National Green Tribunal established in India?

1. 2010 2. 2003
3. 2005 4. 2014

**76.** The Indian National Congress session of 1905 took place in ............ .

1. Madras 2. Calcutta
3. Banaras 4. Lucknow

**77.** In September 2024, who was elected as the Chief Minister of Delhi?

1. Virender Jain 2. Atishi Marlena
3. Arvind Kejriwal 4. Manish Sisodia

**78.** Which of the following waterways of India is navigable by mechanical boats up to Patna and by ordinary boats up to Haridwar?

1. National Waterway 3 (NW 3)
2. National Waterway 2 (NW 2)
3. National Waterway 4 (NW 4)
4. National Waterway 1 (NW 1)

| | | | | | |
|---|---|---|---|---|---|
| **67.** 1 | **68.** 4 | **69.** 1 | **70.** 4 | **71.** 4 | **72.** 3 |
| **73.** 2 | **74.** 4 | **75.** 1 | **76.** 3 | **77.** 2 | **78.** 4 |

**79.** What was the primary strategy adopted by the Indian government in the 1950s for economic development?

1. Rapid industrialisation through centrally prepared five-year plans
2. Developing the agricultural sector as the foundation of the economy
3. Focusing on agricultural expansion and crop yield improvement
4. Encouraging private sector growth in basic and heavy industries

**80.** Right to Education is contained in which of the following Articles of the Indian Constitution?

1. Article 19 2. Article 17
3. Article 51 A 4. Article 21 A

**81.** SONAR technology utilises sound energy for navigation, particularly in underwater environments. What does the acronym 'SONAR' represent?

1. Sound Organized Navigation And Ranging
2. Sound Oscillation Navigation And Ranging
3. Sound Navigation And Ranging
4. Sound Observational Navigation And Ranging

**82.** The National Rural Employment Programme (NREP) was launched during which of the following five year plans?

1. 8th Five Year Plan
2. 7th Five Year Plan
3. 6th Five Year Plan
4. 5th Five Year Plan

**83.** Which of the following does NOT come in the Ghan Vadya category?

1. Gurki 2. Gedi
3. Dandia 4. Harmonium

**84.** Who is the author of the biography 'Manoj Bajpayee: The Definitive Biography', published in March 2024?

1. Tanuja Chaturvedi
2. Mukesh Manjunath
3. Piyush Pandey
4. Anustup Basu

**85.** Which of the following is the name of the new high-quality malaria vaccine, developed by the Serum Institute of India and the University of Oxford, rolled out in Africa from July 2024?

1. R22 2. R21
3. R20 4. R24

**86.** Padma Awards 2024 were conferred to how many women awardees by the President of India?

1. 28 2. 20
3. 30 4. 36

**87.** The Water (Prevention and Control of Pollution) Amendment Bill, 2024, will initially apply to how many states?

1. 4 2. 1
3. 5 4. 2

**88.** When was the Battle of Kanauj fought?

1. 1556 2. 1540
3. 1567 4. 1526

**89.** What is the projected fiscal deficit for the financial year 2024-25, as per the Union Budget?

1. 4.9% 2. 5.1%
3. 4.5% 4. 3.9%

**90.** In October 2024, the Indian Army's Sudarshan Chakra Corps conducted the 'Swavlamban Shakti' Exercise in which state?

1. Bihar 2. Uttar Pradesh
3. Madhya Pradesh 4. Haryana

| | | | | | |
|---|---|---|---|---|---|
| **79.** 1 | **80.** 4 | **81.** 3 | **82.** 3 | **83.** 4 | **84.** 3 |
| **85.** 2 | **86.** 3 | **87.** 4 | **88.** 2 | **89.** 2 | **90.** 2 |

**91.** Which desert is known as the Great Indian Desert?

1. Gobi Desert
2. Arabian Desert
3. Thar Desert
4. Sahara Desert

**92.** The Terai region is best known for:

1. rocky terrain
2. dry soil and sparse vegetation
3. rich forest cover and marshy land
4. salt pans

**93.** The Simhastha Kumbh Mela festival at Ujjain is celebrated on the banks of river ......... .

1. Narmada
2. Shipra
3. Betwa
4. Kuno

**94.** Which of the following is the main purpose of focusing on human development?

1. To ensure that individuals lead healthy, educated and productive lives
2. To promote economic growth only
3. To improve trade relations
4. To increase industrialisation

**95.** Which commander in chief of British army captured Lucknow during the revolt of 1857?

1. Sir Colin Campbell
2. Colonel Oncell
3. William Taylor and Eye
4. General Hugh Rose

**96.** Which of the following groups of states is part of the Great Indian Desert?

1. Rajasthan, Gujarat, Punjab and Haryana
2. Gujarat, Punjab, Haryana and Maharashtra
3. Punjab, Haryana, Rajasthan and Madhya Pradesh
4. Rajasthan, Gujarat, Madhya Pradesh and Uttar Pradesh

**97.** Which of the following banks appointed Amitava Chatterjee as its Managing Director and Chief Executive Officer, effective 30 December 2024?

1. Punjab National Bank
2. State Bank of India
3. ICICI Bank
4. Jammu & Kashmir Bank

**98.** Under which Article of the Indian Constitution can the President of India seek the advisory opinion of the Supreme Court?

1. Article 141
2. Article 143
3. Article 129
4. Article 148

**99.** Kanuma festival is celebrated on which day of Sankranti by Hindus in the south Indian states, especially in Andhra Pradesh and Telangana?

1. Fifth
2. Seventh
3. Second
4. Third

**100.** How many medals and Medallions of Excellence were won by India at WorldSkills Lyon 2024 in France?

1. 8
2. 4
3. 16
4. 12

**101.** The Union cabinet in September 2024 approved Chandrayaan-4 and ......... .

1. Neptune Orbiter Mission
2. Mars Orbiter Mission
3. Venus Orbiter Mission
4. Jupiter Orbiter Mission

**102.** The Indian Councils Act, 1861, initiated the process of decentralisation by restoring legislative powers to which provinces?

1. Punjab and Bengal
2. United Provinces and Assam
3. Bihar and Orissa
4. Bombay and Madras

| | | | | | |
|---|---|---|---|---|---|
| **91.** 3 | **92.** 3 | **93.** 2 | **94.** 1 | **95.** 1 | **96.** 1 |
| **97.** 4 | **98.** 2 | **99.** 4 | **100.** 3 | **101.** 3 | **102.** 4 |

**103.** What role does the Economic Survey 2024 attribute to the tripartite compact in achieving India's development goals?

1. Reduces foreign influence
2. Focuses on self-reliance
3. Increases government power
4. Ensures cooperation between central, state governments and private sector

**104.** Which of the following is a traditional hornpipe instrument of Assam made from buffalo horn?

1. Khol
2. Chang
3. Pongi
4. Pepa

**105.** The British adopted which of the following policies with respect to landlords and zamindars after the Revolt of 1857?

1. The policy of land redistribution
2. The policy of confiscation of property
3. Policies that protected their rights and provided security over their lands
4. The policy of land nationalisation

**106.** In which country was the 44th session of the Codex Committee on Nutrition and Foods for Special Dietary Uses (CCNFSDU) held from 2 October to 6 October 2024?

1. New Zealand
2. Germany
3. Peru
4. Canada

**107.** SBI's loan loss provisions increased by how much percentage in Q3 FY24 year-over-year?

1. 10.75%
2. 13.02%
3. 35.5%
4. 36.05%

**108.** What ideology did the extremists strongly oppose within the Indian National Congress?

1. Nationalism
2. Swadeshi
3. Gradualism
4. Self-governance

**109.** Which of the following vector quantities has the same dimensions as of the scalar quantity 'work'?

1. Angular momentum
2. Gravitational constant
3. Torque
4. Force

**110.** Which of the following Articles states that the Chief Minister shall communicate to the Governor all decisions of the Council of Ministers?

1. Article 163
2. Article 168
3. Article 164
4. Article 167

**111.** On which date did the Constituent Assembly give the third reading of the Constitution?

1. 17 October 1949
2. 14 November 1949
3. 29 August 1947
4. 26 November 1949

**112.** The element ........... is commonly used in aircraft construction.

1. Hafnium
2. Zirconium
3. Osmium
4. Titanium

**113.** Who was the last ruler of the Sayyid dynasty?

1. Mubarak Shah
2. Muhammad Shah
3. Alauddin Alam Shah
4. Khizr Khan

**114.** What is rural development?

1. Improving the quality of life and economic well-being of people living in rural areas
2. Development of urban infrastructure
3. Shifting rural people to urban areas
4. Industrialisation of rural areas

| | | | | | |
|---|---|---|---|---|---|
| **103.** 4 | **104.** 4 | **105.** 3 | **106.** 2 | **107.** 1 | **108.** 3 |
| **109.** 3 | **110.** 4 | **111.** 4 | **112.** 4 | **113.** 3 | **114.** 1 |

**115.** Which Indian state is the leader in solar power generation with its largest installed capacity?

1. Gujarat
2. Karnataka
3. Rajasthan
4. Tamil Nadu

**116.** Who among the following gave sharp criticism of imperialism, termed as 'drain of wealth', which was a milestone in the mainstream Indian independence movement?

1. Bhimrao Ramji Ambedkar
2. Dadabhai Naoroji
3. Zakir Husain
4. Chakravarti Rajagopalachari

**117.** In the context of inheritance of sex chromosomes in humans, which of the following statements is correct?

1. All children inherit a Y chromosome from their father, and the sex is determined by the chromosome inherited from their mother.
2. All children inherit a Y chromosome from their mother, and the sex is determined by the chromosome inherited from their father.
3. All children inherit an X chromosome from their father, and the sex is determined by the chromosome inherited from their mother.
4. All children inherit an X chromosome from their mother, and the sex is determined by the chromosome inherited from their father.

**118.** The famous 'Sam Sand Dunes' region is located in which state of India?

1. Punjab
2. Gujarat
3. Rajasthan
4. Haryana

**119.** What has been a major environmental challenge linked to globalisation in India?

1. Reduction in industrialisation
2. Pollution and overuse of natural resources
3. Decrease in foreign investments due to regulations
4. Increase in deforestation laws

**120.** Which law or principle explains the connection between fluid velocity and pressure in a moving fluid?

1. Archimedes' Principle
2. Boyle's Law
3. Pascal's Law
4. Bernoulli's Principle

## EXPLANATORY ANSWERS

**1. (2):** Arjun's 1 hour's work $= \frac{1}{4}$

Kartik's 1 hour's work $= \frac{1}{48}$

Let Ishan alone can do it in $x$ hours

Then, Ishan's 1 hour's work $= \frac{1}{x}$

According to the question,

$$\frac{1}{4}+\frac{1}{48}+\frac{1}{x}=\frac{1}{3}$$

$$\Rightarrow \frac{12+1}{48}+\frac{1}{x}=\frac{1}{3}$$

$$\Rightarrow \frac{13}{48}+\frac{1}{x}=\frac{1}{3}$$

$$\Rightarrow \frac{1}{x}=\frac{1}{3}-\frac{13}{48}$$

$$\Rightarrow \frac{1}{x}=\frac{16-13}{48}$$

$$\Rightarrow \frac{1}{x}=\frac{3}{48}$$

| 115. 3 | 116. 2 | 117. 4 | 118. 3 | 119. 2 | 120. 4 |
|---|---|---|---|---|---|

$\Rightarrow \frac{1}{x} = \frac{1}{16}$

$\Rightarrow x = 16$

$\therefore$ Ishan alone can do it in 16 hours.

**2. (2):** $41 - [36 - \{48 \div 2 - (5 - 10 \div 2) \div 3\}]$

$= 41 - [36 - \{48 \div 2 - (5 - 5) \div 3\}]$

$= 41 - [36 - \{48 \div 2 - 0 \div 3\}]$

$= 41 - [36 - \{24 - 0\}]$

$= 41 - [36 - 24]$

$= 41 - 12$

$= 29$

**3. (4):** LCM of 9, 11 and 21 = 693

$\because$ Smallest five digit number = 10000

$\therefore$ 693 × 15 = 10,395

$\therefore$ The smallest five digit number is 10,395 which is divisible by 9, 11 and 21.

**4. (1):** $\sqrt{\left(17+\sqrt{\left(56+\sqrt{\left(60+\sqrt{\left(9+\sqrt{(49)}\right)}\right)}\right)}\right)}$

$= \sqrt{17+\sqrt{56+\sqrt{60+\sqrt{9+7}}}}$

$= \sqrt{17+\sqrt{56+\sqrt{60+\sqrt{16}}}}$

$= \sqrt{17+\sqrt{56+\sqrt{60+4}}}$

$= \sqrt{17+\sqrt{56+\sqrt{64}}}$

$= \sqrt{17+\sqrt{56+8}}$

$= \sqrt{17+\sqrt{64}}$

$= \sqrt{17+8}$

$= \sqrt{25}$

$= 5.$

**5. (4):** The average speed of Vishal $= \frac{2xy}{x+y}$

$= \frac{2 \times 104 \times 112}{104 + 112}$

$= \frac{2 \times 104 \times 112}{216}$

$= \frac{1 \times 104 \times 112}{108}$

$= \frac{26 \times 112}{27}$

$= 0.963 \times 112$

$= 107.85$ km/h.

**6. (4):** Ratio of their profit

$= 6 \times 7 : 7 \times 3 : 9 \times 9$

$= 2 \times 7 : 7 \times 1 : 3 \times 9$

$= 14 : 7 : 27.$

**7. (4):** Simple interest for Bank A $= \frac{prt}{100}$

$= \frac{420000 \times 3.5 \times 2}{100}$

$= 4200 \times 7 =$ ₹ 29400

and Simple interest for Bank B $= \frac{prt}{100}$

$= \frac{420000 \times 6 \times 2}{100}$

$= 4200 \times 12 =$ ₹ 50400

$\therefore$ The required positive difference of S.I.

$= 50400 - 29400$

= ₹ 21000.

**8. (1):** Given,

Train A leaves M at 7.30 AM and reaches N at 2.30 PM on the same day.

and Train B leaves N at 7.30 AM and reaches M at 2.30 PM on the same day.

Hence, Train A and B meet at 11:35 AM.

**9. (1):** The distance of journey = Speed × time

$= 56 \times 16 = 896$

$\therefore$ Required speed in 8 hours $= \frac{\text{Distance}}{\text{Time}}$

$= \frac{896}{8} = 112$ km/h

**10. (2):** Given, 40% of $k$ = 1200% of 10 – 10

$\Rightarrow k \times \frac{40}{100} = 10 \times \frac{1200}{100} - 10$

$\Rightarrow \frac{2}{5}k = 120 - 10 = 110$

$\Rightarrow k = 55 \times 5 = 275$

**11. (3):** Let C.P. of 1 article = ₹ 1

Then, C.P. of $x$ articles = ₹ $x$

and M.P. of $x$ articles = ₹ 30

$$\therefore \quad x \times \frac{120}{100} = 30$$

$$\Rightarrow \quad x \times \frac{6}{5} = 30$$

$$\Rightarrow \quad x = 30 \times \frac{5}{6}$$

$$\Rightarrow \quad x = 5 \times 5 = ₹\ 25$$

**12. (4):** By the law of Alligation

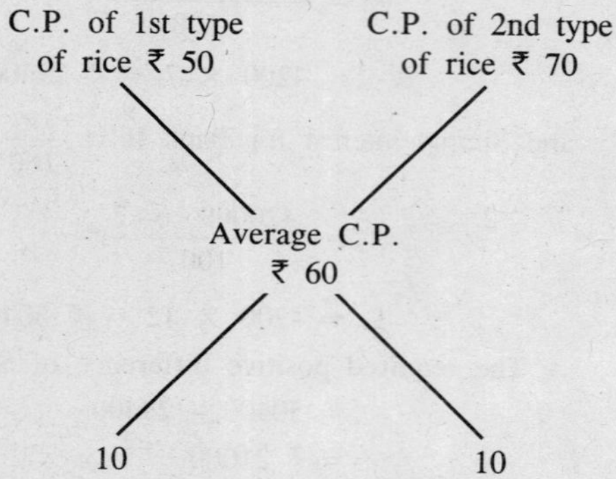


∴ Required ratio of the two types of rice be

Mixed = 10 : 10 = 1 : 1.

**13. (4):** C.P. of 3 items = ₹ 120 + ₹ 150 + ₹ 180
= ₹ 450

and S.P. of 3 items

$$= 120 \times \frac{120}{100} + 150 \times \frac{110}{100} + 180 \times \frac{105}{100}$$

= 144 + 165 + 189

= ₹ 498

∵ Profit = S.P. – C.P.

= ₹ 498 – ₹ 450

= ₹ 48

$$\therefore \text{Profit \%} = \frac{\text{Profit} \times 100}{\text{C.P.}}$$

$$= \frac{48 \times 100}{450} = 48 \times \frac{2}{9}$$

$$= 16 \times \frac{2}{3} = \frac{32}{3} = 10\frac{2}{3}\%$$

**14. (3):** $\frac{0.75^2 - 0.25^2}{2} \times \frac{2.5^2 - 1.5^2}{4} \times \frac{1}{0.25}$

$$= \frac{(0.75-0.25)(0.75+0.25)}{2} \times \frac{(2.5-1.5)(2.5+1.5)}{4} \times \frac{1}{0.25}$$

$$= \frac{0.50 \times 1.00}{2} \times \frac{1.0 \times 4.0}{4} \times \frac{1}{0.25}$$

$$= 0.25 \times 1 \times \frac{1}{0.25}$$

= 1.

**15. (4):** The sum of 8 numbers = 888

$$\Rightarrow \quad \text{Their average} = \frac{888}{8} = 111.$$

**16. (2):** 1 man's 1 day's work = $\frac{1}{30}$

and 1 woman's 1 day's work = $\frac{1}{70}$

∴ (7 women + 3 men)'s 1 day's work

$$= \frac{7}{70} + \frac{3}{30}$$

$$= \frac{1}{10} + \frac{1}{10} = \frac{2}{10} = \frac{1}{5}$$

∴ 7 women and 3 men can complete it in 5 days.

**17. (2):** ∵ Volume of sphere = $\frac{4}{3}\pi r^3$

∴ The volume of spherical shell

$$= \frac{4}{3}\pi \times 13^3 - \frac{4}{3}\pi \times 10^3$$

$$= \frac{4}{3}\pi(13^3 - 10^3)$$

$$= \frac{4}{3}\pi(13-10)(13^2 + 13 \times 10 + 10^2)$$

$$= \frac{4}{3} \times \frac{22}{7} \times 3 \times (169 + 130 + 100)$$

$$= 4 \times \frac{22}{7} \times 399$$

= 88 × 57

= 5016 $cm^3$

[Given, metal of density 9 $g/cm^3$]

$\therefore$ The weight of the shell $= 5016 \times 9g$

$= 45144g$

$= \frac{45144}{1000}$ kg

$= 45.144$ kg.

**18. (2):** Here, 1st term $= a = 2$,

$d$ = common difference $= 2$,

$n$ = number of terms $= 138$

$\because \quad S_n = \frac{n}{2}[2a+(n-1)d]$

$= \frac{138}{2}[2\times 2+(138-1)\times 2]$

$= \frac{138}{2}\times 2[2+137]$

$= 138 \times 139$

$\therefore$ The sum of first 138 even numbers $= 138 \times 139$

$\therefore$ The required Average $= \frac{138\times 139}{138} = 139$.

**19. (2):** Here $h = 14$ cm, diameter of a circular base $= 6$ cm

$\Rightarrow 2r = 6$

$\Rightarrow r = 3$ cm

$\therefore$ The volume of a cone $= \frac{1}{3}\pi r^2 h$

$= \frac{1}{3}\times\frac{22}{7}\times 3^2\times 14$

$= 22 \times 3 \times 2$

$= 132$ cm$^3$.

**20. (2):** $18^{-13} \div 18^{18} \times 18^{-3}$

$= \frac{1}{18^{13}} \div 18^{18} \times \frac{1}{18^{3}}$

$= \frac{1}{18^{13}} \times \frac{1}{18^{18}} \times \frac{1}{18^{3}}$

$= \frac{1}{18^{13+18+3}}$

$= \frac{1}{18^{34}} = 18^{-34}$.

**21. (3):** Two years ago, the price of milk = ₹ 60.

Now, the price of the milk $= 60\times\frac{115}{100}\times\frac{112}{100}$

$= 3\times\frac{115}{5}\times\frac{112}{100}$

$= 3\times 23\times\frac{28}{25}$

$= \frac{1932}{25}$

$= 77.28\%$.

**22. (1):** Let $x$ litres petrol must be poured into the storage tank in order to fill it.

Then, $x\times\frac{100-10}{100} = 56$

$\Rightarrow \quad x\times\frac{90}{100} = 56$

$\Rightarrow \quad x\times\frac{9}{10} = 56$

$\Rightarrow \quad x = \frac{56\times 10}{9} = \frac{560}{9}$

$\Rightarrow \quad x = 62.22$ litres.

**23. (4):** Let the C.P. of an article = ₹ 100

Then, S.P. = 100 + 17 = ₹ 117

Given, the S.P. is double

$\therefore$ New S.P. = 2 × ₹ 117

= ₹ 234

$\therefore$ Profit = New S.P. – C.P.

= 234 – 100

= 134

$\therefore$ The profit will be 134%.

**24. (2):** Given S.P. of the mixture = ₹ 90.2 per kg

$\therefore$ C.P. per kg $= 90.2\times\frac{100}{100+10}$

$= 90.2\times\frac{100}{110} = 90.2\times\frac{10}{11}$

$= 8.2 \times 10$

= ₹ 82

By the law of Alligation:

C.P. per kg of 1st type sugar ₹ 84 | C.P. per kg of 2nd type sugar ₹ 51

Average C.P. per kg of sugar ₹ 82

31 | 2

∴ The required ratio = 31 : 2.

**25. (1):** Let distance between the parallel sides be $x$ cm.

Then, Area of a trapezium

$\Rightarrow \quad = \frac{1}{2}$ (Sum of parallel sides) $\times h$

$\Rightarrow \quad 330 = \frac{1}{2} \times (24 + 20) \times x$

$\Rightarrow \quad 330 = \frac{1}{2} \times 44 \times x$

$\Rightarrow \quad 330 = 22 \times x$

$\Rightarrow \quad x = \frac{330}{22} = \frac{30}{2} = 15$

$\Rightarrow \quad x = 15$ cm.

**26. (4):** Given, the sum of 5 numbers = 655

The average of the first two numbers = 77

∴ The sum of the first two numbers

= 2 × 77 = 154

and the third number = 129

∴ The sum of the first three numbers

= 154 + 129 = 283

∴ The sum of the remaining two numbers

= 655 − 283 = 372

Hence, the average of the remaining two numbers

$= \frac{372}{2}$

= 186

**27. (1):** Let the cost price of goods be ₹ 100

Then, the selling price = 100 + 90 = ₹ 190

Given, discount = 18%

∴ Final selling price $= 190 \times \frac{(100-18)}{100}$

$= 190 \times \frac{82}{100}$

$= 19 \times \frac{41}{5} = \frac{779}{5}$

= 155.8

∴ Profit = Final selling price − cost price

= 155.8 − 100

= ₹ 55.8

His percentage of profit is 55.8%.

**28. (4):** $90 = 2 \times 3^2 \times 5$,

$1020 = 2^2 \times 3 \times 5 \times 17$,

$2340 = 2^2 \times 3^2 \times 5 \times 13$

∴ The greatest common divisor of

90, 1020 and 2340 = 2 × 3 × 5 = 30

**29. (4):** Two years ago the population of the city.

$$= \frac{1,39,650}{\left(1-\frac{2}{100}\right)\left(1-\frac{5}{100}\right)}$$

$$= \frac{1,39,650}{\frac{98}{100} \times \frac{95}{100}}$$

$$= 1,39,650 \times \frac{100}{98} \times \frac{100}{95}$$

$$= 1,39,650 \times \frac{50}{49} \times \frac{20}{19}$$

$$= 2,850 \times 50 \times \frac{20}{19}$$

= 150 × 50 × 20

= 1,50,000.

**30. (1):** Part filled by A in 1 hour $= \frac{1}{12}$

and part filled by B in 1 hour $= \frac{1}{8}$

∴ Part filled by (A + B) in 1 hour

$$= \frac{1}{12} + \frac{1}{8}$$

$$= \frac{2+3}{24} = \frac{5}{24}$$

$\therefore$ The cistern will be filled in $\frac{24}{5}$ hr. $= 4\frac{1}{5}$ hr.

$= 4$ hr. 48 m.

**31. (1):** Given, P = ₹ 8000, $r = 12\%$ p.a.

$\because$ Compounded half-yearly for 2 years.

$\therefore \quad r = 6\%,\ n = 4$

$$\therefore \text{Compound interest} = P\left(1+\frac{r}{100}\right)^n - P$$

$$= P\left[\left(1+\frac{r}{100}\right)^n - 1\right]$$

$$= 8000\left[\left(1+\frac{6}{100}\right)^4 - 1\right]$$

$$= 8000\left[\left(\frac{53}{50}\right)^4 - 1\right]$$

$$= 8000\left[\frac{7890481}{6250000} - 1\right]$$

$$= 8000\left[\frac{1640481}{6250000}\right]$$

$$= 8\times\frac{1640481}{6250} = \frac{4\times 1640481}{3125}$$

$= 4 \times 524.95392$

$= 2099.81568$

$=$ ₹ 2,100

$\Rightarrow$ Required compound interest = ₹ 2,100.

**32. (2):** LCM of 8, 9 and 12 = 72

$\because \quad 72 \times 90 = 6480$

$\therefore$ The least required number should be added

$= 6480 - 6424 = 56.$

**33. (3):** Given, length of a train = 242 m

Speed of a man = 9.5 km/h

Let the speed of the train be $x$ km/h

$\because$ Train crosses a man in the opposite direction

$\therefore$ Relative Speed $= (9.5 + x)$km/h

$$= (9.5 + x) \times \frac{5}{18} \text{ m/s.}$$

$$\therefore \quad \frac{242}{24} = (9.5 + x) \times \frac{5}{18}$$

$$\Rightarrow \quad 9.5 + x = \frac{242\times 18}{24\times 5}$$

$$\Rightarrow \quad 9.5 + x = \frac{242\times 3}{4\times 5}$$

$$\Rightarrow \quad 9.5 + x = \frac{363}{10}$$

$\Rightarrow \quad 9.5 + x = 36.3$

$\Rightarrow \quad x = 36.3 - 9.5 = 26.8$

Hence, the speed of the train $= x = 26.8$ km/hr.

**34. (3):** Let the share of three persons be $16x$, $13x$ and $15x$.

Given, Amount = ₹ 968

$\therefore \quad 16x + 13x + 15x = 968$

$\Rightarrow \quad 44x = 968$

$\Rightarrow \quad x = \frac{968}{44} = \frac{88}{4} = 22$

$\Rightarrow \quad x = 22$

$\therefore$ The difference between the largest and the smallest shares

$= 16x - 13x$

$= 3x = 3 \times 22 = 66.$

**35. (4):** $\frac{62}{4} - 7\times 2.5 + \sqrt[3]{2197}$

$$= \frac{31}{2} - 17.5 + (13^3)^{1/3}$$

$= 15.5 - 17.5 + 13$

$= 28.5 - 17.5$

$= 11.0 = 11.$

**36. (1):** Given, six people are sitting in a straight row facing north

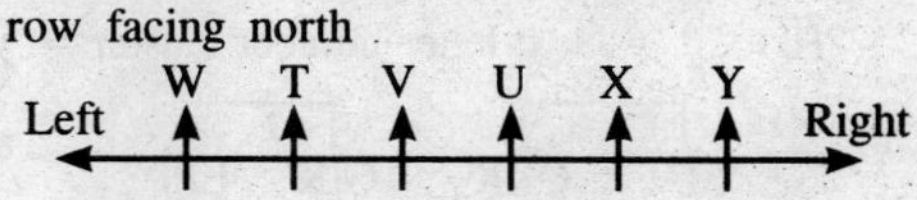


Here, Two people sit between T and X

**37. (2):** Given, Series:

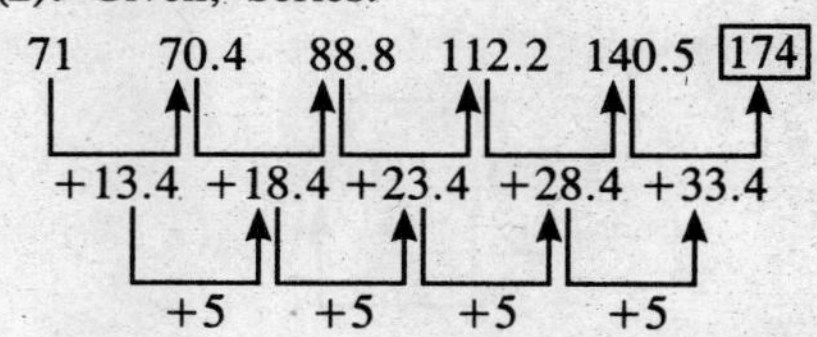


Here, ? = 174 $\Rightarrow$ 174 should come in place of the question mark in the given series.

**38. (2):** Given sets:

(6, 11, 19)

$\Rightarrow 19 - 6 - 2 = 19 - 8 = 11$

(7, 12, 21)

$\Rightarrow 21 - 7 - 2 = 21 - 9 = 12$

Similarly,

(12, 17, 31)

$\Rightarrow 31 - 12 - 2 = 31 - 14 = 17$

$\therefore$ Option (2) is related in the same way as are the numbers of the given sets.

**40. (3):**

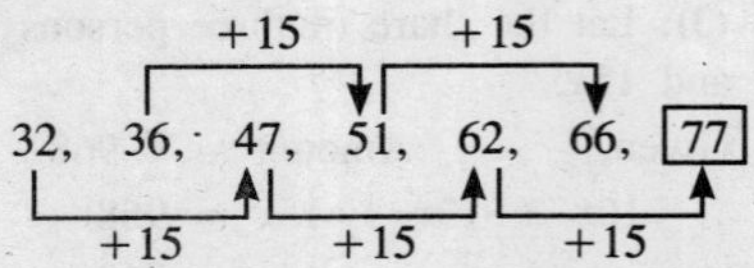


Hence, 77 will come in place of question mark.

**41. (4):** Given Y, A, K, S, E, N and T are sitting around a circular table facing the centre.

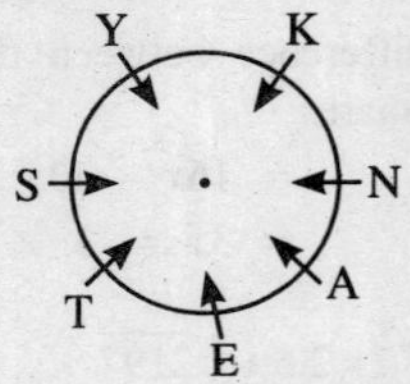


Here, T sits to the immediate left of E.

**42. (1):**

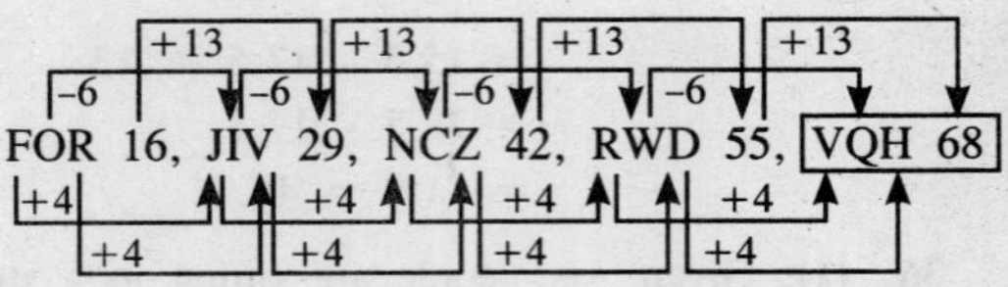


Here, ? = Next letter-number cluster = VQH 68

**43. (4):**

Similarly,

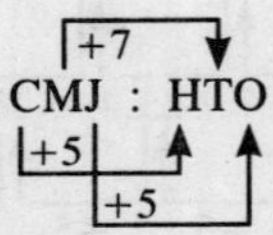


Here, option (4) follows the same pattern as the one followed by the two set of pairs given.

**44. (3):**

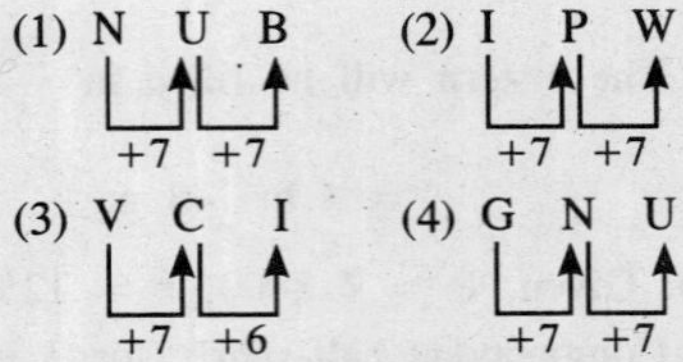


Here, option (3) does not belong to the group.

**45. (1):** Given, the five, three-digit numbers.
458, 652, 483, 617, 456

$\therefore$ The third digit of the highest number (652) = 2

And the second digit of the lowest number (456) = 5

$\therefore$ The resultant = 2 + 5 = 7.

**46. (2):** Given,

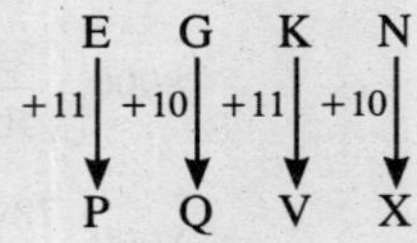


and

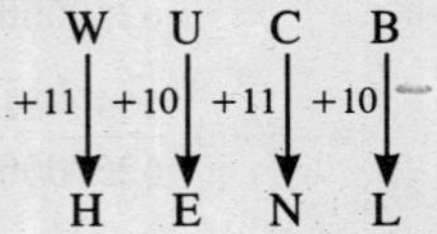


Similarly,

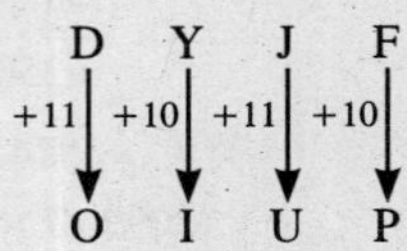


$\therefore$ DYJF is related to OIUP in the same logic.

**47. (3):**

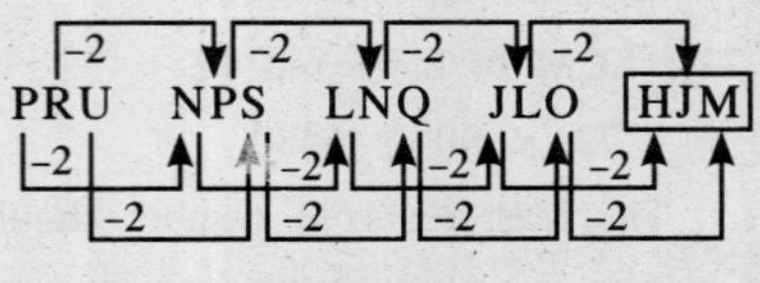


Here, HJM should come in place of the question mark i.e., ? = HJM.

**48. (4):** Given,

'tea and coffee' = 'nm hg bv' ...(*i*)

and 'tea is better' = 'mn vb bg' ...(*ii*)

from (*i*) and (*ii*), we have

'tea' = 'hg'

$\therefore$ 'tea' is coded as 'hg'

**50. (1):** The required result = 74 − 47 = 27.

**51. (3):** Given,

'how was exam' = 'xp or hg' ...(*i*)

and 'exam is tough' = 'fs xp wl' ...(*ii*)

from (*i*) and (*ii*), we get

'exam' = 'xp'

∴ 'exam' is coded as 'xp' in the given language.

**52. (2):** Given, 'MOTION' = '121345' ...(*i*)

and SLOW = '1689' ...(*ii*)

from (*i*) and (*ii*), we get

0 = 1

∴ '1' is the code for '0' in the given code language.

**53. (2):** 86 94 110 142 [206] 334

+8 +16 +32 +64 +128

×2 ×2 ×2 ×2

Here, ? = the missing term = 206.

**54. (4):**

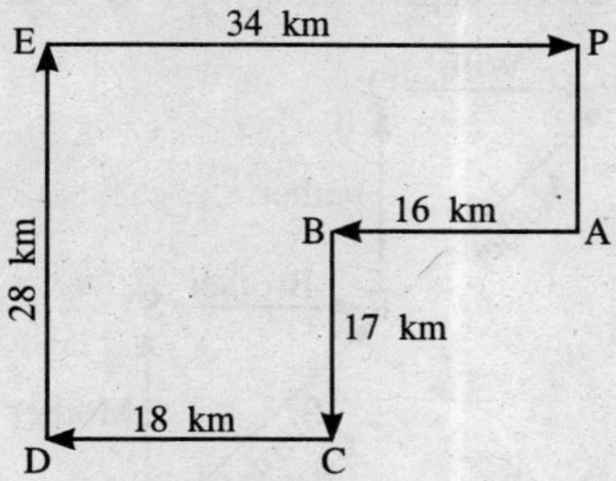


Here, Starting point = A

and Last point = P

∵ AB + CD = 16 + 18 = 34 km

∴ AB + CD = EP = 34 km

and PA + BC = DE = 28 km

⇒ PA + 17 = 28

⇒ PA = 11 km

∴ He should drive 11 km to South direction in order to reach point A again.

**55. (1):** Given, 2935874

∴ 2 9 3 5 8 7 4

+1 –3 –3 –3 +1 –3 +1

3 6 0 2 9 4 5

∴ New number = 3602948

∴ None of the digits will appear more than once in the new number thus formed.

**56. (1):** From given statements.

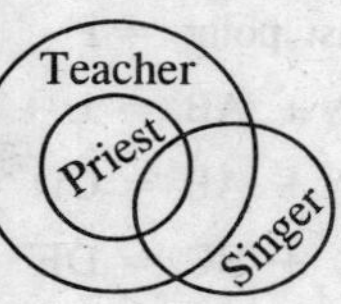


**Conclusions:**

I. Some singers are teachers. (true)

II. Some singers are priests. (true)

Here, Both conclusions I and II follow.

**57. (3):** From given statements:

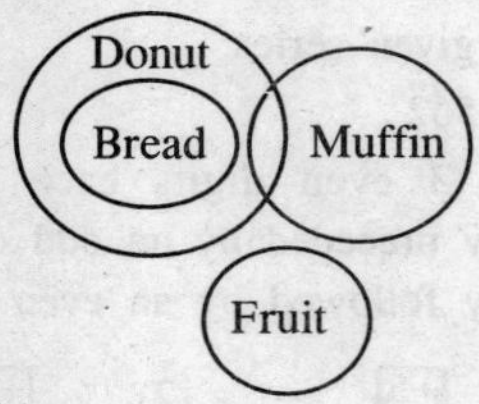


**Conclusions:**

I. No bread is a fruit. (false)

II. Some muffins are breads. (false)

Here, Neither conclusion (I) nor (II) follows.

**58. (4):** Given, All 48 people are standing in a row facing North

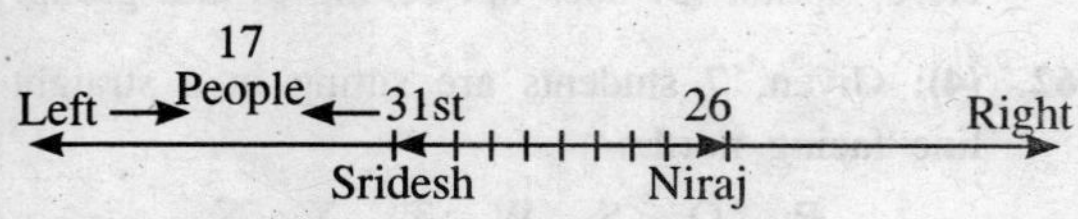


∵ Sridesh is 31st from the right

∴ 48 – 31 = 17 people are left from Sridesh.

and Niraj is 26th from the left end.

∴ 17 + 9 = 26

*i.e.*, 17 + 1 + 7 + 1 = 26

∴ There are 9 – 2 = 7 people between Sridesh and Niraj.

**59. (4):**

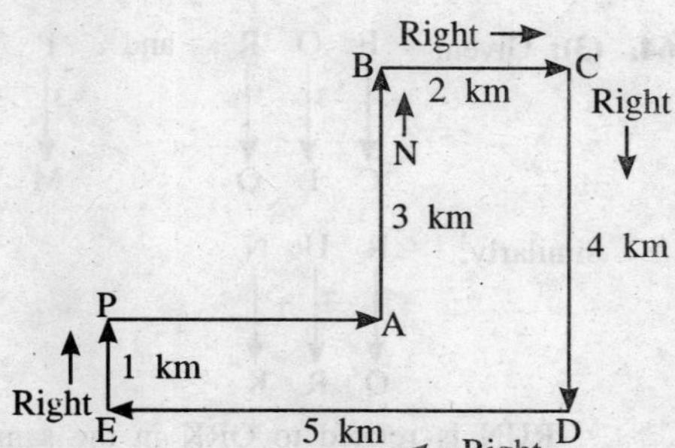

Here, Starting point = A

Last point = P

∵ EP + AB = 1 + 3 = 4 km

∴ EP + AB = CD = 4 km

and PA + BC = DE

⇒ PA + 2 = 5

⇒ PA = 5 − 2 = 3

⇒ PA = 3 km

Mr. Z should drive 3 km towards East direction in order to reach point A again.

**60. (1):** From given series:

786, 726, 562

There are 3 even digits each of which is immediately preceded by an odd digit and also immediately followed by an even digit.

**61. (2):**

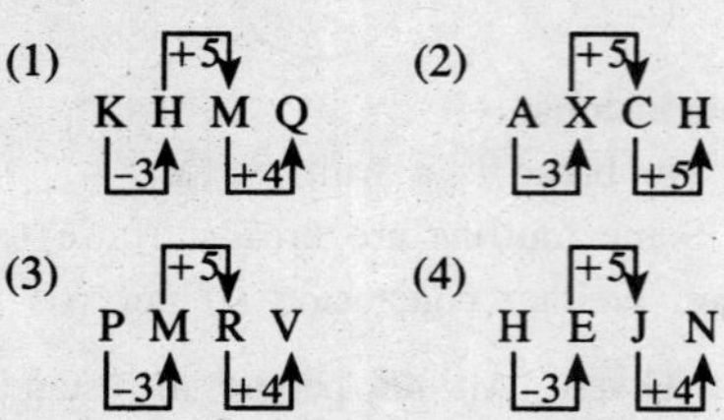


Here, option (2) does not belong to that group.

**62. (4):** Given, 7 students are sitting in a straight line facing north.

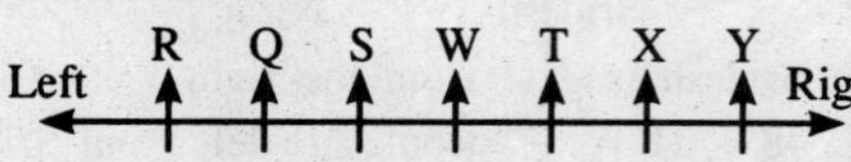


Here, 3 people sit between Y and S.

**63. (4):** Given, all the symbols are dropped

∴ New series: 758243196

Now fifth from the right = 4

**64. (3):** Given,

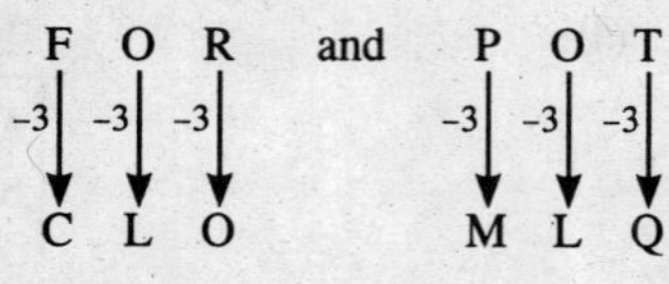


Similarly,

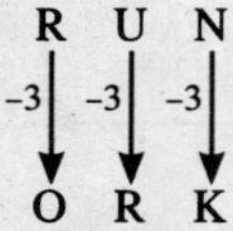


∴ RUN is related to ORK in the same logic.

**65. (1):** The Number of students in Eden's class = 21 + 14 − 1 = 34.

**66. (1):** From the given statements

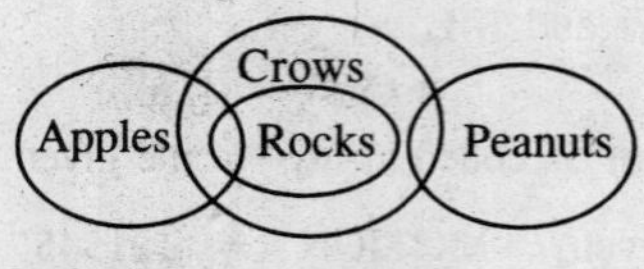


**Conclusions:**

I. Some rocks are peanuts. (False)

II. Some crows are apples. (True)

Here, only conclusion (II) follows.

**67. (1):**

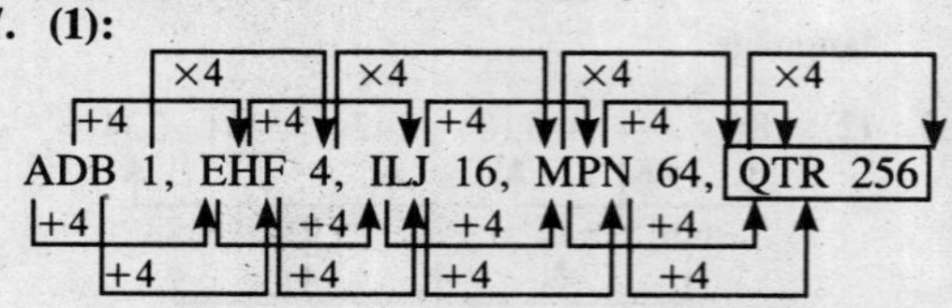


Here, ? = The next-letter-cluster = QTR 256.

**68. (4):** Given, expression = P + Q ÷ R − S × T

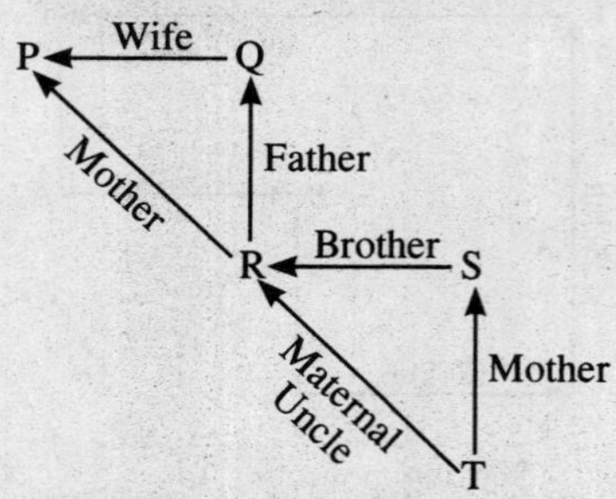


Here, P is the Grandmother of T.

**69. (1):** Given, Expression = F * A : L ? E = N

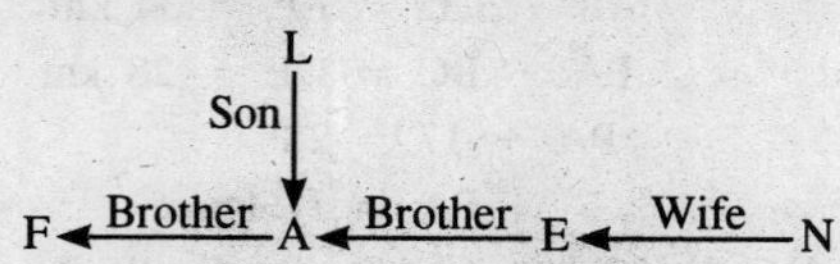


Here, F is the wife's brother of N.

**70. (4):** ∵ Obtain adding 4 to each digit of 49 = 813

∴ Required difference = 813 − 49 = 764.

**71. (4):** NW-1 is the longest national waterway in India, stretching 1,620 km from Allahabad (Prayagraj) to Haldia along the Ganga-Bhagirathi-Hooghly river system. It plays a vital role in inland cargo transport and has been developed under the Jal Marg Vikas Project.

**72. (3):** The Appellate Tribunal for Electricity was established in 2005 under the Electricity Act, 2003. It serves as a statutory body to hear appeals against the decisions of the Central and State Electricity Regulatory Commission, ensuring proper legal oversight in the power sector.

**73. (2):** FDI facilitates the movement of capital, technology, and expertise across borders, encouraging economic growth. It helps build infrastructure, generate employment, and integrate domestic markets with the global economy, unlike import restrictions or tariffs which limit such flows.

**74. (4):** HDFC Bank reported a 15% year-on-year growth in total deposits in Q2 FY25. This reflects increased customer trust and strong financial performance following the merger with HDFC Ltd, significantly boosting its deposit base.

**75. (1):** The National Green Tribunal was established in 2010 under the NGT Act to handle environmental protection and conservation-related legal matters. It provides speedy and specialized adjudication of environmental disputes, helping reduce the burden on traditional courts.

**76. (3):** The Indian National Congress session of 1905 was held at Banaras (now Varanasi) under the presidency of Gopal Krishna Gokhale. This session took place during the time of Lord Curzon's partition of Bengal, and it emphasized moderate methods of protest and national unity.

**77. (2):** In September 2024, Atishi Marlena was elected as the Chief Minister of Delhi following Arvind Kejriwal's resignation amid legal proceedings. A prominent leader from the Aam Aadmi Party, she previously served as Delhi's Education Minister and played a key role in public sector reforms.

**78. (4):** NW-1, running from Prayagraj to Haldia, is navigable by mechanical boats up to Patna and by ordinary boats further upstream to Haridwar. This makes it strategically important for transporting goods in northern India using the Ganga river system.

**79. (1):** In the 1950s, India adopted a centrally planned economic model with the launch of the First Five-Year Plan in 1951. The strategy focused on rapid industrialisation, especially in heavy industries, as guided by the Planning Commission under the influence of Nehruvian socialist policies.

**80. (4):** The Right to Education was made a fundamental right under Article 21A of the Constitution by the 86th Constitutional Amendment Act, 2002. It mandates free and compulsory education for all children aged 6 to 14 years, coming into force from April 1, 2010.

**81. (3):** SONAR stands for Sound Navigation And Ranging. It is a technique that uses sound waves to detect and locate objects underwater. The system sends sound pulses and measures the time it takes for the echo to return after bouncing off an object, helping in navigation and depth measurement.

**82. (3):** The National Rural Employment Programme (NREP) was launched in 1980 during the 6th Five Year Plan (1980–1985). It aimed at generating employment opportunities in rural areas and creating durable community assets like roads and irrigation canals.

**83. (4):** Harmonium does not belong to the Ghan Vadya (idiophonic instruments) category, which includes instruments that produce sound by the vibration of their own body (like Dandia, Gedi, Gurki). Harmonium is a reed instrument that uses air pressure to produce sound and falls under the Sushir Vadya category.

**84. (3):** Piyush Pandey authored "Manoj Bajpayee: The Definitive Biography", published in March 2024. The book chronicles the life and acting journey of Manoj Bajpayee, highlighting his rise from a small-town theatre artist to one of India's most respected actors.

**85. (2):** R21 is the new high-quality malaria vaccine developed by the Serum Institute of India in collaboration with the University of Oxford. It was rolled out in African nations from July 2024 and is considered a significant advancement due to its high efficacy and suitability for mass immunization.

**86. (3):** In the Padma Awards 2024, a total of 30 women were honoured by the President of India for their contributions across various fields including arts, literature, social work, science, and sports. This reflected a strong representation of women achievers in one of the country's highest civilian awards.

**87. (4):** The Water (Prevention and Control of Pollution) Amendment Bill, 2024 is initially applicable to two states—Rajasthan and Himachal Pradesh. These states passed resolutions under Article 252 of the Constitution, allowing the Centre to legislate on their behalf in matters related to water pollution control.

**88. (2):** The Battle of Kanauj, also known as the Battle of Bilgram, was fought in 1540 between Mughal Emperor Humayun and Sher Shah Suri. Humayun suffered a decisive defeat, which led to the temporary loss of the Mughal Empire and the rise of the Sur Empire under Sher Shah.

**89. (2):** According to the Union Budget 2024–25, the projected fiscal deficit for the financial year is 5.1% of GDP. This target reflects the government's focus on fiscal consolidation while still maintaining capital expenditure to stimulate economic growth.

**90. (2):** In October 2024, the Indian Army's Sudarshan Chakra Corps conducted the 'Swavlamban Shakti' military exercise in Uttar Pradesh. The exercise aimed to validate integrated operations, logistics coordination, and operational readiness in line with self-reliant defence capabilities.

**91. (3):** The Thar Desert, also known as the Great Indian Desert, lies mostly in the northwestern part of India, primarily in Rajasthan. It is characterized by arid conditions, sand dunes, sparse vegetation, and extreme temperatures, making it the largest desert in India.

**92. (3):** The Terai region lies at the foothills of the Himalayas and is known for its dense forests, fertile alluvial soil, and marshy lands. The region is home to rich biodiversity and supports both agriculture and wildlife, including national parks like Dudhwa and Valmiki.

**93. (2):** The Simhastha Kumbh Mela in Ujjain is held on the banks of the Shipra River once every 12 years. It is one of the four sites of the Kumbh Mela and holds immense religious significance in Hinduism, attracting millions of pilgrims for ritual bathing.

**94. (1):** Human development focuses on improving people's well-being by expanding their choices and capabilities. It emphasizes access to healthcare, quality education, and meaningful livelihood opportunities, rather than merely measuring economic growth.

**95. (1):** During the revolt of 1857, Sir Colin Campbell, the Commander-in-Chief of the British Army in India, led the military operation to recapture Lucknow from the rebels. His successful campaign marked a turning point in regaining British control over North India.

**96. (1):** The Great Indian Desert, or Thar Desert, primarily spans Rajasthan and extends into parts of Gujarat, Punjab, and Haryana. These states share the arid and semi-arid climatic features associated with the desert, including sandy terrain and low rainfall.

**97. (4):** Amitava Chatterjee was appointed as the Managing Director and CEO of Jammu & Kashmir Bank, effective from 30 December 2024. He brings with him decades of banking experience and has been chosen to lead the institution through its next phase of growth and reforms.

**98. (2):** Under Article 143 of the Indian Constitution, the President can seek the advisory opinion of the Supreme Court on any question of law or fact of public importance. The Court may give its opinion, though it is not binding on the President.

**99. (4):** Kanuma is celebrated on the third day of the Sankranti festival, mainly in Andhra Pradesh and Telangana. It is a festival dedicated to honoring cattle, particularly bulls and oxen, which play an important role in agricultural life.

**100. (3):** India won a total of 16 recognitions at the WorldSkills Lyon 2024 in France, including medals and Medallions of Excellence. This performance showcased India's growing strength in vocational skills across various trades at the global level.

**101. (3):** In September 2024, the Union Cabinet approved both Chandrayaan-4 and the Venus Orbiter Mission. The Venus mission is part of ISRO's long-term planetary exploration program and aims to study the atmosphere and surface characteristics of Venus, which has often been referred to as Earth's twin.

**102. (4):** The Indian Councils Act of 1861 marked the beginning of legislative decentralisation by restoring legislative powers to the Bombay and Madras Presidencies. This enabled these provinces to make laws on certain subjects, laying the foundation for provincial autonomy under British rule.

**103. (4):** The Economic Survey 2024 emphasized a "tripartite compact" involving the Centre, states, and private sector as crucial for achieving development goals. It highlights that coordinated efforts among these entities are necessary to drive infrastructure growth, investment, and public service delivery.

**104. (4):** The pepa is a traditional wind instrument of Assam, made from the horn of a buffalo. It is widely used in the Bihu festival and folk music performances and is known for its sharp and rhythmic sound that complements the dance and drum beats.

**105. (3):** After the 1857 Revolt, the British adopted a conciliatory approach toward zamindars and landlords. They were assured protection of their rights and properties to secure their loyalty, as the colonial administration realized their importance in maintaining political and administrative control.

**106. (2):** The 44th session of the Codex Committee on Nutrition and Foods for Special Dietary Uses (CCNFSDU) was held in Germany from 2 to 6 October 2024. Germany hosts the CCNFSDU regularly as it serves as the host government for this Codex body, which sets international food standards on nutrition-related matters.

**107. (1):** In Q3 FY24, the State Bank of India (SBI) reported a 10.75% year-over-year increase in its loan loss provisions. These provisions are funds set aside to cover potential loan defaults, and the rise reflects SBI's cautious approach amid evolving credit risk scenarios.

**108. (3):** The extremists within the Indian National Congress opposed the ideology of gradualism, which was promoted by the moderates. Extremists demanded immediate self-rule and used assertive methods like Swadeshi and boycott, while rejecting the moderate belief in slow constitutional reforms under British rule.

**109. (3):** Torque, like work, has the dimensional formula $[ML^2T^{-2}]$, and hence shares the same dimensions. However, while work is a scalar quantity representing energy transfer, torque is a vector quantity representing the tendency of a force to rotate an object about an axis.

**110. (4):** Article 167 of the Indian Constitution states that it is the duty of the Chief Minister to communicate to the Governor all decisions of the Council of Ministers relating to the administration of the state and to furnish information as the Governor may call for.

**111. (4):** The Constituent Assembly gave the third and final reading to the Indian Constitution on 26 November, 1949. This date is commemorated annually as Constitution Day (Samvidhan Divas), as it marks the formal adoption of the Constitution, which came into effect on 26 January, 1950.

**112. (4):** Titanium is widely used in aircraft construction due to its high strength-to-weight ratio, excellent corrosion resistance, and ability to withstand high temperatures. These properties make it ideal for use in both airframes and engine components of modern aircraft.

**113. (3):** Alauddin Alam Shah was the last ruler of the Sayyid dynasty, which ruled Delhi from 1414 to 1451. He abdicated the throne in 1451 and retired to Budaun, after which Bahlul Lodi took over Delhi and established the Lodi dynasty.

**114.** **(1):** Rural development involves initiatives aimed at enhancing living standards, infrastructure, healthcare, education, and employment opportunities in rural regions. It focuses on inclusive growth and balanced regional development across the country.

**115.** **(3):** Rajasthan leads India in solar power generation with the highest installed solar capacity. Its vast arid land and high solar irradiance make it ideal for large-scale solar energy projects under the National Solar Mission and state initiatives.

**116.** **(2):** Dadabhai Naoroji was the first to systematically present the 'Drain of Wealth' theory, which exposed how British colonial policies led to the economic exploitation of India. His work, especially in Poverty and Un-British Rule in India, laid the foundation for economic nationalism in the Indian freedom struggle.

**117.** **(4):** In human reproduction, the mother always contributes an X chromosome, while the father contributes either an X or a Y. If the father contributes an X, the child is female (XX); he contributes a Y, the child is male (XY). Hence, the sex is determined by the father chromosome.

**118.** **(3):** The Sam Sand Dunes are located in the Thar Desert near Jaisalmer in Rajasthan. It is a popular tourist destination known for its rolling sand dunes, desert safaris, and vibrant Rajasthan cultural performances, especially during the Desert Festival.

**119.** **(2):** Globalisation in India has led to rapid industrialisation and urbanisation, contributing to environmental issues such as air and water pollution, deforestation, and excessive extraction of natural resources. These challenges strain ecosystems and threaten sustainable development.

**120.** **(4):** Bernoulli's Principle explains that in a moving fluid, as the velocity increases, the pressure decreases. This relationship helps explain various phenomena such as how airplanes achieve lift and why fluids move faster through narrow sections of a pipe.

Previous Paper (Solved)

## Railway Protection Force & Railway Protection Special Force

# RPF/RPSF—CONSTABLE

## Recruitment Exam–2019*

**1.** In which city is the "Hawa Mahal" located?
A. Humpy B. Jaipur
C. Leh D. Aihole

**2.** Which of the following is not a part of Tennis Grand Slam Tournament?
A. Korea Open
B. Wimbledon Open
C. French Open
D. US Open

**3.** Who was the founder of Sikhism?
A. Mahavira
B. Gautam Buddha
C. Makkhali Gosala
D. Guru Nanak

**4.** Who was the founder of Khudai khidmatgar?
A. Shaukat Ali
B. M A Jinnah
C. Ghulam Ahmad Mirza
D. Khan Abdul Ghaffar Khan

**5.** Who organized the court in 1877 to accept Queen Victoria as the Queen of India?
A. Ripon B. Lytton
C. Curzon D. Dalhousie

**6.** Where did Gandhi lead the strike of mill workers since 1918?
A. Champaran B. Bardoli
C. Ahmedabad D. Kheda

**7.** Which of the following countries is the smallest country in West Asia?
A. UAE B. Qatar
C. Kuwait D. Bahrain

**8.** What is the process of transforming a larva into adult undergoing drastic changes?
A. Metamorphosis
B. Transpiration
C. Fermentation
D. Photosynthesis

**9.** In which battle did Tipu Sultan die in 1799?
A. Seringapatam
B. Mangalore
C. Pondicherry
D. Madras

**10.** In which state Sujani embroidery originated?
A. Himachal Pradesh
B. Rajasthan
C. Bihar
D. Manipur

**11.** What is the process of coupling homologous chromosome called?
A. Synopsis B. Diplotene
C. Leptotene D. Diakinesis

**12.** Who has the power to declare a national emergency in India?
A. Supreme Court B. President
C. Cabinet D. Prime Minister

**13.** From which language is the word "ध्यान" taken?
A. Hindi B. Bangla
C. Urdu D. Kashmiri

**14.** What is the 'market value' of all goods and services produced in the country during a year?
A. Gross National Product (GNP)
B. Economic Growth
C. Economic Development
D. Gross Domestic Product (GDP)

* *Exam held on 09-02-2019*

**15.** The term of the Comptroller and Auditor General of India is for:

A. 6 years B. 4 years
C. 7 years D. 5 years

**16.** Which of the following is an artificial waterway flowing from north to south in the landmass of Suez in north-eastern Egypt?

A. Red slug B. Rotaz canal
C. Black canal D. Suez canal

**17.** State emergency is also known as:

A. Chief Minister's rule
B. President's rule
C. Governor's rule
D. Prime Minister's rule

**18.** Who among the following occupies the second highest position in India?

A. Governor B. President
C. Prime Minister D. Vice President

**19.** The game of hockey was started by .............. in India.

A. Russian people
B. British people
C. American people
D. Sri Lankan people

**20.** Indian Statistical Institute was established in ............ city.

A. Delhi B. Bombay
C. Calcutta D. Madras

**21.** What is at the centre of the cricket ground?

A. Pitch B. Long on
C. Long off D. Square leg

**22.** In which of the following games/sports the ball is required to play?

A. Kho-kho B. High jump
C. Karate D. Volleyball

**23.** What is the process of transformation of a substance from solid state to gas state without going through liquid state?

A. Liquefaction
B. Sublimation
C. Evaporation
D. Compression

**24.** Which card is used in a football game to indicate that a player has been sent out of the game?

A. Green card B. Pink card
C. White card D. Red card

**25.** How many subjects are there in the Union List of India currently?

A. 47 subjects B. 97 subjects
C. 100 subjects D. 52 subjects

**26.** The central government appointed a three-member commission on center-state relations headed by:

A. R.S. Sarkaria B. S.V.S. Raghavan
C. K.M. Birla D. J.S. Verma

**27.** From which country does the famous cosmopolitan silk route extend to Europe?

A. China B. Canada
C. USA D. Australia

**28.** In which of the following countries is the Great Artesian Basin located?

A. China B. America
C. India D. Australia

**29.** Which method is used to determine the speed of sound in gas?

A. Resonance wave
B. Kunti's tube
C. Resonance width
D. GM counter

**30.** In which year did "ICC" start limited overs in the Cricket World Cup for the first time?

A. 2000 B. 1975
C. 1983 D. 1947

**31.** Which of the following is an example of conventional energy?

A. Tide B. Natural Gas
C. Solar D. Geothermal

**32.** How many times has a financial emergency been declared in India so far?

A. 2 times B. 1 time
C. Never D. 3 times

**33.** Goods and Services Tax (India) came into force from:

A. June 2016 B. August 2015
C. August 2017 D. July 2017

**34.** The cells of the nervous system that support, protect and nurture neurons are called:
A. Glial cells B. Glyco cells
C. Glycine cells D. Glycol cells

**35.** Which of the following islands has an active volcano?
A. Narcondam island
B. Reunion island
C. Barren island
D. Car Nicobar

**36.** The difference of potential of layer of a diode is called
A. Breakdown barrier
B. Potential hindrance
C. Conductor barrier
D. Voltage barrier

**37.** The Constitution of India adopts universal adult suffrage on the basis of Lok Sabha elections. Every citizen who is not less than ............. has the right to vote.
A. 21 years B. 23 years
C. 18 years D. 25 years

**38.** In which year did the First World War take place?
A. 1927 B. 1914
C. 1905 D. 1935

**39.** Which of the following soil is deposited in the lake of Kashmir valley?
A. Hard soil B. Red soil
C. Carey soil D. Mountain soil

**40.** In which of the following continents is the native place of the species of Eucalyptus tree?
A. Europe B. North America
C. Australia D. Antartica

**41.** Cactus, Acacia and Date tree are characteristic of which vegetable region?
A. Mediterranean forests
B. Tropical grasslands
C. Equatorial rainforest
D. Desert region

**42.** Which of the following important diversity is found in the Himalayan wet forest?
A. Oak B. Mahogany
C. Teak D. Catechu

**43.** Which of the following river is not a tributary of Mahanadi river?
A. Ib B. Musi
C. Mand D. Shivnath River

**44.** Which Ministry of the Government of India launched the "Startup India Scheme"?
A. Ministry of Commerce and Industry
B. Ministry of Agriculture
C. Finance Ministry
D. Ministry of Rural Development

**45.** Atoms and molecules can only emit or absorb energy in the form of discontinuous packets of energy, called
A. Quanta B. Azimuthal
C. Planck constant D. Periodic

**46.** Who is defined as the total number of protons present in the nucleus of an atom?
A. Mass number
B. Isotopic number
C. Atomic number
D. Molecular number

**47.** What is the repetition of sound called due to reflection of sound?
A. Echo
B. Refraction of sound
C. Sound duplication
D. Reflection of sound

**48.** In which state is Farakka barrage located?
A. W. Bengal B. Jharkhand
C. Odisha D. Bihar

**49.** The word 'integrity' was added to the Preamble of the Indian Constitution in the year:
A. 1956 B. 1986
C. 1966 D. 1976

**50.** Who among the following was the Labour Minister in the first cabinet of Independent India?
A. John Matthai B. Jagjivan Ram
C. Asaf Ali D. Liaquat Ali Khan

**51.** Read the following statements and answer the following questions.

Meaning of A4B is A, mother of B
Meaning of A3B is A is sister of B
Meaning of A5B is A, mother of B
Meaning of A7B is A is brother of B

Which of the following equation indicates that P is brother of S?

A. P7Q7R5S B. P7Q5R3S
C. P5Q5R3S D. P5Q7R5S

**52.** Replace the question mark with the appropriate option given as per the logic used in the first pair:
2019:36::2559:??

A. 62 B. 65
C. 64 D. 63

**53.** Find the next number in the series.
10, 19, 37, 64, 100, ?

A. 145 B. 150
C. 140 D. 143

**Directions (Q. No. 54 & 55):** *In this question a passage has been given followed by a statement. Read the passage carefully and decide the statement based on the given passage.*

Saint Nicholas alias Santa Claus is believed to have lived in modern-day Turkey (then considered part of ancient Greece) around 300 B.C. at Patara. He was the elder clergyman of Myra, famous for good deeds among the poor, love for children and gifts to the needy. He is usually depicted as a slim figure wearing the red and golden attire of his religious office. They look beautiful in pictures with a traditional aura - an indicator of good deeds, with a stick or a Bible or both. Here is a glimpse of the developmental story from a religious icon of Santa Claus to the North Pole becoming a divine figure.

**13th Century:** Bishop Nicholas of Myra was declared a saint in the first millennium. By the 13th century, in honour of these, the Dutch celebrated a tradition of putting coins in shoes left outside the homes of the poor. After doing this, he expressed that Saint Nicholas had done all these. Later, Saint Nicholas became the Sinterklaas, and now, the official Sinterklaas of the Netherlands is a bushy figure in white robes, scarlet watch and royal long white hair and beard. Incidentally, it travels by white horse.

**16th Century:** Saint Nicholas is now popular throughout Europe. Dutch Sinterklaases have become Santa Claus in many areas. Every year, the feast of Saint Nicholas or Santa Claus is celebrated on 6th December, which is the death anniversary of the original bishop of Myra (the year is not set, but there is no dispute on the date).

**54. Statements:** In the 13th century, the Dutch Sinterklaas became Santa Claus in many areas.

Select an appropriate option from the following options.

(a) The statement is definitely true.
(b) The statement is probably true.
(c) The statement cannot be determined.
(d) The statement is definitely false.

A. (d) B. (a)
C. (c) D. (b)

**55. Statements:** December 6 is celebrated as a feast for Santa Claus, the death anniversary of Saint Nicholas.

Select an appropriate option from the following options

(a) The statement is definitely true.
(b) The statement is probably true.
(c) The statement cannot be determined.
(d) The statement is definitely false.

A. (a) B. (c)
C. (d) D. (b)

**56.** How many right-angled triangles can be made from the given figure?

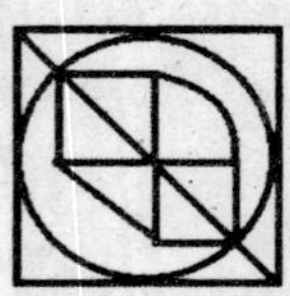

A. 4 B. 10
C. 7 D. 8

**57.** In this question, two conclusions (*i*) and (*ii*) are given after a statement. Assuming the statement to be true, consider the both conclusions together and decide which of these conclusions is logically correct beyond any doubt based on the information given in the statement.

**Statement:** All lights are chargers. All fans are lights.

**Conclusions:**

(*i*) All fans are chargers.
(*ii*) All chargers are lights.

Select the appropriate option from the following options:

(*a*) Only conclusion (*i*) follows.
(*b*) Only conclusion (*ii*) follows.
(*c*) Either conclusion (*i*) or (*ii*) follows
(*d*) Neither conclusion (*i*) nor (*ii*) follows
(*e*) Both conclusion (*i*) and (*ii*) follow

A. (*a*) B. (*b*)
C. (*e*) D. (*c*)

**58.** In this question, two statements showing definite relation are given, followed by three conclusions (*i*), (*ii*), and (*iii*). Assuming the statement to be true, find which conclusion is definitely true.

**Statement:**

$D < I \leq S = P; P > U \geq T = E$

**Conclusions:**

(*i*) $D < P$
(*ii*) $S > E$
(*iii*) $S > T$

A. (*i*) and (*ii*) only
B. (*ii*) and (*iii*) only
C. only (*iii*)
D. All are correct

**59.** In this question, three statements are followed by three conclusions. Assuming the statement to be true, consider the both conclusions together and decide which of these conclusions is logically correct beyond any doubt based on the information given in the statement.

**Statement:** All buds are blossoms. All flowers are blossoms. Some buds are colours.

**Conclusions:**

(*i*) All buds are blossoms.
(*ii*) Some colours are flowers.
(*iii*) Some blossoms are colours.

A. Only (*i*) and (*ii*)
B. Only (*i*) and (*iii*)
C. Only (*ii*) and (*iii*)
D. All follow

**60.** A is niece of B, who is only son of C. D is husband of C. How is A related to C?

A. Grandson B. Son-in-law
C. Son D. Nephew

**61.** *Read the given information carefully and answer the following questions.*

The six students A, B, C, D, E and F are sitting in a row facing north (not necessarily in the same order).

(*i*) C sits on the right side of the person who is sitting second to the left of D.
(*ii*) There are three persons between F and C, and one between E and A who sits at the end of the line.
(*iii*) B and C are not neighbours.

If B changes his position with E and C with A and D with F, then who sits on either end of the line?

A. E, C B. C, D
C. D, F D. A, F

**62.** Four of the following five are similar in some way and therefore form a group. Which is not related to this group?

Liberal, Strict, Easy-going, Tolerant, Lenient

A. Liberal B. Strict
C. Lenient D. Easy-going

**63.** Select the correct water image of the given figure from the options.

HERON

A. HEꓤOИ B. ИOЯƎH
C. HEROИ D. HEꓤON

**64.** Replace the question mark with the appropriate option given as per the logic used in the first pair.

J : Q : : S : ??

A. X B. Y
C. Z D. W

**65.** How many squares are there in the given figure?

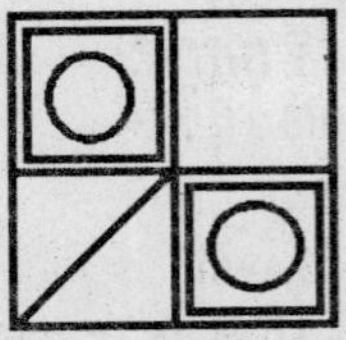

A. 7 B. 9
C. 8 D. 12

**66.** The 6 letters H, I, J, K, L and M are inscribed on the surfaces of a dice as shown below. Which letter is inscribed on the surface opposite to the face of J?

A. K B. M
C. L D. I

**67.** Find out the next number in the series.

10, 24, 52, 108, 220, ?

A. 443 B. 444
C. 442 D. 440

**68.** In a code language, if BRING is coded as UEEJQ, then in the same language CYCLE will be coded as:

A. FBFOH B. FBYOH
C. BFFHO D. BFYHO

**69.** Replace the question mark with the appropriate option given as per the logic used in the first pair.

Sphere : Ball : : Cube : ??

A. Dice B. Dance
C. Eat D. Work

**70.** Four of the following five are similar in some way and therefore form a group. Which is not related to this group?

B, S, Q, Y, C

A. C B. Y
C. S D. Q

**71.** Choose the correct alternative from the following options that make a perfect square (three pictures out of 5 given below):

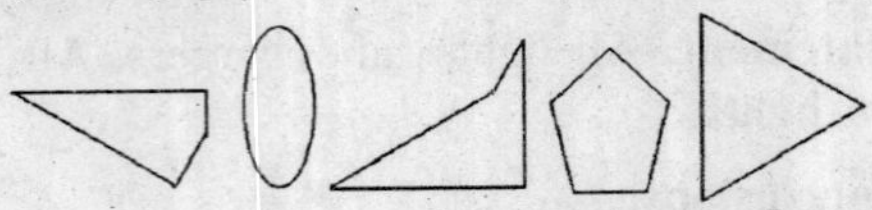

1 2 3 4 5

A. 1, 3 and 5
B. 2, 3 and 5
C. 1, 2 and 4
D. 1, 3 and 4

**72.** Four of the following five are similar in some way and therefore form a group. Which is not related to this group?

PL, IE, FA, OK, NJ

A. OK B. NJ
C. FA D. PL

**73.** Select the upcoming picture from the given series from the options.

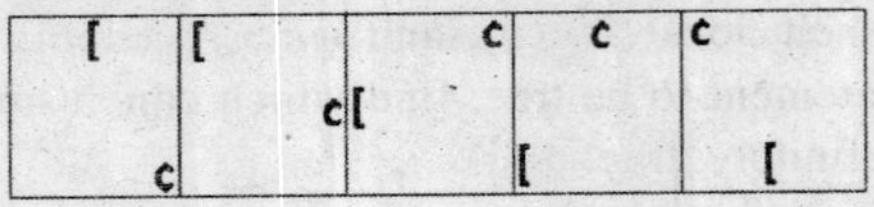

A. 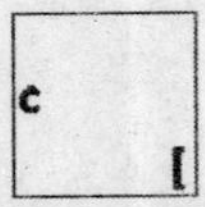 B. 

C. 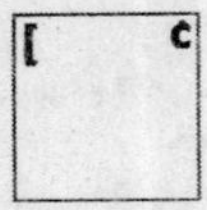 D. 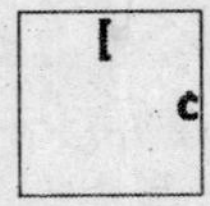

**74.** Pointing to a girl, a woman said, "She has no siblings and I am the sister of her mother's father's son who has two children." How is the girl related to the woman?

A. Cousin
B. Grand-daughter
C. Daughter
D. Neice

**75.** Replace the question mark with the appropriate option given as per the logic used in the first pair.

Jar : Lid : : Bottle : ??

A. Success B. Charger
C. Luck D. Cork

**76.** In this question, the relationship between the various elements is shown in the statement. Two conclusions are given after the statement:

**Statement:** $J < U < D = G \leq E < S$

**Conclusions:**

(*i*) $U < S$

(*ii*) $S < D$

Select the appropriate option from the following options.

(*a*) Only conclusion (*i*) is logical

(*b*) Only conclusion (*ii*) is logical

(*c*) Either conclusion (*i*) or (*ii*) is logical

(*d*) Neither conclusion (*i*) or (*ii*) is logical

(*e*) Conclusion (*i*) and (*ii*) both are logical

A. (*b*) B. (*a*)

C. (*d*) D. (*c*)

**77.** *Read the given information carefully and answer the following questions.*

Six students A, B, C, D, E and F are sitting in a row facing north (not necessarily in the same order).

(*i*) C is sitting to the right of the person who is sitting second to the left of D.

(*ii*) There are three persons between F and C and one between E and A.

(*iii*) B and C are not neigh-bours.

Which of the following statements is incorrect regarding the arrangement?

A. F and A are sitting at the end of the row

B. E sits third to the right of the end of the row.

C. B sits second to the right of F.

D. D and C are not neighbours.

**78.** Select the diagram which completes the figure from the options.

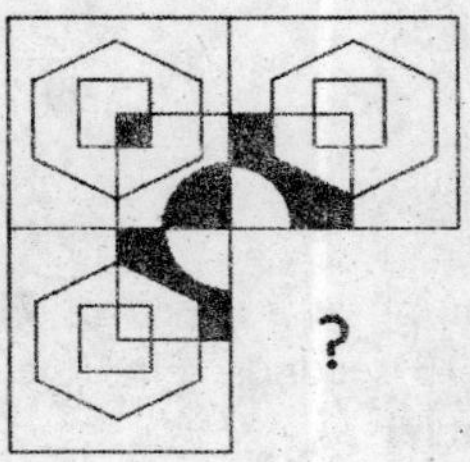

A. 

B. 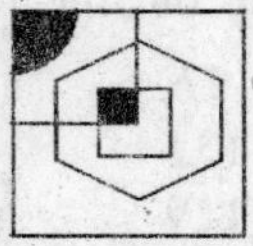

C. 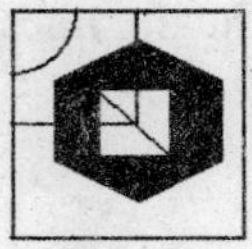

D. 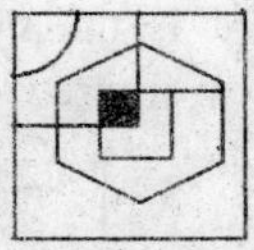

**79.** If the mirror is placed on the shaded line, the correct mirror image of the given figure will be:

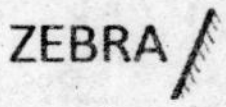


A. 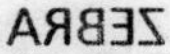

B. 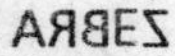

C. 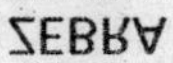

D. 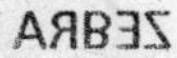

**80.** In a code language, if DISC is coded as 49193, then in the same language what will be the code of FILE?

A. 68125 B. 69135

C. 69125 D. 68135

**81.** In this question, two statements (*i*) and (*ii*) are given after a statement. Assuming the statement to be true, consider the both conclusions together and decide which of these conclusions is logically correct beyond any doubt based on the information given in the statement.

**Statement:** Talking about attendance, Vijay is an excellent student in his college.

**Conclusions:**

(*i*) Vijay will have an outstanding academic record.

(*ii*) Vijay is being appreciated by all his teachers for his regular attendance.

Select the appropriate option from the following options.

(*a*) Only conclusion (*i*) is logical

(*b*) Only conclusion (*ii*) is logical

(*c*) Either conclusion (*i*) or (*ii*) is logical

(*d*) Neither conclusion (*i*) nor (*ii*) is logical

(*e*) Conclusion (*i*) and (*ii*) both are logical

A. (*a*) B. (*b*)

C. (*d*) D. (*c*)

**82.** Find out the next number in the series.

10, 27, 61, 78, 112 ?

A. 131 B. 127
C. 129 D. 133

**83.** What is the number of straight lines in the given figure?

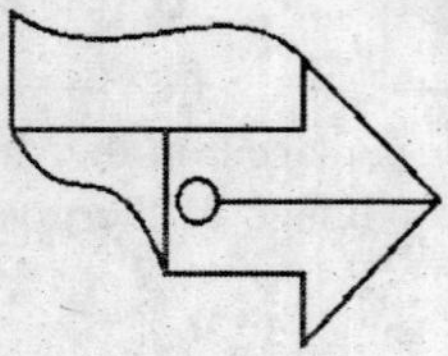

A. 12 B. 15
C. 13 D. 11

**84.** Find out the next number in the series.

20, 47, 74, 101, 128, ?

A. 160 B. 158
C. 155 D. 165

**85.** *Read the given information carefully and answer the following questions.*

Six students A, B, C, D, E and F are sitting in a row facing north (not necessarily in the same order).

(*i*) C is sitting to the right of the person who is sitting second to the left of D.

(*ii*) There are three persons between F and C and one between E and A.

(*iii*) B and C are not neigh-bours.

Who sits to the immediate right of C?

A. E B. A
C. D D. F

**86.** What will be the amount after a period of 2 years at a compound interest rate of 10% per annum at ₹ 18,300?

A. ₹ 23,143 B. ₹ 24,143
C. ₹ 22,143 D. ₹ 25,143

**Direction:** *Study the following graph and answer the question based on it.*

Number of vehicles manufactured by X and Y companies from 2001 to 2006 (in thousands)

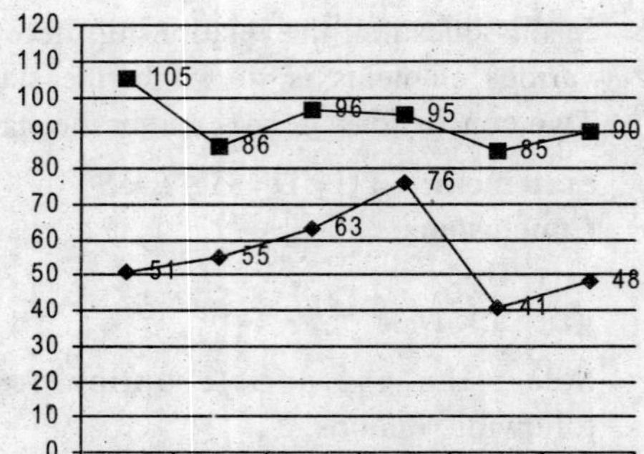


| | 2001 | 2002 | 2003 | 2004 | 2005 | 2006 |
|---|---|---|---|---|---|---|
| X | 51 | 55 | 63 | 76 | 41 | 48 |
| Y | 105 | 86 | 96 | 95 | 85 | 90 |

**87.** Find the difference between the total productions of the two companies in the given years.

A. 223 B. 227
C. 229 D. 225

**88.** Simplify:

$$\sqrt{(91+\sqrt{(76+\sqrt{(45-\sqrt{400})})})}$$

A. 10 B. 29
C. 26 D. 20

**89.** Interest earned after 5 years at a simple interest of 12% per annum on a fixed sum of ₹ 6 is 540. Find the amount invested.

A. ₹ 10,800 B. ₹ 10,700
C. ₹ 10,900 D. ₹ 11,000

**90.** To succeed in the competition, Germilyn needs an average score of 75 in four exams. His marks in the first three exams are 64, 60 and 56. How many marks does he need in the fourth exam to succeed in the competition?

A. 122 B. 120
C. 124 D. 126

**91.** X = 0.3477777 ....., Find the fraction value of X:

A. $\frac{313}{900}$ B. $\frac{313}{99}$
C. $\frac{337}{900}$ D. $\frac{313}{999}$

**92.** A train running at a speed of 79 m/s crosses a signal in 13 seconds. Find the length of the train. (In meters)

A. 1027 B. 1025
C. 1029 D. 1031

**93.** The ratio of the sides of a quadrilateral area is 2 : 3 : 4 : 5 and the perimeter is 770 cm. Find the shortest side. (In cm)
A. 110 B. 120
C. 115 D. 105

**94.** The average weight of a state-level cricket team of eleven players is 117 kg. When the coach is added the average weight increases by 1 kg. What is the weight of a coach?
A. 133 B. 129
C. 131 D. 127

**95.** Printed price on book is ₹ 5,400, a bookseller offers a 10% discount on it. If he still makes a profit of 20%, the purchase price of the book is:
A. ₹ 4,050 B. ₹ 4,150
C. ₹ 4,350 D. ₹ 4,250

**96.** Simplify :
$43 - [10 - (49 \div 7 - (15 - 25 \div 5) \div 10)]$
A. 39 B. 45
C. 29 D. 19

**97.** The LCM of two numbers is 128 and their HCF is 8. If one number is 128, find the other number.
A. 96 B. 108
C. 8 D. 112

**Direction:** *Study the following graph and answer the question based on it.*

Number of vehicles manufactured by X and Y companies from 2001 to 2006 (in thousands).

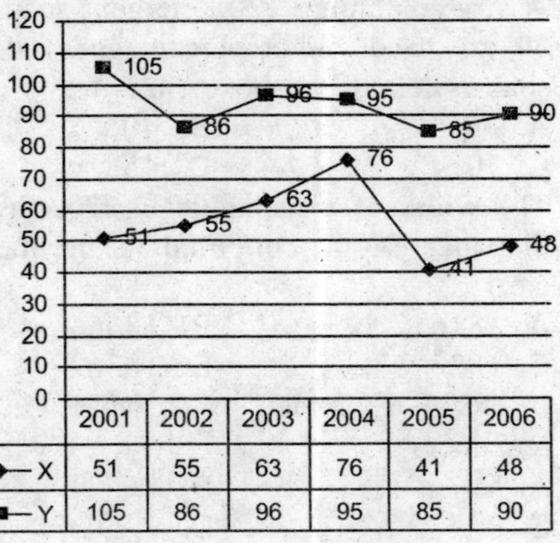


| | 2001 | 2002 | 2003 | 2004 | 2005 | 2006 |
|---|---|---|---|---|---|---|
| X | 51 | 55 | 63 | 76 | 41 | 48 |
| Y | 105 | 86 | 96 | 95 | 85 | 90 |

**98.** The difference between the production of Company X and Company Y was minimal during which of the following years?
A. 2004 B. 2003
C. 2002 D. 2005

**99.** Simplify:
$(82 \times 21 \times 82 \times 21) \div \left(\left(2\left(\sqrt{441} \div 2\right)\right)\right)^2$
A. 3254 B. 7214
C. 6724 D. 3245

**100.** Which of the following numbers is divisible by 12?
A. 18744 B. 19744
C. 17744 D. 16774

**Direction:** *Study the following graph and answer the question based on it.*

Number of vehicles manufactured by X and Y companies from 2001 to 2006 (in thousands).

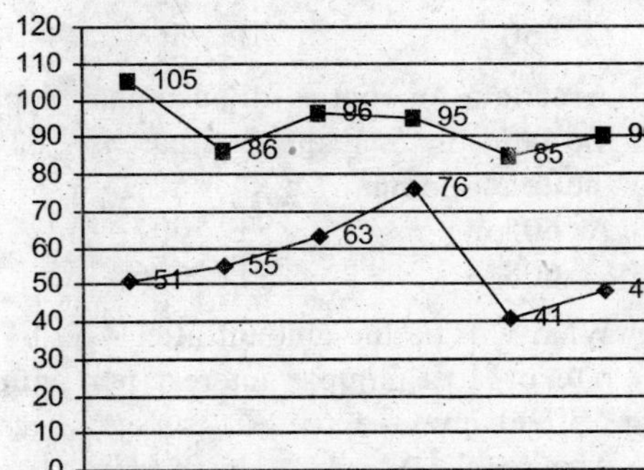


| | 2001 | 2002 | 2003 | 2004 | 2005 | 2006 |
|---|---|---|---|---|---|---|
| X | 51 | 55 | 63 | 76 | 41 | 48 |
| Y | 105 | 86 | 96 | 95 | 85 | 90 |

**101.** What is the difference between the number of vehicles manufactured by the company in 2001 and 2002?
A. 3 B. 4
C. 5 D. 6

**102.** The price of metal piece increases from ₹ 445 to ₹ 534. State the percentage increase. (in %)
A. 30 B. 20
C. 15 D. 25

**103.** The average of 7 numbers is 160. By removing a number, the average remains the same. Find the extracted number.

A. 154 B. 160
C. 156 D. 158

**104.** A shopkeeper paid ₹ 272 for a thing and sold it at ₹ 340. Find the profit percentage earned by the shopkeeper. (in %)
A. 20 B. 35
C. 30 D. 25

**105.** LPG cylinder price increases from ₹ 720 to ₹ 900. What percentage of consumption should be worked out that the amount spent on LPG cylinder remains the same. (in %)
A. 25 B. 30
C. 20 D. 35

**106.** It takes 50 seconds for a train to pass a signal that is at one end of a bridge of 473 meters in length. If the train takes 93 seconds to cross the bridge, find the length of the train. (in metre)
A. 560 B. 555
C. 550 D. 565

**107.** A certain amount is divided into 2 parts in the ratio 6 : 5. If the first part is ₹ 330, find the total amount. (in ₹)
A. 605 B. 607
C. 608 D. 606

**108.** What will be the amount after 4 years at the rate of 13% simple interest per annum on ₹ 5,500 invested? (in ₹)
A. 8,560 B. 8,660
C. 8,360 D. 8,460

**109.** The first part of the Franklin Race completes a speed of 700 mph and the second part of the race at a speed of 1050 mph. Find the average speed of both the parts. (mph-ml/hr.)
A. 850 B. 860
C. 870 D. 840

**110.** Find the area of the equilateral triangle of side 124 cm. (in $cm^2$)
A. $3846\sqrt{3}$ B. $3844\sqrt{3}$
C. $3842\sqrt{3}$ D. $3848\sqrt{3}$

**111.** The ratio of ages of alpha and beta is 2 : 5. If the sum of their ages is 350, find the difference between their ages.
A. 146 B. 150
C. 148 D. 144

**112.** When an item is sold at ₹ 680, then it has a 15% loss. Find the cost price of the item. (in ₹)
A. 780 B. 740
C. 800 D. 760

**113.** The ratio of pen, pencil and eraser in a box is 3 : 2 : 1. If the prices of each pen, pencil and eraser are respectively ₹ 3, ₹ 2 and ₹ 2 and the amount spent on the box is ₹ 795, then find the number of pens in the box.
A. 189 B. 169
C. 159 D. 179

**114.** 25% of 66.67% of 75% of 80% of a number is 6377. Find 40% of that number.
A. 26508 B. 24508
C. 23508 D. 25508

**115.** Find the area of rhombus with diagonals 119 cm and 120 cm. (in $cm^2$)
A. 7150 B. 7120
C. 7130 D. 7140

**116.** A shopkeeper paid ₹ 475 to buy a thing and sold at ₹ 380. Find the loss percentage to the shopkeeper. (in %)
A. 30 B. 25
C. 35 D. 20

**117.** Find the value of X:
$$\sqrt{(30-x)} = \sqrt{(17+\sqrt{1024})}$$
A. 21 B. 19
C. –21 D. –19

**118.** A box containing 120 detergent soaps out of 84 are used. What percentage of detergent soap is left in the box? (in %)
A. 35 B. 40
C. 30 D. 45

**119.** The width of a rectangle is 270 cm and its diagonal is 702 cm. Find its perimeter. (in cm)
A. 1816 B. 1806
C. 1826 D. 1836

**120.** If 15209 is divided by 9, what will be the remainder?
A. 5 B. 8
C. 0 D. 2

# ANSWERS

| 1 | 2 | 3 | 4 | 5 | 6 | 7 | 8 | 9 | 10 |
|---|---|---|---|---|---|---|---|---|---|
| B | A | D | D | B | C | D | A | A | C |
| **11** | **12** | **13** | **14** | **15** | **16** | **17** | **18** | **19** | **20** |
| A | B | C | D | A | D | B | D | B | C |
| **21** | **22** | **23** | **24** | **25** | **26** | **27** | **28** | **29** | **30** |
| A | D | B | D | C | A | A | D | B | B |
| **31** | **32** | **33** | **34** | **35** | **36** | **37** | **38** | **39** | **40** |
| B | C | D | A | C | B | C | B | C | C |
| **41** | **42** | **43** | **44** | **45** | **46** | **47** | **48** | **49** | **50** |
| D | A | B | A | A | C | A | A | D | B |
| **51** | **52** | **53** | **54** | **55** | **56** | **57** | **58** | **59** | **60** |
| A | D | A | A | A | C | A | D | D | B |
| **61** | **62** | **63** | **64** | **65** | **66** | **67** | **68** | **69** | **70** |
| B | B | A | C | A | C | B | D | A | B |
| **71** | **72** | **73** | **74** | **75** | **76** | **77** | **78** | **79** | **80** |
| A | C | A | D | D | B | C | B | A | C |
| **81** | **82** | **83** | **84** | **85** | **86** | **87** | **88** | **89** | **90** |
| C | C | C | C | B | C | A | A | C | B |
| **91** | **92** | **93** | **94** | **95** | **96** | **97** | **98** | **99** | **100** |
| A | A | A | B | A | A | C | A | * | A |
| **101** | **102** | **103** | **104** | **105** | **106** | **107** | **108** | **109** | **110** |
| B | B | B | D | C | C | A | C | D | B |
| **111** | **112** | **113** | **114** | **115** | **116** | **117** | **118** | **119** | **120** |
| B | C | C | D | D | D | D | C | D | B |

## Explanatory Answers

**51.** Checking upon the options,

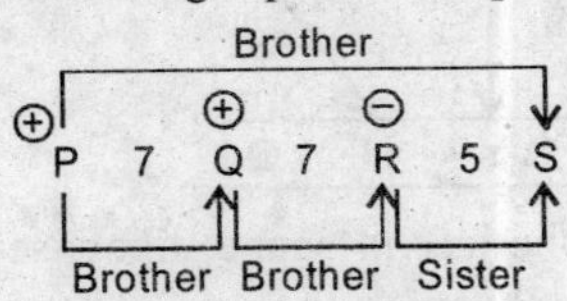


Hence, option (A) is correct.

**52.** 2019 : 36 : : 2559 : ?

As,

$2 + 0 + 1 + 9 = 12 \times 3 = 36$

Similarly,

$2 + 5 + 5 + 9 = 21 \times 3 = 63$

Hence, 63 will come in place of question mark (?)

**53.**

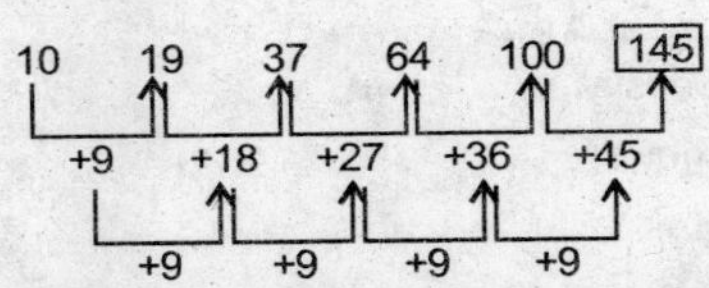


**56.** The given figure will have the following right-angled triangles.

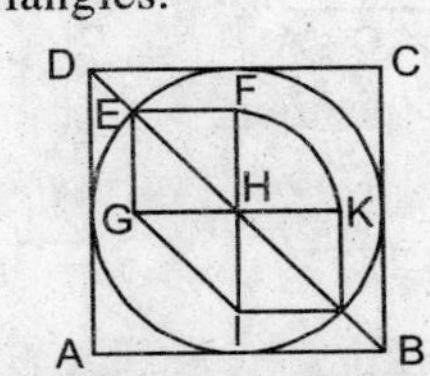


ΔDAB, ΔBCD, ΔEGH, ΔEFH, ΔGHI, ΔHIJ, ΔHKJ

Total = 7.

**57.** 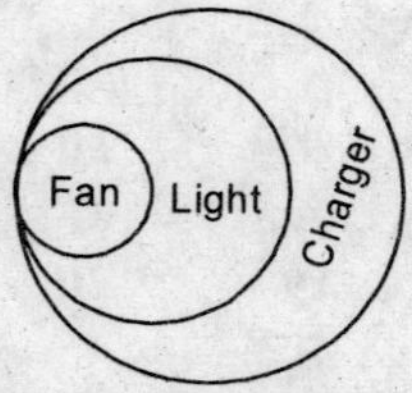


I. All fans are chargers.

**58.** D < I ≤ S = P > U ≥ T = E

S > T

D < P    S > E

(*i*) D < P

(*ii*) S > E

(*iii*) S > T

Hence, all conclusions are correct.

**59.** 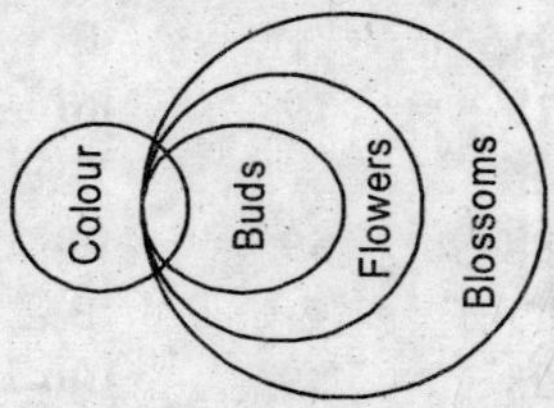


(*i*) All buds are blosoms. (✓)

(*ii*) Some colours are flowers. (✓)

(*iii*) Some blossoms are colours. (✓)

Hence, all logics are compatible.

**60.** 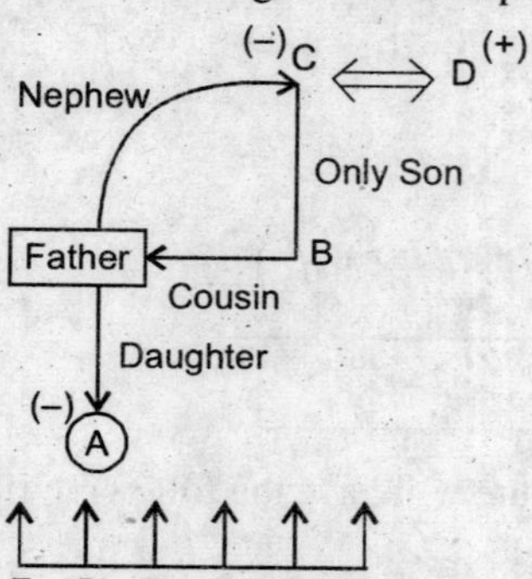


**61.** F B D E C A

On changing position,

D E F B A C

**64.** J : Q : : S : Z

+7    +7

**65.** The given figure has the following squares :

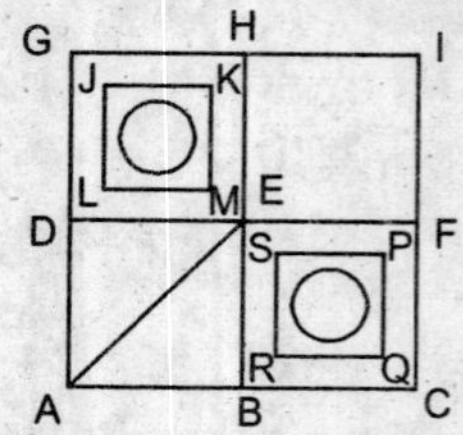


□JKLM, □PQRS, □GDEH, □HEFI, □DEAB, □EFBC, □ACIG

Total square = 7

**66.** 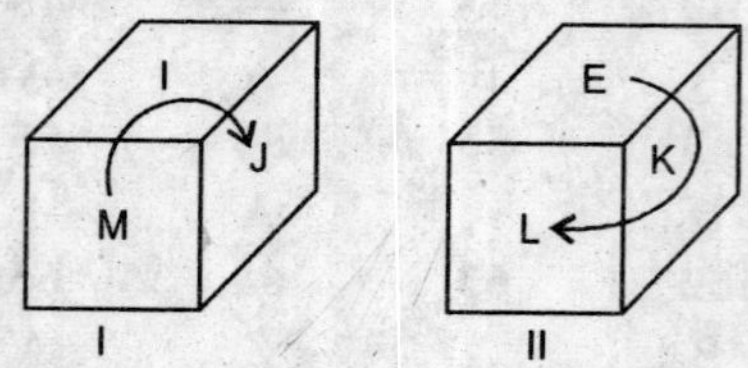


(I) M I J    (II) H K L

M ↔ H

I ↔ K

J ↔ L

**67.** 10  24  52  108  220  444

×2+4  ×2+4  ×2+4  ×2+4  ×2+4

**68.** As,

B R I N G → U E E J Q (+3, +3, –4, +3, +3)

Similarly,

C Y C L E → B F Y H O (+3, +3, –4, +3)

**69.** As the ball is spherical in shape, likewise the dice is cubic in shape.

**70.** B (2)  S (19)  Q (17)  Y (25)  C (3)

Apart from Y, all other letters come in the prime letter in the alphabetical place of English alphabet.

**72.** P L  I E  F A  O K  N J

–4  –4  –5  –4  –4

In the given group, the second letter is 4 places behind the first letter in all groups except FA.

**76.** 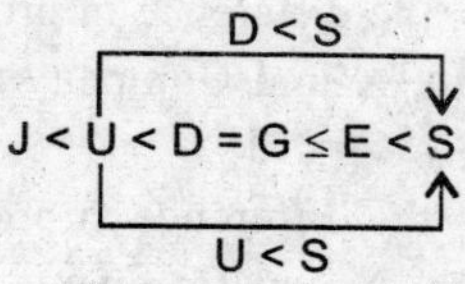


(I) U < S (✓) (II) S < D (✗)

**77.** 

**80.** As,

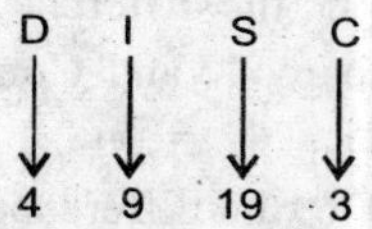


Similarly,

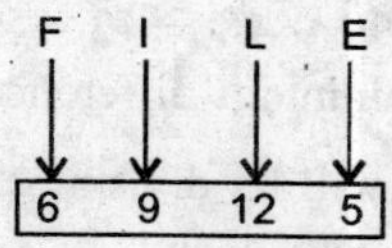


**82.** 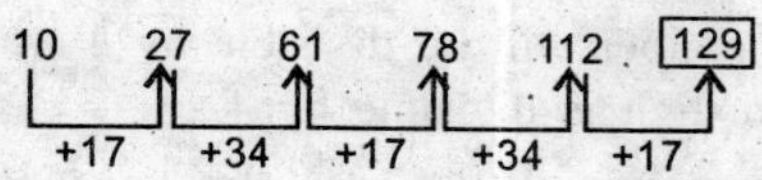


**84.** 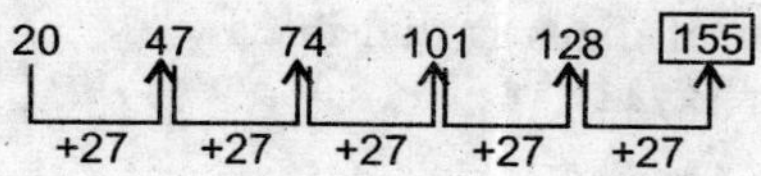


**85.** 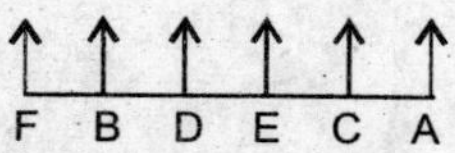


A is sitting just right of C.

**86.** Compound Interest

$$= P\left[\left(1+\frac{R}{100}\right)^{T}\right]$$

$$= 18300\left[\left(1+\frac{10}{100}\right)^{2}\right]$$

$$= 18300\left[\left(\frac{11}{10}\right)^{2}\right]$$

$$= 18300\left[\frac{121}{100}\right] = 22143.$$

**87.** Total production of company X

= 51 + 55 + 63 + 76 + 41 + 48 = 334

Total production of company Y

= 105 + 86 + 96 + 95 + 85 + 90 = 557

Required difference

= 557 − 334 = 223.

**88.** $\sqrt{(91+\sqrt{(76+\sqrt{45-\sqrt{400}}))})}$

$= \sqrt{(91+\sqrt{(76+\sqrt{45-20}))})}$

$= \sqrt{(91+\sqrt{(76+\sqrt{25})})}$

$= \sqrt{(91+\sqrt{(76+5)})}$

$= \sqrt{(91+\sqrt{81})}$

$= \sqrt{(91+9)} = \sqrt{100} = 10$

**89.** Let the sum invested be ₹ $x$

Then, simple interest

$$= \frac{P \times R \times T}{100}$$

$$6{,}540 = \frac{x \times 12 \times 5}{100}$$

$$x = \frac{6540 \times 100}{12 \times 5}$$

$x$ = ₹ 10,900.

**90.** Let, marks in the fourth examination = $x$

Then, $\frac{64+60+56+x}{4} = x$

$180 + x = 300$

$x = 300 - 180$

$x = 120.$

**91.** $X = 0.347777$

$X = 0.34\bar{7}$

$X = \frac{347-34}{900} = \frac{313}{900}.$

**92.** Let, the length of train = $l$ m

Then the speed of train

$$= \frac{\text{distance}}{\text{time}}$$

$$79 = \frac{l}{13}$$

$l = 79 \times 13 = 1027$ m.

**93.** Let, the sides of the quadrilateral be respectively $2x$, $3x$, $4x$ and $5x$.

Then, perimeter of quadrilateral

$= 2x + 3x + 4x + 5x = 14x$

$14x = 770$

$x = 55$

Smallest side $= 2x = 2 \times 55$

$= 110$ cm.

**94.** Let, weight of coach is $x$ kg

$11 \times 117 + x = 12 \times (117 + 1)$

$1287 + x = 1416$

$x = 1416 - 1287$

$x = 129$

Therefore, weight of coach

$= 129$ kg.

**95.** Selling price of the book

$$= 5400\left(1 - \frac{10}{100}\right) = 5400 \times \frac{90}{100}$$

$= ₹\,4860$

$$CP = \frac{100}{100 + \text{Profit\%}} \times SP$$

$$= \frac{100}{100+20} \times 4860 = \frac{100}{120} \times 4860$$

$= ₹\,4050.$

**96.** $43 - [10 - (49 \div 7 - (15 - 25 \div 5) \div 10)]$

According to BODMAS,

$= 43 - [10 - (49 \div 7 - (15 - 5) \div 10)]$

$= 43 - [10 - (7 - 1)]$

$= 43 - [10 - 6]$

$= 43 - 4$

$= 39.$

**97.** 1st number $\times$ 2nd number

$=$ LCM $\times$ HCF

$128 \times$ 2nd number $= 128 \times 8$

$\therefore$ 2nd number $= \frac{128 \times 8}{128} = 8.$

**98.** In the year 2001, the difference in production between Company X and Company Y

$= 105 - 51 = 54$

In the year 2002, the difference in production between Company X and Company Y

$= 86 - 55 = 31$

In the year 2003, the difference in production between Company X and Company Y

$= 96 - 63 = 33$

In the year 2004, the difference in production between Company X and Company Y

$= 95 - 76 = 19$

In the year 2005, the difference in production between Company X and Company Y

$= 85 - 41 = 44$

In the year 2006, the difference in production between Company X and Company Y

$= 90 - 48 = 42$

Therefore, minimum difference in 2004.

**100.** The number will be divisible by 12 which is divisible by both 4 and 3.

A number will be divisible by 4 whose last two digit is divisible by 4.

The number will be divisible by 3 so that the sum of digits is divisible by 3.

(A) 18744

$$\frac{44}{4} = 11$$

Hence, divisible by 4.

$$\frac{1+8+7+4+4}{3} = \frac{24}{3} = 8$$

Hence, it is divisible by 3.

**101.** Number of vehicles manufactured by Company X in 2001 = 51

Number of vehicles manufactured by Company X in 2002 = 55

Required difference = 55 – 51 = 4.

**102.** Percentage increase

$$= \frac{534 - 445}{445} \times 100 = \frac{89}{445} \times 100 = 20\%$$

**103.** Let, number removed is $x$

Then, $x = 160 \times 7 - 160 \times 6$

$x = 1120 - 960$

$x = 160.$

**104.** $$\text{Profit \%} = \frac{SP - CP}{CP} \times 100$$

$$= \frac{340 - 272}{272} \times 100$$

$$= \frac{68}{272} \times 100$$

$$= \frac{6800}{272} = 25\%.$$

**105.** Let, consumption in initial period is $x$ kg

Cost × Consumption = Expenditure

In starting $720 \times 100 = 72{,}000$

By increasing the cost,

$900 \times x = 72{,}000$

$$\therefore \quad x = \frac{72{,}000}{900} = ₹\ 80$$

Per cent decrease in consumption

$$= \frac{100 - 80}{100} \times 100$$

$$= \frac{20}{100} \times 100 = 20\%.$$

**106.** Let, the length of train = $x$ m

∵ The speed of train in both condition is equal

$$\therefore \text{ Speed} = \frac{\text{Distance}}{\text{Time}}$$

$$\frac{x}{50} = \frac{x + 473}{93}$$

$93x = 50x + 23650$

$43x = 23650$

$$x = \frac{23650}{43} = 550 \text{ m.}$$

∴ The length of train is 550 m.

**107.** Let, 1st and 2nd part is $6x$ and $5x$ respectively

Then, $6x = 330$

$x = 55$

∴ Total Amount $= 5x + 6x$

$= 11x + 11 \times 55 = 605.$

**108.** $$SI = \frac{P \times R \times T}{100}$$

$$= \frac{5500 \times 13 \times 4}{100} = 2860$$

Amount = PA + SI

$= 5500 + 2860 = 8360.$

**109.** $$\text{Average speed} = \frac{2S_1S_2}{S_1 + S_2}$$

$$= \frac{2 \times 700 \times 1050}{700 + 1050}$$

$$= \frac{2 \times 700 \times 1050}{1750}$$

= 840 mile/hour.

**110.** Side of equilateral triangle

= 124 cm.

Area of equilateral triangle

$$= \frac{\sqrt{3}}{4}(\text{side})^2 = \frac{\sqrt{3}}{4} \times 124 \times 124$$

$= 3844\sqrt{3}\ \text{cm}^2.$

**111.** Let the age of alpha and beta be $2x$ and $5x$ respectively.

$2x + 5x = 350$

$7x = 350$

$x = 50$

Difference between their ages

$= 5x - 2x = 3x = 3 \times 50 = 150.$

**112.** $$CP = \frac{100}{100 - \text{Loss \%}} \times SP$$

$$= \frac{100}{100 - 15} \times 680$$

$$= \frac{100}{85} \times 680 = ₹\ 800.$$

**113.** Let the number of pen, pencil and eraser in the box be $3x$, $2x$ and $x$ respectively.

Then, the total amount spent on the box

$= 3x \times 3 + 2x \times 2 + x \times 2$

$= 9x + 4x + 2x = 15x$

$15x = 795$

$x = 53$

No. of pen in box $= 3x$

$= 3 \times 53$

$= 159.$

**115.** Area of rhombus $= \frac{1}{2} \times d_1 \times d_2$

$= \frac{1}{2} \times 119 \times 120$

$= 7140 \text{ cm}^2.$

**116.** Loss % $= \frac{\text{CP} - \text{SP}}{\text{CP}} \times 100$

$= \frac{475 - 380}{475} \times 100 = \frac{9500}{475} = 20\%$

**117.** $\sqrt{(30 - x)} = \sqrt{17 + \sqrt{1024}}$

$\sqrt{(30 - x)} = \sqrt{17 + 32}$

$\sqrt{(30 - x)} = \sqrt{49}$

$30 - x = 49$

$x = 30 - 49$

$x = -19.$

**118.** Remaining percentage of soap.

$= \frac{120 - 84}{120} \times 100$

$= \frac{36}{120} \times 100 = 30\%$

**119.** Length of Rectangle $= \sqrt{l^2 - b^2}$

$= \sqrt{(702)^2 - (270)^2}$

$= \sqrt{(702 + 270)(702 - 270)}$

$= \sqrt{972 \times 432}$

$= \sqrt{419904} = 648 \text{ cm}$

Perimeter of Rectangle $= 2(l + b)$

$= 2(270 + 648)$

$= 2 \times 918 = 1836.$

**120.**

```
9) 15209 (1689
   9
   62
   54
    80
    72
     89
     81
      8  ← Remainder
```

Previous Paper (Solved)

## Railway Protection Force & Railway Protection Special Force

# RPF/RPSF—CONSTABLE

## Recruitment Exam–2015*

**1.** Which of these states has the longest international border?
A. Nagaland B. Mizoram
C. Arunachal Pradesh D. Assam

**2.** Which of these fabrics is named after a French dress maker?
A. Linen B. Crepe
C. Georgette D. Chiffon

**3.** Who was the founder of Sikhism?
A. Guru Govind Singh
B. Guru Ram Das
C. Guru Nanak
D. Ranjeet Singh

**4.** Who is the founder of Patna's famous Super 30 Institute that coaches economically backward students for IIT JEE?
A. Anurag Anand B. Sushil Kumar
C. Anand Kumar D. Nitish Kumar

**5.** Shri Narendra Modi is the ____ of India.
A. Speaker of Lok Sabha
B. Prime Minister
C. Leader of Opposition
D. President

**6.** National Unity Day is celebrated in India on ____.
A. 30th January B. 29th August
C. 31st October D. 2nd October

**7.** Which continent is the Giraffe native to?
A. Australia B. Africa
C. America D. Asia

**8.** Sumo is a traditional form of wrestling of which country?
A. China B. Japan
C. Vietnam D. South Korea

**9.** Amir Khusro was the famous poet in the court of ____ .
A. Shah Jahan B. Alauddin Khilji
C. Akbar D. Sher Shah Suri

**10.** Which of these medical conditions is classified into Type-1 and Type-2?
A. Diabetes B. Hepatitis
C. Night Blindness D. Common Cold

**11.** Who is the Commander-in-Chief of the Indian Armed Forces?
A. Prime Minister
B. Vice-President
C. Chief of Army Staff
D. President

**12.** The surface of which of these planets is **not** solid?
A. Jupiter B. Mars
C. Venus D. Mercury

**13.** With which main ingredient is litti, a food item from Bihar, stuffed?
A. Onion B. Potato
C. Vegetables D. Gram Flour

**14.** Which natural phenomenon conducts carbon dioxide fixation in plants?
A. Sunlight B. Rain
C. Thunder D. Cosmic Rays

**15.** Other than cricket which game also has a striker?
A. Ludo B. Kho-Kho
C. Carrom D. Chess

**16.** Islamic state is **not** waging a battle against:
A. Ukraine B. Lebanon
C. Iraq D. Syria

**17.** Which of these places got its name from a local word for mangrove trees?
A. Vrindavan B. Sunderbans
C. Mussoorie D. Madhubani

**18.** Name the Chief Minister of Jharkhand.
A. Babulal Marandi B. Arjun Munda
C. Raghubar Das D. Hemant Soren

* Held on 15-02-2015

**19.** If you are in Red Fort, which city are you visiting?
A. Agra B. Hyderabad
C. Jaipur D. Delhi

**20.** Which of these is **not** a port city on the Arabian Sea?
A. Panaji B. Vishakhapatnam
C. Mumbai D. Mangalore

**21.** Which of these Asian countries is **not** landlocked?
A. Afghanistan B. Laos
C. Mongolia D. Cambodia

**22.** Which was the first hill passenger railway opened in India in 1881?
A. Kalka Shimla Railway
B. Matheran Hill Railway
C. Nilgiri Mountain Railway
D. Darjeeling Himalayan Railway

**23.** What does CO stand for?
A. Carbon B. Carbon monoxide
C. Coal D. Carbon dioxide

**24.** Raslila dance is associated with which God?
A. Lord Shiva B. Lord Ganesha
C. Lord Indra D. Lord Krishna

**25.** Which of the following is an Indian online retail company?
A. Alibaba group B. Amazon
C. eBay D. Jabong

**Directions (26-30):** *Complete the following series each of which follows a certain pattern.*

**26.** 3, 12, 27, 48, 75, 108, ...?...
A. 162 B. 183
C. 192 D. 147

**27.** 49, 121, 169, 289, ...?...
A. 361 B. 529
C. 400 D. 441

**28.** a_ccabc_a_cc_bcc
A. c b c b B. b c b a
C. b a c b D. b b c c

**29.** _cbacb_dbad_adc_.
A. d a c b B. b c a a
C. c c a a D. c b d d

**30.** 2, 3, 4, 6, 8, 12, 16, 24, ...?...
A. 36 B. 30
C. 32 D. 40

**Directions (31-35):** *In the following questions, find the odd one out.*

**31.** A. Nepal B. Germany
C. China D. India

**32.** A. BY B. CV
C. DW D. AZ

**33.** A. 18 B. 27
C. 33 D. 9

**34.** A. Snooker B. Chess
C. Hockey D. Billiards

**35.** A. IFG B. QOP
C. XVW D. ECD

**36.** 24 : 36 :: ? : 72
A. 48 B. 60
C. 56 D. 40

**37.** Convict : Jail :: Lawyer : ...?...
A. Field B. Hospital
C. Office D. Court

**38.** Rabies : Dog :: Ebola : ...?...
A. Fish B. Mosquito
C. Cat D. Bats

**39.** If 26th January, 2015 is Monday what was the day on 26th January, 2011?
A. Tuesday B. Wednesday
C. Thursday D. Monday

**40.** If 'a' means multiplication, 'b' means minus, 'c' means plus and 'd' means division, then 5a 3b 2c [4d 4] = ...?...
A. 6 B. 0
C. 14 D. 12

**41.** GTU : JWX :: CMN : ...?...
A. FQR B. FPQ
C. FPR D. FOP

**Directions (42-45):** *The figure given below consists of three intersecting circles which represent set of players who play Tennis, Badminton and Kabaddi. Each region in the figure is represented by a number.*

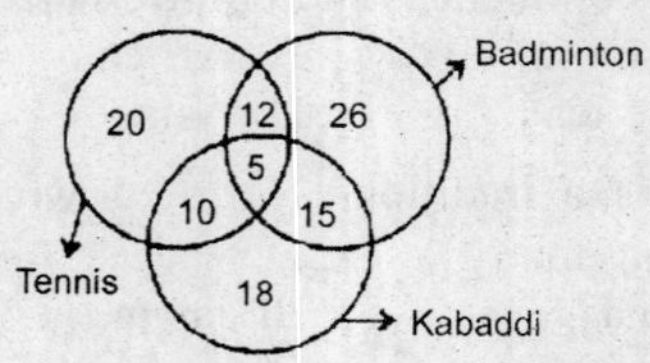


**42.** How many players play Kabaddi?
A. 48 B. 28
C. 38 D. 43

**43.** Which number represents the set of players who play only Tennis?
A. 20 B. 15
C. 5 D. 18

**44.** Which number represents the set of players who play both Tennis and Badminton but not Kabaddi?
A. 10 B. 12
C. 15 D. 5

**45.** Which game is played by least number of players?
A. Tennis B. Badminton
C. Kabaddi D. All the three

**46.** The average of eleven numbers is 30. If average of first ten numbers is 22 then what is the eleventh number?
A. 8 B. 80
C. 30 D. 110

**47.** If 59 is added to a square of a number, the result is 900. What is the number?
A. 30 B. 28
C. 29 D. 27

**48.** If C is to the west of A and B is to the south of A, in what direction is B with respect to C?
A. NW B. SE
C. NE D. SW

**49.** Deepa and Seema together do a work in 6 days. Deepa can complete the same work alone in 9 days. In how many days will Seema complete the work alone?
A. 18 days B. 3 days
C. 12 days D. 15 days

**50.** The population of a city was 70,000, it increased by 8%. What is the population now?
A. 76,000 B. 76,500
C. 76,600 D. 75,600

**51.** What will be the Highest Common Factor of 4, 8 and 12?
A. 1 B. 4
C. 8 D. 2

**52.** If CORRECTION is coded as DPSSFDUJPO, how would EMOTION be coded?
A. FPNUJPO B. FNPUJOP
C. FNPUPOJ D. FNPUJPO

**53.** A motorcycle covers 60 km in 3 hours. Its speed is doubled. What distance will it cover in the next 1 hour?
A. 360 km B. 40 km
C. 60 km D. 120 km

**54.** 75 of $\frac{1}{30} \div \frac{1}{2} = ?$
A. 1.25 B. 2.5
C. 12.5 D. 5

**55.** Ramesh walks 25 metre towards north. He then turns left and walks for 20 metre. He then again turns left and walks for 25 metre. He then turns left and walks for 50 metre. How far is he from his starting position?
A. 30 metre B. 50 metre
C. 120 metre D. 70 metre

**56.** At what % of simple interest per annum will ₹ 400 amount to ₹ 520 in five years?
A. 6% B. 5%
C. 5.5% D. 24%

**57.** The radius of a circular field is 31.5 metre. What is its circum-ference?
A. 198 metre B. 154 metre
C. 237 metre D. 110 metre

**58.** The difference of cubes of two consecutive numbers is 127. What are the numbers?
A. 5 and 6 B. 4 and 5
C. 6 and 7 D. 7 and 8

**59.** The length of a rectangular field is increased by 20% and breadth is decreased by 20%. What is the per cent increase or decrease in its area?
A. 20% increase B. 4% decrease
C. 1% increase D. No change

**60.** Amar is twenty fourth in a queue starting from either end. How many persons are there in the queue?
A. 46 B. 49
C. 47 D. 48

**61.** Ram moves 10 km towards East then moves 10 km right, again moves 10 km right. In which direction is he now from the starting point?
A. north B. west
C. south D. east

**62.** 0.0050 ÷ 0.05 + 0.05 = ?
A. 0.15 B. 0.05
C. 0.16 D. 0.50

**63.** A shirt priced at ₹ 1500 is being sold at a discount of 40% + 60%. What is its price after discount?

A. ₹ 0 B. ₹ 1400
C. ₹ 540 D. ₹ 360

**64.** The sum of two digits of a number is 13. If 9 is subtracted from the number, the digits are interchanged. What is the number?
A. 76 B. 87
C. 78 D. 67

**65.** The sum of four consecutive positive integers is 82, then the smallest one of them is:
A. 20 B. 19
C. 22 D. 21

**66.** Rahul moves 8 km towards West and then turns towards left and travels for 6 km. How far is Rahul from his starting point and in which direction?
A. NE 2 km B. SE 14 km
C. NW 10 km D. SW 10 km

**67.** What is the Lowest Common Multiple of 2, 3 and 7?
A. 42 B. 21
C. 14 D. 6

**68.** There are 1500 students in a school. 15% are Muslims, 7% Sikhs, 8% Christians and remaining are Hindus. How many Hindu students are there in the school?
A. 1470 B. 700
C. 1050 D. 1200

**69.** 20 dogs can eat 20 hens in 10 days. In how many days can 40 dogs eat 40 such hens?
A. 1 B. 20
C. 30 D. 10

**70.** If BANGLE is coded as ELGNAB. How would SANDAL be coded?
A. LADNSA B. LANDAS
C. LADNAS D. LADANS

**71.** If Wednesday falls on 26th January, then what day will it be on the last day of January?
A. Friday B. Monday
C. Sunday D. Thursday

**72.** 60% is equal to:
A. $\frac{6}{9}$ B. $\frac{9}{10}$
C. $\frac{3}{5}$ D. $\frac{7}{9}$

**73.** Average height of a class of 12 students is 180 cm. The average decreases to 179 cm when the height of the class teacher is also added. What is the height of the teacher?
A. 168 cm B. 167 cm
C. 179.5 cm D. 166 cm

**74.** $3 - 1 + 3 \times 6 \div 3 - 1 = ?$
A. 11 B. –3
C. 7 D. 9

**75.** Rishi earned ₹ 83.2 at compound rate of interest 8% per annum over two years. How much did he invest?
A. ₹ 600 B. ₹ 500
B. ₹ 540 D. ₹ 503.2

**76.** If $\frac{1}{4}$ of third-part of a number is equal to 5, then the number is:
A. 15 B. 60
C. 12 D. 20

**77.** If '×' stands for division, '÷' stands for subtraction, '+' stands for multiplication and '–' stands for addition, then:
$6 \times 2 \div 2 - 4 + 2 = ?$
A. 0 B. 4
C. 10 D. 9

**78.** In a group of seven teams, each team plays against one another twice. How many total matches will be played in the group?
A. 49 B. 42
C. 48 D. 28

**79.** A bus travels at a speed of 75 km/hr for 45 minutes and then travels at a speed of 90 km/hr for 45 minutes. What distance will it cover in one and a half hour?
A. 123.75 km B. 165 km
C. 125 km D. 82.5 km

**80.** How many even numbers are there in the following sequence of numbers which are immediately preceded by an odd number but immediately followed by an even number?
5 1 4 7 3 9 8 5 7 2 6 3 1 5 8 6 3 8 5 2 7 4 3 4 9 6
A. Two B. One
C. Four D. Three

**81.** 0.105 + 1.05 + 0.515 + 0.015 = ?
A. 1.685 B. 1.675
C. 1.75 D. 1.785

**82.** Which is the largest fraction?

A. $\frac{3}{4}$ B. $\frac{7}{9}$
C. $\frac{7}{8}$ D. $\frac{9}{10}$

**83.** Average of 8 numbers is 42. If 9 is subtrated from each number then what is the new average?

A. 33 B. 34
C. 25 D. 9

**84.** 

A.  B. 
C.  D. 

**85.** What is the ratio of 20 paise and ₹ 4?

A. 1 : 8 B. 1 : 16
C. 1 : 20 D. 1 : 5

**86.** A shopkeeper sold a shirt for ₹ 728 at a loss of 9%. If he had sold for ₹ 792, what would have been the gain/loss per cent?

A. 8% loss B. 9% profit
C. 1% loss D. 8% profit

**87.** Convert $\frac{9}{10}$ into decimal.

A. 90 B. 1.90
C. 0.09 D. 0.9

**88.** Shyam sold a bag for ₹ 598.9 at a gain of 13%. What was its cost price?

A. ₹ 550 B. ₹ 530
C. ₹ 585 D. ₹ 500

**89.** 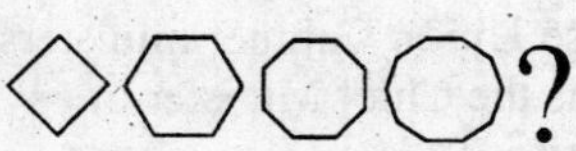

A.  B. 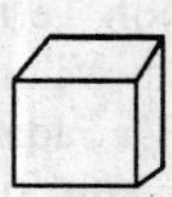
C. 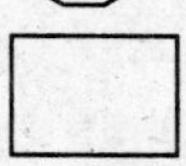 D. 

**90.** In a certain code SEAT is coded as RDZS. How would READ be coded?

A. QDZC B. QDCZ
C. QDZE D. QDZD

**91.** What time will a runner take to run a distance of 8 km at a speed of 15 km/hr?

A. 35 minutes B. 33 minutes
C. 31 minutes D. 32 minutes

**92.** If PERFECTION is coded as EFREPNOITC, how will IMPOSTER be coded?

A. OPIMRETS B. OPMIRETS
C. OPMIERTS D. OPMIREST

**93.** The area of a square field is 196 sq. metre. What would be the length of the rope required to fence the field from any three sides?

A. 56 metre B. 42 metre
C. 52 metre D. 147 metre

**94.** If 40% of a number is 184, then what is the value of 85% of the number?

A. 333 B. 391
C. 380 D. 328

**95.** A TV is bought for ₹ 42,000 and sold for ₹ 49,140. What is the gain per cent?

A. 9% B. 7.14%
B. 17% D. 7%

**96.** For making which sweet is winter melon or white gourd soaked in sugar syrup?

A. Jalebi B. Petha
C. Gulab Jamun D. Murabba

**97.** Which of these is an essential component of most acids?

A. Hydrogen B. Oxygen
C. Helium D. Nitrogen

**98.** Sir Creek is a disputed territory between India and ____.

A. Myanmar B. Nepal
C. Pakistan D. Bangladesh

**99.** Which of these is essential to keep bones strong in the body?

A. Iodine B. Zinc
C. Fats D. Calcium

**100.** How many different kinds of zodiac signs are there in Astrology?

A. 12 B. 16
C. 14 D. 11

**101.** The Nobel Peace Prize for 2014 has been awarded to

A. Kailash Satyarthi
B. Barack Obama
C. Kailash Satyarthi and Tawakkul Karman
D. Kailash Satyarthi and Malala Yousafzai

**102.** The autobiography of which freedom fighter is titled 'Atmakatha' which he wrote during his prison time in Bankipore Jail in Patna?
A. Rajendra Prasad
B. Ram Manohar Lohia
C. Lal Bahadur Shastri
D. Jayaprakash Narayan

**103.** Which was the first element to be artificially produced?
A. Technetium B. Francium
C. Einsteinium D. Promethium

**104.** Who was the host of TV show 'Big Boss 8'?
A. Salman Khan B. Amitabh Bachchan
C. Shah Rukh Khan D. Amir Khan

**105.** Which of the following is **not** a social networking website?
A. Facebook B. hi5
C. Wikipedia D. Twitter

**106.** In the Northern Hemisphere, around which date does the summer solstice occur?
A. 21st June B. 22nd July
C. 23rd May D. 31st March

**107.** Which of these fruits is **not** rich in Vitamin C?
A. Orange B. Kiwi
C. Lemon D. Apple

**108.** Deepika Kumari is associated with which sport?
A. Shooting B. Wrestling
C. Archery D. Football

**109.** Which of these countries is an Archipelago?
A. Laos B. Chile
C. Philippines D. Argentina

**110.** Flight 17, which was shot down over Ukraine was a scheduled international passenger flight to Kuala Lumpur from:
A. Amsterdam B. Moscow
C. Paris D. London

**111.** Manik Sarkar is the Chief Minister of:
A. Assam B. Tripura
C. West Bengal D. Sikkim

**112.** Kaziranga National Park is most famous for:
A. Swamp Deer
B. Wild Ass
C. One-horned Rhinoceros
D. Asiatic Lion

**113.** Which was the last autonomous territory or protectorate to integrate with the Indian union?
A. Puducherry B. Sikkim
C. Diu D. Goa

**114.** Which country will host the 2016 Summer Olympic Games?
A. Argentina B. Russia
C. Japan D. Brazil

**115.** Rann of Kutch is situated in which state?
A. Bihar B. Rajasthan
C. Gujarat D. Maharashtra

**116.** Which new university named after an ancient centre of learning in its vicinity, began its academic session in 2014?
A. Takshila B. Nalanda
C. Pushpagiri D. Vikramshila

**117.** The sign for which mathematical function is the logo of the Red Cross Society?
A. Subtraction B. Multiplication
C. Division D. Addition

**118.** Who was the ruling Governor General of India when the power was transferred from the East India Company to the British Crown?
A. Lord Irwin B. Lord Canning
C. Lord Curzon D. Lord Mountbatten

**119.** Wangchuck dynasty is the ruler of which country?
A. Brunei B. Indonesia
C. Myanmar D. Bhutan

**120.** Which of these Union Cabinet ministers have never served as the Chief Minister of any State or Union Territory?
A. Ram Vilas Paswan
B. D.V. Sadananda Gowda
C. Rajnath Singh
D. Sushma Swaraj

## ANSWERS

| 1 | 2 | 3 | 4 | 5 | 6 | 7 | 8 | 9 | 10 |
|---|---|---|---|---|---|---|---|---|---|
| C | C | C | C | B | C | B | B | B | A |
| **11** | **12** | **13** | **14** | **15** | **16** | **17** | **18** | **19** | **20** |
| D | A | D | A | C | A | B | C | D | B |

| 21 | 22 | 23 | 24 | 25 | 26 | 27 | 28 | 29 | 30 |
|---|---|---|---|---|---|---|---|---|---|
| D | D | B | D | D | D | A | B | A | C |
| **31** | **32** | **33** | **34** | **35** | **36** | **37** | **38** | **39** | **40** |
| B | B | C | C | A | A | D | D | B | C |
| **41** | **42** | **43** | **44** | **45** | **46** | **47** | **48** | **49** | **50** |
| B | A | A | B | A | D | C | B | A | D |
| **51** | **52** | **53** | **54** | **55** | **56** | **57** | **58** | **59** | **60** |
| B | D | B | D | A | A | A | C | B | C |
| **61** | **62** | **63** | **64** | **65** | **66** | **67** | **68** | **69** | **70** |
| C | A | D | A | B | D | A | C | D | C |
| **71** | **72** | **73** | **74** | **75** | **76** | **77** | **78** | **79** | **80** |
| B | C | B | C | B | B | D | B | A | A |
| **81** | **82** | **83** | **84** | **85** | **86** | **87** | **88** | **89** | **90** |
| A | D | A | B | C | A | D | B | A | A |
| **91** | **92** | **93** | **94** | **95** | **96** | **97** | **98** | **99** | **100** |
| D | B | B | B | C | B | A | C | A | A |
| **101** | **102** | **103** | **104** | **105** | **106** | **107** | **108** | **109** | **110** |
| D | A | A | A | C | A | D | C | C | A |
| **111** | **112** | **113** | **114** | **115** | **116** | **117** | **118** | **119** | **120** |
| B | C | B | D | C | B | D | B | D | A |

## Some Selected Explanatory Answers

**27.** $(7)^2 = 49$
$(11)^2 = 121$
$(13)^2 = 169$
$(17)^2 = 289$
$(19)^2 = 361$.

**31.** Except Germany, all others are Asian countries. Germany is in Europe.

**32.** Except CV, all others are pairs of opposite letters.
$B \leftrightarrow Y$ ; $D \leftrightarrow W$ ; $A \leftrightarrow Z$
The opposite letter of C is X.

**33.** Except 33, all others are multiples of 9.

**34.** Except Hockey, all others are indoor games. Again, Hockey is played between two teams consisting of 11 players each.

**36.** $$\frac{24 \times 3}{2} = 36$$
Similarly, $$\frac{48 \times 3}{2} = 72.$$

**37.** Convict is kept in Jail. Similarly, Lawyer practises in Court.

**38.** Rabies is spread through dogs. Similarly, Ebola is spread through bats.

**39.** The number of odd days from 2011 to 2014.
= 1 + 2 + 1 + 1 = 5 days
2012 was a leap year
So, 26th January, 2011
= Monday – 5 = Wednesday.

**42.** The number of players who play Kabaddi
= 5 + 10 + 15 + 18 = 48.

**43.** The number of players who play only Tennis = 20.

**44.** The number of players who play both Tennis and Badminton but not Kabaddi = 12.

**45.** Number of players who play Kabaddi = 48
Number of players who play Badminton = 58
Number of players who play Tennis = 47.

**46.** Eleventh Number
$= 30 \times 11 - 10 \times 22$
$= 330 - 220 = 110$.

**47.** Let, the number be $x$.
According to question,
$$x^2 + 59 = 900$$
$$\Rightarrow \quad x^2 = 900 - 59 = 841$$
$$\therefore \quad x = \sqrt{841} = 29.$$

**49.** Time taken by Seema
= $x$ days (let)
According to the question,

$$\frac{1}{x}+\frac{1}{9}=\frac{1}{6}$$

$$\Rightarrow \quad \frac{1}{x}=\frac{1}{6}-\frac{1}{9}=\frac{3-2}{18}=\frac{1}{18}$$

$$\Rightarrow \quad x = 18 \text{ days.}$$

**50.** Present population of city

$$= P_0\left(1+\frac{R}{100}\right)^T = 70000\left(1+\frac{8}{100}\right)$$

$$= 70000\times\frac{108}{100}=75,600.$$

**51.**
$4 = 2 \times 2$
$8 = 2 \times 2 \times 2$
$12 = 2 \times 2 \times 3$
$\therefore$ HCF $= 2 \times 2 = 4$.

**53.** Speed $= \frac{\text{Distance}}{\text{Time}}=\frac{60}{3}=20$ kmph
New speed $= 2 \times 20 = 40$ kmph
$\therefore$ Required distance = 40 km.

**54.** $? = 75\times\frac{1}{30}\times 2 = 5.$

**56.** S.I. = 520 – 400 = ₹ 120

$$\text{Rate} = \frac{\text{S.I.}\times 100}{\text{Principal}\times\text{Time}}$$

$$= \frac{120\times 100}{400\times 5} = 6\% \text{ per annum.}$$

**57.** Circumference of circle $= 2\pi r$

$$= 2\times\frac{22}{7}\times 31.5 = 198 \text{ metre.}$$

**58.** Of the given options,
$7^3 - 6^3 = 343 - 216 = 127.$

**59.** Required answer

$$= \left(x+y+\frac{xy}{100}\right)\% = \left(20-20-\frac{20\times 20}{100}\right)\%$$

$= -4\%$
Negative sign shows decrease.

**60.** Number of persons in the queue
$= 23 + 23 + 1 = 47.$

**62.**
$$? = 0.0050\times\frac{1}{0.05}+0.05$$
$$= 0.1 + 0.05 = 0.15.$$

**63.** Single equivalent discount

$$= \left(x+y-\frac{xy}{100}\right)\% = \left(40+60-\frac{40\times 60}{100}\right)\%$$

$= (100 - 24)\% = 76\%$
$\therefore$ Required price of shirt = 24% of 1500

$$= \frac{1500\times 24}{100} = ₹\ 360.$$

**65.** Four consecutive positive integers
$\Rightarrow x, x + 1, x + 2, x + 3$
$\therefore x + x + 1 + x + 2 + x + 3 = 82$
$\Rightarrow \quad 4x + 6 = 82$
$\Rightarrow \quad 4x = 82 - 6 = 76$
$\Rightarrow \quad x = \frac{76}{4} = 19.$

**67.** Required LCM $= 2 \times 3 \times 7 = 42$.

**68.** Percentage of Hindu students
= 100 – (15 + 7 + 8)
= 100 – 30 = 70%
$\therefore$ Number of Hindu students

$$= \frac{1500\times 70}{100} = 1050.$$

**70.** The letters of the word BANGLE are coded in reverse order.
$\therefore$ SANDAL $\Rightarrow$ LADNAS.

**71.** There are 31 days in January.
$\therefore \quad 26 + 5 \Rightarrow 31$
Wednesday + 5 days $\Rightarrow$ Monday

**72.** $60\% = \frac{60}{100}=\frac{3}{5}.$

**73.** Decrease in average height = 1 cm.
$\therefore$ Height of teacher $= 180 - 13 \times 1 = 167$ cm.

**74.** $? = 3 - 1 + 3 \times 6 \div 3 - 1$

$$= 3-1+\frac{3\times 6}{3}-1$$

$= 3 - 1 + 6 - 1 = 9 - 2 = 7.$

**76.** Number = $x$ (let)
According to question,

$$\frac{x}{3}\times\frac{1}{4} = 5$$

$$\Rightarrow \quad \frac{x}{12} = 5$$

$$\Rightarrow \quad x = 12 \times 5 = 60.$$

# General Intelligence

## Reasoning Ability

## Chapter 1

# TEST OF ANALOGY

Analogy implies finding corresponding words or pairs. In test of analogy a pair of words/figures with well difined relationship is given and a similar relationship is to be established between two others by selecting from the given answer.

Some examples are given below to make understand the test of analogy.

**Example 1 :**

Cow : Calf : : Lion : Cub

**Ans.** Here Calf is young one of Cow where as Cub is the young one of Lion.

**Example 2 :**

Doctor : Patient : : Lawyer : Client

**Ans.** Here Doctor is to attend the Patient and Lawyer is to attend the Client.

**Example 3 :**

Needle : Sew : : Knife : Cut

**Ans.** A Needle is used for Sewing hence Knife is used for Cutting.

**Example 5 :**

Lizard : Reptile : : Ostrich : Bird

**Ans.** Lizard belongs to the class of Reptile and Ostrich belongs to the class of Bird.

## EXERCISE

**1.** Book : Read : : Pen : ?
A. Publisher B. Stationery
C. Ink D. Write

**2.** Bird : Cage : : Prisoner : ?
A. House B. Police Station
C. Jail D. Court

**3.** War : Death : : Smoke : ?
A. Burning B. Fire
C. Pollution D. Sky

**4.** Apple : Iron : : Grapes : ?
A. Vitamin A B. Vitamin B
C. Vitamin D D. Vitamin C

**5.** Blacksmith : Anvil : : Author : ?
A. Book B. Novel
C. Poem D. Pen

**6.** Rough : Smooth : : Depression : ?
A. Joy B. Happiness
C. Disease D. Mound

**7.** Sun : Shine : : Cloud : ?
A. Rain B. Dark
C. Burst D. Lightning

**8.** Bud : Flower : : Sapling : ?
A. Plant B. Garden
C. Water D. Soil

**9.** Gun : Shoot : : Knife : ?
A. Cut B. Stice
C. Run D. Cuts

**10.** Anger : Rage : : Quarrel : ?
A. Dispute B. Fight
C. War D. Murder

**11.** Attack : Defend : : Sink : ?
A. Float B. Swim
C. Boat D. Water

**12.** Oil : Sunflower : : Plant : ?
A. Twing B. Taste
C. Flower D. Seed

**13.** Gun : Bullet : : Chimney : ?
A. Smoke B. Roof
C. House D. Ground

**14.** Good : Bad : : Rough : ?
A. Plane B. Clean
C. Smooth D. Thick

**15.** Bank : River : : Coast : ?
A. Flood B. Waves
C. Sea D. Beach

**16.** Man : Machine : : Master : ?
A. Slave B. House

C. Manager D. Worker

**17.** Campa : Drink : : Medicine : ?
A. Take B. Swallow
C. Sip D. Taste

**18.** Sharp : Blunt : : Light : ?
A. Heavy B. Dark
C. Empty D. Night

**19.** Adder : Snake : : Crocodile : ?
A. Marsh B. Reptile
C. Ruminant D. Carnivore

**20.** Propellor : Aircraft : : Feathers : ?
A. Neck B. Bird
C. Tail D. Decoration

**21.** Head : Cap : : Finger : ?
A. Nail B. Blood
C. Skin D. Thumb

**22.** Leg : Foot : : Hand : ?
A. Arm B. Thigh
C. Wrist D. Elbow

**23.** Bunch : Key : : Bouquet : ?
A. Pack B. Gift
C. Flower D. Present

**24.** Army : Soldiers : : Galaxy : ?
A. Stars B. Meteor
C. Universe D. Planet

**25.** Water : Thirst : : Food : ?
A. Hunger B. Rice
C. Earn D. Distribute

**26.** Cup : Drink : : Plate : ?
A. Silver B. Dine
C. Fork D. Supper

**27.** Blood : Circulation : : Harmone : ?
A. Egestion B. Control
C. Digestion D. Coordination

**28.** Steel : Bokaro : : Hosiery : ?
A. Calcutta B. Mumbai
C. Kanpur D. Ludhiana

**29.** Bull : Draugut : : Cow : ?
A. Fodder B. Farm
C. Milk D. Livestock

**30.** Cobra : Snake : : Leopard : ?
A. Tiger B. Lion
C. Cat D. Zebra

**31.** Horse : Hay : : Cow : ?
A. Leaves B. Fodder
C. Milk D. Straw

**32.** Movie : Theatre : : Banquet : ?
A. Hotel B. Party
C. Feast D. Supper

**33.** Water : Ocean : : Snow : ?
A. Peaks B. Hail
C. Glacier D. Mountain

**34.** Poison : Socrates : : Crucification : ?
A. Jesus B. Christians
C. Aristotle D. Church

**35.** Tempest : Storm : : Slim : ?
A. Fat B. Plump
C. Slender D. Beautiful

**36.** Chopper : Meat : : Spanner : ?
A. Vegetables B. Cakes
C. Nuts D. Flash

**37.** Kilometre : Distance : : Poundal : ?
A. Density B. Acceleration
C. Force D. Momentum

**38.** Sparrow : Seed : : Silkworm : ?
A. Silic B. Maple
C. Mulberry D. Pine

**39.** Tobacco : Nerves : : Alcohol : ?
A. Liver B. Liquor
C. Head D. Intoxication

**40.** Arm : Forcep : : Leg : ?
A. Thigh B. Ankle
C. Toe D. Foot

**41.** Medicine : Disease : : Surgery : ?
A. Headache B. Tumour
C. Vomiting D. Pain

**42.** Abnormal : Normal : : Mad : ?
A. Good B. Sound
C. Sane D. Perfect

**43.** Die = Punch, Knife = ?
A. Cut B. Sharpen
C. Vegetable D. Murder

**44.** Cloud : Rain : : Snowstorm : ?
A. Hail B. Dew
C. Snow D. Fog

**45.** Beautiful : Ugly : : Brave : ?
A. Coward B. Timid
C. Strong D. Dummy

**46.** Labour = Wage, Clerk = ?
A. Remuneration B. Salary
C. Payment D. Money

**47.** Author : Book : : Poet : ?
A. Novel B. Book
C. Song D. Poem

**48.** Ascorbic Acid : Vitamin : : Glucose : ?
A. Minerals B. Carbohydrates
C. Vitamins D. Proteins

**49.** Life : Death : : Hope : ?
A. Sad B. Despair
C. Pain D. Cry

**50.** Cub : Tiger : : Fawn : ?
A. Stag B. Monkey
C. Ass D. Sheep

# ANSWERS

| 1 | 2 | 3 | 4 | 5 | 6 | 7 | 8 | 9 | 10 |
|---|---|---|---|---|---|---|---|---|---|
| D | C | C | D | D | D | A | A | A | C |
| **11** | **12** | **13** | **14** | **15** | **16** | **17** | **18** | **19** | **20** |
| A | D | A | C | C | A | A | B | B | B |
| **21** | **22** | **23** | **24** | **25** | **26** | **27** | **28** | **29** | **30** |
| A | C | C | A | A | B | D | D | C | C |
| **31** | **32** | **33** | **34** | **35** | **36** | **37** | **38** | **39** | **40** |
| B | A | C | A | C | C | C | C | A | A |
| **41** | **42** | **43** | **44** | **45** | **46** | **47** | **48** | **49** | **50** |
| B | C | A | C | A | B | D | B | B | A |

# EXPLANATORY ANSWERS

**1.** Book is used for Reading, Pen is used for Writing.

**2.** Birds are kept in Cage likewise Prisoners are kept in Jail.

**3.** Second is the Result of first.

**4.** We are getting Vitamin C from Grapes.

**5.** Anvil is used by Blacksmith, Pen is used by Author.

**6.** Second word is antonym of first.

**7.** The Sun gives Shine (Sunrays) whereas Clouds give Rains.

**8.** A Bud blooms into a Flower whereas a Sapling blooms into a Plant.

**9.** The usage of Knife is for Cutting.

**10.** The extreme of Anger is Rage and the extreme of Quarrel is War.

**11.** Second word is antonym of first.

**12.** First item is developed from the second one.

**13.** Second one is the outcome of the first one.

**14.** Second word is antonym of first.

**15.** Coast is the land beside the Sea.

**16.** Machine is made to work by a Man, Slave works under Master.

**17.** Medicine is always Taken.

**18.** The pairs comprise antonyms.

**19.** Crocodile is a Reptile.

**20.** A Propellor helps the Aircraft fly and Feathers help the Bird fly.

**21.** Nails cover the Fingers.

**22.** Wrist is attached to Hand.

**23.** The former in each pair belongs to the latter.

**24.** An Army comprises the Soldiers and a Galaxy comprises the Stars.

**25.** Water satisfies the Thirst of a person and Food satisfies the Hunger of a person.

**26.** Plates are kept of Dine.

**27.** Second is the function of first.

**28.** Ludhiana is famous for Hosiery.

**29.** Bull is a Draughter animal and Cow is Milk animal.

**30.** The second one denotes the family to which the first one belongs.

**31.** The second one is the food for the first one.

**32.** Second is the place where first is held.

**33.** Ocean is moving body of Water, Glacier is moving body of Snow.

**34.** First became the cause of death of the second.

**35.** First is of higher intensity.

**36.** First is the tool applied at the second.

**37.** Poundal is a unit of Force.

38. First feed at the second.
39. Alcohol affects the Liver.
40. The upper portion of Leg is Thigh.
41. Medicine is used to cure disease, Surgery is done to remove Tumour.
42. Second word is antonym of first.
43. We use a Die for Punching and we use a Knife for Cutting.
44. A Cloud gives Rains and a Snowstorm gives Snow.
45. Second word is antonym of first.
46. Clerks are given Salary.
47. Poet writes Poems.
48. Ascorbic Acid is a Vitamin and Glucose is a Carbohydrate.
49. The words in each pair are antonyms of each other.
50. First one is the young offspring of the second one.

## Chapter 2

# SERIES COMPLETION

In this chapter, some series of numbers or Alphabatical letters have been given. A particular pattern is followed and the student has to calculate his answer according to the pattern.

**Example 1 :** Which number will replace the question mark (?) :

2, 5, 9, 19, 37, ?

A. 45 B. 52

C. 69 D. 75

**Ans.** $2 \times 2 + 1 = 5$

$5 \times 2 - 1 = 9$

$9 \times 2 + 1 = 19$

So $37 \times 2 + 1 = 75$ Right Answer is D.

**Example 2 :** Find out the missing number :

0, 3, 8, ?, 24

A. 12 B. 14

C. 15 D. 11

**Ans.** $1^2 - 1$

$2^2 - 1$

$3^2 - 1$

So, $4^2 - 1 = 15$ Right Answer is C.

**Example 3 :** Which number would replace question mark (?) :

7, 12, 19, ?, 39

A. 29 B. 26

C. 28 D. 24

**Ans.** Given sequence follows this pattern :

$7 + 5 = 12$

$12 + 7 = 19$

$19 + 9 = 28$ Hence the Answer is C.

**Example 4 :** Find the odd man out:

3, 5, 7, 11, 13

A. 7 B. 11

C. 9 D. 13

**Ans.** Pattern is : 9 is the only number whose square-root is possible and here, 9 is the odd man out.

**Example 5 :** Find the odd man out:

3, 8, 15, 24, 34, 48, 63

A. 15 B. 24

C. 34 D. 48

E. 63

**Ans.** The, differences between the numbers are 5, 7, 9, 11 .... and so on. So, after 24, there should be (24 + 11), *i.e.*, 35. Hence the odd man is 34.

## EXERCISE

**Complete the Series:**

**1.** 196, 16, 144, 36, 100, 64, ?

A. 36 B. 64

C. 80 D. 100

**2.** 8, 48, 12, ?, 18, 108

A. 52 B. 72

C. 78 D. 64

**3.** 1, 4, 27, 16, 125, ?

A. 36 B. 81

C. 144 D. 216

**4.** 1, 2, 5, 12, 27, 58, 121, ?

A. 246 B. 247

C. 248 D. 249

**5.** 3, 6, 5, 20, 7, 42, 9, ?

A. 54 B. 60

C. 66 D. 72

**6.** 2, 3, 8, 63, ?

A. 1038 B. 1998

C. 3008 D. 3968

**7.** 3, 15, 35, ?, 99, 143

A. 63 B. 69

C. 77 D. 81

**8.** 2, 5, 9, 19, 37, ?

A. 45 B. 52

C. 69 D. 75

**9.** 240, ? 120, 40, 10, 2

A. 240 B. 120

C. 40 D. 10

10. 4, 7, 3, 6, 2, 5, ?
A. 8 B. 1
C. 4 D. 3

11. 1, 5, 8, 10, 11, ?
A. 5 B. 7
C. 9 D. 11

12. ?, 6, 30, 120, 360, 720
A. 3 B. 2
C. 1 D. 0

13. 1, 3, 1, 9, 1, 81, 1, ?
A. 4 B. 1
C. 243 D. 6561

14. 10, 12, 11, 14, 16, 15, ?
A. 18, 20, 19 B. 18, 19, 20
C. 17, 19, 18 D. 21, 23, 24

15. 5, 24, 61, 122, 213, 340, ?
A. 27 B. 61
C. 122 D. 509

16. 7, 28, 63, 124, ?
A. 127 B. 214
C. 215 D. 227

17. 1, 24, 60, 120, ?
A. 210 B. 240
C. 260 D. 215

18. 3, 5, 7, 9, 11, 13, ?
A. 15 B. 17
C. 18 D. 14

19. 3, 9, 27, 81, ?
A. 324 B. 243
C. 210 D. 311

20. 2, 5, 9, ?, 20, 27
A. 14 B. 16
C. 18 D. 20

21. 0, 1, 4, 9, 16, ?
A. 24 B. 20
C. 25 D. 28

22. 30, 29, 27, 24, 20, ?
A. 16 B. 17
C. 15 D. 14

23. 2, 3, 4, 9, 16, 54, 96, ?
A. 486 B. 768
C. 560 D. 324

24. 3, 19, 41, 71, 109, ?
A. 155 B. 157
C. 153 D. 158

25. 2, 12, 36, 80, 150, ?
A. 252 B. 256
C. 216 D. 284

## ANSWERS

| 1 | 2 | 3 | 4 | 5 | 6 | 7 | 8 | 9 | 10 |
|---|---|---|---|---|---|---|---|---|---|
| B | B | A | C | D | D | A | D | A | B |
| **11** | **12** | **13** | **14** | **15** | **16** | **17** | **18** | **19** | **20** |
| D | C | D | A | D | C | A | A | B | A |
| **21** | **22** | **23** | **24** | **25** | | | | | |
| C | C | A | A | A | | | | | |

## EXPLANATORY ANSWERS

1. There are two series :
I : $14^2 - 12^2 - 10^2$ and so on.
II : $4^2 - 6^2 - 8^2$ and so on.
2. $(8 \times 6)\ (12 \times 6)\ (18 \times 6)$
3. $1^3, 2^2, 3^3, 4^2, 5^3, 6^2$
4. $(121 \times 2 + 6)$
5. $(3 \times 2)\ (5 \times 4)\ (7 \times 6)\ (9 \times 8)$
6. $(2)^2 - 1 = 3; (3)^2 - 1 = 8; (8)^2 - 1 = 63, (63)^2 - 1 = 3968$
7. One series is 4, 3, 2, 1. Other (alternate) series is 7, 6, 5, 4.
8. $\times 2 + 1, \times 2 - 1$
9. $(2 \times 5)\ (10 \times 4)\ (40 \times 3)\ (120 \times 2)$
10. Our series is 4, 3, 2, 1. Other (alternate) series is 7, 6, 5, 4.
11. $(1 + 4)\ (5 + 3)\ (8 + 2)\ (10 + 1)\ (11 + 0)$
12. $(1 \times 6)\ (6 \times 5)\ (30 \times 4)\ (120 \times 3)\ (360 \times 2)$
13. $1^2, 3^2, 9^2, 81^2$
14. (10 ... 12) (14 ... 16) ... (18 ...)
15. $(8^3 - 3)$
16. $(2^3 - 1)\ (3^3 - 1)\ (4^3 - 1)\ (5^3 - 1)\ (6^3 - 1)$
17. $(1^3 - 0)\ (3^3 - 3)\ (4^3 - 4)\ (5^3 - 5)\ (6^3 - 6)$
18. difference of 2.
19. $(3 \times 3)\ (9 \times 3)\ (27 \times 3)\ (81 \times 3)$
20. increasing difference 3, 4, 5, 6
21. $5^2$
22. $(30 - 1)\ (29 - 2)\ (27 - 3)\ (24 - 4)\ (20 - 5)$
23. Alternate $(3 \times 3)\ (9 \times 6)\ (54 \times 9)$
24. $(12^2 + 11)$
25. $1^3 + 1^2, 2^3 + 2^2, 3^3 + 3^2, 4^3 + 4^2, 5^3 + 5^2, 6^3 + 6^2$

## Chapter 3

# WRONG NUMBER OUT

In this type of test the candidates are asked to find out one figure which is not similar to any of the others. The given series are either in continuation or in a specific pattern or having some similarity but one of them is different. So we have to find out which number/alphabet is misfit and not following the rubs of the series or having the some properties as that of other, number/alphabet.

**Find the Wrong Number:**

**1.** 1, 3, 5, 7, 8, 11, 13

A. 3 B. 7
C. 9 D. 11

**2.** 3, 7, 11, 15, 17

A. 7 B. 11
C. 17 D. 15

**3.** 7, 26, 63, 124, 210

A. 26 B. 124
C. 210 D. 7

**4.** 24, 51, 33, 42, 72

A. 51 B. 42
C. 72 D. 33

**5.** 14, 6, 8, 16, 21

A. 6 B. 8
C. 16 D. 21

**6.** 24, 27, 31, 33, 36

A. 24 B. 27
C. 31 D. 33

**7.** 8, 13, 21, 32, 47, 63, 83

A. 13 B. 21
C. 32 D. 47

**8.** 3, 10, 27, 4, 16, 64, 5, 25, 125

A. 3 B. 4
C. 10 D. 27

**9.** 15, 16, 22, 29, 45, 70

A. 16 B. 22
C. 45 D. 70

**10.** 1, 3, 7, 15, 27, 63, 127

A. 7 B. 15
C. 27 D. 63

**11.** 11, 5, 20, 12, 40, 26, 74, 54

A. 5 B. 20
C. 40 D. 26

**Replace the Wrong Number:**

**12.** 1, 2, 11, 36, 84

A. 30 B. 28
C. 37 D. 85

**13.** 3, 8, 18, 38, 75

A. 78 B. 75
C. 65 D. 58

**14.** 2, 3, 5, 8, 13, 34

A. 21 B. 25
C. 29 D. 34

**Complete the Alphabet Series:**

**15.** A, Z, B, Y, C, X, ?

A. W B. U
C. V D. D

**16.** AC, CE, DF, EG, ?

A. GF B. GI
C. GK D. GE

**17.** AZ, BY, CX, ?

A. DW B. DU
C. DV D. DX

**18.** YEB : WFD : VGF : SHH : ?

A. QIJ B. QUL
C. TOL D. None of these

**19.** AD, EH, IL, ?, QT

A. LM B. MN
C. MP D. OM

**20.** JE, LH, OL, SQ, ?

A. WV B. WX
C. VW D. XW

**21.** DF, GJ, KM, NQ, RT, ?

A. UW B. YZ
C. XZ D. UX

**22.** CE, GI, KM, OQ, ?

A. TW B. TV
C. SU D. RT
E. UW

**23.** AZ, BY, CX, ?
A. EP B. GH
C. IJ D. DW

**24.** CAT, FDW, IGZ, ?
A. KJA B. KTC
C. LHO D. LJC

**25.** QPO, SRQ, UTS, WVU, ?
A. XVZ B. ZYA
C. YXW D. VWX
E. AZY

## ANSWERS

| 1 | 2 | 3 | 4 | 5 | 6 | 7 | 8 | 9 | 10 |
|---|---|---|---|---|---|---|---|---|---|
| C | D | D | C | D | C | D | C | B | C |
| **11** | **12** | **13** | **14** | **15** | **16** | **17** | **18** | **19** | **20** |
| C | D | A | A | D | B | A | A | C | D |
| **21** | **22** | **23** | **24** | **25** | | | | | |
| D | C | D | D | C | | | | | |

## EXPLANATORY ANSWERS

**1.** $\sqrt{9} = 3$

**2.** 15 has got a fraction $5 \times 3$.

**3.** 7 has got no fraction.

**4.** There are two series with a common difference of 9, *i.e.*, 24, 33, 42 and 51, 42, .... So, 72 is the odd number here.

**5.** 21 is not divisible by 2.

**6.** 31 does not have any fraction.

**7.** 47 is wrong and must be replaced by $(32 + 14) = 46$.

**8.** The correct sequence is $3, 3^2, 3^3 \ldots 4, 4^2, 4^3 \ldots$ 10 should be replaced by 9.

**9.** 22 is wrong and must be replaced by $(16 + 4)$ 20.
The pattern is $1^2 + 2^2 + 3^3 \ldots$.

**10.** 27 is wrong must be replaced by $(15 + 2^4) = 31$.

**11.** The given sequence is a combination of two series (*i*), 11, 20, 40, 74; (*ii*) 5, 12, 26, 54.
40 is wrong and must be replaced by 38.

**12.** The correct sequence is
$1 + (1)^2 = 2, 2 + (3)^2 = 11, 11 + (5)^2 = 36$
So, $36 + (7)^2 = 85$. Hence 84 should be replaced with 85.

**13.** Wrong figure is 75. It must be replaced by 78
$(3\times2+2)\,(8\times2+2)\,(18\times2+2)\,(38\times2+2)$

**14.** Clearly each terms of the series is the sum of preceding terms.
So the term 21 is missing and 34 is a wrong entry.

**15.** The embedded series is A – B – C – D.

**16.** GI is correct choice as the series moves after shipping one alphabet.

**17.** A – B – C – D and W... X...Y...Z are the two series embedded in one another.

**18.** OIJ is the right sequence.

**19.** The first and second letters of each term are moved ahead by four alphabets.

**20.** The first letters of the first, second, third *etc.* terms are moved ahead by two, three and four alphabets, respectively

**21.** There is a gap of one letter between both the letters of first terms, a gap of two letters between both the letters of second terms . . . .

**22.** The letters of each terms are alternate and also the last letter of each term and the first letter of the next term and alternate.

**23.** The first letter if each term is moved by one alphabet forward and the second letter is moved one step backward .

**24.** All the letters of each term are moved by three alphabets forward . . . .

**25.** Each term in the series consists of three consecutive letters in reverse order. The first letter of each term and the last letter of the next term are two series.

## Chapter 4

# LETTER SERIES

In the letter series test, some sequence of alphabets have been given. Based on this sequence, we have to find out next combination of alphabets. Nowadays, two or more than two questions are being asked in this area. Topic itself is very simple and requires a little concentration, Some examples have been given so as to make our readers understand the basic concepts and applications.

**Example :** aab — aab — aab —

A. bba B. abb

C. bab D. aab

E. bbb

**Ans.** Proceed Step by Step

The sequence is aabb, aabb, aabb

Hence Right Answer is (E).

## EXERCISE

**1.** a — ba — cbaac — aa — ba

A. c, c, b, b B. c, a, l

C. c, b, c, b D. b, b, c, c

**2.** ab — baabc — aabcb — abcb —

A. b, c, a, a B. c, b, a, a

C. a, b, c, a D. a, a, c, b

**3.** — ba — ababa — aba — ab

A. a, a, a, b B. a, a, a, a

C. a, b, a, b D. a, b, b, b

**4.** — aba — abaa — baa — ba

A. b, b, b, b B. a, b, b, b

C. a, a, a, a D. b, a, a, a

**5.** ac — baac — b — acbb —

A. b, a, a, b B. a, b, b, c

C. a, a, b, c D. b, b, a, a

**6.** a — bdb — c — ca — acbdb — cac — d

A. a, d, b, d, c, b B. c, d, a, d, a, b

C. a, b, a, d, d, c D. c, b, a, d, b, a

**7.** aa — aaa — aaaa — aaaa — b

A. b, a, a, a B. b, b, a, a

C. b, b, b, b D. b, b, b, a

**8.** aa — aabb — b — aa — aabb — bb

A. b, a, b, b, a B. b, b, b, a, a

C. b, a, b, b, a D. a, a, b, b, b

**9.** ababb — b — b — ab — bb

A. b, b, a, a B. b, b, a, b

C. a, a, b, a D. a, a, b, b

**10.** — bbaaba — ba —

A. b, b, a, a B. a, a, b, b

C. a, b, a, b D. b, a, b, a

**11.** — baabbaa — b — a

A. a, a, b B. a, b, a

C. b, a, b D. b, b, a

**12.** — — abbbab bb — b

A. b, b, a B. a, a, b

C. a, a, a D. b, b, b

**13.** b — bb — abbbab —

A. a, a, b B. b, b, b

C. a, b, a D. a, b, b

**14.** — baa — ba — aab —

A. b, a, b, a B. b, b, a, a

C. a, b, b, b D. b, b, a, b

**15.** — aabb — a — ab — b.

A. b, b, a, a B. a, b, a, b

C. b, a, b, a D. b, c, a, b

**16.** — aa — baa — ab — a

A. a, b, a, b B. b, b, a, a

C. a, b, b, b D. a, a, b, b

**17.** a — baa — aa — ab

A. b,b,b,b B. b,b,a,a

C. a, b, b, a D. a, a, a, a

**18.** — aa — a — baaa —

A. b,a,b,a B. b,b,a,a

C. b,b,a,b D. b,a,b,b

**19.** — a — b — aaab — aa

A. b,b,b,b B. a,a,a,b

C. b,a,a,b D. a,b,a,b

**20.** — b — baaabb — a —

A. a,b,b,a B. a,b,a,b

C. b,a,b,a D. b,a,a,b

**21.** — a — aabb — aab —

A. a,b,b,a B. a,a,a,b

C. b,a,a,b D. b,b,a,b

**22.** — baa — ab — aaa — aaa —

A. b,a,b,a B. a,b,a,b

C. a,a,b,b D. a,a,a,b

**23.** — b — baaa — bba —

A. a,b,b,b B. b,a,a,b

C. a,b,b,a D. b,a,b,a

**24.** — ba — baa — ab — a

A. b,a,a,b B. b,a,b,a

C. a,a,a,b D. a,b,b,b

**25.** baa — a — a — bab — aba

A. a,a,b,b B. a,b,b,a

C. b,b,a,a D. b,b,b,a

## ANSWERS

| 1 | 2 | 3 | 4 | 5 | 6 | 7 | 8 | 9 | 10 |
|---|---|---|---|---|---|---|---|---|---|
| B | B | D | C | D | D | D | A | C | D |
| **11** | **12** | **13** | **14** | **15** | **16** | **17** | **18** | **19** | **20** |
| D | A | D | C | B | A | C | D | D | A |
| **21** | **22** | **23** | **24** | **25** | | | | | |
| D | D | C | D | C | | | | | |

## EXPLANATORY ANSWERS

**1.** *acba, acba, acba, acba*

**2.** *abcba, abcba, abcba, abcba* . . . .

**3.** *ab, ab, ab, ab* . . . .

**4.** *aaba, aaba, aaba* . . . .

**5.** *acbba, acbba, acbba* . . . .

**6.** Series *acbdbbcacad* repeated two times.

**7.** *aab,— aaab, — aaaab, — aaaaab*

**8.** *aab, aab, babb, aab, aab, babb.*

**9.** Series *ababb* repeated three times.

**10.** Series *babbaa* repeated twice.

**11.** Series *bbaa* repeated three times.

**12.** Series *bbab* repeated three times.

**13.** Series *babb* repeated three times.

**14.** Series *abaabb* repeated twice.

**15.** Series *aaabbb* repeated twice.

**16.** Series *aaabba* repeated twice.

**17.** Series *aabaab* repeated twice.

**18.** Series *baaaab* repeated twice.

**19.** *aabbaa* repeated twice.

**20.** Series *abbaa* repeated twice.

**21.** Series *baaabb* repeated twice.

**22.** Series *abaaa* repeated twice.

**23.** Series *abbbaa* repeated twice.

**24.** Series *ababba* repeated twice.

**25.** Series *baaba* repeated three times.

## Chapter 5

# DIRECTION TEST

Direction Test is a test to judge the candidate's ability to understand and find out the four directions correctly and also, the distance covered while he is moving in different directions from a Starting point.

The following figure shows the four main Directions—*N* for North, *S* for South, *E* for East and *W* for West. There are four cardinal directions also — named as *NW, NE, SW* and *SE*.

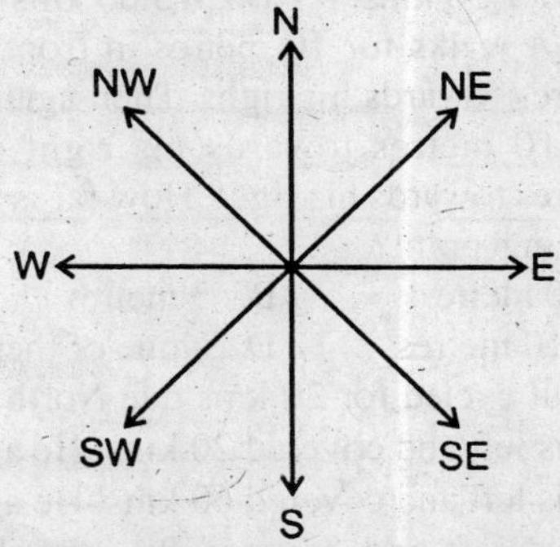


**Example 1 :** Mr. Mohan moves 10 km towards East then again moves 10 km left, again moves 10 km left. How much is the distance from starting point and in which direction he is now?

**Ans.**

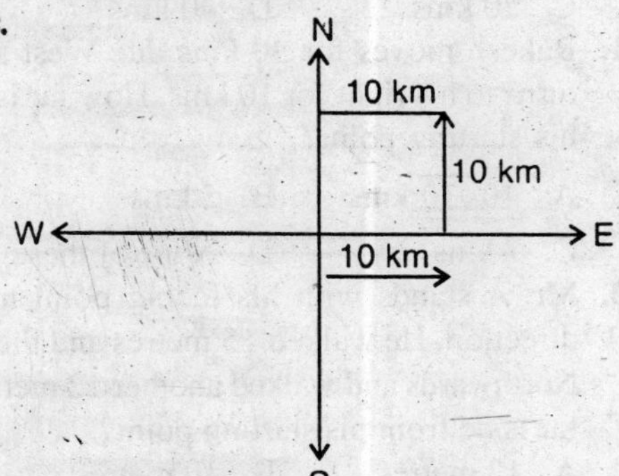


According to the figure Mr. Mohan is in North direction and is 10 km away from the starting point.

**Example 2 :** Mr. Ram left home and cycled 15 km to South thereafter he turned his left and cycled 20 km, again turned left and cycled 15 km and again turned left and cycled 20 km. Where is he at present?

**Ans.**

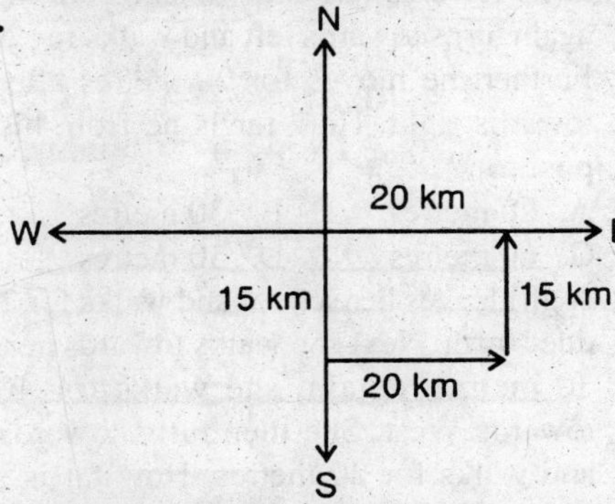


According to the figure Mr. Ram is at the starting point.

**Example 3 :** A boy is looking for his brother. He went 4 km towards East and then turned to his left and went as for as 3 km. He found his brother there. What is the distance from the starting point and the meeting point (where he meet his brother)?

**Ans.**

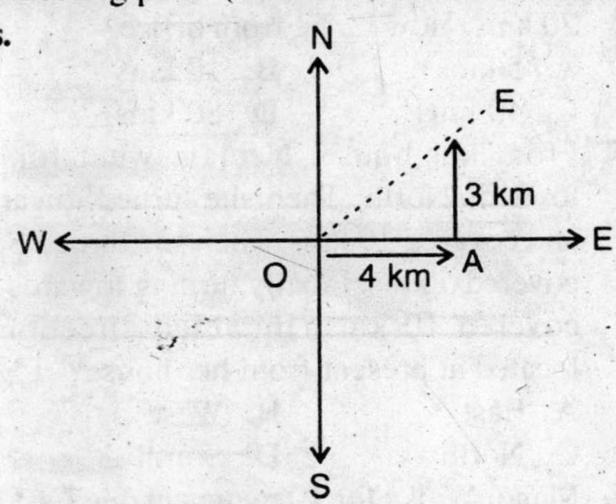


$$OE = \sqrt{OA^2 + AE^2}$$

$$= \sqrt{4^2 + 3^2}$$

$$= \sqrt{16 + 9}$$

$$= 5 \text{ km.}$$

# EXERCISE

1. A man is facing North and turned to his right at an angle of 180°, again he turned right at an angle of 90°. In which direction is he now?

   A. East B. North
   C. West D. South

2. Suresh walks 20 metres towards North. He then turns towards left and walks for 40 metres. He again turns towards left and walks for 20 metres. Further, he moves for 20 metres after turning towards right. How far is he from his starting position?

   A. 20 metres B. 30 metres
   C. 60 metres D. 50 metres

3. A girl leaves her school and walks for 20 metres due North. Next she walks towards her right for 30 metres. Again, she walks for 40 metres towards West. She then turns towards her left and walks for 20 metres. How far is she from her starting point?

   A. 30 metres B. 20 metres
   C. 10 metres D. 15 metres

4. Mohan went for 15 kms towards the West from his office and then turned towards his left and walked for 20 kms. He then turned East and walked 25 kms and finally turning left covered 20 kms. How far he from office?

   A. 5 kms B. 10 kms
   C. 40 kms D. 80 kms

5. From her house, Neelam went for 15 kms towards North. Then she turned towards West and covered 10 kms. Then she turned South and covered 5 kms. Finally turning towards East she covered 10 kms. In which direction, is she located at present from her house?

   A. East B. West
   C. North D. South

6. Manoj Walks for 10 metres in due East and then for 10 metres towards his right. Then every time turning to his left he walks for 5, 15 and 15 metres, respectively. How far is he from his starting point?

   A. 5 metres B. 10 metres
   C. 20 metres D. 23 metres

7. Mr Lokesh moved for 20 kms towards North and turned back to South by distance of 40 kms. He turned towards his left and travelled for 20 kms. Again, he turned towards his left for 10 kms, again moved towards left for 20 kms. How far is he from his starting point.

   A. 10 kms B. 20 kms
   C. 30 kms D. 25 kms

8. Ram moves for 30 kms due East and then turns towards left and travels for 40 kms. How far is Ram from his starting point and in which direction?

   A. *NE* 50 kms B. *SE* 40 kms
   C. *NW* 30 kms D. *WS* 60 kms

9. Mr. *A* walks for 10 metres in front and for 10 metres towards his right. Then again, he walks for 10 metres towards his right and for 10 metres towards his right. How far is he from the starting point?

   A. 0 metre B. 5 metres
   C. 10 metres D. None of these

10. Rahul cycled for 20 kms due North and turned to his left and covered 20 kms. He again turned to his left and covered 60 kms. He again turned to his left and covered 20 kms. Finally, he moved for 40 kms towards his left. How far is he from his starting point?

    A. 0 km B. 5 kms
    C. 20 kms D. 40 kms

11. Rakesh moves for 30 kms due West and then, turns to his right for 10 kms. How far is he from his starting point?

    A. $10\sqrt{10}$ kms B. 5 kms
    C. 7 kms D. None of these

12. Mr. *A* stands with his facing point to the *SE* direction. He walked 15 metres and then turned Northwards and walked another 12 metres. How far is he from his starting point?

    A. 12 metres B. 10 metres
    C. 9 metres D. 5 metres

13. *K* went 10 m towards East and then, turned towards North and walked for another 15 m. Then, he turned towards West and covered 12 m and then, turned towards South and covered

15 m. How far is he from starting point?

A. 2 metres B. 5 metres
C. 6 metres D. 10 metres

**14.** Anil walked for 3 m. towards North and turned towards West and walked for 2 m. Then, he turned towards North and walked for 1 m and then, he turned towards East and walked for 5 m. How far is he from his starting point?

A. 1 metre B. 2 metres
C. 3 metres D. 5 metres

**15.** I went for 15 metres due North. Then, I turned towards South and coverd 5 metres and then, I turned towards East and covered 10 metres. In which direction, am I?

A. East B. West
C. North D. South

**16.** *A, B, C,* and *D* are playing cards. *B* is sitting in front of *D*. *A* is sitting to right of *D*, facing *C*. *D* is facing South. Which direction is being faced by *C*?

A. East B. West
C. North D. South

**17.** *A* and *B* start their journeys in opposite directions. *A* is facing North and walked for 10 kms whereas Mr. *B* walked for 20 kms. Mr. *A* turned to his right and walked for 15 kms. Again, he turned towards his left and covered 10 kms. Mr. *B* turned towards his left for 15 kms and again, towards his left for 20 kms. At what direction, are they meeting?

A. East B. South
C. North D. West

**18.** *A, B, C* and *D* are playing a game of Carrom. *A,C* and *B,D* are partners. *D* is to the right of *C* who is facing West. Then *B* is facing.

A. North B. East
C. South D. West

**19.** If *A* is to the South of *B* and *C* is to the East of *B*, in what diretion is *A* with respect to *C*?

A. *NE* B. *NW*
C. *SE* D. *SW*

**20.** Rakesh's School bus is facing North when he reaches his school. After starting from Rakesh's house, it turns towards right twice and then towards left, before reaching to school. What direction was the bus facing, when it left the bus stop in front of Rakesh's House?

A. North B. South
C. East D. West

**21.** Rinku starts his journey towards West and walked 10 kms then; he moves towards his left 20 kms and again moves towards left for 40 kms. Again, he moves towards left for 20 kms. How for is he from starting point?

A. 20 kms B. 30 kms
C. 40 kms D. 10 kms

**22.** Suresh left his office towards North and covered 15 kms. He turned towards his right and covered 10 kms. Again, he moved towards right and covered 30 kms. How far is he from his starting point?

A. $\sqrt{325}$ B. $\sqrt{275}$
C. $\sqrt{1015}$ D. $\sqrt{513}$

**23.** *A, B, C* and *D* are playing Carrom. *B* is sitting in front of *C* and is facing North. *A* is sitting to the left of *B*. Which direction is being faced by *D*?

A. East B. West
C. North D. South

**24.** Ashok moved towards East and covered 4 kms. He then moved towards South 3 kms. Again he moved his right and covered 7 kms. How far is he from his starting point?

A. $\sqrt{18}$ B. $\sqrt{27}$
C. $\sqrt{25}$ D. $\sqrt{35}$

**25.** Two friends, Ravi and Chavi, left together towards North and covered 10 kms. Ravi turned to his left for 15 kms and again, turned towards left and covered 10 kms. Again he turned towards left for 30 kms. Chavi turned to his right for 15 kms. Again he turned toward right for 10 kms. At which direction, are they meeting again and at what distance?

A. East 15 kms B. West 10 kms
C. North 10 kms D. South 20 kms

## ANSWERS

| 1 | 2 | 3 | 4 | 5 | 6 | 7 | 8 | 9 | 10 |
|---|---|---|---|---|---|---|---|---|---|
| C | C | C | C | C | A | A | A | A | A |

| 11 | 12 | 13 | 14 | 15 | 16 | 17 | 18 | 19 | 20 |
|---|---|---|---|---|---|---|---|---|---|
| A | C | A | D | A | B | A | A | D | D |
| **21** | **22** | **23** | **24** | **25** | | | | | |
| B | A | B | A | A | | | | | |

## EXPLANATORY ANSWERS

**1.**

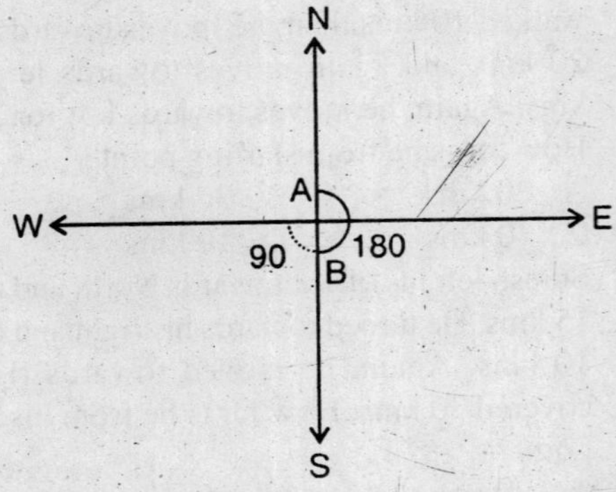


Man turns to his right at an angle of 180°, so he is at point *B* and again he moves towards his right at an angle of 90°, so he is at point *C*. His direction is West.

**2.**

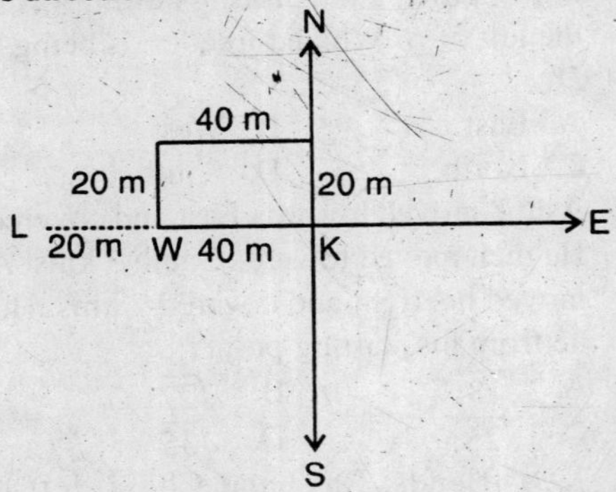


He is at point *L, i.e.,* 60 km from starting point.

**3.**

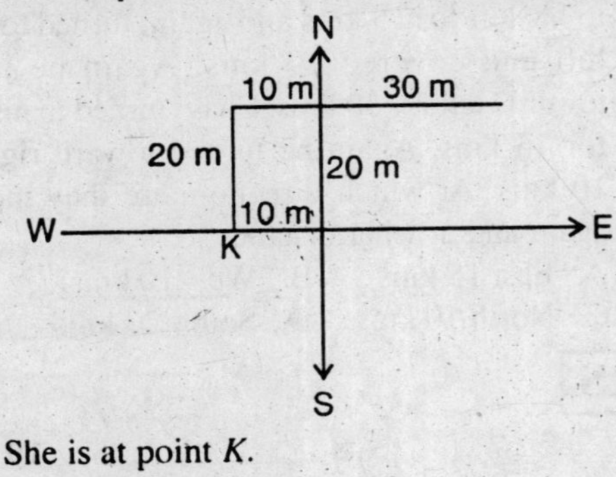


She is at point *K*.

**4.**

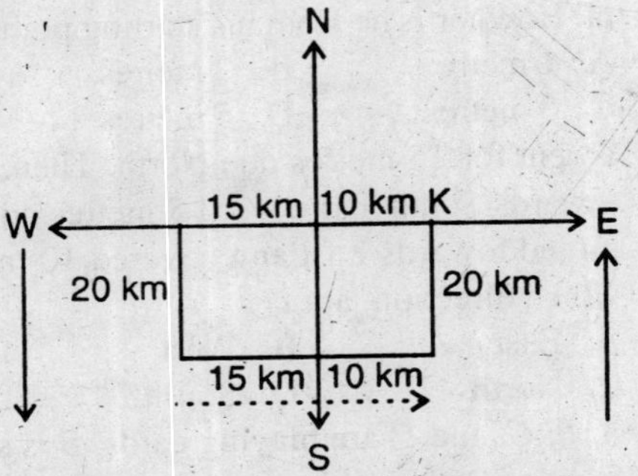


He is at point *K* 10 km from his starting point.

**5.**

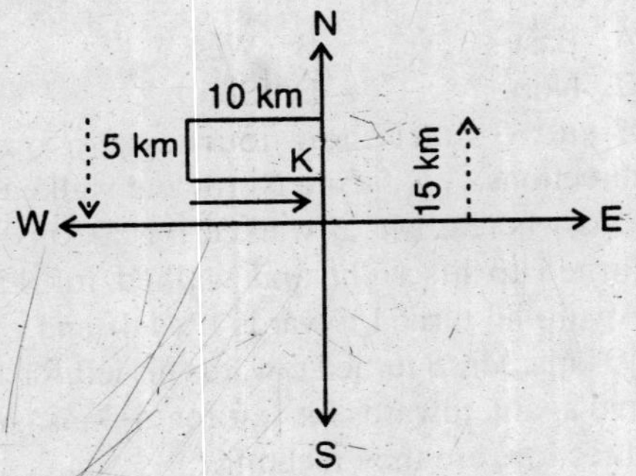


She is at point *K* which is in North.

**6.**

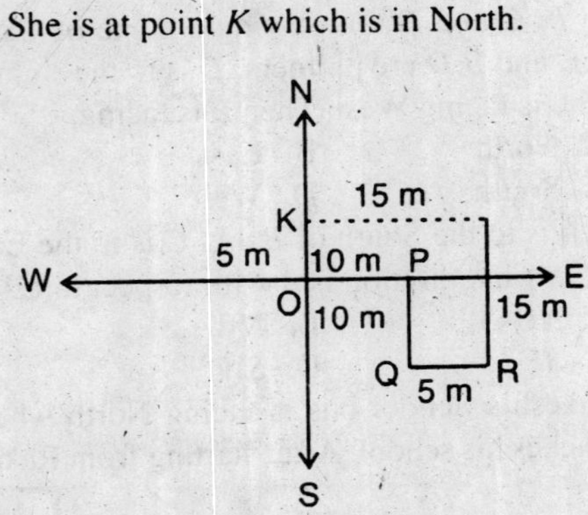


He is at point *K* 5 metres away.

**7.**

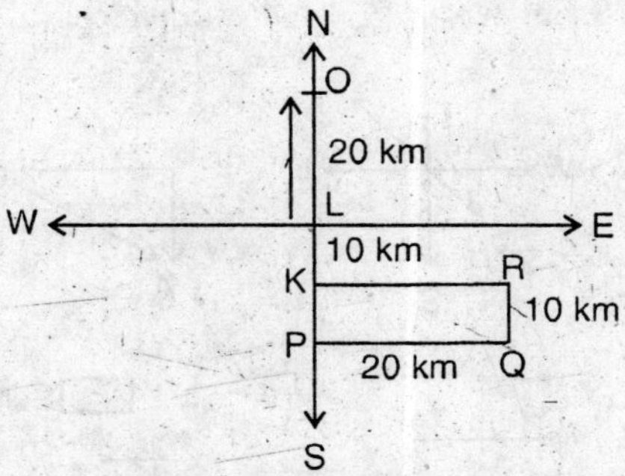


*L* to *O*, *O* to *P*, *P* to *Q*, *Q* to *R*, *R* to *K*.

**8.**

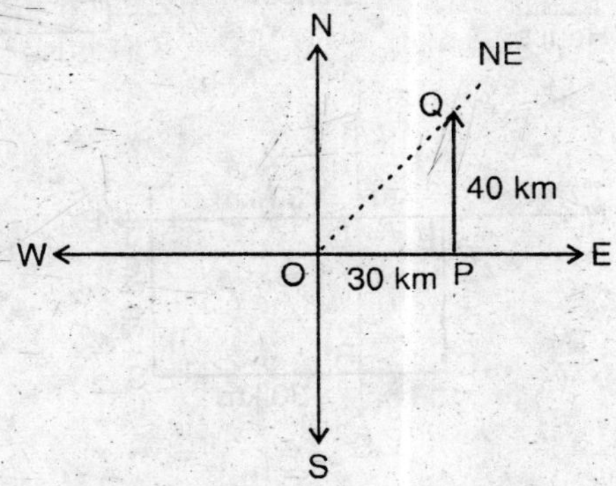


$\sqrt{30^2 + 40^2} = 50$ m.

**9.**

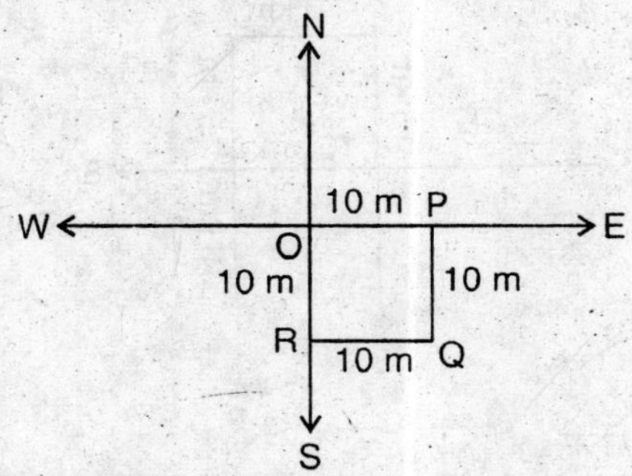


He is at his starting point.

**10.**

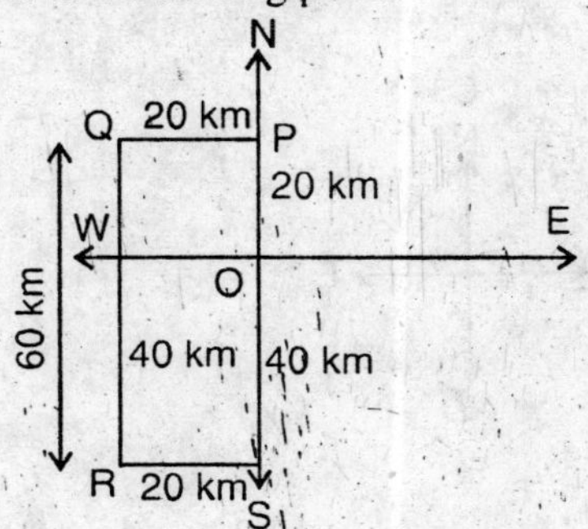


Rahul is at original point.

His journey is *OP*, *PQ*, *QR*, *RS*, *SO*.

**11.**

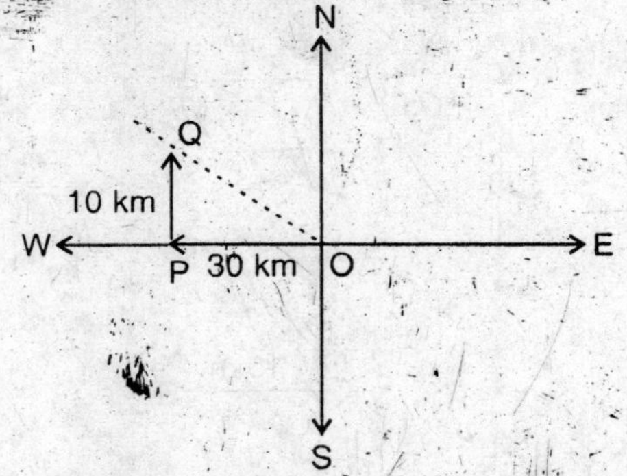


$\sqrt{30^2 + 10^2} = \sqrt{1000} = 10\sqrt{10}$

**12.**

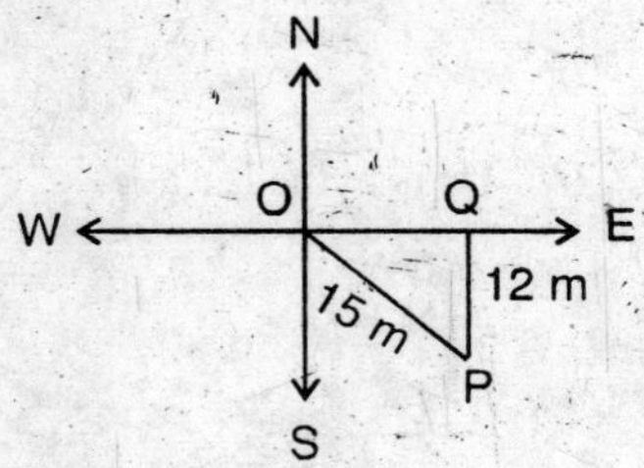


$B = \sqrt{H^2 - P^2} = \sqrt{15^2 - 12^2} = 9$ m.

**13.**

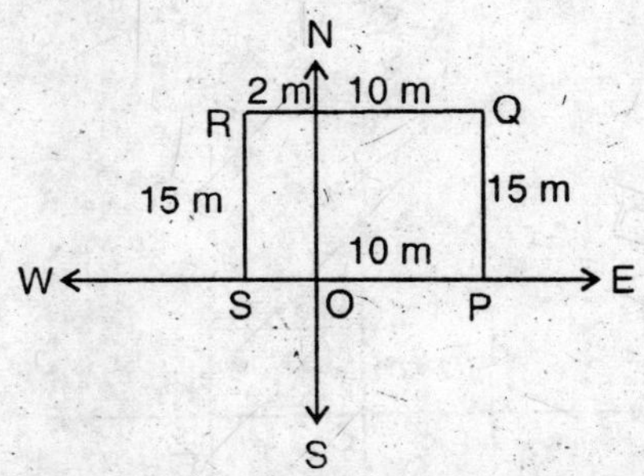


*OP*, *PQ*, *QR*, *RS*. He is at point *S*, 2 metres away from starting point.

**14.**

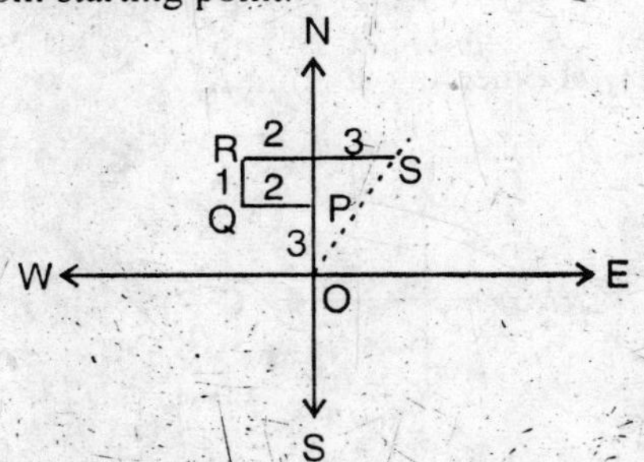


$OP = 3$ m

$PQ = 2$ m
$QR = 1$ m
$RS = 5$ m
$NS = 3$ m

$$OS = \sqrt{NO^2 + NS}$$
$$= \sqrt{4^2 + 3^2}$$
$$= \sqrt{25} = 5 \text{ m.}$$

**15.**

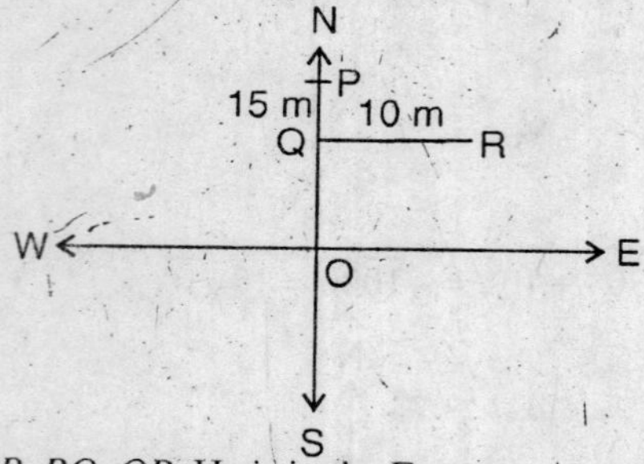


*OP*, *PQ*, *QR*. He is in the East.

**16.**

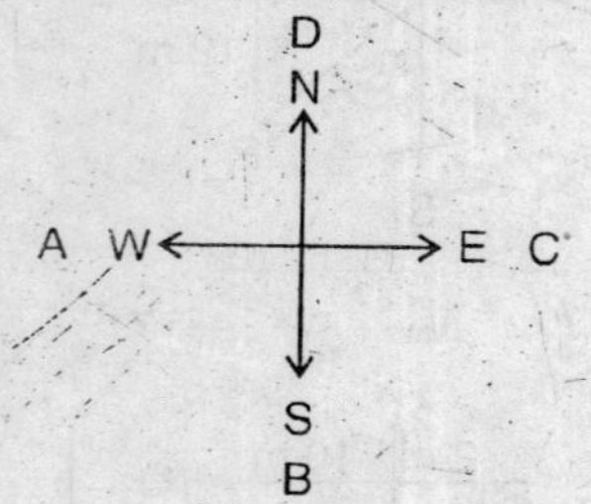


**17.**

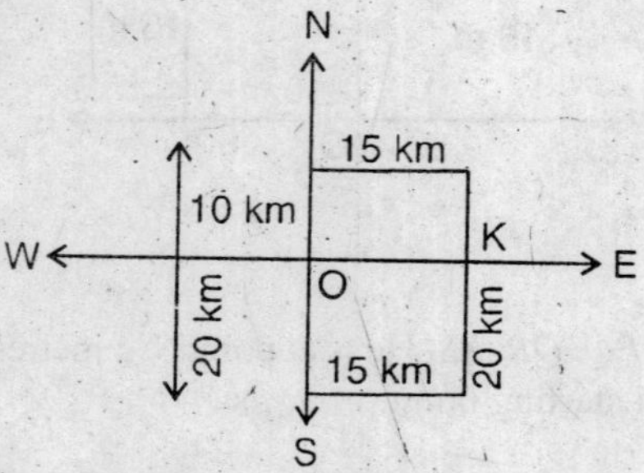


They are meeting at point *K*.

**18.**

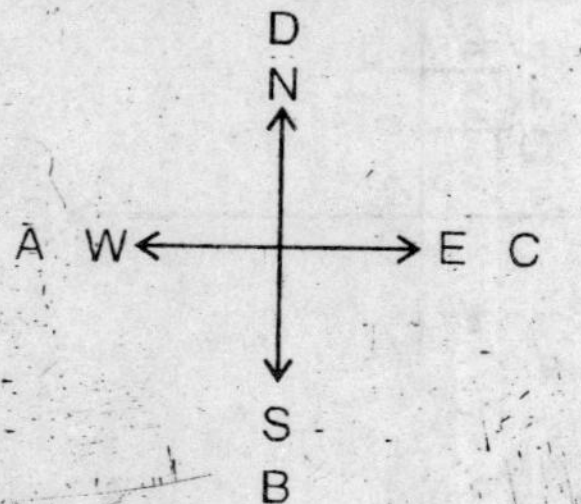


**19.** South-West.

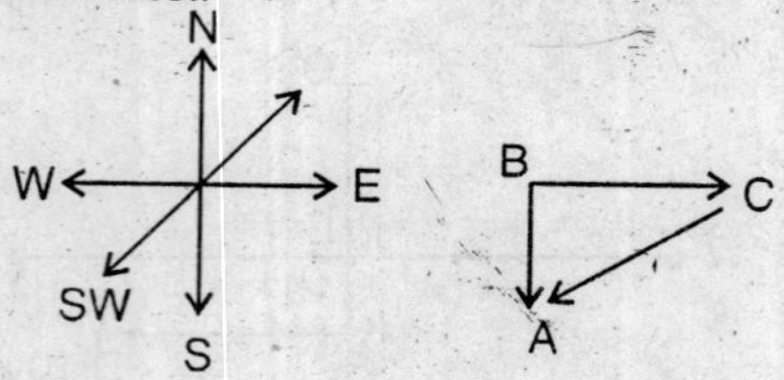


**20.**

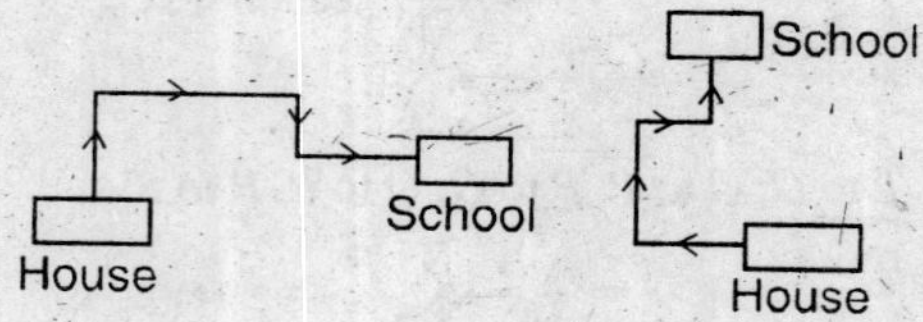


**21.**

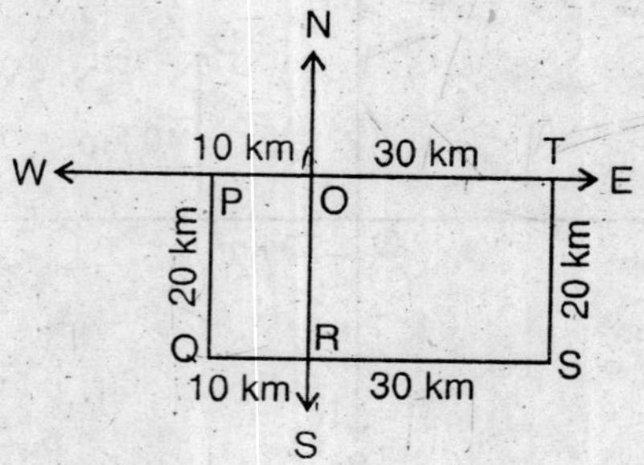


He is at point *T*, *i.e.*, 30 km.

**22.**

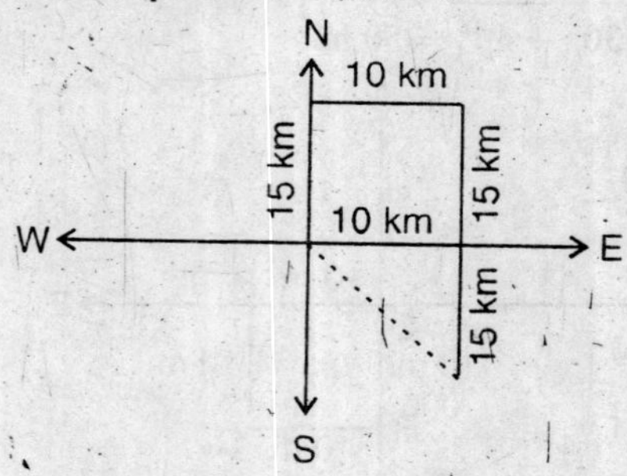


$$\sqrt{325} = \sqrt{10^2 + 15^2}$$

**23.**

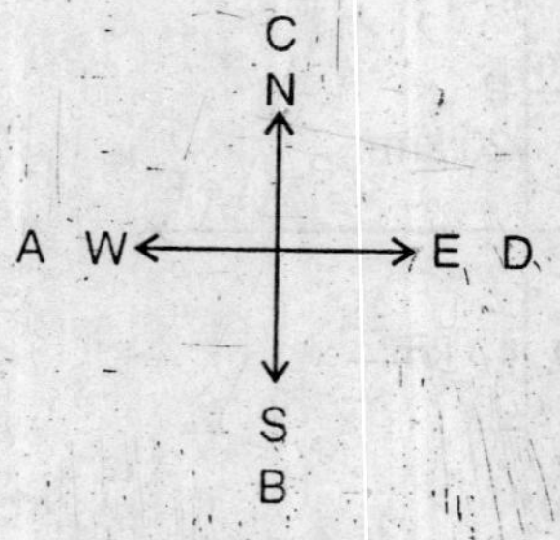

**24.**

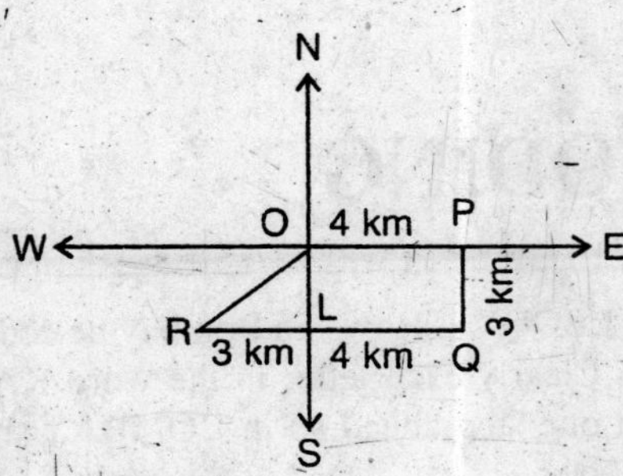


$OP = 4$
$PQ = 3$
$QR = 7$
$LR = 3$

$$RO = \sqrt{3^2 + 3^2} = \sqrt{18}$$

**25.**

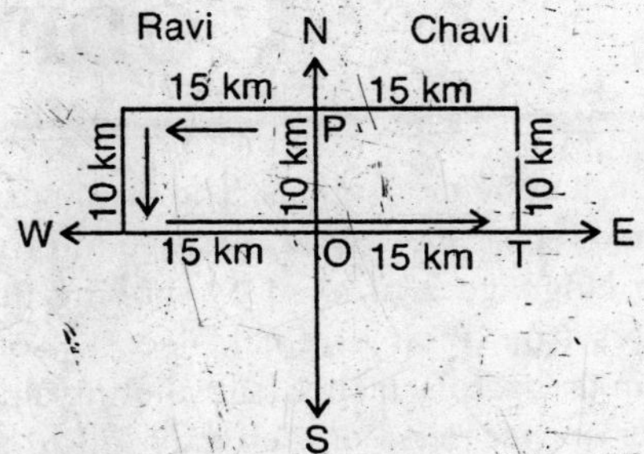


East 15 km At point *T*.

## Chapter 6

# CODING-DECODING

It is a system of signals. The main purpose is to send and recine the coded message information. In this, a language is fromed by moving the letters/ numbers from their original place to some other place in the word/sentence, substituting alphabet for number or vice versa or they may follow any other set/defined pattern.

## ALPHABETS

**Example 1 :** In a certain code, KANPUR has been coded as LBOQVS. How can Bombay be coded?

**Ans.** Clearly each letter in the word KANPUR is moved one step ahead so in BOMBAY the code word will be :

CPNCBZ.

**Example 2 :** According to a certain code, BHART is loded as AIZSS. How NEPAL be coded?

**Ans.** Clearly, in Each word, we are using the previous and next alphabet after the given alphabet. Hence, NEPAL will be Loded as MFOBK.

## EXERCISE

**1.** In a certain code, KANPUR is written as RUPNAK. How could JAIPUR be coded?

A. IJAPRU B. RUPIAJ
C. PURIJA D. RIJAUP

**2.** In a certain code, MASTER is coded as NBTUFS. How could SERVANT be coded?

A. RBSUBOI B. TFSWBOU
C. PQRSTVI D. TFSWAOV

**3.** In a certain code MONKEY is written as XDJMNL. How could TIGER be written?

A. QDFHS B. SDFHS
C. UJHFS D. SHFDQ

**4.** In a certain code, BLOCK is written as AMNDL.How could STREET be written?

A. RUPDDU B. RUQFDU
C. RUQDFU D. RUQFUD

**5.** In a certain code CARROM is written as BZQQNL. How could HOUSE be coded?

A. IPVTF B. TFVPI
C. IPTVE D. IPTVF
E. GNTRD

**6.** In a certain code, LUCK is written as JSAI. How could MUST be coded?

A. KSQR B. KSRQ
C. SKRQ D. KRQS

**7.** In a certain code, CHAMPION is coded as HCMAIPNO. How could NEGATIVE be written in such a code?

A. ENAGITEV B. NEAGVEIT
C. MGAETVIE D. EGAITEVN

**8.** In a certain code DELHI is written as HIELD. How MADRAS is written?

A. ASDRMA B. ASRDAM
C. ADMASR D. MARDAS

**9.** In a certain code, MONDAY is written as OMDNYA. How could FRIDAY be written?

A. RFDIYA B. RFIDAY
C. RFAYID D. AYIDRF

**10.** GOOD has been coded as EMMB. How could BAD be coded?

A. ZYB B. YZB
C. ZBY D. BYZ

## ANSWERS

| 1 | 2 | 3 | 4 | 5 | 6 | 7 | 8 | 9 | 10 |
|---|---|---|---|---|---|---|---|---|---|
| B | B | A | B | E | A | A | A | A | A |

## EXPLANATORY ANSWERS

1. Reverse order of JAIPUR is RUPIAJ.
2. S E R V A N T
   T F S W B O U
   Followed by one alphabet ahead.
3. T I G E R
   Q D F H S
   One alphabet back from the last alphabet.
4. S T R E E T
   R U Q F D U
   One alphabet before and after.
5. H O U S E
   G N T R D
   One alphabet back.
6. L U C K — M U S T
   J S A I — K S Q R
   Two alphabet back.
7. The letters of the word are reversed in order, taking two at a time to obtain the code.
8. D E L H I — M A D R A S
   H I E L D — A S D R M A
   Reverse order of each pair of alphabets.
9. M O N D A Y — F R I D A Y
   O M D N Y A — R F D I Y A
   Position of alphabets is interchanged in pairs.
10. G O O D — B A D
    E M M B — Z Y B
    Two alphabets back.

## NUMBER CODING

**Example 1 :** In a certain code A has been coded as 1, B is 2, C is 3 and so on. How GHAI is coded.

**Ans.**

| A | B | C | D | E | F | G | H | I |
|---|---|---|---|---|---|---|---|---|
| 1 | 2 | 3 | 4 | 5 | 6 | 7 | 8 | 9 |

Clearly the code for GHAI will be 7819.

**Example 2 :** If LEARN is coded as 45896 and TUB as 732. How is BURN coded?

**Ans.** Clearly the code for BURN will be 2396

| L | E | A | R | N | T | U | B |
|---|---|---|---|---|---|---|---|
| 4 | 5 | 8 | 9 | 6 | 7 | 3 | 2 |

## EXERCISE

1. If ROSE is coded as 6821, CHAIR is coded as 73456 and PREACH is coded as 961473, what will be the code for SEARCH?
   A. 246173 B. 214673
   C. 214763 D. 216473
2. If BAD is coded as 214, how is CAGE coded?
   A. 3175 B. 3167
   C. 3716 D. 3617
3. If DIG is coded as 497. How is BIG coded?
   A. 297 B. 479
   C. 792 D. None of these
4. If DIG = 20; BIG = 18, how would CID be written?
   A. 16 B. 18
   C. 21 D. 24
5. If D = 4; COVER = 63, how RING would be written?
   A. 78 B. 48
   C. 38 D. 42
6. If MADRAS is coded as 56, how would KANPUR be coded?
   A. 81 B. 71
   C. 91 D. 75

**(Qs. 7 to 10) :** The following is a certain code :

| 5 | 4 | 7 | 9 | 8 | 3 | 2 |
|---|---|---|---|---|---|---|
| A | P | L | N | O | C | I |

How are the following figures coded?

7. 98745
   A. NOPLA B. ONPLA
   C. NOLPA D. ONALP
8. 47382
   A. LPCOI B. PLCOI
   C. COILP D. OICLP
9. 5479832
   A. APLNOCI B. LNOCIAP
   C. PALNOCI D. APNLOCI
10. 2389745
    A. ICONAP B. ICONLPA
    C. IOCNAP D. ICOLNPA

11. If Black is called is Blue, Blue is called Yellow, Yellow is called Red, Red is called Sky Blue, what is the colour of Sky?
A. Yellow B. Red
C. Blue D. Black

12. If Banana is Apple, Apple is Grapes, Grapes is Mango, Mango is Nuts and Nuts is Guava, which of the following is a Yellow fruit?
A. Mango B. Guava
C. Apple D. Nuts
E. Grapes

13. If Head is Mouth, Mouth is Ear, Ear is Palm, Palm is Elbow, then, what is Ear?
A. Palm B. Ear
C. Head D. Mouth

14. If Rain is Water, Water is Road, Road is Cloud, Cloud is Sky, Sky is Sea, Sea is Path, where do Helicopters fly?
A. Road B. Sea
C. Cloud D. Water

## ANSWERS

| 1 | 2 | 3 | 4 | 5 | 6 | 7 | 8 | 9 | 10 |
|---|---|---|---|---|---|---|---|---|---|
| B | A | A | A | B | A | A | B | A | B |
| **11** | **12** | **13** | **14** | | | | | | |
| B | D | A | B | | | | | | |

## EXPLANATORY ANSWERS

1. R O S E  C H A I R  S E A R C H
6 8 2 1  7 3 4 5 6  2 1 4 6 7 3
2. B A D  C A G E
2 1 4  3 1 7 5
**Code :** A B C D E F G H I
1 2 3 4 5 6 7 8 9
3. D I G  B I G
4 9 7  2 9 7
4. D I G
4 9 7 (4 + 9 + 7)
B I G (2 + 9 + 7)
C I D (3 + 9 + 4)
5. C O V E R = 63; D = 4
RING=18 + 9 + 14 + 7
6. (10 + 1 + 14 + 16 + 21 + 18)
7. NOLPA
8. PLCOI
9. APLNOCI
10. ICONLPA
11. Sky blue is Red. So Red is Right.
12. Because mango is called nuts.
13. Palm, because ear is known as Palms.
14. Because Helicopter fly in Sky which is known as Sea.

## MIXED LETTER CODING

**Example :**

| | | |
|---|---|---|
| Lip | Sip | Tip |
| Flowers | are | Red. |
| Tip | Zip | Kip |
| Shirt | is | Red |
| Sip | Xip | Lip |
| They | are | Good |

What is the code for Flowers, Red and Are?

**Ans.**

Flowers = Lip
Red = Tip
Are = Sip

Common between 1st and 2nd is Red and common code is Tip.

## EXERCISE

1. Lee Pee See means Drink Mango Juice. See Tee Yee means Mangoes are Sour. Pee Nee Yee means Apples are Sweet. Which word denotes *are*?
A. Pee B. Lee
C. See D. Yee

2. Tip Tok Pok means Fast and Accurate. Tok Lok Sok means Dull and Wrong. Zok Tip Tok means Fast and Clever. What is the code for Fast?
   A. Tip B. Tok
   C. Pok D. Zok
3. In a certain code, 247 means Spread Red Carpet, 256 means Dust one Carpet and 236 means One Red Carpet. Which digit means Dust?
   A. 2 B. 3
   C. 5 D. 6
4. In a certain code, 123 means Grass is Green, 345 means Flower is Yellow, 567 means Wear Yellow Colour. What is the code for *Yellow*?
   A. 3 B. 6
   C. 7 D. 5
5. In a certain code, Sunil is written as RVMJK. How RAMESH is written?
   A. QBLFRI B. FRILBQ
   C. BLQIRF D. QBLRIF
6. If Good is written as 347, Bad is written as 743, Right is written as 52347, what will be the code for *Wrong*?
   A. 74325 B. 47325
   C. 74352 D. 74523
7. If
   Right = a e i o u
   Might = p e i o u
   Sight = k e i o u
   Night = l e i o u
   What will be the code for R, M, S, N.
   A. a p k l B. a p d c
   C. l e i o D. a p l k
8. In a certain code, ROAD is written as URDG. How is SWAN written in that code?
   A. VXDQ B. VZDQ
   C. UXDQ D. VZCQ
9. In a certain code, LONDON is written as HPOEPO. Which of the following word is written as CVOHSZ?
   A. MEXICO B. ISLAND
   C. HOLAND D. HUNGRY
10. In a certain code CHAIR is written as EGCHT. How AUDIT is written?
   A. CTFHV B. CSFHV
   C. BTFHV D. CTEHV
11. In a certain code, PROSE is written as PPOQE. How LIGHT is to be written?
   A. LIGFT B. LLGFE
   C. JIEHR D. LGGHT
   E. LGGFT
12. DELHI can be coded as CCIDD. How BOMBAY is written?
   A. AMIWUR B. AMJXVS
   C. MJXVSU D. AJIMJX
13. In a certain code, Sweet is written as 5467, Bitter is written as 7645 and Handsome is written as 1276. What will be code for Ugly?
   A. 7621 B. 6721
   C. 2761 D. 1276
14. In a certain code, RED is written as 27. How will BAD be written?
   A. 8 B. 7
   C. 9 D. 5
15. DEAD is written as 14. How BREAD will be written?
   A. 30 B. 28
   C. 31 D. 36

## ANSWERS

| 1 | 2 | 3 | 4 | 5 | 6 | 7 | 8 | 9 | 10 |
|---|---|---|---|---|---|---|---|---|---|
| D | A | C | D | A | A | A | B | D | A |
| 11 | 12 | 13 | 14 | 15 | | | | | |
| E | B | B | B | A | | | | | |

## EXPLANATORY ANSWERS

1. Yee is common code between second and third, are is also common between second and third sentence.
2. Tip is common between first and third terms whereas are is common in all the three. So Tok means are and Tip means fast.
3. 2 means Carpet. Six is meant for one. So, 5 means Dust.

4. Because 5 is common between second and third codes. Further, Yellow is common between them.
5. S U N I L   R A M E S H
   R V M J K   Q B L F R I
   One alphabet back and one alphabet ahead.
6. Bad is opposite to good, Wrong is opposite to Right. So, 74325 is the right code.
7. i g h t is common in all.
   So, RMSN = apkl
8. Two alphabets missing in between.
9. First alphabet has three alphabets in between with the shipping of one alphabet.
10. One word next and one word back.
11. First alternate is same and then two before.
12. One before two before....
13. Opposite to Handsome.
14. R E D = 27
    18 + 5 + 4 = 27
    B A D = 2 + 1 + 4 = 7.
15. B R E A D
    2 18 5 1 4
    2 + 18 + 5 + 1 + 4 = 30.

# Chapter 7

# LOGICAL VENN DIAGRAMS

## TYPE I

This topic deals with questions, which analyse a candidate's ability to relate a certain group of items and represent them diagrammatically.

**Example 1 :** Teacher (A), Lawyer (B), Doctor (C).

**Ans.** Since all the three are of different categories. Therefore, the Venn diagram will be

**Example 2 :** Kilometre (A), Metre (B), Centimetre (C).

**Ans.** One item belongs to the class of second and second belongs to the class of third. Therefore the diagram will be

**Example 3 :** Chair (A), Table (B), Furniture (C).

**Ans.** Chair and table are separate but the parts of furniture. So, the diagram will be

## EXERCISE

**(Qs. 1 to 6):** *Which of the diagrams correctly represent the items mentioned in each question?*

**1.** Tiger, Deers, Animals.

A. 
B. 
C. 
D. 

**2.** Clerks, Government Employees, Educated persons.

A. 
B. 
C. 
D. 

**3.** Doctor, Cats, Human beings.

A. 
B. 
C. 
D. 

**4.** Banana, Apple, Fruits.

A. 
B. 
C. 
D. 

**5.** Fan, Cooler, Air Conditioner.

A. 
B. 
C. 
D. 

**6.** Brother, Male, Father.

A. 
B. 
C. 
D. 

***Directions for questions 7 to 11:** From the following figures decide, which figure will represent the relationships mentioned in each question.*

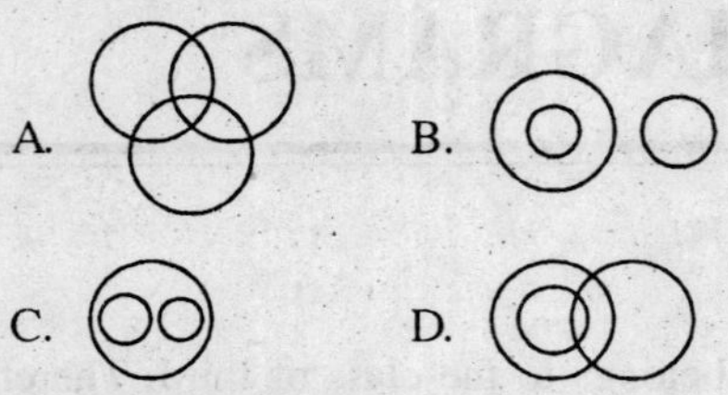


**7.** Women, Mother, Players.
**8.** Poet, Teacher, Men.
**9.** Crow, Sparrow, Birds.
**10.** Campa, Limca, Cold drinks.
**11.** Girls, Students, Atheletes.

***Directions for questions 12 to 21:** Identify the right figure after correlating the terms given in each question.*

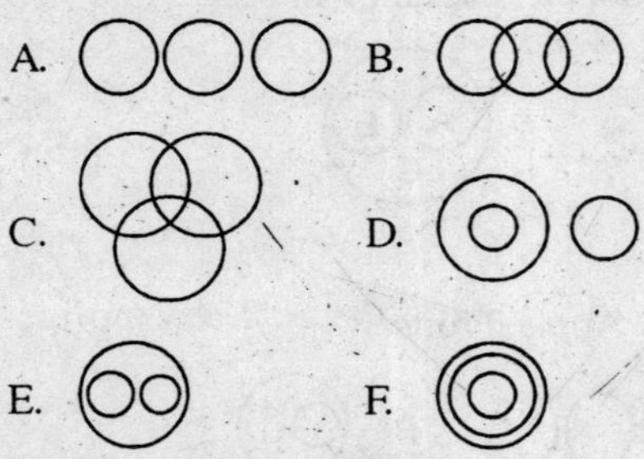


**12.** Haryana, Punjab, Rohtak.
**13.** Carrot, Radish, Vegetable.
**14.** Engineer, Doctor, People.
**15.** Hours, Minutes, Seconds.
**16.** Educated, Brother, Sister.
**17.** Pigeons, Birds, Parrot.
**18.** Diseases, Leprosy, T.B.
**19.** Animals, Men, Plants.
**20.** Biology, Zoology, Botany.
**21.** Science, Physics, Chemistry.

***Directions for questions 22 to 30:** Identify the right figure for satisfying the set of items given in each question.*

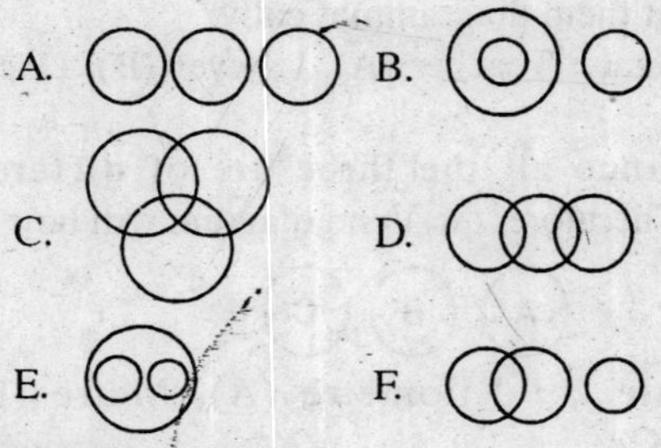


**22.** Yak, Tiger, Animal.
**23.** Tallmen, Shortmen, Indian.
**24.** Society, President, Sceretary.
**25.** Mother, Father, Brother.
**26.** Human beings, Doctor, Teacher.
**27.** Rich, Poor, Men.
**28.** Student, Boys, Girls.
**29.** Pen, Pencil, Stationery.
**30.** Engineer, Doctor, Educated.

## TYPE II

Each Geometrical Figure respresents a certain class.

**Example :**

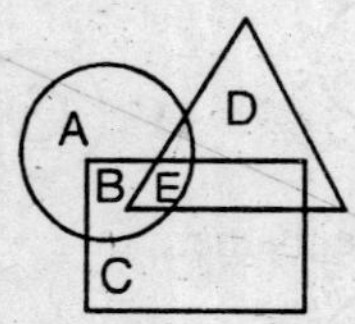


Circle represents Educated
Triangle represents Engineer
Square Represents Villagers.

On the basis of above diagram indicate the following:

1. Alphabet, which represents only the Educated.
2. Alphabet, which represents only Engineer.
3. Alphabet, which represents only Villager.
4. Alphabet, which represents all the three.
5. Alphabet, which represents Villager as well as Educated.

**Solution :**

1. *A* is the point which indicates only Educated.
2. *D* represents triangle which means only Engineer.
3. *C* which is covered by square represents only villagers.
4. *E* covers all the three figures so represent Educated as well as Engineers and Villagers.
5. *B* covers only circle and square therefore, it represents those who are Villagers as well as Educated.

**Question 31 :**

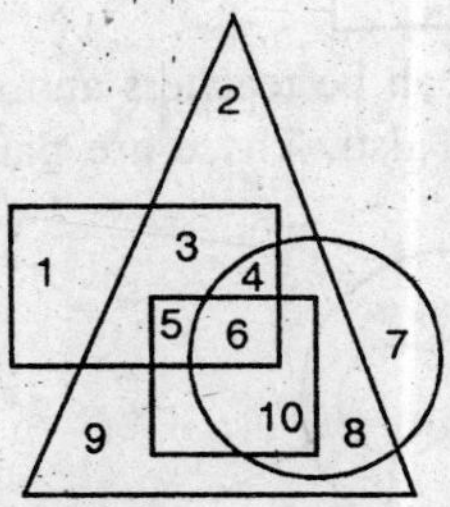


*Directions for questions 31 to 36 : The questions are based on the above diagram.*

1. Rectangle represents Doctors.
2. Triangle represents Villagers.
3. Square represents Graduates.
4. Circle represents Government Employees.

**31.** Which number indicates Doctor as well as Villagers?
A. 1 B. 2
C. 3 D. 6

**32.** Which number indicates only Doctors?
A. 1 B. 7
C. 8 D. 9

**33.** Which number indicates all the four categories?
A. 2 B. 4
C. 6 D. 8

**34.** Which number indicates Doctors, Government Employees and Villagers?
A. 4 B. 6
C. 8 D. 7

**35.** Which number indicates only Graduates?
A. 1 B. 2
C. 7 D. 6

**36.** Which number indicates Graduates, Doctors and Villagers?
A. 5 B. 6
C. 7 D. 8

*Directions for questions 37 to 40 : Refer the following diagram, which indicates the following information in terms of numbers.*

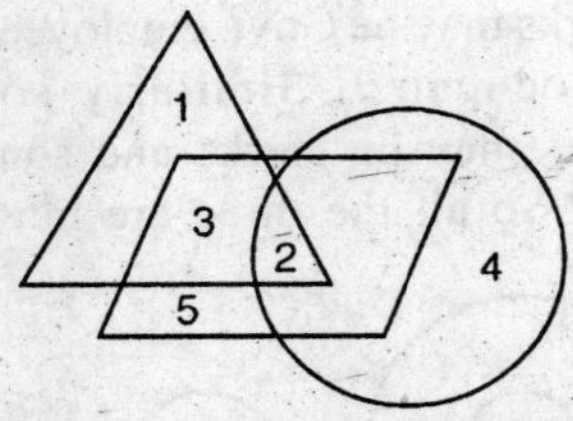


Rectangle represents Lady police. Circle represents Sub Inspector and Triangle represents Graduates.

**37.** Which number indicates Lady police Sub Inspector and Graduates?
A. 1 B. 2
C. 3 D. 4

**38.** Which number indicates Lady police and Graduates?
A. 2 B. 3
C. 5 D. 4

**39.** Which number indicates only Sub Inspector?
A. 5 B. 4
C. 2 D. 1

**40.** Which number indicates Lady police only?
A. 4 B. 5
C. 3 D. 2

## ANSWERS

| 1 | 2 | 3 | 4 | 5 | 6 | 7 | 8 | 9 | 10 |
|---|---|---|---|---|---|---|---|---|---|
| A | C | B | B | A | A | D | A | C | C |
| **11** | **12** | **13** | **14** | **15** | **16** | **17** | **18** | **19** | **20** |
| A | D | E | E | F | B | C | E | A | E |
| **21** | **22** | **23** | **24** | **25** | **26** | **27** | **28** | **29** | **30** |
| E | E | D | E | F | E | E | D | E | E |
| **31** | **32** | **33** | **34** | **35** | **36** | **37** | **38** | **39** | **40** |
| C | A | C | A | C | A | B | B | B | B |

# EXPLANATORY ANSWERS

**1.**

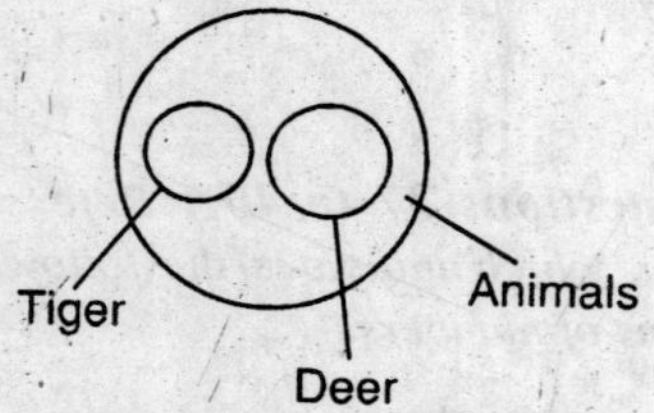


**2.** Some clerks may be Govt. employees and some may be educated. Similarly some Govt. employees may be clerks and some may be educated. So all the three are interrelated to each other.

**3.**

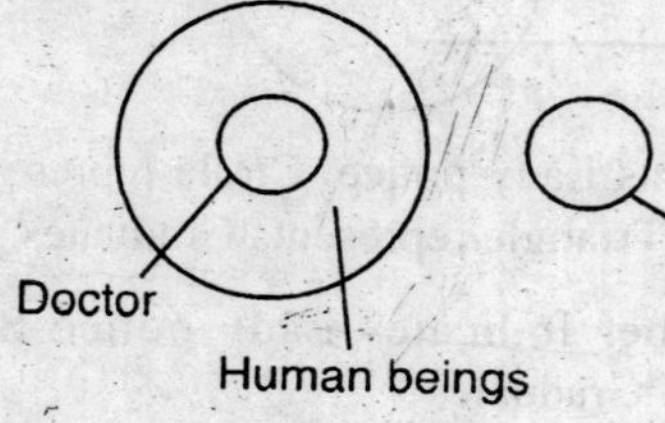


**4.**

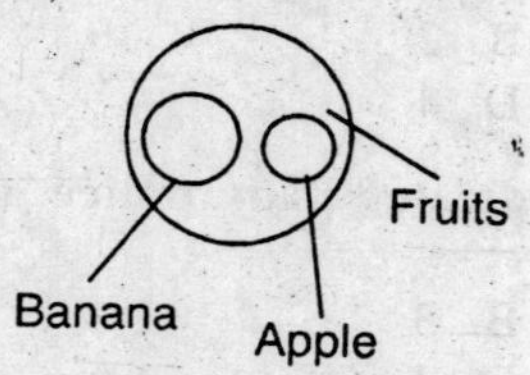


**5.**

**6.** All the three are interrelated to some extent.

**7.** Some mothers and players are women.

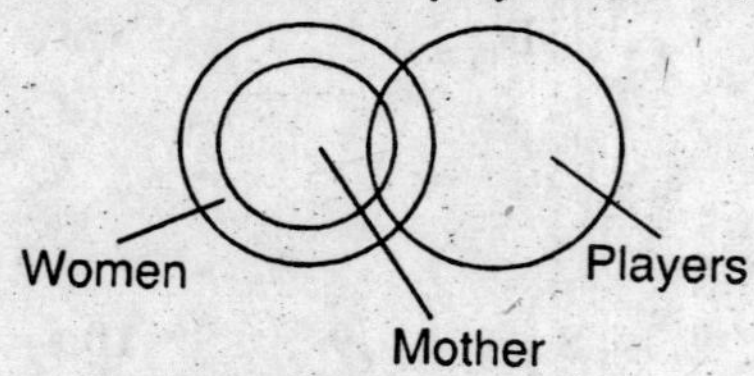


**8.**

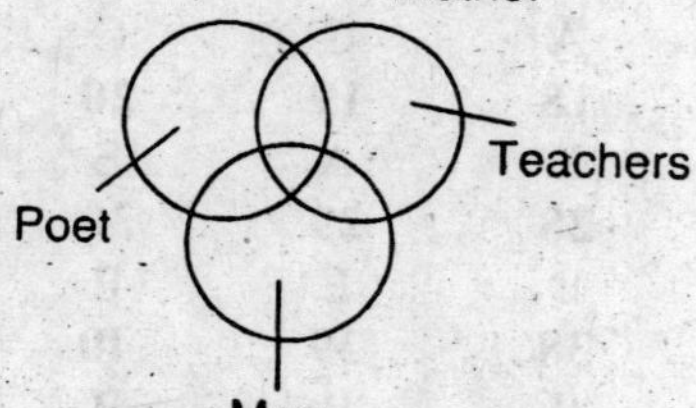


Some poet can be teachers and some teachers can be poet also. These are partly related to each other.

**9.**

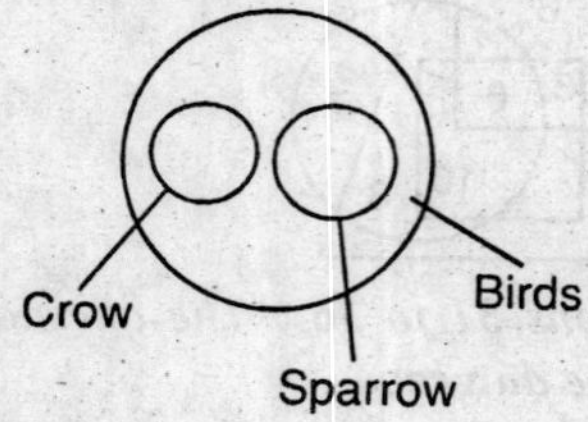


**10.**

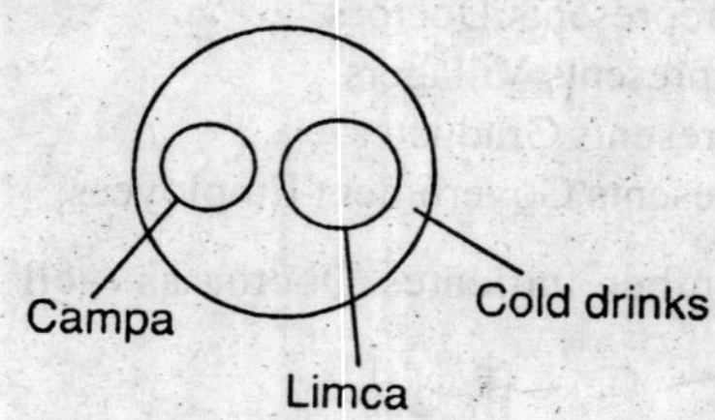


**11.**

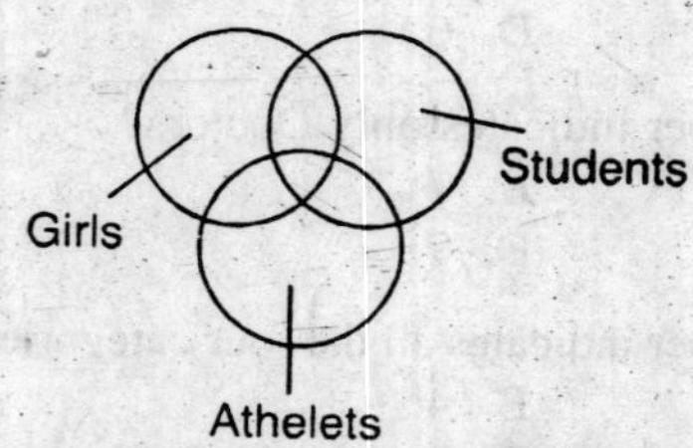


All the three are partly related to each other.

**12.**

**13.**

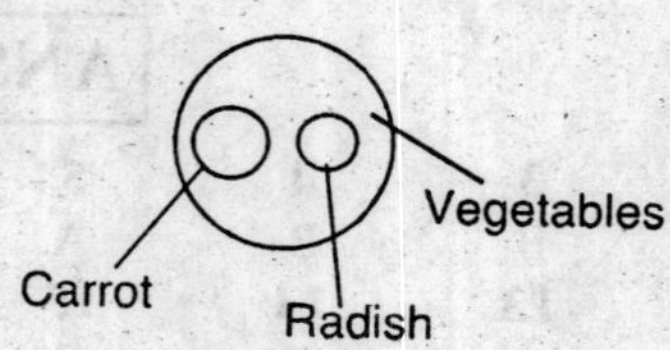


**14.**

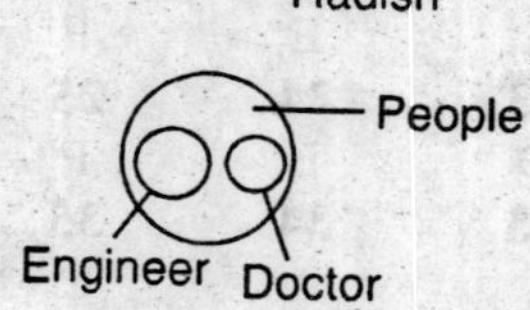

15.
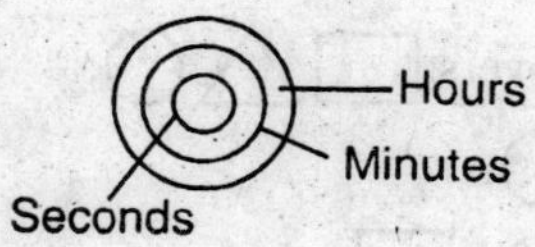


16.
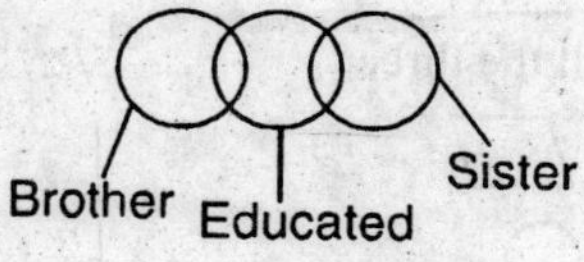


17.

18.
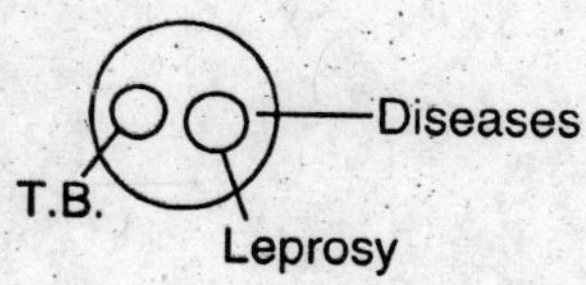


19.
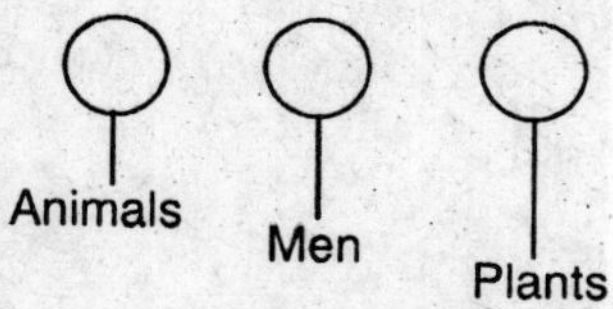


are the three altogether different.

20.
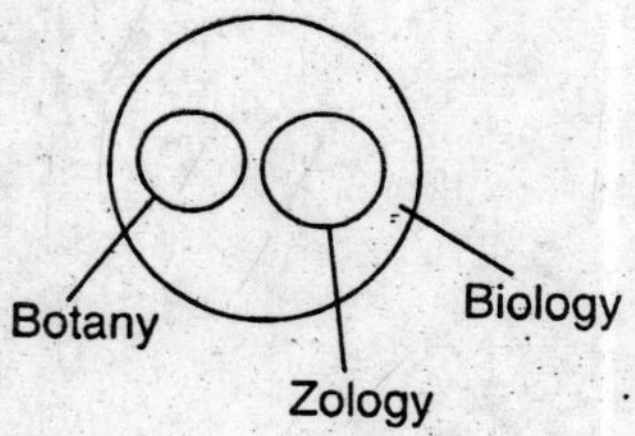


21.
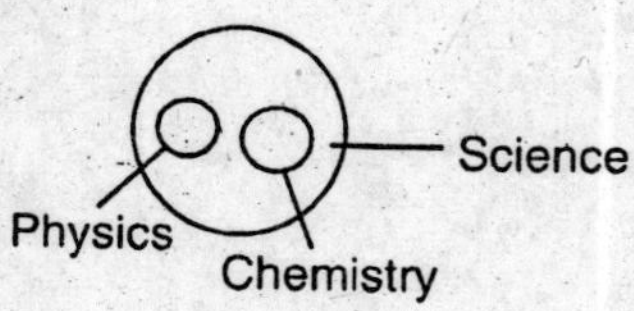


22.
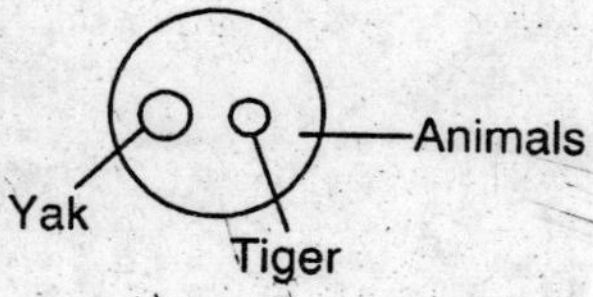


23.
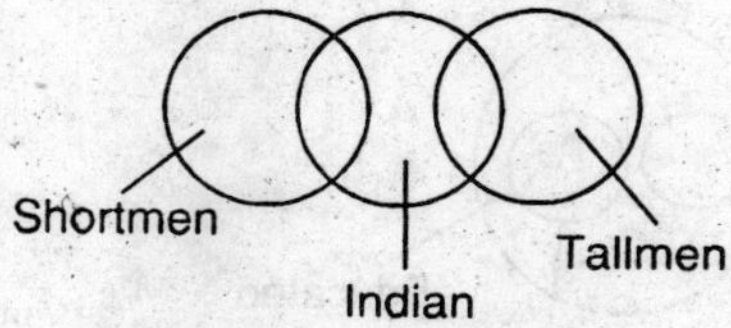


24.
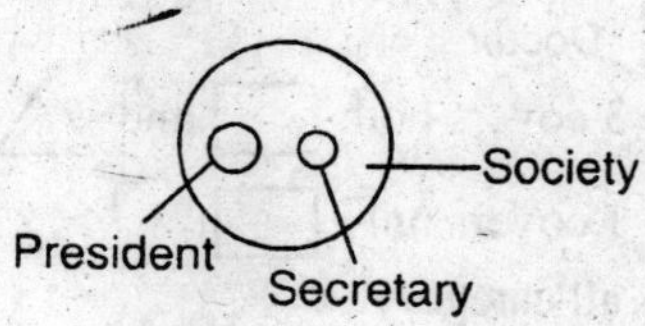


25.
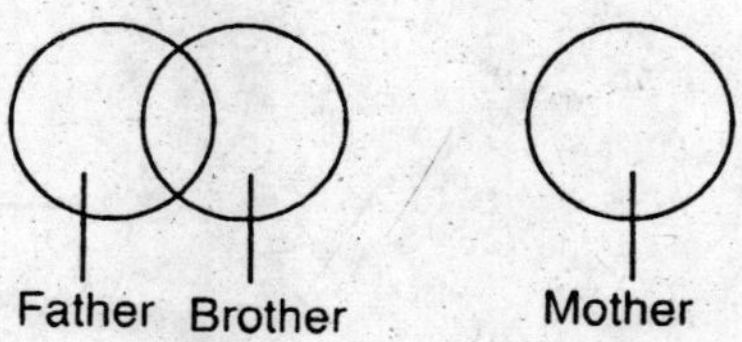


26.
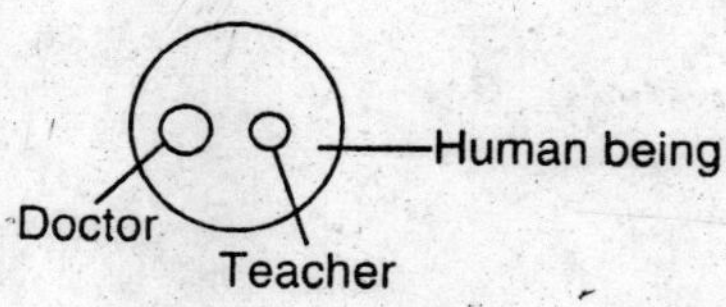


27.
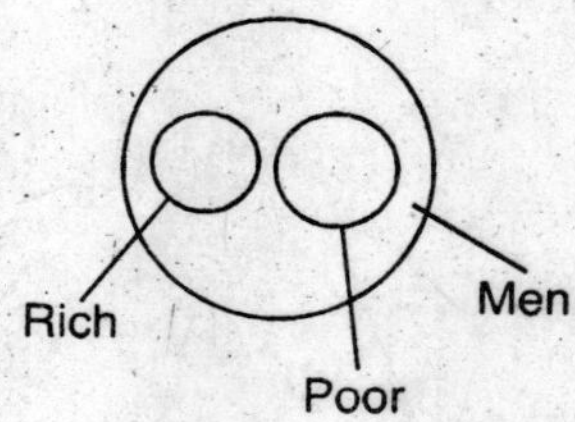


28.
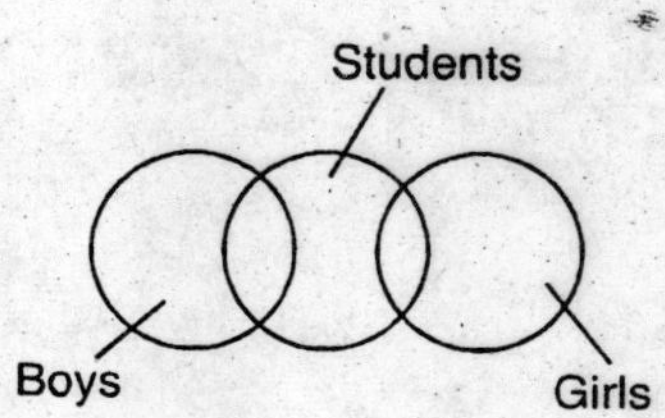


29.
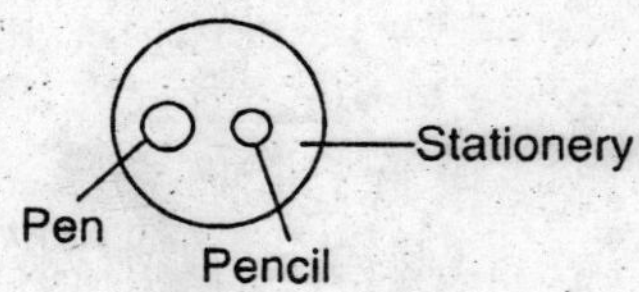

**30.**

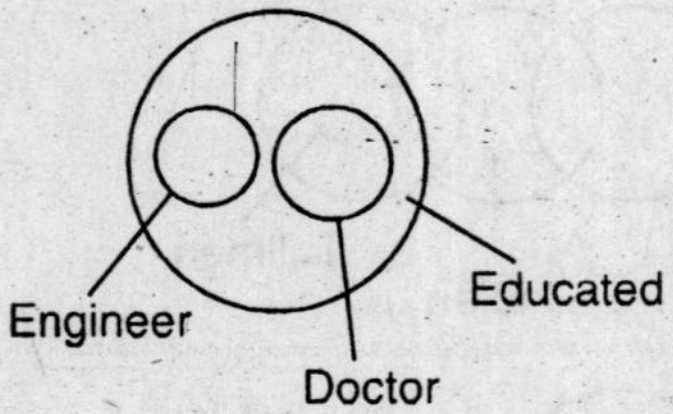


**31.** because No. 3 covers both □ and △.

**32.** because No. 1 covers only □.

**33.** No. 6 covers all category.

**34.** because No. 4 covers □△○.

**35.** It covers only ○.

**36.** It covers □△□.

**37.** No. 2 covers all the three.

**38.** It covers △▱.

**39.** It covers only ○.

**40.** It covers only ▱.

Chapter 8

# BLOOD RELATION

In this type of questions, the success of a student depends upon the knowledge of blood relations. Some of the important relationships have been listed as follows:

| | |
|---|---|
| Father's *or* mother's Son | Brother. |
| Father's *or* mother's Daughter | Sister. |
| Father's *or* mother's Brother | Uncle. |
| Father's *or* mother's Sister | Aunt. |
| Father's *or* mother's Father | Grandfather. |
| Father's *or* mother's Mother | Grandmother. |
| Uncle's or Aunt's Son | Cousin. |
| Brother's Daughter | Niece. |
| Brother's Son | Nephew. |
| Daughter's Husband | Son-in-law. |
| Son's Wife | Daughter-in-law. |
| Husband's or wife's Brother | Brother-in-law. |
| Sister's Husband | Brother-in-law. |

**Example 1 :** Pointing to a photograph, a lady said that his maternal uncle and my maternal uncle both are brothers. What is the relationship of that lady with the person in the photograph?

**Ans :** Clearly, it is the photograph of his son. Because the maternal uncle of his son is the brother of his mother.

**Example 2 :** Introducing a man to her husband, a lady said that he is the brother of the son of her grandfather. What is the relationship of the lady with that person?

A. Uncle B. Brother
C. Grandfather D. Daughter

**Ans :** Obviously, she is the daughter because the son of grandfather is the brother of her uncle.

**Example 3 :** Introducing a man, a woman said, "His wife is the only daughter of my father." How was that man related to that lady?

**Ans :** That lady is the wife of that man because only daughter of my father means she is saying about herself.

**Example 4 :** Introducing a lady, a man said, "She is the only daughter of the only son of his father." How is that man is related to that lady?

**Ans :** That man is the only son of his father and that lady is his only daughter. So, that man is the father of that lady.

**Example 5 :** Pointing towards a person in a photograph, Anshu said, "He is the only son of the father of my sister's brother." How is that person related to Anshu.

**Ans :** Sister's brother is Anshu's brother. But brother's father is her own father. So, the father's son is her brother.

## EXERCISE

**1.** A lady pointed towards a photograph and said that his maternal uncle's sister is the mother of her son. How is the person in photograph related to that lady?
A. Son B. Sister
C. Daughter D. Uncle

**2.** A man said that Sita is the only daughter of his father-in-law. How is Sita related to that man?
A. Wife B. Sister-in-law
C. Daughter D. Sister

**3.** A man said to a woman, "Your only brother's son is my wife's brother." How is the woman, related to the man's wife?
A. Mother B. Aunt
C. Sister D. Can't explained

**4.** Introducing Sita, Ram said, "Her father is the only son of my father." How Ram is related to Sita?
A. Father B. Brother
C. Uncle D. Son

**5.** Introducing a woman, a man said, "Her only brother's son is my wife's brother." How is the woman related to the man's wife?

A. Aunt B. Mother
C. Sister D. Can't explained

**6.** Pointing to a photograph a man said, "Her mother is the only daughter of my father-in-law. What is the relation of the photo with that man?

A. Daughter B. Wife
C. Daughter-in-law D. Can't explained

**7.** $X$ is the mother of $A$ and $B$. $D$ is the wife of $A$ and $C$ is the husband of $B$. What is the relationship of $X$ with $C$?

A. Mother-in-law B. Daughter-in-law
C. Aunt D. None of these

**8.** Both $A$ and $B$ are the children of $X$. Mr. $B$ is $A$'s brother but $A$ is not the brother of $B$. How is $A$ related to $B$?

A. Cousin B. Sister
C. Brother D. Can't explained

**9.** $X$ and $Y$ both are the children of $Z$. If $Z$ is the mother of $X$ and $X$ is the son of $Z$ but $Y$ is not the daughter of $Z$. How are $X$ and $Y$ related?

A. Both are brother B. $X$ is sister of $Y$
C. $Y$ is sister of $X$ D. None of these

**10.** A lady pointed towards a photograph and said that she is the daughter of the son of my father. What is the relationship of that lady with that photograph?

A. Aunt and Niece B. Aunt and her daughter
C. Both are sisters D. None of these

**11.** A boy said to a woman, "Your mother is the wife of my father's elder son." How is that boy related to that woman?

A. Uncle B. Father
C. Brother D. None of these

**12.** Mrs. $X$, a dcotor, was operating a patient and told that the patient is the elder brother of the son of my grandfather. What is the patient to the doctor?

A. Father's elder brother
B. Maternal uncle
C. Uncle
D. None of these

***Directions for questions 13 to 15 : Read the information given below and answer the questions.***

1. $X - Y$ means $X$ is the wife of $Y$
2. $X + Y$ means $X$ is the daughter of $Y$
3. $X \times Y$ means $X$ is the son of $Y$

then about

**13.** $A \times B - C$, which of the following is true?

A. C is the wife of $B$
B. $C$ is the father of $A$
C. $A$ is the daughter of $B$
D. $B$ is the father of $A$

**14.** $X - Y \times T - S$, which of the following is not true?

A. $T$ is the mother of $Y$
B. $S$ is the husband of $T$
C. $Y$ is the daughter of $T$
D. $X$ is the wife of $Y$

**15.** Which statement is correct

A. $A - B$ means $A$ is the brother of $B$
B. $A \times B$ means $A$ is the son of $B$
C. $A + B$ means $B$ is the daughter of $A$

***Directions for questions 16 to 21: Questions are based on the following information :***

There are six members in the family $PQRSTU$. $Q$ is the son of $R$ but $R$ is not the mother of $Q$. $P$ and $R$ are married couple. $T$ is the brother of $R$. $S$ is the daughter of $P$ and $U$ is the brother of $Q$.

**16.** How many male members are there in the family?

A. 1 B. 2
C. 3 D. 4

**17.** Who is the mother of $Q$?

A. $S$ B. $U$
C. $T$ D. $P$

**18.** How many children $P$ have?

A. 1 B. 2
C. 3 D. 4

**19.** Who is the wife of $T$?

A. $P$ B. $U$
C. $Q$ D. None of these

**20.** Which of the following is a pair of females?

A. $PT$ B. $QS$
C. $SU$ D. $PS$

**21.** How is $T$ related to $S$?

A. Father B. Brother
C. Uncle D. None of these

***Directions for questions 22 to 25 : Questions are based on the following information :***

$A + B$ means $A$ is the son of $B$.
$A = B$ means $A$ is the sister of $B$.

$A - B$ means $A$ is the wife of $B$.
$A \times B$ means $A$ is the brother of $B$.
$A \div B$ means $A$ is the mother of $B$.

**22.** What we mean by $X + Z - Y$?
A. $Y$ is the father of $X$
B. $Y$ is the son of $X$
C. $Y$ is the uncle of $X$
D. $Y$ is the brother of $X$

**23.** What we mean by $X \times Z \div Y$?
A. $X$ is the brother of $Z$
B. $X$ is the father of $Y$
C. $X$ is the uncle of $Y$
D. $X$ is the nephew of $Y$

**24.** What we mean by $X = Z + Y$?
A. $X$ is the aunt of $Y$
B. $X$ is the daughter of $Y$
C. $X$ is the niece of $Y$
D. $X$ is the sister of $Y$

**25.** What we mean by $X = Z \div Y$?
A. $X$ is the aunt of $Y$
B. $X$ is the sister of $Y$
C. $Y$ is the niece of $X$
D. $Y$ is the daughter of $X$

## ANSWERS

| 1 | 2 | 3 | 4 | 5 | 6 | 7 | 8 | 9 | 10 |
|---|---|---|---|---|---|---|---|---|---|
| A | A | B | A | B | A | A | B | A | A |
| **11** | **12** | **13** | **14** | **15** | **16** | **17** | **18** | **19** | **20** |
| A | A | B | C | B | A | D | C | D | D |
| **21** | **22** | **23** | **24** | **25** | | | | | |
| C | A | C | B | A | | | | | |

## EXPLANATORY ANSWERS

**1.** Photo's maternal uncle's sister is the mother of her son. So the person in the photo is sister of the lady.

**2.** Father-in-law's only daughter is his wife.

**3.** The woman is man's wife father's sister.

**4.** Ram is Sita's father.

**5.** The woman is man's wife father's sister.

**6.** That photograph is of his daughter.

**7.** Mother-in-law.

**8.** Sister.

**9.** Both are brothers.

**10.** Aunt and niece.

**11.** Uncle.

**12.** Because the grandson is a doctor, and patient is elder brother of his father.

**13.** $A \times B - C$, means $A$ is the son of $B$ who is the wife of $C$ which further means $A$ is the son of $C$. The right answer is $B$.

**14.** $X - Y \times T - S$ means $X$ is the wife of $Y$ who is the son of $T$ and who is the wife of $S$. This means $X$ is the wife of the son of $S$ (the father) *i.e.*, $X$ is the daughter-in-law of $S$. So the right answer is $C$.

**15.** Obviously, $B$ is the right answer.

**(For Qs. 16 to 21)** $Q$ is the son of $R$. But $R$ is not the mother of $Q$ means $R$ is the father of $Q$. $P$ is married to $R$ means $P$ is the father of $Q$. $U$ is the brother of $Q$ means $U$ is the son of $P$ and $R$. $S$ is the daughter of $P$ means $S$ is the daughter of $P$ and $R$. So

**16.** $P$ is the mother hence, she is female.
$Q$ is the son hence male.
$R$ is the father hence male.
$S$ is the daughter hence female.
$T$ is the brother hence male.
$U$ is son hence male. So there are four males.

**17.** Clearly, $P$ is the mother of $Q$. So D is the right answer.

**18.** $P$ have 2 son and one daughter.

**19.** Cannot be determined.

**20.** Because females are the mother $P$ and daughter $S$.

**21.** $T$ is the uncle of $S$.

**22.** $X + Z - Y$ means $X$ is the son of $Z$ who is the wife of $Y$, *i.e.*, $Y$ is the father $X$. So, the answer is A.

**23.** $X \times Z \div Y$ means $X$ is the brother of $Z$ who is the mother of $Y$, *i.e.*, $X$ is the uncle of $Y$. So the answer is B.

**24.** $X = Z + Y$, means $X$ is the sister of $Z$ who is the son of $Y$, *i.e.*, $X$ is the daughter of $Y$. So the answer is B.

**25.** $X = Z \div Y$ means $X$ is the sister of $Z$ who is the mother of $Y$, *i.e.*, $X$ is the aunt of $Y$. The answer is A.

Chapter 9

# CLASSIFICATION (ODD MAN OUT)

The very purpose of this test is to judge the candidate's ability of differentiation. There is a group of certain things in which one is different from the other and that is known as odd man out.

**Example 1 :** A. Green B. Red
C. Blue D. Pink
E. Yellow pale.

**Ans.** Clearly except Pink all are dark colour hence D is the odd man out.

**Example 2 :** A. Butter B. Oil
C. Petrol D. Ink
E. Curd F. Milk

**Ans.** Except milk all are processed things therefore milk is the odd man out.

**Example 3 :** A. Japan B. USA
C. China D. Korea
E. Delhi

**Ans.** Except Delhi all are the names of countries so Delhi is the odd man out.

## EXERCISE

**Find the odd one:**

**1.** A. Potato B. Tomato
C. Lady ringer D. Cucumber
E. Brinjal

**2.** A. Book B. Note Book
C. Pen D. Ink
E. Novel

**3.** A. Horse B. Tiger
C. Elephant D. Lion
E. Dog

**4.** A. River B. Lake
C. Sea D. Pool
E. Pond

**5.** A. Sun B. Moon
C. Star D. Mars
E. Universe

**6.** A. Pineapple B. Orange
C. Malta D. Banana
E. Lemon

**7.** A. Carpenter B. Tailor
C. Blacksmith D. Barber
E. Engineer

**8.** A. Hostel B. Inn
C. Hotel D. Club
E. Motel

**9.** A. Ear B. Heart
C. Lungs D. Kidney
E. Eye

**10.** A. Doe B. Drone
C. Bitch D. Mare
E. Sorceress

**11.** A. Baboon B. Gibbon
C. Chimpanzee D. Gorilla
E. Jaguar

**12.** A. Tiger B. Lion
C. Fox D. Leopard
E. Panther

**13.** A. Botany B. Zoology
C. Physics D. Chemistry
E. Mathematics

**14.** A. January B. March
C. July D. August
E. February

**15.** A. Beijing B. Delhi
C. Pakistan D. Washington
E. Tokyo

**16.** A. Water B. Air
C. Forest D. Hill
E. Garden

**17.** A. Hokey B. Football
C. Cricket D. Pollo
E. Table Tennis

18. A. Broker B. Salesman
C. Customer D. Hawker

**Choose the odd number out:**

19. A. 3 B. 5
C. 7 D. 9
E. 11

20. A. 12 – 4 B. 36 – 6
C. 96 – 12 D. 27 – 3
E. 33 – 9

21. A. 29 B. 38
C. 92 D. 74
E. 54

22. A. 23 – 29 B. 19 – 25
C. 13 – 17 D. 3 – 5

23. A. 4 B. 16
C. 49 D. 64
E. 100

24. A. 3 – 4 B. 4 – 7
C. 5 – 12 D. 20 – 21

**Choose the odd letter group:**

25. A. AC B. JL
C. PR D. TV
E. WX

26. A. AZ B. BY
C. CX D. DW
E. EU

27. A. VWY B. QRT
C. LMO D. JKL
E. DEG

28. A. Wine : Grapes B. Paper : Pulp
C. Shoes : Leather D. Rice : Crop

29. A. Lawyer : Court B. Writer : Book
C. Poet : Poem D. Chemist : Medicine
E. Car : Owner

30. A. Carrot B. Potato
C. Ladyfinger D. Cabbage

# ANSWERS

| 1 | 2 | 3 | 4 | 5 | 6 | 7 | 8 | 9 | 10 |
|---|---|---|---|---|---|---|---|---|---|
| A | E | E | C | E | D | D | D | B | B |
| 11 | 12 | 13 | 14 | 15 | 16 | 17 | 18 | 19 | 20 |
| E | C | E | E | C | E | E | C | D | E |
| 21 | 22 | 23 | 24 | 25 | 26 | 27 | 28 | 29 | 30 |
| E | B | C | D | E | E | D | D | E | A |

# EXPLANATORY ANSWERS

1. Potato is under ground vegetable except others. The right answer is A.
2. All, except Novel, are available at stationery shop.
3. All, except Dog, are wild animal.
4. All, except River, contain stagnant water.
5. All, except Universe, are the part of universe.
6. All, except Banana, are used in juice.
7. All, except Barber, need raw material to work.
8. All, except Club, are staying places.
9. All, except Heart, are in pairs.
10. All, except Drone, are females.
11. All, except Jaguar, are species of monkey.
12. All, except Fox, belong to the cat family.
13. All, except Mathematics, are Science subject.
14. All, except February, have 31days.
15. All, except Pakistan, are capital.
16. All, except Garden, are natural.
17. All are outdoor game.
18. All others earn from customers.
19. 9 is the square of 3.
20. First one is the multiple of second.
21. Except E all other have their sum 11.
22. All, except B, are the pairs of prime numbers.
23. Others are the squares of even numbers.
24. In all other pairs, the numbers are prime.
25. WX of alphabets is continuous pair.
26. They are not in sequence.
27. They are not in proper sequence as others.
28. In all others, second is used in the first one.
29. All others are related to each other for operation.
30. Carrot is used in salad.

Chapter 10

# INSERTING THE MISSING NUMBER

In this type of questions a figure, a set of figures or a matrix is given having a certain character—following a certain pattern. The candidate is required to find out the missing number.

**Example 1 :**

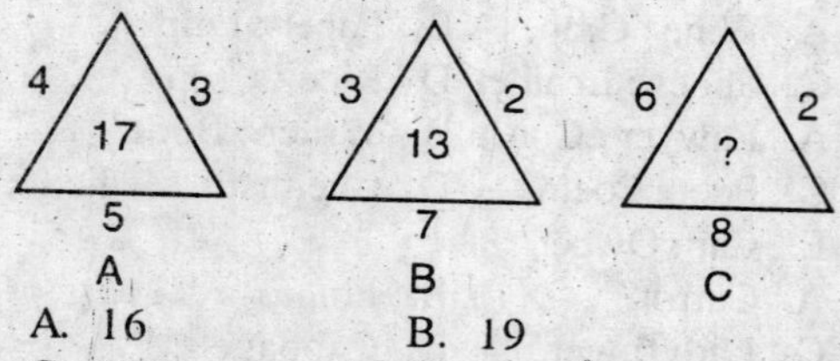


A. 16 B. 19
C. 20 D. None of these

**Ans.** Figure
$A$ $4 \times 3 + 5 = 17$
$B$ $3 \times 2 + 7 = 13$
Like wise $6 \times 2 + 8 = 20$

So the right answer is C.

**Example 2 :**

| ? | 8 | 12 |
|---|---|---|
| 6 | 4 | 8 |
| 5 | 6 | 7 |
| 4 | 2 | 3 |

A. 5 B. 6
C. 7 D. 8

**Ans.** In the second column, $6 + 4 - 2 = 8$
third column, $8 + 7 - 3 = 12$
Like wise $6 + 5 - 4 = 7$

So C is the right answer.

**Example 3 :**

| A | D | H |
|---|---|---|
| F | I | M |
| ? | N | R |

A. K B. N
C. O D. P

**Ans.** The letter in the second and third rows are five steps ahead. So, the missing number is
K (F G H I J K)
1 2 3 4 5

**Example 4 :**

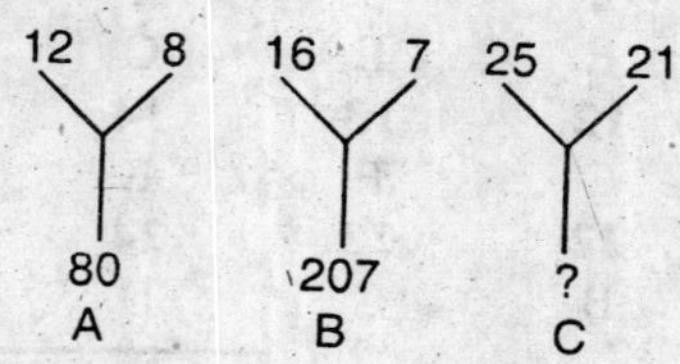


A. 184 B. 210
C. 241 D. 425

in figure
$A = 12^2 - 8^2 = 80$
$B = 16^2 - 7^2 = 207$
$C = 25^2 - 21^2 = 184$

So, A is the right answer.

## EXERCISE

1.

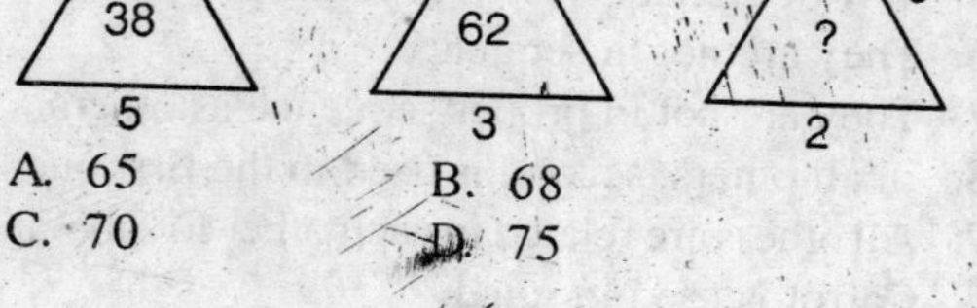


A. 65 B. 68
C. 70 D. 75

2.

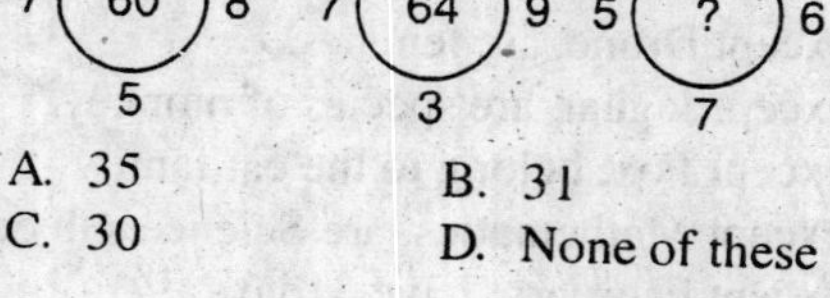


A. 35 B. 31
C. 30 D. None of these

3. 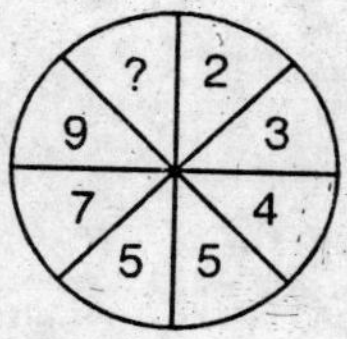


A. 10 B. 11
C. 12 D. 13

4. 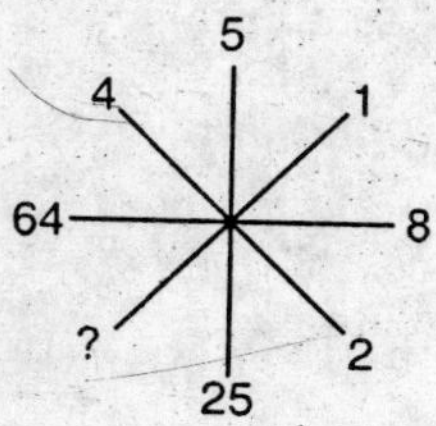


A. 1 B. 2
C. 3 D. 4

5. 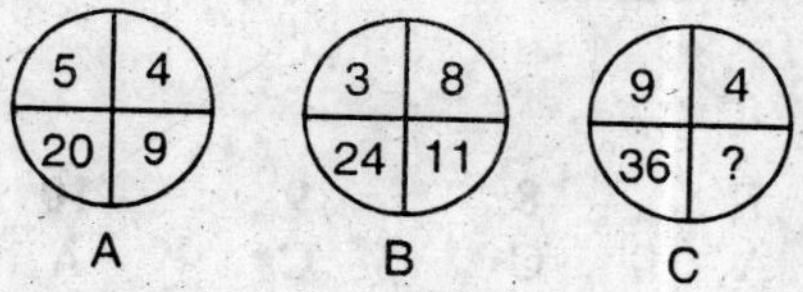


A. 15 B. 36
C. 13 D. None of these

6.

| 6 | 4 | 3 | 21 |
|---|---|---|---|
| 8 | 6 | 5 | 43 |
| 12 | 6 | 2 | ? |

A. 72 B. 70
C. 74 D. 76

7. 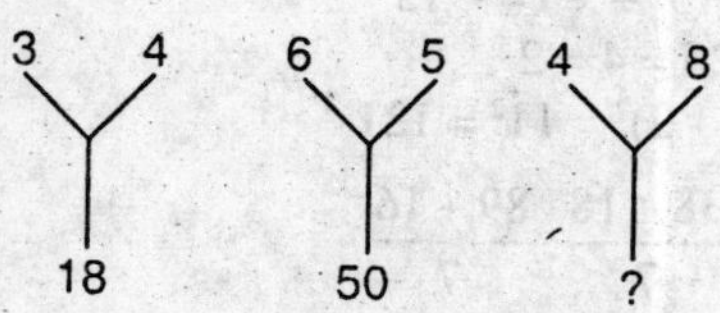


A. 68 B. 78
C. 80 D. 72

8. 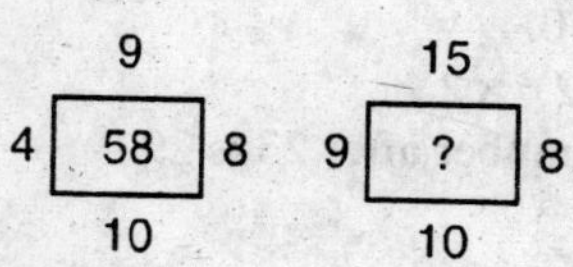


A. 117 B. 100
C. 78 D. 63

9. 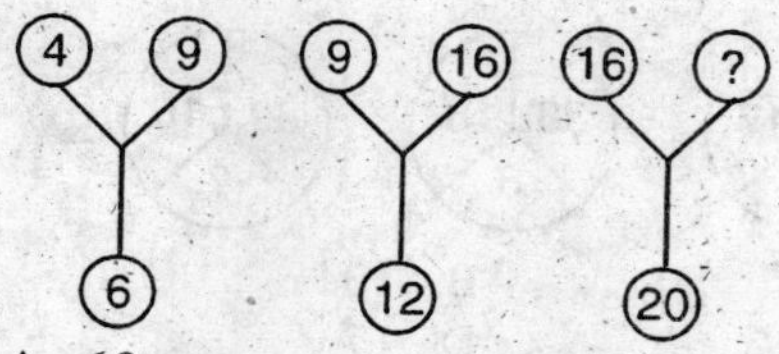


A. 60 B. 50
C. 25 D. 21

10.

| 6 | 11 | 25 |
|---|---|---|
| 8 | 6 | 16 |
| 12 | 5 | ? |

A. 16 B. 25
C. 48 D. 59

11. 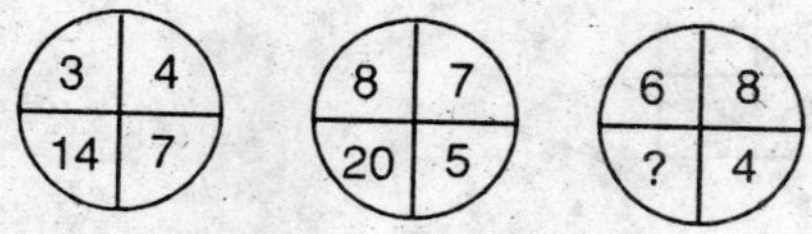


A. 18 B. 20
C. 21 D. 28

12.

| 963 | 2 | 844 |
|---|---|---|
| 464 | ? | 903 |

A. 1 B. 2
C. 3 D. 4

13.

| B | G | N |
|---|---|---|
| D | J | R |
| G | N | ? |

A. U B. V
C. W D. N

14. 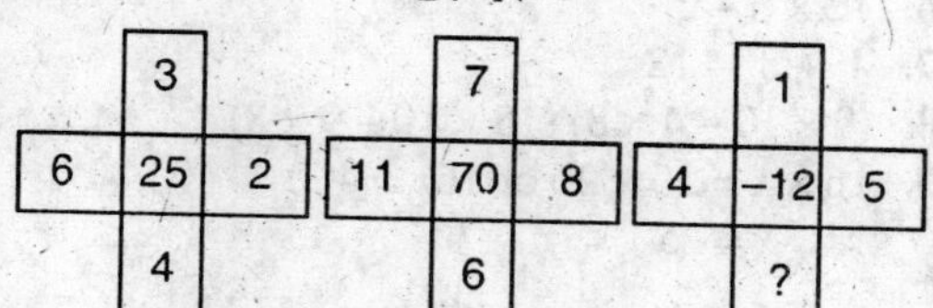


A. 10 B. 6
C. 2 D. 1

15. 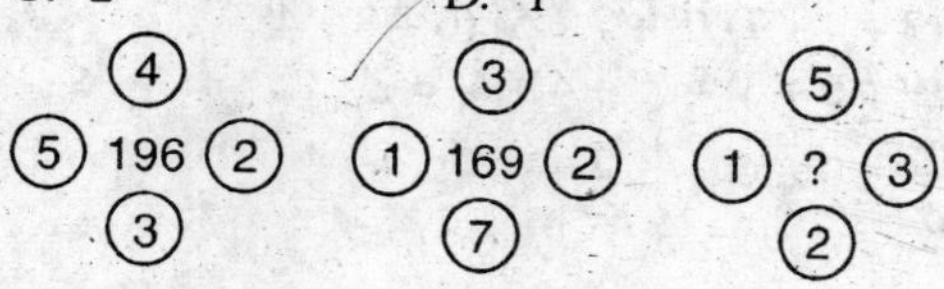


A. 121 B. 144

C. 169 D. 400

**16.**

A. 15 B. 13
C. 19 D. 17

**17.**

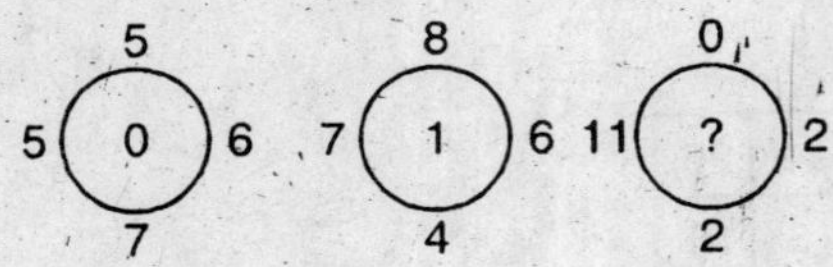


A. 11 B. 0
C. 2 D. 12

**18.**

| 3 | 4 | 5 |
|---|---|---|
| 3 | 7 | 12 |
| 3 | ? | 22 |

A. 11
B. 10
C. 8
D. 9

**19.**

| 3 | 2 | 3 | 75 |
|---|---|---|---|
| 4 | 2 | 2 | ? |

A. 75
B. 72
C. 70
D. None of these

**20.**

| 3 | 5 | 7 |
|---|---|---|
| 11 | 13 | 17 |
| 19 | 23 | ? |

A. 29
B. 31
C. 33
D. None of these

# ANSWERS

| 1 | 2 | 3 | 4 | 5 | 6 | 7 | 8 | 9 | 10 |
|---|---|---|---|---|---|---|---|---|---|
| A | B | B | A | C | B | A | C | C | A |
| **11** | **12** | **13** | **14** | **15** | **16** | **17** | **18** | **19** | **20** |
| A | B | C | C | A | A | A | B | B | A |

# EXPLANATORY ANSWERS

**1.** $5^2 + 6^2 + 2^2 = 65$
**2.** $7 \times 8 + 9 - 5, 7 \times 9 + 4 - 3, 5 \times 6 + 8 - 7$
**3.** In second half no. is 5, 7, 9, 11
**4.** $1^2 = 1$
**5.** $5 \times 4, 5 + 4, 3 \times 8, 3 + 8, 9 \times 4, 9 + 4$
**6.** $12 \times 6 - 2$
**7.** $4^2 + 8^2 - 12$
**8.** $(9 \times 10 - 4 \times 8)\ (15 \times 10 - 9 \times 8)$
**9.** $16 \times x = 20 \times 20$ or $16x = 400$
$\therefore\ x = 25$
**10.** $11 \times 2 + \frac{6}{2}, 6 \times 2 + \frac{8}{2}, 5 \times 2 + \frac{12}{2}$
**11.** $(3 + 4 + 7)\ (8 + 7 + 5)\ (6 + 8 + 4)$
**12.** $(9 + 6 + 3) - (8 + 4 + 4) = 2$
$(4 + 6 + 4) - (9 + 0 + 3) = 2$
**13.** Skipping of alphabets in first column is in the order 1–2; in second column 2–3; in third column 3–4.
**14.** $(1^2 + 4^2) - (5^2 + x^2) = -12$
$x^2 = 29 - 25 = 4 = 2$
**15.** $(1 + 5 + 3 + 2)^2 = 11^2 = 121$
**16.** $\frac{25 + 17}{7}, \frac{38 + 18}{7}, \frac{89 + 16}{7}$
**17.** $= (11 + 2 - 0 + 2) = 11$
**18.** 3 + 4 under 4 is 7.
3 + 7 under 7 is 10.
**19.** $(3 + 3)^2 \times 2; (4 + 2)^2 \times 2$
**20.** The next prime number after 23 is 29.

## Chapter 11

# Number, Ranking and Time Sequence Test

**Number Test**

**Example :** How many 8's are there in the following number series, which are followed or preceded by 2.

8 2 4 5 1 7 2 8 4 8 4 2 2 8 2 6 9 8 2 4 5 8 2 3 7 8 2 5 2 8

A. 5 B. 6
C. 7 D. 8

**Ans.** The number, which comes after, is said to follow and which comes before, is known as precedes. In the given series the total no of 8s is 7, which are followed or preceded by 2.

**Ranking Test**

**Example 1 :** Amit is ranked ninth from the top and thirty-eighth from the bottom in a class. How many students are there in the class.

A. 46 B. 45
C. 47 D. 48

**Ans.** The whole class consists of 8 students who have a rank higher than Amit and Rahul. 37 students who have a rank lower than that of Amit.

So, the total students = 8 + 1 + 37 = 46

**Example 2 :** In a row of students, Anshul is seventh from the left and Madhuri is twelth from the right. If they interchange their positions, Anshul becomes twenty-second from the left. How many students are there in the row?

A. 31 B. 32
C. 33 D. 34

**Ans.** Anshul's new position is twenty-second from left. But it is the same as Madhuri's earlier position, which is 12th from the right.

Thus the Row consists of (21 + 1 + 11) = 33 students.

**Time Sequence Test**

**Example :** Suresh remembers that his brother's birthday is after fifteenth but before eighteenth of February, whereas his sister, Komal, remembers that her brother's birthday is after 16th but before 19th February. On which day in February does Suresh's brother's birthday fall?

A. 16th B. 17th
C. 18th D. 19th

**Ans.** Clearly Suresh's brother's birthday is on the day common to both, *i.e.*, 17th of February.

## EXERCISE

**1.** How many 6s are there in the following number series, which are preceded by 7 but not immediately followed by 9?

6 7 9 5 6 9 7 6 8 7 6 7 8 6 9 4 6 7 7 6 9 5 7 6 3

A. 3 B. 5
C. 4 D. 2

**2.** In the following list of numerals, how many 2s are followed by 1s but not preceded by 4?

4 2 1 2 1 4 2 1 1 2 4 4 4 1 2 2 1 2 1 4 4 2 1 4 2 1 2 1 2 4 1 4 2 1 2 4 1 4 6

A. 2 B. 5
C. 3 D. 4

**3.** How many 7s are there in the following series which are not immediately followed by 3 but immediately preceded by 8?

8 9 8 7 6 2 2 6 3 2 6 9 7 3 2 8 7 2 7 7 8 7 3 7 7 9 4

A. 10 B. 3
C. 2 D. 0

**4.** In the series
6 4 1 2 2 8 7 4 2 1 5 3 8 6 2 1 7 1 4 1 3 2 8 6
How many pairs of alternate numbers have a difference of 2?

A. one B. two
C. three D. four

**5.** How many odd numbers are there in the sequence which are immediately preceded and also immediately followed by even numbers?
5 1 4 7 3 9 8 5 7 2 6 2 1 5 8 6 3 8 5 2 2 4 3 4 9 6

A. 1 B. 2
C. 3 D. 4
E. More than Four

**6.** In a row of trees one tree is fifth from either end of row. How many trees are there in the row?

A. 8 B. 10
C. 9 D. 11

**7.** Ram ranks seventh from the top and twenty eighth from the bottom in a class. How many students are there in the class?

A. 34 B. 36
C. 37 D. 35

**8.** Ramesh ranks twelfth in a class of forty-six. What will be his rank from the last?

A. 35 B. 33
C. 34 D. 37

**9.** Ram is 7 rank ahead of Shyam in a class of 39. If Shyam's rank is 17th from the last, what is Ram's rank from the start?

A. 16th B. 14th
C. 15th D. 17th

**10.** Three persons *X, Y* and *Z* who are standing in a queue. There are five persons between *X* and *Y* and eight persons between *Y* and *Z*. If there are three persons ahead of *Z* and 21 persons behind *X*, what could be the minimum number of persons in the queue?

A. 41 B. 40
C. 28 D. 27

**11.** If the day before Yesterday was Thursday, when would Sunday fall?

A. Tomorrow
B. Today
C. Two days after today
D. None of the above

**12.** How many days will be there from 26th January, 1996 to 15th May, 1996 (both days included).

A. 111 B. 110
C. 112 D. 115

**13.** Sita remembers that her father's birthday was certainly after eighth of December but before 13th of December. Her sister Mohini remembers that their father's birthday was definitely after 9th but before 14th of December. On which date, did their father's birthday fall?

A. 10th
B. 11th
C. 12th
D. on any day in between 10, 11, 12

**14.** If it was Saturday on 17th December, 1982, what will be the day on 22nd December, 1984?

A. Monday B. Tuesday
C. Wednesday D. Sunday

**15.** If the seventh day of a month is three days earlier than Friday, what day will it be on 19th day of the month?

A. Sunday B. Monday
C. Wednesday D. Friday

## ANSWERS

| 1 | 2 | 3 | 4 | 5 | 6 | 7 | 8 | 9 | 10 |
|---|---|---|---|---|---|---|---|---|---|
| C | C | C | B | D | C | A | A | A | B |
| **11** | **12** | **13** | **14** | **15** | | | | | |
| A | A | D | D | A | | | | | |

## EXPLANATORY ANSWERS

**1.** 6 7 9 5 6 9 7 6 8 7 6 7 8 6 9 4 6 7 7 6 9 5 7 6 3

**2.** 4 2 1 2 1 4 2 1 1 2 4 4 4 1 2 2 1 2 1 4 4 2 1 4 2 1 2 1 2 4 1 4 2 1 2 4 1 4 6

**3.** 8 9 8 7 6 2 2 6 3 2 6 9 7 3 2 8 7 2 7 7 8 7 3 7 7 9 4

**4.** (6, 1) (4, 2) (1, 2) (2, 8) (2, 7) (8, 4) (7, 2) (4, 1) (2, 5) (1, 3) (5, 8) (3, 6) (8, 2) (6, 1) (2, 7) (1, 1)

(7, 4) (1, 1) (4, 3) (1, 2) (3, 8) (2, 6) pairs with a difference of 2 are.
(4, 2) (1, 3).

5. 5 1 4 7 3 9 8 5 7 2 6 2 1 5 8 6 3 8 5 2 2 4 3 4 9 6.
6. No. of trees in the row (4 + 1 + 4) = 9
7. Clearly, the number of Students is (6 + 11 + 27) = 34
8. Obviously, his rank is 35 the (46 – 11)
9. Shyam is 17th from the last and Ram is 24th (7 steps ahead), which means that Ram is 16th from the start.
10. There are 40 persons at least
...21... $X$ ...5... $Y$ ...8... $Z$ ...3...
$(21 + 5 + 8 + 3 + X + Y + Z) = 40$ persons.
11. The day before yesterday was Thursday that means today is Saturday and tomorrow will be Sunday.
12. $6 + 29 + 31 + 30 + 15 = 111$
(1996 is a leap year Feb-29)
13. Common days of the sister are 10, 11, 12,
14. **Note :** (1) A year has 365 days.
(2) A year divisible by 4 is a leap year and February is of 29 days, and total days in a year would be 366.
(3) The last day of the year is the same as first day.
(4) If the year is a leap year, then the last day will be one ahead of the first day.
15. As mentioned the 7th day of the month is 3 days earlier than Friday, which is Tuesday. So 14th day is also Tuesday and thus 19th day is Sunday.

## Chapter 12

# Mathematical Operations

In this type of problems, some symbols are given for Addition, Substraction, Multiplication and Division and the problems are to be solved according to the symbols. These symbols are artificial. The candidate has to substitute the real sign and has to solve the question accordingly.

In the solving these type questions BODMAS Formula is used, *i.e.*, the sequence to be followed while solving a question is fixed and bourded by rules in which bracket is solved first and the subtraction performed in the last.

B = Bracket
O = Of
D = Division
M = Multiply
A = Addition
S = Subtraction

**Example 1 :** If + means ÷
– means ×
× means –
÷ means +

Find out the value of $16 \div 8 - 4 + 2 \times 4$ ?

A. 16 B. 28
C. 32 D. 44

**Ans.** Put proper signs in the given equation
$16 + 8 \times 4 \div 2 - 4 = 16 + 8 \times 2 - 4 = 28$
So the answer is B.

**Example 2 :** If *A* means plus, *B* means minus, *C* means division and *D* means multiplication, then 18*A* 12*C* 6*D* 2*B*5 = ?

A. 17 B. 25
C. 27 D. 45

**Ans.** Using proper signs,
$18 + 12 \div 6 \times 2 - 5 = 18 + 2 \times 2 - 5$
$= 18 + 4 - 5 = 17$

Right answer is A.

## ARITHMETICAL REASONING

**Example 1 :** In a Chess tournament each of six players will play every other player exactly once. How many matches will be played during the tournament?

A. 12 B. 15
C. 30 D. 36

**Ans.** Matches of the first player with other 5 players.

Matches of second player with 4 players and so on.

So, number of matches played during the tournament = 5 + 4 + 3 + 2 + 1 = 15

So, B is the right answer.

**Example 2 :** *A, B, C* and *D* play a game of cards. *A* says to *B*, "If I give you 8 cards, you will have as many as *C* has and I shall have 3 less than what *C* has." Also, "If I take 6 cards from *C*, I shall have twice as many as *D* has." If *B* and *D* together have 50 cards, how many cards are with *A*?

A. 40 B. 37
C. 27 D. 23

**Ans.**
$B + 8 = C$ ...(*i*)
$A - 8 = C - 3$ ...(*ii*)
$A + 6 = 2D$ ...(*iii*)
$B + D = 50$ ...(*iv*)

Putting $C = A - 5$ from (*ii*) into (*i*) we have
$B + 8 = A - 5$
or $A - B = 13$ ...(*v*)

Putting $D = 50 - B$ from (*iv*) into (*iii*) we have,
$A + 6 = 100 - 2B$
or $A + 2B = 94$ ...(*vi*)

Solving, (*v*) and (*vi*), we get, $B = 27$
$A = 40$

So, *A* has 40 cards.
Hence, answer is A.

**Example 3 :** A worker may claim Rs. 15 for each km travelled by taxi and Rs. 5 for each km, for which he travells by car. If, in one week, he claimed Rs. 500 for travelling 80 kms, how many kms did he cover by taxi?

A. 40 B. 30
C. 20 D. 10

**Ans.** Let the distance covered by taxi be $x$ km.
Distance covered by car = $(80 - x)$ km.

$$15x + 5(80 - x) = 500$$
$$15x + 400 - 5x = 500$$
$$10x = 100$$
$$x = 10$$

So, the correct answer is D.

## EXERCISE

**1.** If $X$ stands for addition, ÷ stands for subtraction, + stands for multiplication and – stands for division, then $20 \times 8 \div 8 - 4 + 2 =$ ?
A. 80 B. 25
C. 24 D. 5

**2.** If $a$ means plus, $b$ means minus, $c$ means multiplication and $d$ means division, then $18c\ 14a\ 6b\ 16\ d\ 4 =$ ?
A. 63 B. 254
C. 288 D. 1208

**3.** If + means –, – means ×, × means ÷ and ÷ means +, then $15 \times 3 \div 15 + 5 - 2 =$ ?
A. 15 B. 12
C. 10 D. 8

**4.** If $x$ stands for add, $y$ stands for subtract, $z$ stands for divide and $p$ stands for multiply, then what is the value of $(7p3)y\ 6x5$?
A. 5 B. 10
C. 15 D. 20

**5.** If + means ×, ÷ means –, × means ÷ and – means +, what will be the value of
$$4 + 11 \div 5 - 55 = ?$$
A. – 48.5 B. – 11
C. 79 D. 94

*Arithmetical Reasoning*

**6.** Ram is twice as old as Shyam. Three years ago, he was three times as old as Shyam. How old is Ram now?
A. 6 years B. 7 years
C. 8 years D. 12 years

**7.** The age of a mother is twice that of the elder daughter. Ten years hence the age of mother will be three times of the younger daughter. If the difference of the ages of two daughters is 15 years, the age of mother is
A. 50 years B. 55 years
C. 60 years D. 70 years

**8.** A group of 1200 persons comprises captains and soldiers and is travelling in a train. For every 15 soldiers, there is one captain. The number of captains in the group is
A. 85 B. 80
C. 75 D. 70

**9.** Ram cuts a cake into two halves and then, cuts one half into smaller pieces of equal size. Each of the small pieces is of twenty grams (in wieght). If he has seven pieces of the cake in all, what was the weight of the original cake?
A. 120 gms B. 140 gms
C. 240 gms D. 280 gms

**10.** A father is now three times as old as his son. Five years ago, he was four times as old as his son. The age of the son is
A. 12 years B. 15 years
C. 18 years D. 20 years

***Directions for questions 11 to 15: Questions are based on the information given below :***

Data of 450 students who took an examination in Social Sciences, Maths, and Science is given below:

| | |
|---|---|
| Passed in all subjects | 167 |
| Failed in all subjects | 60 |
| Failed in Social Science | 175 |
| Failed in Mathematics | 199 |
| Failed in Science | 191 |
| Passed in Social Science only | 62 |
| Passed in Mathematics only | 48 |
| Passed in Science only | 52 |

**11.** How many students failed in one subject only?
A. 152 B. 144

C. 61 D. 56

**12.** How many students failed in Social Science only?

A. 15 B. 21
C. 30 D. 42

**13.** How many students passed at least in one subject?

A. 450 B. 390
C. 304 D. 167

**14.** How many students failed in two subjects only?

A. 56 B. 61
C. 152 D. 162

**15.** How many students passed in Mathematics and in at least one more subject?

A. 210 B. 203
C. 170 D. 94

## ANSWERS

| 1 | 2 | 3 | 4 | 5 | 6 | 7 | 8 | 9 | 10 |
|---|---|---|---|---|---|---|---|---|---|
| C | B | C | D | D | D | A | C | C | B |
| **11** | **12** | **13** | **14** | **15** | | | | | |
| C | A | B | D | B | | | | | |

## EXPLANATORY ANSWERS

**1.** Using the correct symbols, we have
$20 + 8 - 8 \div 4 \times 2$
$= 20 + 8 - 2 \times 2 = 20 + 8 - 4 = 24$

**2.** Using the correct symbols, we have
$18 \times 14 + 6 - 16 \div 4$
$= 18 \times 14 + 6 - 4 = 252 + 6 - 4 = 254$

**3.** Using the correct symbols, we have
$15 \div 3 + 15 - 5 \times 2$
$= 5 + 15 - 5 \times 2 = 5 + 15 - 10 = 10$

**4.** Using the correct symbols, we have
$(7 \times 3) - 6 + 5 = 21 - 6 + 5 = 20$

**5.** Using the correct symbols, we have
$4 \times 11 - 5 + 55 = 44 - 5 + 55 = 94$

**6.** Let Shyam's present age is $x$ years then Ram's present age is $= 2x$ years. Three years ago Shyam's age $= x - 3$ and Ram's age $= (2x - 3)$
So, $(2x - 3) = 3(x - 3)$
or $2x - 3 = 3x - 9$ or $x = 6$
Hence Ram's present age $= 2 \times 6 = 12$.

**7.** Let the age of elder daughter be $= x$
Then the age of younger daughter $= (x - 15)$
and age of mother $= 2x$
So, $2x + 10 = 3(x - 15 + 10)$
$2x + 10 = 3x - 15$ or $x = 25$
$\therefore$ Mother's age $2x = 25 \times 2 = 50$ yrs.

**8.** Out of every 16 persons there is one Captain
So, number of Captains is $= 1200/16 = 75$

**9.** The seven pieces consist of 6 smaller equal pieces and 1/2 cake piece.
Weight of each small piece = 20 gms.
So total weight of cake $= 2 \times (20 \times 6) = 240$ gms.

**10.** Let the age of son is $= x$
The father's age is $= 3x$
Five years ago father's age $= 3x - 5$
and son's age $= x - 5$
So, $3x - 5 = 4(x - 5)$ or $x = 15$.

**11.** Candidates failed in one subject only = (total number of candidates) – (candidates passed in all subject + candidates failed in all subjects + candidate passed in one subject only).
$= 450 - (167 + 60 + 62 + 48 + 52)$
$= 450 - 389 = 61$.

**12.** Candidates failed in Social Science only = (candidates failed in Social Science) – (candidates failed in all subjects + candidates passed in Science only + candidates passed in Maths only).
$= 175 - (60 + 52 + 48) = 175 - 160 = 15$

**13.** Candidates passed atleast in one subject = (candidates passed in one subject only) + (candidates passed in two subjects only) + (candidates passed in all subjects).
$= 162 + 61 + 167 = 390$

**14.** Candidates failed in two subjects only = candidates passed in one subject only.
$= 62 + 48 + 52 = 162$

**15.** Candidates failed in Science only
= Candidate failed in Science – (candidates pass in Social Science only + Candidates failed in all subjects + Candidates passed in Mathematics only) $= 191 - (62 + 60 + 40) = 21$
Candidates failed in Social Science = 15
$\therefore$ Candidates passed in Maths and atleast one more subjects $= (21 + 15 + 167) = 203$.

## Chapter 13

# ANALYTICAL REASONING

This topic has been introduced to assess or check the analytical knowledge of the candidate. The problems are related to the counting of geometrical figures in a given complete figure.

## EXERCISE

**1.** How many Triangles are there in the figure below?

A. 5 B. 6
C. 8 D. 10

**2.** How many Parallelograms are there in the figure below?

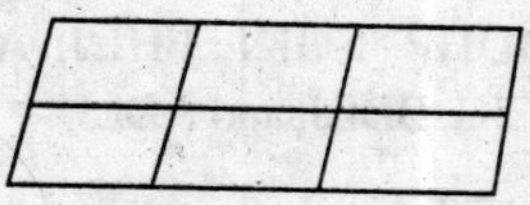

A. 15 B. 18
C. 16 D. 14

**3.** Count the number of Triangles in the following figure :

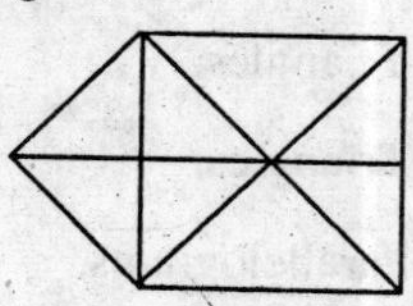

A. 18 B. 16
C. 15 D. 17

**4.** Find out the maximum no. of Squares.

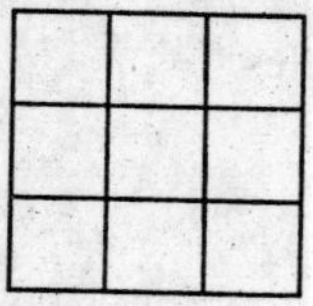

A. 10 B. 13
C. 9 D. 14

**5.** How many Triangles are there in the following figure?

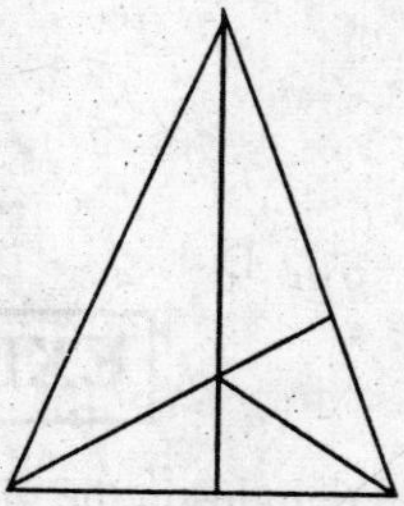

A. 9 B. 10
C. 11 D. 12

**6.** Count the number of Triangles in the following figure?

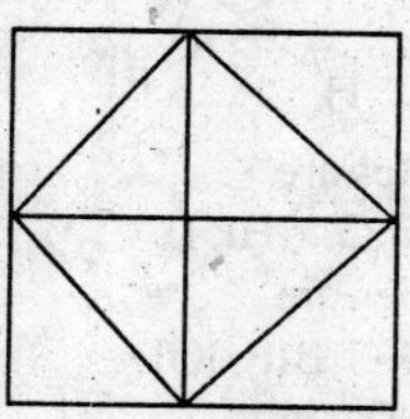

A. 12 B. 10
C. 8 D. 14

**7.** How many Parallelograms are there in the following figures?

A. 30 B. 29
C. 20 D. 12

**8.** How many Triangles are there in the figure?

A. 2 B. 4
C. 3 D. 5

**9.** How many Triangles are there in the figure?

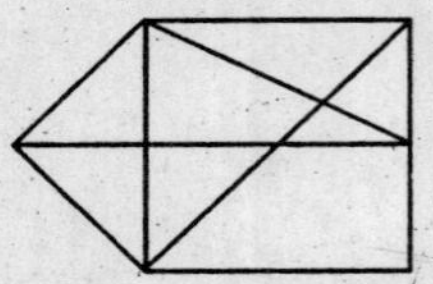

A. 15
B. 14
C. 13
D. 12

**10.** Count how many Circles are there in the figure?

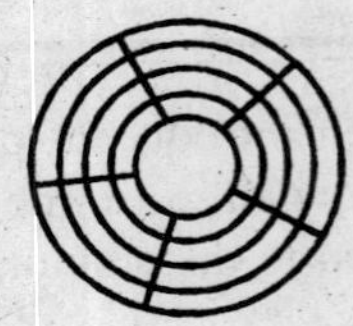

A. 2
B. 4
C. 5
D. 7

# ANSWERS

| 1 | 2 | 3 | 4 | 5 | 6 | 7 | 8 | 9 | 10 |
|---|---|---|---|---|---|---|---|---|---|
| D | C | D | D | D | A | A | B | A | C |

# EXPLANATORY ANSWERS

**1.** There are 10 Triangles in the given figure.

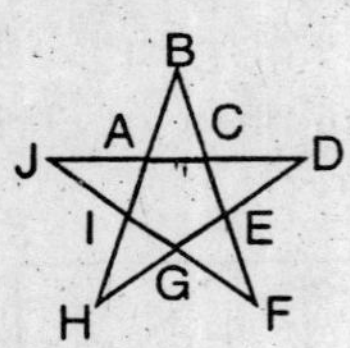


Outer Triangles are
ABC, CDE, EFG, GHI, IJA
Other Triangles are
HBE, HDA, JFC, BIF, JGD
There are 10 Triangles.

**2.** There are sixteen Parallelograms

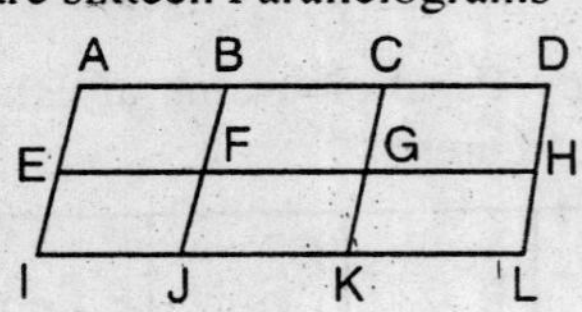


ABFE, BCGF, CDHG, EFJI, FGKJ, GHKL, ACGE, BDHF, EGKI, FHLJ, ABJI, BCKJ, CDLK, ACKI, BDLJ, and ADLI.

**3.** There are 17 Triangles.

Hence D is the right answer.

**4.** There are 4 Squares.

**5.** There are 12 Triangles.

**6.** There are 12 Triangles.

**7.** There are 30 Parallelograms.

**8.** There are 4 Triangles.

**9.** There are 15 Triangels.

**10.** There are 5 Circles.

Chapter 14

# DICE AND CUBES

Problems of Dice and Cubes have become an important part of non-verbal reasoning. This test is meant to judge candidate's ability to solve the problems in a three-dimensional prespective. In this type of problems, you are given different positions of a Cube or Dice and you have to find out the right answer.

**Example 1 :** The following are the different positions of a Cube and you have to find out, which number will come on the face opposite to the face carrying 4?

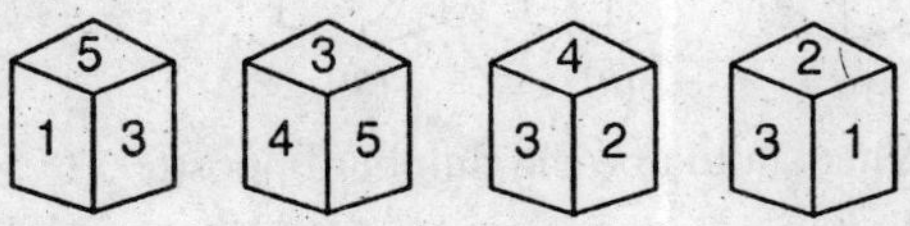


*(i)* *(ii)* *(iii)* *(iv)*

A. 1 B. 6
C. 5 D. 3

**Ans.** (1) 5 and 3 exist with 1.
(2) 5 and 3 exist with 4.
So 1 will be opposite to 4. Hence A is the right answer.

**Example 2 :**

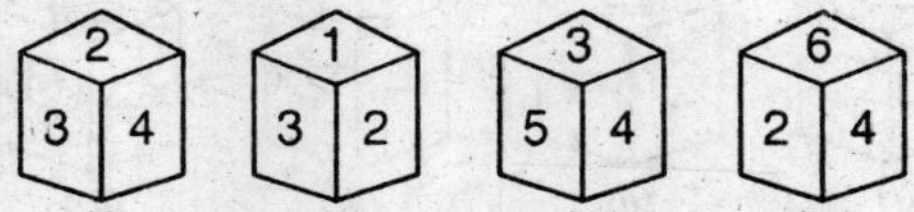


*(i)* *(ii)* *(iii)* *(iv)*

A dice is thrown four times and its four different positions are given below. Find the number on the fall-opposite the few snowing?

A. 3 B. 4
C. 5 D. 6

**Ans.** In the problem figure, No. 2 appears in three dices 1, 2, 4 and also we can see that the number 2, 4 and 1 and 6 appears adjacent to 3. So none of these numbers can be present opposite 2. The only No. is 5 left. So the right answer is C.

## EXERCISE

1. 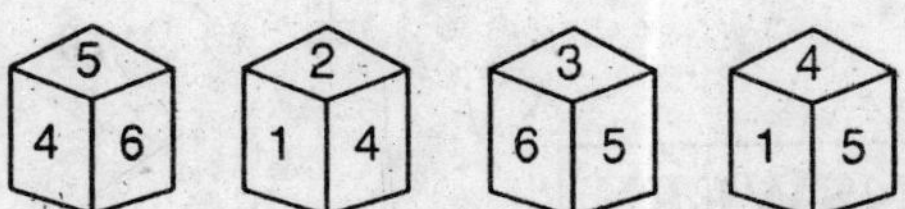


*(i)* *(ii)* *(iii)* *(iv)*

Which number is opposite 3?

A. 1 B. 2
C. 4 D. 6

2. 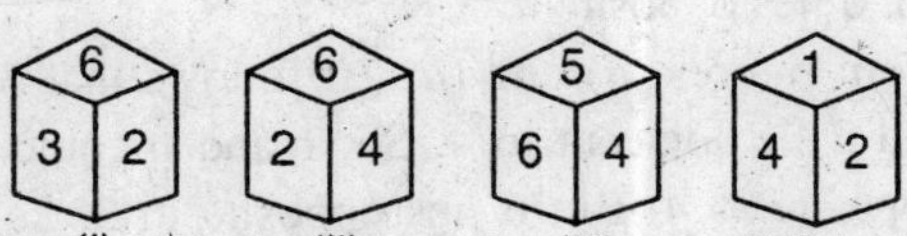


*(i)* *(ii)* *(iii)* *(iv)*

Which number is on the face opposite 6?

A. 1 B. 2
C. 3 D. 4

3. 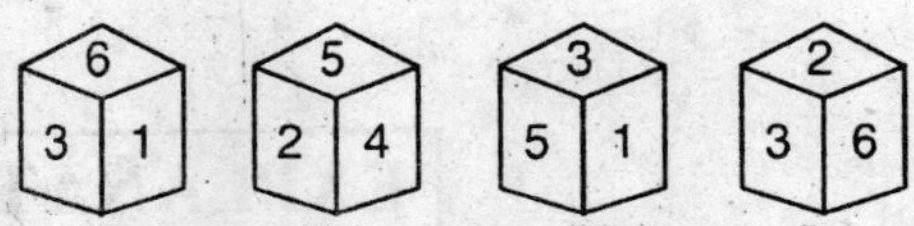


*(i)* *(ii)* *(iii)* *(iv)*

What number is opposite 3?

A. 2 B. 3
C. 4 D. 6

4. 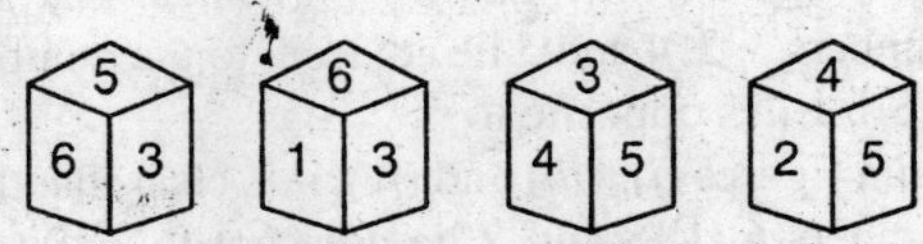


*(i)* *(ii)* *(iii)* *(iv)*

Which number is opposite 6?

A. 1 B. 2
C. 4 D. 5

5. 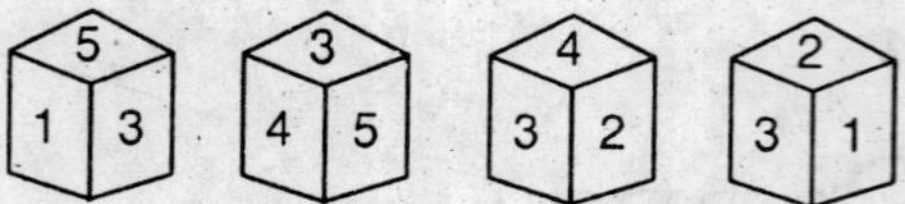

(i) (ii) (iii) (iv)

What number is opposite 4?

A. 1 B. 2
C. 5 D. 6

**Directions :** *Questions 6 to 8 are based on the following illustrations, which are four views of a cube.*

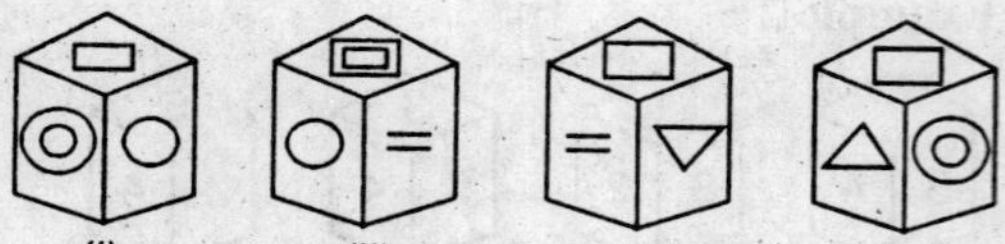

(i) (ii) (iii) (iv)

Study these illustrations carefully and attempt questions 6 to 8.

The symbol at the bottom of (*iv*) is

6. A. ○ B. ◎
C. △ D. ▣

7. The symbol opposite the face having the symbol = is

A. ○ B. △
C. ◎ D. □

8. The symbol opposite the face having triangle is

A. ○ B. ◎
C. = D. ▣

9. If the total number of dots on opposite faces of cubical block is always 7, find the figure which is correct.

A.  B. 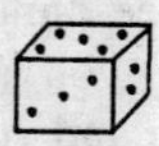

C.  D. 

10. 

(i) (ii) (iii)

What should be the number opposite 3?

A. 1
B. 6
C. 5
D. 4

## ANSWERS

| 1 | 2 | 3 | 4 | 5 | 6 | 7 | 8 | 9 | 10 |
|---|---|---|---|---|---|---|---|---|---|
| C | A | C | C | A | D | C | A | A | B |

## EXPLANATORY ANSWERS

1. From figure (*i*), (*iii*) and (*iv*), we find that the numbers adjacent to 4 are 5, 6, 1 and 2. So, 3 lies opposite to 4.
2. From figure (*i*), (*ii*) and (*iii*), it is clear that the numbers 3, 2, 4 and 5 lie adjacent to the number 6. So, 1 lies opposite to 6.
3. From figures (*i*), (*iii*) and (*iv*), it is clear that the numbers 6, 1, 5 and 2 lie adjacent to 3. So, 4 lies opposite to 3.
4. No. 1, 3 and 5 appear adjacent to 6 so 2 and 4 can appear opposite to 6. The numbers 1, 4, 5 and 6 appear adjacement to 3. So, they cannot appear opposite to 3. The only number is 3 with 2.
5. From figures (*i*), (*ii*) and (*iii*), it is clear that the number 1, 5, 4 and 2 lie adjacent to number 3. So, 6 lies opposite to 3.

   From figures (*ii*) and (*iii*), it follows that 3, 5 and 2 lie adjacent to 4. So, 1 and 6 could be opposite to 4. But 6 lies opposite to 3. So, 1 lies opposite to 4.
6. From figures (*i*), (*iii*) and (*iv*), we observe that the symbols ◎, ○ = and Δ lie adjacent to □. so, □ lies, oppoiste to □.
7. From figures (*ii*) and (*iii*), it is clear that the

symbol □, ○ □ and $\Delta$ lie adjacent to = sign. So, ○ lies oppoiste to =.

**8.** From figures (*iii*) and (*iv*), it follows that the symbol □, = and ○ lies adjacent to $\Delta$. So, one of the symbols ○ or □ can lie opposite to $\Delta$. But □ lies opposite to □. So, ○ lies opposite to $\Delta$.

**9.** Since the sum of the number of dots on opposite faces of the block is always 7, we cannot get 1 dot adjacent to 6 dots, 2 dots adjacent to 5 dots or 3 dots adjacent to 4 dots. So, the figures *b*, *c* and *d* cannot be correct.

**10.** From the three given figures, it is clear that the numbers 1, 2, 5 and 4 appear adjacent to 3. So, none of these can appear opposite to 3. Therefore, 6 appears opposite to 3.

## Chapter 15

# SERIES

This chapter comprises problems based on continuation of figures. There are many types of problems but all of them are based on the same pattern. There is a particular sequence of figures. Candidate has to pick out the next figure from the Answer Figures.

**Example-1 : Problem Figures:**

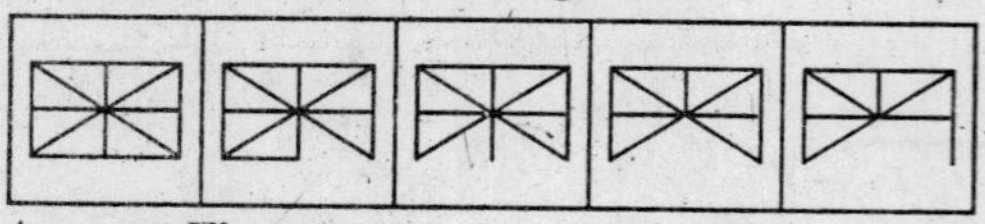

**Answer Figures**

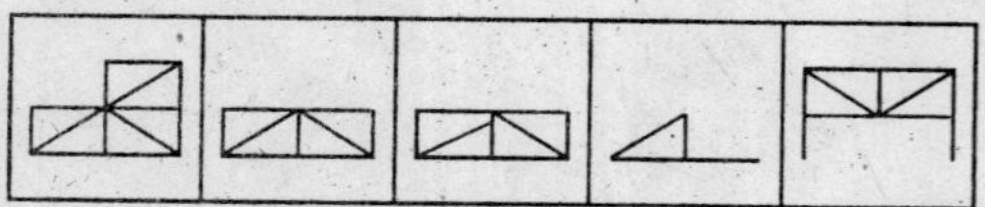

A B C D E

**Answer E :** Problem Figures consist of a rectangle divided into sections. At each step one of the lines is removed. First from the right, then left and then the centre. To continue this pattern, a right diagonal line is removed. In the answer figure a left diagonal line should be removed. Answer Figure 'E' continues the series.

**Example-2 : Problem Figures:**

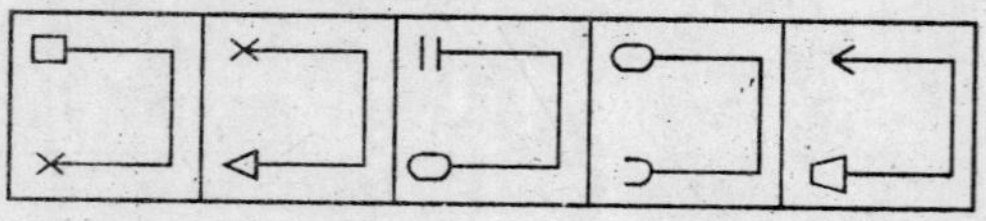

**Answer Figures**

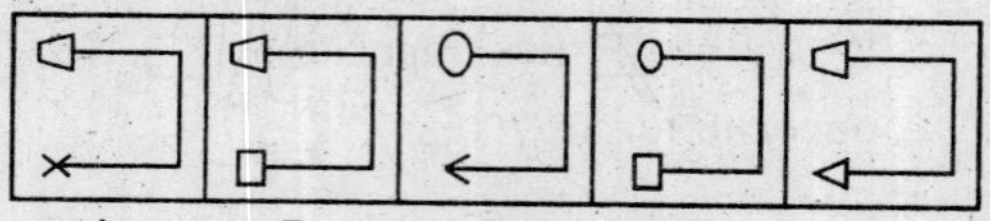

A B C D E

**Answer B :** Observe the series. Figure one corelates to figure two in the manner that the places of both the elements on the left are inter changed and then the element at the bottom is replaced by a new element. Similarly, Figure three corelates to figure four and answer figure 'B' corelates to figure five.

**Example-3 : Problem Figures:**

**Answer Figures**

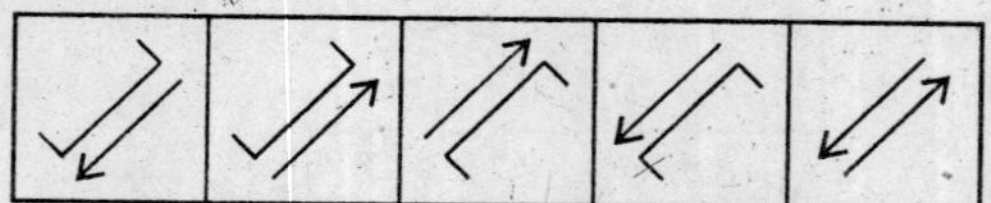

A B C D E

**Answer B :** The two elements are rotated 45° clockwise. Beginning from the top both the elements are changed one by one in a set pattern. Answer figure 'B' continues the series.

## EXERCISE–I

**1. Problem Figures**

**Answer Figures**

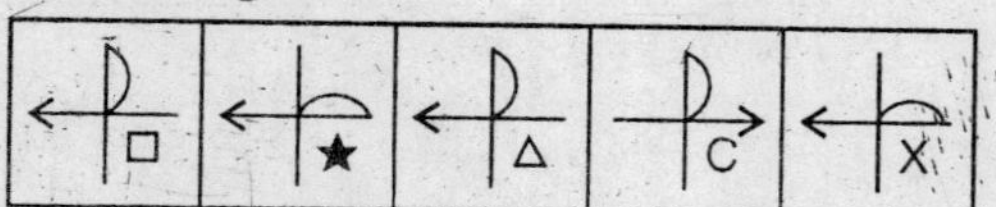

A B C D E

**2. Problem Figures**

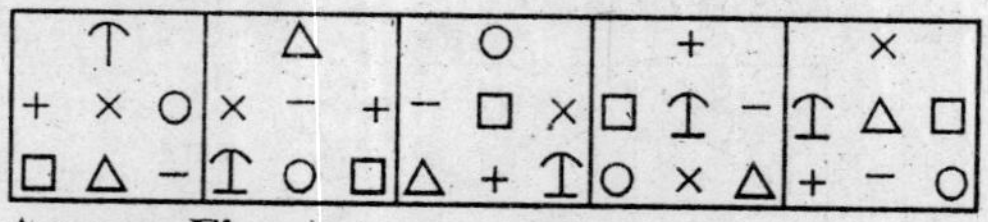

**Answer Figures**

A B C D E

**3. Problem Figures**

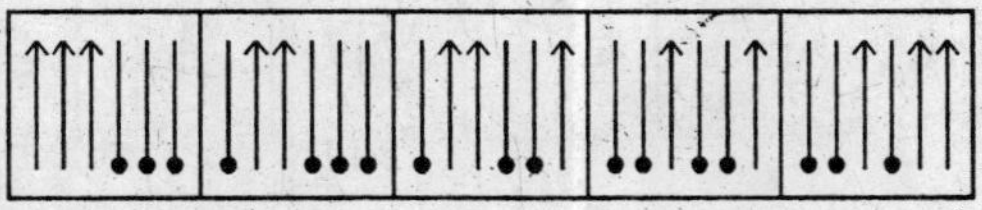

**Answer Figures**

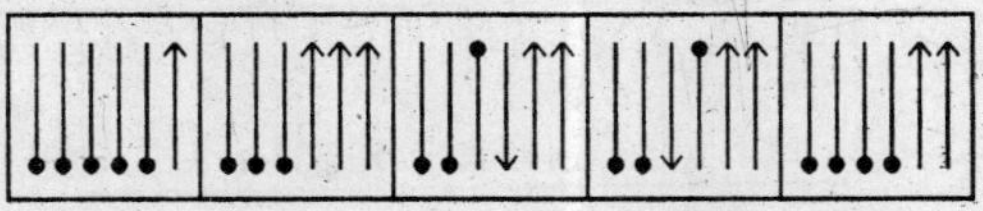

A B C D E

**4. Problem Figures**

**Answer Figures**

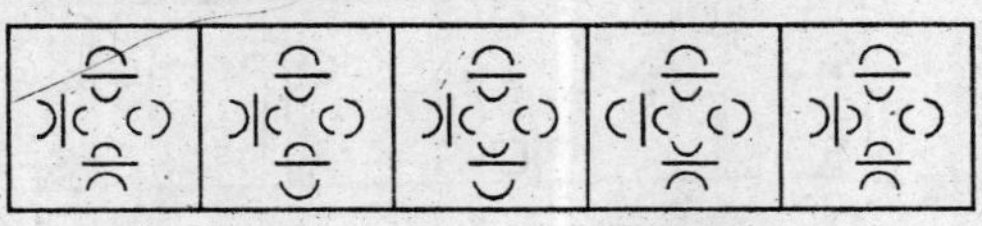

A B C D E

**5. Problem Figures**

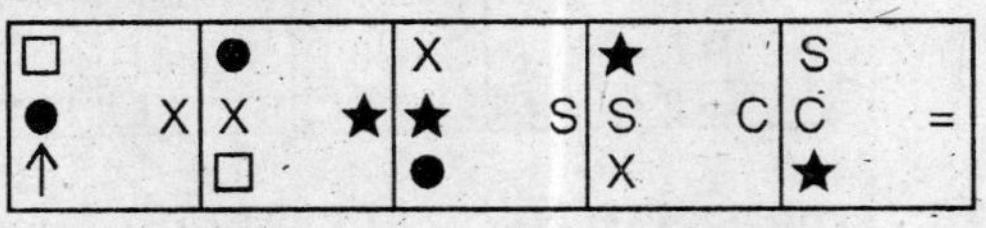

**Answer Figures**

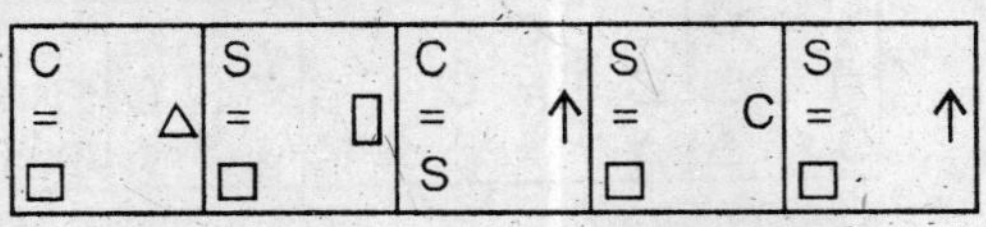

A B C D E

**6. Problem Figures**

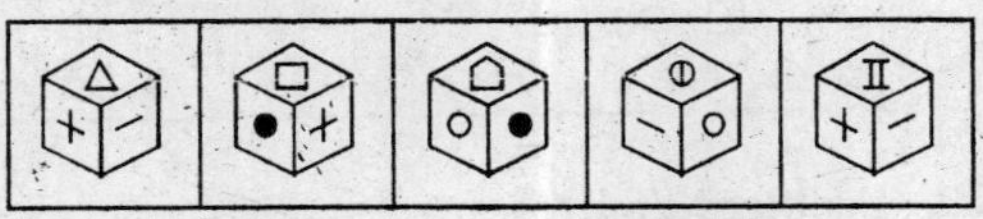

**Answer Figures**

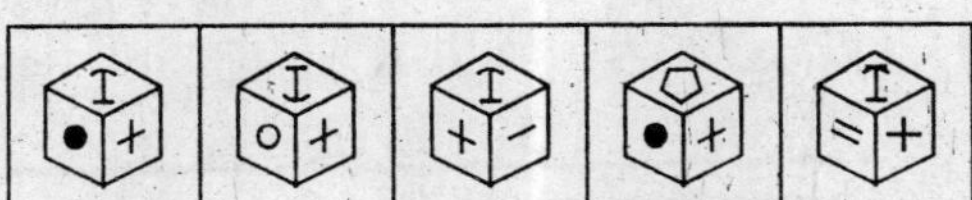

A B C D E

**7. Problem Figures**

**Answer Figures**

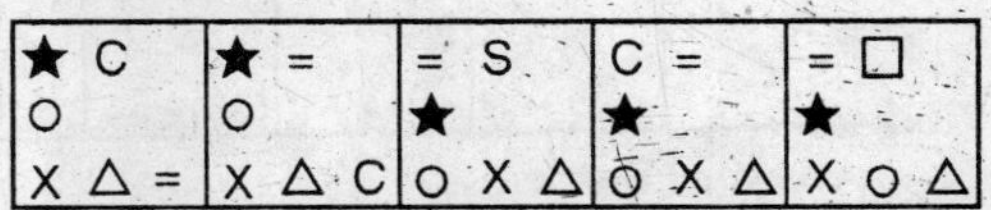

A B C D E

**8. Problem Figures**

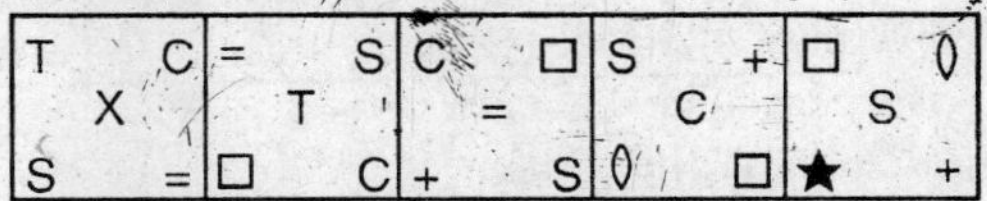

**Answer Figures**

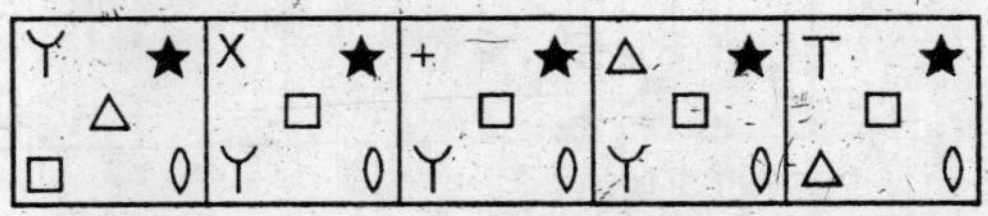

A B C D E

**9. Problem Figures**

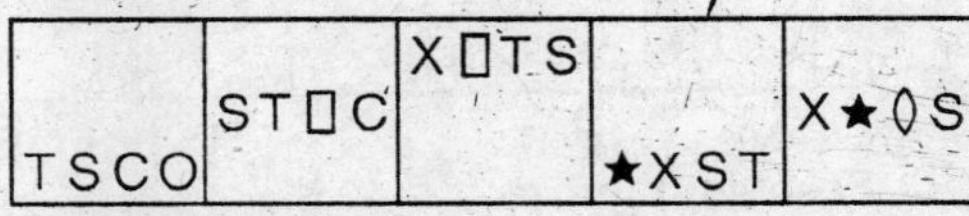

**Answer Figures**

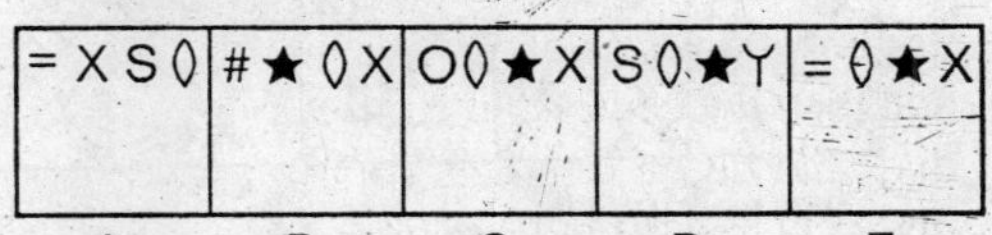

A B C D E

**10. Problem Figures**

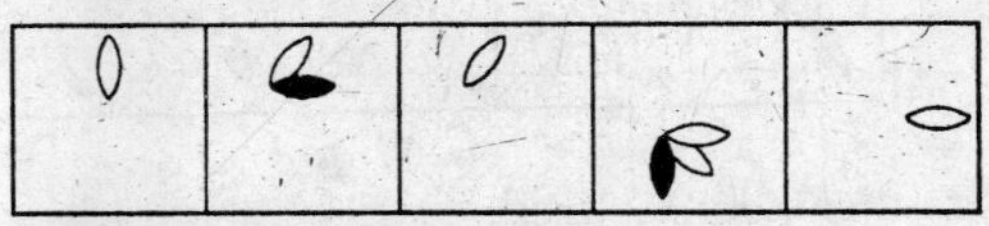

**Answer Figures**

A B C D E

**11. Problem Figures**

**Answer Figures**

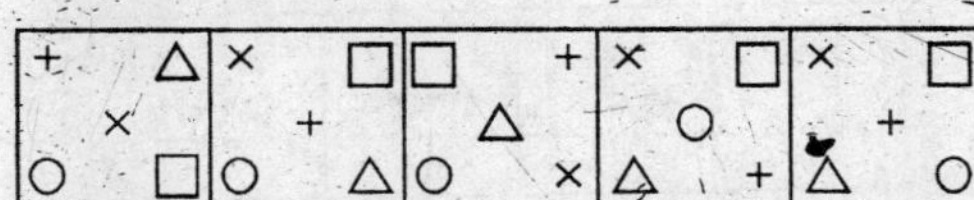

A B C D E

**12. Problem Figures**

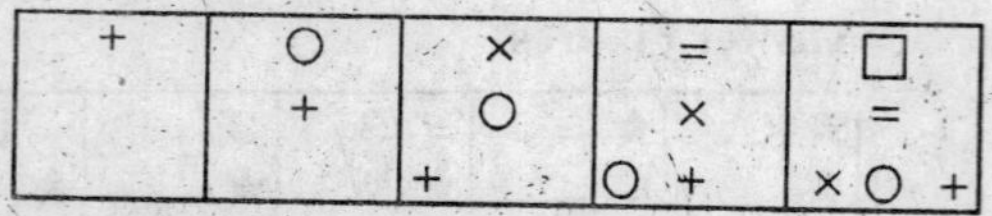

**Answer Figures**

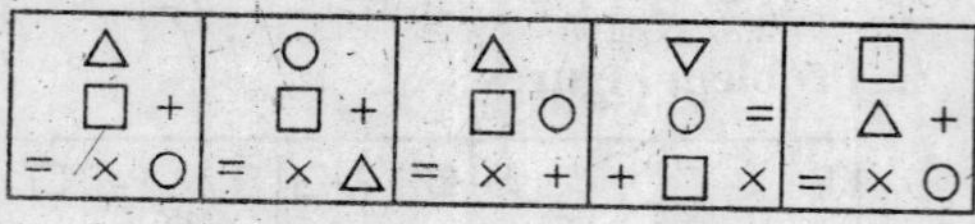

A B C D E

**13. Problem Figures**

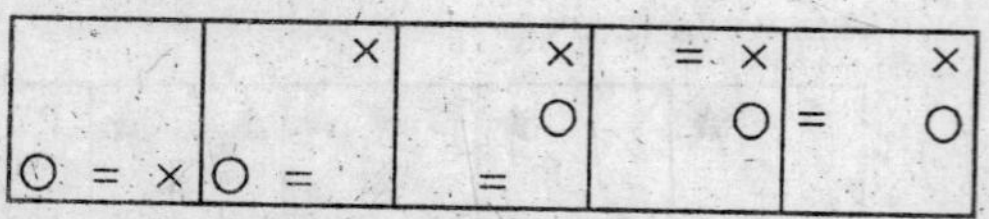

**Answer Figures**

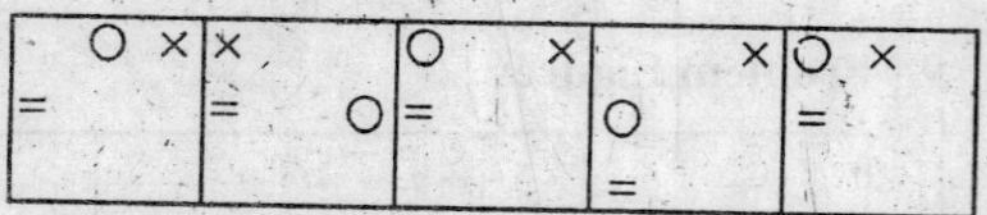

A B C D E

**14. Problem Figures**

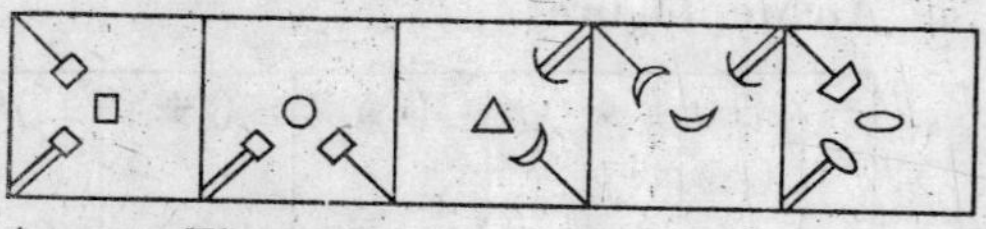

**Answer Figures**

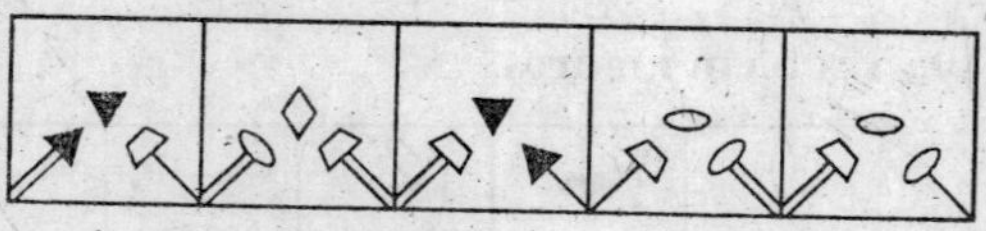

A B C D E

**15. Problem Figures**

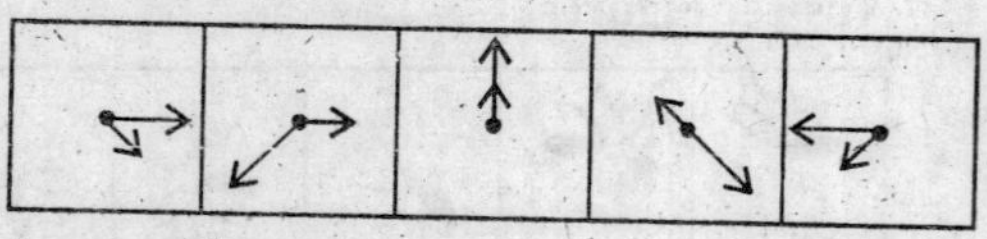

**Answer Figures**

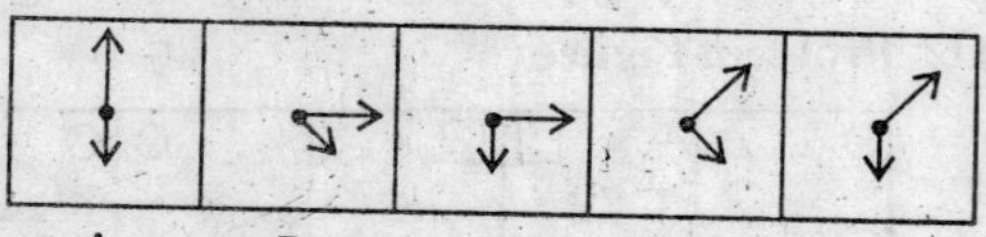

A B C D E

**16. Problem Figures**

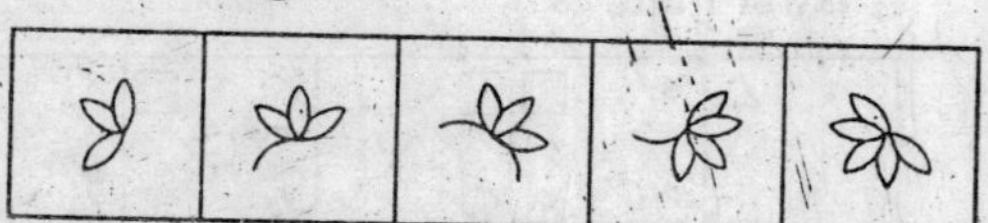

**Answer Figures**

A B C D E

**17. Problem Figures**

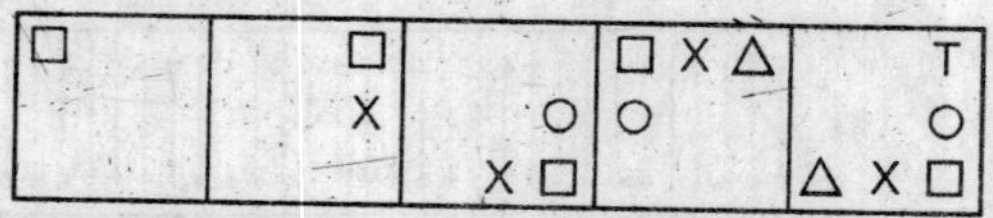

**Answer Figures**

A B C D E

**18. Problem Figures**

**Answer Figures**

A B C D E

**19. Problem Figures**

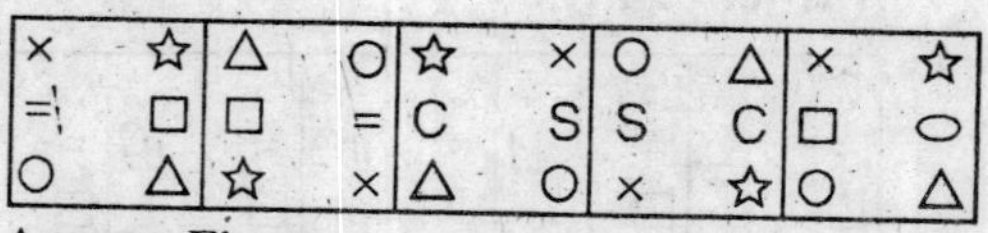

**Answer Figures**

A B C D E

**20. Problem Figures**

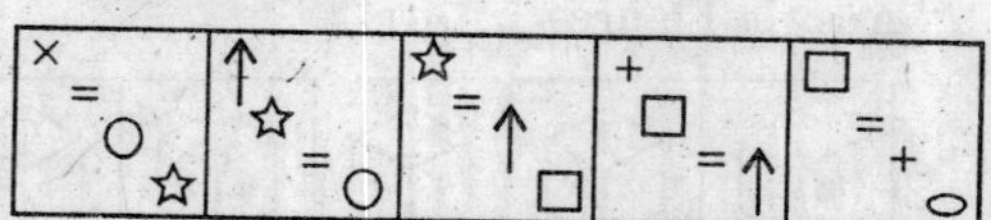

**Answer Figures**

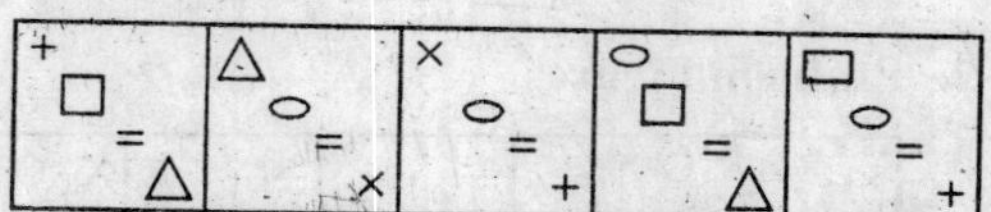

A B C D E

**21. Problem Figures**

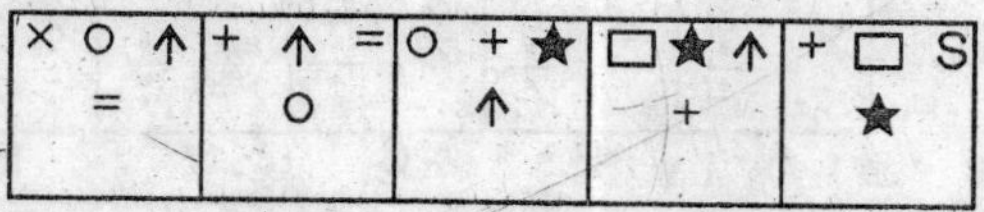

**Answer Figures**

A B C D E

**22. Problem Figures**

**Answer Figures**

A B C D E

**23. Problem Figures**

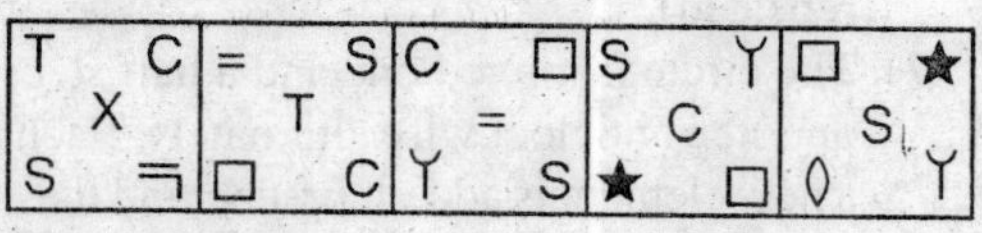

**Answer Figures**

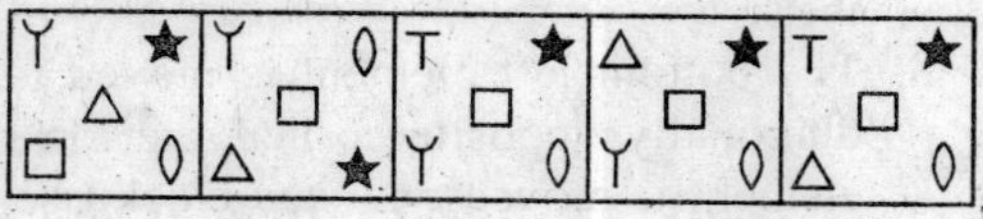

A B C D E

**24. Problem Figures**

**Answer Figures**

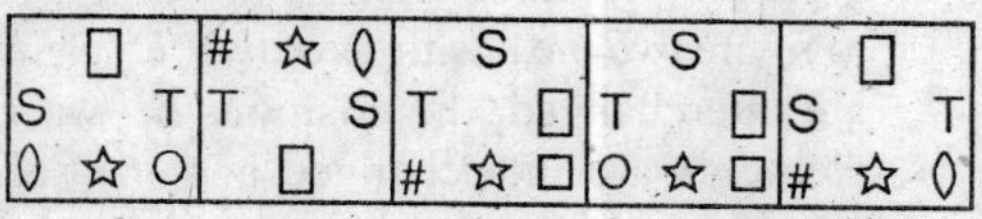

A B C D E

**25. Problem Figures**

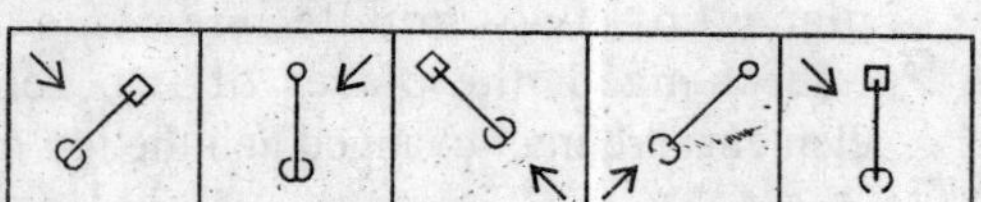

**Answer Figures**

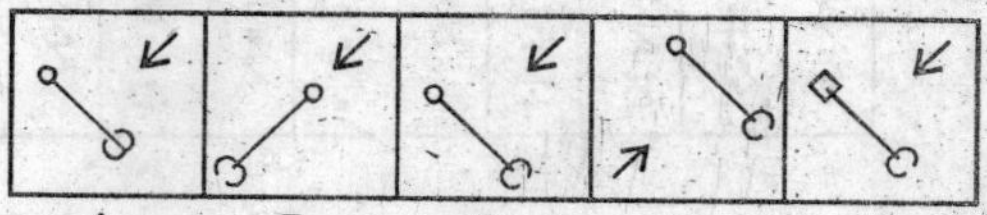

A B C D E

**26. Problem Figures**

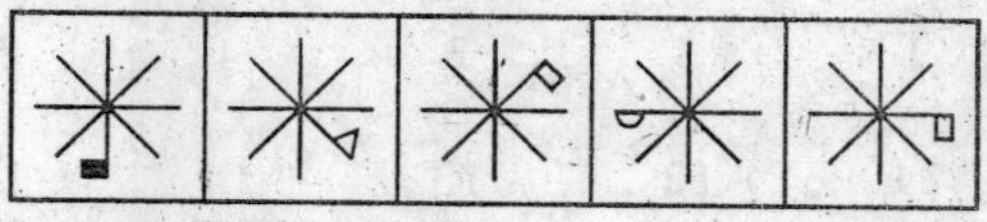

**Answer Figures**

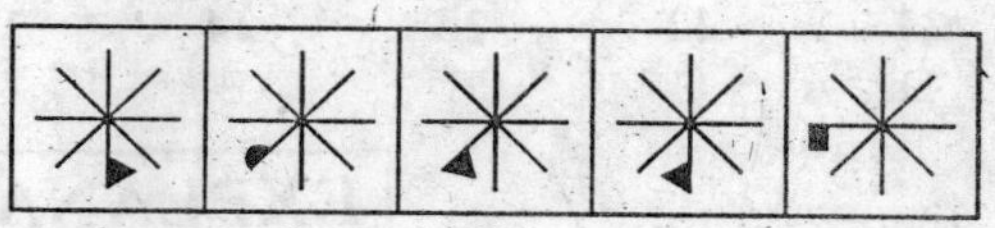

A B C D E

**27. Problem Figures**

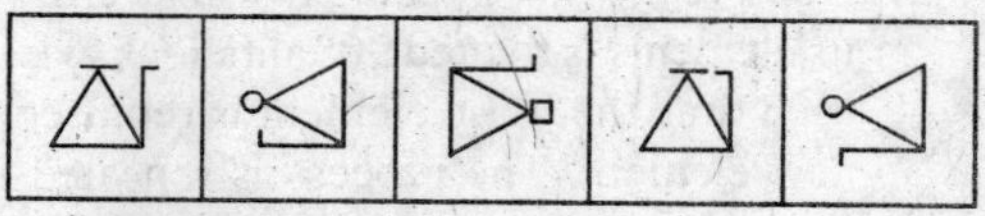

**Answer Figures**

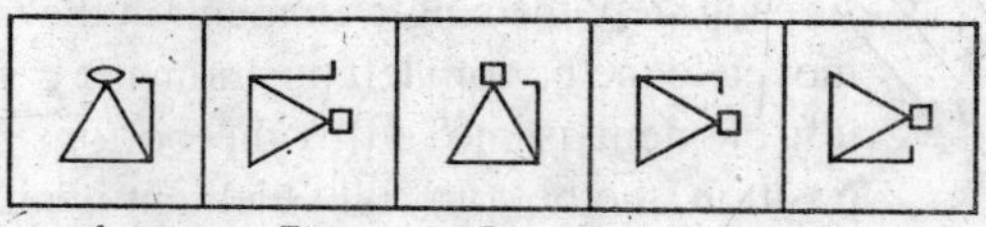

A B C D E

**28. Problem Figures**

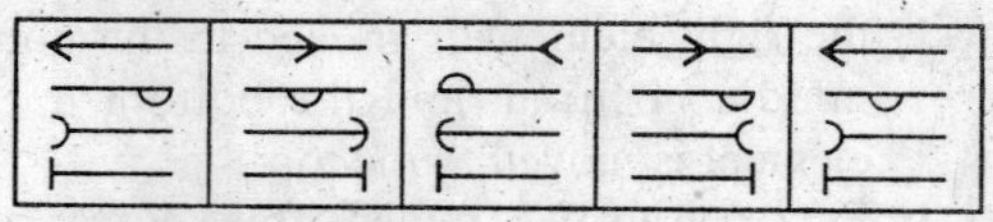

**Answer Figures**

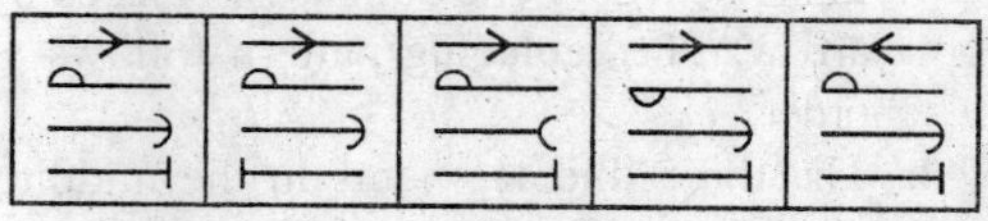

A B C D E

**29. Problem Figures**

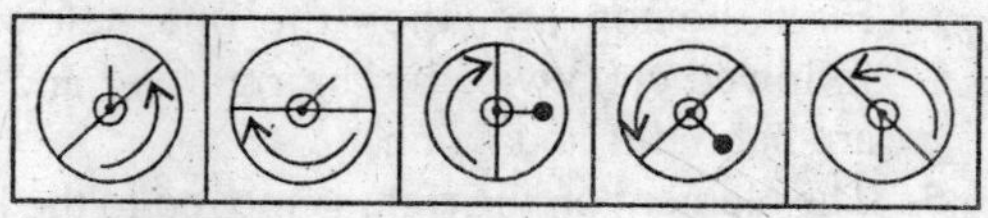

**Answer Figures**

A B C D E

**30. Problem Figures**

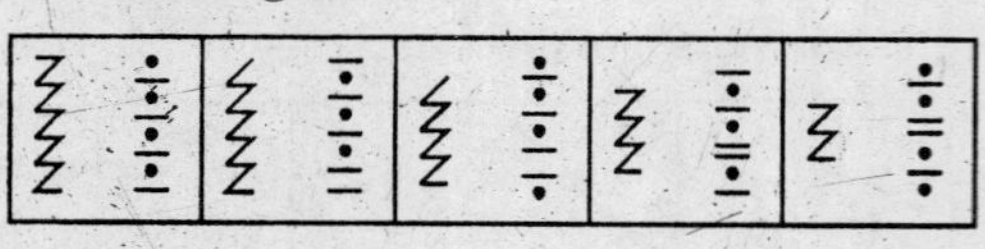

**Answer Figures**

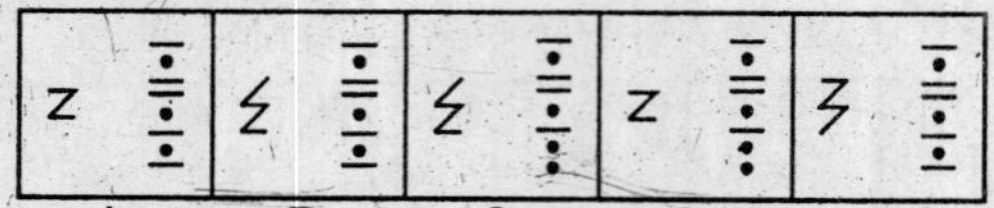

A B C D E

# ANSWERS

| 1 | 2 | 3 | 4 | 5 | 6 | 7 | 8 | 9 | 10 |
|---|---|---|---|---|---|---|---|---|---|
| A | C | E | C | B | E | C | C | E | D |
| **11** | **12** | **13** | **14** | **15** | **16** | **17** | **18** | **19** | **20** |
| B | A | C | B | E | D | A | E | A | E |
| **21** | **22** | **23** | **24** | **25** | **26** | **27** | **28** | **29** | **30** |
| D | C | B | B | C | C | D | A | E | B |

# EXPLANATORY ANSWERS

**1.** Observe the first three figures. The cross with its elements is rotated 90° anticlock-wise and each time the loose element is replaced by a new element. The process is repeated from figure four.

**2.** At each step, the single element on the top is moved to the bottom left position, the bottom left element is moved to the bottom right position, the bottom right element is moved to the centre, the centre element is moved to the left, the left element is moved to the right, the right element is moved to the bottom middle position, and the bottom middle element is moved to the top.

**3.** First, one arrow is replaced by a dot bar, then in the next step one dot bar is replaced by an arrow. The replacing pattern follows a set order.

**4.** The three line segments in the middle are moved on step clockwise. Clockwise, the arcs are turned by 180° one by one in a set order. First the top arc, then the one below it, followed clockwise by the right arc and the arc behind it and so on.

**5.** The element on the right is moved to the left, this middle element is moved up, the top element is moved to the bottom, the bottom element is moved to the right and is replaced by a new element.

**6.** The elements in the sections are moved one step anticlockwise. Only the element in the right section is left untouched while the other two elements are replaced by entirely new elements (none of the earlier elements are repeated).

**7.** The circle is moved one and a half steps and one step anticlockwise alternately. Each time a new element is added, first behind the circle and then ahead of it. Answer figure 'C' follows the series.

**8.** The bottom left element is moved to the diagonally opposite corner, the top right element is moved one step clockwise, the bottom right element is moved to the diagonally opposite corner, the top left element is moved to the centre, and the element in the centre which is replaced by a new element is moved to the bottom left position.

**9.** Note the first three figures. From figure one to figure two the positions of two left elements are interchanged, the positions of two right elements are interchanged and the second element from the right is replaced by a new element. From figure two to figure three the places of two middle elements are interchanged, the places of two corner elements are inter changed and the left most element is replaced by a new element. At each step the elements are moved half way up. The process is repeated from figure four.

**10.** In figures one, three and five the petal is rotated 45° clockwise. In figures two and four the petals are rotated 90° anticlockwise and a new petal added on the right. Answer figure 'D' continues the pattern.

**11.** The places of the circle and one element anticlockwise are inter changed at each step while the places of other three elements are shifted anticlockwise.

**12.** The plus sign is the leading element. At each step a new element is added and all elements follow the plus sign.

**13.** From figure one to figure two, the leading element is moved one step anticlockwise. From figure two to figure three the trailing is moved one and a half steps anticlockwise. From figure three to figure four the left out element is moved two steps anticlockwise. The above process is repeated from figure five.

**14.** Observe the figures. Figure two corresponds to figure one and figure four to figure three. Of the two corner elements the left element is moved to the diagonally opposite corner and the element in the centre is replaced by a new element. Similarly, Answer Figure 'B' corresponds with figure five.

**15.** The smaller arrow is rotated 45° and 90° anticlockwise alternately and the larger arrow is rotated 135° clockwise at each step.

**16.** As the flower is rotated, first half new petal on the left is added and then half on the right is added. Similarly, first the left half petal is completed and then the half petal on the right is completed. Figure 'D' continues the series, half petal on the left is added.

**17.** The square is moved 1, 1, 2, 2 steps clockwise. One new element is added ahead of it and behind it in a set order. To get the answer figure the square should be moved 3 steps clockwise alongwith other elements.

**18.** From figure one to figure two the two top elements and two bottom elements are moved to the second and thirds rows respectively; the elements in the second and third rows are moved to the top and bottom rows respectively; and then the places of top right element and bottom left element are interchanged. From figure two to figure three the movement of elements in the rows is same as above except that in this the places of top left element and bottom right element are interchanged. The above process is repeated.

**19.** From figure one to figure two the position of four corner elements is interchanged diagonally and the places of two middle elements are interchanged. The same rule is applied to figures three and four; and figures five and six.

**20.** First the bottom right element is moved to the second position and the two elements shifted down diagonally while the top most element is replaced by a new element. Then, the top left element is moved to the third position and the two elements shifted up diagonally while the bottom right element is replaced by a new element. The above process is repeated.

**21.** First the top left element is replaced by a new element while the other three elements are rotated anticlockwise. Then the top right element is replaced by a new element while the other three elements are rotated clockwise. The above process is repeated.

**22.** The circle is moved one and a half steps and one step anticlockwise alternately. A new element is added first behind it and then ahead of it in alternate figures.

**23.** At each step the top left element is moved to the centre, the top right element is moved to bottom right position, the two bottom elements are moved to the diagonally opposite corners on the top, and the element in the centre is moved to the bottom left position and is replaced by a new element.

**24.** Alternate figures 1, 3 and 5 have one elements on the top and three at the bottom. Whereas in figures 2 and 4 there are three elements on the top and one at the bottom. Answer figure B continues the series.

**25.** Between figure one and figure four, figure two and figure five, the square is replaced by a circle and vice versa, the direction of the two curves at the base is changed, the arrow is rotated 90° anticlockwise and moved one step anticlockwise. Similarly, answer figure C coordinates with figure three.

**26.** The element is replaced by a new element each time and is moved anticlockwise in increasing numerical order. Also, it is alternately on the right and left side of the spike.

**27.** Observe that figure one and figure four are identical except that one line segment is turned to the opposite direction. The same holds for figure two and figure five. Answer figure D coordinates with figure three.

**28.** The arrowhead is moved to the right end of the line segment and back in a set pattern and its direction is reversed at each step. The semicircle is moved from right end to the left end of the line segment in a set pattern and is placed on the other side. The arc is moved from end to end of the line segment and its direction is reversed in alternate figures. The bottom element is same in alternate figures.

**29.** From figure one to figure two the diagonal with circle and dot bar are rotated 45° clockwise and the direction of the arrow is reversed. Same applies to figure three and figure four. Answer figure E coordinates with figure five.

**30.** One and two line segments from the top are alternately removed from the zig zag pattern on the left. On the right side when a dot is removed a line segment is added at the base and when a line segment is removed, a dot as added; this process is alternate.

## EXERCISE–II

**1. Problem Figures**

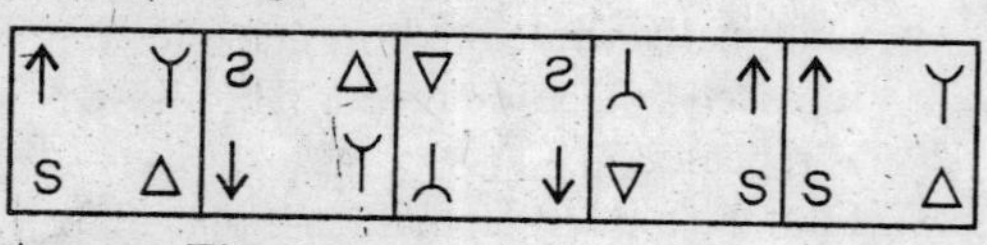

**Answer Figures**

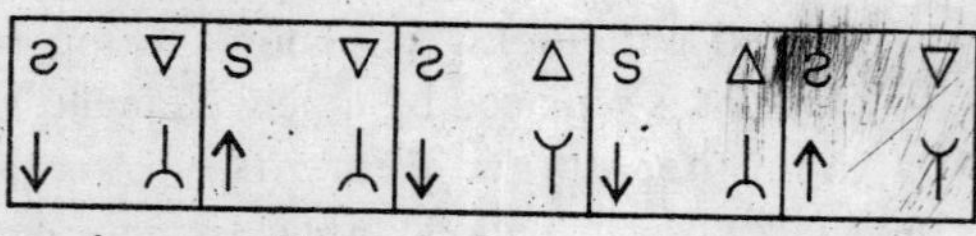

A B C D E

**2. Problem Figures**

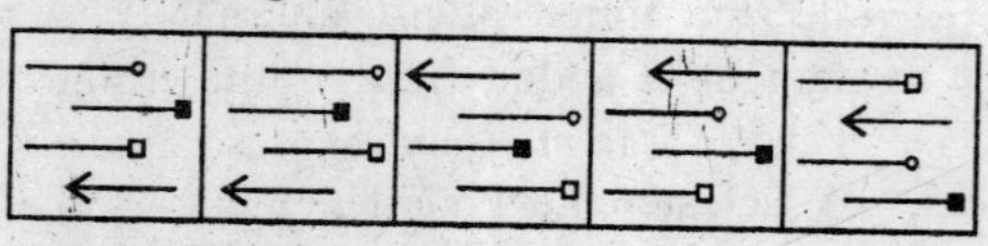

**Answer Figures**

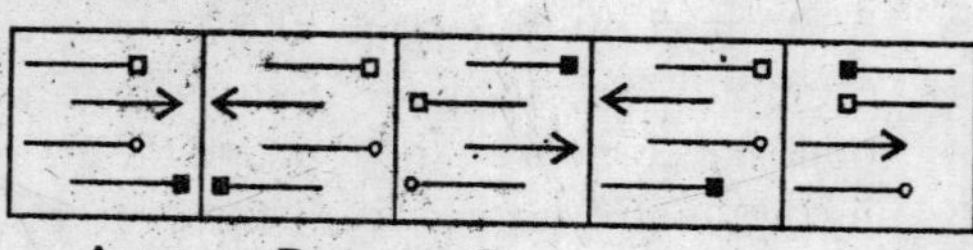

A B C D E

**3. Problem Figures**

**Answer Figures**

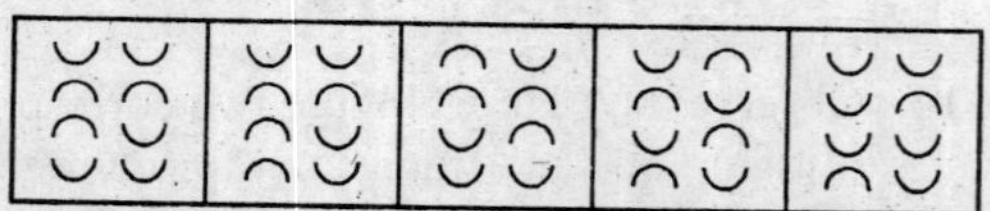

A B C D E

**4. Problem Figures**

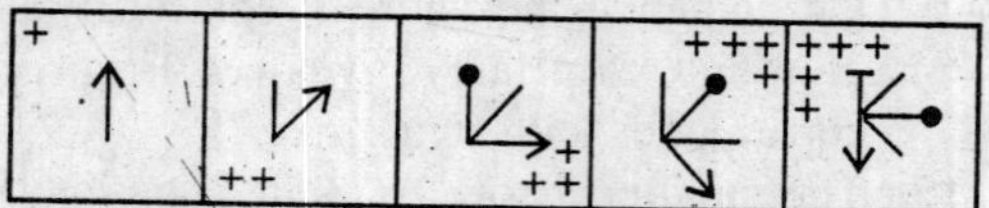

**Answer Figures**

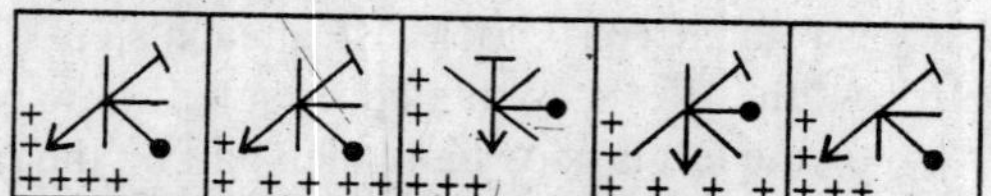

A B C D E

**5. Problem Figures**

**Answer Figures**

A B C D E

6. **Problem Figures**

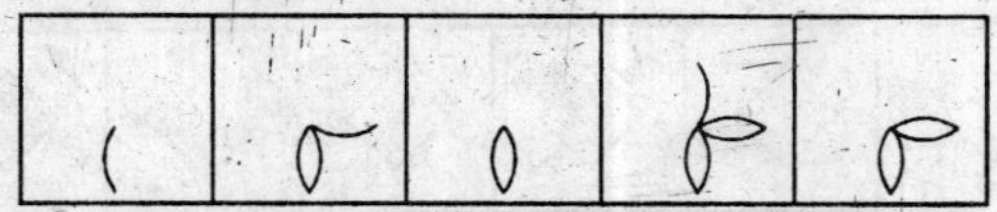

**Answer Figures**

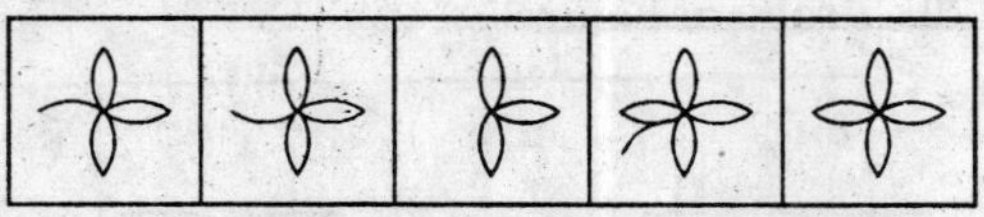

A B C D E

7. **Problem Figures**

**Answer Figures**

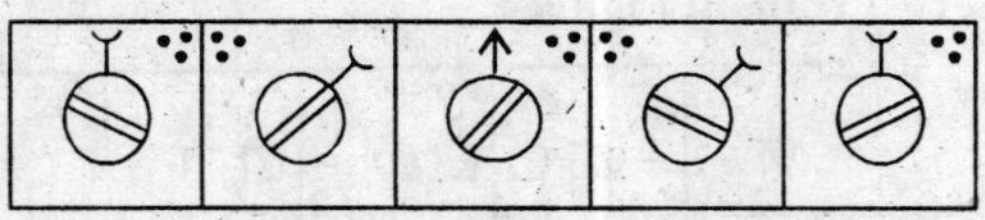

A B C D E

8. **Problem Figures**

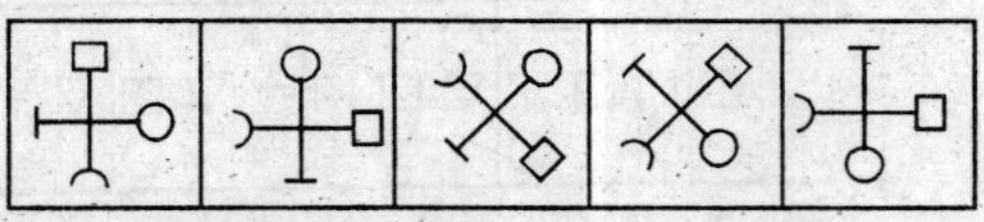

**Answer Figures**

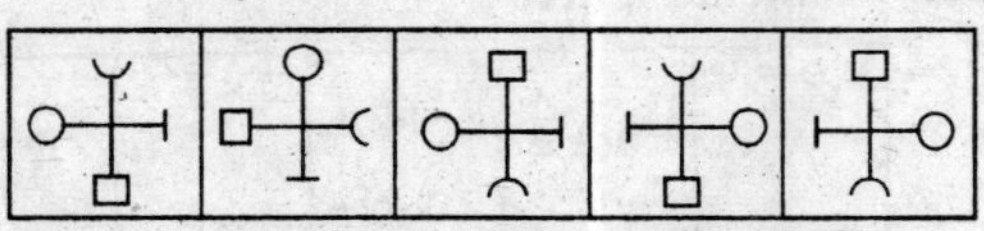

A B C D E

9. **Problem Figures**

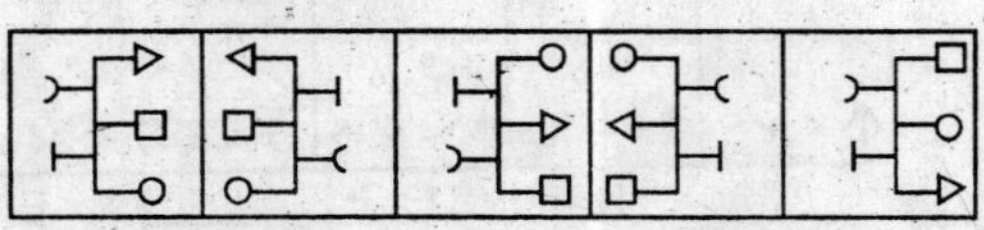

**Answer Figures**

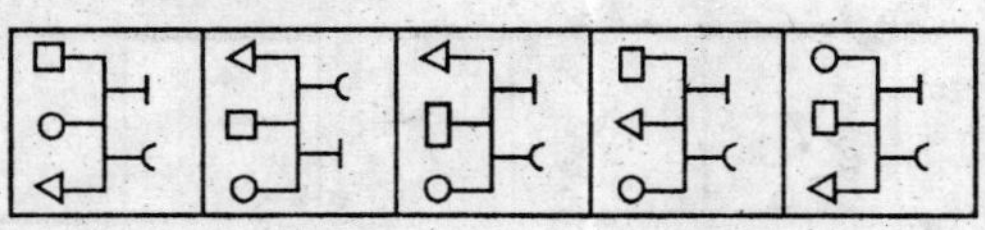

A B C D E

10. **Problem Figures**

**Answer Figures**

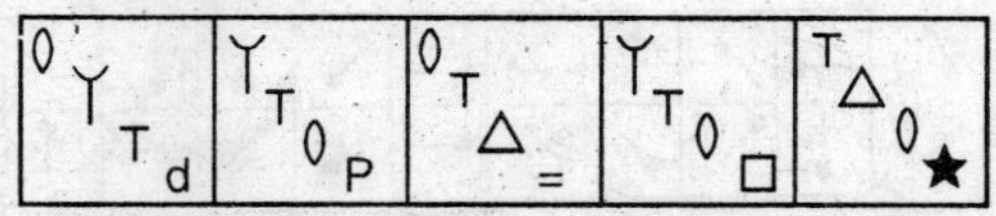


A B C D E

11. **Problem Figures**

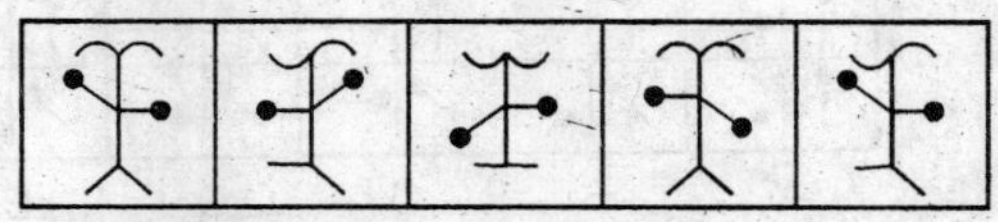

**Answer Figures**

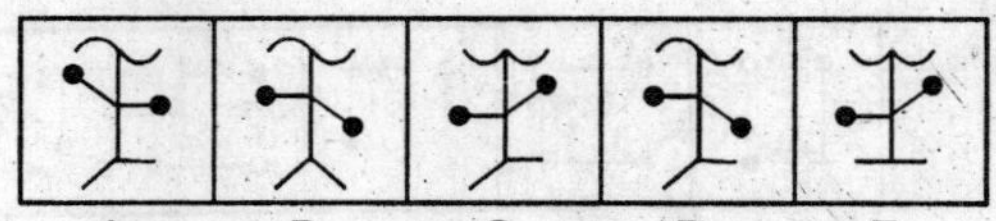

A B C D E

12. **Problem Figures**

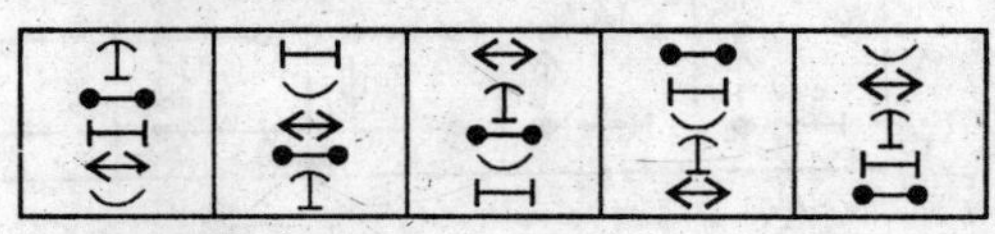

**Answer Figures**

A B C D E

13. **Problem Figures**

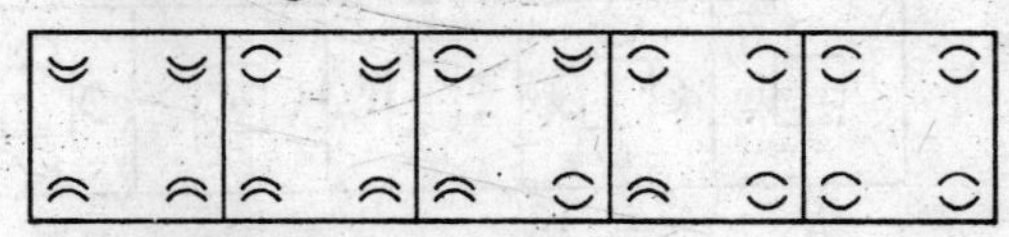

**Answer Figures**

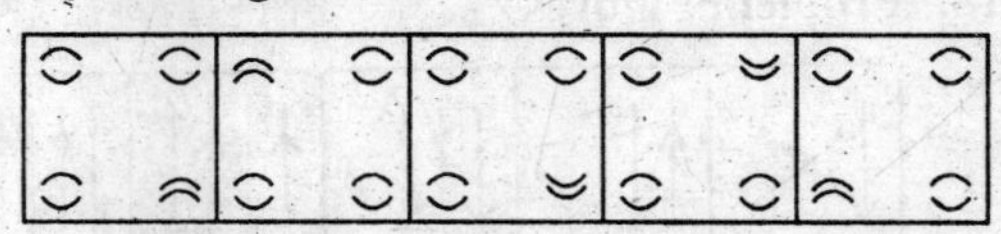

A B C D E

14. **Problem Figures**

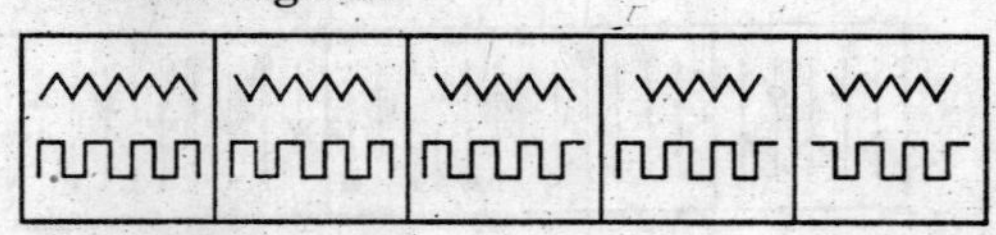

**Answer Figures**

A B C D E

**15. Problem Figures**

**Answer Figures**

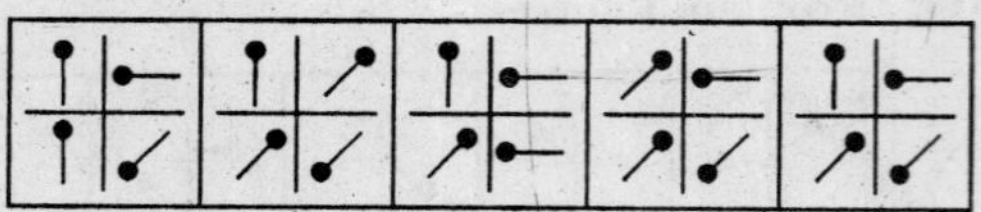

A B C D E

**16. Problem Figures**

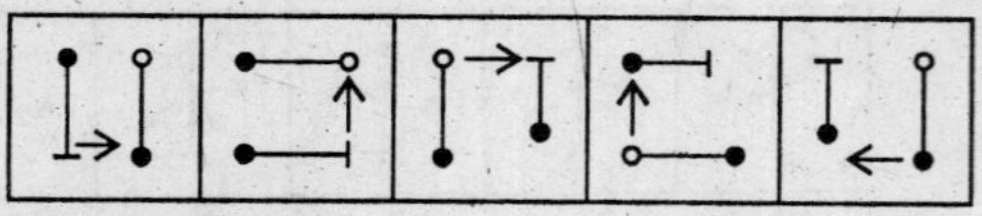

**Answer Figures**

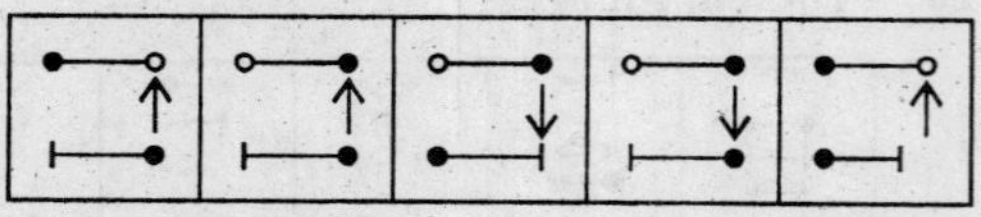

A B C D E

**17. Problem Figures**

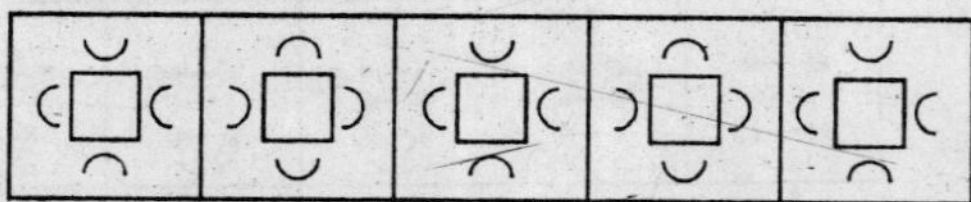

**Answer Figures**

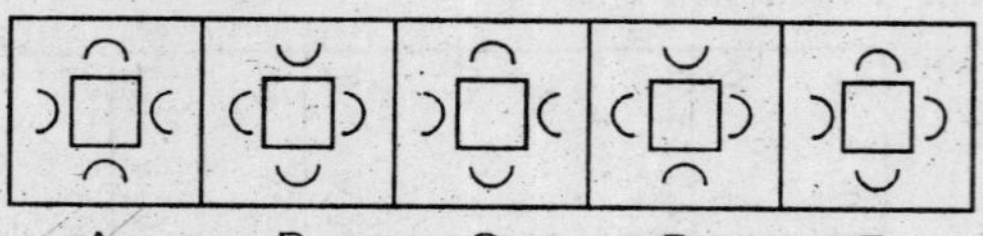

A B C D E

**18. Problem Figures**

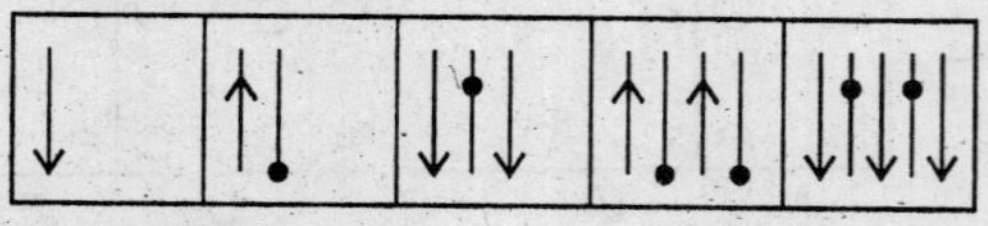

**Answer Figures**

A B C D E

**19. Problem Figures**

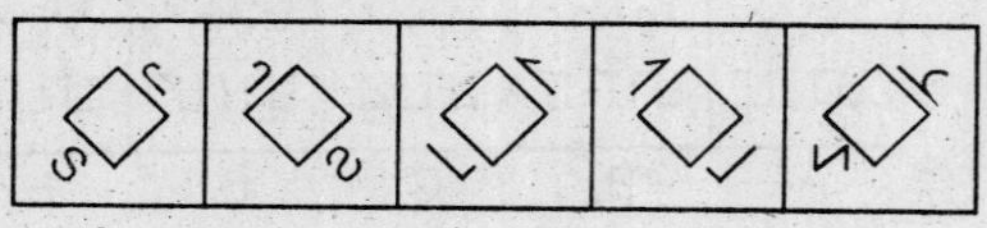

**Answer Figures**

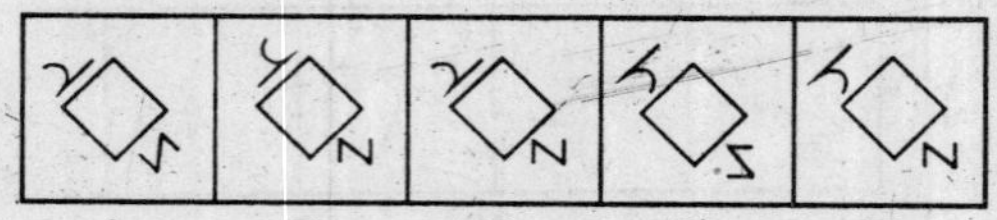

A B C D E

**20. Problem Figures**

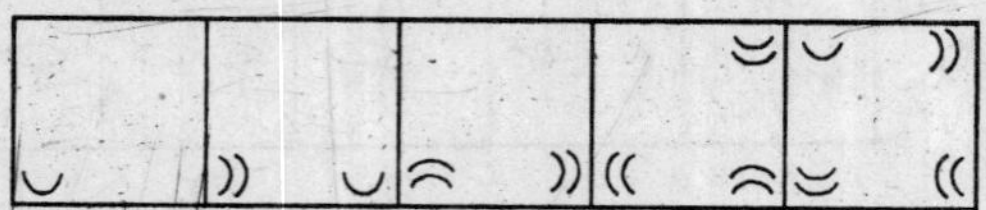

**Answer Figures**

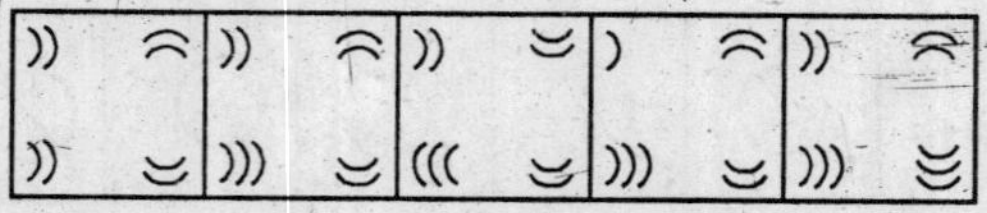

A B C D E

**21. Problem Figures**

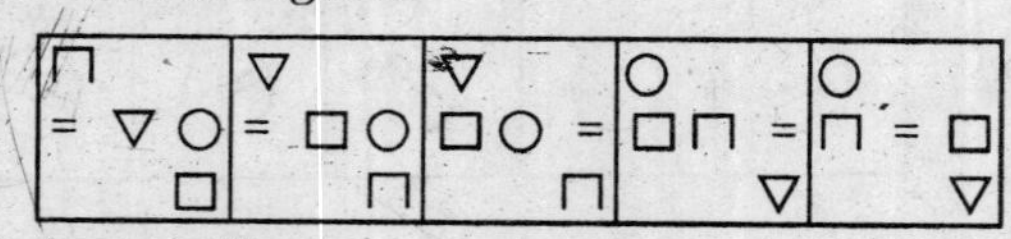

**Answer Figures**

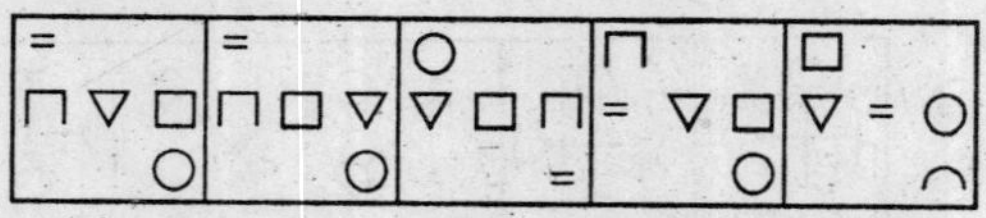

A B C D E

**22. Problem Figures**

**Answer Figures**

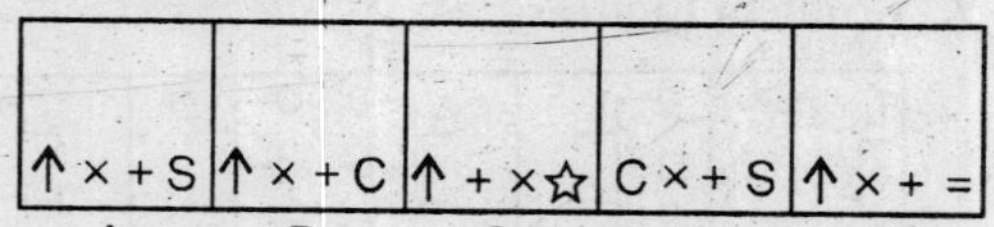


A B C D E

**23. Problem Figures**

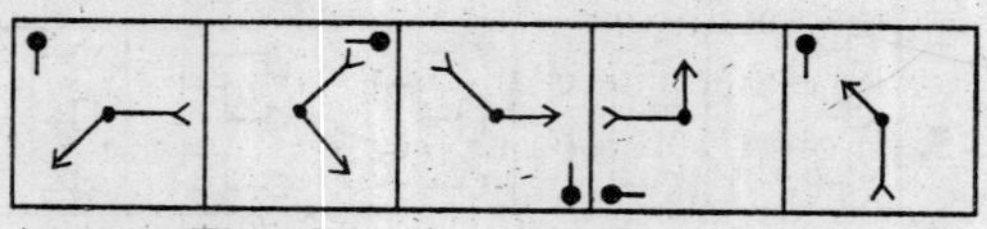

**Answer Figures**

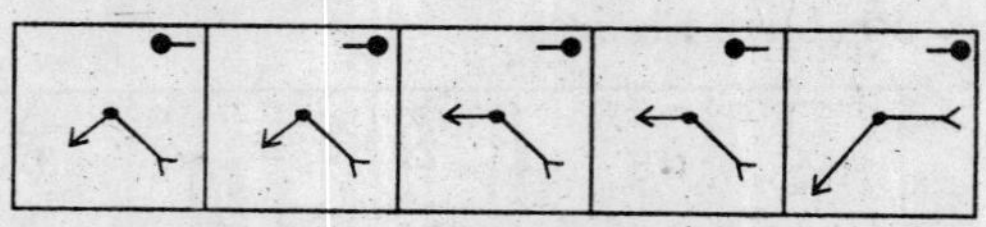

A B C D E

**24. Problem Figures**

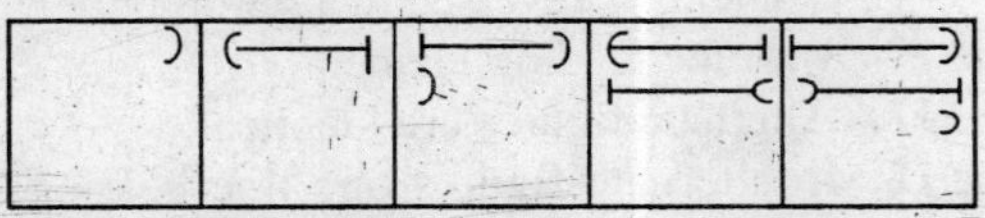

**Answer Figures**

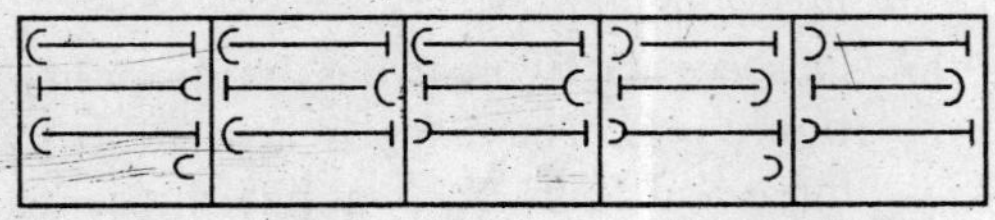

A B C D E

**25. Problem Figures**

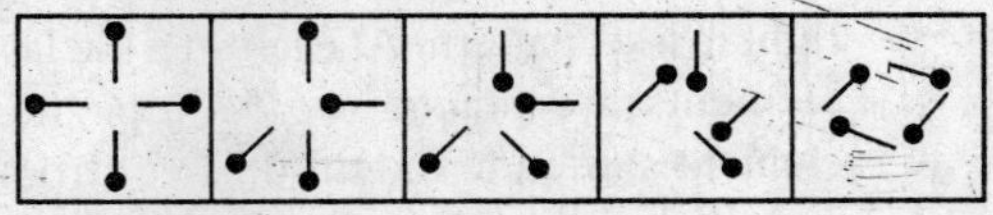

**Answer Figures**

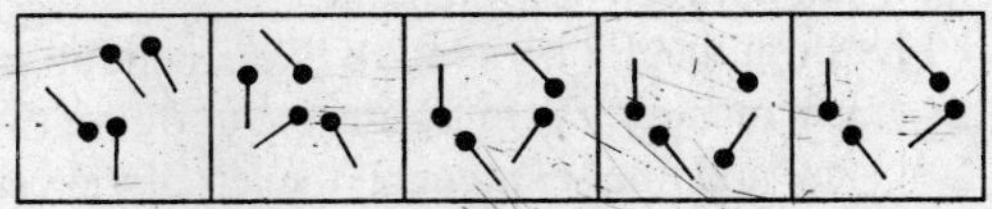

A B C D E

## ANSWERS

| 1 | 2 | 3 | 4 | 5 | 6 | 7 | 8 | 9 | 10 |
|---|---|---|---|---|---|---|---|---|---|
| C | D | B | A | C | E | E | D | A | B |
| **11** | **12** | **13** | **14** | **15** | **16** | **17** | **18** | **19** | **20** |
| E | E | B | A | E | B | E | C | C | B |
| **21** | **22** | **23** | **24** | **25** | | | | | |
| A | B | B | B | E | | | | | |

## EXPLANATORY ANSWERS

**1.** Observe that the series restarts from figure five. Answer figure should be identical to figure two.

**2.** Observe that figures one and two are identical and so are figures three and four. Answer figure should be identical to figure five.

**3.** The right column arcs from bottom to top, and the left column arcs from top to bottom are inverted one by one alternately in a set pattern.

**4.** In alternate figures the arrow is rotated 90° clockwise, one simple line segment and one line segment with busy end are added in a set pattern and the cross is moved to the diagonally opposite corner and one more sign on either side is added.

**5.** From figure one to figure two the elements on the top and bottom right are shifted one step anticlockwise while the places of remaining two elements are interchanged. From figure two to figure three the places of diagonally opposite elements are interchanged while the element in the centre is replaced by a new element. The above steps are repeated.

**6.** The parts of petal are added and removed anticlockwie in the manner plus two, minus one, plus three, minus one; and to continue the series four parts should be added.

**7.** Observe the series. Note that figure one corresponds with figure five in such a manner that the three dots in triangle form are inverted and moved to the diagonally opposite corner, and the arrow is moved to 90° clockwise position. Similarly, answer figure E coordinates with figure two.

**8.** The places of circle and square are interchanged and the places of the arc and line segment are interchanged. Then the cross is rotated 45° clockwise. The above two steps are repeated.

**9.** Figure two is the lateral inversion of figure one except that the places of two elements on one side are interchanged. The same applies to figures three and four. Answer figure A coordinates with figure five.

**10.** The four elements are oscillated from left to right in a set pattern. At each step the last two elements are placed on the top, the first element shifted to the third place (from top) and the last (bottom) element is replaced by an entirely new element.

**11.** Both the dot bars move like a pendulum in a set manner. From figure one to figure two the arc and line segment on the left of the vertical line are moved. From figure two to figure three the arc and line segment on the right of the vertical line are moved. From figure three to figure four both the arcs and the line segments are moved. This process is repeated.

**12.** At each step, beginning from the top, the first, second, third, fourth and fifth (last) elements are moved to the fifth (last), fourth, first, third and second positions respectively.

**13.** One by one, one of the two arcs are inverted in a set order top left, bottom right, top right and bottom left. To continue the series, the remaining arcs will be inverted in the same order.

**14.** From figure one to figure two one line segment on the left of the upper element is removed. From figure two to figure three one line segment on the right of the lower element is removed. From figure three to figure four one line segment on the right of the upper element is removed. From figure four to figure five one line segment on the left of the lower element is removed.

**15.** The dot bars on top left, top right, bottom left and bottom right are rotated 90° anticlockwise, 45° clockwise, 45° clock-wise and 90° anticlockwise respectively.

**16.** All the elements are moved anticlockwise and each time, the direction of one of the elements is reversed in a set order beginning with the leading element.

**17.** Alternate figures are identical.

**18.** In alternate figures one line bearing a dot and the other bearing an arrowhead are added in a set pattern.

**19.** Observe that figure two is the mirror image of figure one. The same is applied to figures three and four. To continue the series, the answer figure should be the mirror image of figure five.

**20.** The arc shapes are turned 90° anticlockwise at each step and two and one arcs are added alternately in anticlockwise manner.

**21.** From figure one to figure two the places of three elements placed diagonally are shifted one place upwards and the top element is placed at the bottom. From figure two to figure three the three elements on the horizontal are shifted one place to the left and the left most element is placed on the extreme right. The above steps are repeated.

**22.** All the elements are moved half way down two steps and then to the top. The positions of two element on the left are interchanged and the positions of two elements on the right are interchanged, while doing so, first the fourth element is replaced by a new element and then the second. The process is repeated.

**23.** In alternate figures the design in the centre is rotated by 135° anticlockwise. The element in the corner is moved clockwise and turned 90° clockwise at each step.

**24.** In alternate figures one 'T' bar and an arc are added in a set pattern.

**25.** Clockwise, from one figure to next, the direction of one element is changed and one element is turned 45° anticlockwise.

## Chapter 16

# CLASSIFICATION

Classification means arranging the given content in groups or classes having qualities of same kind. In classification type questions, the figures or items are sorted out in groups on the basis of their similarities in qualities in shapes, size, pattern, structure, genus, order, species, grade, style, constituents and other specifications, and thus the answer is found out.

**Example-1**

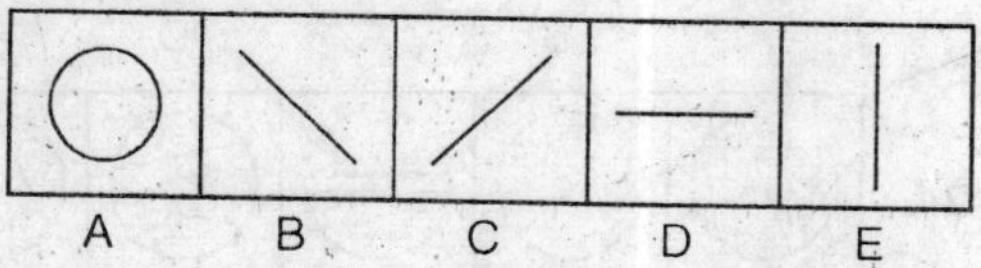

**Answer A :** A is a circle, whereas B, C, D and E are straight lines pointing to different directions. Note that the common characteristic in each of the four figures B, C, D and E is that they are straight lines. Thus, they belong to a class. As against these figures, A is a circle and does not belong to that class.

Therefore, the figure that does not belong to the class is A.

**Example-2**

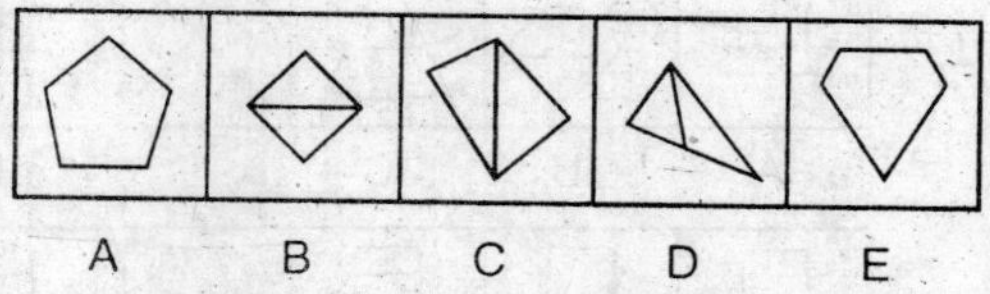

**Answer D :** Figures A, B, C and E are made of 5 straight lines, while D has only four straight lines. Thus A, B, C and E have a common characteristic (they have 5 straight lines each), but D does not have this characteristic. Therefore, D is different from the other four figures.

## EXERCISE

**1.** 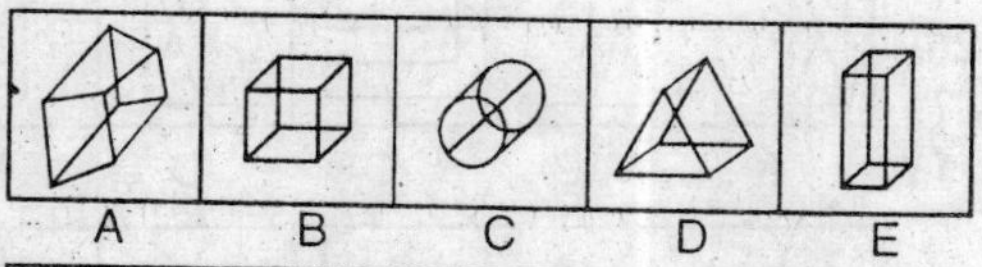

**2.** 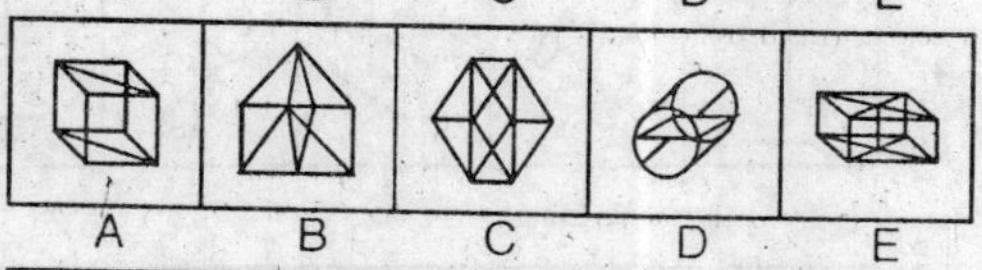

**3.** 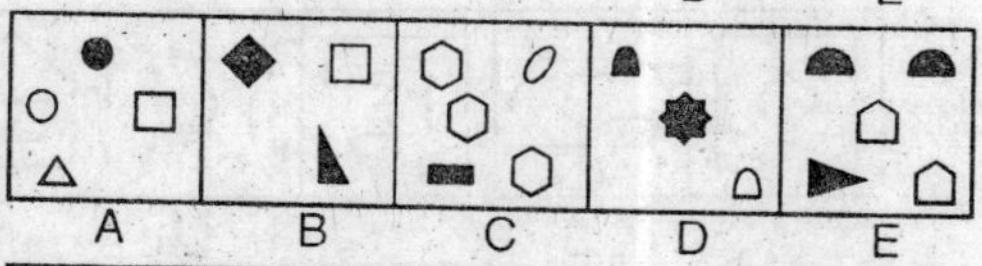

**4.** 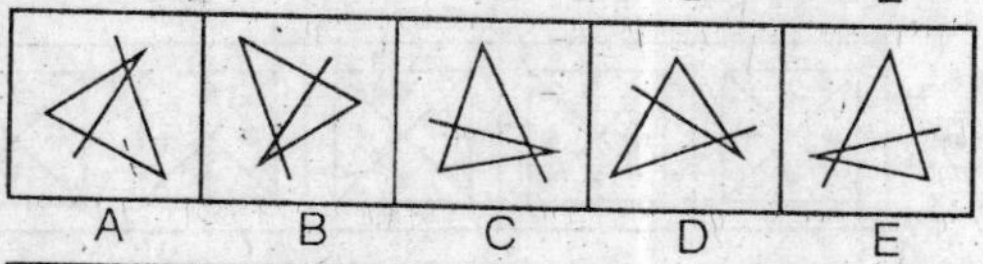

**5.** 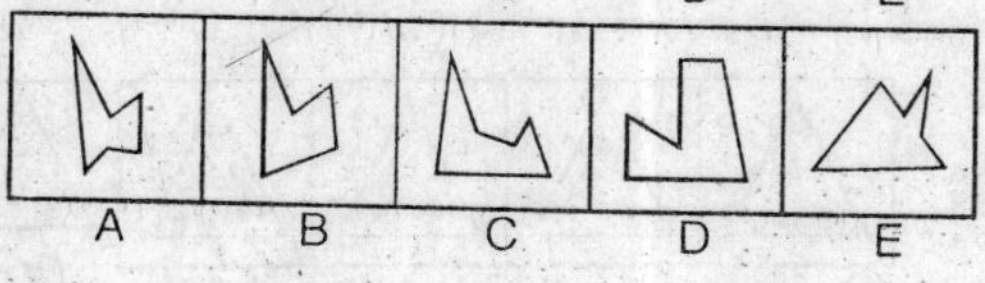

**6.** 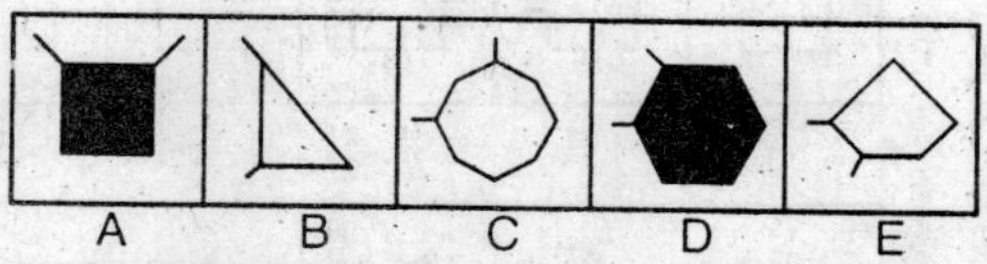

**7.** 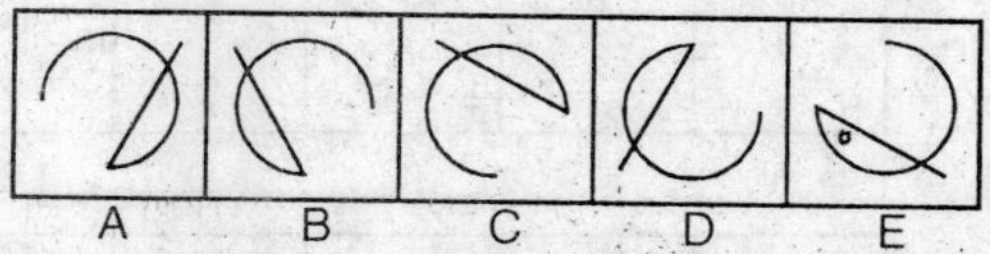

**8.** 

**9.** 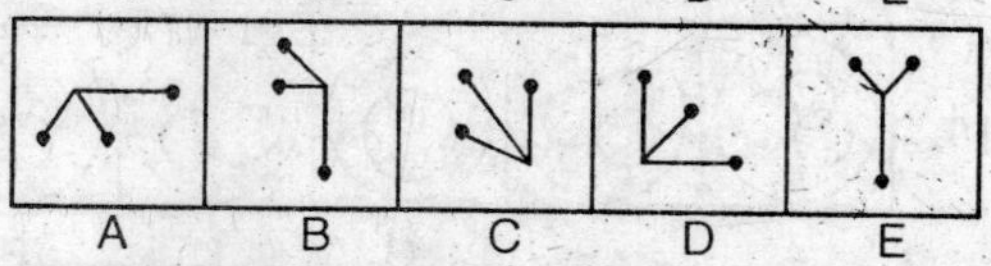

**10.** 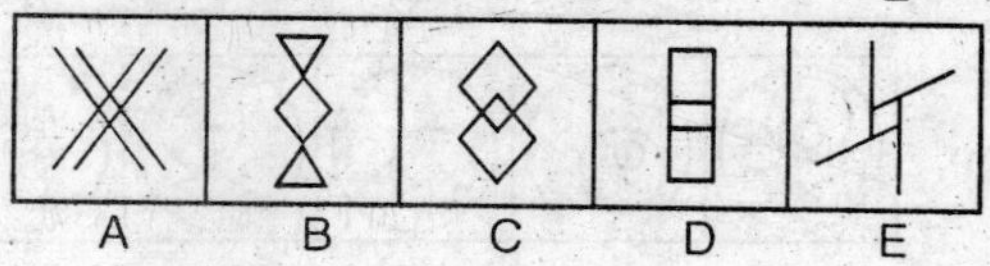

11. 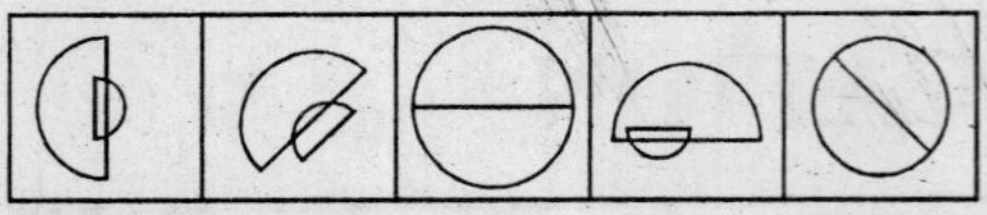

A B C D E

12. 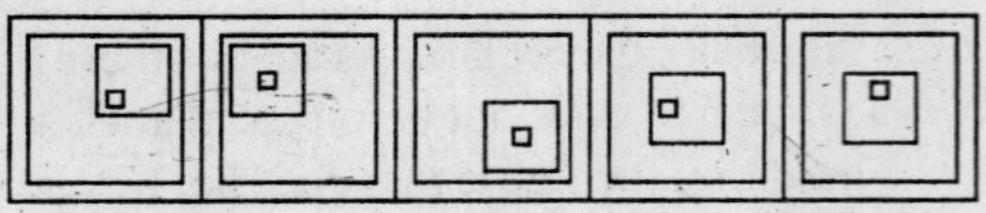

A B C D E

13. 

A B C D E

14. 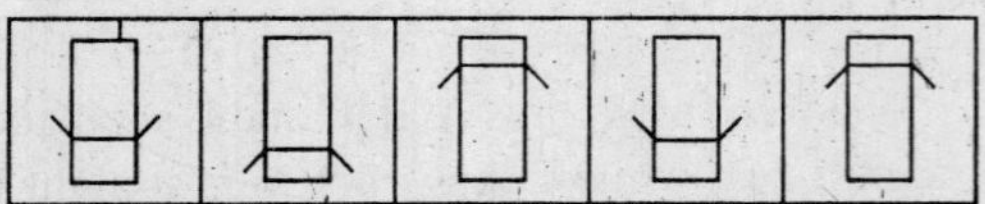

A B C D E

15. 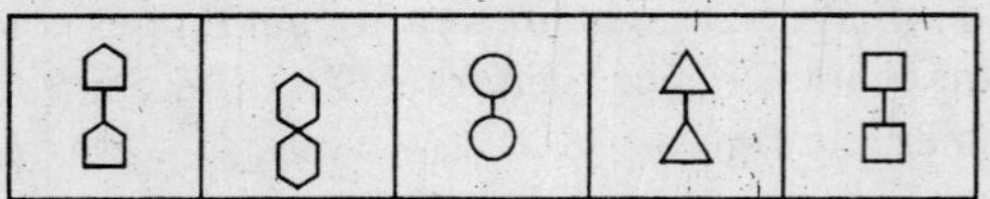

A B C D E

16. 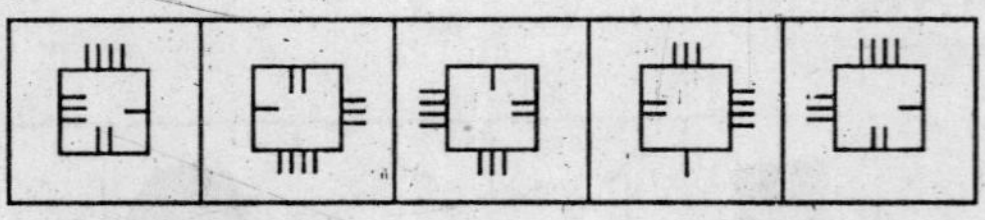

A B C D E

17. 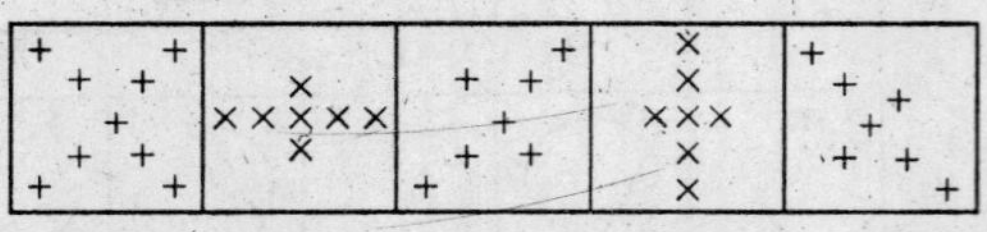

A B C D E

18. 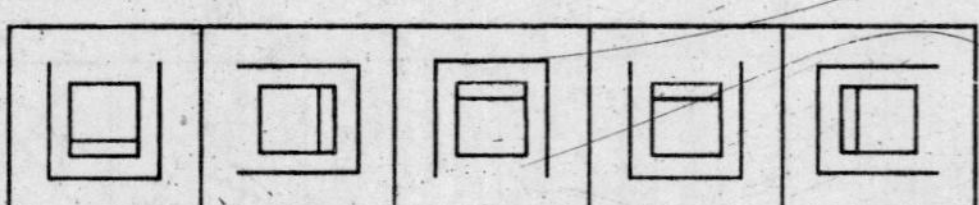

A B C D E

19. 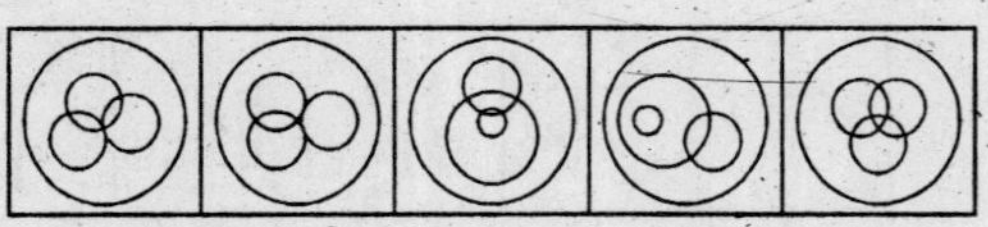

A B C D E

20. 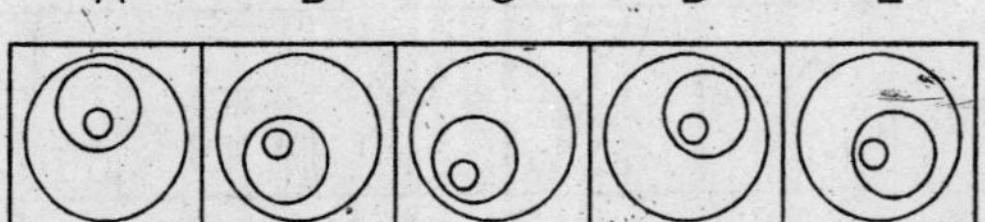

A B C D E

21. 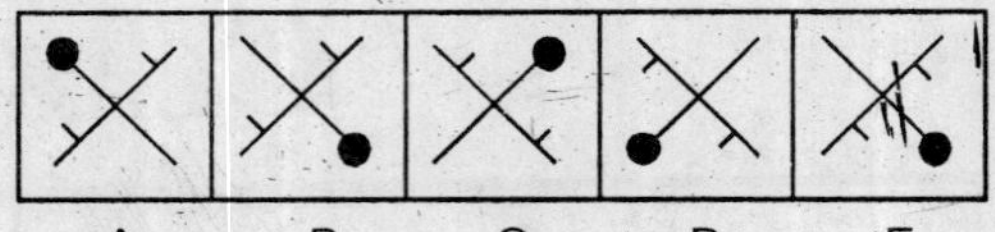

A B C D E

22. 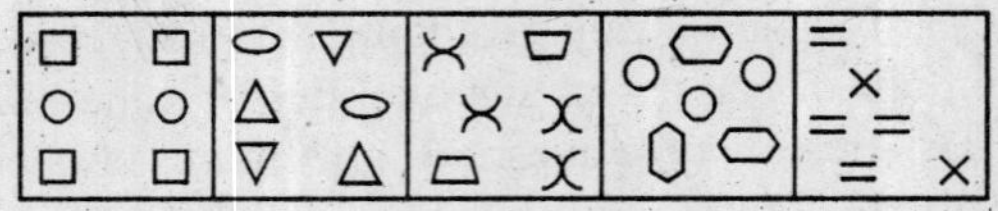

A B C D E

23. 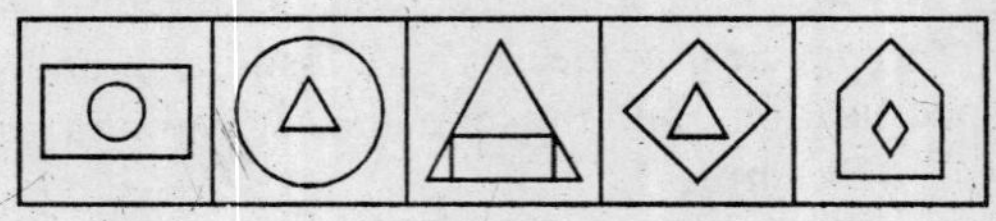

A B C D E

24. 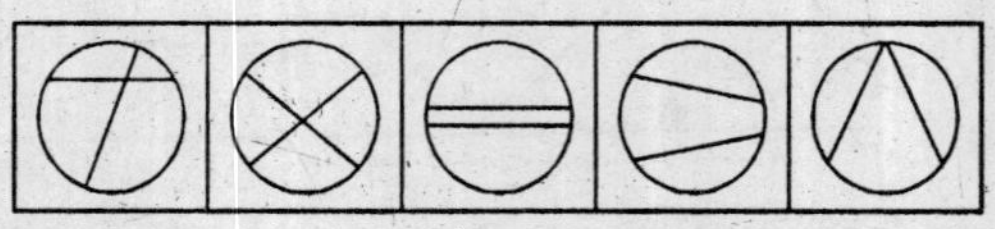

A B C D E

25. 

A B C D E

26. 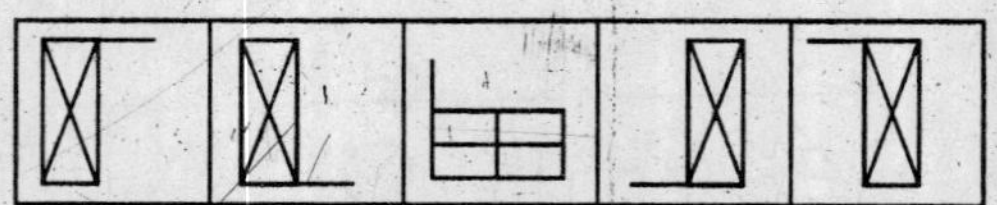

A B C D E

27. 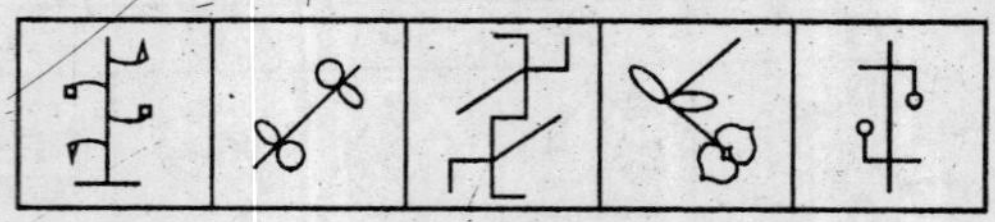

A B C D E

28. 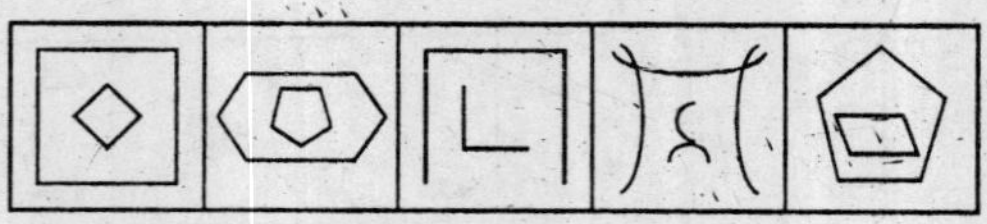

A B C D E

29. 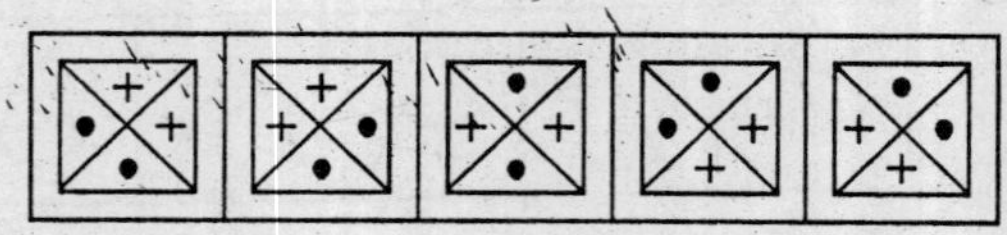

A B C D E

30. 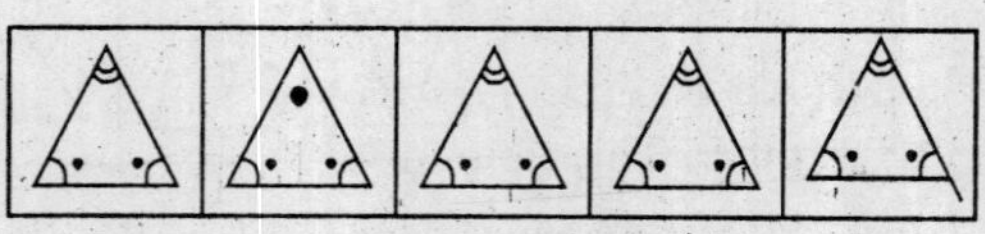

A B C D E

31. 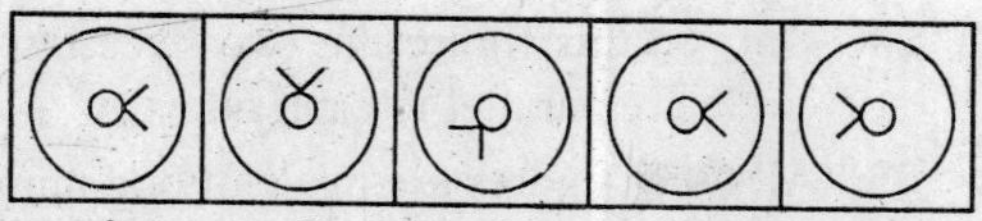

A B C D E

32. 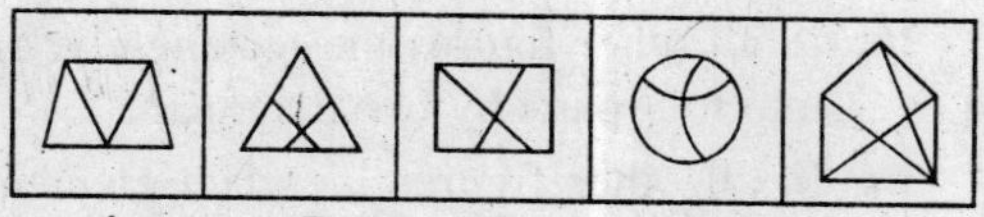

A B C D E

33. 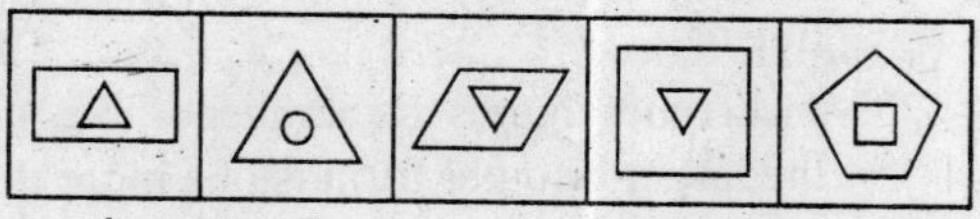

A B C D E

34. 

A B C D E

35. 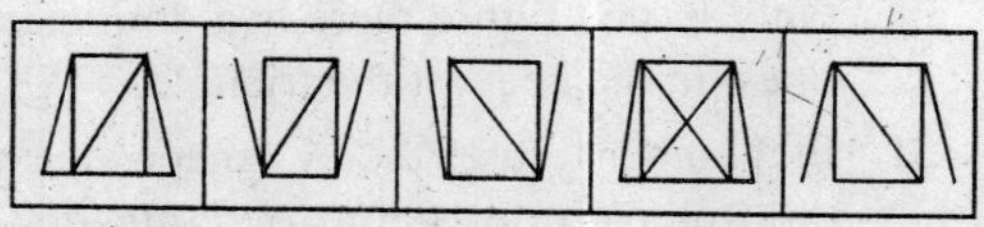

A B C D E

36. 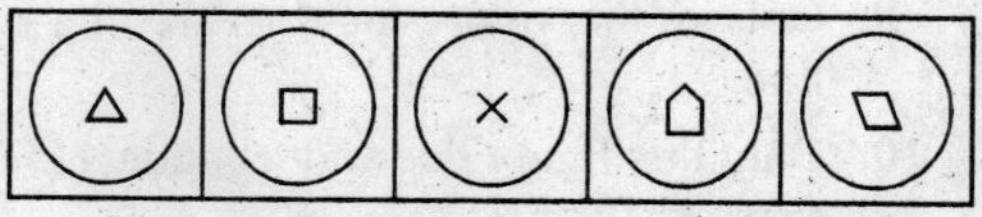

A B C D E

37. 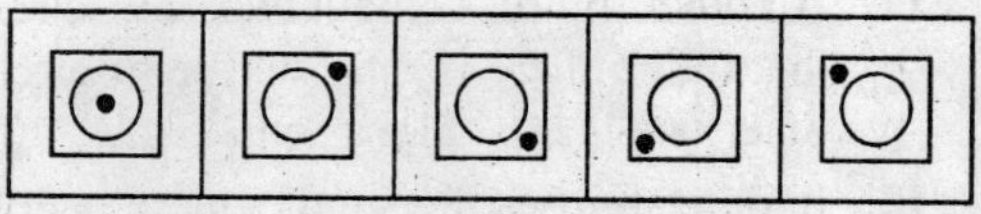

A B C D E

38. 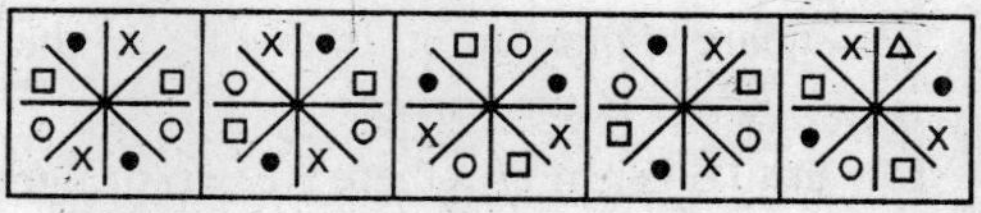

A B C D E

39. 

A B C D E

40. 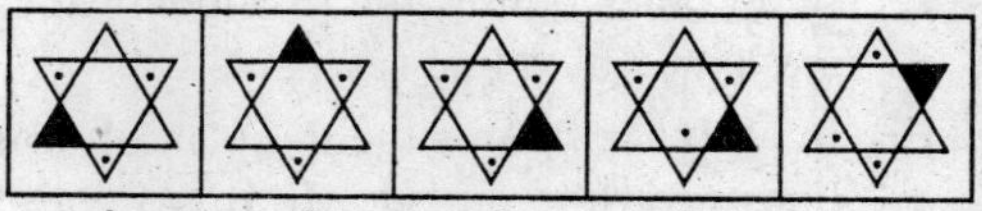

A B C D E

## ANSWERS

| 1 | 2 | 3 | 4 | 5 | 6 | 7 | 8 | 9 | 10 |
|---|---|---|---|---|---|---|---|---|---|
| D | E | E | C | B | C | B | C | D | D |
| 11 | 12 | 13 | 14 | 15 | 16 | 17 | 18 | 19 | 20 |
| D | A | E | B | B | A | A | D | E | C |
| 21 | 22 | 23 | 24 | 25 | 26 | 27 | 28 | 29 | 30 |
| B | D | C | C | D | C | D | A | C | B |
| 31 | 32 | 33 | 34 | 35 | 36 | 37 | 38 | 39 | 40 |
| E | D | B | E | D | C | A | E | A | D |

## EXPLANATORY ANSWERS

1. All other figures have at least two parallel surfaces.
2. Only this figure has been intersected twice.
3. All other figures have either one black or one white design.
4. All other figures can be rotated into each other. This figure is an inverted image of all other figures.
5. All other figures are made of six straight lines.
6. In all other figures the lines are extended from adjacent corners.
7. All other figures can be rotated into each other. In this figure the shape is inverted.
8. Only this figure does not include an acute angle.

9. Only in this figure the dots are in a straight line.
10. Only this figure does not contain a diamond shape in the middle.
11. All other figures contain two semi-circles. In this figure there is only one semi-circle, the other one is less than a semi-circle.
12. In other figures the small square is either in the middle or in the mid of the side of the square containing it. In this figure the small square is in the corner.
13. In all other figures there are two straight lines and three curved lines. In this figure it is opposite.
14. All other figures can be rotated into each other. In this figure the small lines are towards the smaller part of the reetangle.
15. In all other figures the two identical shapes are joined by a line segment.
16. In all other figures the three and four small lines protrude outside. In this figure three lines are inside the square.
17. Only this figure has nine crosses
18. All other figures can be rotated into each other. Only in this figure the smaller part of the contained square is towards the open side of the larger square.
19. Only in this figure all the circles are overlapping each other in equal proportions.
20. In all other figures the innermost cirle is in the centre.
21. All other figures can be rotated into each other. Only in this figure the black circle is not on the side same as of the two small line segments.
22. Only in this figure the two different elements are equal in number.
23. In all other figures the inner figure is not touching the outer figure.
24. Only in this figure the two lines inside the circle are parallel to each other.
25. All other figures are made of odd number of straight lines.
26. In all other figures the rectangle is divided into four parts by two diagonals.
27. In all other figures identical elements are diagonally placed on either side of the middle line.
28. In all other figures the number of lines making the larger or outer form is one more than the number of lines making the smaller or inner form.
29. In all other figures the identical elements are in adjacent sections. In this figure they are in opposite sections.
30. Only in this figure there is a dot, instead of lines, in the apex of the triangle.
31. In all other figures the 'V' shape attached to the inner circle is not touching the outer circle.
32. All other figures are made of straight lines.
33. In all other figures the number of lines making the inner figure is one less than the number of lines making the outer figure.
34. In all other figures the number of curved lines is half the number of straight lines.
35. All other figures are made of seven straight lines.
36. In all other figures the circle contains a closed figure in the centre.
37. In all other figures the dot is outside the circle.
38. Only in this figure there is a triangle instead of circle.
39. In all other figures the single arrow is pointing to the opposite direction of the two arrows.
40. Only in this figures one dot is not inside the triangle.

## Chapter 17

# THE WRONG FIGURE OUT

This type of questions begin with unnumbered figure, followed by five figures, which are numbered from A to E. Then again, unnumbered figure follows the extreme right. One and only one figure out of the figures given does not fit in the series. Therefore, the wrong figure has to be identified.

**Example-1**

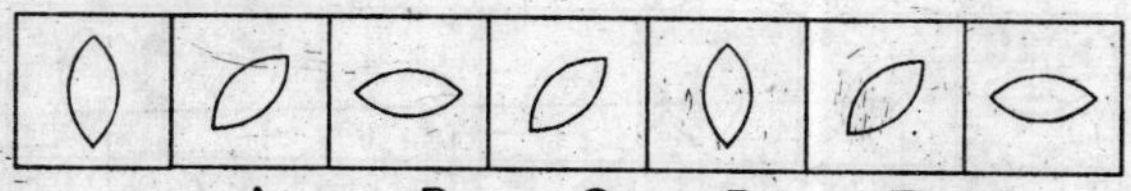

A B C D E

**Answer C :** Observe the pattern of the petal in each box. At each step it is moved 45° clockwise. In figure marked 'C' the petal is moved 45° anticlockwise and this movement does not fit into the order of the given series.

**Example-2**

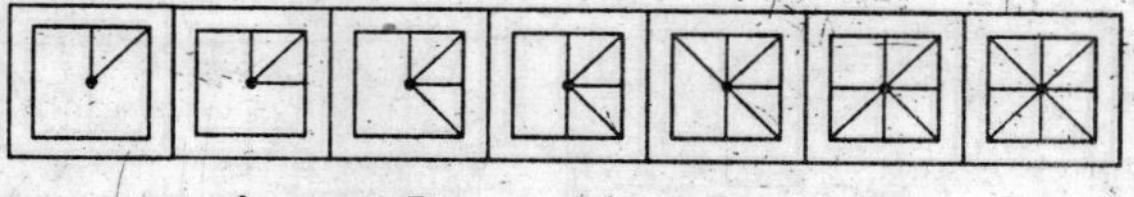

A B C D E

**Answer D :** Note that at each step one line segment is drawn from the centre of the square clockwise in a set pattern. In figure marked 'D' the diagonal line segment should have been touching the bottom left corner instead of the top left corner to fit into the series of the given figures.

## EXERCISE

**1.**

A B C D E

**2.**

A B C D E

**3.**

A B C D E

**4.**

A B C D E

**5.**

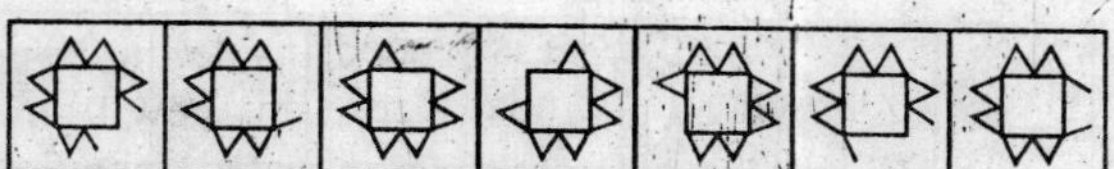

A B C D E

**6.**

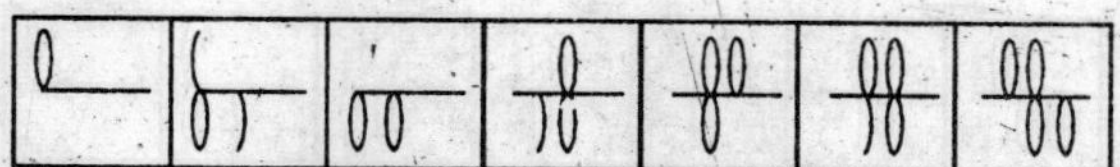

A B C D E

**7.**

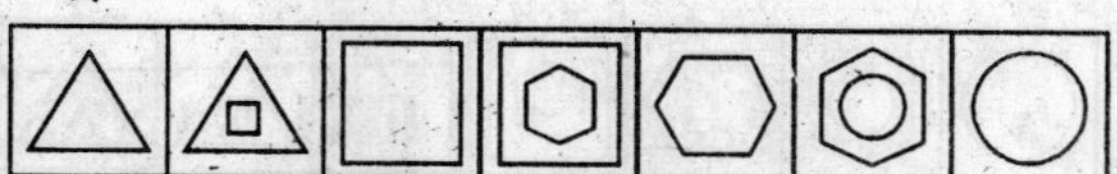

A B C D E

**8.**

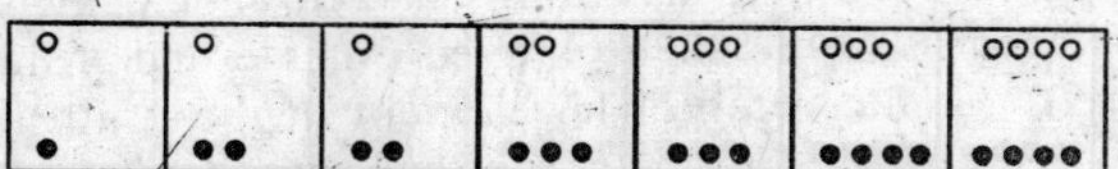

A B C D E

**9.**

A B C D E

**10.**

A B C D E

**11.**

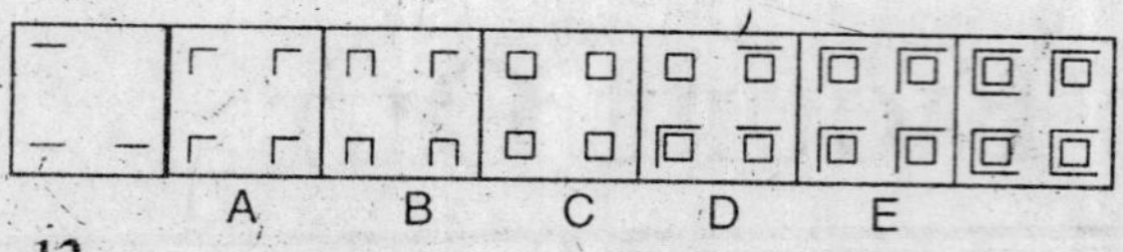


**12.**

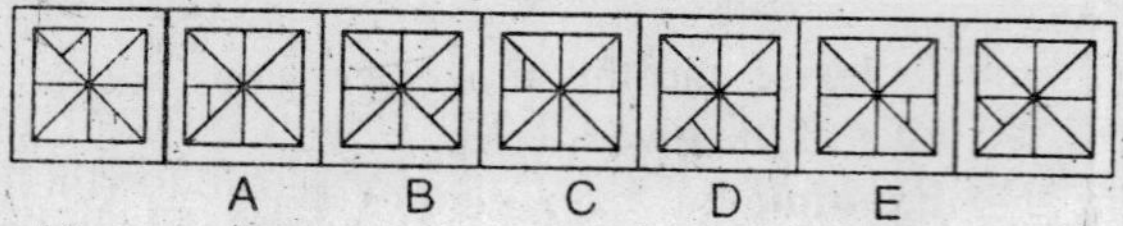


**13.**

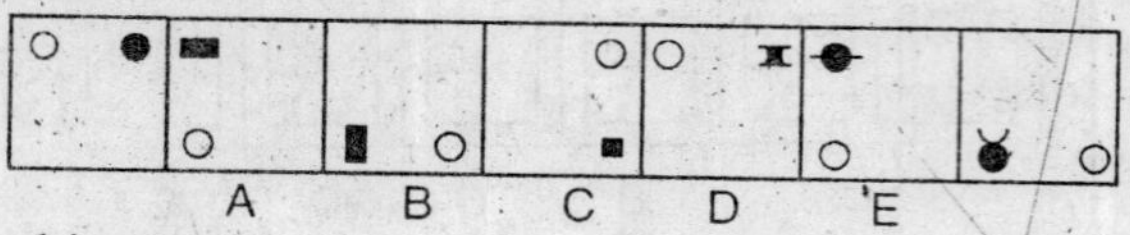


**14.**

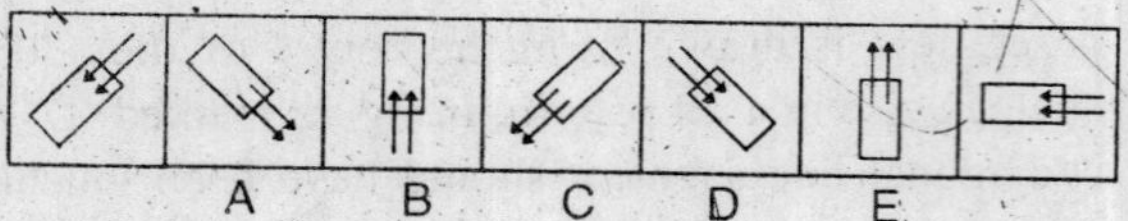


**15.**

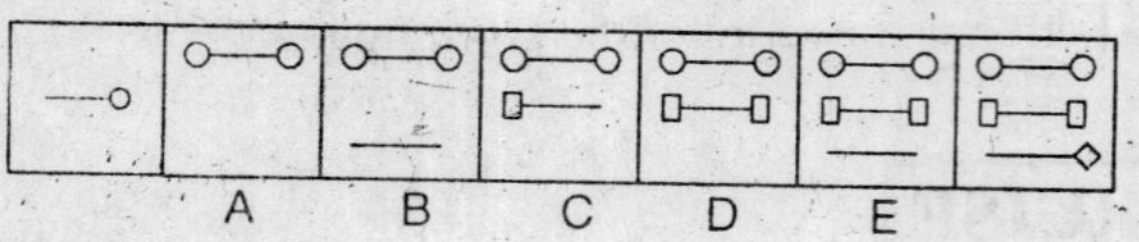


**16.**

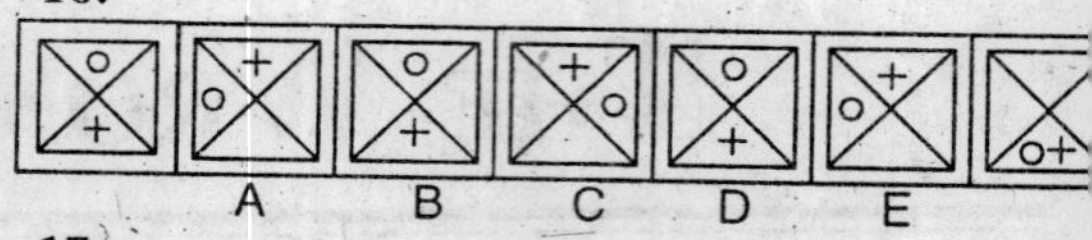


**17.**

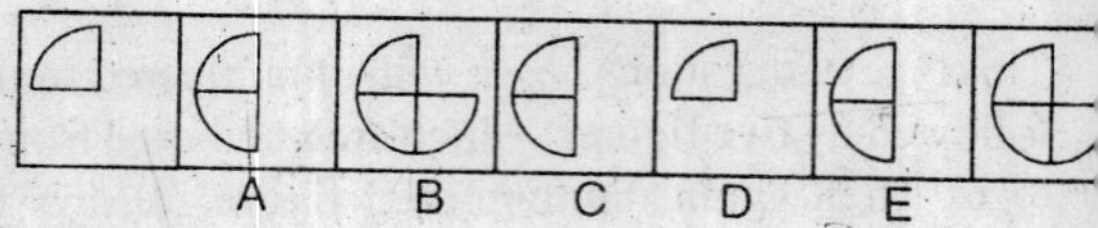


**18.**

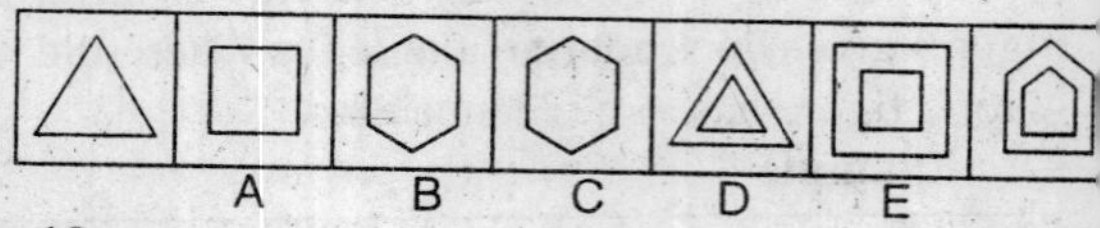


**19.**

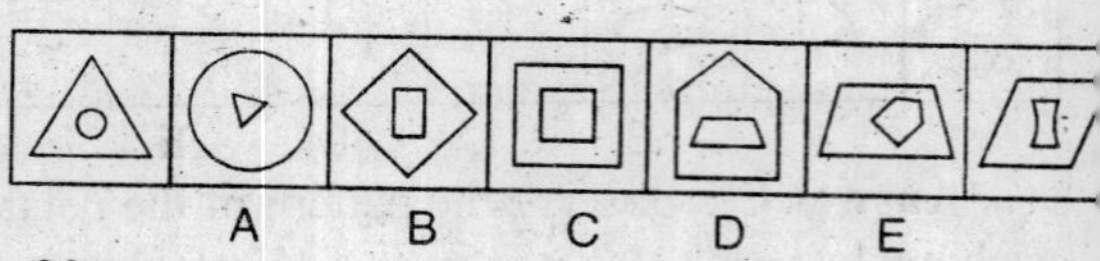


**20.**

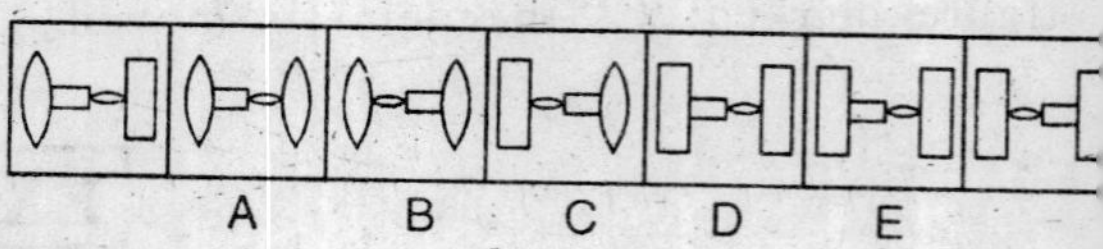


## ANSWERS

| 1 | 2 | 3 | 4 | 5 | 6 | 7 | 8 | 9 | 10 |
|---|---|---|---|---|---|---|---|---|---|
| D | C | C | D | A | A | D | B | C | E |
| **11** | **12** | **13** | **14** | **15** | **16** | **17** | **18** | **19** | **20** |
| D | E | B | A | C | B | C | B | A | D |

## EXPLANATORY ANSWERS

1. The diagonal line is moved anticlockwise and the shade moved outside and inside alternately. The element in the centre is moved to the corner opposite the diagonal and a new element is placed in the centre. In option 'D' there should have been a double arrow instead of square in the centre.
2. The semicircle is moved one step clockwise, and the arrow is moved 90° clockwise, placed in the centre and clockwise corners alternately.
3. The dot is moved 1, 2, 3, 4, 5, 6 steps in the series. In figure 'C' the dot should have been on the vertical line.
4. One and two small lines are added to the figure alternately to complete the human sketch. In option 'D' two lines are added instead of one.
5. First two lines are removed and then two lines are added. The process is repeated. In figure 'A' only one line is removed.
6. Each time half a petal is added to the figure irrespective of the side. In figure 'A' two half petals are added.
7. First a new figure is placed inside the large figure and in the next figure this new figure is enlarged. The process is repeated. In option 'D' the hexagon is tilted, which is wrong.

**8.** One dot and one circle are increased in alternate figures. Figure 'B' should have two circles and two dots.

**9.** In figure 'A' the elements are moved clockwise, the first element is moved to the last and made new. In figure 'B' the elements are moved anticlockwise and new element is added adjacent to the new element in previous figure. This process is repeated from figure 'C' which violates the rule. 'S' shape should have been in place of equal to ( = ) sign.

**10.** The shade is moved 3 steps and 4 steps anticlockwise in alternate figures. After four steps one section clockwise is also shaded. The process is continued. In figure 'E' wrong sections are shaded.

**11.** Five and three lines are added in alternate figures to complete the squares. In figure 'D' four lines are added instead of three.

**12.** The slanting bar is moved three, two and one steps clockwise in alternate figures and the vertical bar is moved one and two steps clockwise in alternate figures. In figure E it is moved four steps clockwise instead of two.

**13.** The circle is moved one step anticlockwise and the other unit which is made new each time is moved behind the circle. In figure 'B' it is not changed.

**14.** The figure is rotated 45° and 90° clockwise in alternate figures and the arrows turned outward and inward alternately. In figure 'A' the rotation is done 90° clockwise instead of 45°.

**15.** The new element is added first on the right and then on the left of the line segment. In option 'C' it is added on the left side of the line segment.

**16.** The plus sign is moved to the diagonally opposite section each time and the circle is moved one step anticlockwise. In option 'B' the plus sign and the circle should have been together in the bottom section.

**17.** One quarter section of the circle is added at each step and the series is repeated from figure D. In option 'C' one section of the circle is missing.

**18.** The number of lines making the figures are increased by one at each step. These figures are doubled from figure D. In figure 'B' there should have been a pentagon instead of hexagon.

**19.** Taking two subsequent figures, the places of two shapes are interchanged. The smaller one is enlarged and the larger one is reduced and tilted 45° clockwise. The process continues with figures B and C. In figure 'A' the triangle is tilted 90° clockwise.

**20.** First the right part is changed, then the candle is laterally inverted and then the left part is changed. The process is repeated by inverting the candle. In option 'D' the right part has also been changed.

# Chapter 18

# ANALOGY

In this type of problems, some relationship is to be established among two figures and on the basis of this relationship, the answer is to be found out from the Answer Figures.

**Example-1 : Problem Figures**

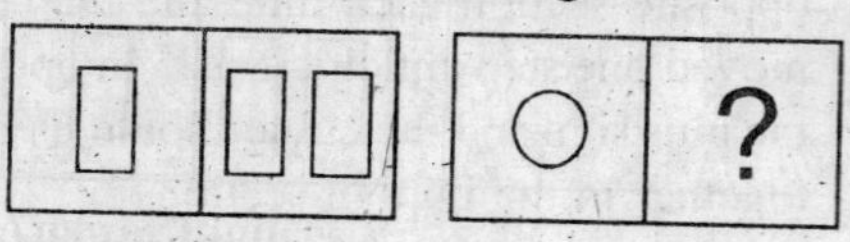

**Answer Figures**

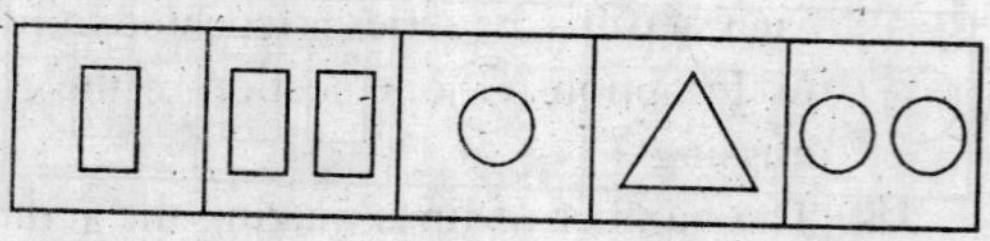

A B C D E

**Answer E :** Observe that the Problem Figures are in two parts. In the first part there are two figures, while in the second part there is one figure followed by a question mark (?). The figures in the first part show a particular relationship and the figures in the second part seek a solution on the basis of this relationship provided in the first part.

The two figures in the first part of the Problem Figures have one and two rectangles respectively. The, first figure has one rectangle whereas the second figure has two rectangles. It means that the relationship between them is—the second figure has double the number of rectangles the first figure has.

The relationship between the two figures in the second part of the Problem Figures must be similar to one that exists between the two figures of the first part of the Problem Figures. i.e. on the same analogy, when the first figure of the second part of Problem Figure has a circle, the second Part must have double the number of circles ie 2 circles.

**Example-2 : Problem Figures**

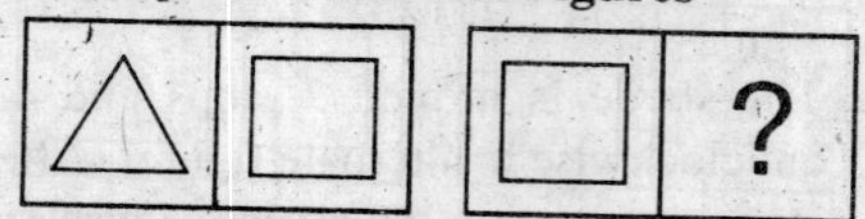

**Answer Figures**

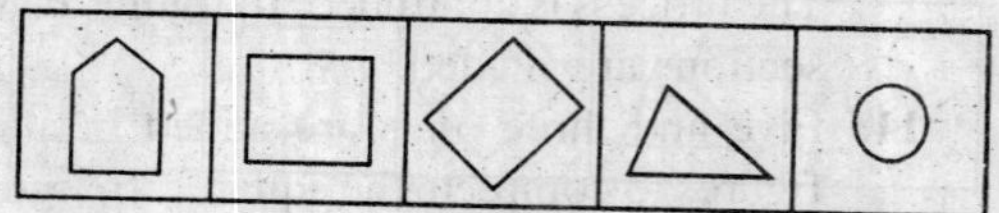

A B C D E

**Answer A :** Study the two figures in the first part of the Problem Figures. They are a triangle and a square. The first figure (a triangle) has three angles and three sides, while the second figure (a square) has four angles and four sides. The relationship between them is—the second figure has one angle and one side more than what the first figure has.

On this analogy the figure to suit in the space marked by ? should be one with 5 angles and 5 sides (one angle and one side more than what the first figure of the second part of the Problem Figures has).

## EXERCISE

1. **Problem Figures**

**Answer Figures**

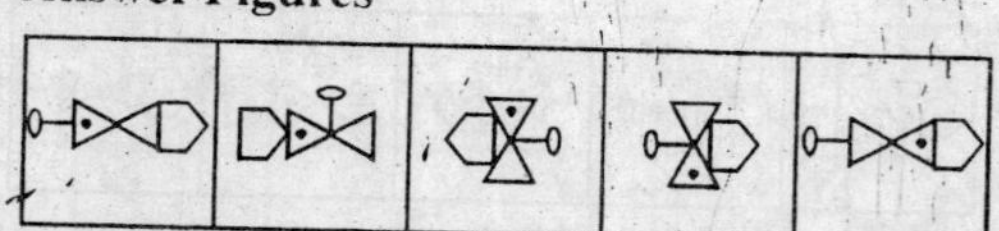

A B C D E

2. **Problem Figures**

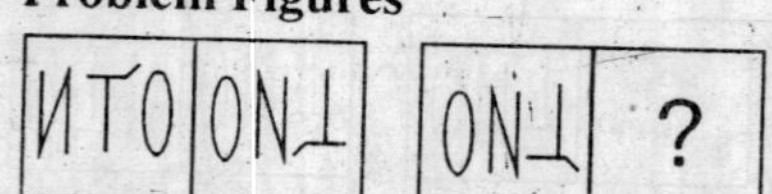

**Answer Figures**

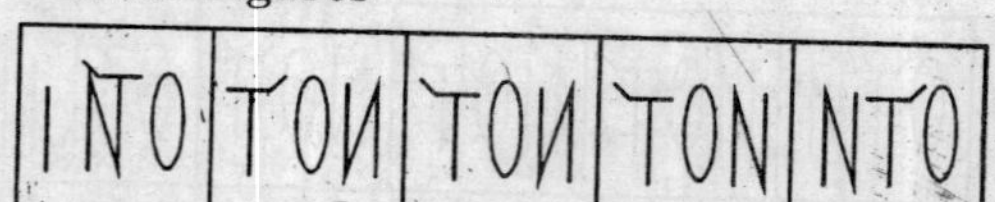

A B C D E

**3. Problem Figures**

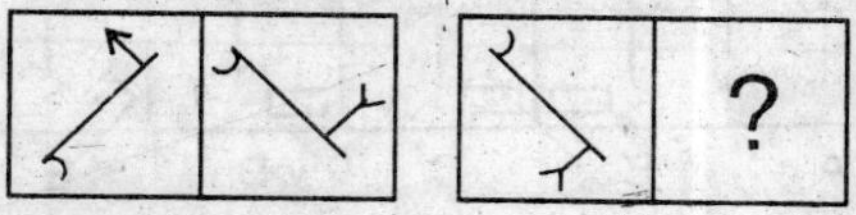

**Answer Figures**

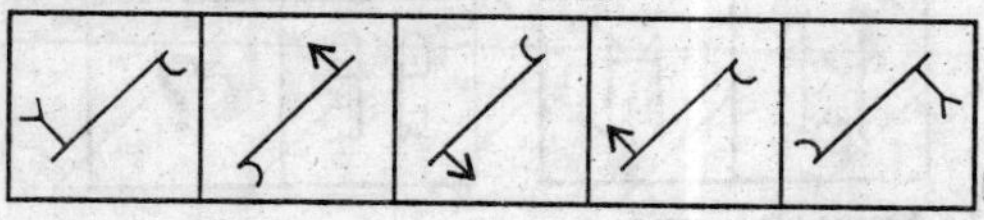

A B C D E

**4. Problem Figures**

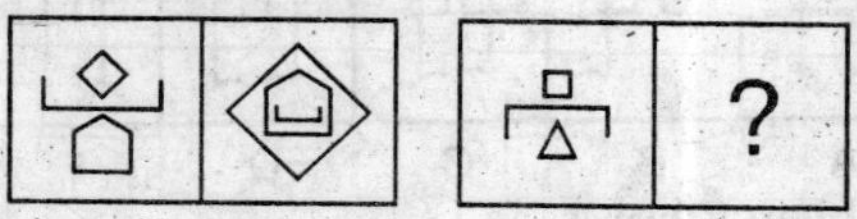

**Answer Figures**

A B C D E

**5. Problem Figures**

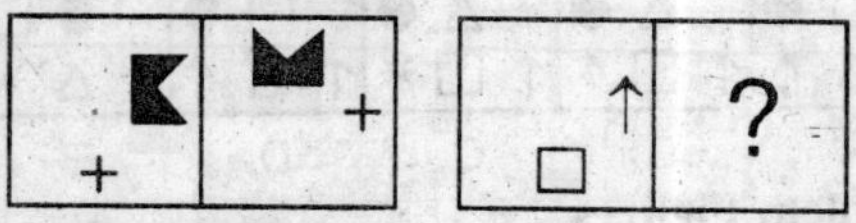

**Answer Figures**

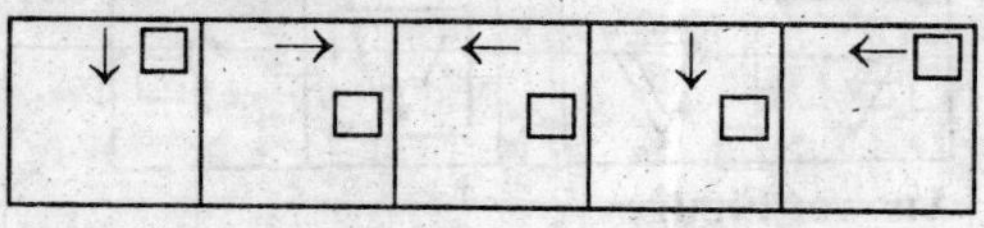

A B C D E

**6. Problem Figures**

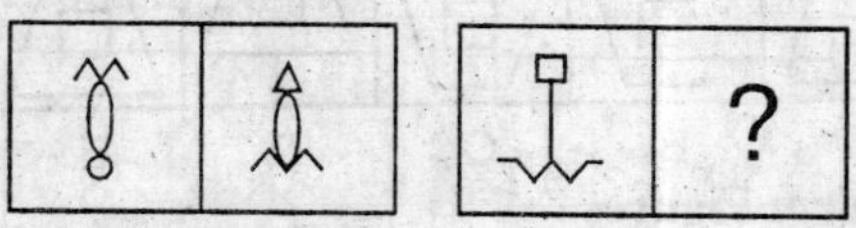

**Answer Figures**

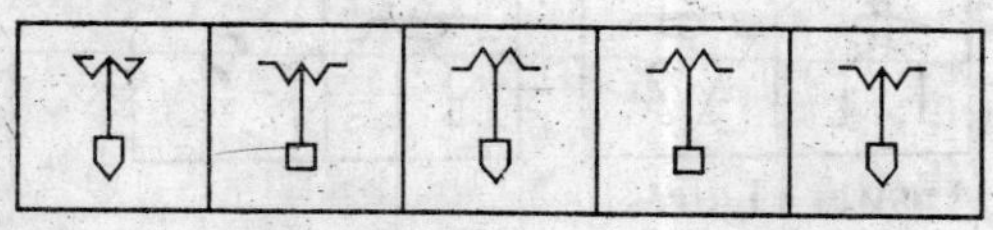

A B C D E

**7. Problem Figures**

**Answer Figures**

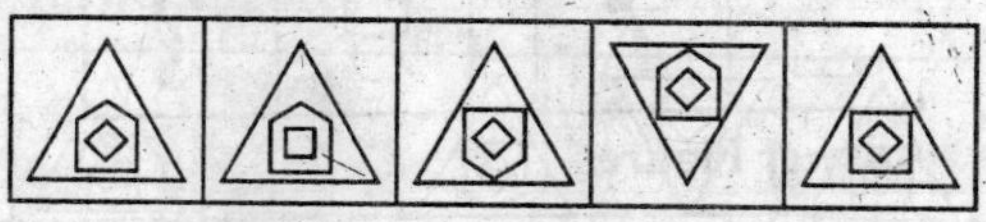

A B C D E

**8. Problem Figures**

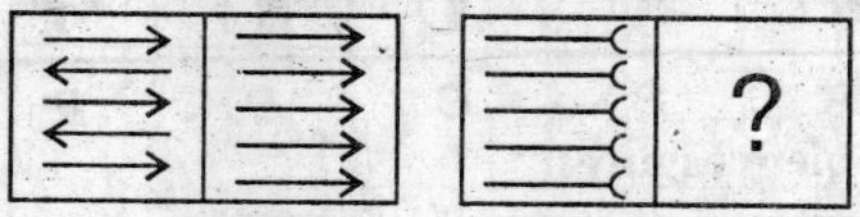

**Answer Figures**

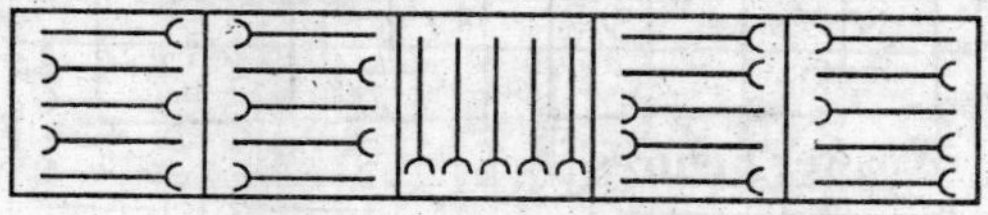

A B C D E

**9. Problem Figures**

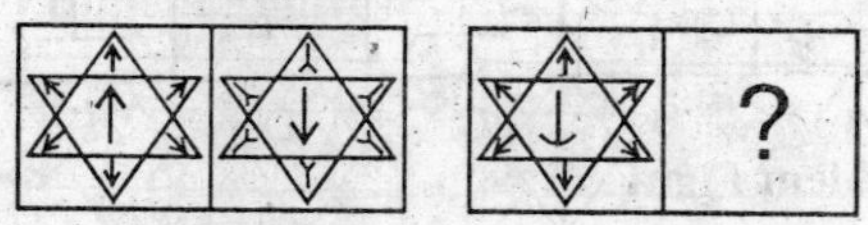

**Answer Figures**

A B C D E

**10. Problem Figures**

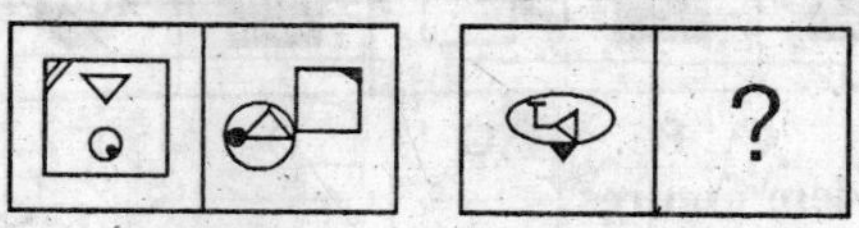

**Answer Figures**

A B C D E

**11. Problem Figures**

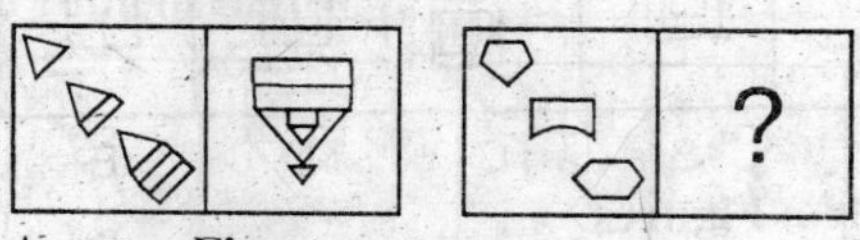

**Answer Figures**

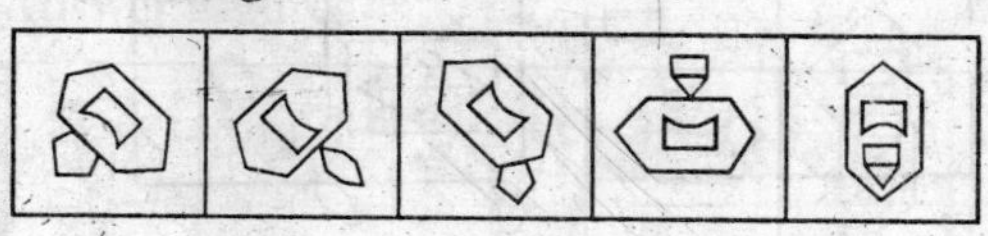

A B C D E

**12. Problem Figures**

**Answer Figures**

A B C D E

**13. Problem Figures**

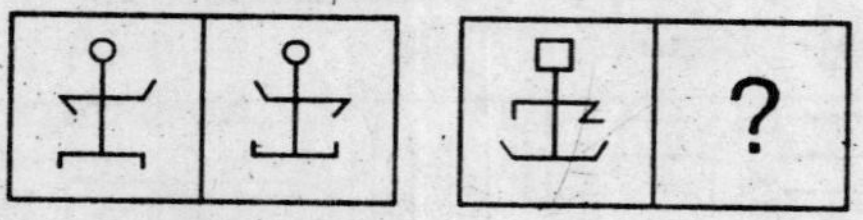

**Answer Figures**

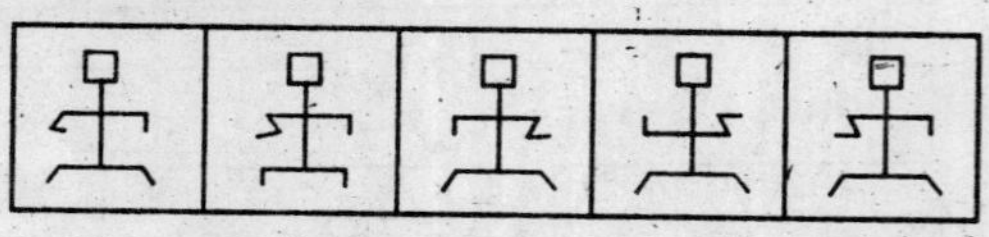

A B C D E

**14. Problem Figures**

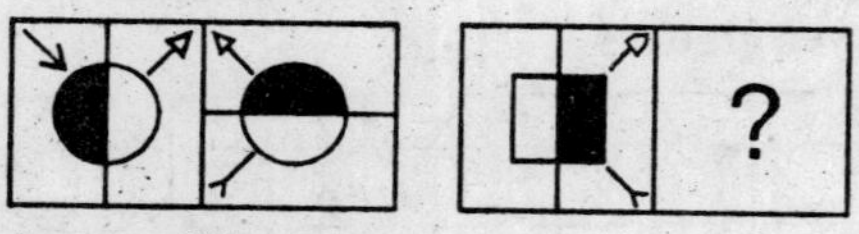

**Answer Figures**

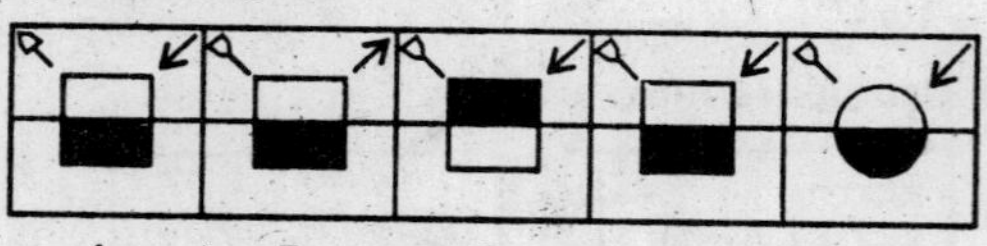

A B C D E

**15. Problem Figures**

**Answer Figures**

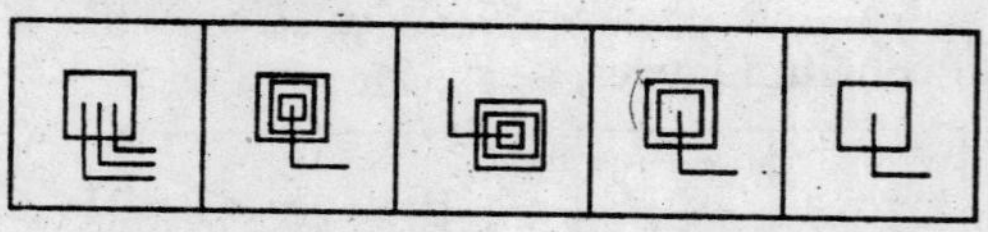

A B C D E

**16. Problem Figures**

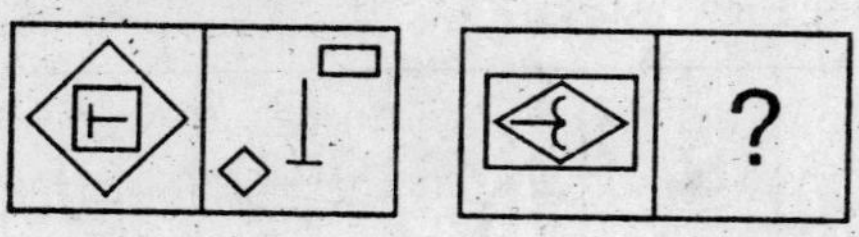

**Answer Figures**

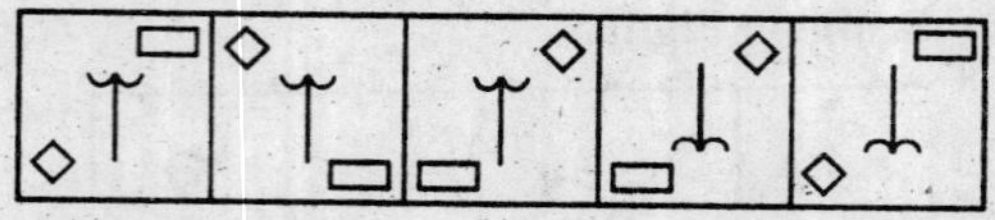

A B C D E

**17. Problem Figures**

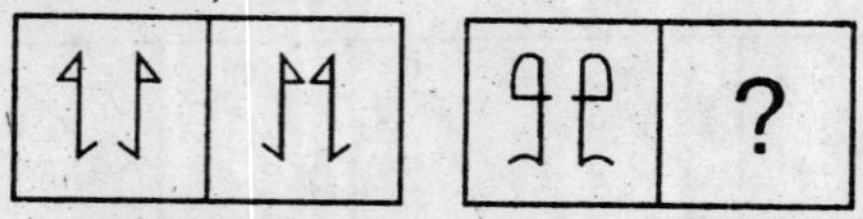

**Answer Figures**

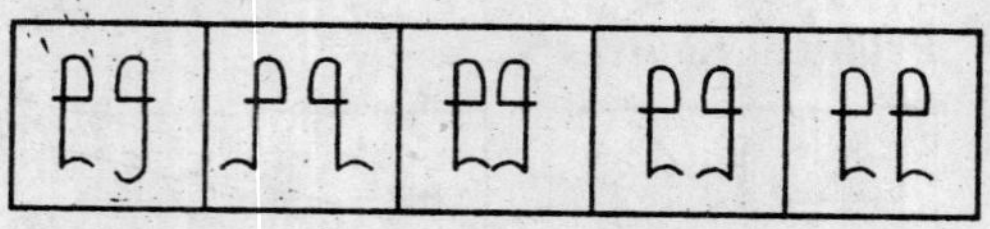

A B C D E

**18. Problem Figures**

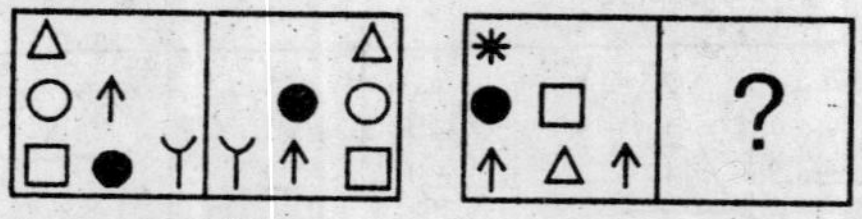

**Answer Figures**

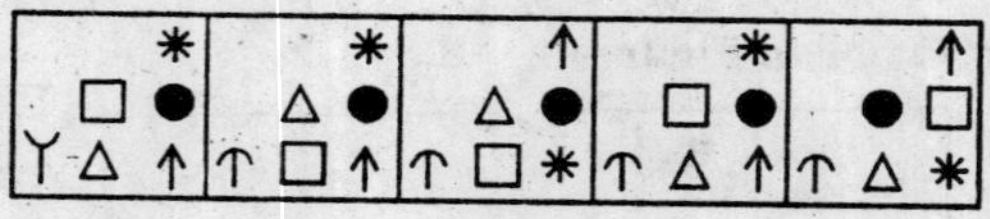

A B C D E

**19. Problem Figures**

**Answer Figures**

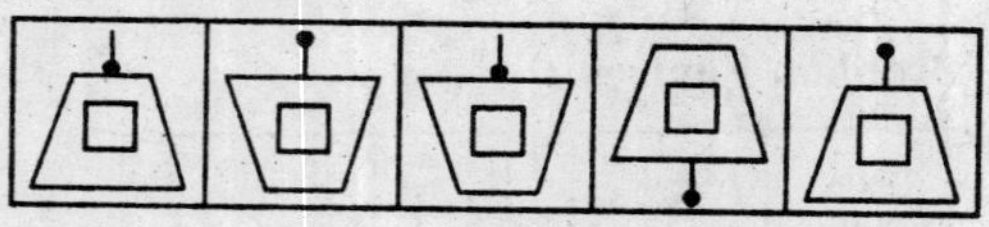

A B C D E

**20. Problem Figures**

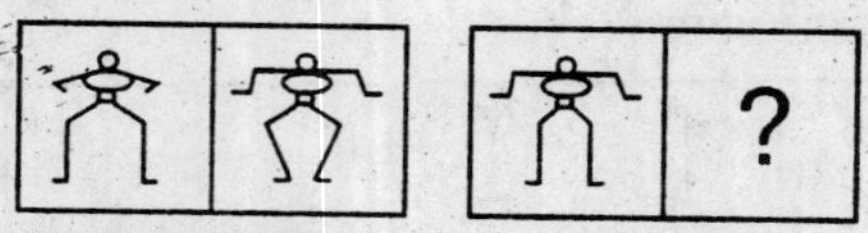

**Answer Figures**

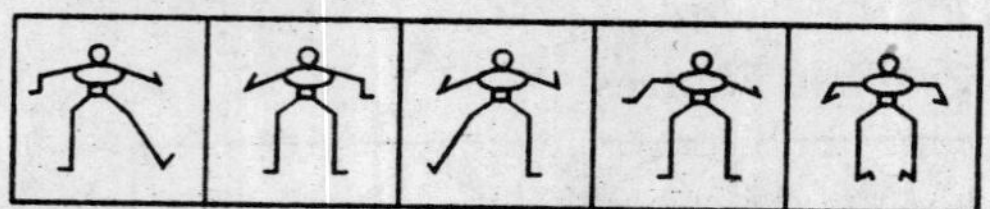

A B C D E

# ANSWERS

| 1 | 2 | 3 | 4 | 5 | 6 | 7 | 8 | 9 | 10 |
|---|---|---|---|---|---|---|---|---|---|
| A | C | D | C | C | E | A | A | B | A |
| **11** | **12** | **13** | **14** | **15** | **16** | **17** | **18** | **19** | **20** |
| C | B | D | D | D | C | D | B | E | B |

# EXPLANATORY ANSWERS

**1.** The element on the right is turned 90° anticlockwise and moved to the centre, the element in the top left corner is turned 90° anticlockwise and attached to the element in the centre on the left, and the element in the bottom left corner is laterally inverted and attached to the element in the centre on the right.

**2.** The element on the extreme right is moved to the extreme left and the other two elements shifted to the right. The T with a bent is turned by 180° and N/N shape is laterally inverted.

**3.** The design is turned 90° clockwise and the lines making the arrowhead are turned in opposite direction.

**4.** The element in the centre is reduced in size, the element at the bottom is enlarged and it encloses the element in the centre, and the element on the top is enlarged and it enclose the other two elements.

**5.** The element at the base is moved one step anticlockwise. The other element is turned 90° anticlockwise and moved one step anticlockwise.

**6.** The places of the elements on the top and at the bottom of the design are interchanged and then one of the elements is made new.

**7.** The innermost design in the first figure is enlarged and made the outermost design in the second figure. The new innermost design is turned by 90°.

**8.** Only the direction of the second element from the top and second element from the bottom is changed.

**9.** The element in the middle of the star is turned upside down. The elements inside the triangles of the star are turned upside down and the lines making the arrowhead are turned in opposite direction.

**10.** There are two small designs enclosed with in a large design. Of these two, the design on the top is turned upside down. The other design is turned 90° clockwise and enlarged to enclose this small design. The large and outer design in figure one is turned 90° clockwise and placed above the other two designs.

**11.** The design in the bottom right is enlarged and turned 135° anticlockwise. The design in the middle is turned 135° anticlockwise and placed inside the enlarged design. The design in the top left is turned 135° anticlockwise and placed at the bottom.

**12.** The design is turned by 180° and then the right half of the top part and left-half of the bottom part are shaded.

**13.** The hands and legs of the figure are turned to the opposite side.

**14.** The figure is turned 90° anticlockwise. The shaded part is unshaded and vice-versa. The lines making the arrowhead are moved to the other end and the other element (triangle/pentagon) is turned upside down.

**15.** The design on the top is made single-lined the design at the bottom is double-lined and then the places of both the designs are interchanged.

**16.** The innermost design is turned 90° anti-clockwise, enlarged the placed in the centre, the outermost design is reduced and placed in the bottom left corner, and the third design is reduced and placed in the top right corner.

**17.** Both the elements in first figure are laterally inverted to get the second figure.

**18.** The three elements on the left are moved to the right side, the single element on the right is moved to the left side and the places of two elements in the middle are interchanged.

**19.** The two enclosed designs are laterally inverted. The design on the top is enlarged and the design at the bottom is placed above it. The large and outer design is reduced and placed inside the lower figure.

**20.** From first figure to the second figure the changes in the symmetrical human sketch are same on either side.

# Chapter 19

# DRAWING INFERENCES

**Directions :** *Below are given some passages followed by several possible inferences which can be drawn from the facts stated in each passage. You have to examine each inference separately in the context of the passage and decide upon its degree of truth or falsity.*

| Mark Answers | If you think... |
|---|---|
| (a) "Definitely True" | the inference properly follows from the statement of facts given. |
| (b) "Probably True" | the inference may be true in the light of the facts given but not definitely true. |
| (c) "Data Inadequate" | from the facts given it cannot be said whether the inference is likely to be true or false. |
| (d) "Probably False" | the inference is probably false in the light of the facts given though not definitely false. |
| (e) "Definitely False" | the inference cannot possibly be drawn from the facts given or it contradicts the given facts. |

### PASSAGE 1

Indian granite industry is in peril in the absence of a uniform policy from the state governments, despite the thrust given by liberalisation policies of the union government. Compared to the remarkable progress in the field during the last three years, the absence of matching policies by state governments had put granite quarry owners and others involved in the industry on the verge of collapse in the international market. The policies differed from state to state, had created problems as far as loyalty, dead rent and duration of lease were concerned.

**1.** Each state having granite quarry has set up its own rules which are contrary to the interest of the industry.

**2.** Till three years ago, granite production in India was not profitable.

**3.** The granite production is largely controlled by individuals.

**4.** The granite produced in India does not match with the quality of international level.

**5.** The union government's liberalisation policy became applicable to granite industry only during the last three years.

### PASSAGE 2

Steel production has always been burdened with costs much higher than in comparable plants overseas. On the one hand custom duty on almost all steel imports has been reduced, on the other excise duty has been raised. Domestic steel products are now uncompetitive which in turn has led to the demand that both the custom and excise rates should be reviewed to prevent sickness in the industry.

**6.** The steel industry in general is making losses as a fall out of the government policy.

**7.** The cost of production of steel in other countries is less than that in India.

**8.** India can compete with the foreign countries in regard to the price of steel with a favourable government policy.

**9.** Foreign steel has become cheaper comparative to domestic steel.

**10.** The government is considering lowering of excise duty on steel products.

### PASSAGE 3

The annual domestic consumption of plastics in India is expected to grow between 2.5 and 3 million tonnes by the end of the Ist balls of the century from the current level of about one million tonnes. The global consumption of plastics now stands at 100 million tonnes. To sustain the present growth pattern, India would need two additional polymer plants of 1,000 tonnes every year till the turn of the Ist half of this century. Entrepreneurs should now think in lines of globalisation and promote projects of international capacity and they would have to look at technology transfer as well as upgradation and strategic and creative alliances.

**11.** The total domestic consumption of plastics in India is about one per cent of the global consumption.

**12.** At present India does not import plastics.

**13.** India lacks in technological capabilities in producing plastics.

**14.** There is an expected growth of about .2 per cent in the plastic consumption every year.

**15.** Potentially India can be one of the major players in the production of plastics in the international market.

## PASSAGE 4

The smaller pesticide formulation units in India operate under heavy constraints such as obsolete technology, small scale of operation and dependence on larger units for raw materials. In view of the loss of expensive material by the smaller units, it is important to either eliminate or reduce losses to the extent possible through innovative and sustainable waste minimisation techniques. Operating profit margins of the units are very low and small adverse conditions land these companies in trouble. Maximum losses suffered by these units are through poor house keeping, sub-optional operating practices, and lack of proper opportunities for recycling waste.

**16.** Smaller units should be operationally self–sufficient so as to minimise losses.

**17.** Recycling of wastes through modern techniques can set off large part of the losses incurred by the smaller units.

**18.** Pesticide units should necessarily be on a large scale to make them economically viable.

**19.** Lack of funds compels smaller units to ignore house keeping.

**20.** Waste management process in India needs modernisation.

## PASSAGE 5

More than a decade of erosion in budgetory support from the Union government, has seriously affected Indian Railways' capacity to finance its plan expenditures. The situation has come to pass where the railways must now think of innovative ways to get longer mileage from its investments. Significantly the resource crunch has had grievous impact on the railways. As a result, it will not be in a position to acquire necessary equipments and this will seriously affect the railways' capacity to serve the needs of the economy in future.

**21.** During the current plan period the railways will not be able to expand its network.

**22.** The fiscal position of railways in the earlier plan period was better than the current plan period.

**23.** Railways had so far believed in traditional ways in generating income.

**24.** Government has shifted its priority from railways to other areas.

**25.** The Union Government has reduced drastically the budgetory support to railways during the last decade.

## PASSAGE 6

As in the case of absolute number of illiterates, the actual number of illiterate females is also increasing with time and faster than the number of male illiterates. More so in the backward states, in the rural areas, and among scheduled castes and scheduled tribes.

The correlation between female illiteracy and infant mortality is equally clear. It is found that mortality was highest in the case of illiterate mothers both in urban and rural areas but much higher in the latter.

**26.** The illitercy rate is higher among females as compared to that of males.

**27.** In terms of absolute numbers there are more male illiterates than female illiterates.

**28.** Infant mortality is correlated more with male than female illiteracy.

**29.**. Infant mortality rate is almost same in urban and rural areas.

**30.** In backward states, the population of scheduled castes and scheduled tribes is more than that in other states.

# EXPLANATORY ANSWERS

**1. *(a)* :** The policies differed from state to state.

**2. *(c)* :** Remarkable progress during the last three years is mentioned in the paragraph but nothing suggests that the production was not profitable.

**3. *(a)* :** There is absence of a uniform policy from the state Governments.

**4. *(c)* :** According to the paragraph, absence of matching policies had put the quarry owners and others involved in the industry on the verge of collapse in the international market. Nothing is mentioned about the granite quality produced in India or of the international level.

**5. *(e)* :** The inference does not relate to the facts given in the statement.

**6. *(d)* :** Government policy alone may not be responsible for the losses. Cost or quality factor may also be responsible.

**7. *(c)* :** The paragraph mentions that steel production in India has always been burdened with costs much higher than in comparable plants overseas. But nowhere in the paragraph it is mentioned that the cost of production of steel is less in other countries.

**8. *(a)* :** If the government reviews its policy, India can definitely compete with the foreign countries in regard to the steel price.

**9. *(a)* :** Customs duty on almost all steel products has been reduced.

**10. *(b)* :** There is a demand that both the customs and excise rates should be reviewed.

**11. *(a)* :** The global consumption of plastics is 100 million tonnes and current level of consumption in India is 1 million tonnes.

**12. *(c)* :** The paragraph does not mention about the import or export of plastics.

**13. *(a)* :** Entrepreneurs would have to look at technology transfer as well as upgradation and strategic and creative alliances.

**14. *(a)* :** The expected growth by end of the Ist half of this century is between 2.5 and 3 million tonnes. India needs 2 additional polymer plants of 1,000 tonnes per year.

**15. *(a)* :** By thinking in lines of globalisation and promoting projects of international capacity India can be one of the major players in the production of plastics in the international market.

**16. *(b)* :** Nowhere in the paragraph it is stated that the losses of the smaller units can be minimised if they are made operationally self–sufficient.

**17. *(a)* :** Lack of proper opportunities for recycling waste is one of the reasons for maximum losses suffered by smaller units.

**18. *(c)* :** The paragraph is about the problems and losses of smaller units. Comparatively, larger units must be facing lesser problems and losses.

**19. *(e)* :** Low profit margins and adverse conditions compels smaller units to ignore house keeping.

**20. *(a)* :** To prevent or eliminate the loss of expensive material by the smaller unit waste management process in India needs modernisation.

**21. *(a)* :** Due to low budget the railways cannot acquire necessary equipments.

**22. *(a)* :** Earlier, there was no need to think of innovative ways.

**23. *(a)* :** Railway budget of the Union Government had supported the Indian Railways for more than a decade.

**24. *(b)* :** Erosion in budgetary support from the Union Government is probably true if the Government has shifted its priority to other areas.

**25. *(a)* :** There has been a grievous impact on the railways.

**26. *(a)* :** The actual number of illiterate females is also increasing with time and faster than the number of male illiterates.

**27. *(c)* :** The passage tells about the increase in number of male and female illiterates but mentions nothing about the present ratio of illiterate males and females.

**28. *(e)* :** Infant mortality is correlated with female illiteracy.

**29. *(e)* :** Mortality is highest in the case of illiterate mothers in rural areas.

**30. *(c)* :** The population figures are not mentioned in the passage.

Chapter 20

# CRITICAL THINKING

**Directions :** *In each question below are given two statements followed by two conclusions numbered I and II. You have to take the two given statements to be true even if they seem to be at variance from commonly known facts and then decide which of the given conclusions logically follows from the two given statements, disregarding commonly known facts. Read both the statements and—*

*Give answer (a) if only conclusion I follows; give answer (b) if only conclusion II follows; give answer (c) if either I or II follows; give answer (d) if neither I nor II follows and give answer (e) if both I and II follows.*

1. *Statements* *I:* All tomatoes are red.
   *II:* All grapes are tomatoes.
   *Conclusions* *I:* All grapes are red.
   *II:* Some tomatoes are grapes.
2. *Statements* *I:* All painters are smiling.
   *II:* Some authors are painters.
   *Conclusions* *I:* All smiling authors are painters.
   *II:* Some authors are smiling.
3. *Statements* *I:* All peons in this office are efficient.
   *II:* Ramu is not efficient.
   *Conclusions* *I:* Ramu is not peon in this office.
   *II:* Ramu should be more efficient.
4. *Statements* *I:* All weavers are hard working.
   *II:* No hard working men are foolish.
   *Conclusions* *I:* No weavers are foolish.
   *II:* Some foolish are weavers.
5. *Statements* *I:* All fishes are cars.
   *II:* All cars are vegetables.
   *Conclusions* *I:* Some vegetables are cars.
   *II:* Some vegetables are fishes.
6. *Statements* *I:* Some dogs are pups.
   *II:* All horses are pups.
   *Conclusions* *I:* Some dogs are horses.
   *II:* Some horses are dogs.
7. *Statements* *I:* All beautiful women are mothers.
   *II:* All mothers are understanding.
   *Conclusions* *I:* All beautiful women are understanding.
   *II:* All mothers are beautiful women.
8. *Statements* *I:* Some toys are tables.
   *II:* No table is black.
   *Conclusions* *I:* Some toys are black.
   *II:* Some toys are not black.

**Directions :** *In each question below is given a statement followed by two assumptions numbered I and II. An assumption is something supposed or taken for granted. You have to consider the statement and the following assumptions and decide which of the assumptions is implicit in the statement. Give answer—*

*(a)* If assumption I is implicit.
*(b)* If assumption II is implicit.
*(c)* If either I or II is implicit.
*(d)* If neither I nor II is implicit.
*(e)* If both I and II are implicit.

9. *Statement* : Apart from the entertainment value of television, its educational value cannot be ignored.
   *Assumptions I:* People take the television to be means of entertainment only.
   *II:* The educational value of television is not realised properly.
10. *Statement* : Ten candidates who were on the waiting list could finally be admitted to the course.
   *Assumptions I:* Wait-listed candidates get admission with difficulty.

*II* : A large number of candidates were on the waiting list.

**11.** *Statement* : In Mumbai, railway trains are indispensable for people in the suburbs to reach their places of work on time.

*Assumptions I* : Railway trains are the only mode of transport available in the suburbs of Mumbai.

*II* : Only railway trains run punctually.

**12.** *Statement* : The mangoes are too cheap to be good.

*Assumptions I* : When the mango crop is abundant, the prices go down.

*II* : The lower the selling price, the inferior is the quality of the commodity.

**13.** *Statement* : Of all the newspapers published in Delhi, 'The Time and Space' has the largest number of readers.

*Assumptions I* : Volume of readership of all the newspapers in Delhi is known.

*II* : No newspaper in Delhi other than 'The Time and Space' has large readership.

**14.** *Statement* : 'Smoking Prohibited'. A notice in a railway compartment.

*Assumptions I* : Some persons like to smoke in the compartment.

*II* : Some persons smoke in the compartment.

**15.** *Statement* : A friend in need is a friend indeed.

*Assumptions I* : Relatives are of no help in difficult circumstances.

*II* : Taking help from a friend is desirable.

**16.** *Statement* : When in Chennai, stay at Hotel 'X' for comfort and good service, because my best friend has recommended it.

*Assumptions I* : My best friend is trustworthy.

*II* : Comfort and good service cannot be expected from all hotels.

# EXPLANATORY ANSWERS

**1.** *(e)* : When all tomatoes are red and all grapes are tomatoes, then all grapes are also red. When all grapes are tomatoes, then some tomatoes must be grapes. Therefore, both conclusions I and II are correct.

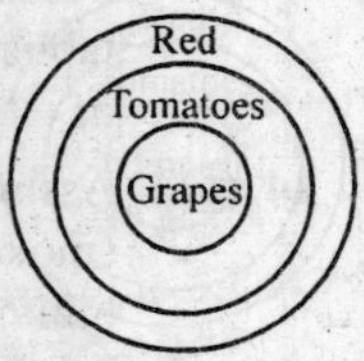


**2.** *(b)* : When all painters are smiling and some authors are painters, then some authors are smiling. Therefore, only conclusion II is correct.

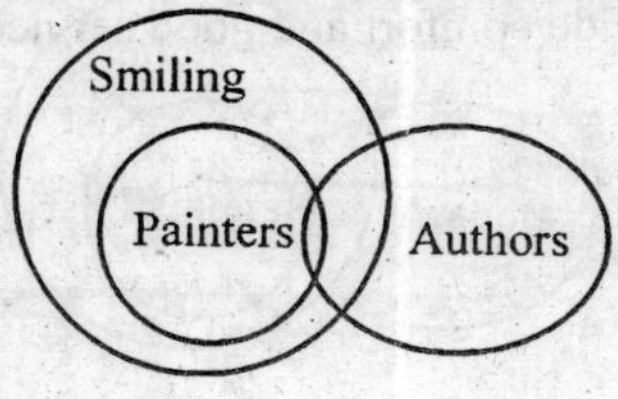


**3.** *(a)* : When all the peons of the office are efficient, then Ramu cannot be a peon in this office. Therefore, only conclusion I is correct.

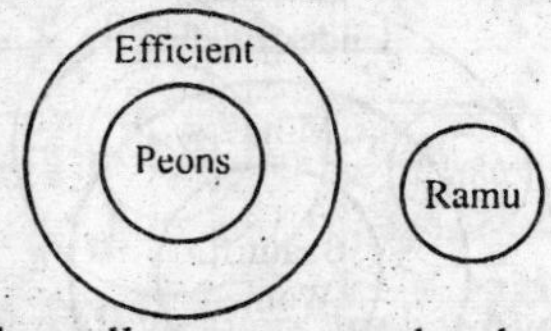


**4.** *(a)* : When all weavers are hardworking and no hardworking men are foolish, then no weavers are foolish. Therefore, only conclusion I is correct.

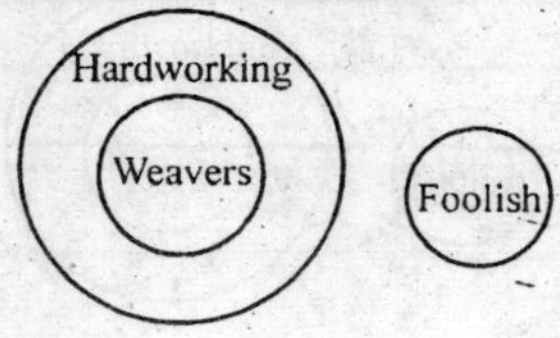

**5. *(e)* :** When all fishes are cars and all cars are vegetables, then all fishes will naturally be vegetables. This means that some vegetables are fishes. And when all cars are vegetables, then some vegetables will be cars naturally. Therefore, both the conclusions I and II are correct.

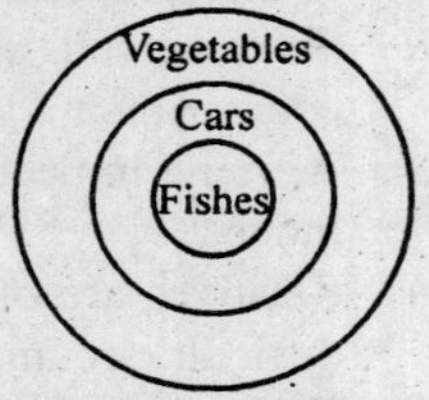


**6. *(d)* :** No relationship can be established between the two statements. Therefore, neither conclusion I nor conclusion II is correct.

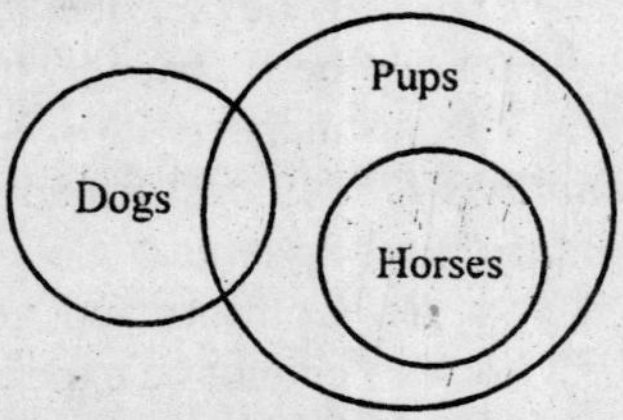


**7. *(a)* :** When all beautiful women are mothers and all mothers are understanding, then naturally all beautiful women are understanding. All mothers need not be beautiful women. Therefore, only conclusion I is correct.

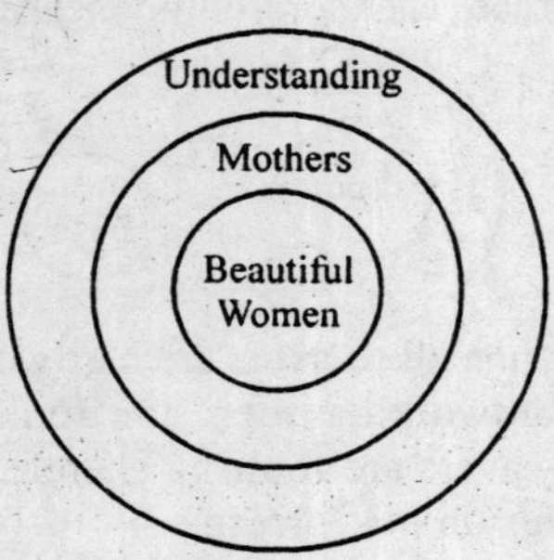


**8. *(c)* :** When some toys are tables and no table is black, then it is indicated that some toys can be black, as all toys are not tables. On the other hand, some toys may not be black. Therefore, there is a possibility that some toys may or may not be black. As such, either conclusion I or conclusion II can be correct.

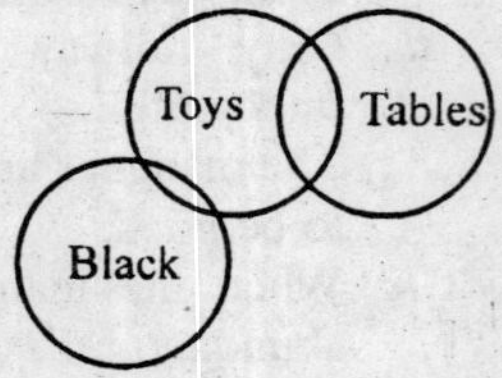


**9. *(e)* :** Both assumptions I and II are implicit.

**10. *(a)* :** Assumption II is not implicit in the statement. Only assumption I is implicit.

**11. *(d)* :** Neither assumption I nor assumption II is implicit in the statement.

**12. *(b)* :** Assumption I is not implicit in the statement, because it states the principle of supply and prices. Only assumption II is implicit which states the principle of price-quality parity.

**13. *(a)* :** Assumption I is implicit in the statement because the largest readership may be established only if the volume of readership of all the newspapers is known.

**14. *(b)* :** Assumption II suggests that some persons smoke in the compartment. 'Smoking Prohibited' is the notice for those persons.

**15. *(d)* :** The statement highlights the criterion of a true friend.

**16. *(e)* :** Both assumptions I and II are implicit because *(i)* the advice is from a trustworthy best friend, and *(ii)* all hotels cannot provide comfort and good service.

# Chapter 21

# EMOTIONAL INTELLIGENCE

Emotional intelligence (EI) refers to the ability to perceive, control, and evaluate emotions. Emotional intelligence (EI) is the area of cognitive ability involving traits and social skills that facilitate interpersonal behavior. Intelligence can be broadly defined as the capacity for goal-oriented adaptive behavior; emotional intelligence focuses on the aspects of intelligence that govern self-knowledge and social adaptation.

Emotional Intelligence that is also called Emotional Intelligence Quotient or (EQ) narrates the capability, capacity, or deftness to understand evaluates, and manages one's emotions.

1. In my group of friends, I am generally aware of how each person feels about the other people in our social circle.
   A. Strongly Agree B. Agree
   C. Disagree D. Strongly Disagree
2. When I am upset, I can usually pinpoint exactly why I am distressed.
   A. Strongly Agree B. Agree
   C. Disagree D. Strongly Disagree
3. While there are some things that I would like to change, I generally like who I am.
   A. Strongly Agree B. Agree
   C. Disagree D. Strongly Disagree
4. When I make mistakes, I often berate and criticize myself and my abilities.
   A. Often B. Sometimes
   C. Rarely D. Almost Never
5. I feel uncomfortable in emotionally charged situations.
   A. Strongly Agree B. Agree
   C. Disagree D. Strongly Disagree
6. I tend to avoid confrontations. When I am involved in a confrontation, I become extremely anxious.
   A. Strongly Agree B. Agree
   C. Disagree D. Strongly Disagree
7. I am generally aloof and detached until I really get to know a person.
   A. Strongly Agree B. Agree
   C. Disagree D. Strongly Disagree
8. I tend to overreact to minor problems.
   A. Often B. Sometimes
   C. Rarely D. Almost Never
9. I feel confident about my own skills, talents, and abilities.
   A. Strongly Agree B. Agree
   C. Disagree D. Strongly Disagree
10. I would describe myself as a good judge of character.
    A. Strongly Agree B. Agree
    C. Disagree D. Strongly Disagree
11. When I am facing an unpleasant task, I tend to:
    A. Make a plan and work on it a little each day
    B. Get it over with as soon as possible
    C. Put it off until the last minute
    D. Don't do it at all
12. Question: During a heated argument, I am more likely to:
    A. Stop the fight and agree to a short break before resuming the discussion.
    B. Shut down and stop responding to the other person.
    C. Give in and apologize in order to quickly end the argument.
    D. Start insulting the other person.
13. When making an important decision, I tend to:
    A. Follow my instincts
    B. Rely on direction from other people
    C. Go with the easiest option
    D. Guess randomly
14. Which of the following statements best describes you?
    A. I have an easy time making friends and getting to know new people.
    B. I get along well with others, but I have to really get to know someone before they become a true friend.
    C. I find it difficult to meet people and make friends.
    D. I cannot make friends.

**15.** You have invested a lot of time and energy into a project for one of your classes. While you feel confident about your work, your instructor gives you a C+ on the project. How do you deal with this situation?

A. Decide the class is stupid and stop putting forth your best efforts.

B. Berate and criticize your own work.

C. Confront the professor and ask for a better grade.

D. Think about ways you could improve the project and apply these ideas to future schoolwork.

**16.** One of your best friends has suffered a miscarriage. How do you respond?

A. Allow your friend to express her feelings and offer your support.

B. Spend time with her, but avoid talking about her loss.

C. Convince her to go out with some friends to get her mind off it.

D. Give her some time to herself.

**17.** One of your co-workers has a habit that annoys you. The problem seems to be getting worse each day. How do you respond?

A. Tell your co-worker what is bothering you.

B. Make a complaint about the behavior to your supervisor.

C. Talk about your coworker beind his back.

D. Suffer in silence.

**18.** You've been feeling stressed out at work and haven't finished projects as quickly as you should. When your boss suddenly assigns you another large project, how to you feel?

A. Anxious about getting all the work done.

B. Overwhelmed by the task before you.

C. Angry that your boss hasn't noticed how overworked you are.

D. Depressed and sure that you can never finish it all.

**19.** If I am scheduled to meet a loved one at a certain time and that person is late, I get worried and eventually start to panic .

A. Frequently B. Sometimes
C. Rarely D. Never

**20.** Others do not want to spend time with me in public because my behavior embarrasses them.

A. Frequently B. Sometimes
C. Rarely D. Never

**21.** I prevent being in situations where I need to show compassion and affection because I feel uncomfortable comforting others.

A. Frequently B. Sometimes
C. Rarely D. Never

**22.** When I am angry, I do not care about what I say or do and end up saying and doing things I regret later and need to apologize for.

A. Frequently B. Sometimes
C. Rarely D. Never

**23.** I feel frequently depressed and unhappy without really knowing why

A. Frequently B. Sometimes
C. Rarely D. Never

**24.** If others point out my mistakes or give me negative feedback about myself, I feel ashamed, embarrassed and then become offensive and angry.

A. Frequently B. Sometimes
C. Rarely D. Never

**25.** Crying makes me feel better so I frequently c when I am angry, ashamed, or embarrassed.

A. Frequently B. Sometimes
C. Rarely D. Never

## ANSWERS

| 1 | 2 | 3 | 4 | 5 | 6 | 7 | 8 | 9 | 10 |
|---|---|---|---|---|---|---|---|---|---|
| B | B | A | B | D | D | C | D | A | B |
| **11** | **12** | **13** | **14** | **15** | **16** | **17** | **18** | **19** | **20** |
| A | A | A | A | D | A | A | A | C | D |
| **21** | **22** | **23** | **24** | **25** | | | | | |
| D | D | D | D | D | | | | | |

## Chapter 22

# TRENDS

**Directions (Qs. 1-36) :** *In the questions given below three alternatives have been given below each one of them. You have to select the right alternative according to your aptitude and mark it in your answer sheet.*

**1.** I like pre-defined rules and regulations—
A. Sometimes B. No
C. Yes

**2.** I found a purse full of money in college premise. I
A. donated the amount among poors
B. gave it to the principal
C. none of these

**3.** I am punctual regarding
A. going to bed B. time
C. meals

**4.** I was travelling on a boat which capsized. Firstly, I
A. rescued others B. saved myself
C. closed by eyes

**5.** When someone asks you for help in odd situations then:
A. you give him/her all possible help
B. you promise him/her help
C. you do not help him/her

**6.** In case my wrist watch is out of order, I
A. would try to repair it myself
B. would give it to watch maker
C. would buy a new watch

**7.** Often I change my opinion in the last moment.
A. Yes B. No
C. Some times

**8.** Generally I am extrovert and well behaved
A. Yes B. No
C. Some times

**9.** I like to use new technique of work
A. Yes B. No
C. Some times

**10.** When someone considers you wrong then:
A. you do not react
B. you consider him/her wrong
C. you try to ward off the misunderstanding on proper occasion.

**11.** The secret of my success is—
A. hard labour B. awakening in night
C. gossiping

**12.** If you are a female and you are talking with a male:
A. You hide your age
B. You are afraid
C. You talk without hesitation

**13.** I do like rules and regulations
A. Yes B. No
C. Some times

**14.** Excellent ideas come to my mind:
A. while working alone
B. while working in group
C. I do not know

**15.** Whenever my little baby cries loudly, then I
A. beat him/her
B. feed milk to him/her
C. make him/her sleep

**16.** When I see a mad person, I
A. approach towards him/her
B. maintain distance from him/her
C. throw stone at him/her

**17.** While driving my car I offer lift who ask for the lift
A. always B. some times
C. never

**18.** When someone tries to convince you then:
A. You get convinced
B. You do not get convinced
C. You hear him/her passionately

**19.** Whenever some one knocks on my closed door then firstly I
A. open the door
B. peep through the lens fitted in the door
C. do not open the door

**20.** I speak to others about my expectation and dreams:
A. rarely B. often
C. sometimes

**21.** Any dispute can be solved by—
A. uarrelling B. count
C. dialogue

**22.** When I do any foolish work then :
A. I feel ashamed
B. I feel proud of my self
C. Nothing happens

**23.** If I were correspondent of any newspaper then I will write on the following subject
A. Cinema and theatre
B. Political events
C. Neither, A nor B

**24.** If I were not human being then :
A. I wish to be a bird
B. I wish to be a horse
C. Can not say

**25.** Suppose, you have worn a new shirt your friend passed a comment that it is not looking good on you. You
A. will change the shirt immediately
B. will take it lightly as it is your style
C. will not change the shirt but feel offended

**26.** I wish to live alone always.
A. Yes B. No
C. Some times

**27.** I want to spend my spare (extra) time :
A. in reading interesting books
B. in reading comics
C. None of these

**28.** Before doing any work I ask myself 'Is it appropriate'?
A. Yes B. No
C. Some times

**29.** If I see the GOD, I will ask for
A. huge wealth B. honesty
C. love

**30.** People call you selfish:
A. Always B. Sometimes
C. Never

**31.** While talking to friends I do not like to express my very personal matters.
A. Yes B. No
C. Sometimes

**32.** Charioteer means
A. selfish B. companion
C. driver of chariot

**33.** Consultation with others helps me to take any decision.
A. Yes B. No
C. I get confused

**34.** Which of the following words is different from others ?
A. probable B. perhaps
C. may be

**35.** After failure:
A. One repents
B. One tries again to succeed
C. Nothing special is happened

**36.** I want to be convinced by arguments
A. Yes B. No
C. Some times

## ANSWERS

| 1 | 2 | 3 | 4 | 5 | 6 | 7 | 8 | 9 | 10 |
|---|---|---|---|---|---|---|---|---|---|
| C | B | B | B | A | B | B | A | A | C |
| 11 | 12 | 13 | 14 | 15 | 16 | 17 | 18 | 19 | 20 |
| A | C | A | A | B | B | B | A | B | A |
| 21 | 22 | 23 | 24 | 25 | 26 | 27 | 28 | 29 | 30 |
| C | A | B | | B | C | A | A | C | C |
| 31 | 32 | 33 | 34 | 35 | 36 | | | | |
| C | C | A | A | B | A | | | | |

## Chapter 23

# SOCIAL INTELLIGENCE

**Directions :** *Each of the following questions is followed by four alternatives. Select the most appropriate answer.*

**1.** In the examination hall, you find that your question paper is too tough to be answered satisfactorily by you. The best thing you can do is:
   A. try cheating from your neighbouring candidate.
   B. leave the paper and walk out.
   C. try attempting those questions first of which you know something.
   D. complain to the examiner about the toughness of the question paper.

**2.** Your best friend is annoyed with you for certain reasons. You will :
   A. try your best to reason out your friend's annoyance.
   B. go out and make new friends.
   C. show indifference.
   D. remind the friend of your good friendship.

**3.** You were invited to a party, but on the day of the party you are informed that the party has been cancelled. You will :
   A. try to find out the reason for its cancellation.
   B. decide that you will never go to that place ever again.
   C. not discuss the matter with anyone.
   D. hold the party at your place instead.

**4.** You find that the cooking gas cylinder is leaking. The first thing you would do is :
   A. switch off the light.
   B. close the knob of the cylinder.
   C. call the fire brigade for help.
   D. alert all the members at home.

**5.** While returning home from a far away place you find that your pocket has been picked. You will :
   A. try to hitch-hike till home.
   B. hire a taxi and pay on reaching home.
   C. go to the nearest police station and lodge a FIR.
   D. call home and ask someone to pick you from the place you make the phone call.

**6.** Your friend has not invited you to his marriage party, will you :
   A. ignore the whole affair?
   B. send him your best wishes?
   C. attend the ceremony?
   D. hold it against him?

**7.** You are interviewed for a new job. Which of the following questions is most important to you?
   A. Remuneration you will be paid.
   B. Opportunities for promotion.
   C. Scope to develop your ideas and use them to improve the working of the organisation.
   D. All the above are equally important.

**8.** You are walking down the street and suddenly you see two hundred–rupee notes on the pavement. What action will you take?
   A. Give the money to beggar.
   B. Pocket it yourself.
   C. Deposit it in the nearest police station.
   D. Leave it where it is.

**9.** You have made some silly mistakes which have been pointed out to you. Will you :
   A. get angry? B. feel miserable?
   C. feel thankful? D. laugh it away?

## ANSWERS

| 1 | 2 | 3 | 4 | 5 | 6 | 7 | 8 | 9 |
|---|---|---|---|---|---|---|---|---|
| C | A | A | B | B | B | D | C | C |

Chapter 24

# PUNCHED HOLE PATTERN-FOLDING & UNFOLDING

**Directions :** *In each one of the following problems, a square transparent sheet with a pattern is given. Figure out from amongst the four alternatives as to how the pattern would appear when the transparent sheet is folded at the dotted line.*

**1.** 

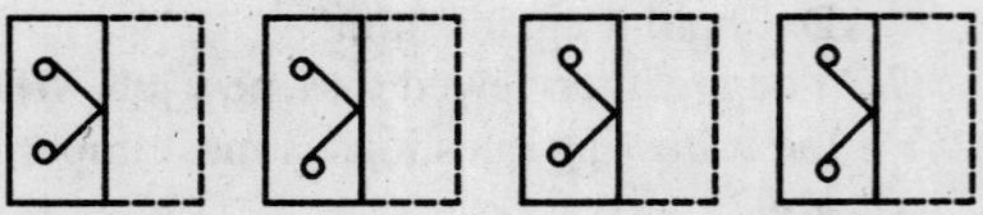

A B C D

**2.** 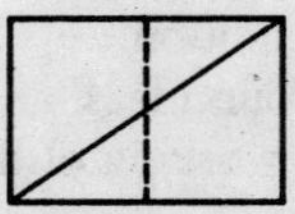

A B C D

**3.** 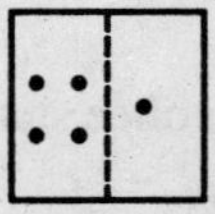

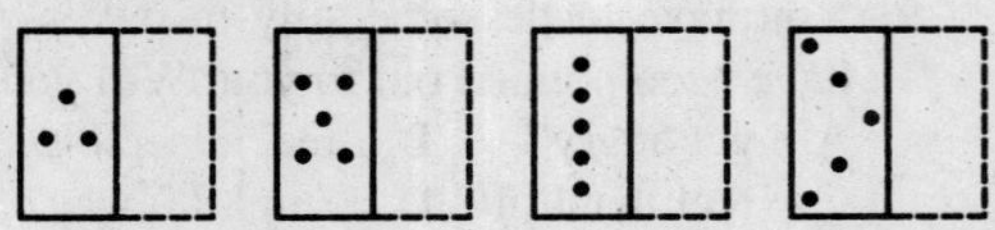

A B C D

**4.** 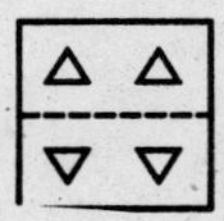

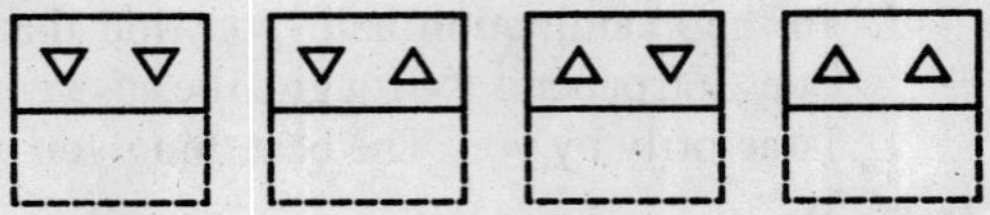

A B C D

**5.** 

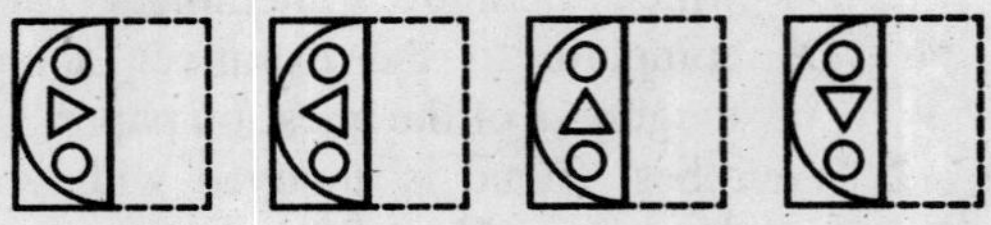

A B C D

**6.** 

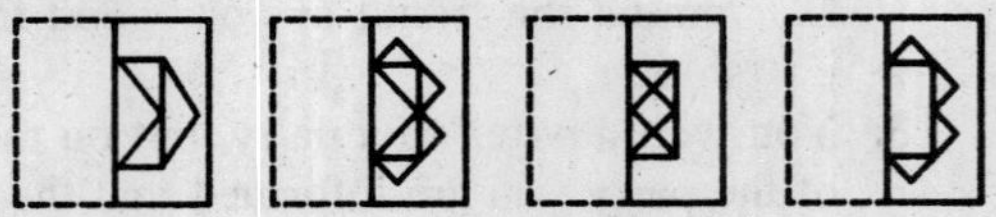

A B C D

**7.** 

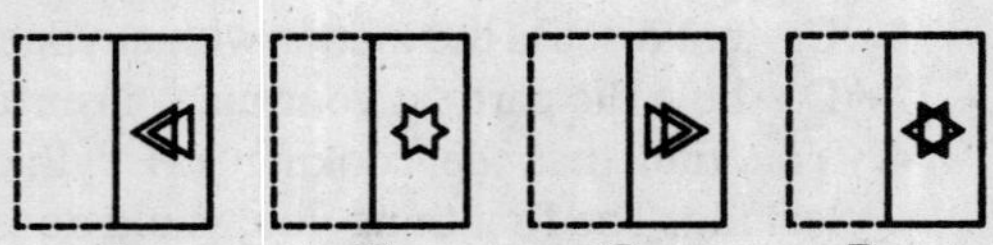

A B C D

**8.** 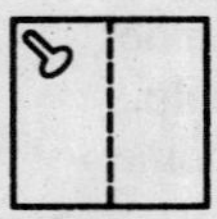

A B C D

9.

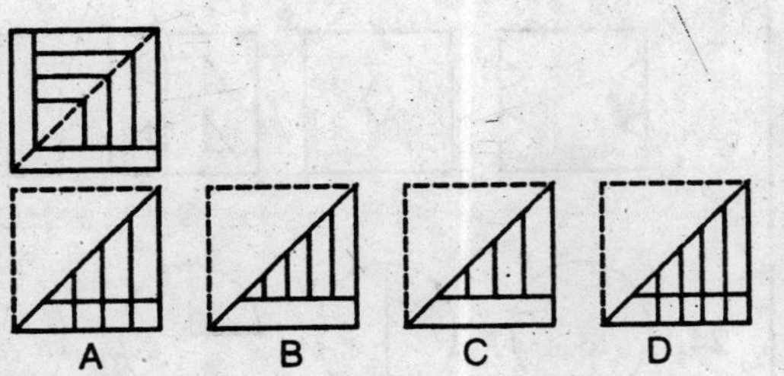


10.

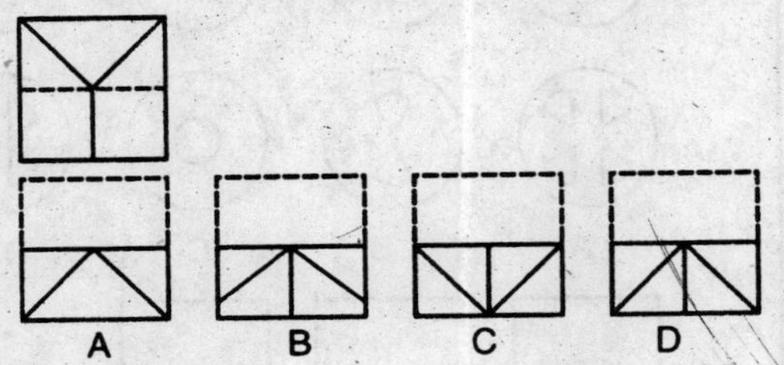


11.

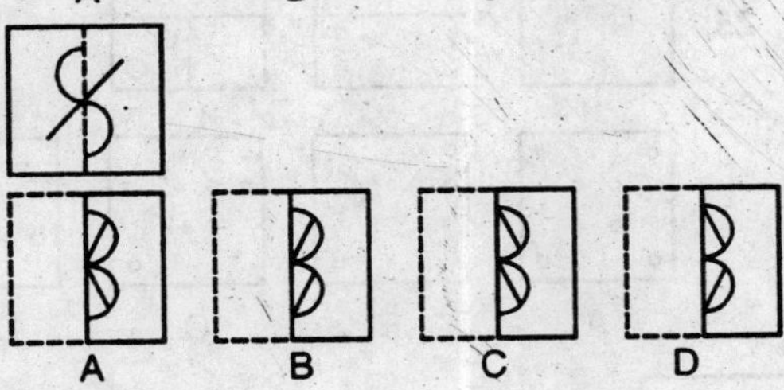


12.

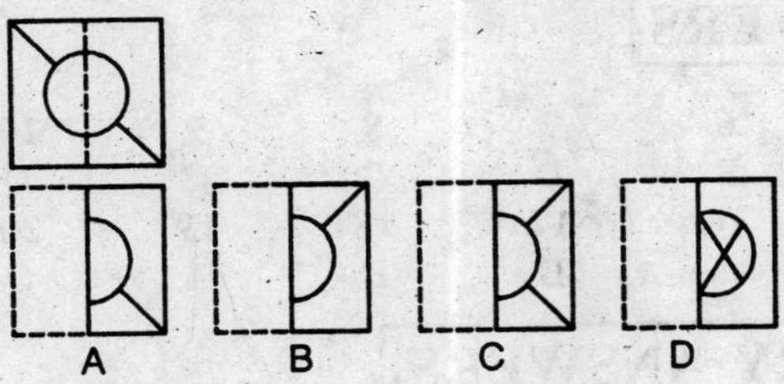


13.

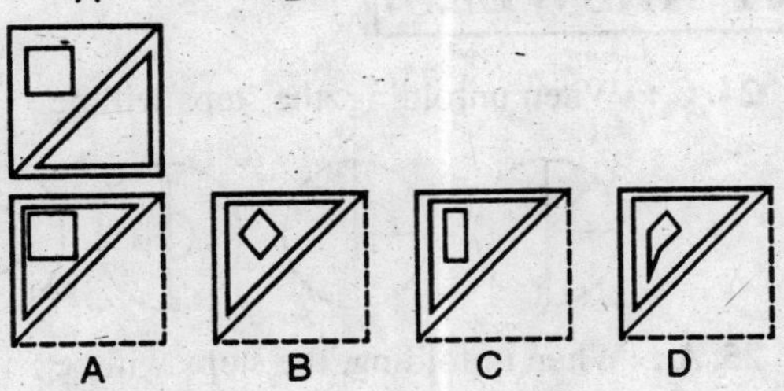


14.

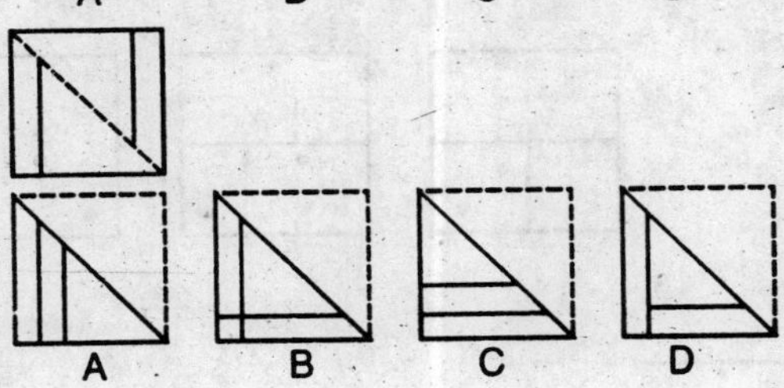


15.

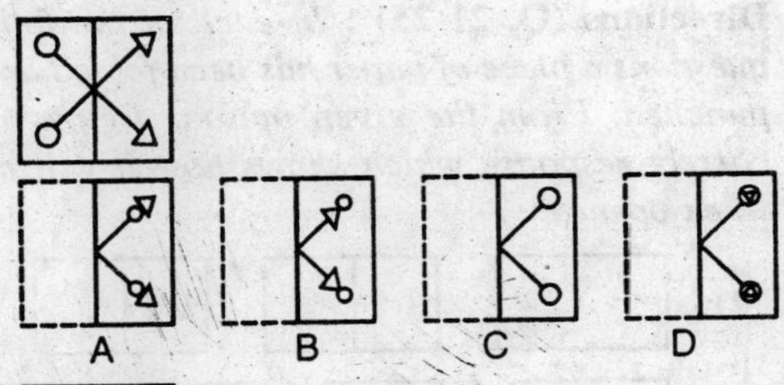


16.

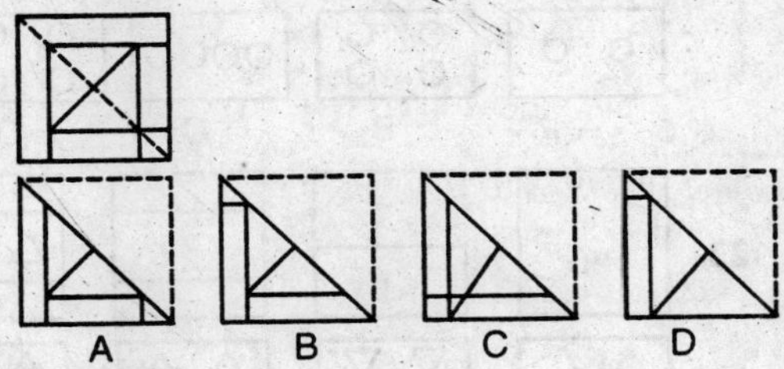


17.

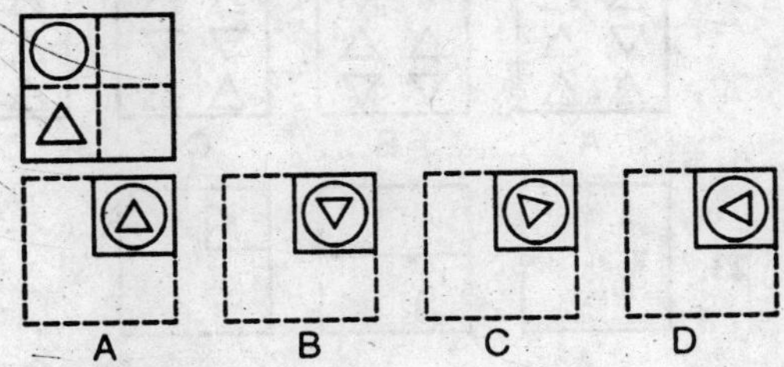


18.

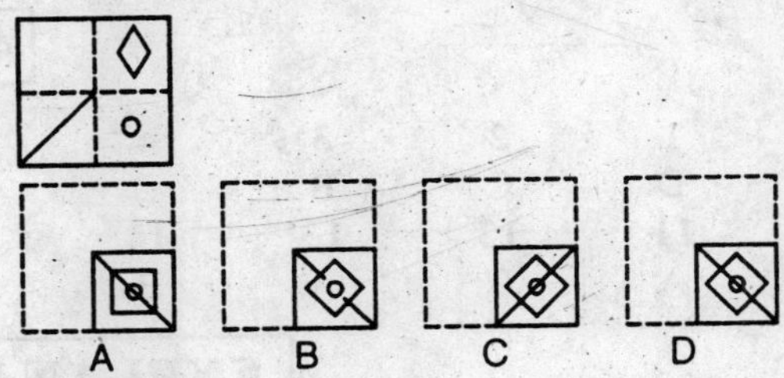


19.

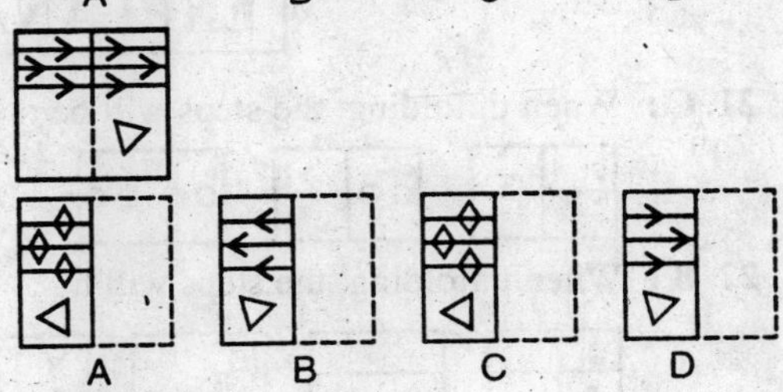


20.

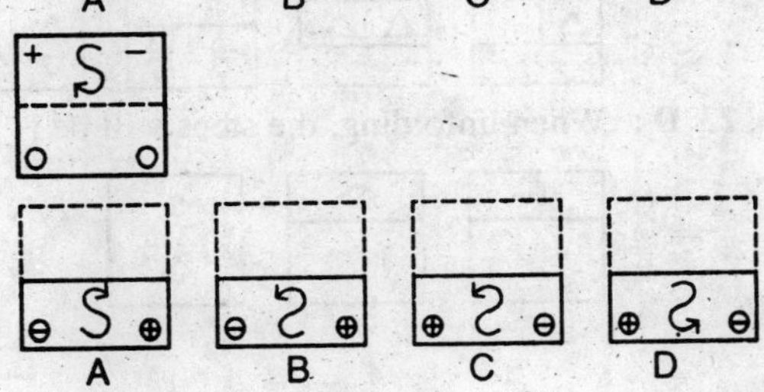

**Directions (Q. 21-25) :** *In each of the following questions a piece of paper has been folded and then punched. From the given options figure out the correct response which shows how it will appear when opened.*

**21.**

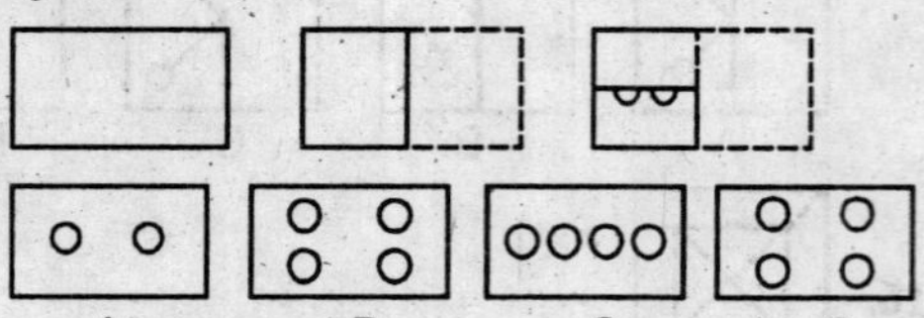

A B C D

**22.**

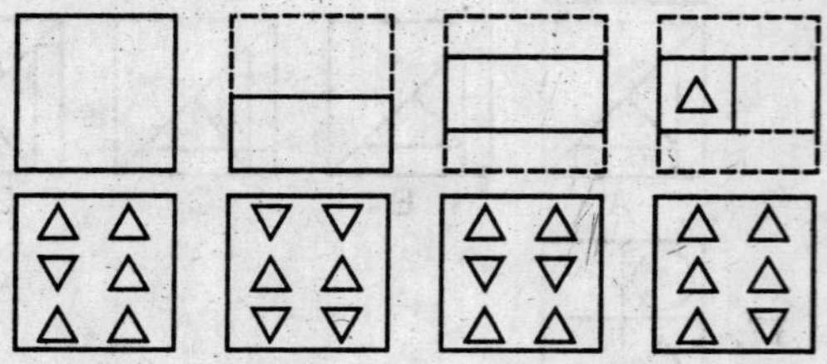

A B C D

**23.**

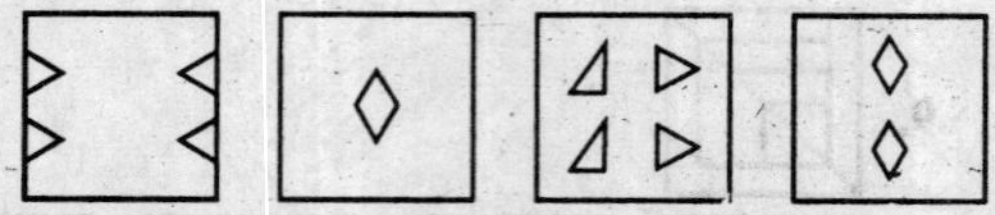

A B C D

**24.**

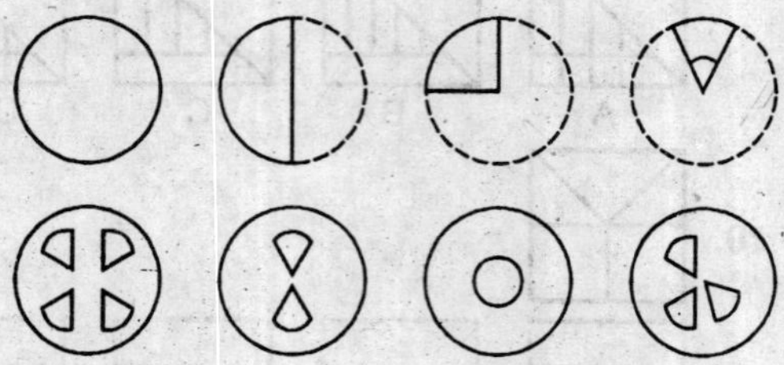

A B C D

**25.**

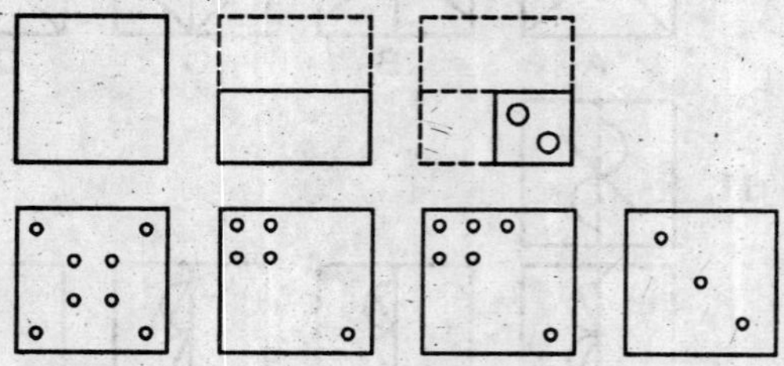

A B C D

## ANSWERS

| 1 | 2 | 3 | 4 | 5 | 6 | 7 | 8 | 9 | 10 |
|---|---|---|---|---|---|---|---|---|---|
| D | C | B | D | B | B | D | B | C | D |
| 11 | 12 | 13 | 14 | 15 | 16 | 17 | 18 | 19 | 20 |
| A | C | A | B | D | A | B | D | A | C |

## EXPLANATORY ANSWERS

**21. C :** When unfolding, the steps will be :

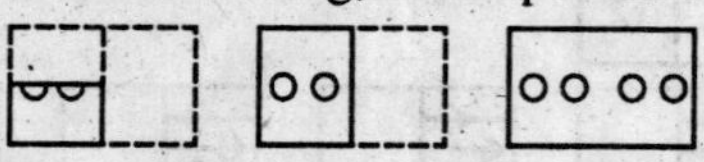

**22. B :** When unfolding, the steps will be :

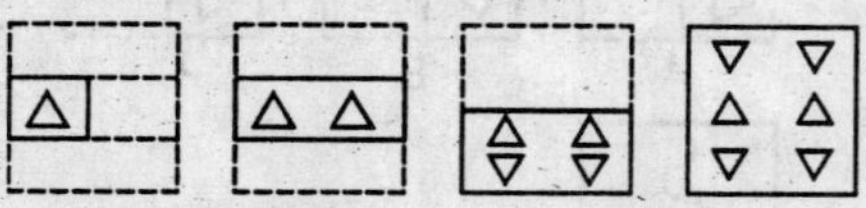

**23. D :** When unfolding, the steps will be :

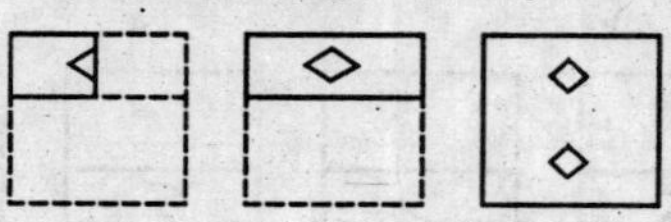

**24. C :** When unfolding, the steps will be :

**25. A :** When unfolding, the steps will be :

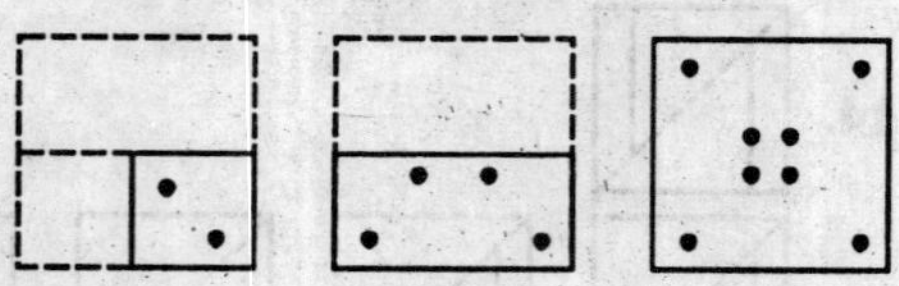

# Chapter 25

# FIGURAL PATTERN-FOLDING & COMPLETION

**Directions :** *In each question, which one of the alternative figures will complete the given figure pattern?*

**1. Pattern** 

**Alternative figures**

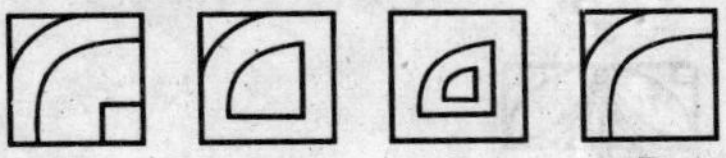

A B C D

**2. Pattern** 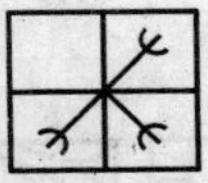

**Alternative figures**

A B C D

**3. Pattern** 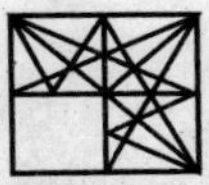

**Alternative figures**

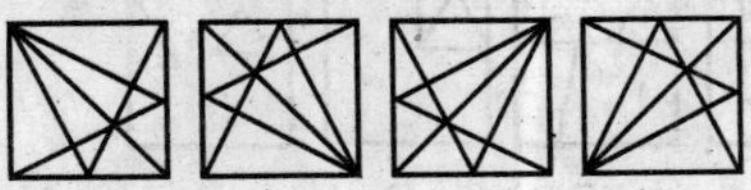

A B C D

**4. Pattern** 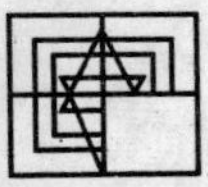

**Alternative figures**

A B C D

**5. Pattern** 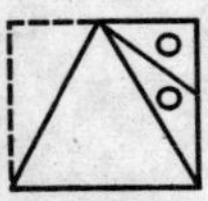

**Alternative figures**

A B C D

**6. Pattern** 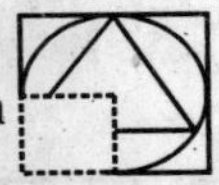

**Alternative figures**

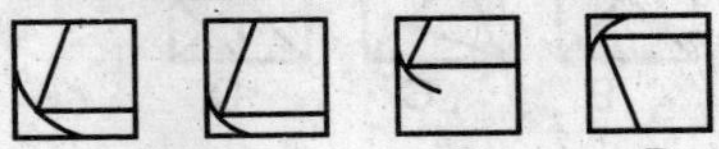

A B C D

**7. Pattern** 

**Alternative figures**

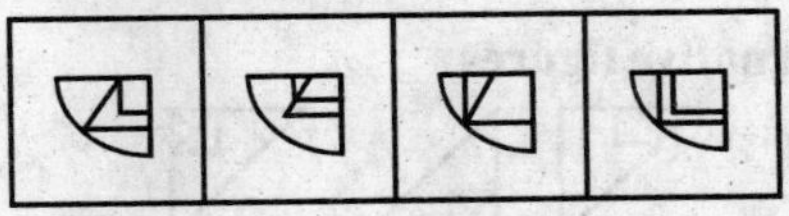

A B C D

**8. Pattern** 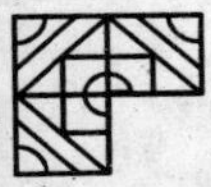

**Alternative figures**

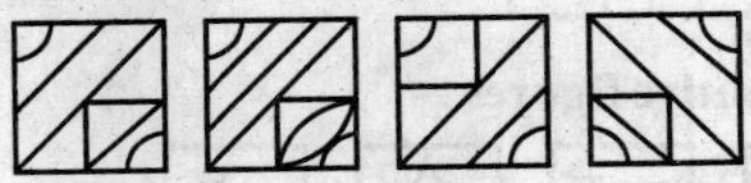

A B C D

**9. Pattern** 

**Alternative figures**

A B C D

**10. Pattern** 

**Alternative figures**

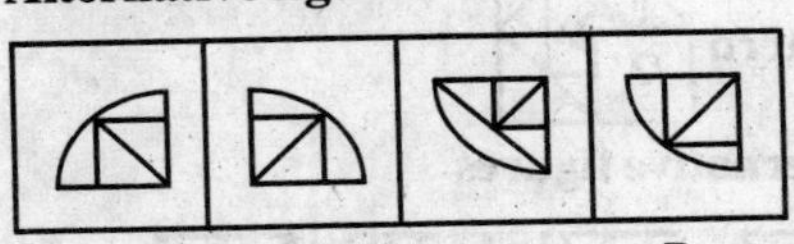

A B C D

**11. Pattern** 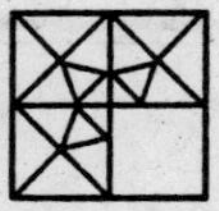

**Alternative figures**

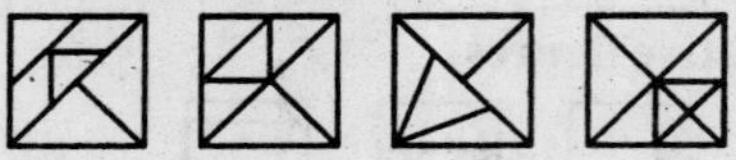

A B C D

**12. Pattern** 

**Alternative figures**

A B C D

**13. Pattern** 

**Alternative figures**

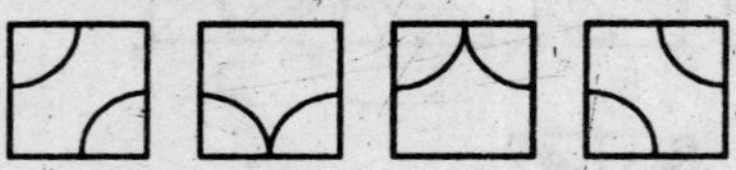

A B C D

**14. Pattern** 

**Alternative figures**

A B C D

**15. Pattern** 

**Alternative figures**

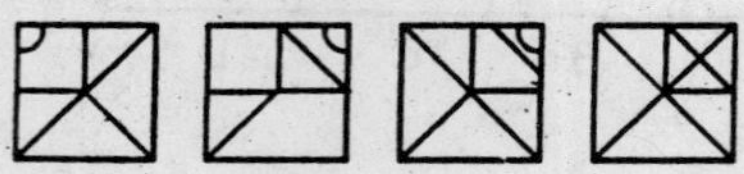

A B C D

**16. Pattern** 

**Alternative figures**

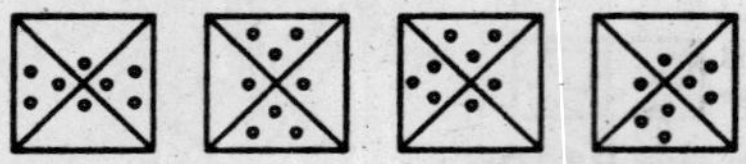

A B C D

**17. Pattern** 

**Alternative figures**

A B C D

**18. Pattern** 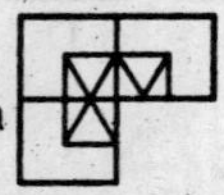

**Alternative figures**

A B C D

**19. Pattern** 

**Alternative figures**

A B C D

**20. Pattern** 

**Alternative figures**

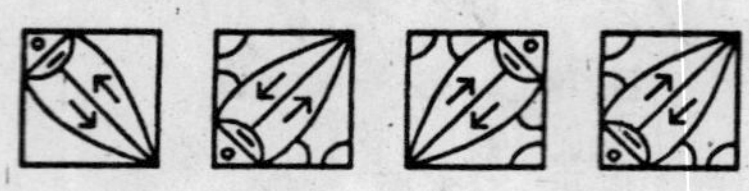

A B C D

# EXPLANATORY ANSWERS

All the completed figures will look like this:

**1. B :** 

**2. A :** 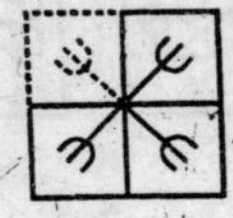

**3. D :** 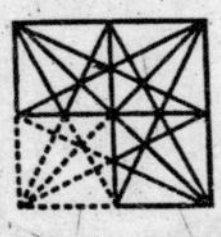

**4. D :** 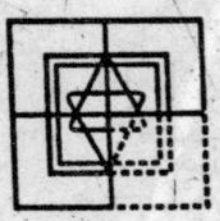

**5. A :** 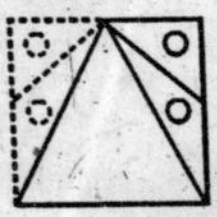

**6. A :** 

**7. B :** 

**8. C :** 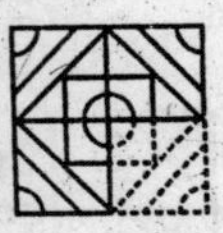

**9. B :** 

**10. C :** 

**11. B :** 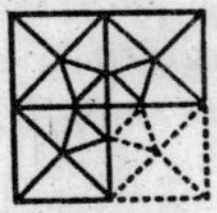

**12. D :** 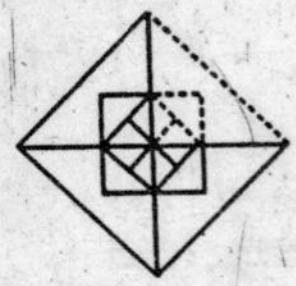

**13. B :** 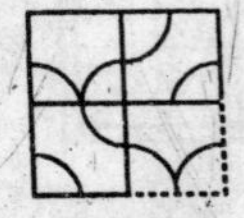

**14. A :** 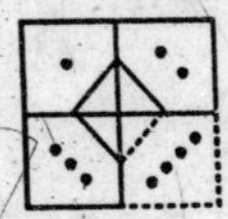

**15. C :** 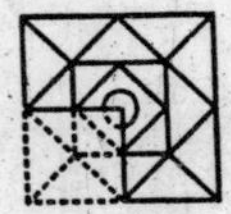

**16. A :** 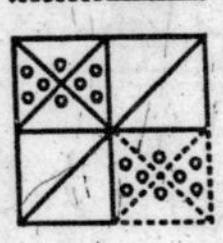

**17. B :** 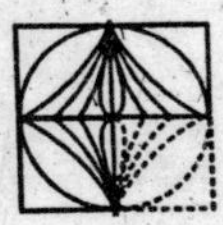

**18. C :** 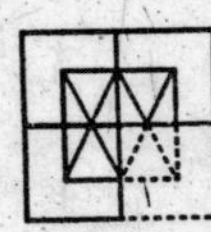

**19. B :** 

**20. D :** 

# Chapter 26

# EMBEDDED FIGURES

**Directions (Qs. 1 to 13) :** *In the questions given below a figure is given. From the given alternatives select the one in which the given figure is embedded.*

**1.** 

A B C D

**2.** 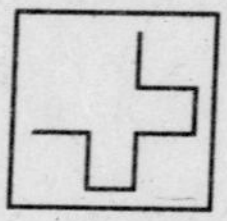

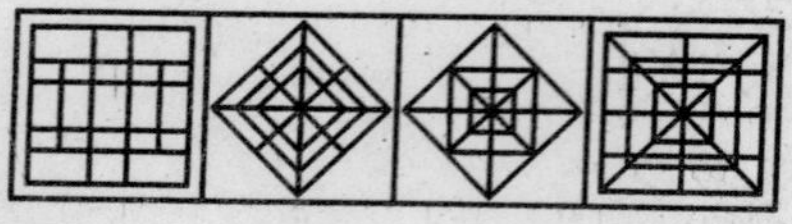

A B C D

[illegible] 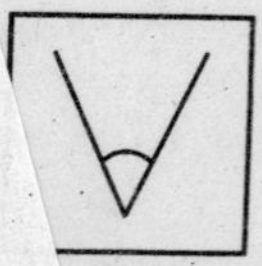

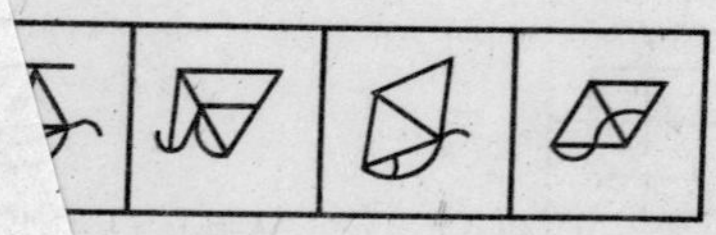

B C D

[illegible] 

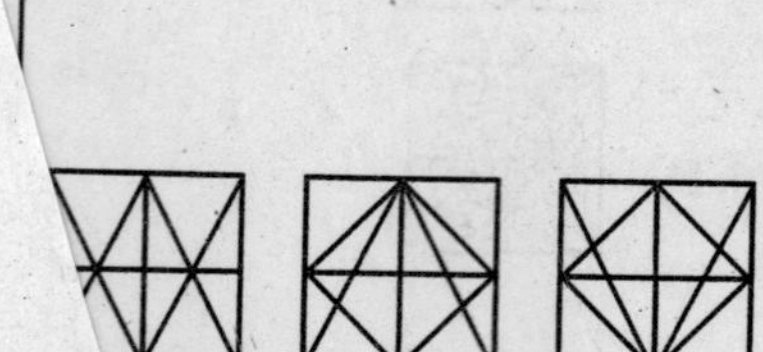

B C D

**5.** 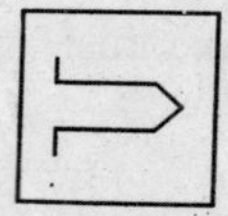

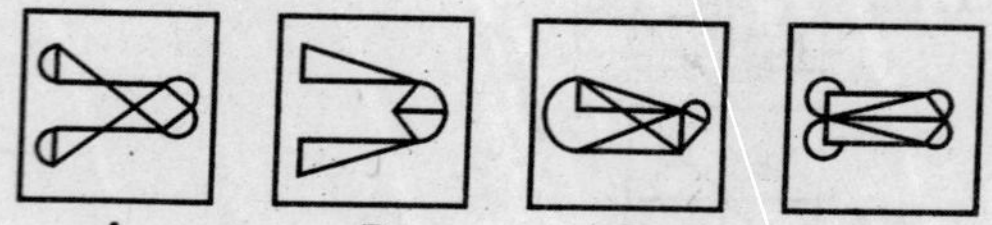

A B C D

**6.** 

A B C D

**7.** 

A B C D

**8.** 

A B C D

**9.** 

A B C D

10.

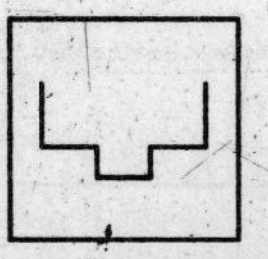

A B C D

11.

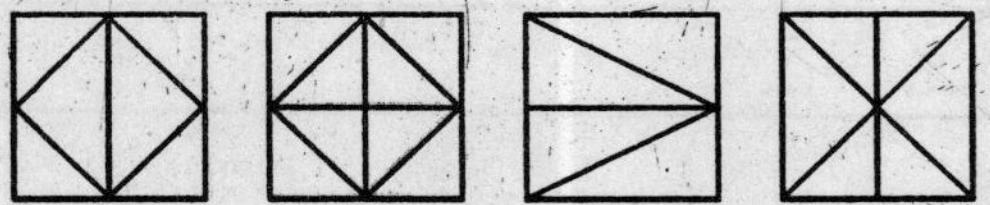

A B C D

12.

A B C D

13.

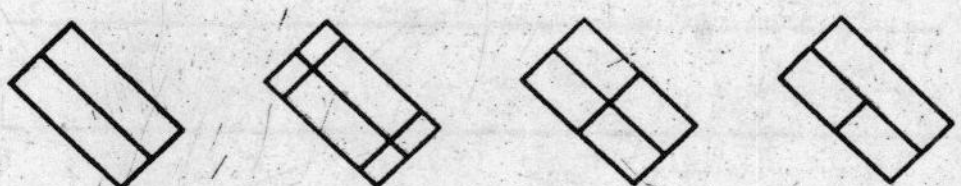

A B C D

## EXPLANATORY ANSWERS

**1. A :** 

**2. A :** 

**3. D :** 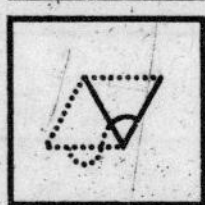

**4. B :** 

**5. A :** 

**6. B :** 

**7. C :** 

**8. A :** 

**9. D :** 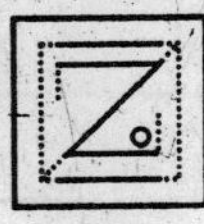

**10. A :** 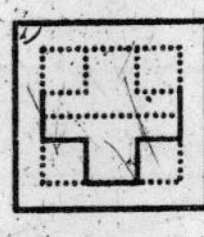

**11. D :** 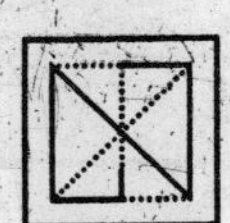

**12. B :** 

**13. D :** 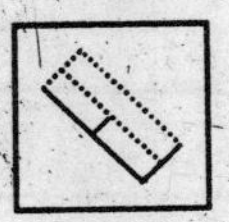

**YOUR SPACE**

# MATHEMATICAL ABILITY

Chapter 1

# NUMBERS

**Natural Numbers :** The numbers like 1, 2, 3, 4. . . . . . . are known as natural numbers.

**Even Numbers :** The numbers, which are divisible by 2, are known as even numbers; *e.g.*, 2, 4, 6, 8, etc.

**Odd Numbers :** The numbers which are not divisible by 2, are known as odd numbers, *e.g.*, 1, 3, 5, 7 . . . . . .

**Prime Numbers :** A number is said to be a prime number if it has only two divisions, namely one and the number itself.

Prime numbers upto 100

2, 3, 5, 7, 11, 13, 17, 19, 23, 29, 31, 37, 41, 43, 47, 53, 59, 61, 67, 71, 73, 79, 83, 89, 97.

**Composite Numbers :** Those numbers which contain more than two different divisions (factors) are called composite numbers; *e.g.*, 4 is a composite number because it is divisible by 1, 2, 4.

**Face Value :** The face value of a digit is the value of the digit itself—whatever it may be.

**Multiplication (Short-cut method)**

**Example 1 :** Multiply $7854 \times 99$

$= 7854 \times (100 - 1)$

$= 785400 - 7854 = 777546$

**Example 2 :** $3618 \times 9999$

$= 3618 \times (10{,}000 - 1)$

$= 36180000 - 3618 = 36176382.$

**Example 3 :** Simplify, $368 \times 746 + 368 \times 254 = ?$

$= 368 \times (746 + 254)$

$= 368 \times 1000 = 368000.$

**Example 4 :** The sum of two numbers is 25 and the difference of their squares is 75. Find the difference between the numbers.

Let the numbers be $x$ and $y$.

Then $\quad x + y = 25$

and $\quad x^2 - y^2 = 75$

$$x - y = \frac{x^2 - y^2}{x + y} = \frac{75}{25} = 3.$$

**Example 5 :** $56747 - (874 + 487 + 5600).$

$= 49{,}786$

**Example 6 :** $6873 + ? = 9820$

Let, $\quad 6873 + x = 9820$

$x = 9820 - 6873 = 2947.$

**Example 7 :** Which one of the following numbers is prime?

(*i*) 331, (*ii*) 481

The square root of 331 is nearly 19. Prime numbers less than 19 are 2, 3, 5, 7, 11, 13 and 17.

Clearly, 331, is not divisible by any of them. So 331 is a prime number.

(*ii*) The square root of 481 is nearly 22

Prime numbers less than 22 are

2, 3, 5, 7, 11, 13, 17, 19

out of these, 481 is divisible by 13. So, 481 is not a prime number.

## EXERCISE

**1.** The local value of 5 in the numeral 4657892 is

A. 5 B. 50,000
C. 10,000 D. Nil

**2.** The face value of 7 in 587689 is

A. 7,000 B. 10,000
C. 7 D. Nil

**3.** $36000 - 888 = 37000 - ?$

A. 3100 B. 1848
C. 1888 D. 1975

**4.** $4658 \times 999 = ?$

A. 4653342 B. 4658000

C. 9987012 D. None of these

**5.** $356 \times 936 - 356 \times 836 = ?$

A. 35600 B. 34500
C. 49630 D. 93600

**6.** $56 \times ? = 2408$

A. 45 B. 53
C. 43 D. 62

**7.** The first Prime number is

A. 1 B. 0
C. 3 D. 2

**8.** The sum of first four Prime numbers is

A. 10 B. 11
C. 16 D. 17

**9.** The largest number of four digits which is exactly divisible by 88, is

A. 9678 B. 8888
C. 9988 D. 9944

**10.** What least number must be subtracted from 13601 to get a number exactly divisible by 87?

A. 49 B. 23
C. 29 D. 31

**11.** Zero is counted as

A. a Whole Number
B. a Prime Number
C. an Integer
D. all of the above

**12.** The greatest among the following is

$\frac{2}{5}, \frac{3}{5}, \frac{11}{5}, \frac{7}{15}, \frac{4}{5}$

A. $\frac{2}{5}$ B. $\frac{11}{5}$
C. $\frac{4}{5}$ D. $\frac{3}{5}$

**13.** In a division sum, the divisor is 12 times the quotient and 5 times the remainder. If the remainder is 48, then the dividend is

A. 240 B. 576
C. 4800 D. 4848

**14.** How many numbers, up to 500, are divisible by 17?

A. 28 B. 30
C. 29 D. 31

**15.** A number, which when divided by 51, leaves a remainder of 19. What is the remainder if the same number is divided by 17?

A. 3 B. 5
C. 2 D. 7

**16.** The largest natural number by which, the product of 3 consecutive even numbers is always divisible, is

A. 16 B. 24
C. 48 D. 96

**17.** $\frac{80}{?} = \frac{?}{20}$

A. 40 B. 400
C. 800 D. 1600

**18.** Find the number, which is nearest to 3006 and exactly divisible by 29.

A. 3100 B. 3016
C. 3121 D. None of these

**19.** A number, which when divided by 779, gives a remainder of 47. By dividing the same number by 19, what would be the remainder?

A. 99 B. 9
C. 8 D. 16

**20.** $106 \times 106 + 94 \times 94$

A. 21032 B. 20032
C. 23032 D. 20072

## EXPLANATORY ANSWERS

**1. B :** The local value of 5 is 50000.

**2. C :** The face value of 7 is 7.
(It is the value of digit itself)

**3. C :** Let, $37000 - x = 36000 - 888$
$x = 37000 - 36000 + 888 = 1888.$

**4. A :** $4658 \times 999 = 4658 \times (1000 - 1)$
$= 4658000 - 4658 = 4653342.$

**5. A :** $356 \times 936 - 356 \times 836 = 356\ (936 - 836)$
$= 356 \times 100 = 35600.$

**6. C :** $56 \times x = 2408$

$$x = \frac{2408}{56} = 43.$$

**7. D :** The first prime number is 2.

**8. D :** $(2 + 3 + 5 + 7) = 17$

**9. D :** Largest number of 4 digits = 9999.

88 ) 9999 ( 113
88
119
88
319
264
55

$\therefore$ Required number is = 9999 – 55 = 9944.

**10. C :** 87 ) 1360 ( 156
87
490
435
551
522
29

$\therefore$ Required number is 29.

**11. A :** Zero is a whole number.

**12. B :** $\frac{2}{5}, \frac{3}{5}, \frac{11}{5}, \frac{7}{15}, \frac{4}{5}$

$$= \frac{6}{15}, \frac{9}{15}, \frac{33}{15}, \frac{7}{15}, \frac{12}{15} = \frac{11}{5}$$

**13. D :** Let the quotient = Q
Remainder = R
Then divisor = 12 Q = 5R
Now, R = 48
Dividend = (20 × 240 + 48) = 4848.

**14. C :** Divide 500 by 17
The quotient is 29
Hence, the number = 29.

**15. C :** Just divide 19 by 17. The remainder is 2. This would lead us to the answer. (Note that the second divisor, *i.e.*, 17, must be the factor of 1st divisor, *i.e.*, 51).

**16. C :** $2 \times 4 \times 6 = 48$

**17. A :** Let $\frac{80}{x} = \frac{x}{20}$

$x^2 = 80 \times 20 = 1600$

$x = \sqrt{1600} = 40.$

**18. B :** On dividing 3006 by 29, the ramainder is 19 which is more than half of 29. So, we have to add (29 – 19) = 10 to the number. So, required number is = (3006 + 10) = 3016.

**19. B :** Number = (779 × K) + 47
where K is quotient.
= (19 × 41 × K) + (19 × 2) + 9
= 19 × (41K + 2) + 9
= 19 × (new quotient) + 9
= Remainder 9.

**20. D :** $106 \times 106 + 94 \times 94 = (106)^2 + (94)^2$

$$= \frac{1}{2}\left[2\left(a^2 + b^2\right)\right] = \frac{1}{2}\left[(a+b)^2 + (a-b)^2\right]$$

$$= \frac{1}{2}\left[(106+94)^2 + (106-94)^2\right]$$

$$= \frac{1}{2}\left[(200)^2 + (12)^2\right]$$

$$= \frac{1}{2}[40000 + 144] = \frac{40144}{2}$$

= 20072.

# Chapter 2

# H.C.F. AND L.C.M.

**HCF :** The **Highest Common Factor** of two or more than two numbers is the greatest number that exactly divides each one of them.

**Example 1 :** Find the HCF of 3556 and 3444.

3444 ) 3556 ( 1
3444
112 ) 3444 ( 30
3360
84 ) 112 ( 1
84
28 ) 84 ( 3
84
×

So, HCF is 28.

**Note :** If HCF of more than two numbers is required, then proceed as follows : ?

A. Find the HCF of any two numbers say $x$
B. Then find the HCF of $x$ and the next number.
C. Proceed in a similar manner with other numbers.
D. In the division exercise of last number, HCF would be found.

**Example 2 :** Find the HCF of 1026, 1215, 2349.

**Solution :** 1215 ) 2349 ( 1
1215
1134 ) 1215 ( 1
1134
81 ) 1134 ( 14
81
324
324
×

Thus HCF of 2349 and 1215 is 81.
Now find the HCF of 81 and 1026.

81 ) 1026 ( 12
81
216
162
54 ) 81 ( 1
54
27 ) 54 ( 2
54
×

Hence, the required H.C.F. is 27.

**LCM :** A number, which can be divided without remainder, by two or more than two numbers, is called a common multiple of those numbers. The least number, which can be divided (without a remainder) by two or more other numbers, is called **Lowest Common Multiple** of all those numbers.

**Example 3 :** Find the LCM of 7, 28, 35, 42

**Solution :**

| | | | | |
|---|---|---|---|---|
| 7 | 7, | 28, | 35, | 42 |
| 2 | 1, | 4, | 5, | 6 |
| | 1, | 2, | 5, | 3 |

$= 7 \times 2 \times 1 \times 2 \times 5 \times 3 = 420.$

**Formula :**

1. Product of two numbers = (their HCF) × (their LCM).

2. $\text{LCM} = \dfrac{\text{Product of the Numbers}}{\text{HCF of the Numbers}}$

3. $\text{HCF of Fractions} = \dfrac{\text{HCF of the Numbers}}{\text{LCM of Denominator}}$

4. $\text{LCM of Fractions} = \dfrac{\text{LCM of the Numbers}}{\text{HCF of Denominators}}$.

**Example 4 :** Find LCM of 852 and 1491.

**Solution :** Find HCF of 852 and 1491 which is 213.

$$\text{LCM} = \frac{\text{Product of Numbers}}{\text{HCF}}$$

$$= \frac{852 \times 1491}{213} = 5964.$$

**Example 5 :** The HCF of two numbers is 4 and their LCM is 576. If one of the numbers is 64, find the other number.

**Solution :** The other number is

$$= \frac{\text{HCF} \times \text{LCM}}{\text{Given number}}$$

$$= \frac{4 \times 576}{64} = 36$$

**Example 6.** Three containers contain milk of volumes 36 litres, 45 liters and 72 litres respectively. What can be the biggest measure to measure all the different quantities?

**Solution :** Find the HCF of all the three quantities.

Biggest Measure = HCF of 36, 45, 72 = 9 litres.

**Example 7 : Find the smallest number that is exactly divisible by 5, 10, 15 and 20.**

**Solution :** Find the LCM of the given numbers.

**LCM of 5, 10, 15, 20 is 60.**

**Example 8.** Find the least number, which when divided by 7, 6, 8, 12 leaves the same remainder 2 in each case.

**Solution :** Required number = LCM of given numbers + 2, which is = 168 + 2 = 170.

## EXERCISE

**1.** Find the HCF of 42, 63, 140

A. 14 B. 9

C. 21 D. 7

**2.** LCM of 22, 54, 108, 135 and 198 is

A. 330 B. 1980

C. 5940 D. 11880

**3.** Which one of the following fractions is greatest of all?

$\frac{7}{8}, \frac{6}{7}, \frac{4}{5}, \frac{5}{6}$

A. $\frac{4}{5}$ B. $\frac{6}{7}$

C. $\frac{5}{6}$ D. $\frac{7}{8}$

**4.** HCF of $\frac{1}{2}, \frac{2}{3}, \frac{3}{4}$ and $\frac{4}{5}$ is

A. 1 B. 12

C. $\frac{4}{5}$ D. $\frac{1}{60}$

**5.** LCM of $\frac{3}{2}, \frac{9}{4}, \frac{6}{16}$ and $\frac{12}{32}$ is

A. $\frac{18}{1}$ B. $\frac{17}{1}$

C. $\frac{36}{1}$ D. $\frac{42}{1}$

**6.** There are four containers having liquid measures as follows:
96 Litres, 528 Litres, 1584 Litres and 2016 Litres. What can be the biggest measure to measure all of them?

A. 48 B. 52

C. 62 D. 58

**7.** Find HCF and LCM of

$\frac{2}{3}, \frac{8}{9}, \frac{32}{81}, \frac{10}{27}.$

HCF A. $\frac{2}{81}$ B. $\frac{3}{81}$

C. $\frac{4}{81}$ D. $\frac{5}{81}$

LCM A. $\frac{160}{3}$ B. $\frac{160}{4}$

C. $\frac{160}{5}$ D. $\frac{160}{6}$

**8.** Arranging the following fractions in the Descending order which one will be the first fraction?

$\frac{2}{3}, \frac{5}{9}, \frac{7}{11}, \frac{3}{7}, \frac{9}{13}, \frac{15}{19}.$

A. $\frac{15}{19}$ B. $\frac{9}{13}$

C. $\frac{7}{11}$ D. $\frac{5}{9}$

**9.** Reduce $\frac{561}{784}$ to lowest terms.

A. $\frac{3}{7}$ B. $\frac{3}{4}$

C. $\frac{5}{8}$ D. $\frac{6}{4}$

**10.** The smallest number, which is divisible by 12, 15, 20 and is a perfect square, is

A. 400 B. 900

C. 1600 D. 3600

**11.** Which one of the following is in ascending

order?

A. $\frac{5}{7}, \frac{7}{8}, \frac{9}{11}$ B. $\frac{9}{11}, \frac{7}{8}, \frac{5}{7}$

C. $\frac{5}{7}, \frac{9}{11}, \frac{7}{8}$ D. $\frac{7}{8}, \frac{5}{7}, \frac{9}{11}$

**12.** LCM of $\frac{3}{4}, \frac{6}{7}, \frac{9}{11}$ is

A. 3 B. 18

C. $\frac{3}{56}$ D. $\frac{9}{28}$

**13.** There are 3 pieces of woodden logs which are 42 m, 49 m and 63 m long. What is the greatest possible length by which these can be measured?

A. 7 m B. 14 m

C. 42 m D. 63 m

**14.** The least number, which when divided by 5, 6, 7 and 8, leaves a remainder 3 but when divided by 9, leaves no remainder, is

A. 1677 B. 1683

C. 2523 D. 3363

**15. The largest number, which exactly divides 210, 315, 147 and 168 is**

**A. 3** **B. 7**

**C. 21** **D. 4410**

**16.** Which one of the following is in the descending order?

A. $\frac{3}{8}, \frac{8}{15}, \frac{11}{23}, \frac{26}{81}$

B. $\frac{26}{81}, \frac{11}{23}, \frac{8}{15}, \frac{3}{8}$

C. $\frac{8}{15}, \frac{11}{23}, \frac{3}{8}, \frac{26}{81}$

D. $\frac{3}{8}, \frac{11}{23}, \frac{8}{15}, \frac{61}{81}$

**17. Five bells begin to toll together and toll respectively at the intervals of 6, 7, 8, 9 and 12 seconds. After how many seconds, will they toll together again?**

**A. 72 seconds** **B. 612 seconds**

**C. 504 seconds** **D. 318 seconds**

**18.** Two numbers are in the ratio of 3 : 4 and the product of their LCM and HCF is 10800. The sum of the numbers is

A. 180 B. 210

C. 225 D. 240

**19.** If the L.C.M. of $x$, $y$ is $z$, then their HCF is

A. $\frac{xy}{z}$ B. $xyz$

C. $\frac{(x+y)}{z}$ D. $\frac{z}{xy}$

**20.** The highest common factor of 70 and 245 is

A. 35 B. 55

C. 45 D. 65

## EXPLANATORY ANSWERS

**1. D :** HCF of 42 and 63 is 21.
HCF of 21 and 140 is 7.
HCF of 42, 63, 140 is 7.

**2. C :** LCM is 5940.

**3. D :** $\frac{7}{8} = 0.875, \frac{6}{7} = 0.857, \frac{4}{5} = 0.8, \frac{5}{6} = 0.833$

So $\frac{7}{8}$ is the greatest.

**4. D :** $\frac{\text{HCF of } 1,2,3,4}{\text{LCM of } 2,3,4,5} = \frac{1}{60}$.

**5. A :** Find $\frac{\text{LCM of } 3,9,6,12}{\text{HCF of } 2,4,16,32} = \frac{36}{2} = \frac{18}{1}$.

**6. A :** Find the HCF
Which is = 48

**7. A :** HCF of given fractions

$= \frac{\text{HCF of } 2, 8, 32, 10}{\text{LCM of } 3, 9, 81, 27} = \frac{2}{81}$

$\text{LCM} = \frac{\text{LCM of } 2, 8, 32, 10}{\text{HCF of } 3, 9, 81, 27} = \frac{160}{3}$

**8. A :** Express them in Decimal form.

$\frac{15}{19}, \frac{9}{13}, \frac{2}{3}, \frac{7}{11}, \frac{5}{9}, \frac{3}{7}$ is descending order.

**9. B :** (Find) HCF of 561, 748, *i.e.*, 187.
Divide numerator and denominator by 187, we get $\frac{3}{4}$.

**10. B :** (Find) LCM of 12, 15, 20, *i.e.*, 60
$60 = 2^2 \times 5 \times 3$

So, required no = 60 × 15 = 900

**11. C :** Decimal form:

$\frac{5}{7} = 0.714,\ \frac{7}{8} = 0.875,\ \frac{9}{11} = 0.818.$

Now, the ascending order is

$\frac{5}{7} < \frac{9}{11} < \frac{7}{8}.$

**12. B :** $\text{LCM} = \frac{\text{LCM of } 3, 6, 9}{\text{HCF of } 4, 7, 11} = \frac{18}{1}$

**13. A :** Greatest possible length is equal to the H.C.F. of 42, 49, 63, which is 7m.

**14. B :** LCM of 5, 6, 7, 8 is 840

Required no. is (840 × 2 + 3) = 1683.

**15. C :** Find the HCF = 21

**16. C :** $\frac{8}{15}, \frac{11}{23}, \frac{3}{8}, \frac{26}{81}$ (Find Decimal form).

**17. C :** LCM of 6, 7, 8, 9, 12 is 504.

**18. B :** Let the number be $3x$ and $4x$.

Their HCF = $x$ and LCM = $12x$.

$\therefore\ 12x \times x = 10800$ or $x^2 = 900$

$x = 30$

So, the numbers are 90 and 120.

The sum of numbers = 210.

**19. A :** $\text{HCF} = \frac{\text{Product of Numbers}}{\text{Their LCM}} = \frac{xy}{}$

**20. A :** The highest common factor of 70 and 245 is

the H.C.F. of bothe numbers.

```
70 ) 245 ( 3
     210
     ---
      35 ) 70 ( 2
           70
           --
            ×
```

Hence, the required HCF = 35.

Chapter 3

# DECIMAL FRACTIONS

Those fractions, in which, denominators are of the power of 10, are called **Decimal Fractions**.

**Example 1 :** $0.64 = \frac{64}{100} = \frac{16}{25}$.

**Addition Rule:** Numbers are to proceed under each other so that the decimal point lies in one column.

**Example 2 :** 427 + 4.027 + 0.427 + 2.0014.

$$\begin{array}{r} 427 \\ 4.027 \\ 0.427 \\ 2.0014 \\ \hline 433.4554 \\ \hline \end{array}$$

**Example 3 :** $0.5 \times 0.05 \times 0.005 \times 50 = ?$

**Solution :** $5 \times 5 \times 5 \times 50 = 6250$

The sum of decimal places of given numbers = six.

So, the required number is = 0.006250.

**Example 4 : Express the following as regular fractions.**

***(i)*** $0.\bar{8}$ ***(ii)*** $0.\overline{92}$ ***(iii)*** $0.\overline{059}$

**Solution :** *(i)* $0.\bar{8} = \frac{8}{9}$ *(ii)* $0.\overline{92} = \frac{92}{99}$

*(iii)* $0.\overline{059} = \frac{59}{999}$.

**Example 5 :** Divide 25 by 0.05.

**Solution :** $\frac{25}{0.05} = \frac{25 \times 100}{0.05 \times 100} = \frac{2500}{5} = 500.$

## EXERCISE

**1.** $0.09 \times 0.008 = ?$

A. 0.072 B. 0.0072
C. 0.00072 D. 0.72

**2.** $0.8 + 0.88 + 0.088 + 8.806$

A. 10.574 B. 10.876
C. 0.086 D. 9.574

**3.** $15.60 \times 0.30 = ?$

A. 4.68 B. 0.458
C. 0.468 D. 0.0468

**4.** $\frac{17.28 \div ?}{3.6 \times 0.2} = 200$

A. 120 **B. 1.20**
**C. 12** **D. 0.12**

**5.** $\frac{0.24 \times 0.35}{0.14 \times 0.15 \times 0.02} = ?$

A. 2 B. 20
C. 200 D. 2000

**6.** The value of $\frac{47}{10000}$ is

A. 0.0047 B. 0.0470
C. 0.00047 D. 0.000047

**7.** $8.32 \times 0.999 = ?$

A. 0.831168 B. 8.31618
C. 8.31168 D. 8.31668

**8.** $\frac{0.5 \times 0.5 \times 0.5 + 0.6 \times 0.6 \times 0.6}{0.5 \times 0.5 - 0.5 \times 0.6 + 0.6 \times 0.6}$

**A. 0.3** **B. 1.1**
**C. 0.1** **D. 0.61**

**9.** $\left(0.\bar{6} + 0.\bar{7} + 0.\bar{8} + 0.\bar{3}\right) = ?$

A. $2\frac{3}{10}$ B. $2\frac{33}{100}$
C. $2\frac{2}{3}$ D. $2.\overline{35}$

**10.** The value of $4.1\dot{2}$ is

A. $4\frac{11}{99}$ B. $5\frac{2}{9}$
C. $4\frac{11}{90}$ D. None of these

# EXPLANATORY ANSWERS

**1. C :** $9 \times 8 = 72$

$\therefore\ 0.09 \times 0.008 = 0.00072.$

**2. A :** 10.574.

**3. A :** 4.68.

**4. D :** Let $\dfrac{17.28 \div x}{3.6 \times 0.2} = 200$

then, $\dfrac{17.28}{x} = 200 \times 3.6 \times 0.2$

$x = \dfrac{17.28}{144} = 0.12$

**5. C :** **6. A :** **7. C :**

**8. B :** $\dfrac{a^3 + b^3}{a^2 - ab + b^2} = (a + b)$

$= 0.5 + 0.6 = 1.1.$

**9. C :** $\dfrac{6}{9} + \dfrac{7}{9} + \dfrac{8}{9} + \dfrac{3}{9} = \dfrac{24}{9} = \dfrac{8}{3} = 2\dfrac{2}{3}.$

**10. C :** The value of $4.1\dot{2}$ is

$4.1\dot{2} = 4 + 0.1\dot{2} = 4 + \dfrac{12 - 1}{90} = 4\dfrac{11}{90}.$

# Chapter 4

# SIMPLIFICATION

During the process of simplification of fractions, we come across the following signs:

(1) B — means brackets ( )

(2) O — of, which means multiplication within brackets

(3) D — means Division (÷)

(4) M — means Multiplication (×)

(5) A — means Addition (+)

(6) S — means Subtraction (–)

In sum, it is denoted by B O D M A S.

**Example 1 :** Simplify

$$4-\left[3-\left\{7-\left(5-\overline{4-3}\right)\right\}\right]$$

**Solution :** $4-\left[3-\left\{7-(5-1)\right\}\right]$

$= 4-\left[3-\left\{7-4\right\}\right]$

$= 4-\left[3-3\right]$

$= 4-0=4.$

**Example 2 :** $27-5+22$

**Solution :** $22+22=44.$

**Example 3 :** $12+12+12\div 12$

**Solution :** $12+12+12\times\frac{1}{12}=12+12+1=25.$

**Example 4 :** $\frac{1}{2}\div\frac{3}{4}\times\frac{3}{4}$

**Solution :** $\frac{1}{2}\times\frac{4}{3}\times\frac{3}{4}=\frac{1}{2}$

**Example 5 :** $\frac{1}{2}\div\frac{2}{3}$ of $\frac{3}{4}$

**Solution :** $\frac{1}{2}\div\frac{1}{2}=1$

**Example 6 :** $\frac{1}{2}\div\frac{2}{3}\div\frac{3}{4}$

**Solution :** $\frac{1}{2}\times\frac{3}{2}\times\frac{4}{3}=1$

**Example 7 :** What is the value of $9989\times 9989-121=?$

**Solution :** $(9989)^2-(11)^2$

$=(9989+11)(9989-11)$

$=10000\times 9978=99780000.$

## EXERCISE

**1.** $171\div 19\times 9=?$

A. 0 B. 1

C. 18 D. 81

**2.** $\dfrac{48-12\times 3+9}{12-9\div 3}=?$

A. 3 B. 21

C. $\frac{7}{3}$ D. $\frac{1}{3}$

**3.** $\dfrac{69-14\times 3+2}{9\times 5-(5)^2}=?$

A. 1.45 B. 2.75

C. 26.5 D. 265

**4.** $\frac{31}{10}\times\frac{3}{10}+\frac{7}{5}\div 20=?$

A. 0 B. 1

C. 100 D. $\frac{107}{200}$

**5.** $\dfrac{[illegible]^{2}\times 18^{4}}{3^{16}}$ is = ?

A. $\frac{2}{3}$ B. $\frac{4}{9}$

C. $\frac{16}{81}$ D. $\frac{32}{243}$

6. $\dfrac{\frac{1}{2} \div 4 + 20}{\frac{1}{2} \times 4 + 20} = ?$

A. $\frac{81}{88}$ B. $2\frac{3}{11}$

C. $\frac{161}{176}$ D. 1

7. $\dfrac{13.75 \times 13.75 - 3.75 \times 3.75}{13.75 - 3.75} = ?$

A. 18.50 B. 16.50

C. 17.50 D. 21.50

8. $9.75 \times 9.75 - 2 \times 4.75 \times 9.75 + 4.75 \times 4.75 = ?$

A. 29 B. 25

C. 28 D. 32

9. $\left(2\frac{2}{19} + \frac{19}{40}\right)^2 - \left(2\frac{2}{19} - \frac{19}{40}\right)^2 = ?$

A. 6 B. 4

C. 7 D. 8

10. $\dfrac{(2.17 + 9.11)^2 + (2.17 - 9.11)^2}{2.17 \times 2.17 + 9.11 \times 9.11} = ?$

A. 3 B. 2

C. 4 D. 6

# EXPLANATORY ANSWERS

**1. D :** $171 \div 19 \times 9 = 171 \times \frac{1}{19} \times 9 = 81.$

**2. C :** Given expression

$= \dfrac{48 - 36 + 9}{12 - 3} = \dfrac{21}{9} = \dfrac{7}{3}$

**3. A :** $\dfrac{69 - 42 + 2}{45 - 25} = \dfrac{29}{20} = 1.45.$

**4. B :** $\dfrac{93}{100} + \dfrac{7}{100} = 1.$

**5. C :** $\dfrac{(3^2)^2 \times (3 \times 3 \times 2)^4}{3^{16}} = \dfrac{3^4 \times 3^8 \times 2^4}{3^{16}}$

$= \dfrac{2^4}{3^4} = \dfrac{16}{81}$

**6. C :** $\dfrac{\frac{1}{2} \times \frac{1}{4} + 20}{2 + 20} = \dfrac{161}{8} \times \dfrac{1}{22} = \dfrac{161}{176}.$

**7. C :** Formula $\dfrac{a^2 - b^2}{a - b} = a + b$

$= 13.75 + 03.75 = 17.50.$

**8. B :** Formula $(a - b)^2 = a^2 - 2ab + b^2$

$= (9.75 - 4.75)^2 = (5)^2 = 25.$

**9. B :** Formula $(a + b)^2 - (a - b)^2 = 4ab$

$= 4 \times \dfrac{40}{19} \times \dfrac{19}{40} = 4.$

**10. B :** $\dfrac{(a + b)^2 + (a - b)^2}{a^2 + b^2}$

$= \dfrac{2(a^2 + b^2)}{(a^2 + b^2)} = 2.$

## Chapter 5

# SQUARE ROOT AND CUBE ROOT

1. The **Square root** of a number is that number which when multiplied by itself, is equal to the given number.

2. A number, whose Square root can be expressed exactly by a whole number, is called a **Perfect Square**.

3. The numbers, whose Square roots cannot be exactly found, are known as **Surds**.

4. Cube root is the quantity of which a given quantity is cube. *e.g.*,

The cube root of 64 is 4 as $4 \times 4 \times 4 = 64$

or $\sqrt[3]{64} = 4$

**Example 1 :** Find the square root of 20736

| | | |
|---|---|---|
| 1 | $2\overline{07}\overline{36}$ | 144 |
| | 1 | |
| 24 | 107 | |
| | 96 | |
| 284 | 1136 | |
| | 1136 | |
| | × | |

So 144 is the square root of 20736.

**Example 2 :** What least number should be added to 2913 to make it a perfect square?

Reasoning : $2913 = (54)^2 - 3$

$\therefore$ 3 must be added

| | | |
|---|---|---|
| 5 | $\overline{29}\,\overline{13}$ | 54 |
| | 25 | |
| 104 | 413 | |
| | 416 | |
| | − 3 | |

So 3 must be added.

**Example 3 :** What least number should be subtracted from 2913 to make the number a perfect square.

**Solution :** $2913 = (53)^2 + 104$

| | | |
|---|---|---|
| 5 | $\overline{29}\,\overline{13}$ | 53 |
| | 25 | |
| 103 | 413 | |
| | 309 | |
| | 104 | |

So 104 must be subtracted.

**Example 4 :** Find the value of $\sqrt[3]{9261}$

**Solution :** $\sqrt[3]{9261} = (3 \times 3 \times 3 \times 7 \times 7 \times 7)^{\frac{1}{3}}$.

| | |
|---|---|
| 3 | 9261 |
| 3 | 3087 |
| 3 | 1029 |
| 7 | 343 |
| 7 | 49 |
| | 7 |

$= 3 \times 7 = 21$

(**Note :** $\sqrt[3]{3 \times 3 \times 3} = 3$ ).

## EXERCISE

**1.** $\sqrt{15625} = ?$

A. 25  B. 125
C. 135  D. 75

**2.** $\frac{\sqrt{?}}{200} = 0.02$

A. 0.4  B. 4
C. 16  D. 1.6

**3.** Evaluate $\sqrt{486} \times \sqrt{6}$.

A. 54  B. 58
C. 68  D. None of these

**4.** The Square root of 133.6336 is

A. 12.56  B. 11.56
C. 13.58  D. None of these

**5.** The sum of squares of two numbers is 26 and

difference is 8. The numbers are

A. 9, 17 B. 3, 17

C. 9, $\sqrt{17}$ D. 3, $\sqrt{17}$

**6.** 27 × 243 is equal to

A. $3^8$ B. $3^9$

C. $3^{10}$ D. $3^{11}$

**7.** $(27)^{-4/3}$ is equal to

A. 81 B. 54

C. $\frac{1}{21}$ D. $\frac{1}{81}$

**8.** $4^4 \times 4^{17} = ?$

A. $8^{17}$ B. $4^{21}$

C. $8^{21}$ D. $4^{13}$

**9.** Evaluate $\sqrt{.4}$ upto four places of decimals.

A. .6378 B. .6324

C. .5879 D. None of these

**10.** If $\sqrt{\frac{x}{169}} = \frac{54}{39}$, then $x$ is equal to

A. 108 B. 324

C. 2916 D. 4800

**11.** $\sqrt{10} \times \sqrt{250} = ?$

A. 46.95 B. 43.75

C. 50.25 D. 50

**12.** The cube root of .000027 is

A. .3 B. .03

C. .003 D. None of these

**13.** $\sqrt{64009} = ?$

A. 803 B. 363

C. 253 D. 347

**14.** $\frac{\sqrt{4375}}{\sqrt{7}} = ?$

A. 24.75 B. 27.25

C. 25 D. 35

**15.** $\frac{\sqrt{1296}}{?} = \frac{?}{2.25}$

A. 6 B. 7

C. 8 D. 9

## EXPLANATORY ANSWERS

**1. B :**

| Divisor | Dividend | Quotient |
|---|---|---|
| 1 | $1\ \overline{56}\ \overline{25}$ | 125 |
| | 1 | |
| 22 | 56 | |
| | 44 | |
| 245 | 1225 | |
| | 1225 | |
| | × | |

**2. C :** Let $\frac{\sqrt{x}}{200} = 0.02$

Then $\sqrt{x} = 200 \times 0.02 = 4$

So, $x = 16$.

**3. A :** $\sqrt{486 \times 6} = \sqrt{6 \times 81 \times 6}$

$= \sqrt{6 \times 6 \times 9 \times 9} = 6 \times 9 = 54.$

**4. B :** $1\overline{33}.\overline{66}\,\overline{36}$

**5. D :** $x^2 + y^2 = 26$, $x^2 - y^2 = 8$

Adding I and II $x^2 = 17$

$x = \sqrt{17}$

$x^2 + y^2 = 26$

$y = \sqrt{9} = 3.$

**6. A :** $= [3 \times 3 \times 3] \times [3 \times 3 \times 3 \times 3 \times 3]$

$= 3^3.3^5 = 3^8.$

**7. D :** $27^{-4/3} = \frac{1}{27^{4/3}} = \frac{1}{\sqrt[3]{(27)^4}} = \frac{1}{3^4}$

$= \frac{1}{3 \times 3 \times 3 \times 3} = \frac{1}{81}.$

**8. B :** $a^x \times a^y = a^{x+y}$ $\therefore 4^4 \times 4^{17} = 4^{21}.$

**9. B :**

| Divisor | Dividend | Quotient |
|---|---|---|
| 6 | .40 | .6324 |
| | 36 | |
| 123 | 400 | |
| | 369 | |
| 1262 | 3100 | |
| | 2524 | |
| 12644 | 57600 | |
| | 50576 | |
| | 7024 | |

$\therefore \sqrt{.4} = 0.6324$

**10. B :** $\sqrt{\frac{x}{169}} = \frac{54}{39}$

$\frac{x}{169} = \frac{54}{39} \times \frac{54}{39}$

$\therefore x = \left(\frac{54}{39} \times \frac{54}{39} \times 169\right) = 324.$

**11. D :** $\sqrt{10} \times \sqrt{250} = \sqrt{10 \times 250}$

$= \sqrt{2500} = 50.$

**12. B :** $(.00027)^{1/3} = \frac{27^{1/3}}{1000000^{1/3}}$

$= \frac{27^{1/3}}{\left(10^6\right)^{1/3}} = .03.$

**13. C :** $\overline{6}\,\overline{40}\,\overline{93}$.

**14. C :**

**15. D :** Let $\frac{\sqrt{1296}}{x} = \frac{x}{2.25}$

$\frac{36}{x} = \frac{x}{2.25}$

$x = \frac{\sqrt{36 \times 225}}{\sqrt{100}} = \frac{6 \times 15}{10} = 9$

# Chapter 6

# PERCENTAGE

1. A fraction with 100 as its denominator is called percentage. So the term-percent means — for every hundred. For examples, a student got 73 marks out of 100. It means he got 73% marks or $\frac{73}{100}$ of the total.

2. When two numbers are given, one of them can be expressed as percentage of other. For example, 20 is what per cent of 50?

If 50 is total then = 20

If it is one = $\frac{20}{50}$

If it is 100 = $\frac{20}{50} \times 100 = 40\%$

So $x$ as a percentage of $y = \frac{x}{y} \times 100$.

**3. Problems related to population**

**I.** If the population of a town is $P$ and its annual increase is $r$ %, then

(*i*) Population after $n$ years = $P\left(1+\frac{r}{100}\right)^n$

(*ii*) Population $n$ years ago = $\frac{P}{\left(1+\frac{r}{100}\right)^n}$.

**II.** If Population is $P$ and annual decrease is $r$%, then

(*i*) Population after $n$ years = $P\left(1-\frac{r}{100}\right)^n$

(*ii*) Population $n$ years ago = $\frac{P}{\left(1-\frac{r}{100}\right)^n}$.

**Example 1 :** Express the following as fractions:

(*i*) 84% (*ii*) 63% (*iii*) 48% (*iv*) 90%

**Solution:** $84\% = \frac{84}{100}$, $63\% = \frac{63}{100}$

$48\% = \frac{48}{100}$, $90\% = \frac{90}{100}$.

**Example 2 :** Express 0.5% as a fraction.

**Solution :** $0.5\% = \frac{0.5}{100} = \frac{5}{1000} = \frac{1}{200}$.

**Example 3 :** Find

(*a*) 80% of 80,

(*b*) 90% of 9, and

(*c*) 3% of 6.

**Solution :** (*a*) 80% of 80 = $\left(\frac{80}{100} \times 80\right) = 64$.

(*b*) 90% of 9 = $\frac{9 \times 90}{100} = \frac{81}{10} = 8.1$.

(*c*) 3% of 6 = $\frac{6 \times 3}{100} = 0.18$.

$\left(\text{Formula } x\% \text{ of } y = \frac{y \times x}{100}\right)$.

**Example 4 :** Fill in the blanks :

(*a*) (.....?.....)% of 90 = 81.

(*b*) (.....?.....)% of 64 = 8.

(*c*) (.....?.....)% of 70 = 49.

**Solution :** (*a*) Let $x$% of 90 = 81

Then $\frac{x}{100} \times 90 = 81$

$x = \frac{81 \times 100}{90} = 90$.

(*b*) Let $x$% of 64 = 8

Then $\frac{x}{100} \times 64 = 8$

$x = \frac{8 \times 100}{64} = 12.5$.

(*c*) $x\%$ of 70 = 49

$$\frac{x}{100} \times 70 = 49$$

$$x = \frac{100 \times 49}{70} = 70.$$

**Example 5 :**

(*a*) What percentage is 150 of 100?

(*b*) What percentage is 10 gms of 1 kg.?

(*c*) What percentage is 150 ml of 35 litres?

**Solution :** (*a*) It is $\frac{150}{100} \times 100 = 150\%$

(*b*) It is $\frac{10}{1000} \times 100 = 1\%$

(*c*) It is $\frac{150}{3500} \times 100 = 4\frac{2}{7}\%$.

**Example 6 :** If the salary of *X* is 20% more than that of *Y*, then how much per cent is the salary of *Y* lower than that of *X*?

**Solution :** The salary of *Y* is less than that of *X* by

$$= \left(\frac{20}{120} \times 100\right)\% = \frac{100}{6} = \frac{50}{3} = 16\frac{2}{3}\%$$

$$\left(\text{Formula}\left(\frac{r}{100+2} \times 100\right)\%\right)$$

**Note :** If the price of a commodity increases by $r\%$, then reduction in consumption so as not to increase the expenditure

$$\left(\frac{r}{100+r} \times 100\right)\%$$

**Example 7 :** If the price of tea is increased by 50%, find the how much percentage, a household should reduce its consumption of tea so the budget remains the same :

**Solution :** $\left(\frac{50}{100+50} \times 100\right)\% = \frac{100}{3} = 33\frac{1}{3}\%.$

**Example 8 :** If the price of sugar falls by 20%, by how much percentage must a household increase its consumption so that budget remains the same?

**Solution :** Increase in consumption :

$$= \left[\frac{20}{100-20} \times 100\right]\%$$

$$= \left(\frac{20}{80} \times 100\right)\% = 25\%.$$

## EXERCISE

**1.** Express as a fraction : $12\frac{1}{2}\%$

A. $\frac{1}{4}$  B. $\frac{1}{8}$

C. $\frac{1}{10}$  D. $\frac{1}{12}$

**2.** What percentage of 80 is 64?

A. 70  B. 60

C. 80  D. 90

**3.** Find 90% of 180.

A. 162  B. 170

C. 160  D. None of these

**4.** Fill in the blanks :

(....?....)% of 60 = 54.

A. 80  B. 70

C. 60  D. 90

**5.** What percentage of $\frac{2}{7}$ is $\frac{1}{35}$?

A. 10%  B. 20%

C. 40%  D. 50%

**6.** 60% of 7[illegible] = ?% of 4200.

A. 20  B. 10

C. 30  D. None of these

**7.** What is 25% of 25% equal to

A. 0.625  B. 6.25

C. 0.00625  D. 0.0625

**8.** The number 0.05 is how much per cent of 20?

A. 25  B. 0.025

C. 0.25  D. 2.5

**9.** The fraction equivalent to $\frac{2}{5}\%$ is

A. $\frac{1}{40}$  B. $\frac{1}{125}$

C. $\frac{1}{250}$ D. $\frac{1}{500}$

**10.** $\frac{30\% \text{ of } 180}{?} = 24$

A. $\frac{3}{10}$ B. $\frac{3}{17}$

C. 1 D. None of these

**11.** Which number is 60% less than 80?

A. 48 B. 42

C. 32 D. 12

**12.** Which number is 125% of 40

A. 50 B. 60

C. 80 D. 320

**13.** What percentage is 3% of 5%?

A. 15% B. 1.5%

C. 0.5% D. None of these

**14.** The population of a town increases 5% annually. If its present population is 84000 what will be the population in 2 years?

A. 92000 B. 92610

C. 93000 D. None of these

**15.** The population of a town increases at the rate of 5% every year. The present population is 8000. When will it become 9261?

A. 5 Years B. 3 Years

C. 1 Year D. None of these

**16.** The price of milk has increased by 60%. In order to restore the original price, the new price must be reduced by

A. $33\frac{1}{3}\%$ B. $37\frac{1}{2}\%$

C. 40% D. 45%

**17.** The price of tea has been reduced by 25%. In order to restore the original price, the new price must be increased by

A. $33\frac{1}{3}\%$ B. $11\frac{1}{9}\%$

C. $9\frac{1}{11}\%$ D. $66\frac{2}{3}\%$

**18.** If Ram secures 50% marks in Hindi and 60% in Science, what percentage of marks did Ram get in both subjects together?

A. 50 B. 55

C. 60 D. None of these

**19.** When the price of a gun was increased by 20% the number of guns sold decreased by 15%. What was the effect on the sales?

A. 4% increse B. 4% decrease

C. 2% increase D. 2% decrease

**20.** A reduction of 20% in the price of sugar enables a person to buy 3.5 kg more for Rs. 77. Find the original price per kg.

A. Rs. 4.00 B. Rs. 4.50

C. Rs. 5.00 D. Rs. 5.50

## EXPLANATORY ANSWERS

**1. B :** $\frac{25}{2} \times \frac{1}{100} = \frac{1}{8}$.

**2. C :** $\frac{64 \times 100}{80} = 80$.

**3. A :** $\frac{180 \times 90}{100} = 162$.

**4. D :** $x \times \frac{1}{100} \times 60 = 54$

$\therefore x = \frac{54 \times 100}{60} = 90\%$.

**5. A :** $x \times \frac{2}{7} \times \frac{1}{100} = \frac{1}{35}$

$\therefore x = \frac{1}{35} \times \frac{7}{2} \times 100 = 10\%$

**6. B :** 60% of 700 is 420 which is 10% of 4200.

**7. D :** $\frac{25}{100} \times \frac{25}{100} = \frac{625}{10000} = 0.0625$.

**8. C :** Let $x$ % of 20 = 0.05

Then $\frac{x}{100} \times 20 = 0.05$ or $x = 0.25$

**9. C :** $\frac{2}{5} \times \frac{1}{100} = \frac{1}{250}$

**10. D :** $\frac{30\% \text{ of } 180}{x} = 24$ or $\frac{54}{x} = 24$

**11. C :** $(80 - 60\% \text{ of } 80) = 32.$

**12. A :** $\frac{40 \times 5}{4} = 50.$

**13. D :** $\left(\frac{3|100}{5|100} \times 100\right)\% = 60\%.$

**14. B :** $84000\left[1+\frac{5}{100}\right]^2 = 84000 \times \frac{441}{400} = 92610$

**15. B :** $9621 = 8000\left(1+\frac{5}{100}\right)^n$

$$\left(1+\frac{5}{100}\right)^n = \frac{9261}{8000} = \left(\frac{21 \times 21 \times 21}{20 \times 20 \times 20}\right)$$

$$= \left(\frac{21}{20}\right)^3 \text{ or } \left(\frac{21}{20}\right)^n = \left(\frac{21}{20}\right)^3$$

Therefore, $n = 3$ years.

**16. B :** Let the original price = Rs. 100

Increased price = Rs 160

Decrease on Rs. 160 = Rs. 60

Decrease on Rs. 100 = $\frac{60}{160} \times 100 = 37\frac{1}{2}\%$

**17. A :** Let the original price = Rs. 100

Reduced price = Rs. 75

Increase on Rs. 75 = $\left(\frac{25}{75} \times 100\right)\%$

$= 33\frac{1}{3}\%$

**18. B :** Total marks 100 + 100 = 200

Total marks obtained = 50 + 60 = 110

$\therefore$ % marks = $\frac{110 \times 100}{200} = 55\%$

**19. C :** $\frac{\text{Increase} \times (\text{Decrease} - \text{Difference})}{100}$

$= \frac{20 \times (15-5)}{100} = 2\%.$

**20. D :**

## Chapter 7

# AVERAGE AND MIXTURE

When we divide the sum of observations or quantities by the number of observations, then the number so obtained is known as **Average**.

**Example 1:** The age of 5 persons is 60, 40, 30, 20, 50. Find the Average age.

**Solution :** Average age is

$$= \frac{(60+40+30+20+50)}{5} = 40 \text{ years.}$$

**Example 2:** Find the average of first five multiple of 4.

**Solution :** $4(1+2+3+4+5) = \frac{4 \times 15}{5} = 12.$

**Example 3:** Ramesh goes to his office on foot at the rate of 8 km per hour but returns home on a bicycle at the rate of 12 km per hour. What is the average-speed?

**Solution :** We whall use the formula $= \frac{2xy}{x+y}$

The Average speed $= \frac{2 \times 8 \times 12}{8+12} = 9.6$ km.

**Example 4:** The average of 3 numbers is 330. The first number is twice the second and thrice the third. Find the middle number.

**Solution :** The average of 3 numbers = 330

So their sum = 330 × 3 = 990

Let first number be $6x$, second be $3x$ and third be $2x$.

So, $11x = 990$

$x = 90$

The numbers are 540, 270, 180

So, middle number is 270.

**Mixtures:** Rule of Mixture:

$$\frac{\text{Quantity of Cheaper}}{\text{Quantity of Dearer}} = \frac{\text{C.P. of Dearer} - \text{M.P.}}{\text{M.P.} - \text{C.P. of Cheaper}}$$

## EXERCISE

**1.** Find the Average score of 5 batsmen when they scored individualy 20, 30, 40, 10 and 0.

A. 20 B. 30
C. 10 D. 5

**2.** The average of 30 results is 20 and the average of other 20 results is 30. What is the average of all the results?

A. 24 B. 25
C. 48 D. 50

**3.** The average of three numbers is 42. The first number is twice the second number and the second number is twice the third number. The difference between the largest and the smallest number is

A. 18 B. 36
C. 54 D. 72

**4.** The average height of 30 boys in a class of 40 boys is 160 cm and that of the remaining boys, is 156 cm. The average height of whole of the class is

A. 158 cm B. 158.5 cm
C. 159 cm D. 159.5 cm

**5.** The average of five numbers is 25. If four of the numbers are 30, 29, 25 and 20, the Average of three larger number is

A. 26 B. 27
C. 28 D. 29

**6.** The average weight of a class of 30 students is 45 kg. If weight of a teacher is included, the average becomes 46 kg. The weight of the teacher is

A. 65 kg B. 66 kg
C. 75 kg D. 76 kg

**7.** The average consumption of vegetables for 7

months is 110 kg and for next five months is 86 kg. The average monthly consumption is

A. 96 kg B. 98 kg
C. 100 kg D. 102 kg

**8.** The average of 25 results is 18, that of first 12 is 14 and that of the last twelve is 17. Find out the 13th result.

A. 28 B. 72
C. 78 D. 85

**9.** Out of four members, the average of first three is 15 and that of the last three is 16. If the last number is 19, the first number is

A. 15 B. 16
C. 18 D. 19

**10.** The Average of all the factors of 60 is

A. 12 B. 6
C. 60 D. 14

**11.** The average age of a husband, his wife and his son, three years ago, was 27 years and that of wife and son, 5 years ago, was 20 years. The present age of the husband is

A. 35 years B. 40 years
C. 32 years D. 45 years

**12.** The average salary of 20 workers in an office is Rs. 1900 P.M. If the manager's salary is added, then the average salary becomes 2000 P.M. What is the manager's annual salary?

A. 24000 B. 25200
C. 45600 D. None of these

**13.** The average expenditure of a man for five months is Rs. 120 and for the next 7 months, it is 130. If he saves Rs. 290 in that year, his monthly average income is

A. Rs. 140 B. Rs. 150
C. Rs. 160 D. Rs. 170

**14.** A batsman makes a score of 87 runs in the 17th innings and thus increases his average by 3. Find the average after 17th innings.

A. 40 B. 32
C. 39 D. 41

**15.** The average of Sita's marks in 7 subjects is 75. Her average in six subjects, excluding Science, is 72. What marks did she get in Science?

A. 72 B. 90
C. 93 D. None of these

**16.** A mixture of 40 litres of milk and water contains 10% water. How much water must be added to make water 20% in the new mixture?

A. 10 litres B. 5 litres
C. 7 litres D. 3 litres

**17.** In what ratio, must a man mix tea at Rs. 1.02 per kg and Rs. 1.44 per kg so as to make the mixture worth Rs. 1.26 per kg.

A. 18 : 24 B. 4 : 3
C. 3 : 4 D. 2 : 5

**18. Milk and water are mixed in a vessel in the ratio of 5 : 2 and in another vessel, in the ratio of 8 : 5. In what ratio, the quantity is taken out from two vessels so as to form a ratio of 9 : 4.**

A. 13 : 2 B. 2 : 7
C. 8 : 5 D. 5 : 8

**19.** In what proportion, must rice at Rs. 3.10 per kg, be mixed with rice at Rs. 3.60 per kg so that the mixture becomes worth Rs. 3.25 per kg.

A. 7 : 2 B. 7 : 1
C. 7 : 3 D. None of these

**20.** In what quantity or ratio, a person should mix three types of wheat, costing Rs. 1.20 per kg, Rs. 1.44 per kg and Rs. 1.74 per kg so that the mix may be worth Rs. 1.41 per kg.

A. 11 : 77 : 7 B. 11 : 7 : 77
C. 7 : 77 : 11 D. None of these

## EXPLANATORY ANSWERS

**1. A :** $\frac{(20+30+40+10+0)}{5} = \frac{100}{5} = 20$

**2. A :** Total of 50 results

$= 30 \times 20 + 20 \times 30 = 1200$

Average $= \frac{1200}{50} = 24.$

**3. C :** Let the 3rd number be $= x$

2nd number be $= 2x$

1st number be $= 4x$

$$\left(\frac{(x+2x+4x)}{3} = 42 \text{ So, } x = 18\right)$$

So largest – smallest $= 4x - x$

$= 72 - 18 = 54$

**4. C :** Average height of the whole class

$$= \frac{30 \times 160 + 10 \times 156}{40} = 159 \text{ cms.}$$

**5. C :** The total of 5 numbers $= 25 \times 5 = 125$

Sum of four number $= 30 + 29 + 25 + 20 = 104$

$\therefore$ 5th number is $= 125 - 104 = 21$

Average of the three large numbers

$$= \frac{30 + 29 + 25}{3} = 28$$

**6. D :** The total weight of the students

$30 \times 45 = 1350$ kg.

Total numbers $= 30 + 1 = 31$

New average $= 46$

New sum $= 46 \times 31 = 1426$ kg.

Weight of the teacher

$= 1426 - 1350 = 76$ kg.

**7. C :** $\frac{110 \times 7 + 86 \times 5}{12} = 100$ kg.

**8. C :** $25 \times 18 - 12 \times 14 + 12 \times 17 = 78$

**9. B :** Sum of four numbers

$15 \times 3 + 19 = 64$

Sum of last three numbers

$16 \times 3 = 48$

$\therefore$ First number $= 64 - 48 = 16.$

**10. D :** Factors of 60 are

1, 2, 3, 4, 5, 6, 10, 12, 15, 20, 30, 60

$$\frac{\text{Sum of all}}{12} = \frac{168}{12} = 14.$$

**11. B :** 3 years ago sum of age $= 27 \times 3 = 81$

Sum of present age $= 81 + 3 \times 3 = 90$

5 years ago sum of age of wife and son $= 20 \times 2 = 40$

Sum of present age $= 40 + 5 \times 2 = 50$

Age of husband $= 90 - 50 = 40$ years.

**12. D :** Manager's Salary P.M.

$= 21 \times 2000 - 20 \times 1900 = 4000$

Manager's annual Salary

$= 4000 \times 12 = 48000$

**13. B : Total income** $= 120 \times 5 + 130 \times 7 + 290 = 1800$

**Average monthly income** $= \frac{1800}{12} = 150$

**14. C :** Average after 17th innings $= x$

Average after 16th innings $= x - 3.$

$\therefore 16(x - 3) + 87 = 17x$

$x = 87 - 48 = 39.$

**15. C :** Marks in Science

$= 7 \times 75 - 6 \times 72 = 93$

**16. B :** Let $x$ should be added. Now, water $=$ (10% of 40) $+ x = 4 + x.$

Mixture $= 40 + x$

$$4 + x = \frac{1}{5} \times (40 + x)$$

$$5x - x = 20$$

$$x = \frac{20}{4} = 5 \text{ litres.}$$

**17. C :** 1.02     1.44

$\searrow$ 1.26 $\swarrow$

$$\text{Ratio} = \frac{0.18}{0.24} = \frac{18}{24} = 3:4.$$

**18. A :**

**19. C :** $\frac{\text{Quantity of cheaper price}}{\text{Quantity of dearer price}} = \frac{35}{15} = \frac{7}{3}.$

$$\frac{\text{Quantity of cheaper}}{\text{Quantity of dearer}} = \frac{\text{CP of dearer} - \text{Mean price}}{\text{Mean price} - \text{CP of cheaper}}$$

**20. D :** Required ratio will be

$$\frac{1.74}{1.41} : \frac{1.44}{1.41} : \frac{1.20}{1.41}$$

$1.2 \times 100 : 1.0 \times 100 : 0.85 \times 100$

$120 : 100 : 85$

$24 : 20 : 17$

Chapter 8

# PROFIT AND LOSS

Profit and Loss is an important concept for every businessman and it is very important to measures it in advance on an approximate basis or otherwise.

The following are the rules regarding Profit and Loss :

(1) Cost Price (C.P.) means the purchase-price at which, the article is purchased.

(2) Selling Price (S.P.) is the price at which, the article is sold in the market.

(3) Profit = S.P. – C.P.

Loss = C.P. – S.P.

**Note :** It is important to note that loss or gain is always measured with cost price as the basis.

$$\text{So Gain \%} = \frac{\text{Gain} \times 100}{\text{C.P.}}$$

$$\text{Loss\%} = \frac{\text{Loss} \times 100}{\text{C.P.}}$$

(4) If an article is sold at a gain of 25%, then

S.P. = (125% of C.P.)

If an article is sold at a loss of 25%, then

S.P. = (75% of C.P.)

(5) $\text{S.P.} = \frac{100 + \text{Gain\%}}{100} \times \text{C.P.}$

Or

$\frac{100 - \text{Loss\%}}{100} \times \text{C.P.}$

(6) $\text{C.P.} = \frac{100}{100 + \text{Gain\%}} \times \text{S.P.}$

Or

$\frac{100}{100 - \text{Loss\%}} \times \text{S.P.}$

**Example 1 :** Find gain or loss percentage when.

1. C.P. = 100
   S.P. = 120
2. C.P. = 100
   S.P. = 75
3. C.P. = 950
   S.P. = 1140
4. C.P. = 1020
   S.P. = 850

**Solution : 1.** Profit = S.P. – C.P.

= 120 – 100 = 20

$$\text{Gain \%} = \frac{\text{Gain} \times 100}{\text{C.P.}}$$

$$= \frac{20 \times 100}{100} = 20\%$$

2. Likewise, $\text{Loss\%} = \frac{25 \times 100}{100} = 25\%$ Loss

3. $\text{Gain\%} = \frac{190}{950} \times 100 = 20\%$

4. $\text{Loss\%} = \frac{170}{1020} \times 100 = 16\frac{2}{3}\%$

**Example 2 :** Find S.P.

1. C.P. = 100 Gain is 25%
2. C.P. = 80 Gain is 20%

**Solution : 1.** $\text{S.P.} = \frac{100 + \text{Gain\%}}{100} \times \text{C.P.}$

$$= \frac{125}{100} \times 100 = 125$$

**2.** $\text{S.P.} = \frac{120}{100} \times 80 = 96$

**Example 3 :** Find C.P. when

(*i*) S.P. = 517 Gain 10%

(*ii*) S.P. = 585 Loss 10%

**Solution :** (*i*) $\text{C.P.} = \frac{100}{100 + \text{Gain\%}} \times \text{S.P.}$

$$= \frac{100}{110} \times 517 = 470$$

(*ii*) $\text{C.P.} = \frac{100}{90} \times 585 = 650$

# EXERCISE

**1.** By selling a vehicle for Rs. 45,000, Mr. Ramesh suffers 25% loss. What was his loss?

A. 15000
B. 17000
C. 12000
D. 10000

**2.** By selling an article for Rs. 1200, 25% profit is earned. If the same article is sold for Rs 1,440, then the gain percentage will be

A. 60% B. 50%
C. 40% D. None of these

**3.** Mohan lost 15% by selling his old fan for Rs. 1,700. At what price, should he sell it so that he gains 15%?

A. 2300 B. 2500
C. 3500 D. None of these

**4.** By selling a radio for Rs 144, a man losses 10%. At what price, should he sell it to gain 10%?

A. 180 B. 176
C. 190 D. 200

**5.** A boy bought some bananas at the rate of 10 bananas for Rs 3 and sold all of them at the rate of 3 bananas for Rs 2. Find the gain or loss.

A. $122\frac{2}{9}$ B. 200
C. 108 D. None of these

**6.** Mr. Cook sold a book at a profit of 12%. If he had sold it for Rs 1.80 more, then he would have gained 18%. Find the C.P.

A. 40 B. 30
C. 45 D. 50

**7.** A man gains 20% by selling an article for Rs. 4.80. What percent would he have gained or lost had he sold it for Rs. 4.30?

A. 7.5% gain
B. 7.5% loss
C. 6.5% gain
D. 6.5% loss

**8.** Mr. *X* sells an article to *Y* at a profit of 20% and *Y* sells it to *Z* at a profit of 25%. If *Z* buys it for Rs. 225, what did *X* pay for it?

A. Rs. 100 B. Rs. 125
C. Rs. 150 D. Rs. 175

**9.** A vendor sells 5 oranges for a Rupee thus gaining 40%. How many oranges did he buy for a rupee?

A. 6 B. 8
C. 7 D. 9

**10.** A person sold watch for Rs. 144 and got a percentage of profit equal to the cost price. Find the cost price of watch.

A. 70 B. 80
C. 60 D. 50

**11.** By selling 100 pens, a shopkeeper gains the S.P. of 20 pens. Find the gain per cent.

A. 20 B. 25
C. 30 D. 40

**12.** A vendor bought toffees at 6 for a Rupee. How many toffees for a Rupee must he sell to gain 20%?

A. 5 B. 6
C. 7 D. 8

**13.** A vendor bought a number of bananas at 3 for a Rupee and sold them at 2 for a Rupee. Find his gain per cent.

A. 30 B. 50
C. 60 D. 55

**14.** A shopkeeper purchases oranges at the rate of 11 oranges for Rs. 10 and sells them at the rate of 10 oranges for Rs. 11. His percentage profit or loss is

A. 21% loss
B. 21% gain
C. 11.5% loss
D. 11.5% gain

**15.** Rakesh sold a watch at a profit of 20%. Had he bought it for 20% less and sold it for Rs 20 less, then he would have gained 20%. The cost price of watch is

A. Rs. 80.25
B. Rs. 81.30
C. Rs. 82.32
D. Rs. 83.33

# EXPLANATORY ANSWERS

**1. A :** C.P. $= \dfrac{100}{100 - \text{loss }\%} \times$ S.P

$= \dfrac{100}{75} \times 45000 = 60{,}000$

Hence, loss = 60,000 – 45000 = 15000.

**2. B :** C.P. $= \dfrac{100}{125} \times 1200 = 960$

Gain = 1440 – 960 = 480

% Gain $= \dfrac{\text{Gain} \times 100}{\text{C.P.}}$

$= \dfrac{480 \times 100}{960} = 50\%.$

**3. A :** C.P. $= \dfrac{1700 \times 100}{100 - 15} = 2000$

S.P. = C.P. $\dfrac{(100 + \text{Gain})}{100}$

$= \dfrac{2000 \times 115}{100} = 2300.$

**4. B :** C.P. $= \dfrac{144 \times 100}{90} = 160$

S.P. $= \dfrac{160 \times 110}{100} = 176.$

**5. A :** C.P. of 30 bananas $= 30 \times \dfrac{3}{10} = 9$

S.P. of 30 bananas $= 30 \times \dfrac{2}{3} = 20$

Gain = 20 – 9 = 11

Gain % $= \dfrac{11}{9} \times 100 = 122\dfrac{2}{9}.$

**6. B :** 118% of cost – 112% of cost = 1.80

Cost of the book $= \dfrac{1.80 \times 100}{6} = 30$

**7. A :** C.P. $= \dfrac{4.8 \times 100}{120} = 4$

S.P. = 4.30, gain = 0.30

% gain $= \dfrac{0.30 \times 100}{4} = 7.5\%$

**8. C :** C.P. of $Z$ = S.P. of Y

$\therefore$ S.P. of $Y$ = 225

C.P. of $Y = \dfrac{225}{125} \times 100 = 180$

C.P. of $Y$ = S.P. of $X$

S.P. of $X$ = 180

C.P. of $X = \dfrac{180 \times 100}{120} = 150$

**9. C :** S.P. of 5 oranges = Re. 1

Gain = 40%

$\therefore$ C.P. of 5 oranges $= \dfrac{100}{100 + 40} \times 1 = \dfrac{5}{7}$

By 5/7 Rs. we get= 5 oranges

For Rs. 1we get $= 5 \times \dfrac{7}{5} = 7$ oranges.

**10. B :**

**11. B : Gain % $= \dfrac{20}{80} \times 100 = 25$**

**12. A :** C.P. of 6 toffees = Re. 1

Gain 20%

$\therefore$ S.P. of 6 toffees $= \dfrac{120}{100} \times 1 = \dfrac{6}{5}$

In Rs. $\dfrac{6}{5}$ he sells 6 toffees

$\therefore$ in Re. 1 he will sell $\dfrac{6 \times 5}{6} = 5$ toffees.

**13. B :** Gain % $= \dfrac{1}{2} \times 100 = 50\%$

**14. B :** C.P. of 11 oranges = Rs. 10

S.P. of 10 oranges = Rs. 11

S.P. of 11 oranges $= \dfrac{11}{10} \times 11 = 12.10$

Gain = 12.10 – 10 = 2.10

% gain $= \dfrac{2.10 \times 100}{10} = 21\%.$

**15. D :**

Chapter 9

# TIME AND WORK

**Rule :** (*i*) If a man can do a work in 10 days, then it is clear that his work for 1 day will be 1/10 of his whole work.

(*ii*) If *A* is twice as good a workman than *B*, then the ratio of work done by *A* and *B* = 2 : 1, and the ratio of time taken by *A* and *B* is 1 : 2,

**Example 1 :** Ram can do a work in 5 days and Shyam can do the same work in 4 days. Then, in how many days, both of them can do the work?

**Solution :** Ram's 1 day's work $= \frac{1}{5}$

Shyam's 1 day's work $= \frac{1}{4}$

So, 1 day's work of both Ram and Shyam

$= \frac{1}{5} + \frac{1}{4} = \frac{9}{20}$

$\therefore$ Both can do it in $\frac{20}{9}$ days

$= 2\frac{2}{9}$ days.

**Example 2 :** *X* and *Y* can dig a tank is 15 days. which *X* alone can dig in 30 days. In how many days, *Y* alone can dig it.

**Solution :** $(X + Y)$'s 1 day's work $= \frac{1}{15}$

*X*'s 1 day's work $= \frac{1}{30}$

*Y*'s 1 day's work $= \frac{1}{15} - \frac{1}{30} = \frac{1}{30}$

So, *Y* alone can dig it in 30 days.

**Example 3 :** *A* can do a work in 20 days, which *B* alone can do in 30 days. If they do it together and get a payment of Rs. 600, then what will be the share of *A* and *B*?

**Solution :** *A*'s 1 day's work $= \frac{1}{20}$

*B*'s 1 day's work $= \frac{1}{30}$

Ratio of shares $\frac{1}{20} : \frac{1}{30} = 3 : 2$

$\therefore$ *A*'s and *B*'s share

A : $600 \times \frac{3}{5} = 360$  B : $600 \times \frac{2}{5} = 240$

## EXERCISE

**1.** Ram can do a piece of work in 30 days while Shyam can do it in 40 days. In how many days, they will finish the work if they do that work together?

A. 70 days  B. $42\frac{3}{4}$ days

C. $27\frac{1}{7}$ days  D. $17\frac{1}{7}$ days

**2.** If 16 persons can complete a piece of work in 5 days, in how many days, 8 persons would be able to do it?

A. 10  B. 7

C. 15  D. None of these

**3.** *X* and *Y* together can do a work in 12 days and *X* alone can do it in 18 days. How many days will be taken by *Y* alone to do it?

A. 40  B. 36

C. 18  D. 20

**4.** *A* and *B* can do a piece of work in 8 days. *B* and *C* can do the same piece of work in 12 days. *A*, *B* and *C* together can do it in 6 days. How much time *A* and *C* will take to finish it?

A. 4 days  B. 8 days

C. 15 days  D. 18 days

**5.** A man can do a job in 10 days. His father takes 15 days and his brother finishes it in 20 days.

They worked together for two days. The man left the job. His father left the job a day earlier than the completion of the work. The number of days for which, the work was carried out, is

A. $7\frac{3}{7}$ day  B. $6\frac{3}{7}$ days
C. $5\frac{3}{7}$ days  D. None of these

**6.** *A* and *B* can together do a piece of work in 15 days. *B* alone can do it in 20 days. In how many days, can *A* alone do it?
A. 30 days  B. 40 days
C. 45 days  D. 60 days

**7.** *A* can do a piece of work in 40 days and worked for 5 days, then *B* finished it in 21 days. In how many days, *A* and *B* together can do it?
A. 12  B. 10
C. 18  D. 15

**8.** *A* and *B* can do a piece of work in 18 days, *B* and *C* in 24 days, *A* and *C* in 36 days. What time will they take if they work together?
A. 12 days  B. 13 days
C. 16 days  D. 26 days

**9.** 12 men or 18 women can reap a field in 14 days. Find the number of days for which, 8 men and 16 women will take to reap it?
A. 5 days  B. 7 days
C. 8 days  D. 9 days

**10.** *A* is twice as good as *B* and together, they finish a piece of work in 14 days. *A* alone can finish the work in
A. 11 days  B. 21 days
C. 28 days  D. 42 days

**11. 8 men can dig a tank in 9 days. If a man works twice as much as a boy, then 4 men and 4 boys can dig a similar tank in**
A. 10 days  B. 12 days
C. 15 days  D. 16 days

**12.** *A* alone can finish a piece of work in 10 days. *B* alone can do it in 15 days. If they together do it then total wages are Rs. 75. A will get
A. Rs. 30  B. Rs. 37.50
C. Rs. 45  D. Rs. 50

**13.** *X*, *Y* and Z can finish a project in 22, 33 and 44 days respectively. If they work jointly, how much time will they take?

A. $10\frac{2}{13}$ days  B. 12 days

C. $17\frac{1}{2}$ days  D. 15 days

**14.** A certain number of men can do a work in 60 days. If 8 more men are added to the existing staff, then the work can be finished in 10 days less. How many men are there?
A. 45  B. 35
C. 52  D. 40

## EXPLANATORY ANSWERS

**1. D :** Both 1 day's work $= \frac{1}{30} + \frac{1}{40} = \frac{7}{120}$

Time taken by them $= \frac{120}{7} = 17\frac{1}{7}$ days

**2. A :** 16 person can do it in 5 days

$\therefore$ 8 person can do it in $= \frac{16 \times 5}{8} = 10$ days

**3. B :** 1 day's work of *X* and $Y = \frac{1}{12}$

1 day's work of $X = \frac{1}{18}$

1 day's work of $Y = \frac{1}{12} - \frac{1}{18} = \frac{1}{36}$

So, *Y* alone can do it in 36 days.

**4. B :** 1 day's work $(A + B) = \frac{1}{8}$ part

1 day's work $(B + C) = \frac{1}{12}$ part

1 day's work $(A + B + C) = \frac{1}{6}$ part

1 day's work of $B = \left(\frac{1}{8} + \frac{1}{12}\right) - \frac{1}{6} = \frac{1}{24}$ part

$\therefore$ 1 day's work *A* and $C = \frac{1}{6} - \frac{1}{24} = \frac{1}{8}$

$\therefore$ Total time taken by *A* and $C = 8$ days

**5. A :**

**6. D :** $A$'s one day's work $= \frac{1}{15} - \frac{1}{20} = \frac{1}{60}$

$\therefore$ $A$ alone can finish it in 60 days.

**7. D :** 5 day's work of $A = \frac{1}{40} \times 5 = \frac{1}{8}$

Remaining work $= 1 - \frac{1}{8} = \frac{7}{8}$ part

In 21 days $B$ finished work $= \frac{7}{8}$ part

1 day's work of $B = \frac{7}{8 \times 21} = \frac{1}{24}$ part

1 day's work of $A$ and $B = \frac{1}{40} + \frac{1}{24} = \frac{1}{15}$

So, time taken by $A$ and $B$ to finish the work = 15 days.

**8. C :**

**9. D :** 12 men = 18 women or

1 man $= \frac{2}{3}$ woman.

$\therefore$ 8 men + 16 women $= \left(8 \times \frac{3}{2} + 16\right)$

= 28 women.

Now 18 women take 14 days

$\therefore$ 28 women taken $= \frac{14 \times 18}{28} = 9$ days

**10. B :** $A : B = 2 : 1$

$(A + B)$'s one day's work $= \frac{1}{14}$

$A$'s one day's work $= \frac{1}{14} \times \frac{2}{3} = \frac{1}{21}$.

So, $A$ alone can finish it in 21 days.

**11. D :** 2 boys = 1 man

$\therefore$ 8 boys + 12 men = 16 men

$12 : 16 :: 9 : x$

$\therefore$ $x = \frac{16 \times 9}{12} = 12$ days

**12. C :** Ratio of $A$ and $B = 3 : 2$

$A$'s share $= 75 \times \frac{3}{5} =$ Rs. 45

**13. A :** $10\frac{2}{13}$ days

**14. D :** Let $X$ men are there.

$X$ men can do the work in 60 days

$X + 8$ men can do the work in 50 days

$\therefore$ $60X = 50X + 400$

$\therefore$ $X = 40$

## Chapter 10

# SIMPLE AND COMPOUND INTEREST

(I) **Simple Interest** (S.I.) = $\frac{P \times R \times T}{100}$.

Here $P$ = Principal
$R$ = Rate
$T$ = Time

(II) $P = \frac{100 \times S.I.}{R \times T}$ ; $R = \frac{100 \times S.I.}{P \times T}$ and

$$T = \frac{100 \times S.I.}{P \times R}$$

**Compound Interest** = $P\left(1 + \frac{R}{100}\right)$

**Example 1 :** At what rate per cent, a sum of money doubles itself in 15 years?

**Solution :** Let $P$ = 100
After 15 years, $A$ = 200
Interest = 100
It implies that 100 is the amount of interest on P = 100.

$$\therefore \text{Rate} = \left(\frac{100 \times 100}{100 \times 15}\right)$$

$$= 6\frac{2}{3}\%$$

**Example 2 :** In how many years, would a sum of money triple itself at the rate of 16% per annum?

**Solution :** Time = $\frac{100 \times 200}{100 \times 16} = 12\frac{1}{2}$ years.

**Example 3 :** A sum of Rs. 500 is invested for 3 years.The rates of interest are $6\frac{1}{2}\%$, $7\frac{1}{2}\%$ and 8%. Calculate the amount of interest.

**Solution :** $\left(6\frac{1}{2} + 7\frac{1}{2} + 8\right)\% = 22\%$

$$\text{Interest} = \frac{500 \times 22 \times 1}{100} = 110.$$

**Example 4 :** Calculate the compound interest when the principle is Rs. 3000 at an interest of 5% per annum for 2 years.

**Solution :** $A = 3000\left(1 + \frac{5}{100}\right)^2$

$$= 3000 \times \frac{105}{100} \times \frac{105}{100}$$

$$= \frac{3}{10} \times 105 \times 105$$

$$= 3307.50$$

Interest = Rs. 3307.50 – 3000
= 307.50.

**Example 5 :** A man deposits Rs. 31250 on fixed deposit terms of 3 years at 12%. If the interest is payable half yearly, how much amount he would receive on maturity?

**Solution :** For half yearly interest, we have
$R = 6$
$n = 3 \times 2 = 6$

$$A = 31250\left(1 + \frac{6}{100}\right)^6$$

$$= 31250\left(\frac{53}{50}\right)^6$$

$$= 31250 \times \frac{53 \times 53 \times 53 \times 53 \times 53 \times 53}{50 \times 50 \times 50 \times 50 \times 50 \times 50}$$

= Rs. 44328.70

# EXERCISE

1. The Compound Interest on Rs. 7500 for 2 years at 4% per annum is
   A. Rs. 632 B. Rs. 602
   C. Rs. 612 D. Rs. 621
2. Simple Interest of a sum at 4% per annum for 2 years is Rs. 80. The compound interest on the same sum for the same period is
   A. Rs. 81.60 B. Rs. 160
   C. Rs. 1081.60 D. None of these
3. Compound interest of Rs. 20480 at $6\frac{1}{4}$% per annum for 2 years and 73 days is
   A. Rs. 3000 B. Rs. 3131
   C. Rs. 2929 D. Rs. 3636
4. What is the principal amount which earns Rs. 132 as compound interest for the second year at 10% per annum?
   A. Rs. 1000 B. Rs. 1200
   C. Rs. 1320 D. None of these
5. The difference between Simple Interest and Compound Interest at the same rate for Rs. 5000 for 2 years is Rs. 72. The rate of interest is
   A. 10% B. 12%
   C. 6% D. 8%
6. A sum of money deposited on C.I. doubles itself in 5 years. It will become eight times its present value in
   A. 15 years B. 20 years
   C. 12 years D. 10 years
7. A tree grows annually by $\frac{1}{8}$th of its height. How much height will it increase after 2 years, if it stands at a height of 64 m today?
   A. 72 cm B. 74 cm
   C. 75 cm D. 81 cm
8. The value of a machine depreciates every year at the rate of 10% of its value at the beginning of that year. If the present value of the machine in Rs. 749, its worth 3 years ago was
   A. Rs. 947.10 B. Rs. 800
   C. Rs. 1000 D. Rs. 750.87
9. Rs. 1600, at 10% per annum compound interest, compounded half yearly amounts to Rs. 1944.81. Find the time period.
   A. 2 years B. 3 years
   C. $1\frac{1}{2}$ years D. $2\frac{1}{2}$ years
10. A sum of money becomes Rs. 6690 after three years and Rs. 10035 after six years on compound interest. The sum is
    A. Rs. 4400 B. Rs. 4445
    C. Rs. 4460 D. Rs. 4520

# EXPLANATORY ANSWERS

**1. C :** Amount = Rs. $\left[7500\left(1+\frac{4}{100}\right)^2\right]$

$\Rightarrow$ Rs. $\left[7500 \times \frac{26}{25} \times \frac{26}{25}\right] = 8112$

$\therefore$ C.I. = 8112 − 7500 = Rs. 612

**2. A :** Principle = Rs. $\left(\frac{100 \times 80}{4 \times 2}\right)$ = Rs. 1000

$\therefore$ C.I. = Rs. $\left[\left\{1000 \times \left(1+\frac{4}{100}\right)^2\right\} - 1000\right]$

= Rs. 81.60

**3. C :** C.I. = $\left[20480 \times \left(1+\frac{25}{4 \times 100}\right)^2 \left(1+\frac{1}{5} \times \frac{25}{4 \times 100}\right) - 20480\right]$

$\Rightarrow \left[\left(20480 \times \frac{17}{16} \times \frac{17}{16} \times \frac{81}{80}\right) - 20480\right]$

= Rs. 2929.

**4. B :** Let $X$ be the principal at the end of the 1st years

Then $\frac{X \times 10 \times 1}{100} = 132$

$X = 1320$

Let $Y$ be the original principal, then

$$1320 = Y\left(1+\frac{10}{100}\right)^1$$

$$\Rightarrow \frac{11}{10}Y = 1320$$

$$Y = 1200$$

**5. B :** $$5000\times\left(1+\frac{R}{100}\right)^2 - 5000 - \frac{5000\times 2\times R}{100} = 72$$

$$\Rightarrow 5000\left[\left(1+\frac{R}{100}\right)^2 - 1 - \frac{R}{50}\right] = 72$$

$$\Rightarrow 1+\frac{R^2}{10000}+\frac{2R}{100}-1-\frac{R}{50} = \frac{72}{5000}$$

$$\Rightarrow R^2 = \frac{72}{5000}\times 10000 = 144$$

$$R = 12\%.$$

**6. A :** Let principal be $P$ and the rate be $r\%$ then, we have

$$2P = P\left(1+\frac{r}{100}\right)^5 \text{ or } \left(1+\frac{r}{100}\right)^5 = 2$$

Let it be 8 times in $t$ year.

Then

$$8\,P = P\left(1+\frac{r}{100}\right)^t \text{ or } \left(1+\frac{r}{100}\right)^t = 8 = 2^3$$

$$= \left(1+\frac{r}{100}\right)^{15}$$

$$t = 15 \text{ years.}$$

**7. D :** Increase Percentage $= \left(\frac{1}{8}\times 100\right)\%$

$$= 12.5\%$$

Height after 2 years $= 64\times\left(\frac{1+25}{2\times 100}\right)^2$

$$= \left[64\times\frac{9}{8}\times\frac{9}{8}\right] = 81 \text{ cm.}$$

**8. C :** $$P\left(1-\frac{10}{100}\right)^3 = 729$$

$$P = \text{Rs.}\left(\frac{729\times 10\times 10\times 10}{9\times 9\times 9}\right) = \text{Rs. } 1000$$

**9. A :** $$1600\left(1+\frac{5}{100}\right)^T = 1944.81$$

$$\Rightarrow \left(\frac{21}{20}\right)^T = \frac{1944.81}{1600}$$

$$= \frac{194481}{160000} = \left(\frac{21}{20}\right)^4$$

$\therefore$ $T = 4$ (half years) or

$T = 2$ years

**10. C :** Let the sum be $P$

Then $$P\left(1+\frac{R}{100}\right)^3 = 6690 \quad \ldots(i)$$

$$P\left(1+\frac{R}{100}\right)^6 = 10{,}035 \quad \ldots(ii)$$

Dividing equation (*ii*) by equation (*i*)

$$\left(1+\frac{R}{100}\right)^3 = \frac{10035}{6690} = \frac{3}{2}$$

or $p\times\frac{3}{2} = 6690$ from (*i*)

or $$P = \frac{6690\times 2}{3} = \text{Rs. } 4460$$

# Chapter 11

# AREA

**rmula**

1. (*a*) Area of a Rectangle = [Length × Breadth]

   (*b*) Length = $\frac{\text{Area}}{\text{Breadth}}$, Breadth = $\frac{\text{Area}}{\text{Length}}$

   (*c*) $(\text{Diagonal})^2 = (\text{Length})^2 + (\text{Breadth})^2$

2. Area of Square = $(\text{Side})^2 = \frac{1}{2}$ $(\text{Diagonal})^2$
3. Area of 4 walls of a room = 2 × (Length + Breadth) × Height
4. Area of a Parallelo gram = (Base × Height)
5. Area of Rhombus = $\frac{1}{2}$ (Product of diagonals)
6. Area of an Equilateral triangle = $\frac{\sqrt{3}}{4}$ $(\text{Side})^2$
7. If *a*, *b* and *c* are the lengths of the sides of a triangle and

$$s = \frac{1}{2}(a + b + c)$$

then, Area of triangle = $\frac{1}{2}$ (Base × Height)

$$= \sqrt{s(s-a)(s-b)(s-c)}$$

9. Area of trapezium = $\frac{1}{2}$ (Sum of parallel sides × distances between them)
10. (*i*) Circumference of circle = $2\pi r$

    (*ii*) Area of circle = $\pi r^2$

    (*iii*) Arc of Sector *ACBO*

$$= \frac{2\pi r\theta}{360}$$

    (Where $\angle AOB = \theta$)

    (*iv*) Area of Sector *ACBO* = $\frac{\pi r^2 \theta}{360}$

    ($\angle AOB = \theta$)

    (*v*) Area of Sector *ACBO* = $\frac{1}{2}$ × Arc AB × *r*

**Example 1:** Find the area of an equilateral triangle, each of whose sides is 12 m long.

**Solution :** Area of the triangle = $\frac{\sqrt{3}}{4}$ $(\text{Side})^2$

$$= \left(\frac{1.73}{4} \times 12 \times 12\right) \text{m}^2 = 62.28 \text{ m}^2$$

**Example 2:** Find the area of a rhombus one side of which measures 20 cm. and one diagonal measures 24 cm.

**Solution :** We know that the diagonal of rhombus biseet each other at right angles so, one side and halves of diagonals form a right angled triangle.

Let $AB$ = 20 cm. and $BD$ = 24 cm.

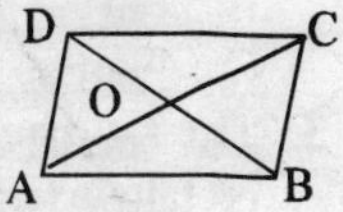


Then $OB$ = 12 cm

$AB^2 = OA^2 + OB^2$

$OA^2 = AB^2 - OB^2$

$OA^2 = (20)^2 - (12)^2 = 256$

$OA = 16$

So, $AC$ = 32 cm.

Hence, Area of rhombus

$$= \frac{1}{2} \times AC \times BD = \left[\frac{1}{2} \times 32 \times 24\right] m^2$$

$$= 384 \text{ cm}^2.$$

**Example 3 :** A Room is 13 m long, 9 m broad and 10 m high. Find the cost of painting the four walls of the room at Rs. 15 per square metre. It being given that the door and windows occupy 40 sq. metres.

**Solution :** Area of 4 walls

= 2 (length + breadth × height)

$\Rightarrow$ [2 (13 + 9) × 10] m² = 440 m²

Area to be painted

(440 – 40) m² = 400 m²

So, cost of painting = Rs. (400 × 15) = Rs. 6000.

**Example 4:** Calculate the circumference and the area of a circle of radius 3.5 cm.

**Solution :** Circumference = $2\pi r$

$$= 2 \times \frac{22}{7} \times 3.5 = 22 \text{ cm.}$$

Area $= \pi r^2 = \left(\frac{22}{7} \times 3.5 \times 3.5\right) \text{cm}^2$

$= 38.5 \text{ m}^2$

**Example 5:** A circular grassy plot of land which is 70 m in diameter, has a path 7 m. wide running round it on its outside. Find the cost of putting gravel on the path at the rate of Rs. 3 per square metre.

**Solution :** Radius of plot = 35 m

Radius of out circle = (35 + 7) = 42 m

Area of path $= \pi \times (42)^2 - \pi \times (35)^2$

$= \pi\left((42)^2 - (35)^2\right)$

$= \frac{22}{7} \times 77 \times 7 \text{ m}^2$

$= 1694 \text{ m}^2$

∴ Cost of gravelling $= \text{Rs. } (1694 \times 3)$

$= \text{Rs. } 5082$

## EXERCISE

1. If the length of a diagonal $AC$ of a square $ABCD$ is 5.2 cm., then area of the square $ABCD$ is
   A. 15.12 sq. cm B. 13.52 sq. cm
   C. 12.62 sq. cm D. 10.10 sq. cm
2. The area of a rectangle, 144 m long, is the same as that of a square having a side 84 m long, then width of the rectangle is
   A. 7 m B. 14 m
   C. 49 m D. cannot be determined
3. The ratio between the length and breadth of a rectangle field is 5 : 4. If the breadth is 20 metres less than the length, the perimeter of the field is
   A. 260 m B. 280 m
   C. 360 m D. None of these
4. If the side of a square is increased by 25%, then by how much percentage does its area get increased?
   A. 125 B. 156.25
   C. 50 D. 56.25
5. If the side of square is doubled, then the ratio of the resulting square of the given square is
   A. 1 : 2 B. 2 : 1
   C. 3 : 1 D. 4 : 1
6. The length of a rectangle is doubled while its breadth is halved. What is the percentage change in area?
   A. 50 B. 75
   C. No change D. None of these
7. The length of a rectangle is increased by 60%. By what per cent, would the width have to be decreased to maintain the same area?
   A. $37\frac{1}{2}\%$ B. 60%
   C. 75% D. 120%
8. If the ratio of the areas of two squares is 9 : 1, then the ratio of their perimeters is
   A. 9 : 1 B. 3 : 1
   C. 3 : 4 D. 1 : 3
9. A hall 20 m long and 15 m broad, is surrounded by a verandah of uniform width of 2.5 m. The cost of flooring the verandah at the rate of Rs. 3.50 per sq. metre is
   A. Rs. 500 B. Rs. 600
   C. Rs. 700 D. Rs. 800
10. The length and breadth of a square are increased by 40% and 30%, respectively. The area of the resulting rectangle exceeds the area of the square by
    A. 42% B. 62%
    C. 82% D. None of these
11. The cost of pasting paper on the four walls of a room is Rs. 48. Each one of the length, breadth and height of another room is double than that room. The cost of pasting paper on the walls of this new room is
    A. Rs. 384 B. Rs. 288
    C. Rs. 192 D. Rs. 96
12. If the radius of a circle is reduced by 50%, its area is reduced by
    A. 25% B. 50%
    C. 75% D. 100%
13. If the diameter of a circle is increased by 100%, its area is increased by
    A. 100% B. 200%
    C. 300% D. 400%
14. The ratio of the radii of two circles is 1 : 3. The ratio of their areas is
    A. 1 : 3 B. 1 : 6

C. 1 : 9 D. None of these

**15.** The area of the largest triangle that can be inscribed in a semicircle of radius $r$ cm is

A. $2r$ cm$^2$ B. $r^2$ cm$^2$

C. $2r$ cm$^2$ D. $\frac{1}{2}r^2$ cm$^2$

**16.** The perimeter of a rhombus is 52 metres, while its longer diagonal has a length of 24 metres. The length of the other diagonal is

A. 5 metres B. 10 metres

C. 20 metres D. 28 metres

**17.** If a square and a rhombus stand on the same base, then the ratio of the areas of the square and the rhombus is

A. greater than 1 B. equal to 1

C. equal to 1/2 D. equal to 1/4

**18.** The ratio of the corresponding sides of two similar triangles is 3 : 4. The ratio of their areas is

A. 4 : 3 B. 3 : 4

C. 9 : 16 D. $\sqrt{3}:2$

**19.** A rectangular carpet has an area of 60 sq. m. Its diagonal and longer side together equal 5 times the shorter side. If diagonal is 13 m long then the length of the carpet is

A. 5 m B. 12 m

C. 13 m D. 14.5 m

**20.** The ratio of the area of a square of side $a$ and the area of an equilateral triangle of side $a$, is

A. 2 : 1 B. $2:\sqrt{3}$

C. 4 : 3 D. $4:\sqrt{3}$

## EXPLANATORY ANSWERS

**1. B :** Area $= \frac{1}{2} \times$ (diagonal) cm$^2$

$= \left(\frac{1}{2} \times 5.2 \times 5.2\right)$ cm$^2$ = 13.52 cm$^2$

**2. C :** Areas of the square = $(84 \times 84)$ m$^2$

Areas of the rectangle = $(144 \times W)$ m$^2$

Width (W) $= \left(\frac{84 \times 84}{144}\right)$ m = 49 m

**3. C :** $5x - 4x = 20$ or $x = 20$

$\therefore$ Length = $(5 \times 20)$ m = 100 m,

Breadth = $(4 \times 20)$ m = 80 m

$\therefore$ Perimeter = 2 (100 + 80) m

= 2 (180) m = 360 m

**4. D :** Let area = 100 m$^2$, Then, side = 10 m

New side = (125% of 10)m $= \left(\frac{125}{100} \times 10\right)$ m

= 12.5 m

New area = $(12.5 \times 12.5)$ m$^2$ = $(12.5)^2$ sq. m.

$\therefore$ Increase in area = $[(12.5)^2 - (10)^2]$ m$^2$

= $[(12.5 + 10)(125 - 10)]$ m$^2$

= $(22.5 \times 2.5)$ m$^2$ = 56.25 m$^2$

$\therefore$ Increase = 56.25%

**5. D :** Let original length = $x$ metres

New length = $2x$ metres.

$\therefore$ Ratio of the area $= \frac{4x^2}{x^2} = \frac{4}{1} = 4:1$

**6. C :** Let length = $l$ and breadth = $b$

Then, area = $l \times b$

New length = $2l$ and new breadth $= \frac{b}{2}$

$\therefore$ New area $= \left(2l \times \frac{b}{2}\right) = lb$

So, there is no change in area.

**7. A :** Initially, let length = $x$ and breath = $y$

Let, new breadth = $z$

Then new length $= \left(\frac{160}{100}x\right) = \frac{8}{5}x$

$\therefore \frac{8}{5}x \times z = xy$ or $z = \frac{5y}{8}$

Decrease in breadth $= \left(y - \frac{5y}{8}\right) = \frac{3}{8}y$

$\therefore$ Decrease Percentage

$= \left(\frac{3}{8}y \times \frac{1}{y} \times 100\right)\%$

$= 37\frac{1}{2}\%$

**8. B :** Let the areas of squares be $(9x^2)$ m$^2$ and $(x^2)$ m$^2$.

Then, their sides are $(3x)$ metres and $x$ metres respectively

$\therefore$ Ratio of their perimetres $= \frac{12x}{4x} = 3:1$

**9. C :** Area of verandah $= [25 \times 20) - (20 \times 15)]\ m^2$
$= 200\ m^2$
$\therefore$ Cost of flooring = (200 × 3.50) = Rs. 700

**10. C :** Let the side of the square = 100 m
New length = 140 m
New breadth = 130 m
Increase in Area
$= [(140 \times 130) - (100 \times 100)] = 8200\ m^2$
Increase percentage
$$= \left(\frac{8200}{100 \times 100} \times 100\right)\% = 82\%$$

**11. C :** Let the dimensions of one room be $l$, $b$ and $h$ metres respectively.
Then, the dimensions of the new room are $2l$, $2b$, $2h$ metres respectively.
$\therefore$ Area of 4 walls of the new room
$= [2 \times (2l + 2b) \times 2h]\ m^2 = 8 \times ((l + b) \times h)\ m^2$
$= 4 \times [2\ (l + b) \times h]$
$= 4 \times$ (area of 4 walls of 1st room)
Required cost = Rs. 4 × 48 = Rs. 192.

**12. C :** Original area $= \pi \times r^2$
$$\text{New area} = \pi\left(\frac{r}{2}\right)^2 = \frac{\pi r^2}{4}$$
$$\text{Reduction in area} = \pi r^2 - \frac{\pi r^2}{4} = \frac{3\pi r^2}{4}$$
Reduction percentage
$$= \left(\frac{3\pi r^2}{4} \times \frac{1}{\pi r^2} \times 100\right) = 75\%$$

**13. C :** $\text{Original area} = \pi\left(\frac{d}{2}\right)^2 = \frac{\pi d^2}{4}$
$$\text{New area} = \pi\left(\frac{2d}{2}\right)^2 = \pi d^2$$
$$\text{Increase in area} = \pi d^2 - \frac{\pi d^2}{4} = \frac{3\pi d^2}{4}$$
$$\text{Increase percentage} = \left(\frac{3\pi d^2}{4} \times \frac{4}{\pi d^2} \times 100\right)$$
$= 300\%$

**14. C :** $\text{Ratio of areas} = \dfrac{\pi r^2}{\pi(3r)^2} = \dfrac{1}{9} = 1:9$

**15. B :** Area of triangle

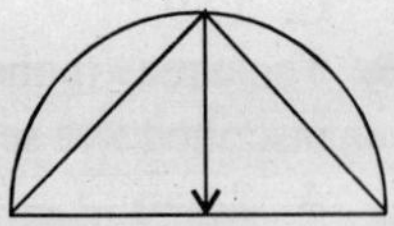

$$= \left[\frac{2}{9} 2r \times r\right] cm^2$$
$= r^2\ cm^2$

**16. B :** Side of the rhombus $= \left(\dfrac{52}{4}\right) = 13$ m

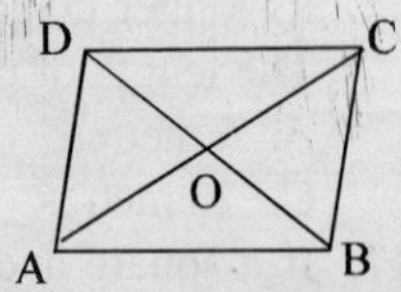

$AB = 13$ m, $AC = 24$,
So $AO = 13$ m
$$OB = \sqrt{AB^2 - OA^2}$$
$$= \sqrt{169 - 144} = 5\ m$$
So $BD = 2 \times OB = 10$ m
Hence other diagonal = 10 m

**17. B :** Let $ABCD$ be the square and $ABEF$ be the rhombus

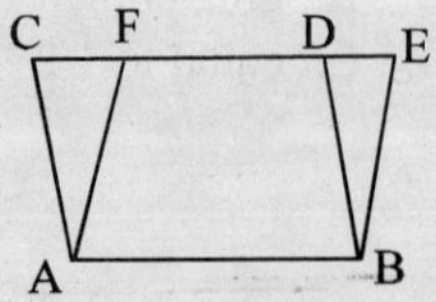

Then, in right triangles $ADF$ and $BCF$ we have,
$AD = BC$ (Side of a square)
and $AF = BE$ (Side of a rhombus)
$\therefore$ $DF = CE$
$[\because DF^2 = AF^2 - AD^2 = BF^2 - BC^2]$
Thus triangle $ADF$ + trapezium $ABCF$
$\Rightarrow$ Triangle $BCE$ + Trap $ABCF$
= Area of sq $ABCD$
$\Rightarrow$ Area of rhombus $ADEF$

**18. C :** Ratio of areas of similar triangles
$\Rightarrow$ Ratio of the squares of corresponding sides
$$= \left(\frac{3x}{4x}\right)^2 = \left(\frac{9x^2}{16x^2}\right) = \frac{9}{16} = 9:16$$

**19. V :** Let bigger side = $l$
Let smaller sides = $b$
and diagonal = $d$ = 13 m (given)
Then, $lb = 60$ and $d + l = 5b$
$d \times b = 60$
$d + l = 56$
$\therefore l \times (d + l) = 300$ or $l \times (13 + l) = 300$
or $l^2 + 13l = 300$ or $l^2 + 13l - 300 = 0$
or $(l + 25)(l - 12) = 0$ $\therefore$ $l = 12$ m

**20. D :** $\text{Ratio of Area} = \dfrac{a^2}{\dfrac{\sqrt{3}a^2}{4}} = \dfrac{4}{\sqrt{3}} = 4:\sqrt{3}$.

# Chapter 12

# VOLUME AND SURFACE AREA

**Volume and Surface Area**

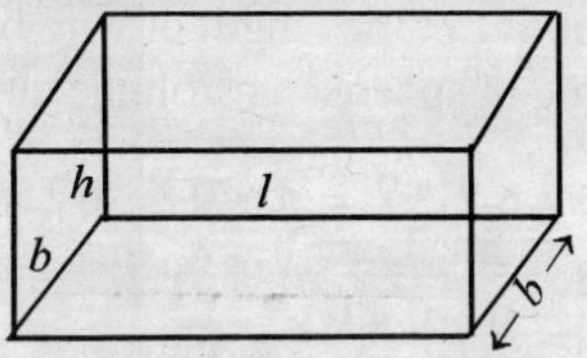


**Formulae**

1. ***Cuboid :*** Let length = $l$, breadth = $b$ and height = $h$ units
   (*i*) Volume of Cuboid = $(l \times b \times h)$ cubic units.
   (*ii*) Whole surface of Cuboid = $2\,(lb + bh + hl)$ sq. unit
   (*iii*) Diagonal of Cuboid = $\sqrt{l^2 + b^2 + h^2}$ units

2. ***Cube :*** Let each edge (or side) of a cube be a units, then
   (*i*) Volume of Cube = $a^3$ cubic units
   (*ii*) Whole surface of the Cube = $6a^2$ sq. units.
   (*iii*) Diagonal of the Cube = $\left(\sqrt{3a}\right)$ units

3. ***Cylinder :*** Let the radius of the base of a cylinder is $r$ units and its height (or length) be $h$.

   (*i*) Volume of the Cylinder
   $= \left(\pi r^2 h\right)$ cubic units
   (*ii*) Curved surface area of the Cylinder
   $= \left(2\pi rh\right)$ sq. unit
   (*iii*) Total surface area of the Cylinder
   $= \left(2\pi rh + 2\pi r^2\right)$ sq. units

4. ***Sphere :*** Let the radius of the sphere be sq. $r$ units.
   (*i*) Volume of Sphere = $\left(\frac{4}{3}\pi r^2\right)$ cubic units
   (*ii*) Surface area of Sphere = $\left(4\pi r^2\right)$ sq.units.
   (*iii*) Volume of Hemisphere = $\frac{2}{3}\pi r^3$ cubic unit
   (*iv*) Curved area of hemisphere = $2\pi r^2$ square units.
   (*v*) Whole surface area of Hemisphere = $3\pi r^2$ square units.

5. ***Cone :*** Let '$r$' be the radius of the base '$h$' be height and '$l$' be the slant height of the cone.

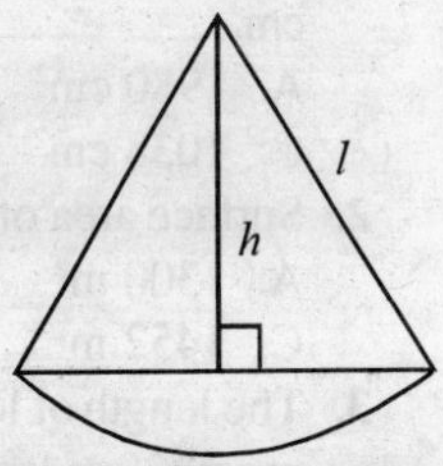


   (*i*) Slant height
   $l = \sqrt{h^2 + r^2}$ units
   (*ii*) Volume of Cone = $\left(\frac{1}{3}\pi r^2 h\right)$ cubic units
   (*iii*) Curved surface area of the Cone = $\pi rl$
   $= \pi r\sqrt{\left(r^2 + h^2\right)}$ square units.

**Example 1 :** Find the length of the largest pole that can be placed in a room, which is 5 m long, 4 metre broad and 3 metre high.

**Solution :** Length of longest pole= length of diagonal $= \sqrt{5^2 + 4^2 + 3^2} = \sqrt{50}$

$= 5\sqrt{2} = 5 \times 1.41 = 7.05$ m

**Example 2 :** Surface area of the cube is 384 cm$^2$. Find its volume.

**Solution :** $6a^2 = 384 \Rightarrow a^2 = 64 \Rightarrow a = 8$

Volume = $8 \times 8 \times 8 = 512$ cm$^2$

**Example 3 :** The capacity of a cylindrical tank is 6160 m³. If the radius of its base is 14 m, find the depth of the tank.

**Solution :** $\frac{22}{7} \times 14 \times 14 \times h = 6160$

$h = 6160 \times \frac{7}{22} \times \frac{1}{14 \times 14} = 10$ m.

**Example 4 :** Find the volume curved, surface area and total surface area of a hemi sphere of radius 21 cm.

Volume $= \frac{2}{3} \times \pi r^3$

$= \frac{2}{3} \times \frac{22}{7} \times 21 \times 21 \times 21 = 19404$ cm³

Curved surface area = $2\pi r^2$

$\Rightarrow \frac{2 \times 22}{7} \times 21 \times 21 = 2772$ cm²

Total surface Area = $3\pi r^2$

$= \frac{3 \times 22}{7} \times 21 \times 21 = 4158$ cm²

**Example 5 :** A copper sphere of diameter 18 cm is drawn into a wire of diameter 4 mm. Find the length of wire.

**Solution:** Let the length of wire be $h$ cm. Then

Volume of sphere= Volume of wire

$\frac{4}{3}\pi \times 9 \times 9 \times 9 = \pi \times 0.2 \times 0.2 \times h$

$h = \frac{4}{3} \times 9 \times 9 \times 9 \times \frac{1}{0.2 \times 0.2} = 24300$ cm

Hence the length of wire = 243 metre

## EXERCISE

**1.** Surface area of cuboid 22 cm by 12 cm by 7.5 cm. is

A. 1980 cm² B. 2076 cm²
C. 1038 cm² D. None of these

**2.** Surface area of a cube is 726 m², its volume is

A. 1300 m² B. 1331 m²
C. 1452 m² D. 1542 m²

**3.** The length of longest rod that can be placed in a room, 20 m long, 16 m broad and 12 m high, is

A. 30 cm B. $15\sqrt{3}$ cm
C. 60 cm D. $20\sqrt{2}$ cm

**4.** A metal sheet, 27 cm long, 8 cm. broad and 1 cm thick, is melted into a cube. The difference between the surface areas of two solids is

A. 284 cm² B. 286 cm²
C. 296 cm² D. 300 cm²

**5.** A river, 2 m deep and 45 m wide, is flowing at the rate of 3 km/h. The amount of the water that runs into the sea per minute is

A. 4500 m³ B. 27000 m³
C. 3000 m³ D. 2700 m³

**6.** If the volume of two cubes are in ratio 8 : 1, the ratio of their edges is

A. 8 : 1 B. $2\sqrt{2}$ : 1
C. 2 : 1 D. None of these

**7.** Two cubes have volumes in the ratio of 1 : 27. The ratio of their surface area is

A. 3 : 1 B. 1 : 8
C. 1 : 9 D. 1 : 18

**8.** The height of a cylinder is 14 cm and its curved surface area is 264 sq. cm. The volume of the cylinder is

A. 308 cm² B. 396 cm²
C. 1848 cm² D. 1232 cm²

**9.** The number of solid spheres, each of diameter 6 cm that could be moulded to form a solid metal cylinder of height 45 cm and diameter 4 cm, is

A. 3 B. 4
C. 5 D. 6

**10.** The radius of a circular cylinder is the same as that of a sphere. Their volume are equal. The height of the cylinder is

A. $\frac{4}{3}$ times that of its radius

B. $\frac{2}{3}$ times that of its radius

C. equal to its radius

D. equal to its diameter

**11.** A right cylinder and a right cone have the same radii and the same volumes. The ratio of the height of the cylinder to that of the cone is

A. 3 : 5 B. 2 : 5
C. 3 : 1 D. 1 : 3

**12.** The volume of a hemisphere is 19404 cubic cm. The total surface area is

A. 2772 sq. cm. B. 4158 sq. cm.
C. 5544 sq. cm. D. 1386 sq. cm.

**13.** The radii of two spheres are in the ratio of 1 : 2. The ratio of their surface areas is

A. 1 : 2 B. 1 : 4
C. 1 : $\sqrt{2}$ D. 3 : 4

**14.** If the volume and surface area of a sphere are numerically the same, then its radius is

A. 1 unit B. 2 units
C. 3 units D. 4 units

**15.** If the radius of a sphere in doubled, then its volume increases by

A. 100% B. 200%
C. 700% D. 800%

**16.** A cylindrical piece of metal of radius 2 cm and height 6 cms is shaped into a cone of same radius. The height of the cone is

A. 18 cms B. 14 cms
C. 12 cms D. 8 cms

**17.** If the volumes of two cones are in the ratio 1 : 4 and their diameters are in the ratio 4 : 5, then the ratio of their heights is

A. 1 : 5 B. 5 : 4
C. 5 : 16 D. 25 : 64

**18.** A cone of height 7 cm and base radius 3 cm is carved from a rectangular block of wood of dimensions 10 cm × 5 cm × 2 cm. The percentage of wood wasted is

A. 34% B. 46%
C. 54% D. 66%

**19.** The percentage increase in the surface area of a cube, when each side is doubled, is

A. 25% B. 50%
C. 150% D. 300%

**20.** A cylinder and a cone have the same height and same radius of the base. The ratio between the volumes of the cylinder and the cone is

A. 1 : 3 B. 3 : 1
C. 1 : 2 D. 2 : 1

## EXPLANATORY ANSWERS

**1. C :** Surface area
$= 2\,(22 \times 12 + 12 \times 7.5 + 22 \times 7.5)\ \text{cm}^2$
$= 264 + 90 + 165 = 1038\ \text{cm}^2$

**2. B :** $6a^2 = 726 \Rightarrow a^2 = 121 \Rightarrow a = 11$ cm
$\therefore$ Volume of the cube $= (11 \times 11 \times 11)\ \text{cm}^2$
$\Rightarrow 1331\ \text{cm}^3$

**3. D :** Length of rod $= \sqrt{20^2 + (16)^2 + (12)^2}$
$= \sqrt{800} \Rightarrow 20\sqrt{2}$ cm.

**4. B :** Volume of sheet $= (27 \times 8 \times 1)\ \text{cm}^3 = 216\ \text{cm}^3$
Volume of cube formed $= 216\ \text{cm}^3$
Edge of cube $= (6 \times 6 \times 6)^{1/3} = 6$ cm
Surface area of original cuboid
$= 2\,(27 \times 8 \times 8 \times 1 \times 27 \times 1)\ \text{cm}^2 \Rightarrow 502\ \text{cm}^2$
Surface area of cube formed $= [6\,(6)^2]$
$= 216\ \text{cm}^2$
Difference in aqreas $= (502 - 216) = 286\ \text{cm}^2$.

**5. A :** Speed per minute $= \dfrac{3 \times 1000}{60}$ m $= 50$ m
Volume of water running per minute
$= (45 \times 2 \times 50)\ \text{m}^2$
$\Rightarrow 4500\ \text{m}^2$

**6. C :** Let their volumes be $8x^3$ and $x^3$, respectively
Then their edges are $2x$ and $x$ respectively
Ratio of their edges = 2 : 1

**7. C :** Let the volumes be $x^3$ and $27x^3$
$\therefore$ Their edges are $x$ and $3x$
Ratio of their surface areas
$8x^2 : 54x^2 = 1 : 9$

**8. B :** $2\pi rh = 264$
$\Rightarrow 2 \times \dfrac{22}{7} \times r \times 14 = 264$
$\therefore r = 3$
So volume $= \pi r^2 h = \dfrac{22}{7} \times 3 \times 3 \times 14\ \text{cm}^2$
$= 396\ \text{cm}^3$

**9. C :** Let No. of spheres are $x$
Then, $x \cdot \dfrac{4}{3}\pi\,(3)^3 = \pi \times 2^2 \times 45$
$36\,x = 180 \Rightarrow x = \dfrac{180}{36} = 5$
$x = 5$

**10. A :** $\frac{4}{3}\pi r^2 = \pi r^2 h \Rightarrow h = \frac{4}{2}r$

$\therefore$ Height = $\frac{4}{3}$ time its radius.

**11. D :** Let the height of cylinder = $h$ and height of cone = $H$

Then $\pi r^2 h = \frac{1}{3}\pi r^2 H$

$$\frac{h}{H} = \frac{1}{3} = 1:3$$

**12. B :** $\frac{2}{3} \times \frac{22}{7} \times r^3 = 19404$

$$r^3 = 19404 \times \frac{7}{22} \times \frac{3}{2} = (21)^3$$

$\therefore$ $r = 21$

Total surface a area = $3\pi r^2$

$$a = 3 \times \frac{22}{7} \times 21 \times 21 = 4158 \text{ cm}^2$$

**13. B :** Let, their radii be $x$ and $2x$

Ratio of their surface areas

$$\frac{4\pi x^2}{4\pi (2x)^2} = \frac{1}{4} = 1:4$$

**14. C :** $\frac{4}{3}\pi r^3 = 4\pi r^2 \Rightarrow r = 3$ units

**15. C :** Original volume = $\frac{4}{3}\pi r^3$

New volume = $\frac{4}{3}\pi (2r)^3 = \frac{32}{3}\pi r^3$

Increase in volume = $\left(\frac{32}{3} - \frac{4}{3}\right)\pi r^3$

$$= \frac{28}{3}\pi r^3$$

Percentage increase in volume

$$= \frac{\frac{28}{3}\pi r^3}{\frac{4}{3}\pi r^3} \times 100$$

$$= \frac{28}{3} \times \frac{3}{4} \times 100 = 700\%$$

**16. A :** $\frac{1}{3}\pi (2)^2 \times h = \pi (2)^2 \times 6 \Rightarrow h = 18$ cm

**17. D :** As the diameters are in the ratio of 4 : 5, so that their radii are in the ratio of 4 : 5.

Let, height be $h$ and $H$

Ratio of volumes= $\frac{1}{4} = \dfrac{\frac{1}{3}\pi (4r)^2 h}{\frac{1}{3}\pi (5r)^2 H}$

$$\frac{1}{4} = \frac{16h}{25H} \text{ or } \frac{h}{H} = \frac{25}{64}$$

or $h : H = 25 : 64$

**18. A :** Total volume = $[10 \times 5 \times 2]$ cm³ = 100 cm²

Curved Volume $= \frac{1}{3} \times \frac{22}{7} \times 3 \times 3 \times 7$

$= 66$ cm²

Wood wasted = (100 – 66) = 34%

**19. D :** Original area = $6a^2$

New area $= 6(2a)^2 = 24a^2$

Increase percentage

$$= \left(\frac{18a^2}{6a^2} \times 100\right)\% = 300\%$$

**20. B :** Ratio of their volumes = $\dfrac{\pi r^2 h}{\frac{1}{3}\pi r^2 h} = \frac{3}{1} = 3:1$

## Chapter 13

# BOATS AND STREAMS

**Note**

(*i*) Direction along the stream is called downstream direction.

(*ii*) Direction against the stream is called upstream direction.

(*iii*) Let, speed of boat in still water be $x$ km/hr and speed of stream be $y$ km/hr.
Then,
Speed of boat in downstream $= (x + y)$ km/hr
Speed of boat in upstream $= (x - y)$ km/hr.

(*iv*) If a man rows in still water at $x$ km/hr and the speed of the current or the stream is $y$ km/hr
Then,
Man's rate with current $= (x + y)$ km/hr
Man's rate against the current $= (x - y)$ km/hr

Rate in still water $= \frac{1}{2}$ [rate with current + rate against the current]

Rate of current $= \frac{1}{2}$ [rate with current − rate against the current]

**Example 1 :** A man rows downstream 30 km and upstream 18 km, taking 5 hours each time. What is the velocity of water?

**Solution :** Man's rate downstream $= \frac{30}{5}$ km/hr
$= 6$ km/hr

Man's rate upstream $= \frac{18}{5}$ km/hr

$\therefore$ Velocity of current $= \frac{1}{2}\left(6 - \frac{18}{5}\right) = 1.2$ km/hr.

**Example 2 :** A man can rows at the speed of 6 km/hr in still water. It takes him twice as long to row up as it takes him to row down the river. Find the rate of stream.

**Solution :** Let the man's rate upstream $= x$ km/hr

Then man's rate downstream $= 2x$ km/hr

Man's rate in still water $= \frac{1}{2}(x + 2x)$ km/hr

$= \frac{3x}{2} = 6$ or $x = 4$ km/hr

Thus man's rate upstream $= 4$ km/hr
Man's rate downstream $= 8$ km/hr

$\because$ Rate of stream $= \frac{1}{2}(8 - 4)$ km/hr $\Rightarrow 2$ km/hr.

**Example 3 :** A man can row 30 km upstream and 44 km downstream in 10 hours. Also, he can row 40 km. upstream and 55 km downstream in 13 hours. Find the rate of current and speed of the man in still water.

**Solution :** Let rate upstream $= x$ km/hr
Rate downstream $= y$ km/hr

$$\frac{30}{x} + \frac{44}{y} = 10 \quad ...(i)$$

$$\frac{40}{x} + \frac{55}{y} = 13 \quad ...(ii)$$

or

$$30u + 44v = 10 \quad ...(iii)$$

$$40u + 55v = 13 \quad ...(iv)$$

Solving (*iii*) and (*iv*), we get $u = \frac{1}{5}$ and $v = \frac{1}{11}$

$\therefore \frac{1}{x} = \frac{1}{5} \Rightarrow x = 5$

$\frac{1}{y} = \frac{1}{11} \Rightarrow y = 11$

Rate in still water $= \frac{1}{2}(5 + 11) = 8$ km/hr

Rate of current $= \frac{1}{2}(11 - 5) = 3$ km/hr

## EXERCISE

**1.** A man can row downstream at 14 km/hr and upstream at 9 km/hr. Man's rate in still water is

A. 5 km/hr B. 23 km/hr
C. 11.5 km/hr D. None of these

**2.** The speed of a boat in still water is 2 km/hr. If its speed upstream is 1 km/hr, then speed of stream is

A. 1.5 km/hr B. 3 km/hr
C. 1 km/hr D. None of these

**3.** A boat goes 40 km upstream in 8 hours and 36 km downstream in 6 hours. The speed of the boat in standing water is

A. 6.5 km/hr B. 6 km/hr
C. 5.5 km/hr D. 5 km/hr

**4.** A man rows upstream 16 km and downstream 28 km taking 5 hours each time. The velocity of the current is

A. 24 km/hr B. 1.2 km/hr
C. 3.6 km/hr D. 1.8 km/hr

**5.** A man can row at the rate of $9\frac{1}{3}$ km/hr in still water and he finds that it takes him thrice as much time to row upstream than the time taken to row downstream the same distance in river. The speed of the current is

A. $3\frac{1}{3}$ km/hr B. $3\frac{1}{9}$ km/hr
C. $1\frac{1}{4}$ km/hr D. $4\frac{2}{3}$ km/hr

**6.** A man can swim at the rate of 3 km/hr in still water. If the velocity of the stream is 2 km/hr, the time taken by him to swim to a place 10 km upstream and back is

A. $8\frac{1}{3}$ hrs B. $9\frac{1}{5}$ hrs
C. 10 hrs D. 12 hrs

**7.** The current of a stream runs at the rate of 4 km an hour. A boat travels for 6 km and come back to the starting point in 2 hours. The speed of the boat in still water is

A. 6 km/hr B. 7.5 km/hr
C. 8 km/hr D. 6.8 km/hr

**8.** A boat moves upstream at the rate of 1 km in 10 minutes and moves downstream at the rate of 1 km in 6 minutes. The speed of current is

A. 1 km/hr B. 1.5 km/hr
C. 2 km/hr D. 2.5 km/hr

## EXPLANATORY ANSWERS

**1. C :** Man's speed in still water

$\Rightarrow \frac{1}{2}(14+9) = 11.5$ km/hr

**2. C :** Let the speed of stream be $x$ km/hr

Then speed upstream = $2 - x$ km/hr

$2 - x = 1 \Rightarrow x = 1$ km/hr

**3. C :** Speed upstream = $\frac{40}{8}$ km/hr

$\Rightarrow$ 5 km/hr

Speed downstream = $\frac{36}{6} = 6$ km/hr

Speed of boat in still water

$\Rightarrow \frac{1}{2}(5+6) = 5.5$ km/hr

**4. B :** Speed downstream = $\frac{28}{5}$ km/hr

$\Rightarrow$ 5.6 km/hr

Speed upstream = $\frac{16}{5} = 3.2$ km/hr

Velocity of current = $\frac{1}{2}(5.6 - 3.2)$

$\Rightarrow$ 1.2 km/hr

**5. D :** Let speed upstream = $x$ km/hr

Then speed downstream = $3x$ km/hr

$\therefore$ Speed in still water $= \frac{1}{2}(x + 3x)$

$= 2x$ km/hr

Speed of current = $\frac{1}{2}(3x - x) = x$ km/hr

$\therefore 2x = \frac{28}{3}$ or $x = \frac{14}{3} = 4\frac{2}{3}$ km/hr.

**6. D :** Speed in downstream = (3 + 2) = 5 km/hr
Speed in upstream = (3 – 2) = 1 km/hr

Them total time taken = $\frac{10}{5} + \frac{10}{1} = 12$ hours

**7. C :** Let the speed in still water be $x$ km/hr

Then $\frac{6}{x+4} + \frac{6}{x-4} = 2$

$\Rightarrow 6\,[x - 4 + x + 4] = 2\,(x^2 - 16)$

$x^2 - 16 = 6x$

$x^2 - 6x - 16 = 0$

$(x - 8)(x + 2) = 0$ So $x = 8$ km/hr

**8. C :** Speed of upstream = 6 km/hr
Speed of downstream = 10 km/hr
$\therefore$ Speed of the current

$\Rightarrow \frac{1}{2}$ (10 – 6) km/hr = 2 km/hr.

## Chapter 14

# PROBLEMS ON AGES

1. Ratio of Vimal's age and Aruna's age is 3 : 5 and sum of their ages is 80 yrs. The ratio of their ages after 10 years will be
   A. 2 : 3 B. 1 : 2
   C. 3 : 2 D. 3 : 5
2. Three years ago the average age of *A* and *B* was 18 years. With *C* joining them average becomes 22. How old is *C* now?
   A. 24 years B. 28 years
   C. 20 years D. 30 years
3. Jayesh is as much younger than Anil as he is older than Prashant. If the sum of ages of Anil and Prashant is 48 years, what is the age of Jayesh?
   A. 20 years B. 24 years
   C. 30 years D. cannot be determined
4. The ratio of the ages of a father and his son at present is 6 : 1. After 5 years, the ratio will become 7 : 2. The present age of the son is
   A. 5 years B. 6 years
   C. 9 years D. 10 years
5. The ratio of Laxmi's age and that of her mother is 3 : 11. The difference of their ages is 24 years. The ratio of their ages after 3 years will be
   A. 1 : 3 B. 2 : 3
   C. 3 : 5 D. None of these
6. 10 years ago, Chandrawati's mother was 4 times older than her daugher. After 10 years the mother will be twice as old as her daughter. The present age of Chandrawati is
   A. 5 yrs B. 10 yrs
   C. 20 yrs D. 30 yrs
7. The age of Mohan's father is 4 times his age. If 5 years ago, father's age was 7 times the age of his son. At present what is the age of Mohan's father?
   A. 35 yrs B. 40 yrs
   C. 70 yrs D. 84 yrs
8. 5 years ago Vinay's age was one-third of the age of Vikas and now Vinay's age is 17 years. What is the present age of Vikas?
   A. 9 years B. 36 years
   C. 41 years D. 51 years
9. Sum of the ages of a son and father is 56 years. After four years, the age of the father will be three times the son's age. Their ages are
   A. 12 yrs, 44 yrs B. 16 yrs, 42 yrs
   C. 16 yrs, 48 yrs D. 18 yrs, 36 yrs
10. Mr. Mohan Lal is 4 times as old as his son. Four years hence, the sum of their ages will be 43 years. The present age of the son is
    A. 5 yrs B. 7 yrs
    C. 8 yrs D. 10 yrs

## EXPLANATORY ANSWERS

**1. A :** $3x + 5x = 80 \Rightarrow x = 10$

Ratio of their ages after 10 years

$3x + 10 : 5x + 10$

$= 40 : 60 \Rightarrow 2 : 3$

**2. A :** Sum of age of *A* and *B*, 3 years ago

$\Rightarrow 18 \times 2 = 36$ yrs

Sum of age of *A*, *B* and *C*

Now $= 22 \times 3 = 66$ years

Sum of ages of *A* and *B* now

$= 36 + 6 = 42$ years

$\therefore$ *C*'s age = (66 – 42) years

$\Rightarrow$ 24 years.

**3. B :** Let Anil's age = *x* years

Then Prashant's age = $(48 - x)$ years

Let the age of Jayesh be '*y*' years

Then

$$y - (48 - x) = x - y$$
$$\Rightarrow 2y = 48$$
$$y = 24 \text{ years.}$$

**4. A :** $\dfrac{6x+5}{x+5} = \dfrac{7}{2} \Rightarrow 2(6x+5) = 7(x+5)$

$\Rightarrow x = 5$

$\therefore$ Son's present age = 5 years.

**5. A :** $11x - 3x = 24$

$\Rightarrow \quad x = 3$

$\therefore$ Ratio of their ages after 3 years

$\Rightarrow [3x + 3 : 11x + 3] = 12 : 26$

$\Rightarrow \quad 1 : 3$

**6. C :** Let Chandrawati's age 10 years ago be = $x$ years and her mother's age = $4x$ years

After 10 years hence—

Chandrawati's mother's age = $4x + 10 + 10$

$= 4x + 20$ years

Chandrawati's age $= x + 10 +$

10

$= x + 20$ years

$4x + 20 = 2(x + 20)$

$2x = 20$

$\Rightarrow x = 10$

So, Chandrawati's present age

$= 10 + 10 = 20$ years

**7. B :** Let Mohan's age be $x$ years

Then his father's age = $4x$ years

$\therefore \quad 4x - 5 = 7(x - 5)$

or $\quad 3x = 30$

$x = 10$

Hence, age of Mohan's father is

$10 \times 4 = 40$ years.

**8. C :** Let present age of Vikas be $x$ years

Then

$17 - 5 = \dfrac{1}{3}(x - 5)$

$x - 5 = 36$

$x = 41$ years

**9. A :** Let the present age of the son and father be $x$ years and $(56 - x)$ years, respectively. Then

$(56 - x + 4) = 3(x + 4)$

$4x = 48$

$x = 12$

So their ages are 12 years, and 44 years, respectively.

**10. B :** Let son's age be $x$ years

Then $(x + 4) + (4x + 4) = 43$

$5x = 35$

$x = 7$ years.

Chapter 15

# TRAIN MOVEMENT

**Note**

(*i*) Time taken by a train $x$ metres long, passing by a signal post or a pole or a standing man is same as the time taken by a train to cover $x$ metres with its own speed.

(*ii*) Time taken by a train, $x$ metres long and passing by a stationary object of length $y$ metres (such as bridge or a tunnel or a platform or a train at rest) is the same as the time taken by a train to cover $(x + y)$ metres with its own speed.

(*iii*) Suppose that two trains or two bodies are moving in the same direction at $u$ km/hr and $v$ km/hr, respectively such that $u > v$. Then their relative speed = $(u - v)$ km/hr. If the relative lengths be $x$ and $y$ km respectively, then time taken by the faster train to cross slower train (moving in the same direction) is = $\left(\dfrac{x+y}{u-v}\right)$.

(*iv*) Suppose two trains or two bodies are moving in opposite directions at $u$ km/hr and $v$ km/hr. Then relative speed = $(u + v)$ km/hr. If their lengths be $x$ and $y$ km, then time taken to cross each other = $\left(\dfrac{x+y}{u+v}\right)$ hr.

(*v*) If two trains start at same time from two points $A$ and $B$ towards each other and after crossing they take $a$ and $b$ hours in reaching points $B$ and $A$, respectively, then

$A$'s speed : $B$'s speed = $\sqrt{b} : \sqrt{a}$

**Example 1 :** A train, 160 m long, is running at 40 km/hr. In how much time, will it pass a platform that is 140 m long.

**Solution :** Speed = $40 \times \dfrac{5}{18}$ m/sec. = $\dfrac{100}{9}$ m/sec.

Distance covered in passing the platform

$\Rightarrow (160 + 140) = 300$ m

Required time taken = $300 \times \dfrac{9}{100} \Rightarrow 27$ sec.

**Example 2 :** A train passes a standing man in 2 seconds and a platform 50 m long in $4\frac{1}{2}$ seconds. Find the length of train and speed of train.

**Solution :** Let speed of train be $x$ km/hr or $\left(\dfrac{5x}{18}\right)$ m/sec.

Let length of train = $y$ metres

$$\frac{y}{\left(\frac{5x}{18}\right)} = 2$$

$$10x = 18y \Rightarrow 5x = 9y$$

$$\text{Also } \frac{y+50}{\left(\frac{5x}{18}\right)} = \frac{9}{2} \Rightarrow 36(y + 50) = 45x$$

$$5x - 4y = 200$$

$$9y - 4y = 200 \Rightarrow y = 40$$

$$5x = 9 \times 40 \Rightarrow x = \frac{9 \times 40}{5} = 72$$

$\therefore$ Speed of train = 72 km/hr

Length of train = 40 m.

**Example 3 :** Two trains, 128 m and 132 m long, are running towards each other on parallel lines at 42 km/hr and 30 km/hr, respectively. In what time, will they be clear of each other from the moment they meet?

**Solution :** Relatives speed = $(42 + 30)$ km/hr

$\Rightarrow \dfrac{72 \times 5}{18}$ m/sec = 20 m/sec

Distance covered in passing each other

= 128 + 132 = 260 m

Required time = $\dfrac{260}{20}$ = 13 sec.

**Example 4 :** Two trains are moving in the same direction at 50 km/hr and 30 km/hr. The faster train crosses a man in the slower train in 18 seconds. Find the length of the faster train.

**Solution :** Relative speed = (50 – 30) km/hr

$$= 20 \times \frac{5}{18} = \frac{50}{9} \text{ m/sec.}$$

Distance covered in 18 second at this speed

$$\Rightarrow 18 \times \frac{50}{9} = 100 \text{ m.}$$

**Example 5 :** A train, 100 m long, takes 9 seconds to cross a man walking at 5 km/hr in the direction opposite to that of the train. Find the speed of train.

**Solution :** Let the speed of the train be $x$ km/hr

Relative speed $\Rightarrow (x + 5)$ km/hr

$$\Rightarrow \frac{5(x+5)}{18} \text{ m/sec}$$

Distances covered in passing the man = 100 m.

$$\therefore \frac{100}{\frac{5(x+5)}{18}} = 9$$

$\Rightarrow 1800 = 45(x + 5)$ or $x =$ 35

## EXERCISE

1. A speed of 16 m/sec. is same as
   A. 40.3 km/hr
   B. 57.6 km/hr
   C. 51.10 km/hr
   D. None of these
2. A train 250 metres long, running with a speed of 50 km/hr, will pass an electric pole in
   A. 30 sec B. 18 sec
   C. 72 sec D. 60 sec
3. A train, 280 metres long, is moving at a speed of 60 km/hr. The time taken by the train to cross a plateform, 220 metres long, is
   A. 20 sec B. 25 sec
   C. 30 sec D. 35 sec
4. A train, 50 metres long, passes a plateform, 100 metres long, in 60 secs. The speed of train is
   A. 10 km/hr
   B. 15 km/hr
   C. 54 km/hr
   D. 100 km/hr
5. A train 100 metres long, running at 36 km/hr, takes 25 seconds to pass a bridge. The length of the bridge is
   A. 150 metres
   B. 144 metres
   C. 90 metres
   D. 540 metres
6. A train, 300 m long, crossed a platform, 900 metres long, in 1 minute and 12 seconds. The speed of train, in km/hr, was
   A. 50 B. 45
   C. 54 D. 60
7. Two trains, 132 metres and 108 metres long, are running in opposite direction, one, at the rate of 32 km/hr and another at the rate of 40 km/hr. From the moment, they will cross each other in
   A. 10 seconds B. 11 seconds
   C. 12 seconds D. 13 seconds
8. A 150 metres long train crosses a man walking at the speed of 6 km/hr in the opposite directions in 6 seconds. The speed of the train in km/hr is
   A. 66 B. 84
   C. 46 D. 106
9. A train passed a pole in 15 sec. and a platform, 100 metres long, in 25 seconds. Its length in metres is
   A. 200
   B. 150
   C. 50
   D. Data inadequate
10. Two stations, $A$ and $B$, are 110 kms apart on a straight line. One train starts from $A$ at 7 A.M. and travels towards $B$ at a speed of 20 km per hour. Another train starts from $B$ at 8 A.M. and travels towards $A$ at a speed of 25 km per hour. At what time, will they meet?
    A. 9 a.m.
    B. 10 a.m.
    C. 11 a.m.
    D. None of these

# EXPLANATORY ANSWERS

**1. B :** 16 m/sec = $\left(16 \times \frac{18}{5}\right)$ km/hr = 57.6 km

**2. B :** Speed of train = $50 \times \frac{5}{18} = \frac{125}{9}$ m/sec.

Time taken by the train to pass the pole

$\Rightarrow 250 \times \frac{9}{125} = 18$ sec.

**3. C :** Speed of train = $60 \times \frac{5}{18} = \frac{50}{3}$ m/sec.

Time taken by the train to cross the platform
= Time taken by it to cover (280 + 220) m

$\Rightarrow 500 \times \frac{3}{50} = 30$ sec.

**4. C :** Distance, covered by train in 10 sec.
= (50 + 100) = 150 m

$\therefore$ Speed = $\frac{150}{10} = 15 \times \frac{18}{5} = 54$ km/hr.

**5. A :** Speed = $36 \times \frac{5}{18}$ m/sec. = 10 m/sec.

Let the length of the bridge = $x$ m

Distance covered = $(100 + x)$ m

Time taken = 25 sec

$\therefore \frac{100 \times x}{25} = 10 \Rightarrow 100 + x = 250$

$\Rightarrow x = 150$ m.

**6. D :** Distance covered in 72 sec = (300 + 900)

Speed = $\left(\frac{1200}{72}\right)$ m/sec = $\frac{50}{3}$ m/sec

$\Rightarrow \frac{50}{3} \times \frac{18}{5} = 60$ km/hr

**7. C :** Relative speed = (32 + 40) km/hr = 72 km/hr

$\Rightarrow 72 \times \frac{5}{18} = 20$ m/sec.

Distance covered in crossing each other

$\Rightarrow$ (132 + 108) m = 240 m

$\therefore$ Time Required = $\left(\frac{240}{20}\right)$ sec.

= 12 sec.

**8. B :** Let the speed of train be $x$ km/hr
Relative speed = $(x + 6)$ km/hr

$\Rightarrow \left((x+6) \times \frac{5}{18}\right)$ m/sec.

$\Rightarrow \frac{150}{6} = \frac{(x+6) \times 5}{18}$

$5x + 30 = 450$

or $x = 84$ km/hr

**9. B :** Let the length of the train be $x$ metre and its speed be $y$ metres/sec.

Then $\frac{x}{y} = 15 \Rightarrow y = \frac{x}{15}$

Now $\frac{x + 100}{25} = \frac{x}{15}$

$\Rightarrow x = 150$ metres.

**10. B :** Suppose that they meet $x$ hrs after 7 A.M.

Distance covered by $A$ in $x$ hrs
= $(20 \times x)$ km

Distance covered by $B$ in $(x - 1)$ hrs
= $25\,(x - 1)$ km

$\therefore 20x + 25\,(x - 1) = 110$ or $45x = 135$

$\Rightarrow x = 3$

So, they meet at 10 A.M.

## Chapter 16

# TIME AND DISTANCE

**Formulae**

(*i*) Speed $= \dfrac{\text{Distance}}{\text{Time}}$

(*ii*) Time $= \dfrac{\text{Distance}}{\text{Speed}}$

(*iii*) Distance = Speed × Time

(*iv*) If a certrain distance is covered at the rate of $x$ km/hr and the same distance is covered at the rate of $y$ km/hr, then the average speed during the whole journey is

$$\left(\frac{2xy}{x+y}\right) \text{ km/hr}$$

(*v*) If the speed of a body is changed in the ratio $a : b$, then the ratio of the time taken change in the ratio $b : a$.

(*vi*) $x$ km/hr $= x \times \dfrac{5}{18}$ m/sec.

(*vii*) $x$ m/sec. $= \left(x \times \dfrac{18}{5}\right)$ km/hr

**Example 1:** Harish covers a certain distance by car driving at 70 km/hr and he returned at the starting point, riding on a scooter at 55 km/hr. Find his average speed for the whole journey.

**Solution :** Average Speed $= \dfrac{2 \times 70 \times 55}{70 + 55}$ km/hr

$= 61.6$ km/hr.

**Example 2:** A man covers a certain distance between his home and office on the scooter, having an average speed of 30 km/hr. He is late by 10 minutes. However, with a speed of 40 km/hr he reaches his office 5 minutes earlier. Find the distance between his home and office.

**Solution :** Let the required distance be $x$ km

Time taken to cover $x$ km at 30 km/hr $= \dfrac{x}{30}$ hrs

Time taken to cover $x$ km at 40 km/hr $= \dfrac{x}{40}$ hrs

Difference in the time taken = 15 m $= \dfrac{1}{4}$ hrs

$$\Rightarrow \quad \frac{x}{30} - \frac{x}{40} = \frac{1}{4}$$

$$\Rightarrow \quad \frac{4x - 3x}{120} = \frac{1}{4}$$

$$\Rightarrow \quad x = 30$$

Hence Required Distance = 30 km.

## EXERCISE

**1.** Speed of 55 m/sec is same as

A. 198 km/hr  B. 11 km/hr

C. $15\frac{5}{18}$ km/hr  D. 275 km/hr

**2.** A man crosses a street, 600 m long, in 5 minutes. His speed in km/hr is

A. 7.2  B. 3.6

C. 10  D. 8.4

**3.** A train is moving with a speed of 92.4 km/hr. How many metres will it cover in 10 minutes?

A. 1540  B. 15400

C. 154  D. 15.4

**4.** A boy goes to school with a speed of 3 km/hr and returns to the village with a speed of 2 km/hr. If he takes 5 hours in all, the distance between the village and the school is

A. 6 km  B. 7 km

C. 8 km  D. 9 km

**5.** A car completes a certain journey in 8 hours. It

covers half the distance at 40 km/hr and the rest at 60 km/hr. The length of journey is

A. 350 km B. 420 km
C. 384 km D. 400 km

6. A train leaves Meerut at 6. a.m. and reaches Delhi at 10 a.m. Another train leaves Delhi at 8 a.m. and reaches Meerut at 11.30. At what time would the two train cross each other?

A. 9.26 a.m. B. 9 a.m.
C. 8.36 a.m. D. 8.56 a.m.

7. A certain distance in covered at a certain speed. If half of this distance is covered in double the time, the ratio of two speeds is

A. 4 : 1 B. 1 : 4
C. 2 : 1 D. 1 : 2

8. A man walking at 3 km/hr crosses a square field diagonally in 3 minutes. The area of the field is

A. 2500 m$^2$ B. 3000 m$^2$
C. 5000 m$^2$ D. 6000 m$^2$

## EXPLANATORY ANSWERS

**1. A :** 55 m/sec = $55 \times \frac{18}{5}$ = 198 km/hr

**2. A :** Speed $= \frac{600}{5 \times 60} = \frac{600}{5 \times 60} \times \frac{18}{5}$ km/hr

= 7.2 km/hr

**3. B :** 92.4 km/hr = $92.4 \times \frac{5}{18}$ m/sec

Distance covered in (10 × 60) sec

$\Rightarrow \left(92.4 \times \frac{5}{18} \times 10 \times 60\right)$ = 15400 m

**4. A :** Let the required distance be $x$ km. Then

$\frac{x}{3} + \frac{x}{2} = 5 \Rightarrow 2x + 3 \qquad x = 30$

$\Rightarrow \qquad x = 6$

**5. C.:** Let the total journey be $x$ km

$\frac{x}{2} \cdot \frac{1}{40} + \frac{x}{2} \cdot \frac{1}{60} = 8 \Rightarrow \frac{x}{80} + \frac{x}{120} = 8$

$\therefore$ $3x + 2x = 1920 \Rightarrow x = 384$ km

**6. D :** Let distance between Meerut and Delhi be $y$ km.

Average speed of the train leaving Meerut

$\Rightarrow \frac{y}{4}$ km/hr

Average speed of the train leaving Delhi

$= \frac{2y}{7}$ km/hr

Suppose they meet $x$ hrs after 6 a.m.

Then $\frac{xy}{4} + \frac{2y(x-2)}{7} = y$

or $\frac{x}{4} + \frac{2x-4}{7} = 1$

$\therefore$ $15x = 44$

$x = \frac{44}{15}$ = 2 hrs 56 m

So trains meet at 8.56 a.m.

**7. A :** Let distance $x$ km be covered in $y$ hrs. Then

1st speed $= \frac{x}{y}$ km/hr

2nd speed $= \frac{x}{2} \div 2y$ km/hr $= \frac{x}{4y}$ km/hr

$\therefore$ Ratio of speeds $= \frac{x}{y} : \frac{x}{4y} = 1 : \frac{1}{4} \Rightarrow 4 : 1$

**8. C :** Speed = $3 \times \frac{5}{18}$ m/sec = $\frac{5}{6}$ m/sec

$\therefore$ Distance covered in (2 × 60) sec

$\Rightarrow \left(\frac{5}{6} \times 2 \times 60\right)$ m = 100 m

$\therefore$ Length of diagonal = 100 m

So Area = $\frac{1}{2}$ (diagonal)$^2$ = $\left(\frac{1}{2} \times 100 \times 100\right)$

$\Rightarrow$ 5000 m$^2$

## Chapter 17

# CHAIN RULE

**Notes:**

(*i*) Method of finding the fourth proportion when other three are given, is called simple proportion of rule of three. Repeated usage of the rule of three is called compound proportion.

(*ii*) **Direct Proportion.** Two quantities are said to be directly proportional if on the increase or decrease of the one the other increases are decreases to the same extent.

*i.e.*, (*i*) More article, more cost and less article less cost

(*ii*) More men more work, less man less work.

(*iii*) **Indirect proportion.** Two quantities are said to be indirectly proportional if on the increase of one the other decreases to the same extent and vice-versa.

(*i*) Less number of days is required to finish a work if more persons are to be employed

(*ii*) More, is the speed, the lesser is the time taken.

**Example 1:** If 36 men can do a piece of work in 25 days, in how many days, will 15 men do it?

**Solution :** Clearly, lesser is the number of men employed, more will be the number of days taken to finish the work.

So, inverse ratio of men is equal to the ratio of time taken.

Let required number of days be $x$, then

$$15 : 36 : : 25 : x$$

or $\frac{15}{36} = \frac{25}{x}$ or $x = \frac{36 \times 25}{15} = 60$

$\therefore$ Required number of days = 60.

**Example 2 :** A contract is to be completed in 56 days and 104 men have put to work, each working for 8 hours a day. After 30 days, $\frac{2}{5}$ th of the work was completed. How many additional men may be employed so that the work may be completed in time, each man now working for 9 hours a day?

**Solution :** Remaining work = $1 - \frac{2}{5} = \frac{3}{5}$

Required Period = 56 – 30 = 26

| | |
|---|---|
| More work, more men | Direct |
| More days, less men | Indirect |
| More hours per day, less men | Indirect |

$$\because \left.\begin{array}{ll} \text{Work} & \frac{2}{5} : \frac{3}{5} \\ \text{days} & 26 : 30 \\ \text{hours} & 9 : 8 \end{array}\right\} : : 104 : x$$

or $x = \frac{3 \times 30 \times 8 \times 104 \times 5}{5 \times 2 \times 26 \times 9} = 160$

So = (160 – 104) = 56 more men must be employed.

**Example 3 :** A garrison of 3300 men had provisions for 32 days, when given at the rate of 850 grams per head. At the end of the 7 days, a reinforcement arrived and it was found that now the provisions will last for 17 days more, when given at the rate of 825 gm per head. What is the strength of reinforcement?

**Solution :** The problem can be put in the form given below :

3300 men taking 850 gm per head have provisions for (32 – 7) for 25 days. Total of men taking 825 gms per head have provisions for 17 days.

Let the number of total men to be $x$. Now less ration per head, more men (Indirect); less days, more men (Indirect proportion)

$$\therefore \left.\begin{array}{ll} \text{Ratio} & 825 : 850 \\ \text{Days} & 17 : 25 \end{array}\right\} : : 3300x$$

$$\therefore 825 \times 17 \times x = 850 \times 25 \times 3300$$

$$x = \frac{850 \times 25 \times 3300}{825 \times 17}$$

$$x = 5000$$

$\therefore$ no. of person in reinforcement

= 5000 – 3300 = 1700 persons

## EXERCISE

**1.** If the rent for grazing 40 cows for 20 days is Rs. 370, how many cows can graze for 30 days on Rs. 111 ?

A. 6 B. 8
C. 5 D. 12

**2.** If six men, working for 8 hours a day, earn Rs. 840 per week, then 9 men, working for 6 hours a day will earn how much per week?

A. Rs. 840 B. Rs. 945
C. Rs. 1620 D. Rs. 1680

**3.** If 20 men, working for 7 hours a day, can do a piece of work in 10 days, in how many days, will 15 men working for 8 hours a day, do the same piece of work?

A. $15\frac{5}{21}$ days B. $11\frac{2}{3}$ days
C. $6\frac{9}{16}$ days D. $4\frac{1}{5}$ days

**4.** 120 men had provision for 200 days. After 5 days, 30 men died due to an epidemic. The remaining food will last for

A. 150 days B. $146\frac{1}{4}$ days
C. 245 days D. 260 days

**5.** 20 men completed one-third of a piece of work in 20 days. How many more men should be employed to finish the rest of the work in 25 more days?

A. 10 B. 12
C. 15 D. 20

**6.** If 12 boys can earn Rs. 240 in 5 days, how many boys can earn Rs. 420 in 21 days?

A. 15 boys B. 5 boys
C. 17 boys D. None of these

**7.** 2 men and 7 boys can do a piece of work in 14 days. 3 men and 8 boys can do the same work in 11 days. 8 men and 6 boys can do 3 times the amount of this work in

A. 21 days B. 18 days
C. 24 days D. 36 days

**8.** If $\left(\frac{4}{5}\right)$ th of a cistern is filled in 1 minute. How much time is required to fill the remaining part of this?

A. 20 seconds B. 15 seconds
C. 12 seconds D. 10 seconds

## EXPLANATORY ANSWERS

**1. B :** More days, less cows (Indirect)
Less rent, less cows (Direct)

$$\left.\begin{matrix}\text{Days} & 30 : 20\\ \text{Rent} & 370 : 111\end{matrix}\right\} :: 18 : x$$

or $$x = \frac{20 \times 111 \times 40}{30 \times 370}$$

$\Rightarrow$ 8 cows.

**2. B :** More mens, more earning (Direct)
Less hours, less earning (Direct)

$$\left.\begin{matrix}\text{Men} & 6 : 9\\ \text{Hours/day} & 8 : 6\end{matrix}\right\} :: 840 : x$$

$$x = \frac{9 \times 6 \times 840}{6 \times 8} = \text{Rs. } 945.$$

**3. B :** Less men, more days (Indirect)
More working hours, less days (Indirect)

$$\left.\begin{matrix}\text{Men} & 15 : 20\\ \text{Working hrs} & 8 : 7\end{matrix}\right\} :: 10 : x$$

$$x = \frac{20 \times 7 \times 10}{15 \times 8} \Rightarrow 11\frac{2}{3} \text{ days}$$

**4. D :** The remaining food is sufficient for 120 men for 195 days
But, Now remaining men = 90
Less men, more days (Indirect)
$\therefore 90 : 120 :: 195 : x$

or $$x = \frac{120 \times 195}{90} = 260 \text{ days.}$$

**5. B :** Works done = $\frac{1}{3}$; work to be done = $\frac{2}{3}$.
Now, more work, more men

More days, less men (Direct) (Direct)

Work $\frac{1}{3} : \frac{2}{3}$ $:: 20 : x$

Days $25 : 20$

$$x = \frac{2}{3} \times 20 \times 20 \times \frac{3}{25} = 32 \text{ men}$$

So, (32 − 20) = 12 more men should be employed.

**6. B :** More money, more boys (Direct)
More days, less boys (Indirect)

Money $240 : 420$

Days $21 : 5$ $:: 12 : x$

$$x = \frac{420 \times 5 \times 12}{240 \times 21} = 5 \text{ boys}$$

**7. A :** (2 × 14) men + (7 × 14) boys

= (3 × 11) men + (8 × 11) boys

or 5 men = 10 boys

1 man = 2 boys

∴ 2 men + 7 boys = 11 boys

and8 men + 6 boys = 22 boys

Now, more boys, less days (Indirect)

More work, more days (Direct)

Boys $22 : 11$

Work $1 : 3$ $:: 14 : x$

$$x = \frac{11 \times 3 \times 14}{22 \times 1} = 21 \text{ days.}$$

**8. B :** Remaining part = $\frac{1}{5}$

Less part to be filled

Less time taken (Direct)

$$\therefore \frac{4}{5} : \frac{1}{5} = 1 : x$$

$$x = \frac{1}{5} \times 1 \times \frac{5}{4} = \frac{1}{4} \text{ minute}$$

= 15 second

Chapter 18

# ALLIGATION OR MIXTURE

**Note**

Cost price of unit quantity of the mixture is called the mean price.

**Rule of Alligation**

It two ingradients are mixed in the ratio then

$$\frac{\text{Quantity of cheaper}}{\text{Quantity of dearer}} = \frac{\text{C.P. of dearer} - \text{mean}}{(\text{Mean Price}) - (\text{C.P. of cheaper})}$$

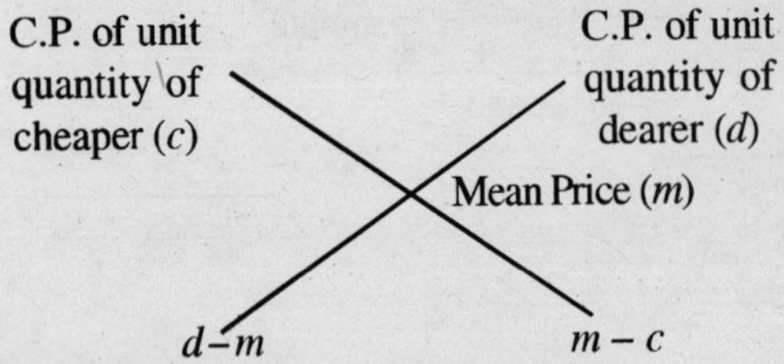


Cheaper quantity : dearer quantity

$= (d - c) : (m - c)$

**Example 1:** In what proportion must rice at Rs. 3.10 per kg. be mixed with rice at Rs. 3.60 per kg, so that mixture be worth Rs. 3.25 per kg?

**Solution :**

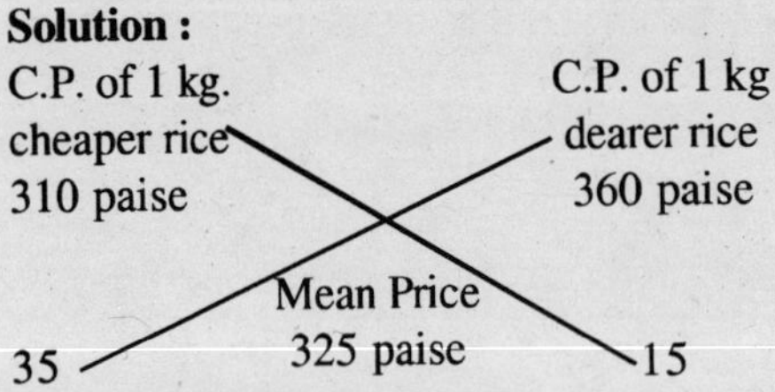


By Alligation Rule, we have

$$\frac{(\text{Quantity of cheaper rice})}{(\text{Quantity of dearer rice})} = \frac{35}{15} = \frac{7}{3}$$

∴ They must be mixed in the Ratio 7 : 3.

**Example 2 :** A man travelled a distance of 80 km in 7 hours partly on foot at the rate of 8 km per hour and partly on bicycle at the rate of 16 km per hour. Find distance travelled by foot.

**Solution :** Average distance travelled in 1 hr.

$\Rightarrow \frac{80}{7}$ km/hr

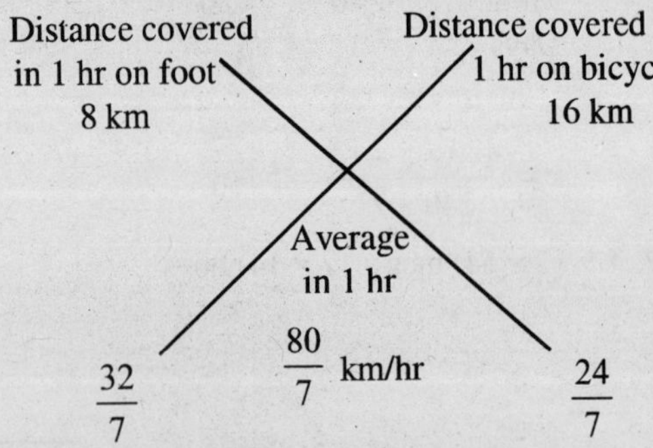


By Alligation Rule, we have

$$\frac{\text{Time taken on foot}}{\text{Time taken on bicycle}} = \frac{32}{24} = 4 : 3$$

Thus out of 7 hours in all he took 4 hours to travel on foot.

Distance covered on foot in 4 hours

$\Rightarrow (4 \times 8)$ km = 32 km.

**Example 3 :** A container contains 80 kg milk. From this container, 8 kg of milk taken out and replaced by water. This process was further repeated two times. How much milk is now contained in the container?

**Solution : Rule:** If amount of liquid left after operations, when the container originally contains $x$ unit of liquid from which, $y$ unit is taken and each time is

$$\left[x\left(1 - \frac{y}{x}\right)^n\right] \text{ units.}$$

**Solution :** Amount of milk left

$$80\left[\left(1 - \frac{8}{80}\right)^3\right] \text{ kg} \qquad = 58.32 \text{ kg.}$$

# EXERCISE

1. A grocer buys two types of rice at Rs. 1.80 and Rs. 1.20 per kg respectively. In what proportion should these be mixed, so that by selling the mixture at Rs. 1.75 per kg. 25% may be gained?
   A. 2 : 1 B. 3 : 2
   C. 3 : 4 D. 1 : 2
2. Rs. 1000 is given on interest in two parts, one part at 6% simple interest and the other part at 8% simple interest. The yearly income is Rs. 75. The sum given at 8% interest is
   A. Rs. 250 B. Rs. 500
   C. Rs. 750 D. Rs. 600
3. Ram mixes 80 kg of sugar worth Rs. 6.75 per kg with 120 kg worth of Rs. 8 per kg. In what rate shall he sell the mixture to gain 20%?
   A. Rs. 7.50 B. Rs. 9
   C. Rs. 8.20 D. Rs. 8.85
4. Two vessels, *A* and *B*, contain milk and water mixture in ratio 5 : 3 and 2 : 3. When these mixtures are mixed to form new mixture containing half milk and half water, they must be taken in the ratio of
   A. 2 : 5 B. 3 : 5
   C. 4 : 5 D. 7 : 3
5. A dishonest milkman offers to sell his milk at C.P. but he mixed it with water and thereby, he gains 25%. The percentage of water in the mixture is
   A. 25% B. 20%
   C. 4% D. None of these
6. In a mixture of 60 liters the ratio of milk and water is 2 : 1. If ratio of milk and water is to be 1 : 2, then amount of water to be further added is
   A. 20 litres B. 30 litres
   C. 40 litres D. 60 litres

# EXPLANATORY ANSWERS

**1. D :** S.P. of 1 kg mixture = Rs 1.75

gain % = 25%

$\therefore$ Mean Price = Rs. $\dfrac{1.75 \times 100}{125}$ = Rs. 1.40

$\because$ Dearer Price : Cheaper Price = 20 : 40 = 1 : 2

**2. C :** Total interest = Rs. 75

Average rate = $\left(\dfrac{100 \times 75}{1000 \times 1}\right)\% = 7\dfrac{1}{2}\%$

$\therefore$ Sum at (6%) : Sum at 8% = $\dfrac{1}{2} : \dfrac{3}{2} \Rightarrow 1 : 3$

Hence sum at 8% = Rs. $1000 \times \dfrac{3}{4}$ = Rs. 750

**3. B :** Total C.P. of 200 kg of mixture

$\Rightarrow$ Rs. (80 × 6.75 + 120 × 8) = Rs. 1500

Average Rate = Rs. 7.50 per kg.

Required Rate = 120% of Rs. 7.50

$\Rightarrow$ Rs. 9 per kg.

**4. C :** Milk in $A = \dfrac{5}{8}$ of whole mixture

Milk in $B = \dfrac{2}{5}$ of whole mixture

Milk in mixture of $A$ and $B = \dfrac{1}{2}$

$\therefore$ By Alligation Rule,

mix $A$ : mix $B = \dfrac{1}{10} : \dfrac{1}{8} = 4 : 5$

**5. B :** Let C.P. of 1 litre of milk be Rs. 1

Then, S.P. of 1 litre lof mixture = Re. 1

gain% = 25%

$\therefore$ C.P. of 1 litre of mixture = Rs. $\left(\dfrac{100}{125} \times 1\right)$

$\Rightarrow$ Rs. 4/5

$\therefore$ Ratio of milk and water = $\dfrac{4}{5} : \dfrac{1}{5} = 4 : 1$

Hence percentage of water in the mixture

$= \dfrac{100 \times 1}{5}\% = 20\%$

**6. D :** Ratio of milk and water in mixture of 60 litres

= 2 : 1

$\therefore$ Quantity of milk = 40 litres

Quantity of water = 20 litres

If the ratio of milk and water is to be 1 : 2, then in 40 litres of milk, water should be 80 litres

$\therefore$ Quantity of water to be added = 60 litres.

# MODEL TEST PAPER

1. If $x^2 + \frac{1}{x^2} = 7$, the value of $x^3 + \frac{1}{x^3}$ is

   A. $\pm 3$ B. $\pm 18$
   C. $\pm 7\sqrt{7}$ D. $\pm 27$

**2.** The value of $\frac{\log 4}{\log 64}$ is

   A. 4 B. 16
   C. $\frac{1}{3}$ D. $\frac{1}{4}$

**3.** $\frac{(0.63)^3 + (0.27)^3}{(0.63)^2 - (0.63 \times 0.27) + (0.27)^2} = ?$

   A. 0.36 B. 0.6
   C. 0.9 D. 1

**4.** The lowest fraction in $\frac{1}{2}, \frac{3}{4}, \frac{5}{6}, \frac{7}{12}, \frac{2}{5}$ is

   A. $\frac{1}{2}$ B. $\frac{2}{5}$
   C. $\frac{3}{4}$ D. $\frac{7}{12}$

**5.** The L.C.M. of $\frac{2}{3}, \frac{4}{3}, \frac{5}{6}, \frac{7}{12}$ is

   A. $\frac{1}{18}$ B. $\frac{1}{36}$
   C. $\frac{35}{9}$ D. $\frac{140}{3}$

**6.** The H.C.F. of three numbers is 12. If they be in the ratio 1 : 2 : 3, the numbers are

   A. 12, 24, 36 B. 10, 20, 30
   C. 5, 10, 15 D. 4, 8, 12

**7.** The number of Prime factors in expression $(6)^{10} \times (7)^{17} \times (11)^{27}$

   A. 54 B. 64
   C. 71 D. 81

**8.** $\sqrt{\frac{0.289}{0.00121}} = ?$

   A. $\frac{170}{11}$ B. $\frac{17}{110}$
   C. $\frac{17}{1100}$ D. $\frac{17}{11}$

**9.** The L.C.M. of 3, 0.09 and 2.7 is

   A. 2.7 B. 0.27
   C. 0.027 D. 27

**10.** $2.\overline{47} + 3.\overline{53} + .\overline{05} = ?$

   A. 6 B. $0.\overline{06}$
   C. $0.\overline{66}$ D. $6.\overline{01}$

**11.** When simplified, the product

$$\left(2-\frac{1}{3}\right)\left(2-\frac{3}{5}\right)\left(2-\frac{5}{7}\right)\ldots\left(2-\frac{999}{1001}\right) \text{ is}$$

equal to

   A. $\frac{991}{1001}$ B. $\frac{1001}{13}$
   C. $\frac{1003}{3}$ D. None of these

**12.** If $\sqrt{24} = 4.899$, then the value of $\sqrt{\frac{8}{3}}$ is

   A. 0.544 B. 2.666
   C. 1.633 D. 1.333

**13.** $\sqrt{12 + \sqrt{12 + \sqrt{12}}} \ldots$ is equal to

   A. 3 B. 4
   C. 6 D. greater than 6

**14.** Which number is 60% less than 80?

   A. 48 B. 42
   C. 32 D. 12

**15.** In an examination, 42% students failed in Hindi and 52% failed in English. 17% failed in both the subjects, the percentage of those who passed in both the subjects, is

   A. 23% B. 27%
   C. 34% D. 40%

**16.** The price of cooking oil has increased by 25%. The percentage of reduction that a family should effect in the usage of cooking oil, so as not to increase the expenditure on this account, is

A. 15% B. 20%
C. 25% D. 30%

**17.** On the reduction of the price of T.V. set by 30%, its sale is increased by 20%. What is the effect of the revenue received by the shopkeeper?

A. 10% increase B. 10% decrease
C. 16% increase D. 16 decrease

**18.** The average weight of 8 persons is increased by 2.5 kg. when one of them, whose weight is 56 kg, is replaced by a new man. The weight of new man is

A. 66 kg B. 75 kg
C. 76 kg D. 86 kg

**19.** The average height of 30 students is 170 cm. When 5 more students joined with a average height of 184 cm, the new average of the whole class will be

A. 172 cm B. 182 cm
C. 162 cm D. 175 cm

**20.** If $A : B = 5 : 7$ and $B : C = 6 : 11$, then $A : B : C$ is

A. 55 : 77 : 66 B. 30 : 42 : 77
C. 35 : 49 : 42 D. None of these

**21.** In a mixture of 60 litres, the ratio of milk and water is 2 : 1. What amount of water must be added to make the ratio 1 : 2 ?

A. 42 litres B. 56 litres
C. 60 litres D. 77 litres

**22.** A circle and a square have same areas. Therefore, the ratio of the side of the square and radius of the circle is

A. $\sqrt{\pi} : 1$ B. $1 : \sqrt{\pi}$
C. $1 : \pi$ D. $\pi : 1$

**23.** Incomes of $A$ and $B$ are in the ratio 3 : 2 and their expenditures are in the ratio 5 : 3. If each one saves Rs. 1000, then A's income is

A. Rs. 3000 B. Rs. 4000
C. Rs. 6000 D. Rs. 9000

**24.** Ram started a business investing Rs. 9000. Five months later, Sudhakar joined him by investing Rs. 8000. If they make a profit of Rs. 6970 at the end of year, Sudhakar's share of profit is

A. Rs. 3690 B. Rs. 1883.78
C. Rs. 2380 D. Rs. 3864

**25.** A horse and a cow were sold for Rs. 12000 each. The horse was sold at a loss of 20% and the cow at a gain to 20%. The entire transaction resulted in

A. no loss or gain
B. a loss of Rs. 1000
C. a gain of Rs. 1000
D. a gain of Rs. 2000

**26.** A bookseller sold his book for Rs. 75 at a profit per cent equal to C.P. The C.P. was

A. Rs. 40 B. Rs. 50
C. Rs. 60 D. Rs. 70

**27.** $A$ can do a piece of work in 10 days and $B$ can do the same piece of work in 20 days. They start the work together. But after 5 days $A$ leaves off. $B$ will do the ramaining piece of work in

A. 5 days B. 6 days
C. 8 days D. 10 days

**28.** 3 men and 4 boys do a piece of work in 8 days while 4 men and 4 boys finish it in 6 days. Then 2 men and 4 boys will finish it in

A. 9 days B. 10 days
C. 12 days D. 14 days

**29.** A cistern (Tank) is normally filled in 8 hours, but takes two hours more to fill because of a leakage in its bottom. If the cistern is full, the leakage will empty it in

A. 16 hrs B. 20 hrs
C. 25 hrs D. 40 hrs

**30.** $A$ is twice as fast as $B$ and $B$ is thrice as fast as $C$ is. A journey covered by $C$ in 42 minutes will be covered by $A$ in

A. 14 minutes B. 54 minutes
C. 63 minutes D. 7 minutes

**31.** Rakesh travels a certain distance at 3 km/hour and reaches late by 15 minutes. If he travels at 4 km/hr, he reaches earlier by 15 minutes. The distance that he has to travel is

A. 4.5 km B. 6 km
C. 7.2 km D. 12 km

**32.** A train crosses a platform, which is 100 metres long, in 60 seconds at a speed of 45 km per hour. The time taken by the train to cross an electric pole is

A. 8 sec B. 1 minute
C. 52 sec D. insufficient data

**33.** The current of a stream runs at the rate 4 km an hour. A boat travels for 6 km and back to the starting point in 2 hours. The speed of the boat in still water is

A. 6 km/hr B. 7.5 km/hr
C. 8 km/hr D. 6.8 km/hr

**34.** Ten years ago, *A* was of an age that was half of the age of *B*. If the ratio of their present ages is 3 : 4, what will be the total of their present ages?

A. 8 years B. 20 years
C. 35 years D. 45 years

**35.** Simple interest on a certain sum for 2 years at 10% per annum is Rs. 90. The corresponding compound interest is

A. Rs. 99 B. Rs. 95.60
C. Rs. 94.50 D. Rs. 108

**36.** The length of a rectangle is increased by 60%. By what per cent, would the width have to be decreased to maintain the same area?

A. $37\frac{1}{2}\%$ B. 60%
C. 75% D. 120%

**37.** A rectangular carpet has an area of 120 sq. m. and a perimeter of 46 m. The length of its diagonal is

A. 15 m B. 16 m
C. 17 m D. 20 m

**38.** The volume of a cube is 512 $cm^3$. Its surface area is

A. 64 $cm^2$ B. 256 $cm^2$
C. 384 $cm^2$ D. 512 $cm^2$

**39.** The maximum length of a pencil that can be kept in a rectangular box of dimensions 8 cm × 6 cm × 2 cm is

A. $2\sqrt{13}$ cm B. $2\sqrt{14}$ cm
C. $2\sqrt{16}$ cm D. $10\sqrt{2}$ cm

**40.** If each edge of a cube is increased by 50%, the percentage increase in the surface area is

A. 50% B. 75%
C. 100% D. 125%

**41.** There are 100 friends in a club. If each one is sending a New Year Greeting Card to the rest of the friends then the total number of cards to be posted in letter-box is

A. 100 B. 10000
C. 9900 D. 9999

**42.** Curved surface area of two spheres are in the ratio of 1 : 4. The ratio of their volumes is

A. 1 : 4 B. $1 : 2\sqrt{2}$
C. 1 : 8 D. 1 : 64

**43.** If radius of a sphere is doubled, then its volume is increased by

A. 100% B. 200%
C. 300% D. 400%

**44.** If 2 boys can earn Rs. 240 in 5 days, how many boys can earn Rs. 420 in 21 days?

A. 15 boys B. 5 boys
C. 17 boys D. None of these

**45.** In what proportion must wheat, at Rs. 1.60 per kg, be mixed with wheat of Rs. 1.45 per kg so that the mixture becomes worth Rs. 1.54 per kg?

A. 2 : 3 B. 3 : 2
C. 3 : 4 D. 4 : 3

**46.** Two vessels, *A* and *B*, contain milk and water, which mixed in ratio, of 5 : 3 and 2 : 3. When these mixtures are mixed to form a new mixture containing half milk and half water, they must be taken in the ratio

A. 2 : 5 B. 3 : 5
C. 4 : 5 D. 7 : 3

**47.** Today is Friday. After 62 days, it will be

A. Friday B. Thursday
C. Saturday D. Monday

**48.** The average of three number is 20. If two of the numbers are 16 and 22, the third number is

A. 18 B. 19
C. 20 D. 22

**49.** $\frac{a}{3} = \frac{b}{4} = \frac{c}{4}$ the value of $\frac{a+b+c}{C}$ is

A. $\frac{1}{2}$ B. $\frac{1}{7}$
C. 2 D. 7

**50.** In a competitive examination, a student scores 4 marks for every correct answer and loses 1 mark for every wrong answer. If he attempts 75 questions and secures 125 marks, then the number of questions he attempts correctly is

A. 35 B. 40
C. 42 D. 46

# ANSWERS

| 1 | 2 | 3 | 4 | 5 | 6 | 7 | 8 | 9 | 10 |
|---|---|---|---|---|---|---|---|---|---|
| B | C | C | D | D | A | B | A | D | D |
| **11** | **12** | **13** | **14** | **15** | **16** | **17** | **18** | **19** | **20** |
| C | C | B | C | A | B | D | C | A | B |
| **21** | **22** | **23** | **24** | **25** | **26** | **27** | **28** | **29** | **30** |
| C | A | C | C | B | B | D | C | D | D |
| **31** | **32** | **33** | **34** | **35** | **36** | **37** | **38** | **39** | **40** |
| B | C | C | C | C | A | C | C | C | D |
| **41** | **42** | **43** | **44** | **45** | **46** | **47** | **48** | **49** | **50** |
| C | C | C | B | B | C | B | D | C | B |

# PRACTICE TEST PAPERS

# MATHEMATICAL ABILITY

## PRACTICE PAPER - 1

**1.** $77.74 + 25.12 - ? = 90.05$
A. 12.51 B. 37.43
C. 12.81 D. 52.62
E. None of these

**2.** $5\frac{1}{2} + 6\frac{1}{4} + 17\frac{1}{2} = ?$
A. 25 B. $\frac{247}{2}$
C. 50 D. 52
E. None of these

**3.** 65% of 260 = ?
A. 250 B. 400
C. 4 D. 169
E. None of these

**4.** $3196.82 - 182 + 0.008 = ?$
A. 3014.812 B. 3014.712
C. 3196.812 D. 3014.828
E. None of these

**5.** $\frac{208 \times 0.08}{4.00} = ?$
A. 1.04 B. 4.16
C. 0.56 D. 52
E. None of these

**6.** $25 \times 2.5 \times 0.25 = ?$
A. 15625 B. 15.625
C. 156.25 D. 1562.5

**7.** 18.25% of 800 = 25% of ?
A. 36.5 B. 146
C. 584 D. 900

**8.** $\frac{1848 \div 44}{3 \times 0.4} = ?$
A. 35 B. 42
C. 5.6 D. 16.8
E. None of these

**9.** $\frac{7}{3} + \frac{3}{7} + \frac{11}{3} + ? = 7$
A. 4/7 B. 3/7
C. 6 D. 1
E. None of these

**10.** Dilip prepared 50 show pieces of sandalwood. The cost of production of each piece was Rs. 10. Apart from this he has to pay Rs. 5 per piece as commission to the selling agent and Rs. 1 per piece to the workshop assistant. What should be the selling price of each article if he wished to sell them at 30% profit?
A. Rs. 14.43 B. Rs. 16.48
C. Rs. 20.80 D. Rs. 84.50
E. None of these

**11.** The simple interest on Rs. 6000 at certain rate of interest for 7 years is Rs. 3780. What is the rate of interest per annum?
A. 6 B. 10.5
C. 7 D. 9
E. None of these

**12.** There would be 10% loss if rice is sold at Rs. 5.40 per kg. At what price per kg. should it be sold to earn a profit of 20%?
A. Rs. 7.20 B. Rs. 7.02
C. Rs. 6.48 D. 6.00
E. None of these

**13.** Eight children and 12 men complete a certain piece of work in 9 days. Each child takes twice the time taken by a man to finish the work. In how many days will 12 men finish the same work?
A. 8 B. 15
C. 9 D. 12
E. None of these

**14.** The ratio of the age of mother to son is 7 : 3 and the sum of their ages is 60 years. What is the difference in their age in years?
A. 42 B. 24
C. 18 D. 4
E. None of these

**15.** Fruit vendor purchased 35 dozen apples at Rs. 10 per dozen. Out of this 2 dozen got rotten and he sold 28 dozen at Rs. 12 per dozen. Remaining apples were sold by him at Rs. 15 per dozen. What profit did he make in this transaction?

A. Rs. 122.50 B. Rs. 61
C. Rs. 56 D. Rs. 41
E. None of these

**16.** A bullock cart has to cover a distance of 80 km in 10 hours. If the bullock cart covers half of its journey in 3/5 time, what should be speed in km/hour to cover the remaining distance in the time left?

A. 8 B. 20
C. 6.4 D. 10
E. None of these

**17.** The average salary of 20 workers in an office is Rs. 1900 per month. If the manager's salary is added the average salary becomes Rs. 2000 p.m. What is the manager's annual salary?

A. Rs. 24,000 B. Rs. 25,200
C. Rs. 45,600 D. 46,800
E. None of these

**18.** Suresh started cycling along the boundries of a square field from corner point *A*. After half an hour he reached the corner point *C*, diagonally opposite to *A*. If his speed was 8 km/h, what is the area of the field in sq. km.?

A. 64 B. 8
C. 4 D. Can't be determined
E. None of these

**19.** Rajesh purchased a plot of land at Rs. 80 per sq. metre through an estate dealer. If the area of the plot was 300 square metre and rate of commission was 3%, what amount Rajesh was required to pay in all?

A. Rs. 24,720 B. Rs. 24,900
C. Rs. 23,380 D. Rs. 23,100
E. None of these

**20.** Satish took a loan at 10% P.A. simple interest. After 4 years he returned the principal along with the interest. If he returns in all Rs. 3500, what is the principal amount?

A. Rs. 3250 B. Rs. 2500
C. Rs. 3150 D. Rs. 2100
E. None of these

**21.** By selling on article for Rs. 460, Mahesh gained 15% profit. What was the cost price of the article?

A. Rs. 391 B. Rs. 400
C. Rs. 529 D. Data inadequate
E. None of these

**22.** Abdul sold 1800 articles in the first month and 2580 articles is the second month. How many articles should he sell in the thrid month so that the average sale in 3 months would be 2300 articles?

A. 2190 B. 3340
C. 2300 D. 2430
E. None of these

**23.** A certain amount was devided between Salim and Rahim in the ratio of 4 : 3. If Rahim's share was Rs. 2400 find out the amount?

A. Rs. 5600 B. Rs. 3200
C. Rs. 9600 D. Rs. 16,800
E. None of these

**24.** 18 binders binds 900 books in 10 days. How many binders will be required to bind 660 books in 12 days?

A. 55 B. 14
C. 13 D. 11
E. None of these

**25.** Some amount out of Rs. 7000 was lent at 6% P.A. and the remaining was lent at 4% P.A. If the total simple interest from both the transactions in 5 years was Rs. 1600, calculate the sum lent at 6% P.A.

A. Rs. 2000 B. Rs. 5000
C. Rs. 3500 D. Can't be determind
E. None of these

**26.** The sum of age of Ram and his mother is 63 years. Four years back his mother's age was 4 times the Ram's age. What is the present age in years of Ram's mother?

A. 44 B. 48
C. 58 D. 52
E. None of these

**27.** *A*, *B* and *C* started a shop by investing Rs. 2700, Rs. 8100 and Rs. 7200. At the end of one year the profit was distributed. If *B*'s share was Rs. 3600, what was their total profit?

A. Rs. 10,800 B. Rs. 11,600
C. Rs. 8000 D. Rs. 12,100

E. None of these

**28.** In a factory the ratio of male workers to female workers was 5 : 3. If the number of female workers was less by 40, what was the total numbers of workers in the factory?

A. 100 B. 500
C. 160 D. 200
E. None of these

**29.** A chair shop's sale increases every month by 10%. If the sale for May was 1000, what would be its sale in August?

A. 1300 B. 1230
C. 1331 D. 1464
E. None of these

**30.** A shopkeeper get 11% profit by selling an object for Rs. 399.60. In order to get 15% profit at what price should the object be sold?

A. Rs. 313 B. Rs. 360
C. Rs. 404 D. Rs. 414
E. None of these

# EXPLANATORY ANSWERS

**1. C :** **2. E :** **3. D :** **4. D :** **5. B**

**6. B :** **7. C :** **8. A :** **9. A :**

**10. C :** Cost of one piece = Rs. 16

Profit = 30%, Sale price = 16 + 30% of 16 = Rs. 20.80.

**11. D :**

**12. A :** Suppose cost price = $k$

$\therefore\ k - 10\%$ of $k = 5.40$

Sale price = 6 + 20% of 6 = 7.20

**13. D :** Since each child takes twice the time taken by man to finish the work.

$\therefore$ 1 man = 2 child

Therefore 8 child and 12 men = 16 men

Since 16 men finish the work in 9 days

1 man finish the work in 144 days

12 men finish the work in $\frac{144}{2} = 12$ days.

**14. B :**

**15. B :** C.P. = 35 × 10 = 350

S.P. = 28 × 12 + 5 × 15 = 411

Profit = 411 − 350 = 61

**16. D :** **17. E :** **18.C :** **19. A :**

**20. B :** Suppose Principal amount = $x$

$$\therefore\ x + \frac{x \times 10 \times 4}{100} = 3500$$

*i.e.*, $x = 2500$

**21. B :** C.P. = $x$

$\therefore\ x + 15\%$ of $x = 460$

*i.e.*, $x + \frac{15x}{100} = 460$

*i.e.*, $x = 400$

**22. E :** **23. A :**

**24. D :** 900 books in 10 days are binded by 18 binders

*i.e.*, 900 book in 1 day are binded by 180 binders.

*i.e.*, 1 book in 1 day is binded

$$= \left(\frac{180}{900}\right) = \frac{1}{5} \text{ binder}$$

$$660 \text{ books in 1 day} = \left(\frac{660}{5}\right) \text{ binders}$$

$$660 \text{ books in 12 days} = \left(\frac{660}{12 \times 5}\right) = 11.$$

**25. A :** **26. B :** **27. C :** **28. C :** **29. C :**

**30. D :** New selling price at which object should be sold $= 399.60 \times \frac{100}{111} \times \frac{115}{100} = 414.$

# PRACTICE PAPER - 2

**1.** In an office there were Grade *A* and *B* officers. Each officers contributed as many rupees as the number of officers in his grade. If the total collection was Rs. 106, what was the total number of officers in the office?

A. 10 B. 14

C. 11 D. Data inadequate
E. None of these

**2.** The price of Scooter and T.V. set are in the ratio of 3 : 2. If the Scooter costs Rs. 6000 more than the T.V. set, what is the price of the T.V. set?
A. 18,000 B. 12,000
C. 6,000 D. 10,000
E. None of these

**3.** How many packets each of 350 gm. can be prepared out of 7.70 kgm. of sugar?
A. 11 B. 22
C. 110 D. 220
E. None of these

**4.** 1/5 of the officers and 1/2 of the supervisors of an institution participated in a conference. If the number of participating officers and supervisors together is 400 what is the total number of officers and supervisors in the institute?
A. 800 B. 1200
C. 680 D. Data inadequate
E. None of these

**5.** Suppose we know that $\sqrt{24}$ is approx. 4.898. What of the following is the best approx. of $\sqrt{\frac{8}{3}}$?
A. 0.544 B. 2.666
C. 1.6333 D. 1.333
E. None of these

**6.** $17 \times 17 \times \frac{1}{51} \div \frac{17}{3} = ?$
A. 0 B. 2
C. $\frac{289}{3}$ D. $\frac{9}{289}$
E. None of these

**7.** $(39 + 13) - (18 + 21) + (9 - 22) = ?$
A. 0 B. 44
C. 42 D. 68
E. None of these

**8.** 60% of 120 = ?
A. 2 B. 72
C. 50 D. 200
E. None of these

**9.** $120.80 \div 40 = ?$
A. 3.2 B. 0.32
C. 0.302 D. 3.02
E. None of these

**10.** $(40)^2 - (30)^2 = 10 \times ?$
A. 1 B. 10
C. 70 D. 690
E. None of these

**11.** $? \div 15 = 0.5$
A. 7.5 B. 0.75
C. 750 D. 0.075
E. None of these

**12.** $\sqrt{4} + (8)^2 = ?$
A. 80 B. 68
C. 18 D. 66
E. None of these

**13.** $\sqrt{\frac{5}{?}} = 5$
A. 1 B. 1/5
C. 5 D. 25
E. None of these

**14.** 15% of ? = 225
A. 15 B. 150
C. 1500 D. 1.5
E. None of these

**15.** $8\frac{1}{2} - 3\frac{1}{4} + 2\frac{3}{4} = ?$
A. $7\frac{3}{4}$ B. 7
C. 8 D. $3\frac{3}{4}$
E. None of these

**16.** $32.32 \div 16 + 0.08 = ?$
A. 2.82 B. 2.02
C. 2.28 D. 2.10
E. None of these

**17.** $74819 + 291 - ? = 61119$
A. 13991 B. 14001
C. 42806 D. 32800
E. None of these

**18.** $57354 - 29999 - 268 - ? = 0$
A. 38197 B. 1555
C. 555 D. 27087
E. None of these

**19.** $170 \times 590 = ?$
A. 100772 B. 10300
C. 107720 D. 10030
E. None of these

**20.** $313131031 \times \frac{1}{31} = ?$
A. 1111 B. 11110

C. 1010101 D. 101011
E. None of these

**21.** If a quarter kg. costs 80 paise, how many paise will 200 grams cost?
A. 16 paise B. 64 paise
C. 100 paise D. 40 paise
E. None of these

**22.** How many days will 36 men take to complete a job which 24 men take 48 days to finish?
A. 72 days B. 36 days
C. 32 days D. 18 days
E. None of these

**23.** Which is the largest of the following numbers?
A. 579.98 B. 579.979
C. 579.1 D. 579.098
E. 579.908

**24.** Which of the following fraction's in descending order?
A. $\frac{7}{16}, \frac{5}{11}, \frac{9}{17}, \frac{4}{7}$ B. $\frac{4}{7}, \frac{9}{17}, \frac{5}{11}, \frac{7}{16}$
C. $\frac{9}{17}, \frac{5}{11}, \frac{7}{16}, \frac{4}{7}$ D. $\frac{4}{7}, \frac{5}{11}, \frac{9}{17}, \frac{7}{16}$
E. None of these

**25.** What should be subtracted from 32575 to make it exactly divisible by 9?
A. 1 B. 2
C. 3 D. 4
E. None of these

**26.** The ratio of $A$'s age to $B$'s age is 4 : 5 and the sum of their ages is 81. What will be the ratio after 9 years?
A. 6 : 5 B. 5 : 4
C. 5 : 6 D. 3 : 4
E. None of these

**27.** The loss incurred on selling an article for Rs. 270 is as much as the profit made when it is sold at 10% profit. What is the cost price of the article?
A. Rs. 90 B. Rs. 110
C. Rs. 363 D. Rs. 300
E. None of these

**28.** If the selling price of 40 articles is equal to the cost price of 50 similar articles, what is the % gain or less?
A. 25% loss B. 25% gain
C. 20% loss D. 20% gain
E. None of these

**29.** The average age of five workers in a store was 36 years. When a new worker joined them, the average age of all of them became 37 years. Therefore how old was the new worker?
A. 37 years B. 42 years
C. 44 years D. Can't be determined
E. None of these

**30.** Ten year ago $B$ was ten times as old as $C$. If the ratio of their present ages is 4 : 1, what is $B$'s present age?
A. 10 years B. 40 years
C. 60 years D. 15 years
E. None of these

## EXPLANATORY ANSWERS

**1. D :** **2. C :** **3. B :** **4. D :** **5. C :**
**6. B :** **7. A :** **8. B :** **9. D :** **10. C :**
**11. A :** **12. D :**

**13. B :** $G.E. = \sqrt{\frac{5}{x}} = 5 \Rightarrow \frac{5}{x} = 25 \Rightarrow x = \frac{1}{5}$

**14. C :** **15. C :** **16. D :** **17. A :** **18. D :**
**19. E :** **20. E :**

**21. B :** $\frac{1}{4}$ kg = 250 gm.
Cost of 250 gm.= 80 paise
Cost of 200 gm. = $\frac{80}{280} \times 200$ = 64 paise

**22. C :** 24 men can finish the job in 48 days
∴ 1 man will finish in 24 × 48 days
*i.e.*, 36 men will finish in $\left(\frac{24 \times 48}{36}\right) = 32$ days

**23. A :** **24. B :** **25. D :** **26. C :**

**27. D :** Suppose cost of article = $x$
S.P. = 270
Loss = $(x - 270)$
∴ $x - 270 = 10\%$ of $x$ or $x = 300$

**28. B :** C.P. of 50 articles = 100
S.P. of 40 articles = 100
*i.e.*, S.P. of 50 articles = 125
Gain on 100 Rs. = 25

**29. B :** **30.C :**

# PRACTICE PAPER - 3

**1.** A number exceeds its 1/7 by 84. What is that number?

A. 12 B. 14
C. 196 D. 98
E. None of these

**2.** What will be 80% of a number whose 200 per cent is 90?

A. 144 B. 72
C. 36 D. 90
E. None of these

**3.** If the length of a rectangle is 5 cms more than its breath and the area is 24 sq. cm, what will be its perimeter?

A. 22 cms B. 30 cms
C. 121 cms D. 60 cms
E. None of these

**4.** If *a, b, c, d* and *e* are five consecutive odd numbers, what is their average?

A. $5(a+4)$

B. $\frac{abcde}{5}$

C. $5(a+b+c+d+e)$

D. Data inadequate

E. None of these

**5.** The sum of two-digit number and the number obtained by interchanging the digits is 99. What is the sum of the two digits of the number?

A. 10 B. 9
C. 18 D. Data inadequate
E. None of these

**6.** $\left(4+\frac{2}{3}\right)\times\left(6+\frac{3}{2}\right)\times 0.5 = ?$

A. 35.5 B. 35
C. 70 D. 175
E. None of these

**7.** $\frac{1}{4}\%$ of ? = 30

A. 120 B. 625
C. 187.5 D. 480
E. None of these

**8.** $\frac{112}{\sqrt{196}}\times\frac{\sqrt{576}}{12}\times\frac{\sqrt{256}}{8} = ?$

A. 8 B. 32
C. 12 D. 16
E. None of these

**9.** 45% of 160 = ?

A. 28 B. 80
C. 88 D. 72
E. None of these

**10.** ? × 15 = 37.5% of 220

A. 82.5 B. 8250
C. 11 D. 5.5
E. None of these

**11.** $\frac{4050}{\sqrt{?}} = 450$

A. 49 B. 100
C. 81 D. 9
E. None of these

**12.** 245.168 − ? = 69.3 + 70.7

A. 105.168 B. 140
C. 175.868 D. 174.468
E. None of these

**13.** $\frac{(28\times 8)+(44\times 4)}{400\div 800} = ?$

A. 400 B. 800
C. 200 D. 1200
E. None of these

**14.** 752 × 25 ÷ 5 = ?

A. 3660 B. 18,800
C. 3650 D. 94,000
E. None of these

**15.** $\frac{4}{135}\times\frac{45}{6}\times\frac{15}{7} = ?$

A. $\frac{10}{21}$ B. $\frac{20}{21}$

C. $\frac{10}{189}$ D. $\frac{21}{20}$

E. None of these

**16.** 492 + 560 + 779 = ?

A. 1731 B. 1931
C. 1831 D. 1631

E. None of these

17. $\frac{?}{169} = 125$

A. 21125 B. 162
C. 138 D. 16225
E. None of these

18. $\frac{1}{2}+\frac{5}{4}+\frac{7}{3}+\frac{15}{12}=?$

A. $\frac{16}{3}$ B. $\frac{16}{6}$
C. $\frac{32}{3}$ D. $\frac{28}{21}$
E. None of these

19. *C*'s mother was four times as old as *C* 10 years ago. After 10 years, she will be twice as old as *C*. How old is *C* today?

A. 5 years B. 10 years
C. 20 years D. 30 years
E. None of these

20. The interest on a certain deposit at 9% p.a. is Rs. 405 in one year. How much will be the additional interest in one year on the same deposit at 10% P.A.?

A. Rs. 40.50 B. Rs. 450
C. Rs. 855 D. Rs. 45
E. None of these

21. When the price of T.V. set increased by 30% the number of T.V. set sold decreased by 20%. What was the effect on the sale?

A. 8% decrease B. 8% increase
C. 4% decrease D. 4% increase
E. None of these

22. A bought paper sheets for Rs. 3600 and spent Rs. 100 on Transport. Paying Rs. 300, he had 330 boxes made, which he sold at Rs. 14 each. What is his profit percentage?

A. 40% B. 60%
C. 180% D. 400%
E. None of these

23. *A*, *B* and *C* together hire a video cassette for a week for Rs. 350. If they use same respectively for 6 hours, 10 hours and 12 hours, then the rent paid by *C* is

A. Rs. 75 B. Rs. 125
C. Rs. 35 D. Rs. 150
E. None of these

24. 18 buckets, each of 8 litres capacity, can fill a tank completely. If the capacity of the bucket would have been 132 litres, than how many buckets would have filled the tank completely?

A. 12 B. 13.5
C. 24 D. Can't be determined
E. None of these

25. The width of a rectangular hall is 3/4 of its length. If the area of the hall is 300 sq. m. then find the difference between its length and the width.

A. 3 B. 4
C. 5 D. 15
E. None of these

26. Anil purchased 120 reams of paper @ Rs. 80 per ream. After purchases, he spent Rs. 280 on transport, 40 paise per ream on octroi duty and Rs. 72 on coolie. What should be selling price per ream in order to get a profit of 8%?

A. Rs. 90 B. Rs. 87.48
C. Rs. 89 D. Rs. 86
E. None of these

27. If the speed of a train is 92.4 km/h, then how many metres are covered by it in 20 minutes?

A. 30,800 m B. 3080 m
C. 308 m D. 30.8 m
E. None of these

28. At simple interest Rs. 800 becomes Rs. 920 in 3 years. If the rate of interest is increased by 3%, then the total amount will become

A. Rs. 92 B. Rs. 1056
C. Rs. 1112 D. Rs. 1182
E. None of these

29. Which of the following figures will replace the (?) in $\frac{?}{36} = \frac{576}{?}$

A. 1,295 B. 24
C. 540 D. 16
E. None of these

30. *A* started a business with Rs. 3000. After 6 months *B* invested Rs. 2000. If at the end of the year, they gain Rs. 2600 then *B*'s share in the profit was

A. 1733 B. 1950
C. 866 D. 650
E. None of these

# EXPLANATORY ANSWERS

**1. D :** **2. C :** **3. A :** **4. E :** **5. B :**
**6. E :** **7. D :** **8. B :** **9. D :** **10. D :**
**11. C :** **12. A :** **13. B :** **14. E :** **15. A :**
**16. C :** **17. A :** **18. A :**

**19. C :** Suppose $C$'s age $= x$

Her mother's age $= y$

$(y - 10) = 4(x - 10)$

$(y + 10) = 2(x + 10)$

$x = 20$

$y = 50$

**20. D :** **21. D :**

**22. E :** C.P. of 330 boxes $= 3600 + 100 + 300 = 4000$

S.P. of 300 boxes $= 330 \times 14 = 4620$

$\therefore$ Profit % $= \frac{620}{4000} \times 100 = 15.5.$

**23. D :** **24. A :** **25. C :** **26. A :** **27. A :**

**28. A :** Interest of Rs. 800 = 120 (in 3 years)

$\therefore$ Rate % $= \frac{100 \times 120}{800 \times 3} = 5\%.$

New rate % $= 5 + 3 = 8\%$

New Amount $= 800 + \left(\frac{8}{100} \times 800 \times 3\right)$

$= 800 + 192 = 992$

**29. E :** $\frac{x}{36} = \frac{576}{x}$

or $x^2 = 36 \times 576 = 6 \times 6 \times 24 \times 24$

or $x = 6 \times 24 = 144$

**30. D :** A's share for 1 month = 3000 × 12= Rs. 36000

B's share for 1 month = 2000 × 6 = Rs. 12000

Ratio of their investment = 36000 : 12000 = 3 : 1

B's share profit $= \frac{1}{4} \times 2600 = 650$

# PRACTICE PAPER - 4

**1.** Each passgenger in a bus deposits an amount equal to the number of passengers travelling for the "Accident aid Fund" while conductor deposits Rs. 15 to make the total amount equal to Rs. 415. How many passengers are there in the bus?

A. 15 B. 20
C. 25 D. 28
E. None of these

**2.** Kamla was married six years ago. Today her age is $1\frac{1}{4}$ times of her age at the time of marriage. The age of her son is $\frac{1}{10}$ times of her present age. What is the age of her son?

A. 2 years B. 3 years
C. 4 years D. 5 years
E. None of these

**3.** The age of $A$ and $B$ are in the ratio of 6 : 5 and sum of their ages is 44 years. What will be the ratio of their ages after 8 years?

A. 5 : 6 B. 7 : 8
C. 8 : 7 D. 14 : 13
E. None of these

**4.** A spends 30% of her income on scooter petrol, $\frac{1}{4}$ of the remaining on house rent and the balance on food. If he spend Rs. 300 on petrol then what is the expenditure on house rent?

A. Rs. 525 B. Rs. 1000
C. Rs. 675 D. Rs. 275
E. None of these

**5.** A Train 100 m. long running @ 50 km/h. crosses a 120 m long train coming from the opposite direction in 6 seconds. What is the speed of other train?

A. 132 km/h B. 83 km/h
C. 60 km/h D. 50 km/h
E. None of these

**6.** The average age of 32 students is 10 years. If the teacher's age is also included, the average increase by one year. What is the age of teacher?

A. 33 years B. 21 years

C. 43 years D. 53 years
E. None of these

7. $4\frac{1}{3} + ? + 2\frac{1}{5} + 6\frac{2}{5} = 16\frac{1}{3}$

A. $3\frac{1}{5}$ B. $3\frac{2}{5}$
C. $4\frac{1}{5}$ D. $3\frac{2}{3}$
E. None of these

8. $\frac{(173-23)\times(37+163)}{(17\times15)-(5\times31)} = ?$

A. 150 B. 200
C. 300 D. 310
E. None of these

9. If $3485 \div 20.5 = 170$; $34.85 \div 2.05 = ?$

A. 1.7 B. 0.17
C. 0.017 D. 17
E. None of these

10. $316.82 + 518.72 + 604.07 = ?$

A. 1429.61 B. 1339.61
C. 1539.61 D. 1440.24
E. None of these

11. $4\frac{4}{2} + 3\frac{3}{5} + 2\frac{6}{5} = ?$

A. $\frac{64}{10}$ B. $\frac{64}{5}$
C. $\frac{96}{10}$ D. $\frac{46}{12}$
E. None of these

12. $47.68 - ? + 16.82 = 43.41$

A. 21.09 B. 11.09
C. 21.19 D. 107.01
E. None of these

13. $22 - \frac{1}{8} + \frac{3}{4} = ?$

A. $21\frac{5}{8}$ B. $22\frac{2}{4}$
C. $22\frac{5}{8}$ D. $22\frac{1}{4}$
E. None of these

14. $3 - \frac{5}{6} + 2\frac{5}{8} - ? = 1$

A. 2 B. 5
C. $3\frac{13}{24}$ D. $\frac{61}{24}$

15. $808 \div 8 \div 0.4 = ?$

A. 25.25 B. 252.5
C. 40.4 D. 202.05
E. None of these

16. 90% of 180 + 200% of 19 = ?

A. 38 B. 162
C. 124 D. 200
E. None of these

17. 22% of 50 = 5 × ?

A. 2.2 B. 10
C. 11 D. 1.1
E. None of these

18. $7.83 - (3.79 - 2.56) = ?$

A. 4.04 B. 1.48
C. 6.06 D. 6.6
E. None of these

19. $212.8 - 18.09 = ?$

A. 193.9 B. 194.71
C. 194.91 D. 193.71
E. None of these

20. $81.23 + 1.79 + 3.07 = ?$

A. 86.29 B. 85.09
C. 85.19 D. 86.19
E. None of these

21. $\frac{\sqrt{100}}{?} = \frac{4}{10}$

A. 100 B. 1000
C. 10 D. 40
E. None of these

22. 12.5% of 1192 = 50% of ?

A. 48 B. 96
C. 24 D. 1200
E. None of these

23. $\frac{(42\times15)+(144\div24)}{(17\times13)-(15.5\times4)} = ?$

A. 4 B. 2.48
C. 6.36 D. 8
E. None of these

24. The length and bredth of a rectangular piece

of land are in the ratio of 5 : 3. The owner spent Rs. 3000 for surrounding it from all the sides @ Rs. 7.50 per meter. What is the difference between the length and breadth?

A. 50 B. 100
C. 200 D. 150
E. None of these

5. The average of runs scored by the 11 players of the cricket team is 60. If the run scored by captain are neglected, the average of run scored by the remaining players increases by 5. How many runs were scored by the captain?

A. 0 B. 10
C. 55 D. 120
E. None of these

6. If the weight of a 15 metre long rod is 25.2 kg., then what will be the weight of a 5 metre long rod of similar shape?

A. 1.68 kg B. 16.8 kg
C. 8.40 kg D. 14 kg
E. None of these

7. *A* salary of Rs. 300 more than *B*'s salary is Rs. 200 more than *C*'s salary. If the total of *B*'s and *C*'s salary is Rs. 1800, then what is the salary of *A*?

A. Rs. 800 B. Rs. 1000
C. Rs. 1300 D. Rs. 3100
E. None of these

**28.** *A, B* and *C* invested Rs. 8000, 4000 and Rs. 8000 respectively in a business. *A* left after six months. If after eight months there was a gain of Rs. 4005, then what will be the share of *B*?

A. Rs. 890 B. Rs. 1780
C. Rs. 1335 D. Rs. 1602
E. None of these

**29.** 15 persons can fill 35 boxes in 7 days. How many persons can fill 65 boxes in 5 days?

A. 13 B. 39
C. 45 D. 65
E. None of these

**30.** $\frac{4}{5}$ of a certain number is 64. Half of that number is

A. 32 B. 40
C. 80 D. 16
E. None of these

# EXPLANATORY ANSWERS

**. B :** **2. B :** **3. C :** **4. E :**

**. E :** If two trains are running in opposite directions then the relative motion of the faster train with respect to the slower train is the sum of their speeds. They will pass each other in a time equivalent to the time taken in travelling distance equal to sum of larger of the train with this relative speed.

**C :** **7. B :** **8. C :** **9. D :** **10. E :**
**B :** **12. A :** **13. C :** **14. E :** **15. B :**
**D :** **17. A :** **18. D :** **19. B :** **20. E :**
**A :** **22. A :** **23. A :**

**A :** $L : B = 5 : 3, \frac{L}{B} = \frac{5}{3}$

$$\therefore\ 2L + 2B = \frac{3000}{7.50} = 400$$

*i.e.,* $L + B = 200$

*i.e.,* $\frac{5B}{3} + B = 200$

*i.e.,* $B = 75$

$L = 125$, and $L - B = 50$

**25. B :** **26. C :** **27. C :**

**28. A :** The rate in which *A, B* and *C* invested $= 8000 \times 6 : 4000 \times 8 : 8000 \times 8 = 3 : 2 : 4$

*B*'s share in a profit $= \frac{2}{9} \times 4005 = 890$

**29. B :**

**30. B :** $\frac{4}{5}k = 64$

*i.e.,* $k = \frac{64 \times 5}{4} = 80$

*i.e.,* $\frac{k}{2} = 40.$

# PRACTICE PAPER - 5

1. $\frac{2}{3}$ of a number is 16 more than forty percent of that number. What is the number?
A. 120 B. 60
C. 180 D. 45
E. None of these

2. 8950.69 – 2685.72 + 157% of 438.28 = ?
A. 7,200 B. 8,400
C. 6,200 D. 6,900
E. 5,800

3. 1678.9 + 132.68 – 6.5 × 16.78 = ?
A. 1712.51 B. 1920.65
C. 1792.51 D. 1702.51
E. None of these

4. The average age of *P, Q, R* at present is 26 years. If *R* is 6 years older than *P*, how old is *Q* now?
A. 28 years B. 32 years
C. 18 years D. Data inadequate
E. None of these

5. The inequality $b^2 - 4 > 7b + 8$ is satisfied if
A. $b \geq 9, b \leq -3$ B. $b \geq 8, b \leq -2$
C. $b = 9, b = -3$ D. $b \geq 8, b \leq -3$
E. $b > 9, b < -3$

6. A amount of money is to be divided among *A*, *B* and *C* in the ratio of 3 : 5 : 12 repectively. If the total share of *A* and *B* together is Rs. 800 less than the share of *C*, what is *A*'s share in it?
A. Rs. 1000 B. Rs. 2400
C. Rs. 600 D. Rs. 1200
E. None of these

7. The breadth of a rectangular plot is increased by 25%. By what percent should the length be decreased to maintain the same area?
A. 25% B. 20%
C. 40% D. 35%
E. None of these

8. When forty per cent of a number is added to another number, the second number increases to its 20%. What is the ratio between the first number and the second number?
A. 1 : 2 B. 2 : 1
C. 1 : 3 D. Data inadequate
E. None of these

9. The average marks obtained by 50 student a class is 55. The average marks obtained those who failed is 45. What is the aver marks obtained by those who passed?
A. 65 B. 70
C. 80 D. Data inadequate
E. None of these

10. 157% of 6529 + ? = 5.6 × 2569 + 2058.
A. 5500 B. 5800
C. 6400 D. 4800
E. 6200

11. Two-fifth of three seventh of one-third number is 30. What is 20% of that number?
A. 105 B. 525
C. 440 D. 620
E. None of these

12. The sum of the digits of a two-digit numb 6 more than the difference between the di of that number. What is definitely the numl
A. 36 B. 63
C. 48 D. Data inadequate
E. None of these

13. A bought a suitcase with 30 per cent disc on labelled price and sold it with 20 per profit on the labelled price. What was percentage profit on the price he bought?
A. 70% B. 85%
C. 65% D. 50%
E. 45%

14. The price of 6 dozens of mangoes is Rs. 1 What will be the price of 215 such mangoe
A. 6400 B. 5,000
C. 48,00 D. 3,600
E. 6,800

15. *A* borrowed some money with 6 p.c. pa si interest for first three years, 8 p.c. pa for the five years and 10 p.c. pa for the period be eight years. If he pays a total interest o 7840 at the end of twelve years, how n money did he borrow?
A. Rs. 12,000 B. Rs. 9,000
C. Rs. 6,000 D. Rs. 8,000
E. None of these

The sum of two numbers is 34 and their product is 288. What is the difference between these two numbers?

A. 2 B. 4
C. 6 D. Data inadequate
E. None of these

The ratio between the breadth and the perimeter of rectangular plot is 1 : 5. If the area of the plot is 2400 square metre, what is its length?

A. 40 metres B. 80 metres
C. 60 metres D. Data inadequate
E. None of these

The ratio between the present ages of *P* and *Q* is 3 : 4. After four years the ratio between their ages will be 11 : 14. What is the present age of *Q*?

A. 18 years B. 24 years
C. 22 years D. Data inadequate
E. None of these

8 men and 12 women can complete a work in 15 days, whereas ten men can complete the same work in 18 days. In how many days will 15 women can complete the same work?

A. 9 days B. 18 days
C. 27 days D. 12 days
E. None of these

5678 – 2305 – 1139 = ?

A. 2504 B. 2324
C. 2054 D. 2334
E. None of these

A's marks in Geography are 30 more than the average marks obtained by him in English and History. If average marks obtained by him in English and History are 45, what are his marks in Geography?

A. 40 marks B. 80 marks
C. 60 marks D. Data inadequate
E. None of these

$5\frac{3}{4}$ of 1460 + $2\frac{1}{3}$ of 178 = ? + $\frac{2}{5}$ of 4138

A. 8,400 B. 6,400
C. 5,800 D. 6,800
E. 7,100

**23.** $4\frac{2}{3}-1\frac{5}{9}+4\frac{8}{6}=?$

A. $8\frac{1}{3}$ B. $8\frac{4}{9}$
C. $7\frac{4}{9}$ D. $6\frac{2}{3}$
E. None of these

**24.** $100 \times 0.2 + 0.01 \times 1000 + 110 = ?$

A. 144 B. 140
C. 141 D. 159
E. None of these

**25.** $\frac{1}{2}+\frac{1}{4}+?=\frac{25}{28}$

A. $\frac{1}{6}$ B. $\frac{1}{7}$
C. $\frac{1}{8}$ D. $\frac{1}{4}$
E. None of these

**26.** $5\frac{2}{3} \div \left(2-\frac{1}{2}\right)=?$

A. $\frac{26}{17}$ B. $\frac{34}{9}$
C. $\frac{38}{3}$ D. $\frac{37}{6}$
E. None of these

**27.** $1 + [\,1 \div \{5 \div 4 - 1 \div (13 \div 3 - 1 \div 3)\}] = ?$

A. 8 B. $\frac{1}{8}$
C. 2 D. 10
E. None of these

**28.** $4 \times 32$ of $75\% \div 3 = ?$

A. 32 B. 45
C. 99 D. 43
E. None of these

**29.** $(242 - 17)^2 - (7 \times 5)^2 = ?$

A. 49400 B. 94400
C. 48400 D. 45000
E. None of these

**30.** 64 of ?% = 20 + 20 of 20%?

A. 47.5 B. 38.6
C. 37.5 D. 37.2
E. None of these

# EXPLANATORY ANSWERS

**1. B :** **2. D :** **3. D :** **4. D :** **5. A :**

**6. C :** Suppose $A = 3k$, $B = 5k$

$C = 12k$

$A + B = C - 800$, $k = 200$

$A$'s share $= 600$

**7. B :**

**8. A :** Let numbers are $x$ and $y$

$\Rightarrow y + 40\%$ of $x = y + 20\%$ of $y$

$\Rightarrow \frac{x}{y} = \frac{1}{2}$

**9. D :** **10. E :** **11. A :**

**12. D :** Let the two-digits number

$10x + y$

$\therefore x + y = 6 + (x - y)$

$\Rightarrow y = 3, x = ?$

**13. A :** Suppose L.P. $= k$

$\therefore$ C.P. $= k - 30\%$ of $k = \frac{7k}{10}$

S.P. $= 12 + 20\%$ of $k = \frac{6k}{5}$

$= \frac{6k}{5} - \frac{7k}{10} = \frac{5k}{10} = \frac{k}{2}$

Profit % $= \frac{k/2}{7k/10} \times 100 = 70$

**14. B :** **15. D :**

**16. A :** $x + y = 34$ and $xy = 288$

$\therefore (x - y)^2 = (x + y)^2 - 4xy$

**17. C :**

**18. B :** $P = 3k$, $Q = 4k$

$\frac{P+4}{Q+4} = \frac{11}{14}$, $k = 6$

$\therefore \quad Q = 24$

**19. E :** **20. E :**

**21. E :** $G = \frac{E+G+H}{3} + 30$ ...

**22. E :** $\frac{E+H}{2} = 45 \Rightarrow E + H = 90$ ...(

$\therefore (i) \Rightarrow G = \frac{90 + G}{3} + 30$

$\Rightarrow G = 90$

**23. B :** **24. B :** **25. B :** **26. B :** **27. C :**

**28. A :** **29. A :** **30. C :**

# General Knowledge & General Awareness

# 1 The Universe

## The Solar System: Some Facts

**nber of Planets:** 8—Mercury, Venus, Earth, Mars, iter, Saturn, Uranus and Neptune.

**rgest most**

| | |
|---|---|
| lassive planet | Jupiter |
| rightest planet | Venus |
| rightest star | Sirius |
| 'astest orbiting planet | Mercury |
| ongest (Synodic) day | Mercury |
| lanet with largest natural satellite | Saturn |
| reatest average density | Jupiter |
| 'allest mountain | Earth |
| trongest magnetic fields | Jupiter |
| lost circular orbit | Venus |
| hortest (synodic) day | Jupiter |
| lottest planet | Venus |
| lo natural satellite | Mercury, Venus |
| lanet with natural satellite with ost eccentric orbit | Neptune |
| owest average density | Saturn |
| reatest amount of liquid n the surface | Earth |

## The Earth: Facts and Data

**nposition of the Earth:** Aluminium (0.4%), phur (2.7%), Silicon (13%), Oxygen (28%), cium (1.2%), Nickel (2.7%), Magnesium %), Iron (35%)

| | | |
|---|---|---|
| urface area | : | 510100500 sq km |
| and Surface (29.1%) | : | 148950800 sq km |
| Ocean Surface (70.9%) | : | 361149700 sq km |
| Type of water | : | 97% salt, 3% fresh |
| Total area of water | : | 382672000 sq km |
| Equatorial diameter | : | 12753 km |
| Equatorial Circumference | : | 40066 km |
| Polar Circumference | : | 39992 km |
| Polar diameter | : | 12710 km |
| Equatorial radius | : | 6376 km |
| Polar radius | : | 6335 km |
| Mass (estimated weight) | : | $594 \times 10^{19}$ metric tons |
| Mean distance from the Sun | : | 149407000 km |
| Earth's orbit speed (around sun) | : | 107320 kmph |
| Period of Revolution (round the sun) | : | 365 days 5 hrs 48 min. 45.51 seconds |
| Time of Rotation (on its axis) | : | 23 hrs 56 min. 4.09 seconds |
| Inclination of the axis (to the plane of the ecliptic) | : | 23º27' |

## Solar Statistics

| | | |
|---|---|---|
| Distance from the Earth | : | 149.8 million km |
| Absolute Visual Magnitude | : | 4.75 |
| Diameter Core | : | 13,84,000 km |
| Temperature | : | 15000000 K |
| Photosphere Temperature | : | 5770 K |

| | | |
|---|---|---|
| Rotation as seen from the Earth (at the equator) | : | 25.38 days |
| Rotation as seen from the Earth (near the poles) | : | 33 days |
| Chemical Composition | : | Hydrogen 71%<br>Helium 26.5%<br>Other elements 2.5% |
| Age | : | About 4.5 billion years |
| Expected lifetime of a normal star | : | About 10 billion years |

## Oceans of the World

| | |
|---|---|
| Pacific | 16,62,41,000 sq km |
| Atlantic | 8,65,57,000 sq km |
| Indian | 7,34,27,000 sq km |
| Arctic | 94,85,000 sq km |

## Longest Rivers

| *Name* | *Country/ Continent* | *Length in Kilometres* |
|---|---|---|
| Nile | Africa | 6650 |
| Amazon | S. Àmerica | 6437 |
| Mississippi-Missouri | USA | 6020 |
| Yangtze-Kiang | China | 5494 |
| Ob-Irtysh | Russia | 5410 |
| Lena | Russia | 4400 |
| Hwang Ho | China | 4344 |
| Niger | Africa | 4180 |
| St. Lawrence | Canada (USA) | 4023 |
| Murray-Darling | Australia | 3780 |
| Volga | Russia | 3690 |
| Indus | Asia | 2900 |
| Danube | Europe | 2850 |
| Orinoco | S. America | 2575 |

## Major Riverside Cities

| *City* | *River* | *Country* |
|---|---|---|
| Alexandria | Nile | Egypt |
| Amsterdam | Amsel | The Netherla |
| Ankara | Kizil | Turkiye |
| Baghdad | Tigris | Iraq |
| Bangkok | Menam | Thailand |
| Belgrade | Danube | Serbia |
| Berlin | Spree | Germany |
| Budapest | Danube | Hungary |
| Cairo | Nile | Egypt |
| Chittagong | Karnaphuli | Bangladesh |
| Karachi | Indus | Pakistan |
| Khartoum | Blue & White Nile | Sudan |
| Lahore | Ravi | Pakistan |
| Lisbon | Tagus | Portugal |
| Liverpool | Mersey | England |
| London | Thames | England |
| Moscow New | Moskva | Russia |
| Orleans | Mississipi | USA |
| New York | Hudson | USA |
| Paris | Seine | France |
| Yangon | Irawadi | Myanmar |
| Rome | Tiber | Italy |

## Major Gulfs of the World

| *Names* | *Areas (Sq. Km.* |
|---|---|
| Gulf of Mexico | 15,44,000 |
| Gulf of Hudson | 12,33,000 |
| Arabian Gulf | 2,38,000 |
| Gulf of St. Lawrence | 2,37,000 |
| Gulf of California | 1,62,000 |
| English Channel | 89,900 |

## Major Mountain Ranges of the Wo

| *Range* | *Location* | *Length (* |
|---|---|---|
| Andes | South America | 7,200 |
| Himalayas-Karakoram-Hindukush | South Central Asia | 5,000 |
| Rockies | North America | 4,800 |

| ange | Location | Length (km) |
|---|---|---|
| reat Dividing ange | East Australia | 3,600 |
| tlas | North West Africa | 1,930 |
| 'estern Ghats | Western India | 1,610 |
| aucasus | Europe | 1,200 |
| laska | USA | 1,130 |
| lps | Europe | 1,050 |

## Largest Deserts of the World

**ubtropical**

| | |
|---|---|
| ahara, North Africa | 94,00,000 sq. km. |
| alahari, Southern Africa | 9,00,000 sq. km. |
| har, India/Pakistan | 2,00,000 sq. km. |
| reat Sandy, Australia | 4,00,000 sq. km. |

**'ool Coastal**

| | |
|---|---|
| tacama, Chile S.A. | 1,40,000 sq. km |

**Cool Winter**

| | |
|---|---|
| Gobi, China | 13,00,000 sq. km. |
| Colorado, Western USA (also called the painted desert) | 3,37,000 sq. km. |

## Atmosphere

### Composition of Gases in Atmosphere

| | |
|---|---|
| Nitrogen | 78.03% |
| Oxygen | 20.99% |
| Argon | 0.93% |
| Carbon dioxide | 0.03% |
| Hydrogen | 0.01% |
| Neon | 0.0018% |
| Helium | 0.0005% |
| Crypton | 0.0001% |
| Xenon | 0.000,005% |
| Ozone | 0.000,0001% |

## World Important Local Winds

**'hinoon:** A warm day wind frequently xperienced on the eastern side of the Rocky Mountains.

**'ohn:** A warm dry wind descending a mountain, s on the north side of the Alps.

**Iaboob:** A sand storm or a dust storm in north nd north-east Sudan near Khartoum.

**agrrio:** It is the tropical cyclone of the 'hilippine Island.

**Loo:** A hot wind which blows in summer season in Indian sub-continent.

**Papasago:** A cold northerly wind sometimes felt on the Mexico plateau.

**Bora:** It is the name given to the cold dry wind experienced particularly in winter along the eastern coast of the Atlantic Ocean and in northern Italy.

**Black Toller:** A hot dust wind which blows in the vast plain of North America.

## Principal Mountain Peaks of the World

| Mountains | Height in Metres | Range | Date of First Ascent |
|---|---|---|---|
| 1. Mount Everest | 8,848 | Himalayas | May 29, 1953 |
| 2. K-2 (Godwin Austen) | 8,611 | Karakoram | July 31, 1954 |
| 3. Kanchenjunga | 8,597 | Himalayas | May 25, 1955 |
| 4. Lhotse | 8,511 | Himalayas | May 18, 1956 |
| 5. Makalu I | 8,481 | Himalayas | May 15, 1955 |
| 6. Dhaulagiri I | 8,167 | Himalayas | May 13, 1960 |
| 7. Mansalu I | 8,156 | Himalayas | May 9, 1956 |
| 8. Chollyo | 8,153 | Himalayas | Oct. 19, 1954 |
| 9. Nanga Parbat | 8,124 | Himalayas | July 3, 1953 |
| 10. Annapurna I | 8,091 | Himalayas | June 3, 1950 |

| Mountains | Height in Metres | Range | Date of First Ascent |
|---|---|---|---|
| 11. Gasherbrum I | 8,068 | Karakoram | July 5, 1958 |
| 12. Broad Peak I | 8,047 | Karakoram | June 9, 1957 |
| 13. Gasherbrum II | 8,034 | Karakoram | July 7, 1956 |
| 14. Shisha Pangma (Gosainthan) | 8,014 | Himalayas | May 2, 1964 |
| 15. Gasherbrum III | 7,952 | Karakoram | Aug. 11, 1975 |

## Types of World Agriculture

**Viticulture**: The cultivation of the vine for production of grapes and wine.
**Pisciculture:** The breeding, rearing and transplantation of fish by artificial means.
**Sericulture:** The raising of silk worms for the production of raw silk.
**Horticulture:** To grow flower front, vegetables on small plots.
**Apiculture:** Bee keeping on a commercial scale for the sale of honey.
**Floriculture:** The cultivation of flowers or flowering plants.
**Mariculture:** Sea farming, or the cultivation of marine plants and animals for commercial purposes.
**Olericulture:** The cultivation of vegetables and kitchen herbs.

## Famous Straits of the World

| Strait | Between | Country |
|---|---|---|
| Malacca Strait | Andaman Sea and South China Sea | Indonesia |
| Palk Strait | Mannar and Bay of Bengal | India-Sri Lanka |
| Magellan Strait | Pacific and South Atlantic Ocean | Chile |
| Dover Strait | English Channel and North Sea | England-France |
| Berring Strait | Berring Sea and Chukasi Sea | Alaska-Russia |
| Sugaroo Strait | Japan Sea and Pacific Ocean | Japan |
| Sunda Strait | Java and Indian Ocean | Indonesia |
| Gibralter Strait | Mediterranean Sea and Atlantic Ocean | Spain |
| Harmuj Strait | Persia and Bay of Oman | Oman-Iran |
| Hudson Strait | Bay of Hudson and Atlantic Ocean | Canada |

## World's Famous Official Documents

**White Paper:** India; **Orange Book:** Netherlands; **Yellow Book:** France; **Green Book:** Italy and Ir
**White Book:** Portugal, China and Germany; **Grey Book:** Japan and Belgium.

## Famous Newspapers of the World

| Newspaper | Place of Publishing | Language |
|---|---|---|
| Daily News | New York (America) | English |
| Guardian | London (Britain) | English |
| Pravada | Moscow (Russia) | Russian |
| Al-Ahram | Cairo (Egypt) | Arabic |
| Merdeca | Jakarta (Indonesia) | Indonesian |
| Times | London (Britain) | English |
| People's Daily | Beijing (China) | Chinese |
| New Statesman | Britain | English |
| Daily Mirror | Britain | English |
| Hindu, Hindustan Times, Times of India, Tribune, Statesman, Indian Express, Economic Times | India | English |
| Hindustan, Nav Bharat Times, Rashtriya Sahara, Dainik Jagaran, Punjab Kesari | India | Hindi |

## Important Boundary Lines

| Boundary Line | Countries |
|---|---|
| Hindenberg Line | Germany-Poland |
| Maginot Line | France and Germany |
| Mannerhein Line | Russia-Finland |
| Mc Mahon Line | India and China |
| Order Niesse Line | Germany-Poland |
| Radcliff Line | India-Pakistan |
| Seigfrid Line | Germany-France |
| Durand Line | Pakistan and Afghani-stan |
| 17th Parallel | The line which defined the boundary between North Vietnam and South Vietnam before the two were united. |
| 38th Parallel | North Korea and South Korea |
| 49th Parallel | U.S.A. and Canada |

## Areawise 10 Big and Small Countries

### 10 Big Countries

| S. No. | Country | Sq. km (Total Portion) sq. km) | Area (Thousand) |
|---|---|---|---|
| 1. | Russia (Europe-Asia) | 17,098,242 | 16,889 |
| 2. | Canada (N. America) | 99,84,670 | 9,221 |
| 3. | China (Asia) | 95,96,961 | 9,327 |
| 4. | U.S.A. (N. America) | 93,72,614 | 9,159 |
| 5. | Brazil (S. America) | 85,14,877 | 8,457 |
| 6. | Australia (S. Pacific) | 77,41,220 | 7,682 |
| 7. | India (Asia) | 32,87,263 | 2,973 |
| 8. | Argentina (S. America) | 27,80,400 | 2,737 |
| 9. | Kazakhstan (Europe-Asia) | 27,24,900 | 2,671 |
| 10. | Algeria (Africa) | 23,81,741 | 2,381 |

### 10 Small Countries

| S. No. | Country | Area (Sq. km) |
|---|---|---|
| 1. | Vatican City (Europe) | 0.44 |
| 2. | Monaco (Europe) | 1.95 |
| 3. | Nauru (Southern Pacific) | 21.10 |
| 4. | Tuvalu | 26.00 |
| 5. | San Marino (Europe) | 61.00 |
| 6. | Liechtenstein (Europe) | 160.00 |
| 7. | Marshall Island (Central Pacific) | 181.00 |
| 8. | St. Kitts and Nevis (Eastern Caribbean) | 261.00 |
| 9. | Grenada (Eastern Caribbean Sea) | 344.00 |
| 10. | Seychelles (Indian Ocean) | 455.00 |

## Populationwise 10 Big and Small Countries

### 10 Big Countries

| S. No. | Country | Population (2026) |
|---|---|---|
| 1. | India | 1,476,630,000 |
| 2. | China | 1,412,910,000 |
| 3. | United States | 349,035,000 |
| 4. | Indonesia | 287,887,000 |
| 5. | Pakistan | 259,300,000 |
| 6. | Nigeria | 242,432,000 |
| 7. | Brazil | 213,563,000 |
| 8. | Bangladesh | 177,818,000 |
| 9. | Russia | 143,394,000 |
| 10. | Ethiopia | 138,902,000 |

### 10 Small Countries

| S. No. | Country | Population (2026) |
|---|---|---|
| 1. | Vatican City | 506 |
| 2. | Niue | 1,822 |
| 3. | Tokelau | 2,691 |
| 4. | Falkland Islands | 3,465 |
| 5. | Montserrat | 4,328 |
| 6. | Saint Helena Ascension and Tristan da Cunha | 5,147 |
| 7. | Saint Pierre and Miquelon | 5,513 |
| 8. | Tuvalu | 9,362 |
| 9. | Wallis and Futuna | 11,113 |
| 10. | Saint Barthelemy | 11,550 |

## Signals/Signs and Meaning

| *Signal/Sign* | *Meaning* |
|---|---|
| Red Triangle | Family Planning |
| Red Cross | Medical Help |
| Red Light | Danger, 'Stop' for the movement of vehicles |
| Green Light | Go |
| Olive Branch | Peace |
| White Pigeon or Dove | Peace |
| Black Strip on Arm | (i) Opposition<br>(ii) Sorrow |
| Black Flag | Opposition |
| Red Flag | (i) Danger<br>(ii) Revolution |
| White Flag | Treaty or Surrender |
| Yellow Flag | Vehicles with patients of contagious diseases |
| Two Bones across with a Skull | Danger of electricity |
| Half mast flown Flag | National mourning |
| Lotus | Sign of civilization and culture |
| Wheel (Chakra) | Sign of Progress |
| A blind folded woman with scale in hand | Sign of Justice |
| Reversed flown flag | National calamity |

## National Emblems of Important Countries

| *Country* | *National Emblem* |
|---|---|
| America | Golden Rod |
| Australia | Kangaroo |
| Ireland | Shamrock |
| Italy | White Lily |
| Israel | Candelabrum |
| Iran | Rose |
| Canada | White Lily |
| Great Britain | Rose |
| Chile | Candor and Huemul |
| Germany | Corn Flower |
| Japan | Chrysanthemum |
| Zimbabwe | Zimbabwe Bird |
| Denmark | Beach |
| Turkiye | Crescent and Star |
| The Netherlands | Lion |
| New Zealand | Kiwi, Fern Southern Cross |
| Norway | Lion |
| Nepal | Kukri |
| Pakistan | Crescent |
| Poland | Eagle |
| France | Lily |
| Belgium | Lion |
| Bangladesh | Water Lily |
| Mongolia | The Soyombo |
| Russia | Double headed eagle |
| Lebanon | Cedar Tree |
| Sudan | Secretary Bird |
| Syria | Eagle |
| India | Lioned Capital |

## Continents : Some Facts

| *Continent* | *Biggest Counrty* | *Highest Peak* | *Longest River* |
|---|---|---|---|
| Asia | China | Mt. Everest (8848 m) | Yangtze Kiang |
| Africa | Algeria | Mt. Kilimanjaro (5895 m) | Nile |
| North America | Canada | Mt. Mckinley (6194 m) | Mississippi Missouri |
| South America | Brazil | Mt. Acancagua (6960 m) | Amazon |
| Europe | Russia | Mt. Elbrus (5642 m) | Ob |
| Australia | Australia | Mt. Coscuisco (2228 m) | Darling |
| Antarctica | — | Vinson Massif (5140 m) | — |

## International Date Line

It roughly corresponds to 180°E or W meridian of longitude which falls on the opposite side of the Greenwich meridian and the date changes by one day (i.e. 24 hours), as this line is crossed. On crossing this line from east to west a day is added, and a day is subtracted on crossing it from west to east.

* * * * *

# 2 World Geography

## Earth

The earth constitutes land, water and air. Land is made up of rocks and soil. It is distributed in continents and islands. The water found in oceans, seas, lakes, etc. occupies about 2/3 of the earth's surface. The earth is surrounded by a cover of air, called atmosphere, which extends up to several hundred kilometres above its surface.

**Shape:** In ancient times people believed that the earth was flat in shape. Greek philosopher Pythagoras (6th century BC) was the first person to declare that the earth was round. After careful measurement, the scientists have found that the earth is slightly oblate (flattened at poles) and not exactly round.

**Motions:** The earth has two motions: *(i) Rotation:* Earth makes a complete round on its axis once each 24 hours (more exactly 23 hours, 56 minutes and 4.09 seconds). It causes days and night on the earth. *(ii) Revolution:* The earth makes a complete round of the Sun in one year. This revolution of earth produces alternate seasons.

***Some Facts:***

1. Equal Day and Night — March 21 and September 23.
2. Longest Day — June 21.
3. Shortest Day — December 22.
4. The sunlight takes eight minutes in travelling from the Sun to the Earth.
5. Average speed of the earth in orbit ---- 66,600 miles (107,220 km) per hour.
6. Earth's equatorial diameter is about 7926 miles (12,756 km).
7. Water (oceans, seas, lakes and rivers) occupies nearly 75 per cent of the surface of the earth.
8. Earth's average distance from the Moon — 2,38,857 miles (3,84,400 km).
9. Earth's average distance from the Sun — 93 million miles (149.4 million km).

**Greenwich Time:** It is the local time of the Greenwich observatory in London on 0° meridian. Greenwich time is international standard time.

**International Date Line:** Half way round the earth from the Greenwich is International Date Line on 180° longitude. It runs down mid-Pacific. It is one day earlier on the east of this line than it is on the west of the line. When it is Monday east of the line, it is Tuesday west of the line.

**Zones:** On the basis of temperature and distribution of solar heat on the surface of the earth, the earth has been divided into five zones: 1. Torrid Zone; 2. North Temperate Zone; 3. South Temperate Zone; 4. Arctic Zone, and 5. Antarctic Zone.

## Continents

Large land masses forming large geographical divisions are called continents. There are seven continents:

1. Asia (29.5%)
2. Africa (20%)
3. Europe (6.5%)
4. North America (16.3%)
5. South America (11.8%)
6. Australia (5.2%), and
7. Antarctica (9.6%).

## Highest Mountain Peaks

1. Everest (Asia-8848 metres)
2. Aconcagua (South America-6960 metres)
3. Mckinley (North America-6194 metres)
4. Kilimanjaro (Africa-5895 metres)
5. Elbrus (Europe-5642 metres)
6. Vinson Massif (Antarctica-5140 metres)
7. Kosciusko (Australia-2228 metres).

## Largest Oceans

1. Pacific Ocean (The largest, covers almost 1/3 of the earth's total area, and the deepest about 6.8 miles at Mariana Trench in western Pacific);
2. Atlantic Ocean, and
3. Indian Ocean.

Other seas and gulfs are — the Mediterranean Sea, South China Sea, Bering Sea, Caribbean Sea, East China Sea, Sea of Japan, North Sea, Baltic Sea, Hudson Bay and Gulf of Mexico.

## Longest Rivers

1. Nile (6650 km-Africa),
2. Amazon (6570 km-South America)
3. Mississippi-Missouri (5970 km-North America)
4. Yangtze Kiang (5470 km-Asia)
5. Ob Irtysh (5150 km-Europe)
6. Congo (4666 km-Africa).

## Great Deserts

1. Sahara (94 lakh sq km-North Africa)
2. Libyan (11.65 lakh sq km-North Africa)
3. Australian (16 lakh sq km-Australia)
4. Gobi (13 lakh sq km-Mongolia)
5. Great Victoria (6,47,000 sq km-Australia)
6. Syrian (5,20,000 sq. km. Arabia)
7. Arabian (23,30,000 sq km Arabia).

## Largest Islands

1. Greenland (21,75,600 sq km)
2. New Guinea (7,77,000 sq km)
3. Borneo (7,25,545 sq km)
4. Malagasy (5,90,000 sq km)
5. Baffin Island (4,76,070 sq km).

## Highest Waterfalls

1. Angel (807 m-Venezuela)
2. Mongefossen (774 m-Norway)
3. Kukenaam (610 m-Venezuela)
4. Ribbon (491 m-USA)
5. King George VI (487 m-Guyana)
6. Upper Yosemite (435 m-USA).

## Major Producers of Crops, Minerals and Industrial goods

**Coal** : China, USA, UK, Germany, Russia Australia and India

**Cocoa** : Ghana, South Africa, West Indies Cote d'Ivaire, Indonesia, Nigeria

**Coffee** : Brazil, Columbia

**Copper** : Chile, USA, Canada, Peru, China

**Cotton** : China, India, USA, Russia, Egypt Brazil, Argentina, Pakistan

**Gold** : China, South Africa, Australia, Canada USA, India

**Grapes** : France, Italy, Portugal, California, USA

**Iron** : China, Australia, Brazil, Russia, USA UK, France, Germany, India, Spain

**Jute** : India, Bangladesh

**Manganese** : China, South Africa, Australia, Brazil

**Petroleum** : USA, Saudi Arab, Venezuela, Russia Iran, Myanmar, UAE

**Rice** : China, India, Indonesia, Bangladesh Vietnam, Japan, Myanmar

**Rubber** : Thailand, Malaysia, Indonesia, Sri Lanka, Vietnam, India

**Silk** : Japan, USA, France, China, India

**Silver** : Mexico, USA, Russia, Peru, India China

**Steel** : China, Japan, USA, Germany, Russia, UK

**Tea** : China, India, Sri Lanka, Kenya Vietnam

**Wheat** : China, India, Russia, USA, Canada Argentina, Australia

**Wool** : Australia, Argentina, New Zealand South Africa

**Tobacco** : China, USA, India, Brazil, Russia Indonesia

**Dimond** : Russia, Botswana, Australia, DR Congo

**Uranium** : Kazakhstan, Canada, Australia

**Thorium** : India, Australia

**Tin** : China, Indonesia, Peru

**Platinum** : South Africa, Russia, Zimbabwe

**Bauxite** : Australia, China, Guinea

## Biggest, Largest, Tallest of the World

| | |
|---|---|
| Largest Desert | Sahara (Africa) |
| Rainiest Place | Mowsynram near Cherrapunjee (Meghalaya, India) |
| Biggest Ocean | Pacific Ocean |
| Deepest Ocean | Pacific Ocean |
| Largest Mammal | Whale |
| Fastest Animal | Cheetah |
| Lightest Substance | Hydrogen gas |
| Longest River | Nile |
| Highest Waterfalls | Salto Angel Falls (Venezuela) |
| Tallest Animal | Giraffe |
| Largest Bird (Land) | Ostrich |
| Hardest Mineral | Diamond |
| Largest Delta | Sunderbans (W.B. India) |
| Largest Art Museum | The Louvre (France) |
| Longest Day | June, 21 |
| Shortest Day | December, 22 |
| Biggest Army | People's Liberation Army, China |
| Largest Salt Water Lake | Caspian Sea |
| Highest Mountain Peak | Everest (8848 metre high) |
| Longest Wall | Great Wall of China |
| Largest Peninsula | Arabia |
| Largest Planet | Jupiter |
| Smallest Continent | Australia |
| Largest Lake | Caspian Sea |
| Deepest Lake | Baikal, 3200 ft. |
| Finest Harbour | Sydney Harbour |
| Smallest Planet | Mercury |
| Largest Continent | Asia |
| Planet nearest to the Sun | Mercury |
| Highest Building | Burj Khalifa, Dubai |
| City largest (Area) | Jiuquan Gansu, China |
| City highest | Wen Chuan (China) |
| Country Biggest | Russia (17075000 sq. km.) |
| Electorate, Largest | India (over 90 crores) |
| Longest Epic | Mahabharat |
| Island, Biggest in the World | Greenland |
| Longest Railway Platform | Shree Siddharoodha Swamiji Railway Station Hubballi, Karnataka (India) |
| Swimming Course | English Channel |

## Currencies of Different Countries

| Country | Currency |
|---|---|
| Australia | Australian Dollar |
| Bangladesh | Taka |
| Belgium | Euro |
| Britain | Pound (Sterling) |
| Myanmar | Kyat |
| Canada | Canadian Dollar |
| Germany | Euro |
| Iran | Rial |
| India | Rupee |
| Sri Lanka | Sri Lankan Rupee |
| China | Yuan |
| Czech Republic | Koruna |
| Denmark | Krone |
| France | Euro |
| Pakistan | Rupee |
| Poland | Zloty |
| Spain | Euro |
| Indonesia | Rupiah |
| Iraq | Dinar |
| Italy | Euro |
| Japan | Yen |
| Mexico | Peso |
| The Netherland | Euro |
| European Union | Euro |
| Sweden | Krona |
| Switzerland | Swiss Franc |
| Turkiye | Turkish Lira |
| U.A.E. | Dirham |
| U.S.A. | Dollar |
| Russia | Rouble |

## Capital of Countries

| Country | Capital | Country | Capital |
|---|---|---|---|
| Austria | Vienna | Indonesia | Jakarta |
| Afghanisatan | Kabul | Iraq | Baghdad |
| Albania | Tirana | Italy | Rome |
| Algeria | Algiers | Ireland | Dublin |
| Andorra | Andorra la Vella | Japan | Tokyo |
| Angola | Luanda | Korea (North) | Pyong Yang |
| Australia | Canberra | Korea (South) | Seoul |
| Azerbaijan | Baku | Kenya | Nairobi |
| Argentina | Buenos Aires | Kuwait | Kuwait |
| Bahamas | Nassau | Laos | Vientiane |
| Bahrain | Manama | Lebanon | Beirut |
| Bangladesh | Dhaka | Mexico | Mexico City |
| Barbados | Bridgetown | Malaysia | Kualalumpur |
| Belarus | Minsk | Morocco | Rabat |
| Belgium | Brussels | Mozambique | Maputo |
| Bolivia | Lapaz | New Zealand | Welington |
| Bulgaria | Sofia | The Netherlands | Amsterdam |
| Bhutan | Thimpu | Panama | Panama City |
| Brazil | Brasilla | Portugal | Lisbon |
| Cambodia | Phnom Penh | Poland | Warsaw |
| Cameroon | Yaounde | Sri Lanka | Colombo |
| Canada | Ottawa | Sweden | Stockholm |
| Chad | N'djamena | Switzerland | Bern |
| Chile | Santiago | Sudan | Khartoum |
| China | Beijing | Sierra Leone | Freetown |
| Cyprus | Nicosia | South Africa | Capetown |
| Columbia | Bagota | Saudi Arabia | Riyadh |
| Croatia | Zagreb | Spain | Madrid |
| Cuba | Havana | Thailand | Bangkok |
| Denmark | Copenhegan | Turkiye | Ankara |
| Ethiopia | Addis Ababa | Russia | Moscow |
| Egypt | Cairo | Azerbaijan | Baku |
| Finland | Helsinki | Armenia | Yerevan |
| France | Paris | Latvia | Riga |
| Germany | Berlin | Ukrain | Kiev |
| Greece | Athens | U.S.A. | Washington |
| Guatemala | Guatemala City | U.K. | London |
| Hungary | Budapest | U.A.E. | Abu Dhabi |
| Iran | Tehran | Vietnam | Hanoi |
| India | New Delhi | Zambia | Lusaka |

## Wonders of the World

**Seven Wonders of the Ancient World:**

1. the Pyramids of Egypt, built in approximately 2700 BC;
2. the Hanging Gardens at Babylon;
3. the temple of Artemis at Emphesus;
4. the statue of Zeus at Olympia;
5. the tomb of Mausolus at Halicarnassus, built in nearly 350 BC;
6. the Colossus of Rhodes, built in nearly 280 BC;
7. the Pharos Lighthouse at Alexandria.

**Seven Wonders of the Medieval World:**

1. the Colosseum of Rome;
2. the Great Wall of China;
3. the Porcelain Tower of Nanking;
4. the Mosque at St. Sophia (Constantinople);
5. Stonehenge;
6. the Catacombs of Rome;
7. the Leaning Tower of Pisa.

**Seven New Wonders of the World:**

1. Taj Mahal of Agra (India);
2. Pyramid at Chichen Itza (Mexico);
3. Machu Picchu (Peru);
4. Statue of Christ The Redeemer (Brazil);
5. Great Wall of China;
6. Roman Colosseum, Italy;
7. Ruins of Petra, Jordan.

## First in the World

| | |
|---|---|
| First Chinese visitor to India | Fahien |
| First foreign invader of India | Alexander, the Great (Greek) |
| First person to climb Mt. Everest | Tenzing Norgay (India) and Edmund Hillary (New Zealand) (1953) |
| First atom bomb dropped at | Hiroshima (Japan) |
| First man in the space | Yuri Gagarin (former USSR) |
| First woman in the space | Valentina Tereshkova (former USSR) |
| First person to walk in the space | Alexei Leonov (former USSR) |
| First person to land on the moon | Neil Armstrong (USA) |
| First and the only woman to have climbed Mt. Everest twice | Santosh Yadav (Indian; May 1992; May 1993) |
| First person on Mt. Everest without oxygen | Phu Dorjee (Indian; May 9, 1984) |
| First person to climb Mt. Everest twice | Nawang Gombu |
| First President of the USA | George Washington |
| First woman Prime Minister | Sirimavo Bandaranaike (Sri Lanka) |
| First person to swim across English Channel | Mathew Webb |
| First woman to swim across English Channel | Gertrude Caroline Ederle |
| First woman to climb Mt. Everest | Junko Tabei (Japan) |
| First woman to climb Mt. Everest alone and without oxygen supplies | Alison Hargreaves (Britain: May 13, 1995) |
| First Aeroplane to fly around the world without refuelling | Voyager (Dec. 1986) |

| | |
|---|---|
| First test-tube Baby | Louise Brown (UK; 1978) |
| First all-talking Film | Jaz Singer (1927) |
| First Secretary-General of the UN | Trygve Lie (Norway: 1946-53) |
| First woman President of the UN General Assembly | Vijayalakshmi Pandit (India: 1953) |
| First woman to reach North Pole | Anna Bancroft (1986) |
| First person to reach North Pole | Robert Peary |
| First person to reach South Pole | Amundsen (1911) |
| First woman to command Spacecraft in space | Ellin Collins |

## Popular Names

| *Popular Name* | *Real Name* |
|---|---|
| Badshah Khan | Abdul Ghaffar Khan |
| Bapu, Father of Nation | M.K. Gandhi |
| Bard of Avon | William Shakespeare |
| Chachaji *or* Panditji | Jawaharlal Nehru |
| Desert Fox | Gen. Rommel (Germany) |
| Desh Bandhu | C.R. Das |
| Father of English Poetry | Geoffrey Chaucer |
| Fuhrer | Adolf Hitler |
| Grand Old Man of India | Dadabhai Naoroji |
| Grand Old Man of Britain | W.E. Gladstone |
| Gurudev | Rabindra Nath Tagore |
| Guruji | M.S. Golwalkar |
| Grand Commoner | Pitt, the younger |
| Iron Man of India | Sardar Patel |
| Lady with the Lamp | Florence Nightingale |
| Lal, Bal, Pal | Lala Lajpat Rai, Bal Gangadhar Tilak, Bipin Chandra Pal |
| Li-Kwan | Pearl Buck |
| Little Corporal *or* Man of Destiny | Napoleon Bonaparte |
| Lokmanya | Bal Gangadhar Tilak |
| Lok Nayak | Jayaprakash Narain |
| Mahamana | Pt. Madan Mohan Malaviya |
| Maid of Orleans | Joan of Arc |
| Maiden Queen | Queen Elizabeth I |
| Man of Blood and Iron | Prince Bismark |
| Netaji | Subhash Chandra Bose |
| Nightingale of India | Sarojini Naidu |
| Priyadarshini | Indira Gandhi |
| Punjab Kesari | Lala Lajpat Rai |
| Wizard of the North | Walter Scott |

## Geographical Surnames

| *Geographical Surname* | *Real Name* |
|---|---|
| Bengal's Sorrow | Damodar River |
| Blue Mountains | Nilgiri Hills |
| China's Sorrow | Hwang-Ho |
| City of Palaces | Kolkata |
| City of Skyscrapers *or* Empire City | New York |
| City of Dreaming Spires | Oxford |
| Cockpit of Europe | Belgium |
| Dark Continent | Africa |
| Emerald Isle | Ireland |
| Eternal City | Rome |
| Forbidden City | Lhasa (Tibet) |
| Gateway of India | Mumbai |
| Gate of Tears | Strait of Bab-el-mandab |
| Gift of the Nile | Egypt |
| Granite City | Aberdeen (Scotland) |
| Hermit Kingdom | Korea |
| Holy Land | Jerusalem |
| Island of Pearls | Bahrain (Persian Gulf) |
| Island of Cloves | Zanzibar |
| Key to the Mediterranean | Gibraltar |
| Land of Five Rivers | Punjab |
| Land of Golden Pagoda | Myanmar |
| Land of Kangaroo | Australia |
| Land of Maple Leaf/Lillies | Canada |
| Land of Midnight Sun | Norway |
| Land of Morning Calm | Korea |
| Land of the Rising Sun | Japan |
| Land of Thousand Lakes | Finland |
| Land of Thunderbolt | Bhutan |
| Land of the White Elephants | Thailand |
| Manchester of the Orient | Osaka (Japan) |
| Pearl of the Antilles *or* Sugar Bowl of the World | Cuba |
| Pink City | Jaipur |
| Playground of Europe | Switzerland |
| Queen of the Adriatic | Venice (Italy) |
| Roof of the World | Pamirs |
| Sick Man of Europe | Turkiye |
| Venice of the North | Stockholm (Sweden) |
| Windy City | Chicago |
| Whiteman's Grave | Guinea Coast of Africa |
| World's Loneliest Island | Tristan de Cunha |

## Countries'/Cities' Names—Old and New

| *Old Name* | *New Name* | *Old Name* | *New Name* |
|---|---|---|---|
| Abyssinia | Ethiopia | Leningrad | St. Petersburg |
| Basutoland | Lesotho | Leopoldville | Kinshasa |
| Bechuanaland | Botswana | Mesopotamia | Iraq |
| British Honduras | Belize | North Rhodesia | Zambia |
| Burma | Myanmar | Nyasaland | Malawi |
| Ceylon | Sri Lanka | Peking | Beijing |
| Zaire | Democratic Republic of the Congo | Persia | Iran |
| Constantinople | Istanbul | Rangoon | Yangon |
| Dahomey | Benin | Salisbury | Harare |
| Dutch East Indies | Indonesia | Siam | Thailand |
| East Pakistan | Bangladesh | South West Africa | Namibia |
| Formosa | Taiwan | Southern Rhodesia | Zimbabwe |
| Gold Coast | Ghana | Turkey | Turkiye |

## IMPORTANT RESIDENCES

• **Buckingham Palace (London):** King/Queen of Britain • **10, Downing Street (London):** Prime Minis Britain • **Elysee Palace (Paris):** President, France • **Rashtrapati Bhawan (New Delhi):** President, In • **White House (Washington):** President, USA • **Vatican (Rome):** Pope

## Important towns situated on the River Banks

| *Town* | *River* | *Town* | *River* |
|---|---|---|---|
| Agra | Yamuna | Leh | Indus |
| Ahmedabad | Sabarmati | London | Thames |
| Ayodhya | Saryu | Lucknow | Gomati |
| Baghdad | Tigris | Nasik | Godavari |
| Berlin | Spree | New York | Hudson |
| Cairo | Nile | Paris | Seine |
| Kolkata | Hooghly | Patna | Ganga |
| Cuttack | Mahanadi | Prayagraj | Confluence of t Ganga and the Yamu |
| Delhi | Yamuna | Rome | Tiber |
| Dibrugarh | Brahmaputra | Srinagar | Jhelum |
| Dublin | Liffey | Surat | Tapti |
| Hardwar | Ganga | Sydney | Murray-Darling |
| Hyderabad | Musi | Varanasi | Ganga |
| Jabalpur | Narbada | Vienna | Danube |
| Kanpur | Ganga | Washington | Potamac |
| Karachi | Indus | Yangon | Irawadi |
| Lahore | Ravi | | |

## Books and Authors

### FOREIGN

| Book | Author | Book | Author |
|---|---|---|---|
| Aesop's Fables | Aesop | Moor's Last Sigh | Salman Rushdie |
| Adventure of Robinson Crusoe | Daniel Defoe | Mother | Maxim Gorky |
| Adventures of Sherlok Holmes | Arthur Conan Doyle | Mother India | Katherine Mayo |
| Alice in Wonderland | Lewis Carrol | Nana | Emile Zola |
| Apple Cart | G.B. Shaw | Ninteen Eighty Four | George Orwell |
| Arabian Nights | Sir Richard Burton | Odyssey | Homer |
| As You Like It | William Shakespeare | Origin of Species | Charles Darwin |
| A Tale of Two Cities | Charles Dickens | Othello | William Shakespeare |
| A Tale of Two Gardens | Octavio Paz | Paradise Lost | John Milton |
| A Thousand Suns | Dominique Lapierre | Paradise Regained | John Milton |
| August Coup | Mikhail S. Gorbachev | Path to Power | Margaret Thatcher |
| Ben Hur | Lewis Wallace | Pickwick Papers | Charles Dickens |
| Candida | G.B. Shaw | Pride and Prejudice | Jane Austen |
| Das Kapital | Karl Marx | Razor's Edge | Somerset Maugham |
| David Copperfield | Charles Dickens | Republic | Plato |
| Divine Comedy | A. Dante | Romeo and Juliet | William Shakespeare |
| Doctor's Dilemma | G.B. Shaw | Round the World in Eighty Days | Jules Verne |
| Famished Road | Ben Okri | Rubaiyat-i-Omar Khayyam | Edward Fitzgerald (Translator) |
| Freedom From Fear | Aung San Suu Kyi | Shape of Things to Come | H.G. Wells |
| Gulistan Bostan | Sheikh Saadi | The Satanic Verses | Salman Rushdie |
| Gulliver's Travels | Jonathan Swift | The Social Contract | Rousseau |
| Hamlet | William Shakespeare | The Tempest | William Shakespeare |
| Iliad | Homer | Time Machine | H.G. Wells |
| Inferno | A. Dante | Tom Sawyer | Mark Twain |
| In Memoriam | Lord Tennyson | Treasure Island | R.L. Stevenson |
| Ivanhoe | Walter Scott | Twelfth Night | William Shakespeare |
| Julius Caesar | William Shakespeare | Uncle Tom's Cabin | H.B. Stowe |
| Lady Chatterley's Lover | D.H. Lawrence | Unto This Last | John Ruskin |
| Lajja | Taslima Nasreen | Utopia | Thomas More |
| Les Miserable | Victor Hugo | Universe Around Us | James Jeans |
| Leviathan | Thomas Hobbes | Vicar of Wakefield | Oliver Goldsmith |
| Lolita | V. Nobokov | War and Peace | Leo Tolstoy |
| Lycidas | John Milton | Wealth of Nations | Adam Smith |
| Mein Kampf | Adolf Hitler | Wonder That was India | A.L. Basham |
| Merchant of Venice | William Shakespeare | Wuthering Heights | Emily Bronte |
| Midnight's Children | Salman Rushdie | | |

### INDIAN

| Book | Author | Book | Author |
|---|---|---|---|
| Abhigyan Shakuntalam | Kalidas | Anand Math | Bankim Chandra Chatterjee |
| Ain-i-Akbari | Abul Fazal | | |

| Book | Author |
|---|---|
| Arthashastra | Kautilya |
| A Suitable Boy | Vikram Seth |
| Bhagwat Gita | Ved Vyas |
| Chidambara | Sumitranandan Pant |
| Devdas | Sarat Chandra Chatterjee |
| Diwan-i-Ghalib | Mirza Ghalib |
| Discovery of India | Jawaharlal Nehru |
| Essays on Gita | Aurobindo Ghosh |
| Eternal India | Indira Gandhi |
| Faces of Everest | Major H.P.S. Ahluwalia |
| Ganadevata | Tarashankar Bandopadhyaya |
| Geet Govind | Jaya Dev |
| Geetanjali | R.N. Tagore |
| Glimpses of World History | Jawaharlal Nehru |
| Godaan | Prem Chand |
| Gul-e-Nagma | Firaq Gorakhpuri |
| Gunahon ka Devta | Dharmveer Bharti |
| Harsh Charita | Bana Bhatta |
| Hindu View of Life | S. Radhakrishnan |
| Idols | Sunil Gavaskar |
| India Divided | Dr. Rajendra Prasad |
| The Judgement | Kuldip Nayyar |
| Juhi ki Kali | Surya Kant Tripathi 'Nirala' |
| Justice of Peace ke Aansu | Janardan Prasad Singh |
| Chand ka Munh Terha Hai | Muktibodh |
| Kapalkundala | Bankim Chandra Chatterjee |
| Kadambari | Bana Bhatta |
| Kagaz Te Kanwas | Amrita Pritam |
| Kamayani | Jai Shankar Prasad |
| Kitni Nawon Mein Kitni Bar | S.H. Vatsyayan |
| Kumar Sambhav | Kalidas |
| Mahabharata | Ved Vyas |
| Malgudi Days | R.K. Narayan |
| Manvini Bhavai | Pannalal Patel |
| Mati Matal | Gopi Nath Mohanty |
| Meghdoot | Kalidas |
| Meri Ekyavan Kavitain | Atal Bihari Vajpayee |
| Meri Sansadiya Yatra | Atal Bihari Vajpayee |
| Mritunjaya | B.K. Bhattacharya |
| Mudrarakshasa | Vishakhadatta |
| My Experiments with Truth | M.K. Gandhi |
| My Own Boswell | M. Hidayatullah |
| My Presidential Years | R. Venkataraman |
| Nisheeth | Uma Shankar Joshi |
| 'No, Sir' | P.G. Mavlankar |
| One Day Wonders | Sunil Gavaskar |
| Panchtantra | Vishnu Sharma |
| Passage to England | Nirad C. Chaudhuri |
| Prison Diary | Jaya Prakash Narayan |
| Raghuvansha | Kalidas |
| Rajtarangini | Kalhana |
| Ramayana | Balmiki |
| Ramcharit Manas | Tulsidas |
| Rukh Te Rishi | Harbhajan Singh |
| Satyarth Prakash | Swami Dayanand |
| Sur Sagar | Surdas |
| The Guide | R.K. Narayan |
| The Insider | P.V. Narasimharao |
| The Post Office — *Dak Ghar* | Rabindra Nath Tagore |
| The God of Small Things | Arundhati Roy |
| Urvashi | Ram Dhari Singh 'Dinkar' |
| Yama | Mahadevi Verma |
| My Country : My Life (Autobiography) | L.K. Advani |
| The Test of My Life | Yuvraj Singh |
| Twenty Years in a Decade | Shah Rukh Khan |

## IMPORTANT BOOKS WRITTEN IN JAIL

| Book | Author |
|---|---|
| My Experiments with Truth | Mahatma Gandhi |
| Glimpses of World History | Jawaharlal Nehru |
| Discovery of India | |
| Gita Rahasya | Lokmanya Bal Gangadhar Tilak |
| Pilgrim's Progress | John Bunyan |
| Bible (in German language) | Martin Luther |
| Les Miserables | Victor Hugo |
| Long Walk to Freedom | Nelson Mandela |

✱ ✱ ✱ ✱ ✱

# 3 Our India

## INDIA : AT A GLANCE

| | | |
|---|---|---|
| Population (2011) | : | 1,21,08,54,977 |
| Capital | : | New Delhi |
| Area | : | 32,87,263 sq km |
| Geographic Location | : | Between 8°4' and 37°6' north latitudes |
| | : | Between 68°7' and 97°25' east longitudes |
| Coastline Length | : | 11098.81 km including the coastline of Lakshadweep, Andaman & Nicobar Islands. |
| Major Languages | : | 22 |
| National Anthem | : | Jana Gana Mana |
| National Currency | : | Rupee (₹) |
| National Animal | : | Tiger |
| National Aquatic Animal | : | Dolphin |
| National Bird | : | Peacock |
| National River | : | Ganga |
| Characteristics of Indian Constitution | : | Socialist, Secular, Democratic, Republic |
| Legislature | : | Bicameral Legislature at the Centre<br>Uni/Bicameral Legislatures in States |
| Executive | : | President, Vice-President and Council of Ministers at the Centre<br>Governor and Council of Ministers in States |
| Judiciary | : | Independent from Executive with Supreme Court at the apex of the hierarchy |
| Total Road Length | : | 66.71 lakh kilometres (March 2024) |

## India: States & Union Territories

| States/Union Territories | Capital | Area in (Sq. Km.) | Language |
|---|---|---|---|
| Andhra Pradesh | Amravati | 1,60,229 | Telugu |
| Arunachal Pradesh | Itanagar | 83,743 | Nyishi, Miji, Wancho etc. |
| Assam | Dispur | 78,438 | Assamese |
| Bihar | Patna | 94,163 | Hindi, Maithili |
| Chhattisgarh | Raipur | 136,034 | Hindi |
| Goa | Panji | 3,702 | Marathi and Konkani |
| Gujarat | Gandhinagar | 1,96,024 | Gujarati |
| Haryana | Chandigarh | 44,212 | Hindi |
| Himachal Pradesh | Shimla | 55,673 | Hindi and Pahari |
| Jharkhand | Ranchi | 79,714 | Hindi, Santhali |
| Karnataka | Bengaluru | 1,91,791 | Kannada |
| Keralam | Thiruvananthapuram | 38,863 | Malayalam |
| Madhya Pradesh | Bhopal | 308,000 | Hindi |
| Maharashtra | Mumbai | 307,713 | Marathi |
| Manipur | Imphal | 22,327 | Manipuri |
| Meghalaya | Shillong | 22,429 | Khasi, Garo and English |
| Mizoram | Aizawl | 21,081 | Mizo and English |
| Nagaland | Kohima | 16,579 | Sema, English |
| Odisha | Bhubaneswar | 155,707 | Odia |
| Punjab | Chandigarh | 50,362 | Punjabi |
| Rajasthan | Jaipur | 3,42,239 | Hindi and Rajasthani |
| Sikkim | Gangtok | 7,096 | Bhutia, Nepali, Lepcha and Limbu |
| Tamil Nadu | Chennai | 1,30,058 | Tamil |
| Telangana | Hyderabad | 1,14,840 | Telugu |
| Tripura | Agartala | 10,491 | Bengali, Kakborak, Manipuri |
| Uttar Pradesh | Lucknow | 2,40,928 | Hindi and Urdu |
| Uttarakhand | Dehradun | 53,484 | Hindi |
| West Bengal | Kolkata | 88,752 | Bengali |
| Jammu and Kashmir | Srinagar (Summer) Jammu (Winter) | 2,22,236* | Kashmiri, Urdu, Dogri |
| Andaman & Nicobar Island | Sri Vijaya Puram | 8,249 | Bengali, Hindi, Nicobarese, Tamil, Telugu, and Malayalam |
| Chandigarh | Chandigarh | 114 | Hindi, Punjabi |
| Dadara & Nagar Haveli and Daman & Diu | Daman | 603 | Gujarati and Hindi |
| Delhi | Delhi | 1483 | Hindi, Punjabi and Urdu |
| Lakshadweep | Kavaratti | 32 | Malayalam |
| Puducherry | Puducherry | 492 | Tamil, Telugu, Malayalam, English and French |
| Ladakh | Leh | — | Ladakhi |

* including areas of Ladakh and illegally occupied by China and Pakistan.

# POPULATION

India's population according to the figures of 2011 census, was 1,21,08,54,977 at the sunrise of March 01, 2011. India's population constitutes nearly 17.5 per cent of the total world population while her geographical area is only 2.42 per cent of the world area. With such a huge population to support on so small an area, the country finds herself in great difficulty in making any significant dent on its poverty and economic backwardness. India's national income, which is barely 2 per cent of the total global income, clearly shows the tremendous strain of population on her economy.

## 2011 Census Highlights

| | | |
|---|---|---|
| Population of India–Total Indian population is 17.7% of total world population | : | 1,21,08,54,977 (Male: 62,32,70,258; Female: 58,75,84,719) |
| Decadal Growth (2001-2011) | : | 17.7 per cent (Males: 17.19 per cent; Females: 18.12 per cent) |
| Hightest Decadal Growth (State-wise) | : | Meghalaya (27.9 per cent) |
| Lowest Decadal Growth (State-wise) | : | Manipur (–18.6 per cent) |
| Most populous State | : | Uttar Pradesh (16.51 per cent of National Population) |
| Density of population | : | 382 persons per sq. km. |
| Most densly populated State | : | Bihar : 1106 per sq. km |
| Sex Ratio | : | 943 females per 1000 males |
| Total Literacy Rate | : | 73% (Males – 80.9%), (Females – 64.6%) |
| Highest Literacy (State-wise) | : | Keralam (94%) |
| Lowest Literacy (State-wise) | : | Bihar (61.8) |

## OTHER DETAILS

### POPULATION OF INDIA

| | | | |
|---|---|---|---|
| 1951 | 36,10,88,090 | 1961 | 43,92,34,771 |
| 1971 | 54,81,59,652 | 1981 | 68,33,29,097 |
| 1991 | 84,64,21,039 | 2001 | 102,87,37,436 |
| 2011 | 1,21,08,54,977 | | |

### DENSITY OF POPULATION (Persons per square kilometre)

| | | | |
|---|---|---|---|
| 1951 | 113 | 1961 | 138 |
| 1971 | 177 | 1981 | 216 |
| 1991 | 267 | 2001 | 324 |
| 2011 | 382 | | |

### ANNUAL COMPOUND RATE OF GROWTH

| | | | |
|---|---|---|---|
| 1941-1951 | 1.25 per cent | 1951-1961 | 1.96 per cent |
| 1961-1971 | 2.22 per cent | 1971-1981 | 2.20 per cent |
| 1981-1991 | 2.14 per cent | 1991-2001 | 1.95 per cent |
| 2001-2011 | 1.64 per cent | | |

## 2011 CENSUS OF INDIA : POPULATION DISTRIBUTION, POPULATION DENSITY AND LITERACY RATE

| S. No. | State/ Union Territories* | Population 2011 | | | Population Density (per sq. km.) | Literacy Rate 2011 | | |
|---|---|---|---|---|---|---|---|---|
| | | Persons | Males | Females | 2011 | Persons | Males | Females |
| | **INDIA** | **1,21,08,54,977** | **62,32,70,258** | **58,75,84,719** | **382** | **73.0** | **80.9** | **64.6** |
| 1. | Jammu and Kashmir | 1,25,41,302 | 66,40,662 | 59,00,640 | 124 | 67.2 | 76.8 | 56.4 |
| 2. | Himachal Pradesh | 68,64,602 | 34,81,873 | 33,82,729 | 123 | 82.8 | 89.5 | 75.9 |
| 3. | Punjab | 2,77,43,338 | 1,46,39,465 | 1,31,03,873 | 551 | 75.8 | 80.4 | 70.7 |
| 4. | Chandigarh | 10,55,450 | 5,80,663 | 4,74,787 | 9,258 | 86.0 | 90.0 | 81.2 |
| 5. | Uttarakhand | 1,00,86,292 | 51,37,773 | 49,48,519 | 189 | 78.8 | 87.4 | 70.0 |
| 6. | Haryana | 2,53,51,462 | 1,34,94,734 | 1,18,56,728 | 573 | 75.6 | 84.1 | 65.9 |
| 7. | Delhi | 1,67,87,941 | 89,87,326 | 78,00,615 | 11,320 | 86.2 | 90.9 | 80.8 |
| 8. | Rajasthan | 6,85,48,437 | 3,55,50,997 | 3,29,97,440 | 200 | 66.1 | 79.2 | 52.1 |
| 9. | Uttar Pradesh | 19,98,12,341 | 10,44,80,510 | 9,53,31,831 | 829 | 67.7 | 77.3 | 57.2 |
| 10. | Bihar | 10,40,99,452 | 5,42,78,157 | 4,98,21,295 | 1,106 | 61.8 | 71.2 | 51.5 |
| 11. | Sikkim | 6,10,577 | 3,23,070 | 2,87,507 | 86 | 81.4 | 86.6 | 75.6 |
| 12. | Arunachal Pradesh | 13,83,727 | 7,13,912 | 6,69,815 | 17 | 65.4 | 72.6 | 57.7 |
| 13. | Nagaland | 19,78,502 | 10,24,649 | 9,53,853 | 119 | 79.6 | 82.8 | 76.1 |
| 14. | Manipur | 28,55,794 | 14,38,586 | 14,17,208 | 128 | 76.94 | 83.58 | 70.26 |
| 15. | Mizoram | 10,97,206 | 5,55,339 | 5,41,867 | 52 | 91.3 | 93.3 | 89.3 |
| 16. | Tripura | 36,73,917 | 18,74,376 | 17,99,541 | 350 | 87.2 | 91.5 | 82.7 |
| 17. | Meghalya | 29,66,889 | 14,91,832 | 14,75,057 | 132 | 74.4 | 76.0 | 72.9 |
| 18. | Assam | 3,12,05,576 | 1,59,39,443 | 1,52,66,133 | 398 | 72.2 | 77.8 | 66.3 |
| 19. | West Bengal | 9,12,76,115 | 4,68,09,027 | 4,44,67,088 | 1,028 | 76.3 | 81.7 | 70.5 |
| 20. | Jharkhand | 3,29,88,134 | 1,69,30,315 | 1,60,57,819 | 414 | 66.4 | 76.8 | 55.4 |
| 21. | Odisha | 4,19,74,218 | 2,12,12,136 | 2,07,62,082 | 270 | 72.9 | 81.6 | 64.0 |
| 22. | Chhattisgarh | 2,55,45,198 | 1,28,32,895 | 1,27,12,303 | 189 | 70.3 | 80.3 | 60.2 |
| 23. | Madhya Pradesh | 7,26,26,809 | 3,76,12,306 | 3,50,14,503 | 236 | 69.3 | 78.7 | 59.2 |
| 24. | Gujarat | 6,04,39,692 | 3,14,91,260 | 2,89,48,432 | 308 | 78.0 | 85.8 | 69.7 |
| 25. | Daman and Diu | 2,43,247 | 1,50,301 | 92,946 | 2,191 | 87.1 | 91.5 | 79.5 |
| 26. | Dadra & Nagar Haweli | 3,43,709 | 1,93,760 | 1,49,949 | 700 | 76.2 | 85.2 | 64.3 |
| 27. | Maharashtra | 11,23,74,333 | 5,82,43,056 | 5,41,31,277 | 365 | 82.3 | 88.4 | 75.9 |
| 28. | Andhra Pradesh | 4,93,86,799 | 2,47,38,068 | 2,46,48,731 | 308 | 67.4 | 74.8 | 60.0 |
| 29. | Karnataka | 6,10,95,297 | 3,09,66,657 | 3,01,28,640 | 319 | 75.4 | 82.5 | 68.1 |
| 30. | Goa | 14,58,545 | 7,39,140 | 7,19,405 | 394 | 88.7 | 92.6 | 84.7 |
| 31. | Lakshadweep | 64,473 | 33,123 | 31,350 | 2,149 | 91.8 | 95.6 | 87.9 |
| 32. | Kerala | 3,34,06,061 | 1,60,27,412 | 1,73,78,649 | 860 | 94.0 | 96.1 | 92.1 |
| 33. | Tamil Nadu | 7,21,47,030 | 3,61,37,975 | 3,60,09,055 | 555 | 80.1 | 86.8 | 73.4 |
| 34. | Puducherry | 12,47,953 | 6,12,511 | 6,35,442 | 2,547 | 85.8 | 91.3 | 80.7 |
| 35. | Andaman & Nicobar Island | 3,80,581 | 2,02,871 | 1,77,710 | 46 | 86.6 | 90.3 | 82.4 |
| 36. | Telangana | 3,51,93,978 | 17,704,078 | 17,489,900 | 308 | 66.5 | 75.0 | 57.9 |

* * * * *

# 4 Indian History

## Famous Sites of Indus Valley Civilization

| Name of Site | Year of Excavation | River/ Sea coast | Discoverer |
|---|---|---|---|
| Harappa (Montgomery–Pakistan) | 1921 | Ravi River | Dayaram Sahney |
| Mohanjodaro (Larkana–Pakistan) | 1922 | Indus River | Rakhal Das Banerjee |
| Chanhudaro (Sindh–Pakistan) | 1931 | Indus River | N.G. Mazumdar |
| Alamgir pur (Meerut – U.P.) | 1952-55 | Hindan River | Yagyadatta Sharma |
| Ropar (Punjab) | 1953 | Sutlej River | Yagyadatta Sharma |
| Rangpur (Kathiabar–Gujarat) | 1953 | Bhabar River | Madho Swaroop Vatsa, Rang Nath Rao |
| Kotdigi (Sindh–Pakistan) | 1953 | Indus River | Fazal Ahmed Khan |
| Lothal (Ahmedabad–Gujarat) | 1954 | Bhogwa River | Rang Nath Rao |
| Kalibanga (Ganganagar–Rajasthan) | 1961 | Ghaggar | Brajwasi Lal |
| Surkotara (Kutch–Gujarat) | 1967 | Ghaggar River | Ravindra Singh Vishta |
| Banawali (Hissar–Haryana) | 1973 | Ghaggar River | Ravindra Singh Vishta |
| Balakote | 1979 | Arabian Sea | George F. Dales |
| Dhaulavira (Gujarat) | 1963-68 | — | J.P. Joshi |
| | 1990-91 | — | Dr. R.S. Vishta |

## Well known Quotations

| | |
|---|---|
| ***"Swarajya is My Birthright"*** | — Bal Gangadhar Tilak |
| ***"Give me blood, I shall give you freedom"*** | — Netajee Subhash Chandra Bose |
| ***"Inqalab Zindabad"*** | — Bhagat Singh |
| ***"Saare Jahan Se Achcha, Hindustan Hamara"*** | — Dr. Mohammed Iqbal |
| ***"Dilli Chalo"*** | — Subhash Chandra Bose |
| ***"Sarfaroshi ki tamanna, Ab Hamare Dil Mein Hai."*** | — Ram Prasad Bismil |
| ***"I am socialist by nature".*** | — Jawahar Lal Nehru |
| ***"Go to Vedas"*** | — Swami Dayanand |
| ***"Aaram Haram Hai"*** | — Jawahar Lal Nehru |
| ***"Jai Jawan, Jai Kisan"*** | — Lal Bahadur Shastri |
| ***"Jai Jawan, Jai Kisan, Jai Vigyan"*** | — Atal Bihari Vajpayee |
| ***"Speak less, work more"*** | — Sanjay Gandhi |
| ***"Vijayee Vishwa Tiranga Pyara"*** | — Shyam Lal Gupta |

| | |
|---|---|
| *"Quit India"* | — Mahatma Gandhi |
| *"Hindi, Hindu, Hindustan"* | — Bhartendu Harishchandra |
| *"Purna Swarajya"* | — Jawahar Lal Nehru |
| *"Every lathi blow inflicted on my body will prove a nail in British coffin"* | — Lala Lajpat Rai |
| *"Jai Hind"* | — Subhash Chandra Bose |
| *"Do or die"* | — Mahatma Gandhi |
| *"Who lives if India dies"* | — Jawahar Lal Nehru |
| *"Vande Mataram"* | — Bankim Chandra Chatterjee |
| *"Jana Gana Mana Adhinayaka Jai Hai"* | —Rabindranath Tagore |
| *"Hate sin, not the sinner."* | — Mahatma Gandhi |
| *"Service of the people is the service of God"* | — Swami Vivekananda |
| *"Truth and non-violence are my God."* | — Mahatma Gandhi |

## Battles and Wars In India

| War | Year | Result |
|---|---|---|
| ***Battle of Kalinga*** | (261 B.C.) | Ashoka defeated the king of Kalinga |
| ***Second battle of Tarain*** | (1192 A.D.) | Muhammad Gori defeated Prithviraj Chauhan |
| ***First battle of Panipat*** | (1526 A.D.) | Babar defeated Ibrahim Lodi |
| ***Battle of Khanwa*** | (1527 A.D.) | Babar defeated Rana Sanga |
| ***Battle of Chausa*** | (1539 A.D.) | Shershah Suri defeated Humayun and became ruler of Delhi |
| ***Second Battle of Panipat*** | (1556 A.D.) | Akbar defeated Hemu |
| ***Battle of Talikota*** | (1565 A.D.) | Allied forces of Bijapur, Bidar, Golkunda and Ahamadnagar defeated the King of Vijay Nagar |
| ***Battle of Haldighati*** | (1576 A.D.) | Some historian say that this battle was indecisive but some say that Rana Pratap was defeated by Akbar |
| ***Battle of Palasey*** | (1757 A.D.) | British forces defeated Nawab of Bengal Sirajudoulla |
| ***Battle of Wandiwash*** | (1760 A.D.) | British forces defeated the French |
| ***Third battle of Panipat*** | (1761 A.D.) | Maratha were defeated by Ahmad Shah Abadali |
| ***Battle of Buxar*** | (1764 A.D.) | British forces defeated the combined forces of Mir Quasim, Shah Alam Mughal empire and Awadh's Nawab |
| ***Third Anglo-Maratha War*** | (1792 A.D.) | Maratha were conclusively defeated |
| ***Fourth Anglo-Mysore War*** | (1799 A.D.) | Tipu Sultan died fighting the British forces |
| ***Second Anglo-Sikh War*** | (1848 A.D.) | British forces annexed Punjab from Sikh rulers |
| ***Indo-China War*** | (1962 A.D.) | China attacked India unilaterally and annexed some area |
| ***Indo-Pak War*** | (1965 A.D.) | Pakistan attacked India but had to suffer severe setbacks |
| ***Indo-Pak War*** | (1971 A.D.) | Pak declare war against India. |

✱ ✱ ✱ ✱ ✱

# 5 Indian Constitution & Polity

Indian Constitution is a comprehensive document and it is the lengthiest written Constitution in the World.

**The Preamble of the Constitution:** "We the people of India, having solemnly resolved to Constitute India into a Sovereign, Socialist, Secular Democratic Republic and to secure to all its citizen.

**Justice:** Social, economic and political.

**Liberty:** Of thought, expression, belief, faith and worship.

**Equality:** Of status and of opportunity, and to promote among them all.

**Fraternity:** Assuring the dignity of the individual and the unity and integrity of the nation.

In Our Constituent Assembly this twenty-sixth day of November, 1949, do Hereby Adopt, Enact and Give to Ourselves This Constitution."

The preamble of the Constitution is the basic philosophy of the Constitution on which it is based. It is the Key of the Constitution. Though it has a limited role legally, whenever there is an ambiguity, the courts refer to the Preamble to get insight into various clauses of the Constitution. The words SECULAR and SOCIALIST were not there in the original Constitution but were incorporated subsequently in 1976 after the 42nd constitutional amendment. The preamble clearly outlines the essential features of our Constitution:

1. The final power lies in the hands of the people.
2. India is a sovereign, socialist, secular, democratic republic.
3. Efforts will be made to give social, economic and political justice.
4. Every citizen of India will have liberty of thought, expression, belief, faith and worship.
5. There will be equality of status and opportunity.
6. The feeling of fraternity among the people will be encouraged.
7. The Unity and Integrity of the nation is of paramount importance.

## SALIENT FEATURES OF THE INDIAN CONSTITUTION

1. The Indian Constitution is a written and detailed one. The framers, considering the political inexperience of the countrymen and complicated situation, deemed it fit to explain the provisions and not leave anything to chance.
2. India is a Sovereign, Socialist, Secular, Democratic republic. The real power vests with the people. They elect their representatives who, in turn, take decisions on their behalf. The country does not encourage any religion and does not interfere in religious affairs. The country is trying to bridge differences between people, varying in social or economic grounds. The country does not have a monarch. We have a President, who is the head of the nation.
3. Indian Constitution has provided a Federal Government. Our Constitution is written and rigid. There is a clear division of powers between the Centre and States. The Supreme Court has been established to give judgements in case of differences between the Centre and States.
4. Indian Constitution has a unitary bias. The Centre has been made powerful than States with more powers in the executive, legislative and financial fields. The entity of States can be dissolved but the Centre will always exist.

5. Parliamentary form of Government has been provided. The head of the nation is President and he is indirectly elected. To advise the President, a Council of Ministers exists. The Council is responsible to the Parliament. The members of Parliament are elected by adult universal suffrage.
6. India has been made a secular country, with no interference in religious affairs.
7. Unlike America, India has single citizenship. People, living in any State, will be citizens of India only.
8. The Indian Constitution has a combination of flexibility and rigidity. Some provisions can be altered by a simple majority in the parliament while a few need ratification by States. Already, over 100 amendments in the Constitution have been made.
9. The Indian Constitution provided for seven fundamental rights, which are essential for all-round development of an individual. These are written and can get remedy from the courts, in case of violation. After 44th amendment, one fundamental right—Right to Property has been deleted.
10. The Indian Constitution envisages fundamental duties for all citizens. All these duties make people aware of their responsibilities towards the nation.
11. The Directive Principles of State Policy are the guidelines and objectives which every state and Central government should aspire. These principles cannot be enforced legally but have the moral backing of people.
12. Independent judiciary is an important achievement of the Constitution. The judiciary has been kept away from executive control. Moreover, rule of law has been applied. The criminal law is same all over the country but personal laws, as per religion and caste, have been allowed.
13. Judicial review has been allowed. So, the legislature and the executive are kept in check. Any transgression on the basic feature of the Constitution is declared null and void by the courts.

## TERRITORY OF THE UNION

India is a Union of States and Union Territories. Parliament has the power to create any State, increase the area of any State, reduce it, change the name or boundaries of any State. However, the President's prior approval is required before the introduction of a bill in the Parliament. The President can consult the concerned State but the view of the latter are not binding.

## CITIZENSHIP

The Constitution provides for a single citizenship. Following categories of persons became citizens of India at the commencement of the Constitution:

1. Persons born and domiciled in India.
2. Persons domiciled in India and either of whose parents was born in India.
3. Persons domiciled in India and residing in India ordinarily for a period of at least five years.
4. Certain categories of people, who had migrated from Pakistan to India.
5. Indians residing abroad but who make an application to acquire Indian citizenship.

The Parliament passed Citizenship Act in 1955, providing for following methods for acquiring Indian citizenship:

1. Citizenship by birth
2. Citizenship by descent
3. Citizenship by registration
4. Citizenship by naturalisation
5. Citizenship by incorporation of territory

The Central Government has the discretion to waive off any or all the conditions of citizenship if it thinks that the applicant has rendered distinguished service to the cause of science, art, philosophy, literature, world peace or human progress in general.

Indian citizenship can be lost by:

(*a*) renunciation;

(*b*) termination — it takes place if a citizen of India voluntary acquires the citizenship of another country; and

(*c*) deprivation — if the Government terminates the citizenship.

Some of the Fundamental Rights belong only to the citizens. They only can contest for the public offices in the country like President, Prime Minister, Chief Minister etc. Indian citizens also get the right to vote.

## SCHEDULES TO THE CONSTITUTION

The Constitution of India originally contained only eight schedules. Presently there are 12 schedules in the constitution.

***First Schedule:*** It consists the list of the States and Union territories. ***Second Schedule:*** This Schedule is related to salary and allowances of the President, Governors, Speaker, Supreme Court and High Court Judges etc. ***Third Schedule:*** Contains forms of oath and affirmation. ***Fourth Schedule:*** Contains allocation of seats to each State and Union territory in the Council of States. ***Fifth Schedule:*** Provides for administration and control of scheduled areas and scheduled tribes. ***Sixth Schedule:*** Provides for administration of Tribal Areas in Assam, Meghalaya and Mizoram. ***Seventh Schedule:*** Distribution of powers and functions between the centre and state governments under three lists. ***Eighth Schedule:*** The languages recognised by Parliament. ***Ninth Schedule:*** It contains laws passed by the Union or States which cannot be taken to courts. ***Tenth Schedule:*** Provisions as to disqualification on the ground of political defection. ***Eleventh Schedule:*** Provisions regarding powers, authority etc. of Panchayati Raj institutions. ***Twelfth Schedule:*** Provisions regarding powers, authority etc. of Municipalities etc.

### Foreign Sources of Indian Constitution

| *Foreign Sources* | *Subject* |
|---|---|
| Britain | Parliamentary system, collective responsibilities of Cabinet |
| America | Fundamental right, Citizenship, Independent Judiciary, Judicial review |
| Canada | Division of powers |
| Ireland | Directive principles |
| Germany | Emergency provisions |
| Russia | Fundamental duties |
| Australia | Concurrent list |

## THE SUPREME COURT

Supreme Court of India, the highest Court of the country, consists of a Chief Justice and some other Judges appointed by the President. The Judges hold office till the age of 65. For appoint-ment as a Judge of the Supreme Court, a person must be a citizen of India and must have been for at least five years as Judge of a High Court or Advocate of a High Court for at least ten years or he must be, in the opinion of the President, a distinguished jurist. The Supreme Court normally sits in New Delhi.

## PARLIAMENT

Parliament is the national legislature of the Indian Union. It consists of two Houses known as the Council of States or the Rajya Sabha and the House of People or Lok Sabha. The President is an integral part of Parliament.

**Rajya Sabha:** The Rajya Sabha is the Upper House of the Parliament and it is constituted of representatives from the States or the Constituent units of the Indian Union. It is a permanent body, one third of its members retiring after every two years. Its maximum strength is 250. Out of these, twelve members are nominated by the President from well-known personalities in the realm of Science, Art, Literature and Social Service. Rest of 238 representatives of the States and Union Territories are elected. Rajya Sabha at present consists of 245 members.

**Lok Sabha:** The Lok Sabha whose life is five years, is the Lower House of Parliament and comprises of members directly elected by the people. The House of the people (Lok Sabha) at present consists of 543 members directly elected from the states and Union Territories. By the 104th amendment of the constitution the reservation for two members of Anglo Indian Community nominated by President have been abolished. The House of the People shall continue for five years (unless sooner dissolved) from the date of its meeting and no longer and the expiry of the said period of 5 years shall operate as dissolution of the House.

**Parliamentary Committees:** There are several Parliamentary Committees to assist the Parliament in its deliberations. These are appointed or elected by the respective Houses of Lok Sabha and Rajya Sabha on a motion made or are nominated by their presiding officers, *i.e.*, the Speaker of Lok Sabha and the Chairman of Rajya Sabha respectively. Broadly, Parliamentary Committees are of two kinds–standing committees and ad-hoc committees. Among the Standing Committees, three are financial Committees:

(*i*) Public Account Committee; (*ii*) Estimate Committee; (*iii*) Public undertaking Committee.

Ad-hoc Committees are appointed as the need arises and cease to exist when the work is over.

**Speaker of Lok Sabha:** Speaker is elected by the Lok Sabha from among its members. The Speaker will have the final power to maintain order within the House of the People and to interpret its rules of procedure. Speaker decides whether a bill is a money bill or a non-money bill.

## Indian States & Union Territories: Allocation of Seats

| S. No. | State/UT | Seats of Lok Sabha | Seats of Rajya Sabha | Legislative Assembly | Legislative Council |
|---|---|---|---|---|---|
| 1. | Andhra Pradesh | 25 | 11 | 175 | 58 |
| 2. | Arunachal Pradesh | 2 | 1 | 60 | |
| 3. | Assam | 14 | 7 | 126 | |
| 4. | Bihar | 40 | 16 | 243 | 75 |
| 5. | Chhattisgarh | 11 | 5 | 90 | |
| 6. | Goa | 2 | 1 | 40 | |
| 7. | Gujarat | 26 | 11 | 182 | |
| 8. | Haryana | 10 | 5 | 90 | |
| 9. | Himachal Pradesh | 4 | 3 | 68 | |
| 10. | Jharkhand | 14 | 6 | 81 | |
| 11. | Karnataka | 28 | 12 | 224 | 75 |
| 12. | Keralam | 20 | 9 | 140 | |
| 13. | Madhya Pradesh | 29 | 11 | 230 | |
| 14. | Maharashtra | 48 | 19 | 288 | 78 |
| 15. | Manipur | 2 | 1 | 60 | |
| 16. | Meghalaya | 2 | 1 | 60 | |
| 17. | Mizoram | 1 | 1 | 40 | |
| 18. | Nagaland | 1 | 1 | 60 | |
| 19. | Odisha | 21 | 10 | 147 | |
| 20. | Punjab | 13 | 7 | 117 | |
| 21. | Rajasthan | 25 | 10 | 200 | |
| 22. | Sikkim | 1 | 1 | 32 | |
| 23. | Tamil Nadu | 39 | 18 | 234 | |
| 24. | Telangana | 17 | 7 | 119 | 40 |
| 25. | Tripura | 2 | 1 | 60 | |
| 26. | Uttar Pradesh | 80 | 31 | 403 | 100 |
| 27. | Uttarakhand | 5 | 3 | 70 | |
| 28. | West Bengal | 42 | 16 | 294 | |

| S. No. | State/UT | Seats of Lok Sabha | Seats of Rajya Sabha | Legislative Assembly | Legislative Council |
|---|---|---|---|---|---|
| 29. | Jammu & Kashmir | 5 | 4 | — | — |
| 30. | Andaman & Nicobar Islands | 1 | — | — | — |
| 31. | Chandigarh | 1 | — | — | — |
| 32. | Dadra & Nagar Haveli and Daman & Diu | 2 | — | — | — |
| 33. | Delhi | 7 | 3 | 70 | — |
| 34. | Lakshadweep | 1 | — | — | — |
| 35. | Puduchery | 1 | 1 | 30 | — |
| 36. | Ladakh | 1 | — | — | — |

### Table of Precedence

1. President
2. Vice-President
3. Prime Minister
4. Governors of States within their respective states
5. Former Presidents

5A. Deputy Prime Minister

6. Chief Justice of India, Speaker of Lok Sabha
7. Cabinet Ministers of the Union, Chief Ministers of States within their respective States, Deputy Chairman NITI Aayog.

   Leaders of opposition in Rajya Sabha and Lok Sabha

7A. Holders of the Bharat Ratna Decoration

8. Ambassadors Extraordinary and Plenipotentiary and High Commissioners of Commonwealth Countries accredited to India

   Chief Ministers of States outside their respective States
9. Judges of the Supreme Court
10. Deputy Chairman Rajya Sabha, Deputy Chief Minister of States

    Deputy Speaker Lok Sabha, Members of the NITI Aayog, Minister of State of the Union and Other Minister in the Ministry of Defence.

## PRESIDENT

The President is the Constitutional head of the Republic of India. He is more or less the titular head of the executive. Really speaking, he is the constitutional head but not the real executive. The real power is vested in the hands of the Council of Ministers.

**Qualifications:** (*i*) Indian citizen, (*ii*) age not less than 35 years, (*iii*) should have qualification for election to Lok Sabha, (*iv*) should not hold any office of profit, (*v*) should not be a Member of Parliament or State Legislature.

**Powers:** He makes appointments to all the constitutional posts. He can address either House of Parliament and dissolve Lok Sabha. All Bills passed by Parliament must receive his assent to become an Act. He issues ordinances when Parliament is not in session. No Money Bill can be introduced in Lok Sabha without his recommendation. He can grant pardon, reprieve or remit punishment and he can commute death sentences, can declare national emergency, state emergency and financial emergency.

**Term and Emolument:** The President holds the office for a period of five years. He is eligible for re-election. He draws a fixed salary per month with various allowances. He is also entitled to rent free official residence called Rashtrapati Bhawan.

## VICE-PRESIDENT

The Vice-President acts as the ex-officio Chairman of the Council of States (Rajya Sabha). He is elected by an electoral college consisting of the members of both Houses of Parliament in accordance with the system of proportional representation by means of the single transferable vote. He must be a citizen of India, not less than 35 years of age, and should be eligible for election as a member of the Council of States. Disputes in connection with election of a president or a vice-president are to be a dealt with in accordance with Article-71. Such disputes shall be decided by the Supreme Court.

## PRIME MINISTER

The Constitution lays down that there shall be a Council of Ministers headed by the Prime Minister to aid and advise the President in the exercise of his functions. The Prime Minister is the head of the Cabinet. Other Ministers are appointed by the President on his advice. He is the leader of the majority party in the Lok Sabha.

## FUNDAMENTAL RIGHTS

Following fundamental rights are enjoyed by every Indian citizen, irrespective of caste, colour, creed and sex:

**1. Right to Equality:** No special privileges, no distinction on grounds of religion, caste, creed and sex.

**2. Right to Freedom:** The right to freedom of expression and speech, the right to choose one's own profession, the right to reside in any part of the Indian Union.

**3. Right to Freedom to Religion:** Except when it is in the interest of public order, morality, health or other conditions, everybody has the right to profess, practice and propagate his religion freely.

**4. Cultural and Educational Rights:** The Constitution provides that every community can run its own institutions to preserve its own culture and language.

**5. Right against Exploitation:** Traffic in human beings and forced labour and the employment of children under 14 years in factories or mines, are punishable offences.

**6. Rights to Constitutional Remedies:** When a citizen finds that any of his fundamental rights has been encroached upon, he can move the Supreme Court, which has been empowered to safeguard the fundamental rights of a citizen (Article 32).

### Jurisdiction and Seat of High Courts

| *Name* | *Year* | *Territorial Jurisdiction* | *Seat* |
|---|---|---|---|
| Allahabad | 1866 | Uttar Pradesh | Prayagraj (Bench at Lucknow) |
| Andhra Pradesh | 2019 | Andhra Pradesh | Amaravati |
| Bombay | 1862 | Maharashtra, Goa, Dadar and Nagar Haveli and Daman and Diu | Mumbai (Benches at Nagpur, Panaji and Sambhajinagar) |
| Calcutta | 1862 | West Bengal and Andaman & Nicobar | Kolkata (Circuit Benches at Sri Vijaya Puram and Jalpaiguri) |
| Chhattisgarh | 2000 | Chhattisgarh | Bilaspur |
| Delhi | 1966 | Delhi | Delhi |
| Gauhati | 1948 | Assam, Nagaland, Mizoram and Arunachal Pradesh | Guwahati (Benches at Kohima, Aizawl and Itanagar) |
| Gujarat | 1960 | Gujarat | Ahmedabad |
| Himachal Pradesh | 1971 | Himachal Pradesh | Shimla |
| Jammu & Kashmir and Ladakh | 1928 | Jammu & Kashmir, Ladakh | Srinagar and Jammu |
| Jharkhand | 2000 | Jharkhand | Ranchi |
| Karnataka | 1884 | Karnataka | Bengaluru (Circuit Benches at Dharwar and Gulbarga) |
| Keralam | 1958 | Keralam & Lakshadweep | Ernakulam |
| Madhya Pradesh | 1956 | Madhya Pradesh | Jabalpur (Benches at Gwalior and Indore) |

| Name | Year | Territorial Jurisdiction | Seat |
|---|---|---|---|
| Madras | 1862 | Tamil Nadu & Puducherry | Chennai (Bench at Madurai) |
| Orissa | 1948 | Odisha | Cuttack |
| Patna | 1916 | Bihar | Patna |
| Punjab and Haryana | 1966 | Punjab, Haryana and Chandigarh | Chandigarh |
| Rajasthan | 1949 | Rajasthan | Jodhpur (Bench at Jaipur) |
| Sikkim | 1975 | Sikkim | Gangtok |
| Uttarakhand | 2000 | Uttarakhand | Nainital |
| Tripura | 2013 | Tripura | Agartala |
| Meghalaya | 2013 | Meghalaya | Shillong |
| Manipur | 2013 | Manipur | Imphal |
| Telangana | 2019 | Telangana | Hyderabad |

## FUNDAMENTAL DUTIES

The fundamental duties for the Indian citizens have been incorporated in the Constitution through the Constitution (42nd) Amendment Act, 1976. These duties are:

(*i*) to abide by the Constitution and respect its ideals and institutions, the National Flag and the National Anthem;

(*ii*) to cherish and follow the noble deeds which inspired our national struggle for freedom;

(*iii*) to uphold and protect the sovereignty, unity and integrity of India;

(*iv*) to defend the country and render national service when called upon to do so;

(*v*) to promote harmony and the spirit of common brotherhood amongst all the people transcending religious, regional or sectional diversities and to renounce practices derogatory to the dignity of women;

(*vi*) to value and preserve the rich heritage of our composite culture;

(*vii*) to protect and improve natural environment including forests, lakes, rivers and wildlife, and to have compassion for living creatures;

(*viii*) to develop the scientific temper, humanism and the spirit of inquiry and reform;

(*ix*) to safeguard public property and to abjure violence;

(*x*) to strive towards excellence in all spheres of individual and collective activity so that the nation constantly rises to higher levels of endeavour and achievement.

(*xi*) who is parent or guardian to provide opportunities for education to his child or, as the case may be, ward between age of six and fourteen years.

## DIRECTIVE PRINCIPLES OF STATE POLICY

The Directive Principles of State Policy are contained in Article 36 to 51 in Part IV of the constitutions. Directive principles are not enforceable through courts. Main aim of Directive principles is to provide social and economic base of a genuine democracy.

**Some Important Directive Principles:**

- Provisions for adequate means of livelihood for all citizens (Art. 39).
- Right to work (Art. 41).
- Right to human condition of work and maternity relief (Art. 42).
- Right to a living wage and condition of work ensuring decent standard of life of worker (Art. 43).
- Common Civil Code (Art. 44).
- Prohibit consumption of liquor (Art. 47).

- Prevent slaughter of useful cattle (Art. 48).
- Organise Panchayati Raj (Art. 40).
- Separate the judiciary from the executive (Art. 50).
- Protect and maintain places of historic monuments (Art. 49).
- International peace (Art. 51).

**Voting Age:** The voting age in the election to the Lok Sabha and State Legislative Assemblies has been reduced from 21 to 18 years by the Constitution (61st) Amendment Act, 1989.

## GOVERNOR

The Governor is appointed by the President and holds office during the pleasure of the President. Apart from the power to appoint the council of ministers, if the governor finds that the government of state cannot be carried on in accordance with the provisions of the constitution (Art. 356), he may send his report to the President who may assume to himself the functions of the government of the state. (This is popularly known as 'President's Rule').

## COUNCIL OF MINISTERS

As in the Centre, there is a Council of Ministers at the State level. It is appointed by the Governor but is responsible to Vidhan Sabha, the lower house of State legislature. The leader of the majority party/group is appointed Chief Minister and other ministers are appointed on his recommendation. The Chief Minister allocates work among the ministers. He can recommend their dismissal, or can bring about changes in the portfolios of the ministers. All the ministers are individually as well as collectively responsible to Vidhan Sabha.

The Chief Minister is first among the equals. Besides appointing his other ministers and allocating work to them, he takes all the major policy decisions. He presides over the Cabinet meetings and all the ministers consult him on important matters. The Chief Minister suggests names for the posts for which the Governor makes appointments in the State. He is the Chief spokesman of the Government and is the communication link between the Government and the Governor.

## STATE LEGISLATURE

For every State there is a legislature comprising the Governor and two houses. However, some legislatures do not have the upper house — the legislative council. The legislative assemblies have the right to pass a resolution to abolish or create the legislative council. It must be passed by a majority of the total membership of the assembly and a two-third majority of the members of the assembly present and voting. The resolution is then sent to the Parliament which makes law, creating or abolishing the Council.

The legislative council cannot have less than forty members and not more than one-third of the strength of the assembly. One-third of the council members are elected by an electoral college, consisting of members of municipalities, district boards and other local bodies. One-third of the council members are elected by assembly members. One-twelfth members are elected by graduates of the State who have been qualified for at least three years. One-twelfth of the members are elected by persons who have been for at least three years engaged in teaching in educational institutions, not lower in standard than that of a secondary school, in the State. The remaining number is filled through Governor's nomination.

The legislative council elections are held on th basis of proportional representation with a singl transferable votes. The candidates have to be abov 30 years of age, voter in any assembly constituenc of the State and is not an employee of the Governmen It is a permanent house, with one-third members retirin every two years. The legislative council of a State i not subject to dissolution.

The legislative assembly is the lower hous and in each State, its members are directly electe by the residents of the State. Legislative Assemb (Vidhan Sabha) of a state consists of not more tha 500 and not less than 60 members (Legislativ Assembly of Sikkim has 32 members vide Artic 371F of the Constitution) chosen by direct electio from territorial constituencies in the state. Th candidate for assembly seats have to be 25 years o age, citizens of India, not disqualified by any cour have his name in the voter list and does not ho any office of profit in the Government. If a member of assembly abstains for 60 days without informing the house, he stands disqualified. If a person is elected from two assembly seats or from one assembly seat and a parliamentary seat, he can retain only one seat.

The tenure of the assembly is five years, but it can be dissolved earlier also. The Governor summons the house regularly, but not more than six months gap can be there between the last meeting of a session and the first meeting of the forthcoming session. Each assembly has a speaker and a deputy speaker who preside over the meetings. One-tenth of the total members or ten members form the quorum, without which the meeting cannot begin.

The State legislatures can make laws on subjects given in the State or Concurrent List. However, some laws have to be approved by the President while some need prior approval of the President, even before introduction in the legislature. During emergency all subjects, and, in case of Rajya Sabha passing a resolution, a particular subject comes under the Parliament's jurisdiction. The legislature passes all financial bills, without which the State Government cannot spend a single paisa. The legislature controls the executive, through no-Confidence motion, adjournment motion, rejecting the budget, proposing changes in the budget or asking questions. Among the two houses, the lower house or legislative assembly is mere powerful as it can even recommend abolition of the upper house. The State Government is also responsible to the assembly and in the field of legislations, its role is paramount.

## THE ATTORNEY GENERAL OF INDIA

The Attorney General of India is the first law officer of the Government of India. Though he is not a member of cabinet he has the right to speak in the House of Parliament, but he has no right to vote. The Attorney General of India shall be appointed by the President and shall hold office during his pleasure. His duty shall be to give advice on such legal matter from time to time as may be referred to him by the President.

## COMPTROLLER & AUDITOR GENERAL OF INDIA (CAG)

The Comptroller and Auditor General of India is guardian of the public purse and it is his duty to see that not a *paisa* is spent out of consolidated fund of India or of a state without the authority of the appropriate legislature. He is appointed by President of India.

**Status**

- Appointed by the President.
- A person with long administrative experience & knowledge of accounts is appointed.
- Holds office for 6 yrs or till 65 yrs of age.
- The President can remove him only on the recommendation of the 2 houses of Parliament (as in case of judge of Supreme Court).

## INTER-STATE COUNCILS

Article 263 provides for inter-state councils. The power of the President to set up Inter-State Councils not only for advising upon disputes but also for investigating and discussing subjects in which some or all of the states, or the Union and one or more of the states have common interest.

## UNION PUBLIC SERVICE COMMISSION (U.P.S.C.)

This Commission is responsible for (i) recruitment to all civil services and posts, under the Union Government by written examinations, interviews and promotions, and (ii) advising the Government on all matters relating to methods of recruitment, principles to be followed in making promotions and transfers. Its Chairman is appointed by the President.

## STAFF SELECTION COMMISSION

The Union Government has constituted the Staff Selection Commission for recruitment to non-technical Group C and some of Group B posts in the central departments and in subordinate offices. The administrative Reforms Commission had recommended the setting up of such a Commission.

* * * * *

# 6 Planning In India

The need for planning was felt in India even before independence. A National Planning Committee was set up by the Indian National Congress as early as 1938. The Planning Commission was set up in 1950. It is an advisory body engaged in the task of meaningful national planning. The main objectives of India's Economic Planning are as follows : (*i*) securing an increase in National Income; (*ii*) achieving a planned rate of investment within a given period to bring the actual investment as a proportion of national income to a higher level; (*iii*) reducing inequality in the distribution of income and wealth; (*iv*) providing additional employment; (*v*) adopting measures to increase agricultural production, manufacturing capacity for producers and a favourable balance of payments.

## Five Year Plans in India

| Plans | Period | Investment (₹ Crore) | Objectives |
|---|---|---|---|
| First Plan | April 1, 1951–March 31, 1956 | 1,960 | Priority to agriculture, electricity and irrigation. |
| Second Plan | April 1, 1956–March 31, 1961 | 4,672 | Development of basic and heavy industries. |
| Third Plan | April 1, 1961–March 31, 1966 | 8,577 | Long term development of India's economy. |
| Annual Plan | April 1, 1966–March 31, 1967 | 2,137 | |
| Annual Plan | April 1, 1967–March 31, 1968 | 2,205 | |
| Annual Plan | April 1, 1968–March 31, 1969 | 2,283 | |
| Fourth Plan | April 1, 1969–March 31, 1974 | 15,779 | Enlarge the income of rural population and supply of goods of mass consumption. |
| Fifth Plan | April 1, 1974–March 31, 1979 | 39,426 | Attain increased self reliance and employment avenues. |
| Annual Plan | April 1, 1979–March 31, 1980 | 12,176 | |
| Sixth Plan | April 1, 1980–March 31, 1985 | 1,09,292 | Removal of unemployment |
| Seventh Plan | April 1, 1985–March 31, 1990 | 2,18,730 | Food work and productivity were the basic priorities. |
| Eighth Plan | April, 1992–March 31, 1997 | 4,95,670 | Raising employment |
| Ninth Plan | April 1, 1997–March 31, 2002 | 9,41,041 | Agriculture and rural development |
| Tenth Plan | April 1, 2002–March 31, 2007 | 14,91,610 | Growth rate 7.8 percent per annum. |
| Eleventh Plan | April 1, 2007–March 31, 2012 | 36,44,718 | Literacy, Employment, Rural development & Transport development. |
| Twelfth Plan | April 1, 2012–March 31, 2017 | 43,33,739 | Long term development of India's economy. |

## INDIA'S AMBITIOUS 15-YEAR VISION PLAN

NITI Aayog has come forward with a draft 15-year vision plan to catapult the country's economy to more than three times as compared to the present day. The new plan is set to replace the centralised five-year plans the country has been following for decades. The new plan is accompanied by shorter sub-plans—a seven-year strategy for 2017-24, and a three-year 'Action Agenda' from 2017-18 to 2019-20. No less than 300 specific action points covering a wide range of sectors have been drawn up as part of the 15 year vision.

The salient features of 15-year vision plan are :

- India aims to more than triple the size of its economy in 15 years with gross domestic product (GDP) expected to rise to ₹ 469 lakh crores from ₹ 137 lakh crore in 2015-16. Per capita GDP is expected to rise by three times to ₹ 3,14,667 in 2015-2016.
- NITI Aayog plans to work closely with staes to boost infrastructure and services, including regions that require special attention. The government made a big push for Goods and Services Tax (GST), urging the state governments to speed up the legislation of state GST bills.
- India's urban population is expected to increase by 22 crores by 2031. The plan is likely to lay emphasis on urban development, taking a note from China's elaborate long-term development agenda.
- The plan envisages a central body for overseeing the implemention of sustainable development goals. Specific goals will cover clean water, removing hunger, climate efforts, responsible consumption, clean energy, quality educaiton, reduced inequality and gender equality, among others.

## NITI AAYOG

The National Institution for transforming India Aayog (NITI Aayog) is a Government of India policy. NITI Aayog seeks to facilities and empower the critical requirement of good governance, which is people-centric, participative, collaborative, transparent and policy-driven.

The started aim for NITI Aayog's creation is to foster involvement and participation in the economic policy-making process by the state Governments of India. It has adopted a "bottom-up" approach in planning which is remarkable contrast to the planning commission's tradition of "top-down" decision-making. The prime minister will serve as chairperson for NITI Aayog.

NITI Aayog was established on 1 January 2015.

### *Members of NITI Aayog*

The NITI Aayog comprises the following:

1. Prime Minister of India as the Chairperson
2. Governing Council comprising the Chief Ministers of all the States and Union territories with Legislatures and lieutenant governors of other Union territories.
3. Regional Councils will be formed to address specific issues and contingencies impacting more than one state or a region. These will be formed for a specified tenure.
4. Experts, specialists and practitioners with relevant domain knowledge as special invitees nominated by the Prime Minister
5. Full-time organizational framework (in addition to Prime Minister as the Chairperson) comprising

   (*i*) *Vice-Chairperson*

   (*ii*) *Members:* Three (3) Full-time

   (*iii*) *Part-time members:* Maximum of two from leading universities research organizations and other relevant institutions in an ex-officio capacity. Part-time members will be on a rotational basis.

   (*iv*) *Ex Officio members:* Maximum of four members of the Union Council of Ministers to be nominated by the Prime Minister.

   (*v*) *Chief Executive Officer:* To be appointed by the Prime Minister for a fixed tenure, in the rank of Secretary to the Government of India.

   (*vi*) Secretariat as deemed necessary.

## FINANCE COMMISSION

Article 280 of the Constitution provides for the appointment of a finance commission every five year. President appoints chairman and members of this commission. Finance commission are to recommend to President the basis for the distribution of the net proceeds of taxes between the centre and the states and the principles which should govern the grants-in-aid to be given to the states out of the consolidated funds of India.

## NATIONAL DEVELOPMENT COUNCIL

The National Development Council, set-up in 1952, consists of representatives of the Central Government as well as the State governments. It is the supreme body insofar as planning is concerned and it determines policies, issues guidelines, reviews working of the plan and finally approves the plan. The Council consists of the Prime Minister (Chairman), all Union Cabinet Ministers, Chief Ministers of all States and Union Territories and the Chairman and members of the NITI Aayog. For matters relating to Plans and planning, the Union Minister of Planning is responsible to the Parliament.

## RESERVE BANK OF INDIA

- It is the Central Bank of the country.
- It was established on April 1, 1935 with a capital of ₹ 5 crore. This capital of ₹ 5 crore was divided into 5 lakh equity shares of ₹ 100 each. In the beginning, the ownership of almost all the share capital was with the non-government share-holders.
- It was nationalized on Jan 1, 1949 as govt. acquired the private share holdings.
- **Governors:** Ist Governor - Sir Smith (1935-37) Ist Indian Governor - C.D. Deshmukh (1948-49)

### Other Financial Institutions

- **Industrial Credit & Investment Corporation of India Bank (ICICI Bank) :** Established in 1955 as a public limited company to encourage and assist industrial units of the nation. It has been converted into a bank with effect from May 3, 2002.
- **Small Industries Development Bank of India (SIDBI) :** Established in 1990; promotes small scale sector.
- **National Bank of Agriculture & Rural Development (NABARD) :** Established on Nov 5, 1982; gives credit facilities to farmers.
- **Export-Import Bank of India (EXIM) :** Set-up on Jan 1, 1982; grants deferred credit to Indian exporters in order to operate in the International market.
- **Industrial Development Bank of India (IDBI) :** Established in 1964; to provide financial assistance to industrial enterprises.
- **Industrial Reconstruction Bank of India (IRBI) :** Set-up in 1971 with the objective of reviving and revitalizing sick industrial units in public and private sectors.

*****

# 7 National Symbols

**State Emblem:** State Emblem of India is an adaptation from the Sarnath Lion Capital of Ashoka. It was adopted by the Government of India on January 26, 1950. In the adapted form, only three lions are visible, the fourth being hidden from the view. The wheel (Dharma Chakra) appears in relief in the centre of the abacus with a bull on the right and a horse on the left. The bell-shaped lotus has been omitted. The words "Satyameva Jayate" meaning "Truth alone triumphs" are inscribed below the Emblem in Devanagari script.

**National Flag:** The National Flag of India is a horizontal tricolour of deep saffron (Kesari), white and dark green in equal proportion. In the centre of the white band there is a wheel in navy blue colour. It has 24 spokes. The ratio of the length and the breadth of the flag is 3 : 2. Its design was adopted by the Constituent Assembly of India on July 22, 1947.

**National Anthem:** Rabindranath Tagore's song 'Jana-gana-mana' was adopted by the Constituent Assembly as the National Anthem of India on January 24, 1950.

*Jana-gan-mana-adhinayaka jaya he,*
*Bharata-bhagya-vidhata*
*Punjab-Sindh-Gujarat-Maratha-Dravida-*
*Utkala-Banga*
*Vindhya-Himachala-Yamuna-Ganga Uchhala-*
*jaladhi-taranga.*
*Tava subha name jage, Tava subha asisa mange,*
*Gahe tava jaya gatha,*
*Jana-gana-mangala-dayak, jaya he Bharata*
*bhagya vidhata,*
*Jaya he, jaya he, jaya he, Jaya jaya jaya,*
*jaya he.*

**National Song:** Bankim Chandra Chatterji's 'Vande Mataram' which was a source of inspiration to the people in their struggle for freedom, has been adopted as National Song. It has an equal status with the National Anthem.

*Vande Mataram*
*Sujalam, suphalam, malayaja-shitalam,*
*Shasya shyamalam, Mataram*
*Shubhrajyotsna,pulkita yaminim,*
*Phulla kusumita drumadalashobhinim,*
*Subhasinim sumadhura—bhashinim,*
*Sukhadam, Varadam, Mataram.*

**National Bird and Animal of India:** Peacock and Tiger; **National Aquatic Animal:** Dolphin; **National Flower:** Lotus; **National Calendar:** It was adopted on March 22, 1957. It has 365 days in the year and the first month of the year is Chaitra.

## Months of the National Calendar

(1) Chaitra, (2) Vaishakha, (3) Jaishtha, (4) Ashadha, (5) Shravan, (6) Bhadra, (7) Ashvina, (8) Kartika, (9) Marga-Shirsha, (10) Pausha, (11) Magha, (12) Phalguna.

* * * * *

# 8 General Science

## INVENTIONS AND DISCOVERIES

### Important Inventions

| *Name of Invention* | *Inventor* | *Nationality* | *Year* |
|---|---|---|---|
| Aeroplane | Orville & Wilbur Wright | U.S.A. | 1903 |
| Ball-Point Pen | John J. Loud | U.S.A. | 1888 |
| Barometer | Evangelista Torricelli | Italy | 1644 |
| Bicycle | Kirkpatrick Macmillan | Britain | 1839-40 |
| Bifocal Lens | Benjamin Franklin | U.S.A. | 1780 |
| Car (Petrol) | Karl Benz | Germany | 1888 |
| Celluloid | Alexander Parkes | Britain | 1861 |
| Cinema | Nicolas & Jean Lumiere | France | 1895 |
| Clock (mechanical) | I-Hsing & Liang Ling-Tsan | China | 725 |
| Diesel Engine | Rudolf Diesel | Germany | 1895 |
| Dynamo | Hypolite Pixii | France | 1832 |
| Electric Lamp | Thomas Alva Edison | U.S.A. | 1879 |
| Electric Motor (DC) | Zenobe Gramme | Belgium | 1873 |
| Electric Motor (AC) | Nikola Tesla | U.S.A. | 1888 |
| Electro-magnet | William Sturgeon | Britain | 1824 |
| Electronic Computer | Dr. Alan M. Turing | Britain | 1943 |
| Film (moving outlines) | Louis Prince | France | 1885 |
| Film (musical sound) | Dr. Le de Forest | U.S.A. | 1923 |
| Fountain Pen | Lewis E. Waterman | U.S.A. | 1884 |
| Gramophone | Thomas Alva Edison | U.S.A. | 1878 |
| Helicopter | Etienne Oehmichen | France | 1924 |
| Jet Engine | Sir Frank Whittle | Britain | 1937 |
| Laser | Charles H. Townes | U.S.A. | 1960 |
| Lift (Mechanical) | Elisha G. Otis | U.S.A. | 1852 |
| Locomotive | Richard Trevithick | Britain | 1804 |
| Machine Gun | James Puckle | Britain | 1718 |
| Microphone | Alexander Graham Bell | U.S.A. | 1876 |
| Microscope | Z. Janssen | Netherlands | 1590 |
| Motor Cycle | G. Daimler | Germany | 1885 |
| Photography (on film) | John Carbutt | U.S.A. | 1888 |
| Printing Press | Johann Gutenberg | Germany | c.1455 |
| Razor (safety) | King C. Gillette | U.S.A. | 1895 |
| Refrigerator | James Harrison & Alexander Catlin | U.S.A. | 1850 |

| Name of Invention | Inventor | Nationality | Year |
|---|---|---|---|
| Safety Pin | Walter Hunt | U.S.A. | 1849 |
| Sewing machine | Barthelemy Thimmonnier | France | 1829 |
| Ship (steam) | J.C. Perier | France | 1775 |
| Ship (turbine) | Hon. Sir C. Parsons | Britain | 1894 |
| Skyscraper | W. Le Baron Jenny | U.S.A. | 1882 |
| Slide Rule | William Oughtred | Britain | 1621 |
| Steam Engine (condenser) | James Watt | Britain | 1765 |
| Steel Production | Henry Bessemer | Britain | 1855 |
| Steel (stainless) | Harry Brearley | Britain | 1913 |
| Submarine | David Bushnell | U.S.A. | 1776 |
| Tank | Sir Ernest Swinton | Britain | 1914 |
| Telegraph | M. Lammond | France | 1787 |
| Telegraph Code | Samuel F.B. Morse | U.S.A. | 1837 |
| Telephone (perfected) | Alexander Graham Bell | U.S.A. | 1876 |
| Television (mechanical) | John Logie Baird | Britain | 1926 |
| Television (electronic) | P.T. Farnsworth | U.S.A. | 1927 |
| Thermometer | Galileo Galilei | Italy | 1593 |
| Transformer | Michael Faraday | Britain | 1831 |
| Transistor | Bardeen, Shockley & Brattain | U.S.A. | 1948 |
| Washing Machine (elec.) | Hurley Machine Co. | U.S.A. | 1907 |
| Zip-Fastener | W.L. Judson | U.S.A. | 1891 |

## Important Discoveries

| Discovery | Discoverer | Nationality | Year |
|---|---|---|---|
| Aluminium | Hans Christian Oerstedt | Denmark | 1827 |
| Atomic number | Henry Moseley | England | 1913 |
| Atomic structure of matter | John Dalton | England | 1803 |
| Chlorine | C.W. Scheele | Sweden | 1774 |
| Electromagnetic induction | Michael Faraday | England | 1831 |
| Electromagnetic waves | Heinrich Hertz | Germany | 1886 |
| Electromagnetism | Hans Christian Oersted | Denmark | 1920 |
| Electron | Sir Joseph Thomson | England | 1897 |
| General theory of relativity | Albert Einstein | Switzerland | 1915 |
| Hydrogen | Henry Cavendish | England | 1766 |
| Law of electric conduction | Georg Ohm | Germany | 1827 |
| Law of electromagnetism | Andre Ampere | France | 1826 |
| Law of falling bodies | Galileo | Italy | 1590 |
| Laws of gravitation & motion | Isaac Newton | England | 1687 |
| Laws of planetary motion | Johannes Kepler | Germany | 1609-19 |
| Magnesium | Sir Humphry Davy | England | 1808 |
| Neptune (Planet) | Johann Galle | Germany | 1846 |
| Neutron | James Chadwick | England | 1932 |
| Nickel | Axel Cronstedt | Sweden | 1751 |
| Nitrogen | Daniel Rutherford | England | 1772 |

| *Discovery* | *Discoverer* | *Nationality* | *Year* |
|---|---|---|---|
| Oxygen | Joseph Priestly C.W. Scheele | England Sweden | 1772 |
| Ozone | Christian Schonbein | Germany | 1839 |
| Pluto (Planet) | Clyde Tombaugh | U.S.A | 1930 |
| Plutonium | G.T. Seaborg | U.S.A | 1940 |
| Proton | Ernest Rutherford | England | 1919 |
| Quantum Theory | Max Planck | Germany | 1900 |
| Radioactivity | Antoine Bacquerel | France | 1896 |
| Radium | Pierre & Marie Curie | France | 1898 |
| Silicon | Jons Berzelius | Sweden | 1824 |
| Special theory of relativity | Albert Einstein | Switzerland | 1905 |
| Sun as centre of solar system | Copernicus | Poland | 1543 |
| Uranium | Martin Klaproth | Germany | 1789 |
| Uranus (Planet) | William Herschel | England | 1781 |
| X-rays | Wilhelm Roentgen | Germany | 1895 |

## Geographical Explorations/Discoveries

| *Place* | *Explorer/Discoverer* | *Nationality* | *Year* |
|---|---|---|---|
| America | Christopher Columbus | Italy | 1492 |
| Hawaii Islands (Sandwich Islands) | Captain James Cook | England | 1778 |
| Newfoundland | John Cabot | England | 1497 |
| New Zealand | Abel Janszoon Tasman | Holland | 1642 |
| North Pole | Robert Peary | USA | 1909 |
| Sea Route to India (via Cape of Good Hope) | Vasco da Gama | Portugal | 1498 |
| South Pole | Roald Amundsen | Norway | 1911 |

## Scientific Instruments

| *Name of Instrument* | *Used for* |
|---|---|
| Altimeter | measuring altitude |
| Ammeter | measuring strength of an electric current |
| Anemometer | measuring the velocity of wind |
| Audiometer | measuring level of hearing |
| Barometer | measuring atmospheric pressure |
| Callipers | measuring the internal and external diameters of tubes |
| Calorimeter | measuring quantity of heat |
| Compass | finding out direction |
| Dynamo | converting mechanical energy into electrical energy |
| Eudiometer | measuring volume changes during chemical reactions between gases |
| Galvanometer | detecting and determining the strength of small electric currents |
| Hydrometer | measuring specific gravity of a liquid |
| Hygrometer | measuring the humidity in the atmosphere |
| Lactometer | measuring the purity of milk |
| Manometer | measuring the gaseous pressure |
| Micrometer | measuring minute distances, angles, etc. |

| *Name of Instrument* | *Used for* |
|---|---|
| Microscope | seeing magnified view of very small objects |
| Periscope | with the help of this instrument an observer in a submarine can see what is going on the surface of the sea |
| Photometer | measuring intensity of light from distant stars |
| Pyrometer | measuring high temperatures |
| Radar | detecting and finding the presence and location of moving objects like aircraft, missile, etc. |
| Radiometer | measuring the emission of radiant energy |
| Rain Gauge | measuring the amount of rainfall |
| Seismograph | measuring and recording the intensity and origin of earthquake shocks |
| Sextant | measuring altitude and angular distances between two objects or heavenly bodies |
| Spectrometer | measuring the refractive indices |
| Spherometer | measuring the curvature of spherical objects/surface |
| Sphygmomanometer | measuring blood pressure |
| Stethoscope | ascertaining the condition of heart and lungs by listening to their function |
| Stroboscope | viewing objects that are moving rapidly with a periodic motion as if they were at rest |
| Tachometer | measuring the rate of revolution or angular speed of a revolving shaft |
| Telescope | viewing magnified images of distant objects |
| Theodolite | measuring the horizontal and vertical angles |
| Thermocouple | measuring the temperature inside furnaces and jet engines |
| Thermometer | measuring human body temperature |
| Thermostat | regulating constant temperature |
| Ultrasonoscope | measuring utrasonic sounds |
| Viscometer | measuring the viscosity of a fluid |
| Voltmeter | measuring potential difference between two points. |

## Diseases and the Parts of Body they Affect

| *Disease* | *Part of body affected* |
|---|---|
| AIDS | Immune system of body |
| Arthritis | Inflammation of joints |
| Asthma | Lungs |
| Cataract | Eyes |
| Conjunctivitis | Eyes |
| Diabetes | Pancreas |
| Diphthcria | Throat |
| Glaucoma | Eyes |
| Eczema | Skin |
| Goitre | Front of the neck (due to enlargement of thyroid gland) |
| Gout | Joints of bone |

| *Disease* | *Part of body affected* |
|---|---|
| Jaundice | Liver |
| Meningitis | Brain or spinal cord |
| Pleurisy | Pleura (inflammation of) |
| Polio | motor neurons |
| Pneumonia | Lungs |
| Pyorrhoea | Sockets of teeth |
| Tuberculosis | Lungs |
| Typhoid | Intestine |
| Malaria | Spleen |
| Leukaemia | Blood |
| Rickets | Bones |

✵ ✵ ✵ ✵ ✵

# 9 Space Research

## First in Space

| | |
|---|---|
| First creator of rules regarding space research | — Isaac Newton |
| First artificial satellite launched in space | — Sputnik-1 (1957) |
| First living being sent in space | — Louika (a dog) |
| Firstever manned spacecraft | — Vostok-I |
| First man in space | — Yuri Gagarin, U.S.S.R. (1961) |
| First woman in space | — Valentina Tereshkova, U.S.S.R. (June 1963) |
| First man who moved in space out of the spacecraft | — Alexi Livonov, U.S.S.R. (June 1965) |
| First person to land on moon | — Neil Armstrong, America (21st July, 1969) |
| First fourwheeled carriage without human being on moon | — Leunokhev-I, U.S.S.R. (1970) |
| First space lab in orbit | — Skylab (America, 1973) |
| First space shuttle | — Columbia (America, 1981) |
| First Indian (man) in space | — Sq. led. Rakesh Sharma (13th April, 1984) |
| First Indian (Woman) in space | — Kalpana Chawla (19th Nov., 1997) |
| First American woman in space | — Sailyride (1983) |
| First spacecraft on Mars | — Pathfinder (6 July, 1997) |
| First woman who lead spacecraft | — Allin Collis (America) |
| First spacecraft without man | — Shenzoo, China (20th Nov. 1999) |
| First country in the world to succeed in an inter-planetary mission on mars in the maiden attempt | — India (MOM Spacecraft) |
| First country to Land on Moon's South Pole | — India (Chandrayaan-3) |

## INDIAN SPACE RESEARCH PROGRAMME

Indian space programme is directed towards self-reliance in the usage of space science and technology for national development. Main thrust is in the areas of:

(*i*) satellite communications for various national applications including telecommunication, TV broadcast and radio networking;

(*ii*) resources survey and management, environmental monitoring and meteorological services through remote sensing; and

(*iii*) development of indigenous satellites and launching of vehicles to achieve the above objectives.

### Space Commission

For promoting a unified development and application of space science and technology for national development, Space Commission and Department of Space were created in 1972 to evolve policies and guidelines to achieve envisaged objectives. Policies framed by Space Commission are implemented through Department of Space (DoS) and Indian Space Research Organisation (ISRO). DoS is also the nodal agency charged with the responsibility of establishing National Natural Resources Management System (NNRMS). The activities of ISRO are carried out by following centres/units.

1. Vikram Sarabhai Space Centre (VSSC), Thiruvananthapuram.
2. Indian Satellite Application Centre (ISAC), Bengaluru.
3. SHAR Centre, Sriharikota (Andhra Pradesh).
4. Space Applications Centre (SAC), Ahmedabad.
5. Liquid Propulsion Systems Centre (LPSC) with its facilities at Bengaluru, Thiruvananthapuram and Mahendragiri.
6. ISRO Telemetry Tracking and Command Network (ISTRAC) with its network of ground stations and Development and Educational Communication Unit (DECU), Ahmedabad.
7. Master Control Facility (MCF), Hassan (Karnataka).
8. National Remote Sensing Agency (NRSA), Secundrabad.

The headquarters of Department of Space and ISRO are located at Bengaluru.

### Background

Indian participation in the field of space research dates back to 1962 when an Indian National Committee for Space Research was set up under the chairmanship of Dr. Vikram A. Sarabhai.

India's practical space activity began with the establishment of the Thumba Equatorial Rocket Launching Station (TERLS) at the Vikram Sarabhai Space Centre (VSSC) in 1963. VSSC had been established a year earlier.

### Progress

Between July 14, 1964 and the end of 1968, India launched over 500 sounding rockets from the TERLS. Scientists from the (erstwhile) U.S.S.R., France, Germany, the United Kingdom and the United States participated in the projects involving these rockets launched for meteorological, ionospheric, serenomic and astronomical studies. Ariane Passenger Payload Experiment (APPLE) satellite was launched at 4.43 PM on June 19, 1981. The 673 kg. satellite was put into orbit by ESAs Ariane launch vehicle under ESA-ISRO joint venture along with two other satellites Meteorite - 2 (European Weather Satellite) and CAT (Ariane Technology Capsule) from Kourou in French Guyana.

### Aryabhatta

India began its experimental satellite missions during the seventies and it ultimately led to the establishment of operational space systems. Aryabhatta, the first Indian satellite was launched in April 1975 by an Intercosmos Rocket of the former U.S.S.R. Aryabhatta had carried on board three scientific payloads.

### Bhaskara

Aryabhatta was followed by two remote sensing satellites, Bhaskara-1 and Bhaskara-2 launched in 1979 and 1981 respectively. The Bhaskaras paved the way for further space programmes.

### Rohini

India's indigenous Satellite Launch Vehicle SLV-3 blasted off from the Sriharikota range (SHAR) on May 31, 1981, on its first development flight. It lifted into orbit the 40 kg Rohini satellite 12 minutes later, travelling at a speed of 28,000 km an hour.

## INSAT SYSTEM

The Indian National Satellite (INSAT) System is a great gift, the Government and the brilliant Indian scientists have given to the people of India, during last two decades of the previous century. India has achieved a lot in its endeavours in space, in these two decades. Through 1980s, India succeeded in establishing operational space system. INSAT was commissioned in 1983 by way of multipurpose satellites. In fact INSAT system is a multipurpose operational satellite system, involving a multi-agency system for inland telecommunications, direct telecasting broadcasting, through satellites, relaying data and meteorological observations.

### Impact of INSAT System

This system has brought about a revolutionary change in the field of telecommunications, weather forecasting and television expansion. In other words, it has had a tremendous impact on the above said three areas and indirectly on all other related areas, benefitting the Indian people, as whole.

✵✵✵✵✵

# 10 Computers

## Introduction

The term computer is derived from the Latin word compute, which means to calculate. A computer is an electronic machine, devised for performing calculations and controlling operations that can be expressed either in logical or numerical terms. In simple terms, a computer is an electronic device that performs diverse operations with the help of instructions to process the information in order to achieve the desired results. A Computer application extends to cover huge area including education, industries, government, medicine, scientific research etc.

A computer is one of the most influential forces available in modern times. Due to its memory, high speed and perfection, its application can be extended to almost infinite levels. Millions of complex calculations can be done in mere fraction of time. Difficult decisions can be made with accuracy for comparatively little cost. Computers are widely seen as instruments for future progress and as tools to achieve substantiality by way of improved access to information by means of video conferencing and e-mail. Indeed computers have left such on impression on modern civilization that we call this era as the information age.

## Computer System

A computer system is a combination of various components. It performs the system functions such as input, processing, output, storage and control. A computer system consists of the following components: 1. Hardware; 2. Software

### Hardware

The physical components of the computer, such as electrical, electronics and mechanical unit are known as the hardware of the computer. That is, the input units, output units and CPU are called hardware. Thus hardware is the equipment involved in the function of a computer. It consists of the components that can be physically handled.

### Software

The computer performs operations like addition, subtraction, multiplication and division only when the user instructs it to do so. The user issues instructions and the CPU acts in accordance with the instructions. The sets of instructions, which control the sequence of operations, are known as programs, and collectively programs are called software. The software can be broadly classified into two types. They are: (a) System Software (b) Application Software.

### Difference between Hardware & Software

***Hardware***

1. It is the physical unit of the computer
2. Hardware understands only machine language, lower level language or binary
3. It works with binary code, the presence or absence of Pulses as 1's or 0's.

***Software***

1. It is a collection of programs to bring the hardware system into operation
2. It is written by a well versed programmer and generally in higher level language which is readable by human being.
3. It is represented by the Higher Level Languages such as BASIC, COBOL, *etc.*,

### System Software

System software consists of several Programs, which are directly responsible for controlling, integrating and managing the individual hardware components of a computer system. They provide basic functionality like file management, visual display and keyboard input which are used by application software. Some examples of system software are operating system, device drivers, language translators, system utilities.

### Application Software

A computer program used to perform a specific task, rather than just managing a computer system. Some examples of application software are word processing, spread sheets, database management systems.

## Two Types of Computer Systems

**Analog Computers :** The analog computers operate by measuring instead of counting. The analog computer works on the supply of continuous electrical signals. The display is also continuous. Its output is in the form of graphs.

**Digital Computers :** These computers work with quantities represented as digits. They operate on discrete quantities. In digital computer, both numeric and non-numeric information are represented as strings of digits. These computers use binary codes, 0's and 1's, to represent the information. The information is given to the computer in the form of discrete electrical signals.

## Input/Output Devices

**Input Devices :** An input device is any machine that feeds data into a computer. For example, a keyboard is an input device. Input devices other than the keyboard are sometimes called alternate devices. Trackballs, mouse and light pens are all alternate input devices.

**Output Devices :** Output is anything that comes out of a computer. Output can be meaningful information or gibberish, and it can appear in a variety of forms - as binary numbers, as characters, as pictures, and as printed pages. Output devices include display screens, loudspeakers, printers, plotters, etc.

## Computer Memory

There are two kinds of computer memory: primary and secondary. Primary memory is accessible directly by the processing unit. RAM is an example of primary memory. As soon as the computer is switched off the contents of the primary memory is lost. You can store and retrieve data much faster with primary memory compared to secondary memory. Secondary memory such as floppy disks, magnetic disk, etc., is located outside the computer. Primary memory is more expensive than secondary memory. Because of this the size of primary memory is less than that of secondary memory.

### Types of Primary Memory

- Random Access Memory (RAM)
- Read Only Memory (ROM)
- Programmable Read Only Memory (PROM)
- Erasable Programmable Read Only Memory (EPROM)

### Cache Memory

To decrease the mismatch in operating speed, a small memory chip is attached between CPU and Main memory whose access time is very close to the processing speed of CPU. It is called CACHE memory. CACHE memories are accessed much faster than conventional RAM. It is used to store programs or data currently being executed or temporary data frequently used by the CPU.

### Types of Secondary Memory

- Magnetic Tape • Magnetic Disk • Floppy Disk
- Optical Disk–1. Compact Disk/ Read Only Memory (CD-ROM), 2. Erasable Optical Disk.

The memory is measured by the following units:

(*a*) **BIT (Binary digit):** It is the smallest possible unit of information. It can be either 0 or 1.

(*b*) **NIBBLE:** Four bits form one nibble.

(*c*) **BYTE:** It is a unit of information consisting of fixed number of bits. It is a combination of 8 bits.

(*d*) **CHARACTER:** It is represented by one byte. It can be a letter, digit, punctuation mark or special characters.

(*e*) **WORD:** The combination of 2 bytes or 4 bytes or 8 bytes is a word.

The data measurement is as follows:

8 bits - 1 byte

1024 bytes - 1 Kilo Byte (KB)

1024 KB - 1 Mega Byte (MB)

1024 MB - 1 Giga Byte (GB)

1024 GB - 1 Tera Byte (TB)

## Word keyboard shortcuts

| Action | Key Stroke |
|---|---|
| Open a file | Ctrl + O |
| New file | Ctrl + N |
| Close a file | Ctrl + W |
| Save As | F12 |
| Save | Ctrl+S or Shift+F12 |
| Print Preview | Ctrl + F2 |
| Print | Ctrl + P |
| Show/Hide paragraph symbols | Ctrl + * |
| Spelling and grammar | F7 |
| Help | F1 |
| Find | Ctrl + F |
| Replace | Ctrl + H |
| Go To | Ctrl + G |
| Select all - entire document | Ctrl + A |
| Select from cursor to beginning of line | Shift + Home |
| Select from cursor to end of line | Shift + End |
| Go to beginning of line | Home |
| Go to end of line | End |
| Go to beginning of document | Ctrl + Home |
| Go to end of document | Ctrl + End |
| Cut | Ctrl + X |
| Copy | Ctrl + C |
| Paste | Ctrl + V |
| Undo | Ctrl + Z |
| Redo | Ctrl + Y |
| Format painter | Ctrl + Shift + C |
| Left alignment | Ctrl + L |
| Center alignment | Ctrl + E |
| Right alignment | Ctrl + R |
| Justified | Ctrl + J |
| Delete previous word | Ctrl + Backspace |
| Apply bulleted list | Ctrl + Shift + L |
| Indent | Ctrl + M |
| Page break | Ctrl + Enter |
| Font face | Ctrl + Shift + F |
| Font size | Ctrl + Shift + P |
| Bold | Ctrl + B |
| Italics | Ctrl + I |
| Underline | Ctrl + U |
| Double underline | Ctrl + Shift + D |
| Word underline | Ctrl + Shift + A |
| Change case | Shift + F3 |
| Subscript | Ctrl + = |
| Superscript | Ctrl + Shift + = |
| Make web hyperlink | Ctrl + K |
| Go to next cell | Tab |
| Go to previous cell | Shift + Tab |
| Go to beginning of column | Alt + PageUp |
| Highlight to beginning of column | Alt + Shift + PageUp |
| Go to end of column | Alt + PageDown |
| Highlight to end of column | Alt + Shift + PageDown |
| Go to beginning of row | Alt + Home |
| Highlight to beginning of row | Alt + Shift + Home |
| Go to end of row | Alt + End |
| Highlight to end of row | Alt + Shift + End |
| Column break | Ctrl + Shift + Enter |
| Copyright © | Alt + Ctrl + C |
| Date field | Alt + Shift + D |
| Go to footnotes | Alt + Ctrl + F |
| Show/Hide ¶ | Ctrl + Shift + 8 |
| Theasaurus | Shift + F7 |

### Operating System

It is the first layer of software loaded into computer memory when it starts up. As the first software layer, all other software that gets loaded after it depends on it for various common core services. In simple words, the operating system organizes and controls the hardware. Examples of operating systems are Windows XP, UNIX, and Linux.

## Programming Languages

Computers are machines. Unfortunately they cannot understand natural languages, such as Hindi, English, Tamil, etc. that human beings speak and understand. Therefore, to give instructions to computers, different languages have been developed. These languages are called computer languages. It is a general purpose language that is designed to combine business and scientific processing features and that can easily learned by novice programmers, yet contains advanced features for experienced programmers.

Computer languages are classified into three categories: 1. Low Level Language; 2. Machine language; 3. High level languages.

### Compiler

A compiler is a kind of translator that translates a program into another program, known as target language. Usually, the term compiler is used for language translator of high-level language into machine language. The compiler replaces single high-level statement with a series of machine language instruction.

### Interpreter

Unlike compilers, an interpreter translates a statement in a program and executes the statement immediately, before translating the next source language statement. Similar to compilers, every interpreted language such as BASIC and LISP has its own interpreters.

## Computer Networks

A **computer network**, often simply referred to as a **network**, is a collection of computers and devices connected by communications channels that facilitates communications among users and allows users to share resources with other users.

### Categories of Network

(*i*) **LAN :** LAN stands for Local Area Network. These networks evolved around the PC revolution. LANs enabled multiple users in a relatively small geographical area to exchange files and messages, as well as access shared resources such as file servers.

(*ii*) **WAN :** WAN stands for Wide Area Network. The interconnection of various LAN's through telephone network, which unites geographically distributed users, is achieved through WAN. In short when we log on to the internet, we become a part of a WAN.

(*iii*) **MAN :** MAN stands for Metropolitan Area Network. It is usually the interconnection between various LAN's in a particular geographical area like a metropolitan city like Bombay.

## Internet

Internet is a communication network which bridges all the small computer networks worldwide as a whole. Internet is based upon Internet technology, in particular World Wide Web (WWW), to build Information System within organization or enterprise to accomplish standardization and automation. Fundamentally, it means network computing environments which let the users share the information through the Internet and Web browsers.

### Characteristics of Intranet

The following are the important characteristics of the Intranet.

(*a*) It is an extended internet-private business networks located outside of the corporate firewall.

(*b*) It can be referred to an intranet that is partially accessible to authorized outsiders.

(*c*) It is a network that uses the internet to link businesses with others that share the common goals.

### E-MAIL

E-mail is an electronic message sent from one computer to another. We can send or receive personal and business-related messages with attachments, such as pictures or formatted documents. We can even send songs and computer programs.

* * * * *

# 11 United Nations

- **Origin:** UN Charter was signed by 50 members on June 26, 1945. It officially came into existence on October 24, 1945.
- **UN Charter:** The Charter is the Constitution of the UN and contains its aims and objectives and rules and regulations for its functioning.
- **Aims and Objectives:** They are security, welfare and human rights.
- **Headquarters:** New York.
- **Flag:** The flag is light blue in colour, and emblazoned in white, in its centre is the UN symbol—a polar map of world embraced by twin olive branches open at the top.
- **Official Languages:** The official languages of the UN are: English, French, Chinese, Russian, Arabic and Spanish. However, working languages are English & French only.
- **Main Organs of the UN:** There are six main organs:
  1. General Assembly
  2. Security Council
  3. Economic and Social Council
  4. Trusteeship Council
  5. International Court of Justice, and
  6. Secretariat.

1. **General Assembly:** It consists of representative of all members of the UN. Each member country has only one vote. It meets once a year and passes UN Budget.
2. **Security Council:** It is the Executive body of the UN and is mainly responsible for maintaining international peace and security. It has 15 members, 5 of which (USA, UK, France, Russia and China) are permanent members. The 10 non-permanent members are elected by General Assembly for two-year term and are not eligible for immediate re-election.
3. **Economic and Social Council:** It has 54 members elected by General Assembly.
4. **Trusteeship Council:** It looks after interest of the people in areas not yet independent and leads them towards self-government.
5. **International Court of Justice:** It has 15 judges, no two of whom may be nationals of the same state. They are elected by General Assembly and Security Council for a term of 9 years. The Court elects its President and Vice-President for a 3-year term.
6. **Secretariat:** It is the Secretariat of the UN and is headed by the Secretary General.

## Years Observed by United Nations

1967 : International Tourism Year
1968 : Human Rights Year
1970 : International Education Year
1972 : International Book Year
1973 : Copernicus Year
1974 : World Population Year
1975 : International Women's Year
1979 : International Year of the Child
1981 : International Year of Disabled
1983 : World Communication Year
1985 : International Youth Year
1986 : International Year of Peace
1987 : International Year of Shelter for the Homeless

1990: International Literacy Year
1992: International Space Year
1993: International Year for World's Indigenous People
1994: International Year of Family
1995: International Year of Tolerance
1996: International Year for Eradication of Poverty
1998: Human Rights Year
1999: Year of Older Persons
2000: Year of the Culture of Peace
2001: International Year of Volunteer
2002: International Year of Eco-tourism
2003: International Year of Fresh Water
2004: International Rice Year
2005: International Year of Sports and Physical Education
2006: International Year of Deserts and Desertification
2008: International Year of Potato
2009: International Year of Astronomy
2010: International Year of Bio-diversity
2011: International Year of Forest
2012: International Year of Cooperatives
2013: International Year of Water Cooperation
2014: International Year of Family Farming
2015: International Year of Soils
2016: International Year of Pulses
2017: International Year of Sustainable Tourism for Development
2019: International Year of Indigenous Languages.
2020: International Year of Plant Health
2021: International Year of Peace and Trust
2022: International Year of Artisanal Fisheries and Aquaculture.
2023: International Year of Millets
2024: International Year of Camelids
2025: International Year of Glaciers Preservation; International Year of Quantum Science and Technology; International Year of Coopera-tives; International Year of Peace and Trust.
2026: International Year of the Woman Farmer; International Year of Volunteers for Sustainable Development; International Year of Rangelands and Pastoralists.

**Present Membership:** At present 193 countries are members of the UNO. South Sudan is the latest entrant to this world organisation.

## Famous International Organisations, Headquarters and Year of Establishment

| *International Organisations* | *Headquarters* | *Year of Establishment* |
|---|---|---|
| United Nations (U.N.) | New York | 1945 |
| International Monetary Fund (I.M.F.) | Washington D.C. | 1945 |
| World Health Organisation (W.H.O.) | Geneva | 1948 |
| Food & Agricultural Organisation (FAO) | Rome | 1945 |
| International Labour Organisation (ILO) | Geneva | 1919 |
| UNESCO | Paris | 1946 |
| International Court of Justice | The Hague | 1945 |
| Universal Postal Union (UPU) | Berne | 1874 |
| International Civil Aviation Organisation (ICAO) | Montreal | 1947 |
| UNIDO | Vienna | 1966 |
| International Atomic Energy Agency (IAEA) | Vienna | 1957 |
| International Finance Corporation (IFC) | Washington D.C. | 1956 |
| United Nations Development Programme (UNDP) | New York | 1965 |
| UNICEF | New York | 1946 |
| International Maritime Organisation (IMO) | London | 1948 |
| World Meteorological Organisation (WMO) | Geneva | 1950 |
| International Telecommunication Union (ITU) | Geneva | 1865 |
| Arab League | Cairo | 1945 |
| Commonwealth of Nations | London | 1931 |
| World Trade Organisation (WTO) | Geneva | 1995 |

| *International Organisations* | *Headquarters* | *Year of Establishment* |
|---|---|---|
| International Development Association (IDA) | Washington D.C. | 1960 |
| International Bank for Reconstruction and Development (IBRD) | Washington D.C. | 1944 |
| World Intellectual Property Organisation (WIPO) | Geneva | 1967 |
| Organisation of Islamic Conference (OIC) | Jeddah (Saudi Arabia) | 1969 |
| Red Cross | Geneva | 1863 |
| Interpol | Lyons | 1923 |
| Asian Development Bank (ADB) | Manila | 1966 |
| North Atlantic Treaty Organisation (NATO) | Brussels | 1949 |
| Association of South East Asian Nations (ASEAN) | Jakarta | 1967 |
| South Asian Association for Regional Cooperation (SAARC) | Kathmandu | 1985 |
| Asia-Pacific Economic Cooperation (APEC) | – | 1989 |
| Organisation for Economic Cooperation and Development (OECD) | Paris | 1961 |
| Organisation of Petroleum Exporting Countries (OPEC) | Vienna | 1960 |
| Common Wealth of Independent States (CIS) | Minsk | 1991 |
| International Olympic Committee (IOC) | Switzerland | 1894 |
| European Union (EU) | Brussels | Changed form of EEC Established in 1958 |
| Amnesty International (AI) | London | 1961 |
| Shanghai Cooperation Organisation (SCO) | Beijing | 2002 |
| BRICS Bank | Shanghai | 2014 |

* * * * *

# 12 First in India

## First in India

| | |
|---|---|
| Nobel Prize for Literature (1913) | Rabindra Nath Tagore |
| Nobel Prize for Physics (1929) | C.V. Raman |
| Nobel Prize for Peace (1979) | Mother Teresa |
| Nobel Prize for Economics (1998) | Amartya Sen |
| Special Oscar award winner (1992) | Satyajit Ray |
| Governor-General of free India (Last also) | C. Rajagopalachari |
| Woman Governor of the State | Smt. Sarojini Naidu |
| Indian Commanders-in-Chief | General K.M. Cariappa |
| Woman Chief Minister of a State | Smt. Sucheta Kripalani |
| Woman President of United Nations General Assembly (1954) | Smt. Vijaylakshmi Pandit |
| President of International Court of Justice | Dr. Nagendra Singh |
| Woman to swim across the English Channel | Ms. Aarti Saha |
| Miss Universe | Miss Sushmita Sen |
| Miss World | Reita Faria |
| Indian to swim across the English Channel | Mihir Sen |
| Field Marshal | S.H.F.J. Manekshaw |
| Indian recipient of Victoria Cross | Khudadad Khan |
| Indian to conquer Mt. Everest | Sherpa Tenzing, May 29, 1953 |
| Indian male cosmonaut (1984) | Rakesh Sharma |
| Indian female cosmonaut | Kalpana Chawla (19 Nov., 1997) |
| Woman to climb Mt. Everest | Miss Bachendri Pal, May 23, 1984 |
| Woman to get Olympic Medal | Karnam Malleswari |
| Indian to address the UN General Assembly in Hindi | Atal Bihari Vajpayee |
| Newspaper | Bengal Gazette, Jan 27, 1780 |
| Postage Stamp issued | In 1852 |
| Telegraph line laid | In 1851, Kolkata; Diamond Harbour |
| Railways run | April 16, 1853; Bombay-Thana |
| Electric Train run | 1925: Bombay-Kurla |
| Atomic Power Station | Tarapore (Maharashtra) |
| Passenger-cum-cargo ship made in India | Harshavardhan |
| Satellite | Aryabhatta (1975) |
| Rocket | Rohini (1967) |
| Atomic Reactor | Apsara (1956) |
| Climb Everest without oxygen | Phu Dorjee (1987) |
| First film (movie) | Raja Harishchandra (1913) |
| First film (talkie) | Alam Ara (1931) |
| Metro Railway | Kolkata Metro Railway |

| | |
|---|---|
| Test-tube baby, scientifically documented | Born on August 6, 1986 at K.E.M. Hospital, Mumbai |
| TV Centre | At Delhi |
| Indian to get an Oscar | Bhanu Athaiya |
| Woman pilot in IAF | Ms Harita Kaur Deol |
| Cellular Phone | Kolkata, August 1, 1995 |
| Women president of Indian National Congress | Smt. Annie Besant |
| President of Indian National Congress | W.C. Banerjee (1885) |
| Indian who passed in I.C.S. Examination | Satendra Nath Tagore |
| Woman chief justice of High Court | Lila Saith (Himachal Pradesh) |
| Woman Foreign Secretary | Chokila Iyyar |

## First Important Officials of India

| | |
|---|---|
| The Governor-General of free India | Lord Mountbatten |
| President | Dr. Rajendra Prasad |
| President (Female) | Pratibha Patil |
| Vice-President | Dr. S. Radhakrishnan |
| Prime Minister | Jawahar Lal Nehru |
| Prime Minister (Female) | Indira Gandhi |
| Deputy Prime Minister | Sardar Vallabhbhai Patel |
| Chief Justice | Harilal J. Kania |
| First Female Judge in Supreme Court | Smt. Meera Sahib Fatima Bibi |
| Speaker, Lok Sabha | Ganesh Vasudeo Mawlankar |
| Woman Speaker of Lok Sabha | Meira Kumar |
| Chief Election Commissioner | Sukumar Sen |
| Indian Commander-in-Chief | General K.M. Cariappa |
| Indian Chief of Army Staff | General Maharaj Rajendra Sinhji |
| Indian Chief of Air Staff | Air Marshal S. Mukherjee |
| Indian Chief of Naval Staff | Vice Admiral Ramdas Katari |
| Chief of Defence Staff (CDS) | General Bipin Rawat |
| Female Minister | Raj Kumari Amrit Kaur (Health Minister) |
| Female Governor | Sarojini Naidu (U.P.) |
| Female Chief Minister | Sucheta Kripalani (U.P. 1963) |
| Finance Commissioner | K.C. Niyogi |
| Leader of Opposition in Lok Sabha (Recognised) | Y.V. Chavan (Congress) |
| Leader of Opposition in Rajya Sabha (Recognised) | Kamalapati Tripathi (Congress) |

## Highest, Biggest, Largest & Longest in India

| | |
|---|---|
| Award for Gallantry, Highest | Param Vir Chakra |
| Award, highest civilian | Bharat Ratna |
| Bank with largest number of branches | State Bank of India |
| River bridge, Longest | Bhupen Hazarika (across Lohit River : Assam 9.15 km) |
| Cantilever Span Bridge, Largest | Howrah Bridge (Kolkata) |
| Cattle Fair, Largest | Sonepur Fair (Bihar) |
| City, Most Populous | Mumbai |
| Corridor, Longest | Ramanathaswamy Corridor, Tamil Nadu (1,220 mt.) |
| Desert, Largest | Thar (Rajasthan) |
| Dam, Longest | Hirakud Dam (Odisha) |
| Dam, Highest | Tehri Dam on Bhagirathi river in Uttarakhand (855 ft.) |

| | |
|---|---|
| Delta, Largest | Sunderban (12,872 Sq. km.) |
| Dome, Largest | Gol Gumbaz (Bijapur) |
| Gateway, Highest | Buland Darwaja at Fatehpur Sikri (54 m.) |
| Lake, Largest (Fresh water) | Wular Lake (Kashmir) |
| Literacy, Highest | Keralam |
| Museum, Largest | Indian Museum (Kolkata) |
| Mosque, Biggest | Jama Masjid (Delhi) |
| Peak, Highest | K-2 (8,611 mt.) |
| Railway Platform, Longest | Shree Siddharoodha Swamiji Railway Station Hubballi, Karnataka (1507 mt.) |
| Railway Bridge, Largest | Vembanad Bridge, Kerala (4.6 km) |
| River, Longest | The Ganga river (2,525 km.) |
| Rainfall, Highest (annual mean) | Mowsynram near Cherrapunji (Meghalaya) |
| Road, Longest | NH-44 (3,745 km) |
| Rock-cut Temple, Largest | Kailash Temples, Ellora (Maharashtra) |
| State, maximum forest cover | Madhya Pradesh |
| State, Largest (area) | Rajasthan (3,42,239 sq. km.) |
| State, Most Populous | Uttar Pradesh (19,98,12,341) |
| State with Maximum density of population | Bihar (1106 persons per sq. km.) |
| Tunnel, Longest (Road) | Dr. Shyama Prasad Mukherjee Tunnel (J & K—9.28 km) |
| Tunnel, Longest (Railway) | T-50 Tunnel (Khari-Sumber section) (12.77 kms) (J&K) |
| Waterfall, Highest | Kunchikal Waterfall, Karnataka (455 m.) |
| Zoo, Largest | Arignar Anna Zoological Park, Chennai, Tamil Nadu |
| Man-made Lake, Largest | Govind Sagar (Bhakra) |

## Indian Banks

- **Reserve Bank of India:** It was established in 1935 and nationalised in 1949. It is the Central Bank of the country and issues all currency notes except one rupee note. It acts as a banker to the Government and exercises control over other commercial banks in the country. Headquarters of Reserve Bank of India is in Mumbai.
- **The State Bank of India:** Largest commercial bank was nationalised in 1955. Till September 2025, State Bank of India has 22,500 branches in India and world.
- **Nationalisation of Banks:** The Government of India on July 19, 1969, took over 14 biggest commercial banks incorporated in the country. On April 15, 1980, six more banks were nationalised. In March 1994, the Parliament passed the Banking Regulation (Amendment) Bill, 1994 which inter alia provided for establishment of private sector banks. Till March 2026 there were 12 public sector banks including SBI in India.

## Insurance

- **Life Insurance Corporation of India:** Since September 1, 1956, when the L.I.C. of India was established, life insurance business in India is transacted by the Corporation and, in a restricted sphere by the Posts and Telegraphs Department of the Government of India and by some State Governments.
- **General Insurance Corporation of India:** It was established in November, 1972 and with effect from January, 1974 the erstwhile 107 Indian and Foreign insurers were grouped by this corporation into four operation companies, namely National Insurance, New India Assurance, Oriental Insurance and United India Insurance.

* * * * *

# 13 Cultural Activities

## AKADEMIES

There are three akademies for promotion of creative art.

1. **Lalit Kala Akademi, New Delhi:** Established in 1954, the Lalit Kala Akademi strives for the popularisation of Indian art within the country and in various countries of the world through exhibitions, publications, workshops and camps. Every three year it organises the Triennale India, an international exhibition. It publishes research papers on Indian arts. Besides organising seminars, it honours eminent artists. The Akademi has set up regional centres called Rashtriya Lalit Kala Kendras at Lucknow, Kolkata, Chennai and Bhubaneswar and a small office at Mumbai.
2. **Sangeet Natak Akademi, New Delhi:** The Sangeet Natak Akademi, set-up in 1953, aims at the promotion and development of dance, drama and music. It holds seminars and festivals, presents awards to the eminent artists and extends financial assistance to traditional teachers and scholarships to students. It also operates a scheme of exchange of troupes.
3. **Sahitya Akademi, New Delhi:** The Sahitya Akademi, established in 1954, has the main functions of development of Indian letters, setting up high literary standards, translation of literary works of one Indian language into other Indian languages, publication of books on history of literature and criticism, bibliographies and reference books. The Akademy has regional offices at Mumbai, Kolkata, Bengaluru and Chennai.
4. **National School of Drama:** It is one of the top theatre training institutes in the world and only one of its kind in India. It was set up in 1959 under Sangeet Natak Akademi but was later made autonomous organisation in 1975.

## SCULPTURE

Archaeological Survey of India, set up in 1861, is responsible for preservation and maintenance of sculptures and historical monuments and manages a number of archaeological museums.

National Archives of India, established in 1891, it is the official custodian of all non-current records of permanent value of the Government of India and its predecessor bodies.

## MUSEUMS

They are repositories of the cultural heritage and conserve and preserve historical technical and other materials against decay and transmit them to posterity as records of history.

## MUSIC

**Main Schools of Classical Music:** There are two main schools of classical music, namely, the Hindustani and the Carnatic. The Hindustani school of classical music is in vogue in north-western India, eastern India and northern parts of the South India.

**Musical Instruments:** They are: Tabla, Mridangam, Pakhawaj, Chandai, Dholak, Veena, Sitar, Sarod, Gootuvadhyam, Sarangi, Flute, Nadaswaram, Shehnai, Shringi and Turahi.

## DANCE

India has a very rich tradition of tribal, folk and classical dances.

## Classical Dance

| Dance | State | Famous Artists |
|---|---|---|
| Bharat Natyam | Tamil Nadu | Yamini Krishnamurthy, Rukmini Devi Arundale, Swapna Sundari, Sonal Mansingh, Vaijanti Mala, Mrinalini Sarabhai, Chandralekha, Indrani, Ram Gopal, Bal Saraswati |
| Kathakali | Keralam | Gopinath, K.K. Nayar, Kunju-Kurup, T.K. Chandu |
| Kuchipudi | Andhra Pradesh | Sapna Sundari, Raja Reddy, Shobha Nayar, Radha Reddy, Vedantam Satyanarayan, Vimpanti Chinna Satyam. |
| Kathak | North India | Birju Maharaj, Gopi Krishna, Shambhu Maharaj, Sitara Devi, Vishnu Sharma, Durga Lal, Shobhana Narayan |
| Odissi | Odisha | Kelucharan Mahapatra, Indrani Rehman, Madhavi Mudgal, Protima Bedi, Samyukta Panigrahi, Sonal Mansingh, Debudas |
| Manipuri | Manipur | Uday Shankar, Bipin Singh, Suryamukhi, Darohra Jhaveri |

## Famous Folk-Dance

| State | Folk Dance |
|---|---|
| Andhra Pradesh | Dandari, Banjara |
| Assam | Bihu, Keli Gopal, Sataria |
| Bihar | Chhau, Magahi, Durga dance |
| W. Bengal | Kirtan, Kalatri, Asweabadh, Brita, Kalidance |
| Chhattisgarh | Saila, Karama, Bhagoria |
| Gujarat | Garba, Rasalila, Tippani, Dandia, |
| Haryana | Damyal, Lahoor |
| Himạchal Pradesh | Dussehra dance, Hikat, Notio |
| Jammu and Kashmir | Dumhal |
| Jharkhand | Jhau, Ghumakudia, Jadur, Sarhul, Soharai, Karama, Vaima, Loojhari, Jat-Jatin, Vidayat |
| Karnataka | Yakshagan, Dolu Kunitha |
| Keralam | Mohini Attam, Padayuni |
| Madhya Pradesh | Lota Nritya, Jawara |
| Maharashtra | Tamasha, Dahi Handi, Gof, Deepak Dindi |
| Manipur | Dhol Cholam |
| Meghalaya | Nongakarem |
| Nagaland | Bamboo dance |
| Odisha | Chhau, Maya Shabari, Dalachai |
| Punjab | Gidda, Bhangra, Panihari |
| Rajasthan | Thumar, Kathaputali, Tera Tali |
| Tamil Nadu | Terukalathu, Kabalatam, Kargam, Pulivesham |
| Tripura | Hazagiri |
| Uttar Pradesh | Rasalila, Nautanki, Thali, Dhurang, Jhumela, Huraka, Bol. |
| Uttarakhand | Kajari, Karan |
| Goa | Dhode Modini |

## Musical Instruments and Artists

| *Musical Instrument* | *Artists* | *Musical Instrument* | *Artists* |
|---|---|---|---|
| Flute | Hari Prasad Chaurasia, Panna Lal Ghosh, T.R. Mahalingam, N. Ramani, Vijaya Raghava Rao | Sitar | Pandit Ravishankar, Vilayat Khan |
| | | Santur | Shiv Kumar Sharma |
| | | Rudraveena | Zia Mohiuddin Dagar |
| Tabla | Allah Rakha, Gudai Maharaj, Latif Khan, Zakir Hussain | Pakhawaj | Govind Rao, Anokhe Lal, Kanthi Maharaj |
| | | Mridanga | Palghat R. Raghu, U.S. Burman |
| Violin | Lalgudi Jayaraman, L. Subramaniam, M.S. Gopal Krishnan, S. Subrahmaniam, V.G. Jog, N. Rajan | Harmonium | Purushottam Walawakar, M. Dhaulpuri |
| | | Guitar | Pt. Vishnu Mohan Bhatt, Brij Bhushan Kalra |
| Shehnai | Bismilla Khan, Imrat Khan | Ghatam | T.H. Vinayakaram |
| Sarod | Ali Akbar Khan, Amjad Ali Khan, Alauddin Khan, Saren Rani, Brij Narayan | Janjira | V. Nagarajan |
| | | Symphony | Jubin Mehta |

## Wild Life Sanctuary in India

India is rich in flora and fauna. However, due to increasing population and industrial and commerci activities, there has been acute pressure on forests. The Government has taken several steps to check t sharp fall in the number of these species. Among the measures are declaration of certain habitats national parks and sanctuaries. 107 national parks and 574 sanctuaries have been established till Augu 2025, important ones being given below:

**Assam:** Kaziranga National Park (know for one-horn Rhinoceroses); Manas Sanctuary.

**Jharkhand:** Hazaribagh National Park; Betla Tiger Reserve Palamau.

**Gujarat:** Valvadar National Park, Bhavnagar; Marine National Park, Gir Forests.

**Himachal Pradesh:** Rohla National Park; Motichur Sanctuary.

**Jammu & Kashmir:** Dachigam Sanctuary.

**Karnataka:** Bandipur National Park; Bannargheta National Park, Bangalore; Nagorhole National Park Coorg; Ranganthitto Bird Sanctuary.

**Keralam:** Eravikulam Rajmallay National Park, Idduki; Periyar Game Sanctuary.

**Madhya Pradesh:** Kanha National Park; Bandhavgarh National Park, Shahdol; Shivpuri National Park

**Maharashtra:** Taloba National Park, Chandrapur; Panch National Park, Nagpur; Borivali Nationa Park, Mumbai; Nawagaon National Park, Bandara; Melghat National Park.

**Manipur:** Reibul Lamjao National Park.

**Odisha:** Simlipal, Tiger Sanctuary.

**Rajasthan:** Sariska Sanctuary; Ghana Bird Sanctuary, Ranthambhor Sanctuary.

**Sikkim:** Khangchandzenda National Park, Gangtok.

**Tamil Nadu:** Vedanthangal Bird Sanctuary; Guindy National Park, Chennai; Mudumalai Sanctuary Kalakad-Munden Thurai Reserve.

**Uttar Pradesh:** Chandraprabha Sanctuary; Dudhwa National Park, Lakhimpur.

**West Bengal:** Jaldapara Sanctuary; Sunderbans.

**Uttarakhand:** Corbett National Park; Nainital.

# 14 Awards

## NATIONAL AWARDS

★ **Bharat Ratna:** This is India's highest civilian award. It is given for exceptional work on art, literature, science and recognition of public service of the highest order. Government servants are not eligible for it.

★ **Padma Vibhushan:** This award is given for exceptional and distinguished service in any field, including service rendered by Govt. servants.

★ **Padma Bhushan:** This award is given for distinguished service of a high order in any field, including service rendered by Govt. servants.

★ **Padma Shri:** This award is given for distinguished service in any field, including service rendered by Government servants.

## GALLANTRY AWARDS

★ **Param Vir Chakra:** The highest award for bravery or some daring and pre-eminent act of valour or self-sacrifice in the presence of the enemy, whether on land, at sea or in the air.

★ **Mahavir Chakra:** It is the second highest decoration and is awarded for acts of conspicuous gallantry in the presence of the enemy, whether on land, at sea or in the air.

★ **Vir Chakra:** It is the third in order of awards given for acts of gallantry in the presence of enemy, whether on land, at sea or in the air.

★ **Ashok Chakra:** This medal is awarded for the most conspicuous bravery or some daring or pre-eminent act of valour or self-sacrifice on land, at sea or in the air but not in the presence of enemy.

★ **Vishishta Sewa Medal:** It is awarded to personnel of all the three Services in class I, II and III in recognition of distinguished service of the "most exceptional" and "exceptional" and a "high" order respectively. Prefixes *Parma* and *Ati* are added before first two categories of medals respectively.

★ **Jeewan Raksha Padak:** Awarded for meritorious acts or a series of acts of a human nature displayed in saving life from drowning, fire and rescue operations in mines etc.

### National Sports Awards

★ **Major Dhyan Chand Khel Ratna Award:** The scheme was launched in the year 1991-92 with the objective of honouring sportspersons to enhance their general status and to give them greater dignity and place of honour in society. Under this scheme, an amount of ₹ 25 lakh is given as award for the most spectacular and outstanding performance by a sportsperson over a period of four years immediately preceding the year in which award is to be given.

★ **Dronacharya Award:** Dronacharya Award is an award presented by ministry of youth Affairs and Sports, Government of India for excellence in sports coaching. The Dronacharya (Lifetime) awardees gets ₹ 15 lakh and Dronacharya (Regular) awardees gets ₹ 10 lakh a bronze statuette of Dronacharya and scroll of honour. The award was instituted in 1985.

★ **Arjuna Award:** The Arjuna Awards are given by the ministry of youth Affairs and sports, government of India to recognize outstanding achievement in National sports. Instituted in 1961 the award carries a cash prize of 15,00,000 a bronze statue of Arjuna and a scroll.

★ **Arjuna Award (Lifetime):** Arjuna Award (Lifetime) is India's highest award for lifetime achievement in sports and games, given by the ministry of youth Affairs and sports, government of India. The award is initiated in 2002. The award carries a cash prize of ₹ 10,00,000 a plaque and a scroll of honour.

★ **Maulana Abul Kalam Azad Trophy:** This trophy was instituted in 1956-57. The top overall performing university in the inter-university tournaments is given the Maulana Abul Kalam Azad (MAKA) Trophy, which is a rolling trophy. A small replica of the MAKA Trophy is also awarded for retention by the university. In addition, the university also gets a cash prize of ₹ 15 lakh. The second and third best universities also receive cash awards amounting to ₹ 5 lakh and ₹ 3 lakh respectively.

## Other Awards

★ **Jnanpith Award:** Awarded to outstanding authors of creative literature in any of the Indian languages recognised by the Constitution of India. It was sponsored by the Bharatiya Jnanpith a culturo-literary society founded in 1944 by Shanti Prasad Jain, an eminent industrialist.

★ **Sahitya Akademi Award:** It is awarded for outstanding literary works and comprises a cash prize of ₹ 1,00,000 in each of the 22 languages mentioned in the Eighth schedule of the Constitution and Rajasthani and English that it supports and a copper plaque.

★ **Saraswati Samman:** The award is given by K.K. Birla Foundation to an outstanding author for his literary work in any Indian language mentioned in the Eighth Schedule of the Constitution and published during the last 10 years.

★ **Dada Saheb Phalke Award:** The prestigious Dada Saheb Phalke Award is given to the persons for outstanding contribution to the growth and development of Indian cinema. First presented in 1969, the award was introduced by the government of India to commemorate Dadasaheb Phalke's contribution to Indian Cinema. Phalke, who is popularly known as and often regarded as a the Father of Indian Cinema was an Indian film-maker who directed India's first-length feature film, Raja Harishchandra. The first recipient of the award was actress Devika Rani, who was honoured at the 17th National film Awards.

★ **Indira Gandhi Award:** The award has been instituted for promoting national integration and understanding amongst the religious groups, communities and ethnic groups of India.

★ **Bhartendu Harishchandra Awards:** The Bhartendu Harishchandra Awards were instituted in 1983, by the Ministry of Information and Broadcasting for original Hindi writing on any subject in mass communications like journalism, publication, advertising, broadcasting films, etc.

## INTERNATIONAL AWARDS

★ **Nobel Prizes:** The most prestigious award in the world is supported by the Nobel Foundation of US. This award was set up in 1900 under the will to Alfred Bernhard Nobel (1833-96). Alfred Nobel was an unmarried, Swedish scientist and chemical engineer who discovered Nitroglycerin ($C_3H_5N_3O_9$) and its use in the manufacture of dynamite in 1966. The interest accrued on the fortune left by him is divided annually among the persons who have made outstanding contribution in science, literature, peace and economics. Swedes found out about the prizes only after his death in 1896. When they read his will in which he had donated the annual income from his fortune to support the awards. In his will he ordered that 'the most worthy shall receive the prize, whether he is Scandinavian or not. This led to his criticism as being unpatriotic for not reserving the prizes only for Swedes.

***Nobel Foundation's Prize Awarding Bodies***

(*i*) The Royal Swedish Academy of Sciences, awards the Nobel prize in Physics and Chemistry.

(*ii*) The Nobel Assembly of Karolinska Chirugical Institute. Sweden, awards the Nobel Prize in Medicine and Physiology.

(*iii*) The Swedish Academy awards the Prize in Literature.

(*iv*) The Committee of the Norwegian Parliament awards the Prize for Peace.

(*v*) The Bank of Sweden awards the Nobel Prize in Economics.

★ **Ramon Magsaysay Award:** The Raman Magsaysay Award, named after a Philippines President, who died in an air crash in 1957, is given annually to Asian nationals or institutions who have made worthy contributions to public service, community leadership, journalism, literature and the creative arts and international understanding. It carries a gold medal, a certificate and US$ 50,000.

★ **Pulitzer Prize:** Instituted in 1970 and named after the US publisher Joseph Pulitzer (1847-1911). It is conferred annually in the United States for accomplishment in journalism, literature and music under the management to the Pulitzer Prize Board at Columbia University.

★ **Man Booker Prize:** Instituted in 1968, it is the highest literary award set up by the Booker Company and the British Publishers Association along the lines of the Pultizer Prize, of USA, worth £ 20,000 (1992). Since 2002, it has been known as the **'Man Booker Prize'**, reflecting the sponsorship by an investment company, the Man Group plc. The winner receives £ 50,000 and both the winner and the shorlisted authors are guaranteed a world wide readership plus a dramatic increase in book sales.

★ **Oscar Awards:** The annual Oscar presentation has been held since 1929. After three-quarters of a century of recognizing excellence in cinema achievement, the annual presentation of the Oscars has become the Academy of Motion Picture Arts and Sciences' most famous activity.

★ **Kalinga Award:** The award given for popularisation of science is an international award conferred annually by the United Nations Educational, Scientific and Cultural Organisation (UNESCO) to a person with a distinguished career of service in the interpretation of science and research to the public. The award was instituted in 1952 at the initiative of Mr Biju Patnaik the founder of the Kalinga Foundation Trust in Odisha.

★ **Grammy Award:** The Grammy Foundation was established in 1989 to cultivate an awareness, appreciation and advancement of the contribution of recorded music American culture from the and technical legends of the past to the still unimagined musical breakthroughs of the future generations of the music professionals. The Grammy Foundation works in partnership with its founder, the Recording Academy, to bring national attention to important issues such as the value and impact of music and arts education and the urgency of preserving our rich cultural legacy.

## Highest Honours of Some Countries

| *Country* | *Highest Honour* |
|---|---|
| India | Bharat Ratna |
| Pakistan | Nishan-e-Pakistan |
| Kuwait | Mubarak-Al-kabir Medal |
| Saudi Arabia | Shah Abdul Aziz Medal |
| Argentina | The Order of Sona Martin |
| Nicaragua | Augusto-Caesar Sandino Order |
| Vietnam | The order of the Golden Star |
| Hungary | The Order of Banner |
| Britain | Member of British Empire, Victoria Cross |
| Japan | Order of Moulovenice Sun |
| Denmark | Order of Diana Brog |
| France | Legend of Honour |
| America | Presidential Medal of Freedom |
| Germany | Pore Lee Merit Iron Cross |
| The Netherlands | Netherlands Lion |

✸ ✸ ✸ ✸ ✸

# 15 Sports

## Important Cups & Trophies

### International

| | | | |
|---|---|---|---|
| *American Cup* | Yacht Racing | *Walker Cup* | Golf |
| *Ashes* | Cricket | *Westchester Cup* | Polo |
| *Benson and Hedges* | Cricket | *Wightman Cup* | Lawn Tennis |
| *Canada Cup* | Golf | *World Cup* | Cricket |
| *Colombo Cup* | Football | *World Cup* | Hockey |
| *Corbitton Cup* | Table Tennis (Women) | *Reliance Cup* | Cricket |
| *Davis Cup* | Lawn Tennis | *Rothman's Trophy* | Cricket |
| *Derby* | Horse Race | *William's Cup* | Basketball |
| *Grand National* | Horse Streple Chase Race | *European Champions Cup* | Football |
| *Jules Rimet Trophy* | World Soccer Cup | *Eisenhower Cup* | Golf |
| *King's Cup* | Air Races | *Essande Champions Cup* | Hockey |
| *Merdeka Cup* | Football | *Rene Frank Trophy* | Hockey |
| *Ryder Cup* | Golf | *Grand Prix* | Table Tennis |
| *Swaythling Cup* | Table Tennis (Men) | *Edgbaston Cup* | Lawn Tennis |
| *Thomas Cup* | Badminton | *Grand Prix* | Lawn Tennis |
| *Uber Cup* | Badminton (Women) | *World Cup* | Weightlifting |
| *U. Thant Cup* | Tennis | | |

### National

| | | | |
|---|---|---|---|
| *Agarwal Cup* | Badminton | *C.K. Naidu Trophy* | Cricket |
| *Agha Khan Cup* | Hockey | *Chakola Gold Trophy* | Football |
| *All India Women's Guru Nanak Championship* | Hockey | *Divan Cup* | Badminton |
| *Bandodkar Trophy* | Football | *Deodhar Trophy* | Cricket |
| *Bangalore Blues Challenge Cup* | Basketball | *Duleep Trophy* | Cricket |
| *Barna-Bellack Cup* | Table Tennis | *D.C.M. Cup* | Football |
| *Beighton Cup* | Hockey | *Durand Cup* | Football |
| *Bombay Gold Cup* | Hockey | *Dhyan Chand Trophy* | Hockey |
| *Burdwan Trophy* | Weightlifting | *Dr. B.C. Roy Trophy* | Football (Junior) |
| *Charminar Trophy* | Atheletics | *Ezra Cup* | Polo |
| *Chadha Cup* | Badminton | *F.A. Cup* | Football |
| | | *G.D. Birla Trophy* | Cricket |
| | | *Ghulam Ahmed Trophy* | Cricket |
| | | *Gurmeet Trophy* | Hockey |

- *Guru Nanak Cup* : Hockey
- *Gyanvati Devi Trophy* : Hockey
- *Holkar Trophy* : Bridge
- *Irani Trophy* : Cricket
- *I.F.A. Shield* : Football
- *Indira Gold Cup* : Hockey
- *Jawaharlal Challenge* : Air Racing
- *Jaswant Singh Trophy* : Best Services Sportsman
- *Kuppuswamy Naidu Trophy* : Hockey
- *Lady Rattan Tata Trophy* : Hockey
- *MCC Trophy* : Hockey
- *Moinuddaula Gold Cup* : Cricket
- *Murugappa Gold Cup* : Hockey
- *Modi Gold Cup* : Hockey
- *Narang Cup* : Badminton
- *Nehru Trophy* : Hockey
- *Nixan Gold Cup* : Football
- *Obaidullah Gold Cup* : Hockey
- *Prithi Singh Cup* : Polo
- *Rani Jhansi Trophy* : Cricket
- *Ranji Trophy* : Cricket
- *Rangaswami Cup* : Hockey
- *Ranjit Singh Gold Cup* : Hockey
- *Rajendra Prasad Cup* : Tennis
- *Ramanujan Trophy* : Table Tennis
- *Rene Frank Trophy* : Hockey
- *Radha Mohan Cup* : Polo
- *Raghbir Singh Memorial* : Football
- *Rohinton Baria Trophy* : Cricket
- *Rovers Cup* : Football
- *Sanjay Gold Cup* : Football
- *Santosh Trophy* : Football
- *Sir Ashutosh Mukherjee* : Football
- *Subroto Cup* : Football
- *Scindia Gold Cup* : Hockey
- *Sahni Trophy* : Hockey
- *Sheesh Mahal Trophy* : Cricket
- *Todd Memorial Trophy* : Football
- *Tommy Eman Gold Cup* : Hockey
- *Vittal Trophy* : Football
- *Vizzy Trophy* : Cricket
- *Vijay Merchant Trophy* : Cricket
- *Wellington Trophy* : Rowing
- *Wills Trophy* : Cricket

## Sports Measurements

- *Badminton Courts:* 44 ft. by 20 ft. (doubles) 44 ft. by 17 ft. (singles)
- *Boxing Ring:* 12 ft. by 28 ft. Sq.
- *Cricket Pitch:* 22 yards (distance)
- *Derby Course:* 1½ miles. (2.4 km)
- *Football Field:*
  (a) Length : 100 – 120 yards.
  Breadth: 50 – 56 yards.
  (b) Rugby : 100 yards by 75 yards
- *Hockey Ground:* 100 yards by 55 to 60 yards
- *Lawn Tennis Court:* 78 ft. by 36 ft. (double), 78 ft. by 28 ft. (single)
- *Marathon Race:* 26 miles, 385 yards
- *Polo Ground:* 300 yards by 200 yards (if boarded)
- *Golf:* Hole 4½ inches in diameter.

## Sports Terms

- **Badminton:** Mixed doubles; Deuce; Drop; Smash; Let; Foot work; Setting.
- **Base Ball:** Pitcher; Put out, Strike; Home; Bunt.
- **Billiards:** Cue; Jigger; Pot; Break; In Baulk; In Off; Cannons.
- **Boxing:** Upper cut; Round; Punch; Bout; Knock down; Hitting below the belt; Ring.
- **Bridge:** Finesse; Dummy; Revoke; Grand Slam; Little Slam; No Trump; Rubber.
- **Chess:** Bishop, Gambit; Checkmate; Stalemate.
- **Cricket:** L.B.W. *(leg before wicket)*; Creases, Popping-creases; Stumped; Bye; Leg-Bye; Googly; Hattrick; Maiden over; Drive; Bowling; Duck; Follow-on; No ball; Leg Break; Silly point; Cover point; Hit-wicket; Late-cut; Slip; Off-spinner.
- **Football:** Off Side; Block; Drop-kick; Penalty-kick (or *goal kick*); Corner-kick; Free-kick; Dribble; Thrown-in; Foul.
- **Golf:** Boggy; Foursome; Stymic; Tee; Put; Hole; Niblic; Caddie; Links; The green; Bunker.
- **Hockey:** Carried; Short Corner; Bully; Sticks; Off side; Roll in; Striking Circle; Under-cutting.
- **Horse racing:** Jockey; Punter.
- **Polo:** Bunker; Chukker; Mallet.
- **Tennis:** Back hand drive; Volley; Smash; Half-volley; Deuce; Service; Let; Grand Slam.

## Name of Playing Compound of Different Games

| *Name of Compound* | *Related Sports* | *Name of Compound* | *Related Sports* |
|---|---|---|---|
| Court | Lawn Tennis, Badminton, Netball, Hand ball, Volleyball, Squash, Kho-Kho, Kabaddi | Pool | Swimming |
| | | Alley | Bowling |
| | | Mat | Judo, Karate II |
| Diamond | Baseball | Arena | Horse Riding |
| | | Vellodrum | Cycling |
| Ring | Boxing, Skating, Wrestling, Circus, Riding display | Field | Polo, Football, Hockey |
| | | Track | Athletics |
| Course | Golf | Pitch | Cricket, Rugby |
| Board | Table Tennis | Rink | Ice Hockey |

## National Sports and Games of Some Countries

| | | | |
|---|---|---|---|
| Australia | Cricket | Spain | Bull Fighting |
| Canada | Ice Hockey | USA | Baseball |
| England | Cricket and Rugby Football | China | Table Tennis |
| Russia | Chess | Malaysia | Badminton |
| Scotland | Rugby Football | Pakistan | Hockey |

## OLYMPIC GAMES

First of all these games were held by the Greeks in 776 B.C. on Mount Olympus in honour of the Greek God Zeus. In this way, the history of Olympic Games is about twenty eight hundred years old. These games continued to be held every four years until 394 A.D. When these games were stopped by a royal order of the emperor of Rome. The modern Olympic Games which started in Athens in 1896, are the result of the devotion and dedication of a French educator Baron Pierre de Coubertin and the first Olympic meet in the modern series was held in 1896 in Athens, the Capital of Greece. Since then, they are being held every four years except for breaks during world wars. The Olympic flag is white in colour with five coloured rings, each ring symbolic of a continent. Summer as well as winter Olympics are held in the same year.

## COMMONWEALTH GAMES

The Commonwealth Games are held every four years, in the year in which Asian Games are held. All the Commonwealth Countries (former colonies of Britain) can take part in it. The first Commonwealth Games were held in 1930 at Hamilton (Canada).

## ASIAN GAMES

After the Second World War, most of the Asia Countries gained independence. On the lines of Ol ympic Games, Asian Games were planned every fou years. India hosted the first Asian Games in 1951

## CRICKET WORLD CUP

The first Cricket World Cup was organised i England in 1975. A separate women's Crick World Cup has been held every 4 years since 197 Australia is the winner of 2023 Cricket World Cu

## HOCKEY WORLD CUP

The first Hockey World Cup was organised i Barcelona (Spain) in 1971. Women's Hockey Wor Cup has been held since 1974.

## FOOTBALL WORLD CUP

The Football World Cup is organised by FIF (Federation of International Football Association The World Cup is called 'Jules Rimet Cup' nam after the name of FIFA President Jules Rimet. T first Football World Cup was organised in Urugu in 1930.

## Personalities Associated with Sports

- **Athletics:** Carl Lewis, Linford Christy, Ben Johnson, Calvin Smith, Edwin Moses, Sergei Bubka, Sebestian Coe, Rosa Mota, Harold Schmidt, Milkha Singh, P.T. Usha, Shiny Abraham, Jesse Owens, Jyotirmoy Sikdar.
- **Boxing:** Cassius Clay (Mohammad Ali), Joe Frazier, Mike Tyson, Larry Holmes, Frank Bruno, Henry Cooper, Archie Moore, Evander Holyfield, George Foreman.
- **Badminton:** Prakash Padukone, Syed Modi, Dinesh Khanna, Jamie Paulson, Nandu Natekar, Liem Swie King, Saina Nehwal, P.V. Sindhu.
- **Billiards:** Wilson Jones, Geet Sethi, Michael Ferreira, Pankaj Advani.
- **Chess:** Boris Spausky, Gary Kasparov, Anatoly Karpov, Victor Korchonoi, Vishwanathan Anand, Konern Humpy, Parveen Thipsay.
- **Cricket:** Sunil Gavaskar, Bishen Singh Bedi, Kapil Dev, Mohd. Azharuddin, Sachin Tendulkar, G.R. Vishwanath, Lala Amarnath, Ajit Wadekar, B.S. Chandrashekhar, E.A.S. Prasanna, S. Venkatraghvan, Don Bradman, Richard Hadlee, Gary Sobers, Ian Botham, Vivian Richards, Clive Llyod, Dilip Sardesai, Charles Griffith, Imran Khan, Mushtaq Mohammad, Geoff Boycott, Tony Greg, Wasim Akram, Richie Benaud, Michael Holding, Greg Chappell, Javed Miandad, Vijay Manjrekar, M.A.K. Pataudi, S.M.H. Kirmani, Bill Lawry, Clive Rice, Mark Taylor, Joel Garner, Arjuna Ranatunga, Arvinda De'Silva, Saurav Ganguly, Virat Kohli, M.S. Dhoni, Ajit Agarkar, Jacques Kallis, John Traicos, W.R. Hammond, Sanath Jaisurya.
- **Hockey:** Dhyan Chand, Ashok Kumar, Ajit Singh, Pargat Singh, Pritpal Singh, Zafar Iqbal, Shankar Laxman, Mervyn Fernandes, Mohammad Shahid, R. Charlesworth, Balbir Singh, Terry Walsh, Kishan Lal, Udlam Singh, Dhanraj Pillai.
- **Football:** Pele, Diego Maradona, Franz Beckenbour, Socrates, Raud Gullit, Garry Linekar, Emilo Butraguino, Coreca, P.C. Bannerji, Arunlal Ghosh, Chuni Goswami, Davor Suker, Ronaldo, Rivaldo, Deschamps.
- **Tennis (Lawn):** Bjorn Borg, Jimmy Connors, John Mcenroe, Ivan Lendl, Pete Sampras, Billie Jean Kings, Chris Evert Lloyd, Martina Navratilova, Steffi Graf, Stefan Edberg, Andre Agassi, Michael Chang, Boris Becker, Leander Paes, Vijay Amritraj, Anand Amritraj, Jaideep Mukherjee, Rod Laver, Roy Emerson, Naresh Kumar, Premjit Lall, Martina Hingis, Mary Pierce, Jana Novotna, Rozer Federer.
- **Golf:** Greg Norman, Jack Nikalus, Sandy Lyle, Seve Bellestros, Nick Faldo, Nick Price, Sher Ali, Jeeve Milkha Singh, S. Choudhary, R.K. Pitamber, Vikramjit Singh.
- **Gymnastics:** Nadia Comaneci, L. Latynina, V. Kaslavska, E. Szebo, W. Kim. Y. Ma, Y. Shrusunova, Daniela Silivas, A. Braglia, V. Chukarin, N. Andrianov, Sergi Kharkhov.
- **Swimming:** Arti Gupta, Arun Kumar Shaw, Baidyanath, Mihir Sen, Aarti Saha, Mark Spitz.
- **Wrestling:** Dara Singh, Bhim Sen, Mukhtiar Singh, Sudesh Kumar, Chandagi Ram.

## Stadia in Various Cities of India

- **Delhi:** Ambedkar Stadium, Arun Jaitley Stadium, Jawaharlal Nehru Stadium, Indira Gandhi Indoor Stadium, Shivaji Stadium, National Stadium.
- **Mumbai:** Brabourne Stadium, Wankhede Stadium.
- **Kolkata:** Eden Gardens, Salt Lake Stadium, Ranjit Stadium, Subhas Sarovar.
- **Chennai:** Nehru Stadium, Chidambaram Stadium, Chepauk.
- **Cuttack:** Barabati Stadium.
- **Kanpur:** Green Park.
- **Jamshedpur:** Keenan Stadium.
- **Nagpur:** Vidarbha CA Ground
- **Jaipur:** Swai Mansingh Stadium
- **Gwalior:** Roop Singh Stadium
- **Vadodara:** Moti Bagh Stadium
- **Patna:** Moin-ul-Haq Stadium
- **Hyderabad:** Lal Bahadur Stadium
- **Patiala:** Yaduvindra Stadium.
- **Bengaluru:** Chinnaswami Stadium.
- **Siliguri:** Kanchenjunga Stadium.
- **Vishakhapatnam:** Indira Priyadarshini Stadium.

* * * * *

# 16 National/International Days

**JANUARY**

| | |
|---|---|
| Infant Protection Day | : January 7 |
| African National Congress Foundation Day | : January 8 |
| NRI Day (India) | : January 9 |
| World Laughter Day | : January 10 |
| National Youth Day (India) | : January 12 |
| Army Day (India) | : January 15 |
| Indian Tourism Day | : January 25 |
| Republic Day (India); International Customs Day | : January 26 |
| Martyrs' Day (India); World Leprosy Eradication Day | : January 30 |

**FEBRUARY**

| | |
|---|---|
| World Wetlands Day | : February 2 |
| World Marriage Day | : Second Sunday of February |
| Valentine Day (World) | : February 14 |
| Mother Tongue Day (World) | : February 21 |
| National Science Day (India) | : February 28 |

**MARCH**

| | |
|---|---|
| International Women's Day; | : March 8 |
| World Disabled Day : World Consumer Rights Day | : March 15 |
| World Forestry Day; International Day for Elimination of Racial Discrimination | : March 21 |
| World Day for Water | : March 22 |
| World Meteorological Day | : March 23 |
| World TB Day | : March 24 |

**APRIL**

| | |
|---|---|
| National Maritime Day (India) | : April 5 |
| World Health Day | : April 7 |
| World Aviation and Cosmonautics Day | : April 12 |
| World Haemophilia Day | : April 17 |
| World Heritage Day, | : April 18 |
| Earth Day (World) | : April 22 |
| World Book and Copyright Day | : April 23 |

**MAY**

| | |
|---|---|
| Workers' Day (International Labour Day) | : May 1 |
| Press Freedom Day; World Asthma Day | : May 3 |
| World Red Cross Day | : May 8 |
| World Mother's Day (2nd Sunday of May) | : May 8 |
| World Thalassaemia Day | : May 9 |
| National Technology Day | : May 11 |
| International Nurses Day | : May 12 |
| International Day of the Family | : May 15 |
| World Telecommunication Day | : May 17 |
| Anti-Terrorism Day | : May 21 |
| Commonwealth Day | : May 24 |
| Anti-Tobacco Day | : May 31 |

**JUNE**

| | |
|---|---|
| International Day of Innocent Children Victims of Aggression | : June 4 |
| World Environment Day | : June 5 |
| Father's Day (3rd Sunday of June) | : June 19 |
| International Yoga Day | : June 21 |
| International Day Against Drug Abuse & Illicit Trafficking | : June 26 |

## JULY

| | |
|---|---|
| Doctors' Day | : July 1 |
| American Independence Day | : July 4 |
| World Zoonosis Day | : July 6 |
| World Population Day | : July 11 |

## AUGUST

| | |
|---|---|
| World Breast Feeding Week | : August 1-7 |
| International Friendship Day | : August 3 |
| Hiroshima Day | : August 6 |
| World Senior Citizen's Day | : August 8 |
| Quit India Day; Nagasaki Day | : August 9 |
| Indian Independence Day | : August 15 |
| International Day of the World's Indigenous People | : August 18 |
| Sadbhavna Divas (India) | : August 20 |
| National Sports Day (India) | : August 29 |

## SEPTEMBER

| | |
|---|---|
| World Yoga Day | : September 2 |
| Teachers' Day | : September 5 |
| World (International) Literacy Day | : September 8 |
| Hindi Day (India) | : September 14 |
| All India Flag Day | : September 15 |
| World Ozone Day | : September 16 |
| Alzheimer's Day (World) | : September 21 |
| Day for Peace & Non-Violence (UN) | : September 21 |
| Rose Day (Welfare of Cancer Patients) World Heart Day | : September 22 |
| International Tiger Day | : September 25 |
| World Tourism Day | : September 27 |

## OCTOBER

| | |
|---|---|
| International Day for the Elderly People | : October 1 |
| Gandhi Jayanti, International Day of Non-Violence | : October 2 |
| World Animal Day | : October 2 |
| World Vegetarian Day | : October 2 |
| World Habitat Day | : October 3 |
| World Animal Welfare Day | : October 4 |
| World Post Office Day | : October 9 |
| National Post Day (India) | : October 10 |
| World Allergy Awareness Day | : October 11 |
| UN International Day for Natural Disaster Reduction | : October 13 |
| World Standards Day | : October 14 |
| World Food Day | : October 16 |
| International Day for the Eradication of Poverty | : October 17 |
| UN Day | : October 24 |
| World Development Information Day | : October 24 |
| Infants Day | : October 27 |
| World Thrift Day | : October 30 |
| National Integration Day (India) | : October 31 |

## NOVEMBER

| | |
|---|---|
| Legal Services Day | : November 9 |
| Children's Day (India) | : November 14 |
| Diabetes Day | : November 14 |
| National Epilepsy Day | : November 17 |

## DECEMBER

| | |
|---|---|
| World AIDS Day | : December 1 |
| World Disabled Day | : December 3 |
| International Volunteer Develompent Day | : December 5 |
| Armed Forces Flag Day (India) | : December 7 |
| Human Rights Day (World) | : December 10 |
| National Energy Conservation Day | : December 14 |
| Farmer's Day | : December 23 |

* * * * *

# 17 Multiple Choice Questions

1. The part of the Sun, which is visible during eclipses only, is known as
   A. photosphere
   B. chromosphere
   C. corona
   D. all the parts are visible with naked eye
2. Sphygmomanometer is used for
   A. measuring the brain pulse of a patient
   B. measuring the systolic and diastolic blood pressures of man
   C. measuring the amount of blood in a human body
   D. measuring the haemoglobin count in a human body
3. The most abundant gas in air is
   A. nitrogen B. hydrogen
   C. oxygen D. ozone
4. The most commonly found acid in nature is
   A. hydrochloric acid
   B. sulphuric acid
   C. lactic acid
   D. acetic acid
5. This bomb is used to destroy living beings but would not damage the buildings and other property
   A. napalm bomb
   B. neutron bomb
   C. hydrogen bomb
   D. None of the above
6. Electrical energy is measured in terms of units which are also termed as
   A. KW B. KWH
   C. WH D. KVAR
7. In cold countries, the radiator water of cars is mixed with glycerol. This is done to
   A. increase the specific heat of water
   B. reduce the freezing point of water
   C. improve the engine efficiency
   D. glycerol is not added in radiator water
8. If the Richter scale shows a value of 7.2, then the seismograph indicates
   A. an earthquake of low intensity
   B. an earthquake of very high intensity
   C. an earthquake of moderate intensity
   D. either A or C
9. The theory of origin of species is based primarily on
   A. the process of biological evolution
   B. the process of natural selection
   C. the evolution of life from the oceans
   D. the evolution of man from apes
10. Common coal used in our households is
    A. Anthracite B. Bituminous coal
    C. Lignite D. All of the above
11. Some recent findings on moon, which point out towards the possibility of settlement of man on moon, include
    A. nil atmospheric gases
    B. ice reserves on the poles
    C. micro-organisms
    D. None of the above
12. Viagra is a medicine for
    A. treatment of AIDS
    B. treatment of female fertility
    C. treatment of male impotency
    D. treatment of Lukaemia
13. Rickets is a disease which is caused by the deficiency of
    A. Vitamin A B. Riboflavin
    C. Vitamin C D. Vitamin D
14. When a ship enters waters of the sea from a river, then its level
    A. rises as the sea water is saline and hence bouyancy force is more

B. decreases as ocean is a large mass of water
C. remains the same as water is the same for the river and the sea
D. None of the above

**15.** The major constituent of pearl is
A. calcium carbonate
B. calcium oxide and ammonium chloride
C. organic mass
D. calcium carbonate and silica

**16.** A healthy person needs ..... calories per day.
A. 2200 B. 2400
C. 2500 D. 1800

**17.** The value of one (marine) Naut is
A. 1951 metre per hour
B. 1852 metre per hour
C. 2305 metre per hour
D. 1860 metre per hour

**18.** Acid and base combine to form
A. salt and nitrogen
B. nitrogen and oxygen
C. salt and water
D. acid and alkali

**19.** Cellulose could be obtained from
A. wood and cotton B. silk and cotton
C. paper and silk D. wood and silk

**20.** ELISA test is done for the detection of
A. cancer B. AIDS
C. diabetes D. None of the above

**21.** Triple Antigen, prevents
A. small pox, malaria, whooping cough
B. tetanus, diphtheria, small pox
C. whooping cough, tetanus, polio
D. diphtheria, tetanus, whooping cough

**22.** A freely falling body
A. would fall towards the surface of the earth
B. would have no weight
C. would have one half of its original weight
D. None of the above

**23.** If the motor neurons of the spinal cord of a child are damaged, then he would develop the following disease.
A. Rickets B. Polio
C. Diphtheria D. Jaundice

**24.** Which one of the following is not a part of the balanced diet?
A. Vitamins B. Carbohydrate
C. Proteins D. Alcohol

**25.** Which statement is not correct in connection with human physiology?
A. The length of the small intestine is 7 metres and its diameter is 2.5 cm.
B. There are 639 muscles in a human body
C. An infant breathes 45 times per minute whereas a six year old child breathes 25 times per minute
D. The weight of the adult human brain is nearly 700 gms

**26.** The bottles of beer are not kept in the deep freezer because
A. beer is an alcohol which could burst under conditions of low temperature
B. alcohol could damage the deep freezer due to its corrosive action if the bottles break accidently
C. water content in beer gets converted into ice which expends (after change of state from water to ice) and this could lead to bursting of beer bottles
D. the low temperature could degrade the beer and hence, it may not good remain for consumption

**27.** Rocket works on the basis of
A. principle of conservation of momentum
B. principle of relativity
C. principle of conservation of mass
D. principle of conservation of energy

**28.** Which one of the following groups is more closely related from the viewpoint of taxonomy?
A. silverfish, starfish, cuttlefish
B. earthworm, seahorse, hookworm
C. housefly, dragonfly, butterfly
D. None of the above

**29.** Red blood corpuscles are produced in
A. liver B. spleen
C. bone marrow D. kidneys

**30.** The disease for which the first oral drug has been developed for treatment.
A. Cancer B. Pneumonid
C. Small pox D. Plauge

**31.** E-comm is a short form of
A. Engineering Commercial
B. Electronic Commercial
C. Electronic Commerce
D. None of the above

**32.** High AC voltages are used for transmitting electric power because
A. at high voltages, current is low and hence, losses are low
B. the transmission of power is quicker
C. the high voltages a consume lesser materials for transmission
D. None of the above

**33.** There is a hole in the boat through which, water is seeping into the boat. Just before the boat capsizes
A. water level would decrease
B. water level would increase
C. water level would remain the same
D. None of the above

**34.** During which month, the rate of rotation of the earth on its axis is the fastest?
A. December
B. May
C. the rate of rotation is fixed
D. It is fastest when the earth is closest to the Sun.

**35.** The time taken by the Sun rays to reach the earth is
A. 9 minutes B. 10 minutes
C. 7 minutes D. 8 minutes

**36.** The outer planets are
A. Moon, Earth, Mercury, Venus
B. Jupiter, Saturn, Uranus, Earth, Mars
C. Jupiter, Uranus, Saturn, Neptune
D. None of the above

**37.** According to the astrophysicists
A. the universe is mobile and expanding
B. the universe is heading for a collision with another universe
C. the universe is stationary
D. the doomsday of universe is near due to the formation of many new black holes

**38.** Which is popular as the White City?
A. New York B. Belgrade
C. Bangalore D. Bab-el-mandab

**39.** The national currency of Haiti is
A. Rupiah B. Gourde
C. Quetzal D. Dong

**40.** Which one is not a news agency of India?
A. UNI
B. PTI
C. Hindustan Samachar
D. Reuters

**41.** The abundant element of the earth's atmosphere is:
A. Oxygen B. nitrogen
C. hydrogen D. $CO_2$

**42.** The first talking movie of India was ..... and the first silent movie of India was .....
A. Aan, Aawara
B. Raja Harish Chandra, Alamara
C. Alamara, Raja Harish Chandra
D. Purana Mandir, Raja Harish Chandra

**43.** Hair becomes grey because
A. rays of the Sun force it to become grey
B. the quantity of melanin is reduced in human body with growing age
C. there is a lack of vitamins in the body due to growing age
D. None of the above

**44.** Salaries of Supreme Court judges are drawn from:
A. Law Ministry Grants
B. Consolidated Fund of India
C. Home Ministry Grants
D. Parliamentary Grants

**45.** The term "Paper-gold" is associated with
A. deficit budgeting
B. loans from the World Bank
C. Special Drawing Rights (SDRs) from the IMF
D. None of the above

**46.** TRAI refers to
A. Terresteral Remote Sensing Authority of India
B. Telecommunication Research Authority of India
C. Transport Regulatory Authority of India
D. Telecom Regulatory Authority of India

**47.** NSDL is an organisation in India which
A. provides security to depositors
B. accepts deposits from recognised bodies

C. provides data security for on-line computer systems
D. None of the above

**48.** The enzyme pepsin converts
A. proteins into peptones
B. fats to amino acids
C. carbohydrates to sugars
D. proteins to amino acids

**49.** Who among the following is not a winner of the PVC?
A. Bana Singh
B. Nirmal Jeet Singh Sekhon
C. Somnath Sharma
D. Shanti Swaroop Rana

**50.** Which one of the following pairs is not correct?
A. Narmada – Betul district
B. Krishna – near Mahabaleshwar
C. Chambal – near Mhow
D. Godavari – Nashik district

**51.** The Japanese art of flower arrangement is known as
A. Bonsai
B. Ongami
C. Ikebota
D. None of the above

**52.** The meaning of the Latin word *Vive Rex* is
A. Long live the king!
B. Let the Nation Live
C. A middle course
D. Nothing wrong here

**53.** The permanent station of India in Antarctica is known as
A. *Vikalp*
B. Antarctica India Station
C. *Maitri*
D. *Dakshin Yamunotri*

**54.** A man dies due to electrocution because
A. electric current passes through his body to earth which leads to sudden contraction and expansion of muscles (including heart muscles) and this, alongwith development of heat in the body, leads to heart failure.
B. there is no resistance offered by the body
C. the body allows the current to flow through the blood which cannot circulate any longer
D. None of the above

**55.** "Blue Dwarfs" are
A. members of the Russian circus
B. warriors of Mongolia
C. young stars of the universe
D. naval officers in the high seas

**56.** What is a fly leaf?
A. thin paper sheet for making packaging material
B. a blank page at the beginning or end of a book
C. a marker in a book
D. a sheet of paper next to the main title of the book

**57.** Who is associated with the theory of inheritance of acquired characters?
A. Spencer
B. Mandeleev
C. Lamarck
D. All of the above

**58.** Ligaments and tendons in the body are made up of
A. skeletal tissue
B. muscular tissue
C. connective tissue
D. epithelial tissue

**59.** A cell membrane is
A. completely permeable
B. impermeable
C. semi-permeable
D. None of the above

**60.** The tenure of the non-permanent members of the UN Security Council is
A. one year
B. three years
C. two years
D. there is no fixed tenure

**61.** Why proper earthing is necessary?
A. It reduces the consumption of electricity
B. It allows the current to flow through the earth wire and into the earth, thus protecting the person
C. It allows the appliance to operate efficiently
D. None of the above

**62.** Which one of the following items has not been included in the minimum needs programme?
A. unemployment allowance
B. rural water supply
C. rural electrification
D. adult education

**63.** This is not the principle organ of digestion and absorption in the human body.
A. small intestine B. stomach
C. large intestine D. Both A and B

**64.** Which are the two stars which appear as morning stars in the Eastern sky and evening stars in the Western sky?
A. Jupiter and Mars
B. Mars and Venus
C. Saturn and Mercury
D. Mercury and Venus

**65.** Which planet rotates on its axis from East to West?
A. Mercury B. Jupiter
C. Earth D. Venus

**66.** The chemical compound present in the stone of human kidney is
A. calcium phosphate
B. calcium carbonate
C. silica
D. calcium oxalate

**67.** Which one of the following diseases would be caused by bacterial infection?
A. tetanus B. rabies
C. cancer D. malaria

**68.** India On-line Limited is
A. an advertising agency
B. a reservation office
C. an information service
D. an internet services provider

**69.** CTBT is related to
A. economic sanctions imposed by the USA on India
B. the codename of Pokharan-II blasts
C. the nuclear test ban treaty which India is being forced to adhere to
D. codename of Pakistani nuclear arsenal

**70.** The disagreement between Lok Sabha and Rajya Sabha is solved by:
A. setting up Joint Select Committee
B. dissolving Lok Sabha
C. setting up adjudication committee
D. calling a joint session

**71.** The national anthem was written by ..... and was translated into English by .....
A. Bankim Chandra Chatterji, Aurobindo Ghosh
B. Rabindra Nath Tagore, Aurobindo Ghosh
C. Bankim Chandra Chatterji, Rabindra Nath Tagore
D. the national anthem was originally written in English and was translated later

**72.** The tear in human body is a solution of :
A. Sodium hydroxide and sodium chloride
B. Calcium bicarbonate and sodium chloride
C. Magnesium bicarbonate and sodium hydroxide
D. Sodium bicarbonate and Magnesium chloride

**73.** The drug seroxat is
A. a new medicine for treating the lepers.
B. a new medicine developed by British scientists and is used for the treatment of shyness and social phobia
C. is anti-AIDS therapy developed by France
D. is an antacid developed in India under guidance of WHO

**74.** What is "Bermuda Triangle" sometimes referred to as the "Grakeyard of ships", located?
A. in the South Pacific ocean
B. in the North Atlantic ocean
C. in the Indian ocean
D. in the Arctic ocean

**75.** The theory propounded by Nobel laurate Professor Amartya Sen–is commonly known as
A. The Famine Economics
B. The Theory of Economic Divide
C. The Amartya Sen Shift
D. The Amartya Sen Divide

**76.** Which is known as the Electronics City of India?
A. Tumkoor B. Secunderabad
C. Bhopal D. None of the above

**77.** The main objective behind the creation of concept of *Navratnas* in the public sector was

A. to increase the control of the PSUs over economy
B. to boost local manufacturing and exports in the core sectors
C. to improve the functional autonomy
D. to improve their image and efficiency by giving them high status

**78.** The North American seaport on the Pacific side is
A. Baltimore B. Boston
C. New York D. Seattle

**79.** The old name of Harare was
A. Sam B. Rhodesia
C. Salisbury D. Batavia

**80.** The famous Prince of Wales Museum is located in
A. Mumbai B. Kolkata
C. Vadodara D. Bangalore

**81.** Who invented Atom Bomb (Uranium Fission)?
A. A W Haffmann
B. Otto Hahn
C. A Einstein
D. None of the above

**82.** The first ever woman to go into space was
A. Kalpana Chawla
B. Valentina Tereshkova
C. Mary Pierce
D. None of the above

**83.** The highest mountain peak in India is
A. K-2 B. Everest
C. Kanchanjunga D. Makalu-I

**84.** The "Garden City" of England is
A. Portsmouth B. Manchester
C. Kent D. Warwickshire

**85.** *Habeas Corpus* is
A. an order of the International Court of Justice
B. a type of writ issued by a High Court or Supreme Court against illegal detention of a person.
C. the petition of a lawyer in the Supreme Court on behalf of his client for bail against the orders of any other court in India
D. None of the above

**86.** If impeachment motion is passed by the American Senate against the US President, he would have to
A. leave office and all his assets created by him during Presidency
B. leave office, lose his pensions, security cover and all those benefits that are accorded to a retired US President
C. jailed for five years and will not get any benefits.
D. retire honourably with all his benefits, compensations, assets and pensions remaining intact

**87.** Who appoints the non-permanent members of the UN Security Council?
A. the permanent members
B. the General Assembly
C. the International Court of Justice
D. None of the above

**88.** The Preamble of the Constitution was amended by:
A. 1st amendment B. 26th amendment
C. 42nd amendment D. 44th amendment

**89.** NNP is equal to
A. GNP + Depreciation
B. GNP – Depreciation
C. GNP + Exports
D. GNP – Exports

**90.** The official airline of Australia is
A. SIA B. Lufthansa
C. Modiluft D. None of the above

**91.** Which one of the following types of coal contains a higher percentage of carbon than the rest?
A. Bituminous Coal B. Lignite
C. Anthracite D. Peat

**92.** Ten Commandments were revealed by God to:
A. Abraham B. Moses
C. Jesus D. Peter

**93.** Kalinga in older days, is now known as:
A. Odisha B. Kohima
C. Karnataka D. Maharashtra

**94.** Bihu festival is celebrated in:
A. Gujarat B. Assam
C. Bihar D. West Bengal

**95.** Milk is an example of
A. gel B. emulsion
C. suspension D. mixture

**96.** The President can dissolve the Lok Sabha before expiry of its term, on the advice of:
A. Prime Minister
B. Speaker
C. Vice-President
D. Election Commissioner

**97.** The State Emblem of India is taken from:
A. Patna
B. Sarnath
C. Bodh Gaya
D. Kolkata

**98.** Tughlaq dynasty occupied Delhi throne after decline of:
A. Suri dynasty
B. Slave dynasty
C. Lodhi dynasty
D. Khilji dynasty

**99.** Governors of states are:
A. appointed by Chief Ministers
B. appointed by the President
C. elected by members of Legislative Assembly
D. elected by people

**100.** The partition of Bengal was carried out by:
A. Lord Curzon
B. Lord Minto
C. Lord Canning
D. Lord Ripon

**101.** The Air Force Day falls on
A. October 10 B. October 9
C. September 5 D. October 8

**102.** MAD stands for
A. Most Active Disease
B. Mica Aluminium Duo
C. Mutually Assured Death
D. Mutually Assured Destruction

**103.** "Disguised Unemployment" means
A. more persons employed for a job that only a few could accomplish
B. people without any technical jobs
C. woman without jobs in rural areas
D. employment of children in factories

**104.** In India, an active volcano is situated at
A. Lakshadweep
B. Chhotanagpur Plateau
C. Andaman and Nicobar
D. Malawa Plateau

**105.** The first country to establish trade relationships with India was
A. England B. France
C. Holland D. Portugal

**106.** Which has the highest share of electrical power generation in India?
A. thermal power
B. nuclear power
C. hydro-power
D. naphtha-based and gas-based power

**107.** The great ocean liner, known to be the best and luxurious during her times, sank in the year
A. 1902 B. 1912
C. 1908 D. 1889

**108.** Who among the following is known as the Indian Napoleon?
A. Chandra Gupta Maurya
B. Bindusar
C. Samudra Gupta
D. Harshvardhana

**109.** Time gap between two sessions of Parliament cannot exceed:
A. 3 months B. 6 months
C. 1 year D. no fixed gap

**110.** In which state, Panchayati Raj was introduced for the first time?
A. Bihar
B. Punjab
C. Rajasthan
D. Andhra Pradesh

**111.** Which one is not a national duty?
A. Respect the Constitution
B. Respect the President
C. Defend the country
D. Protect natural environment

**112.** Treaty of Seringapatam was signed between:
A. Tipu Sultan and Nawab of Hyderabad
B. Tipu Sultan and English
C. Tipu Sultan & Rani of Jhansi
D. Tipu Sultan and French

**113.** NHRC stands for
A. National Hydro Research Committee
B. National Handicapped Rahabilitation Council
C. National Human Rights Commission
D. None of the above

**114.** "Water water everywhere but not a drop to drink" who stated these lines in a poem?
A. John Milton
B. Samuel Taylor Coleridge
C. Lord Byron
D. P.B. Shelley

**115.** Rabindranath Tagore gave up his knighthood after:
A. Jallianwala Bagh Tragedy
B. Introduction of separate electorates
C. Bengal faminine
D. Bengal Partition

**116.** Which country is known as the land of golden wool?
A. India B. Turkiye
C. Australia D. Myanmar

**117.** BIFR stands for
A. Bilateral and International Foreign Regulation
B. Board of Industrial Financial Resurrection
C. Board of Industrial and Financial Reconstruction
D. None of the above

**18.** Pinaca is a
A. drug for curing AIDS
B. multi-barrel rocket system
C. fighter aircraft developed by HAL
D. codename of the nuclear test operation carried out on May 11, 1998

**19.** Vice-President is ex-officio:
A. Member of Rajya Sabha
B. Chairman of Rajya Sabha
C. Member of Lok Sabha
D. Speaker of Lok Sabha

**20.** Vitamin C is not available in this food in sufficiently large quantities.
A. lemon B. tomato
C. cod liver oil D. fresh fruits

**21.** This book was not written in a jail
A. *Glimpses of World History* – J L Nehru
B. *The Bible* (German) – Martin Luther
C. *Les Miserables* – Victor Hugo
D. *Yama* – Mahadevi Verma

**122.** Who among the following can be removed from office through impeachment by Parliament?
A. Speaker of Lok Sabha
B. Prime Minister
C. President of India
D. Vice-President of India

**123.** The following is not the function of the liver.
A. to store excesssive sugar in the form of glycogen
B. the produce an antidote for neutralising poison
C. to manufacture red blood corpuscles
D. to purify the blood through bile

**124.** A fascist is a person whose views are extremely
A. left-winged B. rational
C. right-winged D. liberal

**125.** The famous mathematician and a professor of Astronomy designed this building in London
A. Westminister Abbey
B. St Paul's Cathedral
C. Stock Exchange
D. Tower of London

**126.** Which one of the following sounds cannot be heard by a human ear?
A. 30,000 vibrations per second
B. 10,000 vibrations per second
C. 1,000 vibrations per second
D. 300 vibrations per second

**127.** A weather balloon may not be inflated completely on the ground because
A. it cannot withstand the atmospheric pressure if inflated fully
B. if the balloon is inflated fully on ground, fuel consumption would be higher
C. the air inside the balloon expands as it rises and hence, the balloon could get burst
D. None of the above

**128.** Which one of the following vitamins is stored in the liver?
A. Vitamin C

B. Vitamin $B_{12}$
C. Vitamin A
D. Vitamin K and Vitamin A

**129.** All of the following are plant products except
A. silk B. cork
C. hemp D. linen

**130.** Which one of the following organs in the human body is known as "Adam's Apple"?
A. thyroid B. liver
C. thymus D. adrenal

**131.** Insecticides or medicines could be harmful
A. to the insects and weeds as they kill them instantaneously upon consumption
B. to the habitat as the environment could become polluted due to excessive usage of chemicals in our crop management processes
C. to the human beings and animals who consume the food adulterated by the insecticides and weedicides
D. to the transporters and movers of the crops who could inhale noxious fumes of insecticides and weedicides

**132.** Name the assassin of John Lennon
A. Art Buchwald
B. Lee Oswald
C. Mark David Chapman
D. None of the above

**133.** Which one of the following is not a sprinter?
A. Marion Jones
B. Florence Griffith Joyner
C. Ben Johnson
D. Susie O' Neill

**134.** Which of the following is called the "Gateway to the Pacific"?
A. Suez Canal
B. Bering Sea
C. Panama Canal
D. Gulf of Alaska

**135.** Which one of the following statements is true regarding the treaty on banning the landmines?
A. the USA does not want to sign the CTBT
B. the treaty was kept open for signatures in Ottawa in December, 1997.
C. India has already signed it
D. A and B are true

**136.** Disease that affects many people of different countries is termed as:
A. Sporadic B. Epidemic
C. Endemic D. Pandemic

**137.** The famous Gandhian, who was also known as the "Frontier Gandhi," is
A. Liaqat Ali Khan
B. Yusuf Khan
C. Khan Abdul Ghaffar Khan
D. Abdul Wali Khan

**138.** Which one of the following is an alloy?
A. copper B. lanthanum
C. bronze D. uranium

**139.** World Environment Day is celebrated on
A. June 4 B. June 5
C. June 7 D. March 5

**140.** This country is the largest producer of cotton in the world.
A. India B. China
C. Egypt D. the USA

**141.** International Youth Day is observed on ____.
A. August 11th B. August 10th
C. August 12th D. August 9th

**142.** The temples of Khajuraho were built by
A. Chalukyas B. Pallavas
C. Rashtrakutas D. Chandelas

**143.** National Remote Sensing Agency (NRSA) is located at:
A. Hyderabad
B. Bengluru
C. Thiruvananthapuram
D. Gadanki, near Tirupati

**144.** The clones for ....... and ....... have been developed.
A. man, cow B. crow, sheep
C. rat, cat D. sheep, rat

**145.** AWWA stands for
A. All Women Welfare Association
B. Army Wives Welfare Association
C. Airport Weather and Welfare Authority
D. None of the above

**146.** The popular book *The Gift of Time* by Jonathan Schell, deals with

A. the lewid affair of Bill Clinton and Monica Lewinsky
B. the elimination of nuclear weapons from the world
C. Indo-US relationships
D. the deteriorating environment in industrial America

**147.** How can a person move on a hard icy surface?
A. he should use roller skates
B. he should hop, sneeze, jump and step in the direction which is opposite to the direction of his required movement
C. he should hop, sneeze, jump and step in the direction in which the movement is required
D. he should skid on his knees and hands

**148.** Which states are deriving benefits from the Tungbhadra project?
A. Tamil Nadu, Karnataka, Kerala
B. Tamil Nadu only
C. Andhra Pradesh and Tamil Nadu
D. Tamil Nadu, Andhra Pradesh, Karnataka

**149.** The famous 'Lucknow Pact' was signed between the Congress and the Muslim League in:
A. 1913 B. 1916
C. 1914 D. 1915

**150.** Pyroclastics are
A. non-toxic gases
B. lava flows
C. fragments of hot rock and spattering lava
D. pollutant chemicals from a leather factory

**151.** Which one of the following is not a sedimentary rock?
A. slate B. limestone
C. clay D. sandstone

**152.** Oketa is
A. used to define human-induced climatic changes
B. used to describe increasing drought periods of high magnitudes
C. a unit to describe the prevailing cloudiness
D. None of the above

**153.** The following state produces the maximum quantities (85 percent) of raw silk in India
A. Kerala B. Jammu and Kashmir
C. Karnataka D. Tamil Nadu

**154.** Salal Hydro Electric Project is situated on the river
A. Beas B. Jhelum
C. Chenab D. Sutlej

**155.** Which of the following cities is located along the side of river Seine?
A. Belgrade B. Paris
C. Lisbon D. Budapest

**156.** What is the name of the bell used at the Lloyds in London?
A. The Great Bell B. The Charmer
C. The Tower Bell D. Lutine

**157.** What are "The Hagiographs?"
A. These are the poems written by Lord Byron
B. These are the holy writings of Jewish scriptures
C. These are the geographical lines representing same rainfall levels
D. None of the above

**158.** Which one of the following forms would provide the lowest protection?
A. Patent B. Trademark
C. Copyright D. Logo

**159.** The twenty-fifth State of India is
A. Goa B. Nagaland
C. Mizoram D. Delhi

**160.** What does the 17th Parallel line separate?
A. South and North America
B. North and South Korea
C. South and North Yemen
D. South and North Vietnam

**161.** Operation Flood-II, the prestigious milk products revolution of India, was initiated on
A. October 1, 1979 B. October 2, 1979
C. January 26, 1979 D. October 2, 1978

**162.** After World War I, the peace treaty was signed in:
A. Geneva B. Versailles
C. Paris D. Venice

**163.** Potassium chloride is given to the patient for
A. curing his bleeding gums
B. reducing his cholestrol level
C. reducing his blood pressure
D. alleviating his arthiritis pain

**164.** What is notation?

A. It is another word for "Mutually Assured Destruction"

B. It is the Latin deformation of the phrase "to swim"

C. It is a term used to denote the growth of illeterate masses

D. None of the above

**165.** The hideout of Adolf Hitler in the mountains was

A. Stuttgart B. Heidelberg

C. Berchtesgaden D. Both A and C

**166.** Who stated, "Where wealth accumulates decay?"

A. J M Keynes B. Adam Smith

C. Frederic Engels D. Oliver Goldsmith

**167.** Who was the national leader who wrote History of India on the walls of the Andaman Cellular Jail?

A. Ambedkar B. Vir Savarkar

C. Nandlal Bose D. Jyotiba Phule

**168.** The USA does not possess the following space shuttle

A. Columbia B. Atlantis

C. Challenger D. Discovery

**169.** The term "White Elephant" is used to denote

A. very bright and white item

B. very costly and expensive item

C. an item or a head that is very costly to maintain

D. an item or a head that is a part of the national economic budget of a country

**170.** Kolar Gold Mines are in this state.

A. Karnataka B. Bihar

C. Odisha D. Madhya Pradesh

**171.** Which is the morning star?

A. Pluto

B. Venus

C. Neptune

D. None of the above

**172.** Which one of the following is not an alkali?

A. sodium hydroxide

B. calcium carbonate

C. magnesium hydroxide

D. sodium sulphate

**173.** Polar ice is melting due to greenhouse effect. This would lead to

A. more melting of the polar glaciers and hence, subsequent submerging of land areas of earth

B. increasing temperatures on polar caps

C. reduction in temperature of ocean waters and rise in temperature of the Arctic circle waters as well as those of the Antartic circle waters

D. no impact

**174.** *India 2020* is a book written by

A. Trilok Gurtu

B. Khushwant Singh

C. P Chidambaram

D. A P J Abdul Kalaam

**175.** The Panama Canal connects:

A. The Pacific and Atlantic Oceans

B. The Pacific and Arctic Oceans

C. The Atlantic and Arctic Oceans

D. The Atlantic and Indian Oceans

**176.** The following are single cell structures

A. Paramaecium B. Amoebia

C. Both A and B D. None of A or B

**177.** 'The Last Supper' was painted by:

A. Picasso B. Francis Bacon

C. Michaelangelo D. Raphael

**178.** The plants, which can resist high temperatures, are known as

A. thermophilic B. thermophobic

C. thermoduric D. Both A and B

**179.** Which one of the following vaccines is used for controlling tuberculosis among the cattle?

A. Cell Culture Vaccine

B. Goat Tissue Adapted Vaccine

C. Adjuvant Vaccine

D. BCG Vaccine

**180.** Which one of the following chemicals is carcinogenic if inhaled?

A. carbon dioxide

B. suspended particulate matter

C. lead oxide

D. sulphur dioxide

**181.** What is a "Tenurial System?"

A. It is a system that identifies the ownership of land and the relationship of the land owner with the actual cultivator

B. It identities the land size and the *modus-operandi* of its usage
C. It identifies the ownership of the land
D. None of the above

**182.** Pulses are deficient in
A. methionine B. lysine
C. leusine D. iso-leusine

**183.** Which types of roses are grown in India for industrial applications?
A. R Centripetala and Bushra Rose
B. R Damascena Var Bifera
C. Rosa Damascena
D. A, B and C

**184.** Why sprinkler irrigation is preferred over other methods of irrigation?
A. It is a cheap method and does not require canal-digging and canal maintenance
B. It uses water effectively and water resolves are optimally utilised
C. It does not require well-digging measures which are costly
D. It supplies water only to those fields where the same is required

**185.** The size of clay particles is
A. greater than 0.2 mm
B. 0.02 mm – 0.2 mm
C. 0.002 mm – 0.02 mm
D. less than 0.002 mm

**186.** Which one of the following plants is of great medicinal value?
A. Ranwolfia Serpentiana
B. Thea Sinesis
C. Coffea Robusta
D. Ficus Religiosa

**187.** Biological control agents of soil borne plant pathogens act by
A. rapidly repleting nutrients and thereby, causing starvation and death of the pathogen
B. secreting toxic metabolitics
C. direct parastism or predation on the pathogens
D. All of the above

**88.** Nearly 80 percent of sugarcane in India is planted during
A. July – December B. May – August
C. June – August D. December – April

**189.** Soluble salt content of soil is determined by measuring its
A. pH Value
B. organic matter content
C. Sulphur content
D. electrical conductivity

**190.** Operation Flood is related to ..... whereas development of fisheries is related to .....
A. white revolution, black revolution
B. white revolution, blue revolution
C. green revolution, blue revolution
D. blue revolution, green revolution

**191.** An upper air wind system with very high velocities in certain parts of the atmosphere is called
A. Cyclone B. Anticyclone
C. Jet stream D. Tsunami

**192.** "Mixed Farming" refers to
A. farming by traditional and modern methods
B. agriculture and dairy farming clubbed together
C. farming without synthetic fertilisers but with traditional manure
D. farming with synthetic fertilisers and with traditional manure

**193.** The main constituent of *Gobar Gas* is
A. butane B. carbon monoxide
C. methane D. octane

**194.** Speed of sound waves is maximum in
A. solids B. liquids
C. gases D. vacuum

**195.** When a body gets positively charged, it actually
A. gains electrons
B. loses electrons
C. becomes a donor of ions
D. becomes a receptor of ions

**196.** Which type of nerves carries impulses from the sense organs in response to the stimulus?
A. sensory B. motor
C. secretory D. None of the above

**197.** Which gas does not pollute air (for human and animal consumption)?
A. carbon monoxide B. nitrogen dioxide
C. sulphur dioxide D. carbon dioxide

**198.** The human brain sends and receives signals as
A. electrical impulses
B. chemical impulses
C. motor movements
D. either A or B

**199.** "Foot and Mouth" disease attacks
A. cattle
B. pigs and cattle
C. sheep and pigs
D. cattle, sheep and pigs

**200.** While returning to earth, the spacecraft has a total communication blackout. The reason is
A. during the re-entry period, the density of the plasma generated by the intense functional heat is so high that the operational frequencies used for communication become much lesser than the plasma cut-off frequency, thus resulting in a total blackout
B. the electromagnetic waves present in the space above the earth temporarily overpower the communication system of the aircraft, thus completely crippling its operation and transmission
C. the force of gravity counters the radiowaves emitted by the aircraft
D. None of the above

**201.** The first winning stroke in Lawn Tennis gives the player:
A. 2 points B. 1 point
C. 10 points D. 15 points

**202.** Which of the following game is played for stipulated period of 70 minutes?
A. Hockey B. Football
C. Rugby D. Basketball

**203.** Who is the winner of World Cup Football-2022?
A. Brazil B. Argentina
C. Germany D. France

**204.** Arjuna Award has been instituted for outstanding contribution in the field of
A. Social Service
B. Games and Sports
C. Literature
D. Art and Music

**205.** Murugappa Gold Cup is associated with:
A. Football B. Polo
C. Hockey D. Bridge

**206.** Jimmy Connors and Geoff Boycott are related with following games respectively:
A. Tennis, Football B. Tennis, Cricket
C. Chess, Cricket D. Football, Hockey

**207.** What is the ratio of the width to the length of the National Flag of India?
A. 2 : 4
B. 3 : 5
C. 2 : 3
D. 3 : 4

**208.** Surat is located on the banks of:
A. Narmada B. Tapti
C. Godavari D. Yamuna

**209.** The term 'Steeple Chase' is associated with which of the following games
A. Polo B. Tennis
C. Horse Racing D. Cricket

**210.** Who is known as Father of India's "White Revolution" and "Operation Flood"?
A. Dr. Verghese Kurien
B. J.B. Kripalani
C. Baba Amte
D. Har Gobind Khorana

**211.** The first Olympic games were revived by ..... in 1896 at Athens
A. Lord Welsley
B. Queen Elizabeth-I
C. Baron Piere de Cubertin
D. None of the above

**212.** The national game of the USA is
A. swimming B. baseball
C. athletics D. None of the above

**213.** Jules Rimmet Cup is associated with
A. hockey B. archery
C. football D. table tennis

**214.** The approximate weight of a cricket ball is
A. 5.25 Oz B. 6.30 Oz
C. 7.20 Oz D. 8.25 Oz

**215.** The number of players on each side in a basketball match is
A. 10 B. 6
C. 5 D. 8

**216.** The first woman in the history of US open Championship to have played 100 matches, is:
A. Martina Navaratilova
B. Chris Evert
C. Steffi Graf
D. Helena Sukova

**217.** Swaythling Cup is associated with
A. World Table Tennis Tournament (men)
B. World Table Tennis Tournament (university)
C. World Table Tennis tournament (women)
D. World Hockey Tournament (university)

**218.** Which one of the following is not a cricket - playing nation?
A. West Indies B. Zimbabwe
C. Kenya D. Columbia

**219.** The first recipient of Major Dhyanchand Khel Ratna Award was
A. Geet Sethi B. N Kunjurani Devi
C. V Anand D. P K Garg

**20.** The first Olympic Games were held at Olympia (Greece) in the year:
A. 300 BC B. 776 BC
C. 500 BC D. 394 AD

**21.** Which of the following is the National Game of Spain?
A. Bull fighting B. Baseball
C. Rugby D. Golf

**22.** 'Ashes' is the name of a series between ..... and ..... and it relates to .....
A. Pakistan, Australia, Hockey
B. India, England, Cricket
C. England, Australia, Cricket
D. New Zealand, Australia, Cricket

**23.** The term "Butterfly Stroke" is associated with
A. Kabaddi B. Wrestling
C. Polo D. Swimming

**24.** The Australian Open Tennis Women's Championship (2026) was won by
A. C. Martinez
B. Garbine Muguruza
C. Elena Rybakina
D. Serena Williams

**25.** 'Gambit' is a term normally associated with
A. Bridge B. Chess
C. Billiards D. Polo

**226.** 'Bunker' and 'Chukker' are the two terms associated with
A. Polo B. Rowing
C. Bungey Jumping D. Ice Hockey

**227.** A Lawn Tennis court measures
A. 78 feet by 28 feet
B. 79 feet by 29 feet
C. 76 feet by 26 feet
D. 70 feet by 24 feet

**228.** 'Breast stroke' is related with:
A. Polo
B. Tennis
C. Golf
D. Swimming

**229.** Which one of the following has been entrusted with the responsibility of training coaches in various disciplines of sports?
A. Tata Football Academy
B. Ministry of Human Resource Development
C. Netaji Subhash Institute of Sports
D. Lakshmibai National College of Physical Education

**230.** ICC Men's T20 World Cup 2026 was won by
A. Australia
B. Pakistan
C. India
D. New Zealand

**231.** Governor will act on the advice of Council of Ministers while
A. Dissolving the Legislative Assembly
B. Appointing the Chairman of the State Public Service Commission
C. Recommending for President's Rule in the State
D. Returning a bill for reconsideration

**232.** Who was the first deaf & dumb swimmer in the world to swim 30 km Gibralter strait?
A. Des Renford
B. Mihir Sen
C. Arti Pradhan
D. Taranath Shenoy

**233.** The height of the net in the centre of the tennis court is
A. 3 feet, 5 inches
B. 3 feet, 2 inches
C. 2 feet, 8 inches
D. 2 feet, 6 inches

**234.** 'Canon' is a sports term associated with the following game.
A. Billiards B. Volleyball
C. Shot-Put D. Table Tennis

**235.** The Himalayan Mountaineering Institute is located in
A. Leh B. Darjeeling
C. Kohima D. Dispur

**236.** The diameter of a golf hole is
A. 4.36 inches B. 4.50 inches
C. 5.63 inches D. 4.75 inches

**237.** The total distance of a Marathon Race is ..... miles and ..... yards.
A. 29, 388 B. 26, 380
C. 26, 385 D. 25, 372

**238.** The first woman, who won six gold medals in a single Olympics tournament, was
A. Evelyn Ashford
B. Florence Griffth Joyner
C. Kristin Otto
D. Susi Susanti

**239.** In which year on account of a decree issued by Roman Emperor the Olympic Games were ceased to be played?
A. 350 AD B. 394 AD
C. 300 BC D. 384 AD

**240.** Putney (UK) is a place most frequently associated with
A. swimming B. horse racing
C. boat rowing D. polo

**241.** Dipa Karmakar is associated with which sports?
A. Gymnastics
B. Boxing
C. Badminton
D. Cricket

**242.** The term 'Finesse' is normally associated with this game.
A. Chess B. Bridge
C. Snooker D. Rowing

**243.** The following trophy is not associated with cricket.
A. Ranji Trophy
B. Rohintan Baria Trophy
C. C.K. Naydu Trophy
D. Jules Rimet Trophy

**244.** Who is the first Indian to take a Hat-trick in an International Test Match?
A. Kapil Dev
B. Jasu Patel
C. Harbhajan Singh
D. B.S. Chandrashekhar

**245.** When and where the first Asian Games were held?
A. 1955, Seoul B. 1951, New Delhi
C. 1954, Manila D. 1970, Bangkok

**246.** Ryder Cup is famous trophy of:
A. Badminton B. Golf
C. Lawn Tennis D. Shooting

**247.** What is the measurement of a Golf Hole?
A. 3½ inch in diameter
B. 4½ inch in diameter
C. 7½ centimeter in diameter
D. 10 inch in diameter

**248.** The Supreme Court of India was set up by the
A. Regulating Act, 1773
B. Pitts India Act, 1784
C. Charter Act, 1813
D. Charter Act, 1833

**249.** K Sasikaran is well known as a
A. table tennis player
B. swimmer
C. chess player
D. football player

**250.** Where is the Head Quarter of Asia Development Bank?
A. Washington B. Paris
C. Manila D. Canberra

**251.** In which of the following years 'Nobel Prizes' were instituted?
A. 1910 B. 1905
C. 1901 D. 1911

**252.** The writer who refused the Nobel Prize for Literature was:
A. Winston Churchill
B. Prem Chand
C. Jean Paul Sartre
D. None of the above

**253.** Which country awards the Noble Prize?
A. USA B. India
C. Russia D. Sweden

**254.** In which of the following years Arjuna Awards were instituted
A. 1951 B. 1971
C. 1961 D. 1965

**255.** National Awards for Popularising Science was instituted in the year
A. 1981 B. 1985
C. 1987 D. 1988

**256.** The Government of which state has instituted the 'Tansen Samman'?
A. Madhya Pradesh B. Uttar Pradesh
C. Gujarat D. Maharashtra

**257.** Who among the following has not been awarded the Bharat Ratna?
A. Indira Gandhi
B. Mahatma Gandhi
C. Sardar Patel
D. Dr. Radha Krishnan

**258.** Who returned the award of 'Sir' given by the British government in protest against the "Jallianwala Bagh Massacre" on April 13, 1919?
A. Prem Chand
B. Thomas Roe
C. Rabindra Nath Tagore
D. Dada Bhai Nauroji

**259.** Nobel Prize is not awarded in the following disciplines
A. Chemistry and Physics
B. Literature and Peace
C. Economics and Medicine
D. Geography and Space Research

**260.** In which year Nehru Award for International Understanding instituted
A. 1965 B. 1969
C. 1974 D. 1964

**261.** Dada Saheb Phalke Award is given for:
A. Drama B. Films
C. Social Welfare D. Literature

**262.** 'Pulitzer' prizes are awarded to Americans for excellence in
A. Films B. Journalism
C. Medicine D. Social Work

**263.** C.V. Raman received Nobel Prize in the year
A. 1934 B. 1931
C. 1932 D. 1930

**264.** Saraswati Samman is awarded by
A. Government of India
B. Sahitya Academy
C. K.K. Birla Foundation
D. Lalit Kala Akademi

**265.** On which day every year National Awards for Teachers are announced?
A. August 15 B. September 5
C. November 19 D. November 14

**266.** The National Award given to the distinguished sportsmen/women in India is known as
A. Dronacharya Award
B. Param Vir Chakra
C. Arjun Award
D. Nehru Award

**267.** The prestigious Ramon Magsaysay Award was instituted in the memory of Mr Ramon Magsaysay who was
A. the Secretary – General of UN
B. the Commander of NATO in Europe
C. the President of the Philippines
D. the President of Cambodia

**268.** The Kalinga Prize is awarded by UNESCO but it was founded by an Indian. His name is
A. Biju Patnaik
B. Sharad Pawar
C. C V Raman
D. Piloo Modi

**269.** Who was the first Indian to receive the World Food Prize
A. Dr. M.S. Swaminathan
B. Dr. Amrita Patel
C. Dr. Verghese Kurien
D. None of these

**270.** Jesse Owens Global award is given in the field of:
A. Literature B. Sports
C. Science D. Journalism

**271.** Nobel Alfred Bernhard after whom Nobel Prizes are given was:
A. Engineer B. Doctor
C. Chemist D. Pilot

**272.** Grammy Awards are given in the field of
A. painting B. architecture
C. music D. rock dance

**273.** The highest civilian award of India is
A. *Padma Vibhushan*
B. *Padma Shri*
C. *Bharat Ratna*
D. *Param Vir Chakra*

**274.** The highest military award of India is
A. Shaurya Chakra
B. Param Vishisht Sewa Medal
C. Param Vir Chakra
D. Kirti Chakra

**275.** The first ever B R Ambedkar National Award was given to
A. Baba Amte
B. T Shiv Shankar Pillai
C. International Red Cross
D. National Institute for Social Work and Social Sciences

**276.** 'Victory Medal' is awarded in:
A. UK B. USA
C. Russia D. France

**277.** Which one of the following is not a Shram Award
A. Shram Bhushan
B. Shram Dev
C. Shram Devi
D. Shram Vir

**278.** The Rashtriya Vigyan Puraskar is awarded in how many Categories?
A. 2 B. 3
C. 4 D. 5

**279.** Neeraj Chopra is associated with which game?
A. Badminton
B. Javelin Throw
C. Hockey
D. Wrestling

**280.** First Miss World Competition was established by 'Miss World Incorporation' in the year
A. 1941 B. 1950
C. 1951 D. 1957

**281.** The size of an Olympic medal is ..... mm and thickness is ..... mm.
A. 50, 2.5 B. 60, 3.0
C. 60.5, 3.5 D. 55.2, 2.5

**282.** "Dhanwantari Award" is given in the field of
A. swimming
B. Bharata Natyam
C. cinema
D. medicine

**283.** Which is the most ancient musical instrument of India?
A. Tabla B. Veena
C. Flute D. Sitar

**284.** Which is the second Highest Civilian award in India?
A. Padma Vibushan
B. Padma Shri
C. Bharat Ratna
D. Ashok Chakra

**285.** Gandhiji started the Dandi March for
A. Poorna Swaraj
B. Home-rule
C. Protest against the imposition of Salt Tax
D. Responsible Government

**286.** The second highest gallantry award in India is:
A. Padma Bhushan
B. Vir Chakra
C. Mahavir Chakra
D. Ashok Chakra

**287.** 'Mubarak-Al-Kabir' medal is the highest honour of
A. Kuwait B. Iran
C. Afghanistan D. Iraq

**288.** Bharatendu Harish Chandra awards are given annually for:
A. best local self administration
B. showing kindness and generosity of unusual kind
C. promoting original writing in Hindi
D. None of the above

**289.** Rigveda is divided into how many Mandals?
A. 10 mandals B. 7 mandals
C. 15 mandals D. 20 mandals

**290.** GST has been implemented from:
A. January 1, 2017
B. July 1, 2017
C. January 1, 2018
D. April 1, 2018

**291.** Which tax can be levied by Gram Panchayat?
A. Sales Tax
B. Land Revenue
C. Custom Duty
D. Tax on local fairs

**292.** Oscar award is related to
A. books
B. politics
C. European Community
D. films

**293.** USB stands for
A. Unique Serial Bus
B. Universal Serial Bus
C. Unary Serial Bus
D. Universal Secondary Bus

**294.** Out of the Gallantry awards — PVSM, AVSM and VSM — the most exceptional medal is
A. PVSM
B. AVSM
C. VSM
D. All have equal recognition status

**295.** *Jeewan Raksha Padak* is awarded for
A. bravery in the battle front
B. fine display of vocal music skills
C. saving the life of human beings
D. None of the above

**296.** Who is not eligible for Bharat Ratna?
A. A government official
B. A sportsperson
C. A film actress
D. A Prime Minister

**297.** Jamnalal Bajaj award is given in the field of
I. Social Work
II. Fine Arts
III. Application of Science and Technology
IV. Literature
A. I and II B. I, II and III
C. II and IV D. I and III

**298.** In which year Indira Gandhi Peace Prize was instituted?
A. 1985 B. 1984
C. 1986 D. 1987

**299.** Borlaug Award was instituted for recognising outstanding contribution in the field of:
A. Ecology B. Medicine
C. Agriculture D. Journalism

**300.** Except Dr. Nelson Mandela, who is the other non-Indian so far honoured with Bharat Ratna
A. Dr. Julius Nyerere
B. Helen Hint
C. Hideki Yuka
D. Khan Abdul Ghaffar Khan

**301.** The book "*The Insider*" is written by
A. Madhav Rao Scindia
B. Nana Patekar
C. Shobha De
D. P V Narasimha Rao

**302.** *India Wins Freedom* was written by
A. Dadabhai Nauroji
B. Ashfaqulla Khan
C. Sarojini Naidu
D. Maulana Abul Kalam Azad

**303.** *A Tale of Two Cities* is, in fact, the story of two famous cities. Those cities are
A. Paris and New York
B. London and New York
C. London and Paris
D. Stockholm and New York

**304.** *Ben Hur* was penned by
A. Lewis Wallace
B. Lord Byron
C. William Shakespeare
D. None of the above

**305.** *Panchatantra* was written by
A. R K Narayan B. R K Laxman
C. Vishnu Sharma D. None of the above

**306.** Arundhati Roy has been awarded the prestigious
A. Booker's Prize – 1997
B. Jnanpeeth Award – 1997
C. Sahitya Akademi Award – 1998
D. None of the above

**307.** Who wrote *Odyssey?*
A. George Orwell B. Homer
C. Dom Moraes D. None of the above

**308.** Which one of the following was not written by Shakespeare?
A. *As You Like It*
B. *Mcbeth*

C. *Hamlet*
D. *A Farewell to Arms*

**309.** Lewis Carol wrote a masterpiece. What is its name?
A. *Don Quixote*
B. *Alice in Wonderland*
C. *Adventures of Robinson Crusoe*
D. *Great Expectations*

**310.** The *Tamil Ramayana* is the work of
A. Tulsidas B. Jayangondar
C. Kambar D. Veda Vyas

**311.** In *Shrimad Bhagwat Geeta,* Lord Krishna teaches his disciple Arjuna to
A. rise to the occasion and fight with his near and dear ones
B. withdraw from the battlefield
C. do his duty and not to expect anything in return
D. attack the enemy in a planned and meticulous approach

**312.** Who wrote *Origin of Species?*
A. Charles Darwin
B. Alexander Flaming
C. G.B. Shaw
D. D.H. Lawrence

**313.** The poet and the well-known friend of Prithvi Raj Chauhan, who wrote *Prithvi Raj Raso,* was
A. Harisena B. Vishnu Datt
C. Chand Bardai D. None of the above

**314.** The first book was printed in India in the year 1561. Its name was
A. *The spiritual Compendium of the Christian Life*
B. *Aain-e-Akbari*
C. *Babur Nama*
D. *Ram Charit Manas*

**315.** The famous book *Runs and Ruins* was written by
A. Sir Donald Bradman
B. Sunil Gavaskar
C. Kapil Dev
D. Richard Hadlee

**316.** Adam Smith wrote the following famous book
A. The Wreck
B. Dr Zhivago
C. The Wealth of Nations
D. Tarzan of the Apes

**317.** H G Wells is known as a
A. poet
B. science-fiction writer
C. thriller-fiction writer
D. essay writer and critic

**318.** Tukaram wrote his devotional songs in this language
A. Urdu B. Gujarati
C. Hindi D. Marathi

**319.** Our ancient scholars and writers used this language for their social, religious and political books and works
A. Tamil
B. Sanskrit
C. Urdu
D. Hindi *(Devanagari)*

**320.** *Gora* is the hero of a book written by Rabindra Nath Tagore. What is the name of the book?
A. *Geetanjali* B. *Patanjali*
C. *Gora* D. *Twelfth Night*

**321.** Shylock is
A. the villain *in A Pound of Flesh* by William Shakespeare
B. an old Jew who is a famous hero of the Israeli nation
C. the hero of *Miranda,* written by William Shakespeare
D. the comic character of *Alice In the Wonderland* by Lewis Caroll

**322.** The following was a famous Hindi author and story-writer
A. Shobha De B. Aruna Asaf Ali
C. Mahadevi Verma D. Amrita Pritam

**323.** *Mudrarakshasa* was composed by
A. Vishakhadatta B. Bhavabhuti
C. Sivananda D. Jayadeva

**324.** *Razor's Edge* was written by
A. Toni Morrison
B. Saul Bellow
C. W Somerset Maugham
D. None of the above

25. *Sakharam Binder* is a famous play written by
A. Anil Barve B. Vijay Tendulkar
C. V S Naipaul D. Tasleema Nasreen

26. The major work of Sir Isaac Newton is
A. *Principia*
B. *Heritage*
C. *Human knowledge*
D. *I Dare*

27. The hero of *The Jungle Book,* written by Rudyard Kipling, is
A. the lion
B. Mowghuli
C. the father of Mowghuli
D. there is no hero

8. Who stated, "Peace hath her victories, no less renowned than war?"
A. Alfred Lord Tennyson
B. William Shakespeare
C. John Milton
D. None of the above

9. Macawber is a character who was created by
A. Thomas Hardy
B. P G Wodehouse
C. Charles Dickens
D. J W Von Goethe

0. *Pride and Prejudice* was written by
A. Anton Chekhov B. Maxim Gorky
C. Jane Austen D. Anthony West

1. *In the Afternoon Time* is the English translation of the autobiography of the famous poet, Harivansh Rai Bachchan. The autobiography was translated into English by
A. Vikram Seth
B. Dr Rupert Snell
C. William Faulkner
D. P D Tandon

2. Who is the author of the book *The Celestine Vision?*
A. Paul Hockins B. Salman Rushdie
C. Joseph Conrad D. James Redfield

. The author of the famous book *Blue Mountain Revisited* is
A. Charles Kingsley B. Virginia Woolf
C. Arthur Koestler D. Peter Topkins

. Homer was the great poet of the following language
A. Italian B. Greek
C. Arabic D. French

335. When is the Human Rights Day observed every year?
A. $10^{th}$ April
B. $10^{th}$ September
C. $10^{th}$ December
D. $12^{th}$ December

336. *Godaan* was written by Munshi Prem Chand and it depicts
A. the methodology for taking adequate care of the cows
B. exploitation of simple rural folk by the rich landlords of rural India
C. the mutiny of 1857 in which, Indians refused to bite the *Kartoos* made with cow beef
D. None of the above

337. Manu wrote a book during ancient times in which, he divided the Aryan society into four distinct classes. What was the name of the book?
A. *Arthashastra* B. *Manusmriti*
C. *Moti Mahal* D. *My Truth*

338. R. Venkataraman wrote *My Presidential Years.* What was the main theme of the book?
A. It described the aristocratic procedures being followed in the *Rashtrapati Bhawan* during his tenure as President
B. It described the power equations and ploys in the centre and in the states during his term
C. It described how he felt caged while he was President due to a load of procedures and formalities
D. It explained the machinations of the political party which was in power during his tenure as President

339. The hero of the play cried in the end, "Et Tu, Brute!" and died. Which is the play and who is the author?
A. The Wealth of Nations — Adam Smith
B. Mein Kempf — Adolf Hitler
C. Julius Caesar — William Shakespeare
D. None of the above

**340.** Don Veto Corleone was the undisputed king of the underworld in this novel. This masterpiece was also converted into a film in which Al Pacino played the role of the Don. What is the name of the novel and that of the author?
A. *A Farewell to Arms* — E Hemingway
B. *The Godfather* — Mario Puzo
C. *From Here to Eternity* — James Jones
D. *Dialogue with Death* — Arthur Koestler

**341.** *Gypsy Camp Vanishes Into the Blue* was a famous blockbuster movie made by the erstwhile USSR. The original story was written by a famous author. His name is
A. Leo Tolstoy
B. Anton Chekhov
C. Maxim Gorky
D. Leon Uris

**342.** The total number of *Puranas* written during the Vedic age is
A. 22
B. 9
C. 18
D. 25

**343.** In computer network terminology. WAN stands for
A. World area network
B. Wide area network
C. Wide array net
D. Wireless area network

**344.** The first woman in the world to have climbed Mt. Everest twice is
A. Bachendri Pal
B. Molly Chacko
C. Santosh Yadav
D. Theresia Kiesl

**345.** According to *The Ramayana,* who received the last teaching lessons from the knowledge-able Ravana while he was on his death-bed?
A. Rama
B. Sugreeva
C. Laxmana
D. Both A and C

**346.** He was a German but he saved many a Jew from the cruel hands of the Nazis. A movi was made on this theme which won th coveted Oscar Prize. The book and the autho are
A. *Operation Shylock* — Philip Roth
B. *Schindler's List* — Thomas Keneally
C. *The Rescue* — Joseph Conrad
D. *The Slave* — Isaac Bashevis Singer

**347.** He was the favourite assistant of Sherloc Holmes, the famous character created b Arthur Conan Doyle. His name is
A. Zhivago
B. Watson
C. Hawkins
D. Hector

**348.** 'New Silk Route' is a rail route which link China with the European Country ______.
A. Germany
B. France
C. Italy
D. None of the above

**349.** He wrote *Sharmili*, *Gaylord* and *Kati Patan* His novels were written in Hindi and some them have been converted into films also. H name is
A. Gita Mehta
B. B N Mullick
C. Nirad C Chaudhary
D. Gulshan Nanda

**350.** Pt. Shiv Kumar Sharma is an exponent of
A. Mandolin
B. Santoor
C. Sitar
D. Veena

## ANSWERS

| 1 | 2 | 3 | 4 | 5 | 6 | 7 | 8 | 9 | 10 |
|---|---|---|---|---|---|---|---|---|---|
| C | B | A | D | B | B | B | B | B | A |
| **11** | **12** | **13** | **14** | **15** | **16** | **17** | **18** | **19** | **20** |
| B | C | D | A | A | C | B | C | A | B |

| 21 | 22 | 23 | 24 | 25 | 26 | 27 | 28 | 29 | 30 |
|---|---|---|---|---|---|---|---|---|---|
| D | B | B | D | D | C | A | C | C | C |
| 31 | 32 | 33 | 34 | 35 | 36 | 37 | 38 | 39 | 40 |
| C | A | A | C | D | C | A | B | B | D |
| 41 | 42 | 43 | 44 | 45 | 46 | 47 | 48 | 49 | 50 |
| B | C | B | B | C | D | A | A | D | A |
| 51 | 52 | 53 | 54 | 55 | 56 | 57 | 58 | 59 | 60 |
| D | A | C | A | C | B | C | A | C | C |
| 61 | 62 | 63 | 64 | 65 | 66 | 67 | 68 | 69 | 70 |
| B | A | C | B | D | D | A | C | C | D |
| 71 | 72 | 73 | 74 | 75 | 76 | 77 | 78 | 79 | 80 |
| B | B | B | B | C | D | C | D | C | A |
| 81 | 82 | 83 | 84 | 85 | 86 | 87 | 88 | 89 | 90 |
| B | B | A | C | B | B | B | C | B | D |
| 91 | 92 | 93 | 94 | 95 | 96 | 97 | 98 | 99 | 100 |
| C | B | A | B | B | A | B | D | B | A |
| 101 | 102 | 103 | 104 | 105 | 106 | 107 | 108 | 109 | 110 |
| D | D | A | C | D | A | B | C | B | C |
| 111 | 112 | 113 | 114 | 115 | 116 | 117 | 118 | 119 | 120 |
| B | B | C | B | A | C | C | B | B | C |
| 121 | 122 | 123 | 124 | 125 | 126 | 127 | 128 | 129 | 130 |
| D | C | D | C | B | A | C | C | A | A |
| 131 | 132 | 133 | 134 | 135 | 136 | 137 | 138 | 139 | 140 |
| C | C | D | C | D | D | C | C | B | B |
| 141 | 142 | 143 | 144 | 145 | 146 | 147 | 148 | 149 | 150 |
| C | D | A | D | B | B | B | D | B | C |
| 151 | 152 | 153 | 154 | 155 | 156 | 157 | 158 | 159 | 160 |
| A | C | C | C | B | D | B | A | A | D |
| 161 | 162 | 163 | 164 | 165 | 166 | 167 | 168 | 169 | 170 |
| B | B | C | B | C | D | B | C | C | A |
| 171 | 172 | 173 | 174 | 175 | 176 | 177 | 178 | 179 | 180 |
| B | D | A | D | A | C | C | C | D | C |
| 181 | 182 | 183 | 184 | 185 | 186 | 187 | 188 | 189 | 190 |
| A | A | D | B | D | A | D | D | D | B |
| 191 | 192 | 193 | 194 | 195 | 196 | 197 | 198 | 199 | 200 |
| C | B | C | A | B | A | D | B | D | A |
| 201 | 202 | 203 | 204 | 205 | 206 | 207 | 208 | 209 | 210 |
| D | A | B | B | C | B | C | B | C | A |
| 211 | 212 | 213 | 214 | 215 | 216 | 217 | 218 | 219 | 220 |
| C | B | C | A | C | B | A | D | C | B |
| 221 | 222 | 223 | 224 | 225 | 226 | 227 | 228 | 229 | 230 |
| A | C | D | C | B | A | A | D | C | C |
| 231 | 232 | 233 | 234 | 235 | 236 | 237 | 238 | 239 | 240 |
| A | D | B | A | B | B | C | C | B | C |
| 241 | 242 | 243 | 244 | 245 | 246 | 247 | 248 | 249 | 250 |
| A | B | D | C | B | B | B | A | C | C |

| 251 | 252 | 253 | 254 | 255 | 256 | 257 | 258 | 259 | 260 |
|---|---|---|---|---|---|---|---|---|---|
| C | C | D | C | C | A | B | C | D | D |
| 261 | 262 | 263 | 264 | 265 | 266 | 267 | 268 | 269 | 270 |
| B | B | D | C | B | C | C | A | C | B |
| 271 | 272 | 273 | 274 | 275 | 276 | 277 | 278 | 279 | 280 |
| C | C | C | C | D | B | B | C | B | C |
| 281 | 282 | 283 | 284 | 285 | 286 | 287 | 288 | 289 | 290 |
| B | D | C | A | C | C | A | C | A | B |
| 291 | 292 | 293 | 294 | 295 | 296 | 297 | 298 | 299 | 300 |
| D | D | B | A | C | A | D | C | C | D |
| 301 | 302 | 303 | 304 | 305 | 306 | 307 | 308 | 309 | 310 |
| D | D | C | A | C | A | B | D | B | C |
| 311 | 312 | 313 | 314 | 315 | 316 | 317 | 318 | 319 | 320 |
| C | A | C | A | B | C | B | D | B | C |
| 321 | 322 | 323 | 324 | 325 | 326 | 327 | 328 | 329 | 330 |
| A | C | A | C | B | A | B | C | C | C |
| 331 | 332 | 333 | 334 | 335 | 336 | 337 | 338 | 339 | 340 |
| B | D | D | B | C | B | B | C | C | B |
| 341 | 342 | 343 | 344 | 345 | 346 | 347 | 348 | 349 | 350 |
| C | C | B | C | C | B | B | A | D | B |

* * * * *

2606-SP